Habermas on Law and Democracy

PHILOSOPHY, SOCIAL THEORY, AND THE RULE OF LAW

General Editors

Andrew Arato, Seyla Benhabib, Ferenc Fehér,
William Forbath, Agnes Heller, Arthur Jacobson, and Michel Rosenfeld

Habermas on Law and Democracy

Critical Exchanges

EDITED BY

Michel Rosenfeld and Andrew Arato

UNIVERSITY OF CALIFORNIA PRESS

Berkeley   Los Angeles   London

This book is a print-on-demand volume. It is manufactured
using toner in place of ink. Type and images may be less
sharp than the same material seen in traditionally printed
University of California Press editions.

University of California Press
Berkeley and Los Angeles, California

University of California Press
London, England

Copyright © 1998 by The Regents of the University of California

Library of Congress Cataloging-in-Publication Data

Habermas on law and democracy : critical exchanges / edited by Michel
Rosenfeld and Andrew Arato.
    p.   cm. — (Philosophy, social theory, and the rule of law ;
6)
   Includes bibliographical references and index.
   ISBN 0-520-20466-2 (alk. paper)
   1. Law—Philosophy.   2. Sociological jurisprudence.   3. Democracy.
4. Habermas, Jürgen.   I. Rosenfeld, Michel, 1948–   . II. Arato,
Andrew.   III. Series.
K355.H333   1998   97-26887
                                                                 CIP

Printed in the United States of America

For Susan, Maïa, and Alexis
—M. R.

For Jean
—A. A.

CONTENTS

PART SEVEN • HABERMAS RESPONDS
TO HIS CRITICS

ACKNOWLEDGMENTS

This book represents the culmination of an extraordinary interdisciplinary and intercontinental intellectual journey. The essays included here originated at a conference held at the Benjamin N. Cardozo School of Law on September 20 and 21, 1992, in which Jürgen Habermas and thirty-two scholars from the United States, Germany, and many other countries, representing the fields of law, philosophy, sociology, and political science, engaged in two days of intense, open, and wide-ranging discussion of virtually every major subject addressed by Habermas in *Between Facts and Norms: Contributions to a Discourse Theory of Law and Democracy.* The Cardozo conference, which took place at the time of the publication of the original German version of *Between Facts and Norms,* thus constitutes the first in-depth discussion of Habermas's book.

The editors wish to thank above all Jürgen Habermas who graciously agreed to participate at the Cardozo conference, where he delivered the keynote address, entitled "Paradigms of Law," which is the first essay in this book. During the rest of the conference, Habermas spent very long hours closely listening and thoroughly responding to the thirty or so presentations made on various aspects of his book, in an intense and most enriching dialogue. Finally, subsequent to the conference, on receiving the papers written by the participants, Habermas generously agreed to provide the written reply that is included as the last essay in this volume.

Many thanks are also due to Bill Rehg for his translation of "Paradigms of Law" and of Habermas's "Reply," to which he kindly turned as soon as the original was completed.

The editors wish to thank Linda Goebel, a student in the Class of 1998 at the Cardozo School of Law for her very able assitance in preparing the index to this volume.

It would not have been possible to organize an international gathering of the magnitude of the Cardozo conference without receiving significant financial support. Fortunately, the conference was able to count on the generous assistance of the Jacob Burns Institute for Advanced Legal Studies at Cardozo, the Goethe House/German Cultural Center, and the Friedrich Ebert Foundation, for which the editors are very grateful.

Introduction

Habermas's Discourse
Theory of Law and Democracy

Jürgen Habermas's much-awaited *Between Facts and Norms: Contributions to a Discourse Theory of Law and Democracy* is a monumental work of philosophy and social theory that aims at reconciling law and justice as well as democracy and rights. Through a reconstructive approach grounded in his discourse theory, Habermas places law at the center of a web that links morals, law, and politics in a way that substantially perfects the Kantian project undertaken by John Rawls in *A Theory of Justice*.

Between Facts and Norms is at once a work of sharp critical analysis and dazzling synthetic breath. In it, Habermas provides a rich critique of the main contemporary German and American trends in jurisprudence and constitutional theory and offers a challenging alternative building on his theory of communicative action[1] and expanding on his discourse ethics.[2] Reminiscent in scope and ambition of Max Weber's sociology of law[3] and Hegel's philosophy of law,[4] *Between Facts and Norms* is a work that raises as many questions as it answers. Undoubtedly, *Between Facts and Norms* will remain for the foreseeable future at the center of debates in legal and democratic theory.

The essays published in this volume originated in the first comprehensive and in-depth public discussion of all major aspects of *Between Facts and*

---

1. *See* JÜRGEN HABERMAS, THE THEORY OF COMMUNICATIVE ACTION (Thomas McCarthy trans., 1984 & 1987).

2. *See* JÜRGEN HABERMAS, MORAL CONSCIOUSNESS AND COMMUNICATIVE ACTION (Christian Lenhardt & Shierry W. Nicholsen trans., 1990).

3. *See* MAX WEBER, ECONOMY AND SOCIETY (Guenther Roth & Clause Wittich eds. & Ephraim Fischoff et al. trans., 1968).

4. *See* G. W. HEGEL, PHILOSOPHY OF RIGHT (T. M. Knox trans., 1967).

Norms, which took place at a conference held on September 20 and 21, 1992, at the Benjamin N. Cardozo School of Law in New York City, in which Jürgen Habermas and all the other authors included in this volume participated. The first essay in the present collection, "Paradigms of Law," presented by Habermas as the keynote address at that conference, provides a succinct summary of Habermas's case in favor of his discursively grounded proceduralist paradigm of law, which constitutes the centerpiece of *Between Facts and Norms.* The final essay in this collection, Habermas's thorough and systematic reply to the essays written by the other conference participants, not only furthers the fruitful dialogue between Habermas and his critics but also provides many valuable new insights concerning some of the most salient issues tackled in *Between Facts and Norms,* and thus amounts to a veritable companion to that book.

Habermas's ambitious project to reconcile law, rights, justice, and democracy arises in the context of the deep divisions characteristic of contemporary pluralistic constitutional democracies. In the face of widely diverging conceptions of the good and significant disagreement over fundamental values, the relationship between law and ethics as well as that between law and politics becomes increasingly problematic. Moreover, jurisprudential attempts to deal with these difficulties have touched on a wide selection of alternatives, without striking a satisfactory balance between the various disparate strands typically prevalent within contemporary polities. At one extreme, one finds those, like several proponents of the Critical Legal Studies movement, who tend to collapse law into politics and who deem legal norms sufficiently porous or contradictory to suit the aims of those who wield the greatest political power.[5] At the other extreme are those who conceive law as independent and essentially severable from ethics and politics. The most prominent advocate of this position is Niklas Luhmann whose legal autopoiesis casts law as a self-referential system that remains normatively closed.[6] Consistent with Luhmann's approach, the actual content of legal norms does not much matter, provided law—conceived as a system of rules—manages to stabilize expectations and thus reduces complexity and uncertainty in dealings among social actors.[7]

Neither of the above-mentioned extremes is satisfactory. First, differ-

---

5. The relevant Critical Legal Studies literature is vast, but the following articles stand out as being among the best: Duncan Kennedy, *The Structure of Blackstone's Commentaries,* 28 BUFFALO L. REV. 205 (1979); and Roberto M. Unger, *The Critical Legal Studies Movement,* 96 HARVARD L. REV. (1983).

6. *See, e.g.,* Niklas Luhmann, *Operational Closure and Structural Coupling: The Differentiation of the Legal System,* 13 CARDOZO L. REV. 1419 (1992).

7. *See* NIKLAS LUHMANN, A SOCIOLOGICAL THEORY OF LAW 31–40 (Martin Albrow ed. & Elizabeth King & Martin Albrow trans., 1985); NIKLAS LUHMANN, ESSAYS ON SELF-REFERENCE 14–15, 232–33 (1990).

ences between polities that strive to adhere to the rule of law and those that do not, amply demonstrate that law is not merely reducible to politics. And, second, even if one concedes that stabilizing expectations constitutes the overriding purpose of private law, it is difficult to accept that the principal purpose of public law in general and of the legal/constitutional protection of fundamental rights in particular[8] would be the same.

Another way to deal with the problematic nexus between law, ethics, and politics is through adaptation of the Kantian dichotomy between the right and the good in order to subsume the basic framework of the legal system— or, at least, the fundamental underpinnings of the constitutional order—to the right. The foremost and most influential systematic effort in that direction is obviously the political philosophy of John Rawls as elaborated in his *Theory of Justice*, and its closest counterpart in the realm of jurisprudence is found in the legal and constitutional theory of Ronald Dworkin.[9] Both Rawls and Dworkin seek to set the normative unity and cohesion of the polity above the realm of contested conceptions of the good, but both are forced to make such major sacrifices along the way as to seriously undermine the force of their ultimate conclusions.

Rawls resorts to his notorious hypothetical contract concluded behind a veil of ignorance to combine the respective strengths of Rousseau and Kant at a higher level of abstraction.[10] But in the course of this process, all differences between persons are set aside, with the consequence that all the hypothetical social contractors become interchangeable. Accordingly, the hypothetical social contract becomes reducible to a solipsistic individual act, and the principles of justice that emerge from this process come closer to being incompatible with any conception of the good than to being in harmony with most of them.

Dworkin, in contrast, forswears the abstract realm of hypothetical agreements,[11] but cannot thereby avoid the twin pitfalls of contingency and excessive abstraction. Dworkin embraces a liberal-egalitarian position that is steeped in the Kantian tradition inasmuch as it predicates that rights trump goods. From the standpoint of the legitimacy of law or legal interpretation, however, Dworkin would be hard pressed to justify that his liberal-egalitarian rights are more legitimate than liberal-libertarian or conservative rights, or even than those goods that loom as normatively paramount within ethical theories committed to the priority of goods over rights, if it were not for his assertion that the U.S. Constitution happens to have

8. *See* Michel Rosenfeld, *Autopoiesis and Justice*, 13 CARDOZO L. REV. 1681 (1992).
9. *See* RONALD DWORKIN, TAKING RIGHTS SERIOUSLY (1977) and LAW'S EMPIRE (1986).
10. *See* JOHN RAWLS, A THEORY OF JUSTICE 11 (1971).
11. *See* RONALD DWORKIN, *The Original Position, in* READING RAWLS 16–53 (Norman Daniels ed., 1976).

codified liberal-egalitarian rights and principles.[12] But this latter assertion makes Dworkin's theory doubly vulnerable: on the one hand, it can be dismissed as merely parochial since it depends on contingent historical facts lacking any import beyond the United States; on the other hand, Dworkin's conclusions regarding the American Constitution may be attacked as being historically unwarranted.

By tying the legitimacy of law to liberal-egalitarianism, Dworkin infuses law with a moral dimension and thus avoids the respective extremes of Critical Legal Studies and legal autopoiesis. Moreover, by combining his moral conception of law with the historically grounded process of common law adjudication on the basis of precedents, Dworkin constructs a theory of legal interpretation that avoids the twin pitfalls of unavoidable indeterminacy and purely circular self-referentiality. Furthermore, through a highly abstract analysis of the role of judges, and through reliance on the model of the superhuman judge Hercules, Dworkin advances the thesis that hard cases can be given a single right answer.[13] However, not only is this thesis counterintuitive, but Dworkin's Hercules operates at such a high level of abstraction that the isolated and exclusively monological process through which he arrives at the "right answer" seems of little relevance from the standpoint of the interpretive responsibility of real-life judges.

A further consequence of liberal theories such as those of Rawls and Dworkin, which place rights above goods, is the exacerbation of the tension between democracy and rights. Indeed, maintaining the priority of liberal rights often requires setting aside widely supported policies. One attractive way of overcoming this tension and of surmounting the limitations of monological reasoning is through recourse to communitarianism—or more precisely, to deliberative, republican-minded communitarianism, such as that articulated by Frank Michelman.[14] The chief virtue of such communitarianism is that it grounds legal norms in a dialogical process embedded in a well of commonly shared values and commitments in ways that seem apt to defuse the tension between democracy and rights.

While undoubtedly attractive, the communitarianism in question proves ultimately unsatisfactory in that it tends to unduly minimize the clash among competing conceptions of the good typical within contemporary pluralistic polities. For precisely that reason, notwithstanding his significant common affinities with it, Habermas cannot settle on such communitarianism. More generally, Habermas's philosophical and jurisprudential project

12. In addition to the above-cited works by Dworkin, see generally his FREEDOM'S LAW: THE MORAL READING OF THE AMERICAN CONSTITUTION (1996).

13. *See* DWORKIN, TAKING RIGHTS SERIOUSLY, *supra* note 9, esp. chs. 4 and 13.

14. *See* Frank Michelman, *Law's Republic,* 97 YALE L.J. 1493 (1988); *The Supreme Court, 1985 Term—Foreword: Traces of Self-Government,* 100 HARVARD L. REV. 4 (1986).

in *Between Facts and Norms* can be understood in terms of seeking to integrate what is most attractive about theories such as those of Rawls, Dworkin, and Michelman without falling prey to their respective shortcomings. Because of his moorings in the Kantian tradition and his steadfast commitment to proceduralism, Habermas's project is best viewed as a quest to perfect Rawls's contribution presented in *A Theory of Justice*, in ways that allow for genuine dialogue and consideration of differences that divide social actors while narrowing the gap between democracy and rights. Furthermore, Habermas's quest seeks to avoid recourse to dilution of the grip of commonly shared normative constraints in ways reminiscent of the evolution of Rawls's own theory from the comprehensive view espoused in *A Theory of Justice* to the more modest proposal for reliance on the contingencies of an "overlapping consensus" that lies at the core of his more recent views as expressed in *Political Liberalism.*[15]

Consistent with his overall objectives, Habermas conceives of laws's legitimacy as stemming from its being at once self-imposed and binding.[16] Moreover, laws that can be genuinely said to be both self-imposed and binding would bridge the gap between democracy and rights. Also, as Habermas insists that all persons subjected to laws must be treated as free and equal actors, laws that are at once self-imposed and binding must successfully reconcile legal and factual equality. In the first essay in this volume, entitled "Paradigms of Law," Habermas zeroes in on the centerpiece of his theory of law, by focusing on three paradigms designed to simultaneously satisfy legal and factual equality. The first of these, the "liberal-bourgeois" paradigm promotes a formal conception of law and reduces justice to the equal distribution of rights. Habermas considers this paradigm inadequate inasmuch as it cannot generate factual equality under current conditions. For its part, the second paradigm, the social welfare paradigm, which is geared to achieving material equality, does so in a way that sacrifices dignity and autonomy. To overcome these deficiencies, Habermas proposes his proceduralist paradigm, which allows for the simultaneous satisfaction of legal and factual equality through deployment of the discourse principle in a way that establishes the requisite nexus between self-legislation and law as binding.

The remaining contributors to this volume concentrate on the most salient issues raised by Habermas's conception of law and democracy, with each of them focusing on certain aspects or implications of Habermas's theory.

Andrew Arato maintains that the important idea of a procedural legal paradigm has not been developed by Habermas with sufficient clarity and

---

15. *See* JOHN RAWLS, POLITICAL LIBERALISM (1993).
16. *See* Habermas, BETWEEN FACTS AND NORMS *supra,* Ch. IX.

in terms of all its potential implications. After exploring the different interpretations given by Habermas, each focusing on alternative meanings of the concept of reflection, Arato considers the possible meanings of this paradigm for new legal institutions and practices.

Jacques Lenoble argues that the procedural paradigm put forth by Habermas is very important but cannot be adequately developed on the basis of Habermas's own theory of communication. Replacing notions of consensus and coming to an understanding with convention and undecidability, Lenoble suggests ways to remedy the weaknesses in Habermas's critique of civic republicanism and in his theory of adjudication.

Michel Rosenfeld presents Habermas's proceduralism as the culmination of a trend that relates back to Hobbes through Kant and Rawls. Rosenfeld argues that all proceduralism must ultimately be grounded on substantive values and that Habermas's proceduralism must be qualified as ultimately derivative. Rosenfeld then seeks to illustrate the limitations of Habermas's proceduralism by demonstrating that the discourse principle is vulnerable to certain kinds of feminist objections.

Thomas McCarthy situates Habermas's conception of law within his broader normative theory. Moreover, McCarthy criticizes Habermas's important distinction between ethical and moral discourse as being problematic beyond the purely analytical level. In particular, argues McCarthy, the distinction in question is likely to be misleading in contexts marked by pervasive and irreconcilable cultural differences. McCarthy proposes an alternative model of conflict resolution in which coming to an agreement is but one possibility. As McCarthy sees it, other such possibilities include mutual respect for positions that remain irreconcilable and democratic decision making with the aid of fair procedures.

Niklas Luhmann raises a fundamental question that goes to the heart of Habermas's use of the discourse principle to achieve a procedural justification of law. Consistent with discourse theory, a legal norm is justified if all those who would be subject to it *could* agree to it as participants in a rational discourse. Luhmann, however, argues that the combination of Habermas's rejection of metaphysics and of the fact that not all those to be affected by a law could actually participate in the requisite discussion undermines the discourse principle. What the latter requires can only be known when a decision is reached, but no such decision could ever be reached if all those affected by it had to partake in it.

Gunther Teubner approaches Habermas's discourse principle from the standpoint of the postmodern fragmentation of rationality into an unwieldy multiplicity of discourses. According to Teubner, unlike in Habermas's preceding works in which he embraced the unity of discourse, in *Between Facts and Norms* he accepts the multiplicity of discourses and deals with the problem of collisions among discourses through a theory of discourse compatibility. In Teubner's view, recourse to compatibility does not provide a viable solution, as the problem of multiple discourses is not accurately captured in terms of the dichotomy between a hierarchy and a heterarchy of discourses. Ultimately, argues Teubner, each discourse—including law—seeks to reconcile the others from the perspective of its own fragmented and partial position.

Arthur Jacobson evaluates Habermas's conception of law in terms of the distinction between static and dynamic jurisprudence. According to Jacobson, Habermas eschews the greater potential of dynamic jurisprudence to ground legal rights within the static confines of positivism and the jurisprudence of right. Moreover, argues Jacobson, by seeking to link rights to democracy through his discourse principle, Habermas eviscerates rights of their most promising and disruptive potential.

Michael Power insists that in spite of apparent discrepancies, there is a continuity that links Habermas's early works, such as *Knowledge and Human Interests*,[17] to *Between Facts and Norms*. Power asserts that it is Habermas's recourse to the "counterfactual imagination" that accounts for such continuity. Counterfactuals make it possible to fill the gap between the reconstruction of a practice as possessing a cogent meaning and the empirical manifestations of such practice. Counterfactuals, moreover, allow for either critical theory or building a "reflective equilibrium," depending on whether a current practice is criticized in terms of its realizable potential or whether it is normatively vindicated in terms of its approximation to such potential. In Power's estimation, in *Between Facts and Norms* Habermas is more drawn to reflective equilibrium than to critical theory.

Robert Alexy investigates whether Habermas's theory of legal discourse is adequate as an account of the rationality of adjudication. Relying on the distinction drawn by Habermas between "discourse of justification" and "discourse of application," Alexy argues that though the distinction is correct, it is empty and prone to be misunderstood. Accordingly, Alexy concludes that the only way to solve the problem of rationality in adjudication is through a theory of legal discourse in which such discourse emerges as a special case of general practical discourse.

Although a proponent of Habermas's discourse theory, which he helped to elaborate, Klaus Günther is critical of the status of negative rights in Habermas's theory. Departing from the commonly shared idea of the right of withdrawal from (public) communication as a way of grounding the rights of private autonomy in the discourse model, Günther argues *contra* Habermas that it is impossible to neglect negative rights even on the most abstract level of the analysis of the system of rights. This is because, accord-

17. *See* JÜRGEN HABERMAS, KNOWLEDGE AND HUMAN INTERESTS (Jeremy J. Shapiro trans., 1971).

ing to Günther, legal norms necessarily produce an artificial gap that makes recourse to negative liberty necessary.

William Rehg focuses on the application of Habermas's discourse theory to institutional contexts. According to Rehg, by tying legitimacy virtually exclusively to the discourse principle, Habermas underestimates the import of time-constrained decision making. Consistent with this, Rehg concludes that Habermas falls to perceive the legitimating potential of majority rule or of fair legal procedures.

William Forbath criticizes Habermas for his failure to refer to the insights of the American Legal Realists, and in particular to their account of the relations between state and society and law and the economy. According to Forbath, Habermas has an unduly narrow conception of the economy that prevents him from realizing that market and property relations can be fairly radically reorganized without threatening freedom or efficiency. As a consequence of this, concludes Forbath, Habermas's theory lacks sufficient critical bite.

Richard Bernstein, like McCarthy, argues that the distinction between ethical and moral discourse cannot be maintained in the context of democratic procedures and institutions. But whereas McCarthy is concerned with ethical conflict and multicultural recognition, and is apprehensive about seeking an overly thick "overlapping consensus," Bernstein maintains that Habermas's conception does not adequately stress democratic ethos. If Habermas's democratic theory is at all convincing, it is due to its reliance on substantial ethical commitments to democracy. Although Habermas has recognized this to some extent, he has repeatedly insisted on the priority and separability of a moral discourse that is not reducible to the self-reflection of a given political community.

Frank Michelman rejects Habermas's characterization of his civic republicanism as presupposing a thick, substantial consensus as a sine qua non of important political decisions. Michelman insists that the participatory impulse in his theory is necessarily linked to a liberal-pluralist view of the actual conditions in complex societies. To the extent that the discourse paradigm and his own views diverge, therefore, this is due, according to Michelman, to Habermas's unwarranted insistence that questions of justice can be in any way detached from the specific collectivities in which they arise.

Ulrich Preuss explores the tensions between law and politics and concludes that neither the liberal nor the welfare state paradigms accounts for this relation of law and power. He construes Habermas's effort to build a procedural paradigm as an attempt to account for law as the mechanism through which social power is democratized and administrative power legitimated. Without rejecting the distinction between the moral and the ethical, Preuss raises several critical questions designed to elucidate whether the distinction in question is likely to be fruitful for legal and democratic theory. In particular, Preuss inquires whether apparently irreconcilable ethical differences could be tamed in institutional contexts through transformation into pragmatic conflicts of interests.

Both András Sajó and Bernhard Schlink focus on the uses of Habermas's theory of institutionalized procedures in relation to the practice of constitutional courts. Sajó makes fruitful use of the idea of the materialization of law under modern welfare states for the analysis of constitutional courts. Moreover, by referring to a series of German cases, he demonstrates the legal plausibility of Habermas's idea of using the public sphere to redress the failure of the classical separation of powers in the face of a previously uncontrollable administrative machinery. Sajó concludes that constitutional adjudication must and does take into account a politically mediated public opinion. Schlink, on the other hand, argues that Habermas's theory has no direct relevance to the practice of the German Constitutional Court. In Schlink's conception, the judicial process and constitutional adjudication loom as largely independent from democratic processes and public opinion shifts.

Habermas's "Reply" constitutes the last essay in this volume. It addresses various criticisms against his theory of law and further elaborates and amplifies some of the key points developed in *Between Facts and Norms*.

Most of the essays included in this volume were originally published in a special symposium issue of the *Cardozo Law Review*. The editors wish to thank the *Law Review* for agreeing to the publication of these essays in the present volume.

Michel Rosenfeld
Andrew Arato
December 1996

PART ONE

Habermas's Proceduralist Paradigm of Law

ONE

Paradigms of Law

Jürgen Habermas*†

Among legal scholars expressions such as "social ideal" or "social model," and even "social vision," have become generally accepted ways of referring to the images of society inscribed in a legal system. Such expressions refer to those implicit images of one's own society that guide the contemporary practices of making and applying law. These images or paradigms provide the background for an interpretation of the system of basic rights. In other words, they orient the project of realizing an association of free and equal citizens. A paradigm is discerned primarily in paramount judicial decisions, and it is usually equated with the court's implicit image of society. For example, Friedrich Kübler speaks of the "social construction of reality" that underlies judgments of facts in legal discourse, that is, how factual courses of events and the functioning of social systems are described and evaluated by judges.[1] As early as 1931, Otto Kahn-Freund examined the "social ideal" of the Supreme Labor Court (*Reichsarbeitsgericht*) during the Weimar Period from the perspective of ideology critique.[2] Two decades later Franz Wieacker introduced the equivalent concept of the "social model" for descriptive purposes when he deciphered the liberal paradigm of law in the classical statute books of private law.[3] In elaborating the paradigm of bour-

*Professor Emeritus, University of Frankfurt, Germany.
†Translated by William Rehg.
    1. *See* Friedrich Kübler, Über die praktischen Aufgaben zeitgemäßer Privatrechtstheorie 9 (1975).
    2. Otto Kahn-Freund, *Das soziale Ideal des Reichsarbeitsgerichts, in* Arbeitsrecht und Politik 149 (Thilo Ramm ed., 1966).
    3. *See* Franz Wieacker, *Das Sozialmodell der klassischen Privatrechtsgesetzbücher und die Entwicklung der modernen Gesellschaft, in* Industriegesellschaft und Privatrechtsordnung 5 (1974).

geois formal law, Wieacker's famous study simultaneously clarified the background in contrast to which the "materialization" of law during the last one hundred years could emerge.[4] This *social transformation of law* was initially thought of as a process in which a new instrumental understanding of law, one related to social-welfare conceptions of justice, was superimposed on the liberal model of law, which it suppressed and finally supplanted. German jurisprudence has perceived this process, which dissolved the classical unity and systematic organization of the legal order, as a "crisis of law." In the first part of this Article, I will introduce the two paradigms of formal and materialized law in their standard versions. The second part examines the recent criticism of welfare-state paternalism in order to introduce a third paradigm of law—the proceduralist paradigm. The proceduralist paradigm is more appropriate for complex societies than the two paradigms that have competed up to now. Finally, this Article uses the example of feminist legal theory to elucidate an important aspect of this new paradigm—the internal connection between the private or social autonomy of the individual legal person and the public or political autonomy of citizens in democratic opinion- and will-formation.

I.

The welfare-state model emerged from the reformist critique of bourgeois formal law. According to this model, an economic society institutionalized in the form of private law (above all through property rights and contractual freedom) was separated from the sphere of the common good and the state, and left to the more or less spontaneous working of market mechanisms. This "private law society" (*Privatrechtsgesellschaft*) was tailored for the autonomy of legal subjects who, primarily as market participants, would seek and find their happiness by pursuing their own particular interests as rationally as possible. Since the principle of legal freedom implied equal protection for all persons, this principle seemed to satisfy the normative expectation that, by delimiting spheres of individual liberty through guarantees of a negative legal status, social justice could be concomitantly produced. The right of *each person* to do as he or she pleases within the limits of general laws is legitimate only under the condition that these laws guarantee equal treatment. This legitimating force, found in equal treatment, appeared, from a liberal point of view, to be already guaranteed through the formal universality of legal statutes, that is, through the grammar and the semantic form of conditional legal programs. In any case, this form of abstract and general law was typical for the norms of bourgeois private law

4. *See id.*

that confer powers and impose prohibitions.[5] However, the expectation of social justice was implicitly linked with the demarcation of nondiscriminatory *conditions for the actual exercise* of those liberties granted by legal norms regulating contracts, property, inheritance, and association. This expectation tacitly relied on a certain image of society. Primarily, it depended on economic assumptions about equilibrium in market processes (with entrepreneurial freedom and consumer sovereignty). Corresponding to these were sociological assumptions about the distribution of wealth and an approximately equal distribution of social power, which was supposed to secure equal opportunities for exercising the powers conferred by private law. If freedom in "the capacity to own and acquire property" is to fulfill justice expectations, then an equality of "legal ability" must exist.

Of course, these and similar background assumptions of the liberal model soon proved vulnerable to substantive criticisms. This led to a reformist praxis which, however, was based not on a change in the normative premises, but only on a more abstract version of them. It was the same system of basic rights that now, with a changing image of society, led to a different reading. Under the conditions of an organized capitalism dependent on the government's provision of public infrastructure and planning, and with a growing inequality in economic power, assets, and social opportunities, the objective legal content of subjective private rights became visible. In such a changed social context, the universal right to equal individual liberties could no longer be guaranteed through the negative status of the legal subject. Rather, it proved necessary, on the one hand, to specify the content of the existing norms of private law and, on the other, to introduce new categories of basic rights grounding claims to a more just distribution of socially produced wealth and a more effective protection from socially produced dangers. From a normative point of view, both the materialization of private law and the new category of social entitlements are *justified in a relative sense,* namely in relation to an equal distribution of individual liberties. As Robert Alexy explains, materialization results from the fact "that legal freedom, that is, the legal permission to do as one pleases, is worthless without actual freedom, the real possibility of choosing between the permitted alternatives."[6] Social entitlements, on the other hand, are due to the fact "that under the conditions of modern industrial society the actual freedom of a large number of rights-bearers does not have its material basis in an environment they control, but essentially depends on government activities."[7]

---

5. This form was also typical for the corresponding individual rights that imposed certain interventionary duties on an administration bound by law.

6. ROBERT ALEXY, THEORIE DER GRUNDRECHTE 458 (1985).

7. *Id.*

Notwithstanding their different legal traditions, we observe this change from formal to materialized law in all modern societies. In a recent study using the example of American tort law, Henry J. Steiner has supplied convincing evidence for the paradigm shift to be observed in the adjudication of liability:

> What this common law change does express is not then a radical shift in political or legal premises, but rather a trend in liberal thought from the vision and ideology of a more individualistic society stressing a facilitative state framework for private activity to the vision and ideology of a more managerial, redistributive, and welfare state.[8]

If we list the combinations of features with which cases of liability in business transactions were once described—*and therewith interpreted*—from a liberal viewpoint, and compare these features with how such cases are described and interpreted today in view of welfare regulations, we obtain the following table:

The Liberal View	Today's View
unique	statistical
individual, personal	category, impersonal
concrete, anecdotal	generalized, purged of detail
occasional, random	recurrent, systemic
isolated conduct	part of an activity
unforeseeable (in the particular)	predictable (in the aggregate)
wait and see, fatalism	manageable, planning through insurance and regulation

If one reads the table in the given sequence (from top to bottom), then the difference in the patterns of interpretation appears as a change in perspective that an observer makes in moving from the action level to the system level of description: on the left side, the individual actor in his natural setting, that is, in a contingently changing environment, provides the point of reference; with his individual liberty, he also has to carry the responsibility for the consequences of his decisions. On the right side, the statistically described interrelationships of a system constitutes the point of reference; here the doubly contingent decisions of the involved parties, together with their consequences, are taken as dependent variables. If, on the contrary, one reads the table in reverse order (from the bottom up), then the difference in patterns of interpretation appear as a shift in the actor's perspective: according to the liberal market model, society repre-

8. Henry J. Steiner, Moral Argument and Social Vision in the Courts: A Study of Tort Accident Law 9 (1987).

sents the result of spontaneous forces and thus is something like a "second nature" that resists the influence of individual actors. From the vantage point of the regulatory welfare-state, however, society loses precisely this quasi-natural character. As soon as system conditions vary beyond a certain level determined by the "limits of social tolerance," the state is held accountable for crisis conditions perceived to result from its own deficits in planning and intervention.

The welfare-state model appears in different versions, depending on whether one credits the state with a wide range of possibilities for direct political intervention in a society at its disposal, or whether one conceives it more realistically as one system among several, which must restrict itself to a narrow range of indirect steering inputs. But both readings of the welfare-state model assume a competition between two agents, the state and those subject to it, who dispute each other's scope for action. One might say the welfare-state model *pays for* the agency of the state at the expense of the autonomous status of individual actors. What is awarded to the state in capacities for social regulation seemingly must be *taken*, in the form of private autonomy, from individuals caught in their systemic dependencies. From this point of view, the state and private actors are involved in a zero-sum game—what the one gains in competence the other loses. According to the liberal model, the subjects of private law, who once acted within the framework of their equally distributed liberties, were limited only by the contingencies of their quasi-natural social situation. Today, they run up against the paternalistic provisions of a superior political will that intervenes in these social contingencies and regulates social processes with the intention of providing the actual preconditions for an equal exercise of individual liberties.

The welfare-state provides services and apportions life opportunities by guaranteeing social security, health care, housing, income provisions; education, leisure, and the natural bases of life, it grants each person the material basis for a humanly dignified existence. A welfare-state with such overwhelming provisions, however, almost inevitably tends to impose supposedly "normal" patterns of behavior on its clients. This normalizing pressure obviously runs the risk of impairing individual autonomy, precisely the autonomy it is supposed to promote by providing the factual preconditions for the equal opportunity to exercise negative freedoms.

II.

The dangers of such welfare paternalism provided *one* incentive for seeking a new legal paradigm that avoids the complementary weaknesses of both the paradigms of formal and materialized law. I would like to propose a *proceduralist understanding of law* that is centered on the procedural conditions of the democratic process. According to this view, the legal order is structured neither by the measure of individual legal protection for private-autonomous market participants nor by the measure of comprehensive social security for the clients of welfare-state bureaucracies. Although it is supposed to provide or guarantee both of these, they do not form the paradigmatic cases. In the proceduralist paradigm of law, the vacant places of the economic man or welfare-client are occupied by a public of citizens who participate in political communication in order to articulate their wants and needs, to give voice to their violated interests, and, above all, to clarify and settle the contested standards and criteria according to which equals are treated equally and unequals unequally. This move enlarges the perspective that previously restricted our view of the social functions of negative freedom and legally protected private autonomy. Both the welfare-state and the liberal paradigms share the *productivistic image* of a capitalist industrial society.

In the liberal view, the private pursuit of personal interests is what allows capitalist society to satisfy the expectation of social justice, whereas in the social-welfare view, this is precisely what shatters the expectation of justice. Both views are fixated on the question of whether it suffices to guarantee private autonomy through individual liberties, or whether, to the contrary, the *conditions for the genesis* of private autonomy must be secured by granting welfare entitlements. Both views lose sight of the internal connection between private and political autonomy, and thus lose sight of the democratic meaning of a legal community's self-organization. The still unresolved dispute between these two parties is focused on specifying the material preconditions for the equal status of legal persons as *addressees* of the legal order. However, if we start from a fully developed concept of private and public autonomy, legal persons are autonomous only insofar as they can understand themselves at the same time as *authors* of the law to which they are subject as addressees. The subtle connections that link legitimacy to private and public autonomy require further explanation.

A well-served private autonomy helps "secure the conditions" of public autonomy just as much as, conversely, the appropriate exercise of public autonomy helps "secure the conditions" of private autonomy (i.e., secure the "fair value" of private liberties). This mutual dependency, or circular relationship, is manifested in the genesis of valid law. This is because legitimate law emerges from, and reproduces itself only in, the forms of a constitutionally regulated circulation of power, which should be nourished by the communications of an unsubverted public sphere that in turn is rooted in the associational network of a liberal civil society and gains support from the core private spheres of the lifeworld. Public sphere and civil society, the centerpiece of the new image, form the necessary context for the generation and reproduction of communicative power and legitimate law. With this conception, the burden of normative expectations in general shifts from the level of *actors'* qualities, competences, and opportunities to the *forms of communication* in which an informal and noninstitutionalized opinion- and will-formation can develop and interact with the institutionalized deliberation and decision making inside the political system. In place of the zero-sum game between competing initiatives of private and governmental actors, we reckon instead with the complementary forms of communication found in the private and public spheres of the lifeworld, on the one hand, and in political institutions, on the other. Given this image, the normative intuition behind a self-organizing legal community can be restated as follows: a legal order *is* legitimate to the extent that it equally secures the co-original private and political autonomy of its citizens; at the same time, however, it *owes* its legitimacy to the forms of communication in which civic autonomy alone can express and prove itself. This is the key to a proceduralist understanding of law. After the formal guarantee of private autonomy has proven insufficient, and after social intervention through law also threatens the very private autonomy it means to restore, the only solution consists in thematizing the connection between forms of communication that *simultaneously* guarantee private and public autonomy *in the very conditions from which they emerge.*

In introducing the proceduralist paradigm of law, I begin with three premises: (i) the way back, advertised by neoliberalism as a "return of civil society and its law,"[9] is blocked; however, (ii) the call for the "rediscovery of the individual" is provoked by a welfare-state juridification that threatens to twist the declared goal of restoring private autonomy into its opposite[10]; and finally, (iii) the social-welfare project must neither be simply continued along the same lines nor be broken off, but rather it must be pursued at a higher level of reflection.[11] The intention is to tame the capitalist economic system, that is, to "restructure" it socially and ecologically in such a way that the deployment of administrative power can be simultaneously brought under control. From the standpoint of effectiveness, this means training the administration to employ mild forms of indirect steering; from the standpoint of legitimacy, it means linking the administration to communicative power and immunizing it better against illegitimate power. This path to

9. *See* Ernst J. Mestmäcker, *Wiederkehr der bürgerlichen Gesellschaft und ihres Rechts*, 10 RECHTSHISTORISCHES J. 177 (1991); *see also* Ernst J. Mestmäcker, *Der Kampf ums Recht in der offenen Gesellschaft*, 2 RECHTSTHEORIE 273 (1989).

10. Spiros Simitis, *Wiederentdeckung des Individuums und arbeitsrechtliche Normen*, 2 SINZHEIMER CAHIERS 7 (1991).

11. JÜRGEN HABERMAS, *The New Obscurity: The Crisis of the Welfare State and the Exhaustion of Utopian Energies*, in THE NEW CONSERVATISM: CULTURAL CRITICISM AND THE HISTORIANS' DEBATE 48, 64–69 (Shierry W. Nicholsen ed. & trans., 1989).

realizing the system of rights under the conditions of a complex society cannot be adequately characterized in terms of a specific legal form—reflexive law—that the procedural paradigm of law would privilege in a manner similar to the way liberal and welfare paradigms once favored their corresponding legal forms—formal and materialized law.[12] Rather, the choice of the respective legal form must in each case remain bound to the original meaning of the system of rights, which is to secure the citizens' private and public autonomy *uno actu:* each legal act should at the same time be understood as a contribution to the politically autonomous elaboration of basic rights, and thus as an element in an ongoing process of constitution making.

What is meant by this internal connection between private and political autonomy? The social-welfare critique of bourgeois formal law directs attention to the dialectic between the legal and the actual freedom of the *addressees* of law, and hence focuses primarily on the implementation of basic social rights. Actual equality is gauged by the observable social effects that legal regulations have for those affected, whereas legal equality refers to the latter's power to decide freely according to their own preferences within the legal framework. The principle of legal freedom engenders actual inequalities, since it not only permits, but also facilitates the differential use of the same rights by different subjects; it thereby fulfills the legal presuppositions for the autonomous pursuit of private life plans. To this extent, legal equality cannot coincide with actual equality. On the other hand, the requirement of equal legal treatment is contradicted by those de facto inequalities that discriminate against specific persons or groups by reducing their opportunities to utilize equally distributed individual liberties. Insofar as welfare compensations establish equal opportunities to make equal use of legal powers, compensation for material inequalities in life circumstances and power positions helps realize legal equality. To this extent, the dialectic between legal and actual equality has been an inconspicuous motor of legal development for quite some time.

This relation grows into a *dilemma,* however, when welfare regulations, employing criteria of equal treatment in an attempt to secure an actual equality in living situations and power positions, achieve this goal only under conditions or with instruments that, as far as the presumptive beneficiaries are concerned, also severely *limit* the vulnerable areas in which individuals can autonomously pursue a private life plan. This point is reached when statutory regulations on work and family life *force* employees or family

---

12. *See* Gunther Teubner, *Substantive and Reflexive Elements in Modern Law,* 17 LAW & SOC'Y REV. 239 (1983); *see also* Gunther Teubner, *Regulatorisches Recht: Chronik eines angekündigten Todes,* 54 ARCHIV FUR RECHTS- UND SOZIALPHILOSOPHIE 140 (1990). *But see* Eckard Rehbinder, *Reflexive Law and Practice, in* STATE, LAW, AND ECONOMY AS AUTOPOIETIC SYSTEMS: REGULATION AND AUTONOMY IN A NEW PERSPECTIVE 579 (Alberto Febbrajo & Gunther Teubner eds., 1992).

members to conform their behavior to a "normal" work relation or a standard pattern of socialization; when the recipients of other compensations *pay* for these with dependence on normalizing intrusions by employment offices, welfare agencies, and housing authorities; or when they must accept court decisions that directly intervene in their lives; or when collective legal protection, the right to unionize, and so on, provide an effective representation of interests only at the cost of the freedom to decide by organization members, who are condemned to *passive followership and conformity.* Each of these critical cases concerns the same phenomenon: the act of satisfying the material preconditions for an equal opportunity to exercise individual liberties alters living situations and power positions in such a way that the compensation for disadvantages is associated with forms of tutelage that convert the intended *authorization* for the use of freedom into a *custodial supervision.*

It is also clear that in such aforementioned cases, materialized law is stamped by an ambivalence of guaranteeing freedom and taking it away, an ambivalence that results from the dialectic of legal and actual equality and hence issues from the structure of this process of juridification. Still, it would be rash to describe this structure itself as *dilemmatic.*[13] For the criteria by which one can identify the point where empowerment is converted into supervision are, even if context-dependent and contested, not arbitrary.

III.

In concluding this Article, I will use feminist legal theory to elucidate the proceduralist paradigm. The feminist discussion focuses on developments in law where the dialectic of legal and actual equality has intensified in an interesting way. The problems connected with the equal treatment of men and women make one aware that the sought-for liberation should not be understood simply as welfare benefits in the sense of a just social share. Rights can empower both men and women to shape their own lives autonomously only to the extent that these rights also facilitate equal participation in the practice of civic self-determination, because only the affected persons themselves can clarify the "relevant aspects"—the standards and criteria—that define equality and inequality for a given matter.

The classical feminism stemming from the nineteenth century understood the equality of women primarily as equal access to existing educa-

---

13. *See* 2 JÜRGEN HABERMAS, THE THEORY OF COMMUNICATIVE ACTION 361–73 (Thomas McCarthy trans., 1987) (proposing a distinction between law as institution and law as medium—contrasting socially interactive norms with legal forms of the political system—which cannot be maintained).

tional institutions and occupational systems, to public offices, parliaments, and so forth. The liberal rhetoric of implementing formal rights was intended to uncouple the acquisition of social status as much as possible from gender, and to guarantee women opportunities in the competition for education, jobs, income, social standing, influence, and political power, regardless of the outcome. Liberal politics was supposed to bring about the inclusion of women in a society that hitherto had denied them fair chances to compete. The difference between the sexes supposedly would lose its social relevance once the differential access to the relevant spheres was overcome. However, to the extent that the formal equality of women was implemented in some important social spheres, the dialectic of legal and actual equality was also felt, leading to special regulations, primarily in welfare, labor, and family law. Here, liberal justifications were relinquished in favor of welfare-type arguments. Good examples are found in the protective norms pertaining to pregnancy and maternity, or to custody rights and divorce cases. Such norms and rights cluster around the clear biological differences connected with reproduction. The same holds for special regulations in the criminal law dealing with sex offenses. In these areas, the feminist legislation followed the social-welfare program of promoting equality in women's legal status via compensations for disadvantages, whether "natural" or "social."

Since the late sixties, however, a reawakening feminist movement has directed public attention to the *ambivalent consequences* of the more or less successfully implemented programs. Welfare-state paternalism has in many cases assumed a literal meaning. This has occurred, for example, to the extent that legal provisions for pregnancy and maternity have only increased the risk of women losing their jobs; to the extent that protective labor laws have generally reinforced segregation in the labor market or the over-representation of women in lower wage brackets; to the extent that a liberalized divorce law has only confronted women with the burdening effects of divorce; or to the extent that neglected interdependencies between regulations of welfare, labor, and family law have led to the further accumulation of gender-specific disadvantages through negative feedback loops. To the extent that such things have occurred, a materialization of law directed at the real discrimination against women has had the opposite effect. The statistical findings on the "feminization of poverty" have been alarming, and not simply in the United States.

From a juridic point of view, one reason for this reflexively generated discrimination lies in the *overgeneralized classifications* used to label disadvantaging situations and disadvantaged groups of persons. What is meant to promote the equal status of women in general often benefits only one category of (already privileged) women at the cost of another category, because gender-specific inequalities are correlated in a complex and obscure manner with membership in other underprivileged groups (social class, age, ethnicity, sexual orientation, etc.). However, an important role is played by the fact that legislation and adjudication arrive at "false" classifications, not because they are altogether blind to contexts, but because their perception of context and gender is guided by an *outmoded paradigmatic understanding of law*. This is the more or less unarticulated issue common to the various currents of radical feminism since the seventies. The feminist movement objects to the premise underlying both the welfare-state and the liberal politics of equality, namely the assumption that equal entitlements of the sexes can be achieved within the existing institutional framework and within a culture dominated and defined by men.

Each special regulation, intended to compensate for the disadvantages of women in the labor market or workplace, in marriage or after divorce, in regard to social security, health provisions, sexual harassment, pornography, and so forth, rests on an interpretation of differences in gender-specific living situations and experiences. To the extent that legislation and adjudication in these cases are oriented by traditional interpretive patterns, regulatory law consolidates the existing *stereotypes of gender identity*. In producing such "normalizing effects," legislation and adjudication themselves become part of the problem they are meant to solve. As long as the "normal work relation" of the fully employed male serves as the standard for "deviations" that need to be offset, women are forced by compensatory regulations to adapt to institutions that *structurally* disadvantage them.

What impact do these considerations have for the paradigmatic understanding of law? My thesis is this: the pressure towards assimilation that is exerted on women by both the social-welfare and the liberal politics of equality—a pressure felt precisely where those programs succeed—ultimately comes from the fact that gender differences are not conceived as relationships involving two *equally* problematic variables and *in need of interpretation*. Differences are instead seen as deviations—as gender-dependent, indeed feminine, exceptions from supposedly unproblematic male standards. Of course, the two legal paradigms which concur in their premises lead to different consequences. Whereas the social-welfare paradigm makes special legal allowances for the divergences and freezes them as such, the liberal market model tends to ignore and trivialize actual inequalities. This explains why current feminist critique once again revolves around the issue of gender-dependent *differences*.[14]

---

14. Doctrinally speaking, two alternative paths to sex equality for women exist within the mainstream approach to sex discrimination, paths that follow the lines of the sameness/difference tension. The leading one is: be the same as men. This path is termed "gender neutrality" doctrinally and the single standard philosophically. It is testimony to how substance becomes form in law that this

Feminist critique misses its real target, however, if it locates the mistake in the "sameness/difference approach" as such, and hence in the dialectic of legal and actual equality driven by the imperative of equal treatment. This is true of approaches that, in rejecting the conventional paradigmatic understanding of "rights," also throw out the idea of realizing rights *in any way*.[15] The theory of rights is not necessarily connected with an individualistic contraction of the concept of rights.[16] If one starts with an intersubjective concept of rights, the real source of error is easily identified: public discussions conducted inside the arenas of those who are immediately affected must first clarify the aspects and criteria under which differences between the experiences and living situations of (specific groups of) women and men become relevant for an equal opportunity to take advantage of individual liberties. Institutionally defined gender stereotypes must not be assumed without question. Today, these social constructions can be formed only in a conscious, deliberate fashion; they require the *affected parties themselves* to conduct public discourses in which they articulate the standards of comparison and justify the relevant aspects. Accordingly, private autonomy cannot be secured without simultaneously promoting public autonomy.

Gender identity and gender relations are social constructions that crystallize around biological differences, yet vary historically. In women's struggle for equality, one can clearly observe that the rights meant to guarantee the autonomous pursuit of a personal life project cannot be adequately formulated at all, unless the relevant aspects for defining equal and unequal treatment are convincingly articulated and justified beforehand by the affected parties themselves. The classification of gender roles and gender-related differences touches elementary layers of a society's cultural self-understanding. Radical feminism has emphasized the reflexive, fallible, and essentially contestable character of this self-understanding. Therefore, competing views about the identity of the sexes and their relation to each

---

rule is considered formal equality. . . . To women who want equality yet find themselves "different," the doctrine provides an alternative route: be different from men. This equal recognition of difference is termed the special benefit rule or special protection rule legally, the double standard philosophically. It is in rather bad odor, reminiscent . . . of protective labor laws.
CATHERINE A. MACKINNON, *TOWARD A FEMINIST THEORY OF THE STATE* 219–20 (1989).

15. *See id.* at 215–50; CAROL SMART, FEMINISM AND THE POWER OF LAW 138–59 (1989); IRIS M. YOUNG, JUSTICE AND THE POLITICS OF DIFFERENCE 97–121 (1990).

16. *See* SEYLA BENHABIB, *Feminism and the Question of Postmodernism, in* SITUATING THE SELF: GENDER, COMMUNITY AND POSTMODERNISM IN CONTEMPORARY ETHICS 203–41 (1992) (arguing against the contextualist and skeptical interpretation of political discourse on the part of poststructuralist feminism).

other must be open to public discussion. Even the feminist avant-garde does not have a monopoly on definition. Like intellectuals, spokeswomen can be sure they prejudge nothing and that they treat no one as an inferior only if all those affected have an effective opportunity to voice their demands for rights on the basis of concrete experiences of violated integrity, discrimination, and oppression. The concrete relations of recognition, mirrored in the mutual attribution of rights, always emerges from a "struggle for recognition"; this struggle is motivated by the suffering incurred by, and the passionate indignation against, concrete cases of denigration and disrespect.[17] As Axel Honneth has shown, experiences of insults to human dignity are what must be articulated in order to attest to those aspects and criteria under which equals should be treated equally and unequals treated unequally in a given context.[18] This contest over the interpretation of needs cannot be delegated to judges and officials, nor even to political legislators.

The important consequence of this, for our purposes, is the following: no regulation, however sensitive to context, can *adequately* concretize the equal right to an autonomous private life, unless it simultaneously strengthens the effectiveness of the equal rights to exercise political autonomy, that is, the right to participate in forms of political communication that provide the sole arenas in which citizens can clarify the relevant aspects that define equal status. The insight into this *connection between private and public autonomy* underlies the reservations that contemporary feminism has with regard to an instrumental model of politics oriented exclusively to results; it explains the importance that feminism places on "identity politics," that is, on the consciousness-raising effected in the political process itself.

According to this proceduralist understanding, the realization of basic rights is a process *that secures the private autonomy of equally entitled citizens only in step with the activation of their political autonomy.*

17. *See* AXEL HONNETH, STRUGGLE FOR RECOGNITION: THE MORAL GRAMMAR OF SOCIAL CONFLICTS (Joel Anderson trans., 1995).
18. *See id.*

TWO

Procedural Law and Civil Society

Interpreting the Radical Democratic Paradigm

Andrew Arato*

Jürgen Habermas has remained faithful to the heritage of Critical Theory—to the method and perspective of immanent social criticism. His concept of a "procedural legal paradigm" is fully intelligible only in the context of this background.[1] It means first and foremost enlightenment in contemporary society with a normative project in mind: the actualization of the system of rights in the fullest sense. The paradigm concept helps to reconstruct the background assumptions of two historical forms of the *Rechtsstaat,* the liberal constitutional state and the liberal democratic welfare state of the present period. With respect to the second, the goal of theory is diagnosis that should help to orient action.

Paradigms are based on the rational reconstruction of forms of consciousness, filtered and synthesized into theory. The construction of both liberal and welfare state paradigms refers to social totalities that are subjected to critique. This critique, however, is not conceived as a mere confrontation of norm and fact, ought and is, but presupposes rather that elements of rationality are already present in the two relevant types of society: that principles of justice are in part embedded in actual institutions, and actual institutions are linked up with elements of justice. Combining differentiated dimensions of validity and facticity, law and the legal order are the guarantees of the possibility of "immanent criticism."[2] Those of us who still value aspects of the project of critical theory can only applaud such a

*Professor of Sociology, New School for Social Research, New York.
1. BETWEEN FACTS AND NORMS: CONTRIBUTIONS TO A DISCOURSE THEORY OF LAW AND DEMOCRACY (1996).
2. T. W. ADORNO, *Cultural Critique and Society, in* PRISMS (1981).

forthright reintroduction of its main methodological themes on the level of legal theory.

There are, however, many unresolved problems in the conception. Most important, we do not know what exactly is the referent of the procedural or radical democratic paradigm. We can be sure that Habermas is not proposing a structuralist theory in which there is complete historical discontinuity and normative incommensurability between epistemic formations.[3] Although the term "paradigm" is taken from Thomas Kuhn's *Structure of Scientific Revolutions,* the model Habermas actually uses is clearly a developmental one in the tradition of German Idealism. Each paradigm seeks to encompass the previous one whose critique plays an important role in new paradigm construction. The welfare state model incorporates the stress on subjective autonomy and the institutions of the constitutional state; similarly the procedural model seeks to continue, if in a reflective and critical manner, the welfare statist attempt to balance formal legal equality with greater factual equality. Thus in a sense we do know what the procedural paradigm is all about: it is equivalent to what Habermas elsewhere has called the continuation of the welfare state on a higher level of reflection (*auf höherer Reflexionsstufe*).[4]

The solution, however, seems to imply that the three paradigms are not fully parallel, or even that there is not strictly speaking a "procedural paradigm" of law. After all, the welfare state model is not simply identified as the continuation of the liberal paradigm on a "higher level of reflection." The reason why such identification would be misleading is that the legality of the welfare state, specifically the establishment of purposive forms of legal reasoning, the materialization and particularization of law, and the shift of emphasis toward the administration and the courts involve a large-scale (even if not complete) replacement of the hypothetical programs, the formal and general laws, and the legislative orientation of the liberal paradigm. What is in particular unclear in Habermas's conception, however, is whether the procedural paradigm can be said to involve any new legal institutions and practices at all.

Of course, a procedural paradigm cannot be developed in a manner fully parallel to its predecessors simply because the three paradigms have different relations to time. The liberal paradigm is a matter of the past; Habermas considers all neoliberal attempts to return to it to be futile and counterproductive. The welfare state paradigm is a matter of the present, and as such it too can be empirically described, if only in an open-ended manner. The

---

3. MICHEL FOUCAULT, THE ORDER OF THINGS (1970).

4. *Die Krise des Wohlfahrstaates und die Erschöpfung utopischer Energien, in* DIE NEUE UNÜBERSICHTLICHKEIT 157 (1985).

procedural paradigm, even if some of its elements were to be found in the present, could only be a future-directed project, part of a long-term strategy of democratization. For this reason it cannot be the object of the sociology of law in the same sense as its predecessors. Such an asymmetry of course is part and parcel of the situation faced by any critical theory of society with "emancipatory intentions."

Nevertheless, Habermas does not satisfy himself with a critical project about whose eventual institutions nothing definite can be said. There are in fact two directions in which he tries to determine the specificity of the procedural paradigm. Both are linked to the idea of reflection. The liberal as well as the welfare state model represent attempts to establish private and public autonomy, whose meaning is given by the idea of democratic legitimacy and fundamental rights. Without proper reflection about the meaning of these terms, however, private and public autonomy are understood within both paradigms as a zero sum game, while democracy and constitutional rights are generally viewed in terms of potential conflict and antagonism. The process of reflection Habermas has in mind leads first and foremost to an understanding of the "co-originality" and complementarity of public and private freedom, democracy, and rights. Moreover, the liberal and welfare statist models can be said to focus on the output side of the legal system, on the two different types of laws produced. The procedural model, however, seems to focus on the interaction among democratic citizens and the input side of lawmaking involving the publics of state and civil society. Habermas sees this difference as the token of the democratic radicalism of his proposal. Thus the context for the reflection he stresses is not merely theoretical but public political interaction. Yet it is not clear what difference reflection rooted in democratic process can make for legal outcomes.

There is a second sense in which the procedural paradigm can be said to involve self-reflection. The liberal paradigm understood itself as the rule of law, as the only form of the actualization of the system of rights. Similarly, the welfare paradigm, as we see in T. H. Marshall's classical synthesis, was understood by its advocates as the full actualization of the system of rights in a set of entitlements, social rights, without which civil and political rights remained privileges of economic and educational elites.[5] The advocates of neither paradigm were aware of the ambiguities of each from the point of view of securing autonomy. The defenders of the first were unaware of the role of private power in producing the unfreedom of those formally entitled to have rights; the partisans of the second were equally blind to the consequences of intervention by public power. Habermas does not associate the procedural paradigm with a new set of rights. He links it instead to a

5. *Citizenship and Social Class,* in CLASS, CITIZENSHIP AND SOCIAL DEVELOPMENT (1965).

full development of the implications of the system of rights inherited from liberalism and the welfare state.

To be sure, the welfare state already inherited liberal rights of personhood, of communication, and of political rights as well as due process. The difference the procedural paradigm is supposed to make in this context is based on the promise that the democratic process of reflection it promotes, with the implied participation of all specifically concerned, would allow the adoption and application of precisely the social rights necessary for the functioning of all rights. This process of reflection would help the legislature, the administration, and the courts to identify and protect the "context-sensitive thresholds" where the provision of social rights providing the material prerequisites of private autonomy do not yet establish entitlements and rights claims that might damage, through new forms of dependence and control, the autonomy rights they were meant to protect.[6] Such is one way to understand Habermas's argument that the procedural paradigm cannot be distinguished by a legal form in the way that the earlier paradigms have privileged formal and material law respectively, but rather by a context-related choice among legal forms with the aim of securing the system of rights.[7] Thus in this understanding the new paradigm would be distinguished by the application of procedures of democratic reflection to the determination of the meaning of rights. The substantive gain of a radical democratic procedure would be, in other words, a more coherent and more consistent establishment and application of fundamental rights.

But from another point of view this supposed radicalism might still be purchased at the cost of a possible conservatism that involves a moderation of Habermas's own earlier critique of welfare state "juridification." A decade and a half ago, using the distinction between law as institution and law as medium, Habermas pointed to new forms of law in the areas of school policy and family law that allow the autonomous self-application of legal norms by concerned constituencies. Thus, in the two contexts at least, bureaucratically applied welfare state types of legalization or juridification (*Verrechtlichung*) disruptive of horizontal solidarity and local autonomy could be avoided.[8] The distinction is rejected in the current work, and the examples are gone.[9] It may very well be that Habermas is right in doing away with a distinction that implies that socially integrative norms ("law as institution") and laws of the political system ("law as medium") are different sets of laws. All modern law integrates society, and arguably at least all laws are products of the political system. But with this said we cannot eliminate

6. *See id.*
7. *See supra* note 1 at 410.
8. 2 THEORY OF COMMUNICATIVE ACTION 356–73 (1987).
9. *See supra* note 1 at 562, fn. 48.

the question whether there are in the epoch of the welfare state legal forms that could be privileged elements of a future legal paradigm, just as the elements of materialized law noticed already by Max Weber[10] could become more central in the welfare state. Even if enacted through the political system, the elements of school and family law once mentioned by Habermas could anticipate the unfolding of a legal order in which self-regulation by those concerned could in part take the place of both administrative regulation and deregulation.

They are in fact so regarded by theorists of "reflexive law," from whom Habermas has sought to distance himself.[11] Teubner's stress to be sure was always on soft forms of legal regulation of *economic* actors that would be compatible with their self-regulation, the application of procedures to procedures of bargaining and management. This is what he called not only reflexive but also procedural law, in the sense of the self-application of legal procedures.[12] Exactly in this sense, which does involve specific legal forms, the importance of procedural law has been noticed by earlier analysts of welfare state juridification like Marshall and Unger.[13] Interestingly, these two theorists considered procedural law as typified by collective bargaining regulation an early and inadequate form of the materialization of law, because procedural law remained fundamentally formal (Unger) and because it could not guarantee the desirable level of the equality of outcomes (Marshall). And indeed collective bargaining arrangements in themselves could not establish welfare state protections that would be even relatively inclusive. Habermas's suspicions concerning an elevation of procedural law to a replacement of welfare state juridification may have something to do with this state of affairs.[14]

---

10. II ECONOMY AND SOCIETY (1978).

11. *Cf.* Guenther Teubner's earlier essay *Substantive and Reflexive Elements in Modern Law*, *in* 17 LAW AND SOCIETY REV. 2 (1983), and *After Legal Instrumentalism? Strategic Models of Post-regulatory Law*, *in* DILEMMAS OF LAW IN THE WELFARE STATE (Guenther Teubner ed., 1986). I believe Habermas's reservations concerning Teubner's work have to do above all with rejection of the autopoietic garb in which these the latter's came to be represented.

12. Strictly speaking, Teubner's reflexive law is not self-referring in the sense of being literally applied to itself. Some constitutional rules regulating constitutional law making like amendment rules are fully self-referring. Constitutional provisions that establish a constitutional court, which would have to be interpreted by the same court, is a second relevant example. These may be the purest form of reflexive law. See H. L. A. HART, *Self-referring Laws*, *in* ESSAYS IN JURISPRUDENCE AND PHILOSOPHY (1983). On the distinction between reflection and reflexivity, *see* NIKLAS LUHMANN, *The Self-thematization of Society*, *in* THE DIFFERENTIATION OF SOCIETY (1982).

13. *See* LAW IN MODERN SOCIETY 194–96, 212 (1976).

14. In 1981, however, he considered the procedural type of welfare-state regulation less ambiguous from the point of view of guaranteeing freedom than top down substantive intervention. *See* 2 THEORY OF COMMUNICATIVE ACTION 361–62 & esp. 364 (1987).

But what if the elements of procedural law to which we can point today were anticipations of arrangements that could become far more general than procedural interpretation of labor contracts, which in any case carries little hope of equalization in the current period of economic globalization? Habermas points to such a possibility when he discusses the role of public hearings monitoring administrative decisions, compensating for a failing system of the classical separation of powers. Instead of seeking to inhibit the administration through formal and general laws, which is no longer possible, instead of proposing that the legislature mandate the specific contents of interventions, which cannot be done, Habermas is here defending a model of bringing the procedures of administrative activity under the control of public procedures on the output side, where those concerned are able to discern and call to attention the unwanted side effects of intervention.[15]

Granted, again we are only given by Habermas a rather isolated example of what could be construed as a new legal form of a new legal paradigm, and even that unintentionally. But the discussion of judicial review, as András Sajó shows[16] can provide us with additional materials. As he argues, following Habermas's own discussion, the vast expansion of quasi-legislative activity of constitutional courts can be itself seen as a form of juridification of the epoch of the welfare state, even if at times, especially in the beginning, judicial interventions sought to interfere with the establishment of welfare state policy. As in the case of applying the vague, blanket standards (*Generalklauseln*) typical for all legal instrumentalism,[17] constitutional court judges today in the United States and Germany at least rely on interpretive principles that leave significant latitude for the introduction of particular judicial philosophies and political intentions. Here too the materialization of law has by now become ambiguous, on the verge of weakening the legitimacy of constitutionalism itself. And here too one can show the futility of any return to a self-imposed model of judicial passivity where a tradition of active constitutional review has been established. Thus it makes sense to argue, as Habermas seems to, that constitutional courts can only be controlled through processes of public reflection about their role and concerning their decisions. The question is whether such public control can be given a legal form (as the Teubner conception might imply) or whether we must be content in this context with the diffuse influence of weak publics as Habermas seems to maintain.

15. *See supra* note 1 at 440–41.
16. ANDRÁS SAJÓ, *Constitutional Adjudication in Light of Discourse Theory, in* 17 CARDOZO L. REV. 4–5, pt. I, 1193ff. & ch. 17, this vol.
17. For a good recent discussion, *see* WILLIAM SCHEUERMAN, BETWEEN THE NORM AND THE EXCEPTION ch. 4 & passim (1994).

We should certainly welcome Habermas's interpretation of democratic procedure as the source of legal legitimacy, not in terms of a state-centered theory as in liberalism and republicanism both, but in terms of a decentered, civil society–based conception that focuses on the forms of communication between the unrestricted but weak societal and necessarily restricted but relatively strong political public spheres. I consider it remarkable that exactly at the time when Habermas has redefined his notion of public in this sense,[18] many others are still trying to reinvent his earlier theory under the heading of "strong publics" or seek to interpret the idea of "deliberative democracy" in a way that would simply dress up a variety of democratic fundamentalisms in Habermasian terms. Habermas of course has for a long time sought to distance himself from all sociologically primitive assumptions about any formalized politics that gravitate either toward authoritarian attacks on parliamentarianism or incoherent utopias or both. The theory of civil society, in part derived from his own earlier work, now gives him a radical democratic alternative compatible with his normative assumptions and the challenge of complexity.[19]

The conception of the civil public sphere is central to contemporary prospects of democratization, yet it helps to avoid such politically irrelevant illusions as the conversion of state policy making into a fully deliberative process, or the radical democratization of all spheres of life. As for Talcott Parsons, for Habermas too procedural law becomes above all law "of" (even if not created by) an autonomous civil society, just as formal law is oriented to the autonomy of the market economy, substantive law is oriented to the freedom of the state to intervene.[20] A procedural understanding of constitutional politics would in this conception mean the influence of "weak" but formally unrestricted civil publics on processes of constitutional lawmaking and interpretation that would have the task of democratically "controlling" all instances capable of exercising a part of the constituent power, especially judicial review of legislation. Precisely to the degree one does not claim

18. One that comes very close to the civil society-oriented perspective worked out by Jean Cohen and myself, to which he generously refers. See *supra* note 1 at 367–70 and JEAN COHEN & ANDREW ARATO, CIVIL SOCIETY AND POLITICAL THEORY (1992).

19. See *supra* note 1 at ch. 8.

20. In my view, such a law would also be "for" civil society, if it were incorporated in constitutions in order to limit and regulate the associations, publics, and even initiatives of civil society as traditional constitutionalism has regulated the state. Such a limit may be the requirement of open membership, internally democratic procedures, publicity of deliberations, accountability of officeholders, financing rules, specific relationship to state institutions, etc. But in this case as well as the state, limits can empower institutions both by guaranteeing their internal and external legitimacy and by pinpointing the channels where they can regularly and openly exert public influence on policy making.

constituent or legislative *power* for the civil public, its critical activity and political *influence* can be made legitimate within a constitutional democracy.

Two obvious objections can be made against this conception. First, it may only describe what we in the United States already have, and thus would be hard to represent as a critical theory.[21] Second, and more important, a democratic model relying on only weak publics may be too weak and may not even amount to a politics to the extent that influence cannot reliably contribute to the production of binding decisions.

In answer to the second objection, one inevitably answers the first as well. The concept of the public sphere should be seen as a double one, distinguishing not only organizationally but in terms of their very structure between civil publics and the publics of formal political institutions: parliaments and courts (and possibly the administration?). The latter, the formal political publics, produce binding decisions and in this sense are indeed "strong" publics. They nevertheless involve social, formal, and temporal limits to open-ended communication. In parliaments and courts, for example, only persons with a specific status can speak, following procedural and temporal limitations. Given the pressures of decision such limits do not exclude and may indeed preserve the possibility of deliberation.[22] But the deliberation of such bodies remains restricted; the publicity of formal political institutions is normatively deficient. From the point of view of a discourse theoretical understanding of democratic legitimacy, such restriction of communication can be justified only to the extent that we can see formal political publics as particularly sensitive outposts within the structure of the state to processes of public communication in civil society. The extent of such sensitivity is, however, an empirical matter, one very much open, in my view, to institutional design. Thus the politics of civil society should be seen as a dualistic one, aiming at both expansion of the civil public that can influence state actors and the redesign of state institutions.[23] In no really existing democracy can these mutually dependent tasks be said to be complete.

The current revival of constitutional discussion and constitutional poli-

---

21. *See* BARRY FRIEDMAN, *Dialogue and Judicial Review,* in 91 MICH. L. REV. 577ff. (1993).

22. Paradoxically, the exclusion of the public at large can foster the deliberative character of such bodies. Constitutional assemblies may be a case in point, as the instructive contrast between the Philadelphia Convention and the Constituent Assembly of 1789–91 demonstrates. ANDREW ARATO, *Forms of Constitution Making and Theories of Democracy,* in 17 CARDOZO L. REV. 2 (1995). For a somewhat different view, JON ELSTER, *Constitutional Bootstrapping in Philadelphia and Paris,* in CONSTITUTIONALISM, IDENTITY, DIFFERENCE AND LEGITIMACY (Michel Rosenfeld ed., 1994).

23. *See* CIVIL SOCIETY AND POLITICAL THEORY as well as HABERMAS, BETWEEN FACTS AND NORMS 370ff.

tics, a veritably international phenomenon, has put institutional design and redesign on the agenda almost everywhere. In the United States at least, legitimation problems of judicial review play a major (though no longer the exclusive) role in this discussion.[24] Unlike in Germany, it yet has to be noticed in this country that criticisms of judicial activism that may come from all political directions have to do with the dysfunctions of the welfare state paradigm on the constitutional level. Nevertheless, in line with Habermas's own interpretation of his theory, one might point to the extensive discussion itself as the way the civil public seeks to influence and bring within new limits the constitutional politics of judges. Such a model might be called the continuation of the activist practice of judicial review on a "higher level of reflection," involving no new legal institutions or procedures.

The project of the dualistic politics of civil society, however, should be somewhat more ambitious in the area of constitutional law. Public discussion and criticism can and should aim at influencing the pattern of decisions, but also the institutional matrix within which the decisions take place. In the latter context, the recent focus of the American discussion on constitutional revision and the need to change amendment procedures, which from a formal point of view represent the only democratic check on the constituent powers of judicial review, is especially important.[25] So are ongoing discussions concerning constitution making and redesign in Eastern and Western Europe, Latin America, and Africa.[26] In many cases constitution making is only part of catching up with what others already have. But an increasing number of discussions are about legal issues and institutions that can no longer be adequately conceptualized within either the liberal or the welfare state paradigms. Not only constitutional review but also the question of social rights and social bargaining fall into this group. So do questions of an ecological constitutionalism. Discussions of electoral rules and minority rights, finally, raise important questions about inclusion in the formal and civil publics, respectively, and as such give a procedural form to redistributive questions. In all these areas there are institutional choices and the possibility of new design combinations. It is in this sense that potential developments in constitutional law give us some good reasons to believe that the procedural paradigm can develop its own legal materi-

24. ANDREW ARATO, *Slouching Toward Philadelphia?* in 3 CONSTELLATIONS 2 (1996).

25. See especially B. ACKERMAN, *We the People* (1991), a text that Habermas reads in a somewhat tendentious manner; and SANFORD LEVINSON, ed., RESPONDING TO IMPERFECTION (1995); ARATO, *supra* note 24. My own criticisms of Ackerman do not have anything to do with the "vitalism" that Habermas seems to notice in his text.

26. ULRICH PREUSS, CONSTITUTIONAL REVOLUTION (1995); GIOVANNI SARTORI, COMPARATIVE CONSTITUTIONAL ENGINEERING (1994).

als and that it need not become entirely dependent on the materials of its predecessors.[27]

Of course, with this said we need not, unreflectively, put procedural law in a privileged position of a new paradigm with respect to other legal resources. We may still say with Habermas that what would be above all characteristic of the procedural paradigm is that it would rely on democratic reflection to choose among *three* types of legal forms: formal, substantive, and procedural. But on reflection we should see that procedural law now has a double status in the conception, unlike that of formal and materialized law. It represents not only a new form of law but also a new framework within which the choice of legal forms is to be made. For this reason it is a good idea to insist on the "reflexivity" of procedural law.

It should be stressed that the idea of procedural law is somewhat flattened to mean only democratic procedure as such, even the vastly expanded democratic procedure Habermas has in mind. While perhaps deficient from the point of view of democratic theory, the idea of reflexive law is more complex: the application of procedures to procedures, or the stimulation of the transformation of procedures by establishing new, metaprocedures.[28] Reflexive law in this sense represents a legal form especially suited to combine three advantages: nonintrusive, postregulatory regulation, a renewed formal structure preserving the integrity of the legal medium, and the normatively desirable combination of freedom and regulation. Keeping these desiderata in mind, constitutional lawmaking, redesign, and interpretation may very well represent reflexive legality par excellence.

Constitutionalism of course reinforces by definition the liberal rule of law. Whatever we may say about the eclipse of formal and general rules, the domain of secondary rules represents an important preserve within which they have survived, and should survive in the future as well. Constitutionalism is not, however, merely the extension and generalization of the rule of law, but its reflexive version: the procedures of the rule of law dedicated to the preservation of the rule of law. We know that the idea of the rule of law was originally ambiguous, and could be interpreted in terms of the rule of the lawmaking body that exercises sovereign powers.[29] The extension of the idea of the rule of law rather than men, initially directed against

---

27. Habermas welcomes the current opening up of constitutional politics but does not integrate it into his conception. *See* BETWEEN FACTS AND NORMS 390–91 where he refers to the writings of Dieter Grimm and Ulrich Preuss.

28. To Habermas such reflexive law is not the specific legal form to which the procedural paradigm refers; indeed he seems to think of this form as representing only a "more realistic" type of welfare state regulation.

29. FRANZ NEUMANN, *The Change of the Function of Law in Modern Society, in* THE DEMOCRATIC AND AUTHORITARIAN STATE ([1937] 1957).

the arbitrary rule of the executive power, could not be reliably guarded against turning into its opposite: the rule of a specific body of men, this time the legislature. The problem could be solved only by constitutionalism, since it relocates sovereign power on a metapolitical level and binds both legislature and executive to the constitution.[30] Similarly, it could be argued, welfare state intervention on behalf of rights generates a form of political power that is as great a potential threat to rights as was parliamentary sovereignty. Just as the extension of the formal structures of the rule of law can be solved only on the metapolitical constitutional level, it may be the case that the extension of the substantive goals of the welfare state beyond thresholds that have recently emerged can be achieved only on this higher level. At issue is not the constitutionalization of social rights. We need to explore the extent to which constitutional redesign can also help to deal with policy problems that have become intractable in the context of both liberal and welfare state paradigms. In other words, we must investigate the possibility of a constitutionalism that would serve the material goals of the welfare state by establishing the limits of bureaucratic intervention and creating incentives for self-regulation.

Of course, constitutional politics is legitimate today only as democratic procedure, and this means in a constitutional democracy that democratic procedures are applied to democratic procedures themselves. It is to Habermas's credit that he brought our attention to the nonformalized "procedures" of a democratic civil society in the process of the constitution of democracy.[31] But we need to pay equal attention to the formalized procedures of the political system, both as the target of civil influence and as the framework within which the rules of a future procedural paradigm must be enacted.

---

30. *See* F. Hayek, The Constitution of Liberty ch. 12 (1960).
31. See *supra* note 1 at 444–45.

THREE

Law and Undecidability

Toward a New Vision of the Proceduralization of Law

Jacques Lenoble†

I. INTRODUCTION: LEGAL THEORY AND THE RADICALIZATION OF DEMOCRACY

In the model of the liberal state, legal formalism and belief in the rationality of free citizens were the keys to social rationality. With the emergence of the welfare state and its reliance on interventionism, the role of administration has evolved in nonformalistic ways. Rationality became a matter of expertise.

Today, new cracks in the grand edifice of modern reason are reappearing almost daily, and these come in addition to the undermining wrought earlier by the demonstration of the radical finitude of all human knowledge. With these new problems, a new paradigm of the state is emerging. The increasing complexification of the environment seems to make norms flexible, fluid, and unsure. Formal criteria are increasingly replaced by procedural and pragmatic methods. Without sinking into relativism, we must modify our procedures to reorganize an irreducible "indetermination" in the most rational way.

As we assess the theoretical framework put forward by Jürgen Habermas,

*Professor of Law and Director of the Center for Philosophy of Law, Université Catholique de Louvain, Belgium.

†Translated from the original French by Richard Perry, Assistant Professor of Social Ecology, University of California at Irvine, and former fellow of the Center for Philosophy of Law of the University of Louvain. Professor Perry acknowledges the invaluable assistance of Catherine St. Clair, a 1993 graduate of the University of California at Irvine.

This paper is a new and shorter version of an earlier essay. I would like to thank Louis-Leon Christians, member of the Center for Philosophy of Law of the University of Louvain, for his most helpful work on this new text; see also for new developments, J. LENOBLE, DROIT ET COMMUNICATION (1994).

we must wonder whether or not he has failed to meet the challenge of these contemporary developments by having remained so devoutly committed to his "unitary" vision of the three "worlds"—the objective world, the social world, and the subjective world—which are presupposed by human beings as the constitutive horizon of their discourse.

This question touches every aspect of Habermas's vision of law and democracy. Indeed, it is precisely because he remains so bound to the classical conceptions of democracy and law that Habermas has failed to recognize the profound transformations that we cannot ignore today if we are to confront the growing crisis of political representation in Western liberal democracy.

The classical theory of democracy was based on the idea of a possible guaranty of the rationality of state actions, built on a twofold distinction between right and good and between justification (legislative function) and application of law (administrative and judicial functions). This theory of rational guaranty remained even in a welfare state context but now becomes a focus of controversy.

Democracy is facing a new transition: the organization of the radical uncertainty of present normativity. This reorganization of normative complexity, which will cut into the classical distinctions cited above, will be founded more and more on a method of regulated negotiation. The radical evolution of the judicial signifies this new rationality. Based on an apprehension of rational uncertainty, judicial review becomes more pragmatic and associates new actors to its mission. A new paradigm is emerging and is progressively replacing both the earlier paradigm of formalist legal theory linked to the classical liberal state and that of the substantive, policy-oriented view of law associated with the welfare state: the paradigm of procedural law.

A major expression of this orientation is constituted by Habermas's works. Habermas's hypothesis of the proceduralization of law constitutes a clear advance in democratic rationality when compared to the two available traditional models for a modern legal order, the model of liberal formalist legalism and the model of the welfare state. However, there are numerous possible interpretations of the proceduralization of law, and the choice among these interpretations is tied to specific, fundamental philosophical commitments. For the purposes of this essay, it is the interpretation that Habermas himself has given to the procedural model of law and to the conception of rationality underlying it which calls for a sharply critical reassessment.

A major import of Habermas's vision of the proceduralization of law is expressed in his claim that the new paradigm he advocates is capable of adequately embodying precisely the conception of law and politics toward which we are bound to be guided by a philosophically rigorous understanding of the limits of modern reason. Given such claims, it is therefore no less than fair that we inquire, first of all, whether Habermas's thesis does in fact provide us with a more profound understanding of the recent changes in Western society and, second, whether his vision is really capable of answering the numerous critiques of the modern rationalist project that have dominated the intellectual debates of the past quarter century. Furthermore, we must ask how Habermas's thesis proposes to meet the double challenge to the classic conceptions of law that both the United States and Europe are confronting today: (a) how to regulate the market and the administrative apparatus of the bureaucratic state and (b) the question of identity and the consequences of multiculturalism for the rule of law in our modern societies.

Surely, Habermas's project is itself also motivated by a keen awareness of the need to get beyond the classical visions of law that have characterized the liberal state and the welfare state. But is the theory of law he proposes really adequate to the stakes currently at issue?

In my view, the answer to this question must be a negative one. Furthermore, the inadequacy of the conception of law proposed by Habermas is felt not only at a theoretical level; it also entails very real practical consequences. From the descriptive as well as from the normative perspective, it is my belief that Habermas utterly fails to grasp the importance of the stakes involved in the necessary transformation of the legal model of the welfare state. Let me briefly elaborate here the twofold thesis that I will develop later: (a) I share Habermas's view that the recent developments in our Western democracies call for the emergence of a new, third paradigm of law and that this paradigm must be grounded in a better understanding of the limits of human reason. Further, I agree with Habermas that this new legal paradigm must be conceptualized in procedural terms. A procedural approach signifies the withdrawal of the traditional theories on the democratic rationalization of the society. It is more respectful of the radical limits of human reason. The most recent researches (analytic or hermeneutic) have pointed out that practical reason is replacing theoretical reason, obviating the drive to determine the keys of a certainly valid knowledge. A new theory of communication whose purpose is to redefine pragmatic rational constraints has progressively replaced the ancient theory of knowledge. (b) However, it is Habermas's own interpretation of the proceduralization of law that appears to me to be mistaken. This error derives from his flawed, overly idealized conception of communicative action, more specifically, from his excessively idealized view of speech act theory. Habermas's works fail to perceive the pragmatical limits of reason. Beyond the normative pretensions bound to a pragmatic idealization, a second dimension must be found: the pragmatic "undecidability" of the interlocutor intention. This misunderstanding of linguistic exchange is reflected in the conception of law that Habermas advocates; it is because he is mistaken about linguistic action in general that Habermas's theory proves inadequate to the task of accounting for the practical logical work in legal judgment. This inadequacy in his concept of law then itself leads Habermas to a view of proceduralization that fails to appreciate the stakes that are in fact at issue today.

Because he focuses on a view of proceduralization that is almost exclusively "cultural," based only on a strengthening of the public space, Habermas fails to accommodate within his theoretical model the crucial transformations in administrative law and in the legal regulation of the market that are already in progress elsewhere.

To elucidate this twofold inadequacy of Habermas's theory, my analysis unfolds in three stages. In the first stage (section I), I address the fundamental philosophical arguments that underlie Habermas's position and seek to show what is problematic about them. Then (in section II), I show how Habermas's philosophical confusion is reflected in his theory of law and, more precisely, in his concept of legal judgment (in the distinction between justification and application), and in his view of the role of the constitutional judge. Finally (in section III), I show how the inadequacies of Habermas's theory of law lead to corresponding inadequacies in his conception of the proceduralization of law and, ultimately, to the inadequacies in the vision of deliberative democracy to which it is tied. At the same time, I will take the opportunity to sketch the main ideas of a more satisfactory conception of the proceduralization of law and of the state.

The paradigm of proceduralization is not univocal. If the Habermasian model makes up for a lot of inadequacies of the Luhmannian functionalist model, it fails to move beyond formalism and remains bound to the classical idealization of human reason. Our thesis expounds a cognitive model of proceduralization: to reinforce the role of the public space is not enough; it is necessary to develop a new cognitive "apparatus" to perceive complexity and new structures of review, to make up for the insufficiencies of a too simple public space resort.

II. LAW AND THE UNDECIDABILITY OF LANGUAGE: THE PHILOSOPHICAL AMBIGUITY OF JÜRGEN HABERMAS

Habermas's conception of the theory of law and democracy is utterly linked to his underlying philosophical commitments. Thus any serious critique of his vision must necessarily take careful account of the philosophical arguments on which his legal and political analyses are grounded. This is all the more the case because the arguments that are traditionally advanced against Habermas so often misunderstand the "subtlety" of his philosophical positions. Furthermore, Habermas has developed his analyses very much in view of the classical formulations put forward by his deconstructionist critics; by this, I mean that his "rationalism" does not in fact exhibit the sort of naïveté to which his critics too often reduce his views in their characterizations. In my opinion, if we are to understand precisely where the philosophical weaknesses in Habermas's reasoning lie, and if we are to understand to what extent they account for the weaknesses in his legal theory and in his theory of the changes our model of democracy calls for, I will need to review briefly the essential elements of his legal thinking. This summary will allow us to discern how his positions grow out of the theory of language that Habermas has developed. I will then be able to disentangle the confusion that, in my view, characterizes Habermas's underlying philosophical assumptions.

A. *Law and Modernity*

Habermas's views on law can be summarized in four points. The first three points concern the principal legal consequences of the great historical transformation that gave birth to modern society. Modern law can only be understood in the general historical context/background of the "modernization" and "rationalization" of our societies, because the rationality of law and the rationalization of society are closely linked to one another. Because they have relied on a defective conception of the rationalization of society, the theoretical "models" that until now have presided over the organization and functioning of modern law have become quite obsolete. Habermas believes that a new paradigm is required, one that is founded on a better understanding of the demands of the modern project of reason. It is to the introduction of this new paradigm that Habermas devotes the fourth point of his vision of law.

1. First, modernity signifies the loss of the traditional mode of legitimation (grounded in the conformity with a common "social ethos") and its replacement by two other modes for the integration of social behaviors. The first of these modes is "communicative"; the second is "systemic." The communicative mode implies that the norms established to resolve conflicts between individuals or groups can no longer draw their validity solely from agreements arrived at by communication among the members of the group. The rationality of the norm is no longer "substantial" but "procedural" since it derives from a respect for the argumentative rules that define the discussion. The systemic mode of behavioral integration means that social integration, in the "technical" spheres of material production (i.e., economic activity) and of the material organization of the collectivity (i.e., administrative activity), will henceforth be carried out autonomously within each of the two spheres by the operation of a univocal code. These codes are, respectively, money in the economic subsystem and power in the sub-

system of state administration. The internal regulation of these two "subsystems" will thus be able to be assured in the most efficacious manner possible, without being subjected to the hazards and indeterminacy of an ever-precarious, intersubjective communicative exchange.

This new communicative "nature" requires, according to Habermas, a twofold modification of our understanding of law. The first of these shifts concerns the question of the law's validity. From now on, natural law theory and classical legal positivism are equally to be rejected. Both natural law and positive law thinkers fail to understand that law must derive its validity from the fact of its "legality" alone, and therefore that the link law maintains with the question of its legitimacy must be conceived as exclusively procedural, or, to be more precise, it must be conceived in terms of communicative action. The law is only legitimate insofar as its development and elaboration result from an equal participation of all citizens in the discussion that leads to its adoption by the polity. This is what the principles of democracy mean for the fields of law and politics, namely, a principle of discussion as a precondition for the rationality of any discussion aimed at reaching consensus on norms. Modern law, as the price of its legitimacy, must therefore ensure respect for the fundamental rights of individuals. This is a consequence of the fundamental right to participate in the public debate over the justification of norms. This consequence follows also from the principles of liberty and equality, which are the necessary correlates of the fundamental right of public participation.

To adopt such a communicative interpretation of the conditions of legitimacy of modern law will also, as Habermas maintains, enable us to recognize the error of the functionalist analyses put forward by Niklas Luhmann and Gunther Teubner. Under democracy, a strategic attitude toward legal rules has as its condition of possibility another attitude, one of participation in the discussion that has led to the adoption of the rule—for each individual is at the same time both subject to the legal rule and its participant-author. In regard to these two aspects of legal subjectivity, each of which in democratic theory presupposes the other, rational attitudes can be different (either strategic or communicative) without being mutually contradictory.

But the transformation brought about by modernity in our understanding of the legitimacy of norms requires still a second modification, in this case in the organization of particular legal procedures. In contrast to a posttraditional morality that would imply a form of justification subordinate to a potentially interrupted process of discussion, the law must ensure its own effective application to best assure successful social integration. It must therefore structure its own institutionalization so as to generate collectively constraining decisions whose application is not at the mercy of the ethical or moral motivations of its subjects. This fact, Habermas explains, provides an explanatory principle for the distinguishing characteristics of the modern state.

2. The concept of communicative reason that permits Habermas to define the nature of modern law, when considered from another angle, also helps to articulate the logical distinction that differentiates the legislator's discourse from the discourse of the judge. It is because legal theory has not correctly understood the concept of reason under modernity that it has never clearly perceived, Habermas says, the logical specificity of the operation of applying a legal rule.

From a communicative reason perspective, Habermas can reject the classical vision of a judge who is trapped within the sterile binary choice presented by positivist legal theory, that is, between a syllogistic formalism on the one hand and a skeptical "realism" on the other. Beyond its insurmountable indeterminacy at the semantic level, the discourse of adjudication is constrained by a *pragmatic* logic that obliges the judge to justify her reasoning in a manner quite different from the reasoning of the legislator. Therefore, according to Habermas, the "discourse of application" of a legal rule possesses a specific rationality of its own that makes it impossible to reduce it to the legislator's "discourse of justification." Whatever one may think of the ultimate truth of the Legal Realist critique, the pragmatics of judicial discourse allow us to bring to view its underlying integrational presuppositions that validate—though now on the basis of quite different arguments—the traditional intuition of jurists according to which the justification and the application of a legal rule are not simply two rational operations of the same nature. I will elaborate later on Habermas's characterization of the rational constraints that are specific to adjudication.

3. A similar line of reasoning leads Habermas to reinterpret those analyses of the role of the constitutional judge which currently prevail in both German and American constitutional doctrine. I will later elaborate on Habermas's view in order to show its limitations. For now, let me simply recall Habermas's basic position regarding the "neorepublican" and "communitarian" analyses put forward by certain leading American constitutional scholars, most notably by Frank Michelman. Having failed to grasp the complexity of the form of communicative rationality that is specific to the "disenchanted" normative discourse of modernity, the communitarians are unable to imagine any normative framework for politics and law other than that of the premodern, Aristotelian model of the legal subject's unreflective sense of identification with and belonging to a community inscribed within a collectively shared and lived ethical tradition. To put forward such a vision as a serious proposal is to ignore not only the irreducible ethical pluralism of modern societies but also to forget the differentiation between law (politics) and morality that has developed as an integral aspect of modernity. This forgetting results, Habermas constantly empha-

sizes, in an unjustifiably hypertrophied role for the constitutional judge in Michelman's "republican" vision, which is accompanied by a misconception of the role of moral argument in the legal and political discourse of a democracy, as it should be understood. I will take up this argument in some detail later. For now, we simply need to bear in mind that for Habermas the discourse of the constitutional judge must always be thought of in light of the distinction between application and justification, and that this distinction must define the framework for all judicial activity, even where the judge is acting to review the enactments of the legislator for their conformity with the principles of constitutional democracy.

4. What Habermas calls the paradigm of the proceduralization of law can be deduced in its entirety from the preceding discussion. For Habermas, the two paradigms of law that have been predominant in Western democratic societies up to now—the formalist paradigm of liberal law and the policy-driven legal paradigm of the welfare state—remain fettered to an inadequate conception of modern rationality. Of course, Habermas acknowledges that each of these paradigms has in its own way attempted to rationalize modern society and to promote its own version of the values of liberty and equality that distinguish the democratic project. But the model of rationalization that is implicit to both of them rests on an incorrect and reductionist vision of rationality. Rational action is conceptualized from the beginning solely on the model of goal-directed rational action, and it is thus marked by an utter misappreciation of that form of rationality which is specific to communicative action.

This reductionist vision is reflected in the functions and objectives that each of these paradigms assigns to law. To respect private autonomy (in the liberal vision of law) or to want to create the conditions of a real equality for free and autonomous subjects (in the project of the welfare state) are both undeniably important objectives. But they remain insufficient.

If an improvement is expected from this proceduralization of law, it is not the prospective result of a transformation of modes of regulation specific to the market or to the administrative regime[1] but rather it is in the prospect of a strengthening of citizens' means of expression and participation in the justification of the rules of law that are supposed, in quite clas-

---

1. Habermas's fundamental idea is that modern law enables subsystems such as the market and the regulatory administrative apparatus to be subordinated to the normative constraints imposed on them in a sense from the outside, that is, imposed by the law, or more precisely, imposed by the popular will as democratically expressed through procedures settled in a communicative fashion. Modern law must then be understood as that which permits the mutual articulation of the "system" and the "lifeworld" (the "system" is to be understood as made up of two subsystems, i.e., the market, which is steered through the medium of money, and the administrative apparatus, which is steered through the medium of power; contrasted to the system is the lifeworld, which is socially integrated by communication).

sical fashion, to be subsequently imposed on the "strategic" action of public and private actors. A better understanding of the role of the citizen as actor in the process of elaboration and justification of the law should lead to an improvement of the modes of participation in the cultural public space which is connected with but antecedent to political acts by the legislator. In other words, the inadequacy of law—as it has been highlighted by the emergence of the procedural paradigm of law—is essentially a problem of the public modes for the elaboration and justification of norms laid down by the legislator and not a problem in the modes of application of these norms—or in the modes of regulation linked to the application function.

In the last part of my discussion (see *infra*, section III), I will show how a conception of the proceduralization of law and deliberative democracy such as Habermas's misses not only the transformations already under way in our legal systems in the United States and in Europe but also those changes that will require a radical reinterpretation of our democratic system. In any event, before continuing my critique, I will have to locate the "cause," at the underlying conceptual or philosophical level, that has led Habermas to his "reductionist" and "idealist" misconception of the proceduralization of law. This "cause" resides in the conception of language on which Habermas has based his whole theory of law and democracy. As the preceding discussion has shown, the grand vision of modern law that Habermas has developed rests in its entirety on his concept of communicative action. This concept itself rests on a pragmatic theory of discourse, that is, on a particular interpretation of speech act theory.

B. *Two Conceptions of Idealization in Language*

Certainly at least since the end of the eighteenth century (for was it not Kant himself who best expressed it in his *Transcendental Dialectic?*), philosophy has repeatedly demonstrated the radical impotence of all human knowledge in its effort to construct a complete description of the laws of this determinate system.[2] The classic epistemological binary opposition is thereby set up which places on one side the "objective truth" of the universe's global organization, accessible only to God or to "Laplace's demon," and which places on the other side the irreducible fact of our human fini-

---

2. Recall that for Kant, this impotence was a matter not of some "factual" impossibility but rather of impossibility by virtue of "law." Kant's *idée regulatrice* did not constitute in this sense an ideal toward which one is to strive. This "ideal" was an impossibility for human knowledge; we can only know those phenomena given us in spatiotemporal experience (our intuition of the senses). The *idée regulatrice* is to be conceived as "regulating" the use of our understanding. From this point, the theory of the analogies of experience (see *infra*) follows. It is at this last level that we note the effects of the Kantian assumption of an objective world conceived as a stable and unitary system.

tude. In this classical conception, the scientist may concede that "determinist description may be inaccessible in practice, yet it serves no less as a limit condition which is to define the series of progressively more accurate descriptions."[3] But in such a context, the assumptions of determinism and of a stable, unitary organization of the universe remain "by law" the assumptions adjudged necessary for all scientific knowledge. Such necessary assumptions constitute, to adopt Kant's language, an *idée regulatrice* (regulative idea) within whose horizon of sense theoretical knowledge organizes itself.

It is precisely this supposition that is being called into question today. From the idealized model of a unitary universe that is stable and determinate in its unfolding, we must move to a conception of the universe as an unstable system whose course is indeterminate and is only "measurable" by relying on probabilistic notions, such as a roll of the dice.

This metaphor of the roll of the dice best expresses—analogically[4]—the way to think of language and law. A metaphorical image of "liars' poker" might express this sense even more succinctly. Indeed, beyond the idea of unforeseeability associated with the image of playing dice, what is important for us to highlight here is the idea of undecidability: in a poker game, one cannot know for certain whether one's partner is bluffing or telling the truth. As in a poker game, every speech act is riddled with a radical undecidability. This fact does not cast doubt on the element of idealization that accompanies all language; but it does force us to reexamine the way it has classically been understood, just as contemporary physics obliges us to reexamine Kant's formulation of the idea of a stable and unitary system that governs scientific knowledge. Despite the important advances achieved by Habermas's pragmatic turn, such a reexamination in the face of new evidence is precisely what he refuses to undertake, insofar as he remains devoutly committed to his classical conception of the presuppositions of

---

3. ILYA PRIGOGINE & I. STENGERS, LA NOUVELLE ALLIANCE 128 (1986).

4. Two comments are necessary at the start of this discussion. First, my use of the metaphor of the roll of the dice (or of the poker game) is to be handled with caution. It is purely *heuristic* and is not intended to describe adequately the precise nature either of linguistic communication or of law. Like all metaphors, this one seeks only to illustrate with the help of an expressive image the basic idea that I wish to develop, namely, that law must be reconceptualized starting from a concept of linguistic communication that takes the fact of undecidability as its foundational logic. Next, my reference to contemporary developments in theoretical physics must be interpreted in the same way. This reference permits me to present in a concrete and instructive fashion the much-needed questioning of the ideas of unity and stability on the basis of which Kant conceptualized the wager for reason and Habermas has modeled his view of linguistic communication (for Habermas, communicative action presupposes, in an ideal sense, that partners in communication come to agreement over a unique meaning). In other words, I in no way intend to posit, as it may seem that I have done by referring to scientific discourse, that legal discourse should "correspond" to a better comprehension of the "real."

reason. The Kantian notion of the wager for reason—which Habermas shares—leads to a view of linguistic communication that utterly fails to take into account its inherent undecidability. The thesis I now wish to develop derives from the profound implications of this failure. The importance for law of the idea of undecidability as illustrated by a metaphor such as gambling on a roll of the dice or in a poker game will be analyzed later (*cf. infra* section III), but what should be immediately apparent is its stark difference from the metaphor of the chess game dear to such positivists as H. L. A. Hart, or from Dworkin's chain novel metaphor.

As we have seen, the concepts of deliberative democracy and the "procedural" rationality of modern law are analyzed by Habermas starting from his foundational notion of communicative action. Communicative action is itself conceived from the start as a model type, that is, as an idealized linguistic exchange in which a hearer arrives at a yes or no response to a validity claim in a speech act that has been uttered by a speaker. For Habermas, this idealized model of a linguistic exchange—to the extent that it aims at a mutual comprehension—is informed by a quite specific logic that renders the communicative act irreducible to a merely teleological model of action oriented toward success alone.[5] This is the essential reason why Habermas has chosen to anchor his political and legal theory in a theory of language conceived as a formal, universal pragmatics. Without going into great detail here, I will need to summarize the essential elements of his theory of language to show precisely how it remains marked by a classical, idealized conception of reason.

According to Kant's theory of reason, one thing that we can observe in the scientific and moral judgments of human beings is a deployment of reason that rests on a simple wager; this is the wager for reason (which also, as we shall see, serves as evidence for the Kantian concept of the *idée regulatrice*).

The currency in which this wager for reason is supposed to cash out is made up of what Kant calls, apropos of scientific knowledge,[6] the analogies of experience: the principles of causality and reciprocal action.

Against David Hume's idea that analogy consists of a more or less approximate resemblance, Kant puts forward a concept of analogy that he

---

5. The concepts of speech and of mutual comprehension are constitutive of one another. We are able to analyze the formal-pragmatic characteristics of the attitude oriented toward mutual comprehension by taking as our model the attitudes of the parties taking part in such an interaction where, in the simplest case, one of them utters a speech act and the other, in response to this act, takes a yes or no position. JÜRGEN HABERMAS, 1 THÉORIE DE L'AGIR COMMUNICATIONNEL 297 (Jean-Marc Ferry trans., 1987).

6. According to Kant, the same mechanism, *mutatis mutandens*, informs both practical and aesthetic knowledge. See J. Lenoble, *Droit, raison pratique, et analogie: L'enjeu actuel d'une relecture de Kant*, 31 PHILOSOPHIE 213–41 (1992).

formulates with a necessary philosophical rigor. Analogy, then, is an identity of relation between dissimilar realities, the "human" reality accessible to experience and the "noumenal" reality beyond experience. Kant tells us that it is by distinguishing between two levels in this way—between the dissimilarity at the level of realities and the similarity at the level of relations—that we can hope to gain a richer, more productive philosophical understanding. The Kantian theory of the *idées regulatrices* is closely tied to this distinction between the two levels and to his redefinition of Hume's looser notion of analogy.

We cannot give any experiential content to the Ideas of Reason or derive from them any theoretical knowledge. A simple *foyer imaginaire* (imaginary locus) linked to the movement of Reason, the Idea of Reason (God, the Subject and the System) does not, for all that, lose all usefulness: it exercises a regulative function. The fact that a categorical schematization of Reason is impossible does not render impossible any meaningful discourse about it. This is precisely what conceptualizing the analogical relation has allowed us to grasp: that parallel to the dissimilarity of realities (the unconditioned and the conditioned), there does exist an identity of relation.

Surely, ever since Kant, the notion of consciousness must be considered suspect. Have we not witnessed plentiful evidence of the multiple constraints that compel us to regard the gap between consciousness and its aim toward Reason as unbridgeable? The idea of a possible correlation between consciousness and a real "object" of which it must give an account appears utterly chimerical to our contemporaries. But, as Habermas tells us, this realization does not necessarily oblige us to abandon the hypothesis of the wager for reason. Indeed, there is something else which today allows us to affirm it. Now, our understanding of reason is no longer grounded on a notion of an individual consciousness that mirrors an external objective world, but rather it is grounded on a new understanding of linguistic communication. Surely, no guarantee of the determinacy of the meaning of our speech is to be hoped for in the semantic relationship between language and the world. But this indeterminacy of meaning at the semantic level is, in a sense, made up for by a "determinability" of meaning at the pragmatic level.

In speech, partners in a conversation do effectively come to an agreement on a common validity claim under the constraint of the law of the best argument. The speaker utters a claim that he judges to be valid, and his hearer either accepts the claim or reinitiates the exchange by proposing a counterclaim. In either case it is Reason that always remains the goal. But this aim at an ultimate shared validity is no longer to be understood as grounded in the ever-illusory pretension of an individual consciousness to "represent" an external reality.

The law of the best argument plays much the same role as Kant's analogies. It expresses an identity of relation that holds within the domain of what is specifically human. Every speech act that a speaker puts forward to be accepted or rejected by a conversation partner contains an element of idealization (this is the illocutionary dimension inherent to all linguistic action). This element of idealization plays the same "cognitive" function as the "schematism" of scientific reason or the "typicality" of practical reason. This idealization is associated in Kantian theory with the analogy between the human experiential world and the suprasensible or ideal world.

Every effort to arrive at an agreement through the medium of language implicates a striving toward the ideal. This striving takes the form of a wager, a wager that offers a procedural means to arrive at a rational agreement. Although its conclusions remain always potentially subject to challenge, human argumentation is to function much as a Kantian "analogy" that cognitively produces the constitutive relations of a purely ideal model of universal consensus.

It is at this point that Habermas's paradigm shows its similarity to the Kantian paradigm, and it is here too that it reveals its similar weaknesses. Habermas at once grants too much to linguistic communication and demands too much of it. Far be it from me to deny, as the "deconstructionists" might do, the functioning of the element of idealization that is an inevitable aspect of every speech act. However, this idealization cannot be thought of as providing a model that generates, even in a simply regulative fashion, some sort of mechanism that produces rational knowledge. All communicative action, even when conceptualized as an ideal type, is so thoroughly informed by a constitutive *undecidability* that it cannot hope to yield any sort of model that offers an effective procedure. In this sense, no analogy can be drawn; the undecidability of speech acts is such that not only is knowledge of the ideal as undemonstrable as it is in Kant's theory—where the suprasensible reality is unknowable—but in communicative action, what remains equally undecidable even at the level of an ideal speech situation is the very relation that is to ratify its success.

As Kant and Habermas have correctly pointed out, the irreducible gap between the actual and the ideal must be incorporated into the wager for the ideal that is a constitutive element of every speech act. But, in addition, the wager must also take account of the internal structural undecidability of the ideal itself. Even in an ideal speech situation, there is no assurance of the success of any communicative act. This fact leads to an inversion of Habermas's model. The empirical success of an actual communicative act is not an analogical reflection of some mechanism that is operative in an ideal communicative act. To the contrary, its success is grounded in the capacity of conventionally substitutional mechanisms to ward off, insofar as they are able, the fundamental undecidability of linguistic exchanges inherent in the very nature of all speech acts. We must remember that this fact does not eliminate the structuring function played by the *foyer imaginaire* that arises from the aim toward the ideal. But we must conceive of this structuring function in relation to the fundamental undecidability that permeates not only knowledge of the ideal but also the internal structure of the ideal speech situation itself. In this sense, a fundamental indeterminacy riddles not only the semantic relations of language but also the pragmatics of discourse. This fact obliges us to modify sharply Habermas's dichotomies between consensus and compromise, between strategic action and communicative action, and between particular interests and general interests; we must also reexamine Habermas's notion of pragmatic determinacy and, with regard to law, his distinction between application and justification, as well as his ultimate conception of the proceduralization of law. But let me describe more fully Habermas's approach to the pragmatics of discourse before considering what modifications to it are called for.

Habermas's entire chain of reasoning rests on two interrelated assumptions: the first assumption concerns the necessary link between the "illocutionary" dimension of a speech act and its claim to validity; the second assumption concerns the distinction between the illocutionary act (the communicative act) and the perlocutionary act (the teleological or strategic act). The first assumption derives from the logical argument of the performative contradiction. Habermas's ethics of communication—that is to say, the constraint that results from the mere fact of respecting the logic inherent in the illocutionary act—is a simple transposition of the normative constraints that derive from the pragmatic presuppositions that operate within the simple fact of carrying out an illocutionary act. In making this transposition however, Habermas does not take into account a logical distinction that is essential here; this is the distinction between paradox and undecidability.[7]

As Pierre Livet has correctly pointed out,[8] although it is paradoxical to say "I lie," it is by no means paradoxical to say "I do not lay claim either to truth or to falsehood" or, in other words, "I am undemonstrable." Every human interchange that takes place through the medium of speech acts is affected by this sort of strictly logical undecidability. A simple example will

7. I must acknowledge here the theoretical debt I owe to the work of Pierre Livet, which has allowed me to clarify the theses that Andre Berten and I first put forward in our book DIRE LA NORME, DROIT, POLITIQUE, ENONCIATION (1990). The logic of enunciation that we developed in this book has greatly benefited from contact with Livet's notion of "pragmatic" undecidability.

8. *See Les limites de la communication, in* LES ETUDES PHILOSOPHIQUES, nn. 2–3 (1987); *Limitations Cognitives et Communication Collective, in* INTRODUCTION AUX SCIENCES COGNITIVES (Daniel Andler ed., 1992); *Des Limitations Cognitive de la Communication a ses Limites Collectives, in* PRAXIS ET COGNITION 235ff. (1992).

show this clearly.[9] When I make a promise—given that I do carry out the act that I have promised to perform—it will be impossible for anyone to decide whether I have fulfilled the promise out of respect for the commitment I have made or because I am animated by some other motive that is altogether contingent to my promise. Yet the conditions of satisfaction of the speech act constituted by my promise would imply that I fulfill my promise for the motivation of respecting the promise I have made. Habermas does not deny the semantic indeterminacy of any utterance's pretension to validity. But, in his view, this sense of semantic indeterminacy can be simply counterbalanced by bringing to light the pragmatic constraints that are always at work in human linguistic interaction. These constraints derive from the mere fact that anyone who performs an illocutionary act thereby inscribes himself within a language game that is governed by the logic of the "truth claim."

Two consequences follow from the realization that all linguistic communication is "logically" rooted in the undecidability of its link to validity. The first consequence is the communicative "wager." This is a renewed version of Donald Davidson's principle of charity. I will never obtain a sure guarantee or a positive proof that allows me to demonstrate that a communicative situation is "open" and thus that my interlocutor is respecting the rules and constraints of the language game of reasoned argumentation. The success of a speech act always rests on the impossibility of obtaining any guarantee of its success. But that is not all. The only possible logic is not one that presents a binary alternative between validity and nonvalidity. Surely every speaker presupposes his or her discourse to be justified: it is in this sense that every speech act presupposes a link to validity; that is, by virtue of its illocutionary force, it entails a claim to validity. In this sense, we see once again that there is an element of idealization immanent to every speech act, a transcendence that is immanent to the discourse itself.

However, to have said this is hardly to have gotten to the bottom of the logical properties of human discourse. Rather than aspire to an absolute and externally verifiable semantic truth, a pragmatically grounded theory simply shows us that every speaker speaks only under a nondemonstrable presupposition of this regulatory horizon of discourse. He acts "as if." This "as if" is acknowledged in the fact that a speaker can only aspire to validity.

9. This proposition calls for elaboration that would manifestly exceed the scope of the present essay. See, most notably, the above-mentioned articles by Pierre Livet. I will simply mention in passing the various degrees of undecidability that are functions of the diverse forms of communicative action. But undecidability, in a strong sense, is always at issue in speech acts. This suggests, at the level of a working hypothesis, that this undecidability is bound up with the self-referential aspect of performative acts. On this self-referentiality, *see* DIRE LA NORME.

From the simple fact of this aspiration, however, arise the pragmatic constraints that are inherent to a language game governed by procedures of reasoned argumentation.[10] This pattern of a dialectical opposition between relativism and dogmatism that then resolves itself in the critical synthesis of a relationship that is "reflective" of validity can be taken as defining the modern paradigm of reason. Habermas remains completely caught in this model, even though the very fact that he has gotten beyond the older model of the philosophy of consciousness has shed a great deal of light on the sociopolitical implications of such a paradigm.

In any case, this familiar modern dialectic no longer suffices. Habermas has not drawn all of the conclusions that follow from his intention to displace the classical model of the philosophy of consciousness in favor of his discursive model. Habermas takes into account only one of the constitutive axes of linguistic exchange—the axis of validity.[11] This axis is brought to light when we analyze the presuppositions that are evident to the speaker in the reflexivity of his relation to his utterance.

But there also exists a second axis, the fundamental asymmetry of linguistic exchange, linked to the conversational position of the hearer. It is a mistake to analyze this second position simply as a mirror image of the speaker's position, though this is an assumption common to all analyses of language that take as their point of departure the theoretical model of George Herbert Mead. In all such models, the hearer is never conceived as anything but an alter ego into whose place the speaker must project himself if he wishes to respect the constraint of intersubjectivity. Surely, this is a necessary constraint that permits us to escape the trap of dogmatism rightly denounced by Kant. But this first constraint is insufficient to account for all the implications linked to the play of intersubjectivity.

In effect, what is specific to the hearer's position is the impossibility of determining the speaker's relation to validity. I can never be certain whether one who speaks does so for some contingent personal reason or for the reason that he believes what he says. Undecidability is a consequence of the pragmatic wager itself, of the very fact of making an utterance.

It is in this sense that the logic of undecidability is pragmatic and no longer semantic. Suppose that I ask someone whom I have ordered to close the door whether he has done so because of the fact that I have ordered

10. The most important of these constraints is the one that requires that participants submit to the law of the best argument. In addition, the process of reasoned argumentation is specified according to the type of validity aimed at: truth in the case of theoretical discourse, rightness in the case of practical, political, juridical, ethical, or moral discourse, and honesty in the case of discourse about the self.

11. In this, Habermas resembles all other leading thinkers of modernity. But this is only to be expected given that the analysis of reason from the perspective of discourse is very recent.

him to do it. A confirmation from the person to whom I have addressed my order may always be interpreted as his effort to counter the anxiety manifested by my request and not as effective confirmation that he has carried out my order because of the fact that I have ordered him. Every demand for confirmation creates in itself the conditions for its own refutation. The success of any speech act (such as the order in the example just cited above) is undecidable, but the fact that it is undecidable is true.[12]

Contrary to what Habermas believes, the actual, daily success of our speech acts presupposes that one abandons the illusory belief that an idealized argumentative exchange will lead to an agreement on a unique and valid proposition. In this sense, we could say "we never *are in* agreement," but rather "we *come to* an agreement." Actual agreement can only be achieved with the help of conventional substitutes. These are conventional reference points that permit us to construct agreements. By definition, these agreements are always unstable since any recourse to conventions exposes at the same time—if we pay close attention to the logical nature of the operation—the purely conventional and precarious character of the agreement's foundations.

Here we can see once again, if we look at communicative action from a

---

12. Surely, one might object, this undecidability shows that one can never determine whether one's conversation partner is acting according to a "strategic" or a "communicative" rationality (to take up Habermas's terminology). But is it not then paradoxical to posit this "undecidability" as "true"? If the success of communicative action is undemonstrable, should we not regard this claim of undecidability as itself undecidable? Indeed, does the presupposition of a true undecidability not imply that there exists at least one successful communication, one that leads to a conclusion of undecidability? From this perspective, should we not be allowed to "wager" as much on decidability as on undecidability? And does actual communicative practice not give us any indications that would justify our betting on the decidability of a communicative act rather than on its undecidability? Surely, if we follow this line of reasoning, we might well conclude that even though the decidability of communicative action is not "demonstrable," it is certainly "arguable" once we abandon an exclusively demonstrative view of reason? This line of argument is unacceptable not so much because of Bertrand Russell's argument that a reflexive move of this sort, to apply undecidability to the proposition of undecidability itself, would be a logical error linked to a confusion of the levels of language; for the purposes of this discussion, this line of reasoning is unacceptable because it fails to grasp the shift of levels between semantics and pragmatics. I am certainly obliged to put aside as undecidable the proposition that declares the success of any speech act to be an undecidable question. But who cannot see that by the same token, I am presupposing the truth of undecidability itself? This is a pragmatic implication. To avoid a performative contradiction, I have to posit as true the statement that declares the success of any communicative act to be undecidable. We escape from the infinite regress through the pragmatic fact itself. In other words, the so-called semantic paradox that would consist of positing as true the undecidability of "all" communication is resolved pragmatically. It is for this reason that we can maintain the logical necessity of acknowledging the undecidability of the success of all communicative action, even at the level of an ideal speech situation.

certain angle, the "model" of the vanishing structure dear to contemporary physics; every agreement creates in itself the conditions of its own potential dissolution.

Next, the fact of undecidability also helps to show the inevitable "blurring" of the classical distinctions. Classical thought has always tended to treat as conceptually discrete and autonomous entities each pole of several celebrated binary oppositions: semantics is opposed to pragmatics, strategic rationality is opposed to communicative rationality, and the speaker's position is opposed to the hearer's position. The implication of undecidability is that it will be necessary in each instance to crosscut, interweave, and conjoin the two poles (see *infra* for further discussion).

Finally, undecidability leads in practice to a valorization of Habermas's ultimate objective, that is, his vision of a broadened communication and a reinforcement of the space of public debate. But I would assert that this objective implies that, contrary to Habermas, we must bring to light the precise, logical nature of human linguistic exchange. Habermas's excessively idealistic view of the idealization of discourse leads, on the contrary, to the sort of dogmatic effects that we shall see exemplified in his position on law (in his distinction between application and justification) and in his conception of the proceduralization of law and the state. It is indeed by bringing to light the purely conventional character of the substitutes by the aid of which actual agreements are arrived at that we create the most radical conditions for a potential reexamination of the social reference points on which we have heretofore relied. The ever-present potential of reinitiating the broadest possible public communication is in effect the only way to "respect" the precarious character of the purely conventional grounds of actual social agreements. This also helps us to demystify the inevitably precarious, "nondogmatizable" nature of the "conventions" with the aid of which agreements are always arrived at.[13] Furthermore, this also helps us to see to what extent the "normative" conditions of communication itself—the conditions of liberty and equality among the participants in the discussion—are conditions to respect if we intend to respect the logical consequences of the strictly conventional, and therefore precarious, character of the existing conventions. In this sense, the relativist position misses the consequences of the idealization that accompanies every speech act. I shall return to this point below.

Now that I have explored three important consequences of undecidability, let us take up once again our line of inquiry on the relationship between undecidability and idealization in linguistic action.

I am in no position to satisfy the commonsense understanding implied

---

13. Of course, the undecidability of communicative action itself implies the ever-possible elaboration of decision-making substitutes in order to counterbalance this undecidability.

by the success of any communicative act (*cf.* David Lewis's "common knowledge"). It is in this sense that we can say that communicative action functions precisely at the cost of our being unable to know whether our partners in conversation consider themselves bound by the constraints of validity.

The logic of linguistic communicative exchange requires, then, two presuppositions: first, that there is an inevitable relationship between the speaker and a claim to validity; and second, that there is an implicit or explicit acknowledgment of the impossibility of a communicative act whose success is guaranteed, even at the level of the ideal.

How are we to reconcile the apparent contradiction of these two necessary presuppositions? No doubt, one may assert that the notion of the communicative wager, or of the "as if" associated with the Kantian *idée regulatrice,* presents a synthesis of the two presuppositions. We can clearly see that this is not the case. To act as if the communication were successful still does not imply an acknowledgment of the impossibility of any guarantee of the success of a communicative action. A person who undertakes a communicative act can be likened to a scientist who cannot find any experiment that will either confirm or disconfirm his hypothesis. When we communicate through the medium of language, we must necessarily wager on a communicative act that is ever precarious because its success is never guaranteed.

Contrary to the classical idea, the new idea of truth—the inevitable horizon of our discourse—must be associated with the idea of the impossibility of guaranteeing an accord between conversation partners. Reasoned argumentation cannot assume any certainty of closure or of decidability—not only at the empirical level as in the modern theory of reason but also at the level of the ideal. All linguistic communication is irreducibly gripped by instability; the existence of some ideal guarantee can never be assumed. In the one case, we bet on the existence of a guarantee. In the other, we bet on a success that we know is never guaranteed. The nature of the bet is not the same.

Undoubtedly, the idealization of validity (the validity claim) informs every speech act, in theoretical discourse as well as in practical discourse. But this idealization no longer rests on the presupposition of an ideal agreement necessary to the postulated validity. On the contrary, we have demonstrated the undecidability of a speech act's success. What ensures its possible actual success is the specifically human resort to conventional substitutes.

It is not, then, exclusively at the "opening" stage of communication that the question of the undecidability of speech acts arises. This also means that the success of a linguistic exchange cannot be entirely determinable by rational procedures. The notion of a bet, if we take it quite seriously as being fundamentally linked to the undecidability of language, must also signify that the determination of truth, correctness, or veracity—the three

kinds of validity put into play by every "illocutionary" speech act, according
to Habermas—cannot, *even ideally*, be interpreted as rationally determinable, or therefore as an indication of the uniqueness of reason. Fundamentally, it is here that we see the need to abandon the idea of successful communication as a model of actual communication. We must therefore
invert the assumptions that Habermas has placed at the root of his conception of the idealization immanent within all linguistic communicative exchange. Undecidability calls into question this classical interpretation; we
need to regard the claim to validity and the plural character of validity as
reconcilable, even if the idea may seem counterintuitive. Undoubtedly,
each linguistic actor is inscribed within the horizon of a necessarily unique
validity. But there is nothing that logically allows one to determine that
reasoned argument, even as ideally conceived, would logically imply the
construction of a unique validity. To make any such assumption, in effect,
would be to misunderstand the undecidability of the link between validity
and the speech act.

We are now better prepared to show explicitly the gap that this notion
of undecidability both permits and constrains in its relation to the modern
paradigm of reason as it was constructed by Kant, and within which Habermas continues to work despite his wishes to free himself from it.

The Kantian concept of the *idée regulatrice* was not constructed in light
of the clear distinction between paradox and undecidability.[14] If we remain
bound simply to the range of performative contradictions, as do Habermas
and Karl Otto Apel, or merely to the play of conditions of possibility as in
Kant's theory (it does not matter here that Apel and Habermas have ques-
tioned the philosophy of consciousness), it is inevitable that we have to posit
the necessity of a horizon in terms of validity conceived in the mode of
uniqueness.

Of course, the Ideas of Reason are not themselves demonstrable; they
themselves are only the effect of a wager. This wager is authorized, we could

14. Along with Pierre Livet, let us clearly distinguish between nondecidability, undecidability, and paradox. A proposition is nondecidable when one can neither prove it nor refute
it. A proposition is undecidable when one falls into a contradiction as soon as one tries either
to prove it or to refute it. But, in the latter case, the fact of its unfalsifiability or undecidability
remains true. Finally, paradoxes are nondecidable propositions such that attempts to validate
them turn out to be self-refuting, without ever arriving at stability, the fixed point of undecidability. As mentioned earlier in the text, Pierre Livet takes the classical liar's paradox as an
excellent example. On one hand is the proposition, "I am lying," which is paradoxical. On the
other hand is the self-describing proposition, "I am undemonstrable," which is undecidable.
The undecidability of performatives is of this latter type. When I say, "I order you to close the
door," any request for confirmation of the fact that the addressee of the order has carried it
out because it was so ordered—which is a constitutive element of the communicative intention, as Searle has shown—itself re-creates the conditions of doubt. One is confronted with
the sort of undecidability that we will call *pragmatic*.

say, by that which is performatively "attested" by the very fact of the judgment of the subject of consciousness. Thus, to take only the example of scientific knowledge, it is quite possible to practice scientific research without wagering on the idea that the world is a system governed by laws, that is, without presupposing the objective world to be a place of truth.

It is this particular understanding of the wager that must be called into question today. It is not a matter of calling into question the idea of the wager for reason itself or, what amounts to the same thing, of questioning the element of idealization contained in language.

Every speech act implies reference to a horizon of validity. We follow the Kantian paradigm on this point, though in other terms, Habermas is correct to link meaning and validity. However, the reference to this horizon of validity is not exhausted in the simple phenomenon of what is performatively attested within the position of the speaker. Once we have acknowledged the argument from the performative contradiction (or, what comes to the same thing, the argument for the inescapable presence of an element of idealization in language), there are two possibilities for how we are to conceive the presupposition of this horizon, and ultimately for how we are to conceptualize the wager for reason. Either one presupposes that the idea of validity implies uniqueness or, to the contrary, one assumes that it implies plurality, that is, a changing structure of the reference itself. In this latter perspective, the "path of reason" is no longer thought of in terms of a path toward a unique pole always identical to itself. This last idea is surely counterintuitive if we refer merely to the perspective of what I necessarily presuppose when I put forward a judgment. Yet the recent analysis of pragmatics enables me to show that the speaker's perspective must be complemented by the characteristics of the hearer's position. It is impossible for the hearer to know whether the speaker is playing the language game constrained by validity. The argument from the performative contradiction is no longer sufficient here. Undoubtedly, the proposition "I am lying" is contradictory (the skeptic's paradox). But undecidability is formulated differently.

The more refined distinction between paradox and undecidability permits us to accept Kant's argument while rejecting its assumption of the uniqueness of validity: the horizon of language, or its element of idealization, must integrate by *law/right*, or *ideally* what it is not decidable. We must not, however, deny the element of idealization implicit in language—and the "ethical" constraints on normative discourse that follow from it (a respect for the requirements of equality and liberty on which any broadened communication must depend).[15] But we must conceptualize the nature

15. Two qualifications are called for here. First of all, these normative constraints linked to the logic of communicative action are not grounded in any "foundation" in moral na-

of idealization very differently from the way Kant and Habermas have viewed it.

The only way to respect the double constraint on every communicative exchange is to maintain the vision of a possible plural validity. This means, much as we saw earlier in the recent research on unstable systems in physics, that what is called into question is the idea of the uniqueness of the world that we all presuppose and construct as the horizon of our discourse. We must therefore regard as open, and as ultimately undecidable, the question of whether the ever-possible failure of a process of reasoned argumentation is due to contingent causes or to ontological reasons. In other words, we must question Habermas's notion of a difference between compromise and consensus.

This fact does not condemn us to a skeptical decisionism. The principle of reasoned argumentation remains in effect but without any assurance of success, even at the level of the ideal. Any search for a common accord is likely to be polarized into incommensurably opposed positions because both parties are striving for a single, unique validity.

The new approach to the pragmatics of discourse obliges us, as we have already said, to sharply modify a number of Habermas's distinctions. Habermas is right to differentiate between the illocutionary act and the perlocutionary act, especially if the perlocutionary act is reduced, as in Habermas's theory, to a speech act in which language is instrumentalized to mask the speaker's real intentions from the hearer. But Habermas's is a reductive view both of the illocutionary act and of strategic action.

This reductive, idealized conception of communicative action leads Habermas to misunderstand the dimension of constitutive intentionality of the illocutionary act and of the perlocutionary effects that follow from it. This communicative intention, which cannot be reduced to the masked intention of Habermas's model of the perlocutionary act, reveals the structural undecidability of every speech act.

Two other fundamental distinctions of Habermas's theory must be modi-

---

ture. The obligation that is brought to light is a logical constraint and not a moral one. This "logical" necessity of the nature of linguistic communication can always be obscured by any behavior, either individual or collective, that privileges, consciously or unconsciously, a dogmatic interpretation. Let us remember then that it is in relation to the logical obligation to respect the constraints linked to a broadened communication that the criteria are defined which enable us to get beyond the strictly relativist or skeptical positions. Of course, these criteria imply a radical semantic indeterminacy. However, they are made up of pragmatic reference points that are needed by any social group which seeks to respect the consequences of a communicative rationality, as it is "properly understood." As we shall see, this is the sense that seems to be guiding the contemporary developments in law and the function of the judiciary in our societies.

fied: the distinction between universalizable interest and private interest and the distinction between semantic indeterminacy and pragmatic determinability. First, the distinction that Habermas places at the foundation of his cognitivist approach to matters of morality must be rethought. Contrary to what he asserts, it is not plausible to assume an idealized discussion that would ensure that we will arrive at a consensus on universalizable interests. Granted, every practical discussion implies the goal of agreeing on universalizable interests, wherever these are involved. In this sense, I believe along with Habermas that every practical discussion implies the analytical distinction between private and universal interest, between purely practical (pragmatic) norms, on the one hand and ethical or moral norms, on the other, and the distinction between interest and law and an interest and a right (I shall return to this point). However, this does not have any determining force for the actual debate. We cannot in fact assume some ideal discussion that would lead to accord over what is universal and what is private. In this sense, moreover, no agreement, not even an ideal one, will ever be other than a compromise: there is nothing that allows us to posit the necessary presupposition of an ideal consensus on universalizable interests. As a speaker, I can only posit the existence of a space for the universal. But, if we are not to ignore the implications of the undecidability of communicative action, we cannot just assume the existence of a successful consensus on universalizable interests, even at the purely ideal consensus level. That is to say that, contrary to what Habermas maintains, the distinction between private and universal is not only affected by the inability of human knowledge to define the content of the universal, the problem is that *this distinction, even if thought of as pure idealization, is itself undecidable.* I shall return to this distinction in the course of my critique of Habermas's views on American "republicanism" in constitutional theory. This is why Habermas is wrong, in my opinion, to conceptualize his model of democracy and the proceduralization of law from the standpoint of moral discourse, wrong, that is, to take as the point of departure for his theory a consensus on universalizable interests used as a model for practical discussion. What he misses is the specific character of the pluralism that distinguishes contemporary democracy. Here, we see once again the consequences of Habermas's idealism insofar as he remains committed to his conception of the wager for reason grounded in the classical model of a unique validity and of the objective world as a stable system. In the manner of unstable systems, agreements on norms in our societies must be conceived as coding to a "plural" model of the right. No discussion, not even a discussion concerning interests that are seen as universalizable, not even a discussion conducted in an ideal speech situation under the constraint of the requirement for justification and in compliance with the law of the best argument, will ever be anything but an undecidable and therefore unstable compromise.

That is to say, agreements that are successful in practice must always rely on conventional substitutes. Certainly, these substitutes themselves must be thought of in light of the model of undecidable discourse. The greatest risk indeed would be to interpret this undecidability in a relativist fashion that would lead, in the best case, to a deconstructionist skepticism and, in the worst case, to Hobbes's positivism. If the modern wager for reason, defined by Kant and taken up again by Habermas, must be reenvisioned so as to integrate within it an undecidability that is not only semantic but also pragmatic, by the same token we must not forget the inevitable wager for reason itself. Every communicative act is inescapably caught in two dimensions, by the claim to validity as well as by the impossibility of confirming or disconfirming the success of its communicative intention. To try, as Habermas does, to ward off the latter by resort to conventional substitutes amenable to a guaranteed determinability would run the risk of not taking into account the former. A twofold danger must then be avoided. The first, the notion of an ideal communicative action that reduces human finitude merely to our inability to reach the ideal, ignores the pragmatic undecidability that riddles the ideal itself. The second is the opposite position that imagines that any convention that ensures decidability is acceptable. We must join both of these positions into one, or rather go beyond them. The democratic experience distinguishes itself from other political forms by its normative requirement to envision the social bond and the modes of social integration as functions of a normative representation of the finite character of human reason. It follows from this that every regulation of human action must be subject to the requirements of reasoned debate because it is the only way to meet the demand for a "foundation" of validity or justification for the norm. In the reverse situation, it is necessary to implement mechanisms to ward off the undecidability of this communicative action while making sure that these cannot be disconnected from the procedural requirements. In this sense, no conventional substitute itself can guarantee decidability. There is always the possibility that any supposed foundation can be challenged in such a way as to maintain the sense that no convention can have a foundation. A convention cannot itself be placed in the position of a foundation. It is this fact that calls into question Habermas's "calculable" model of strategic action within the market and administrative systems. It is in this sense as well that the contemporary evolution of law can be understood, and that the model of the proceduralization of law and politics must be understood. But before I outline the fundamental requirements of a correct conception of the much-needed proceduralization of law in light of a wager for reason reenvisioned on the basis of pragmatic undecidability, let us look at the shortcomings of Habermas's theory of law.

II. THE SHORTCOMINGS OF HABERMAS'S THEORY OF LAW

I can now return to Habermas's conception of law. As we have seen above, it can be reduced to four main points concerned primarily with the questions of *validity*, of the rationality of *legal judgment*, of the nature of *constitutional justice*, and finally of the *procedural law paradigm*. How, at each of these four different levels, do we perceive the effects of the excessively idealistic conception of the wager for reason within which Habermas remains imprisoned? How must his conception of law be reformulated if we are to do justice to the pragmatic undecidability of all linguistic communication?

A first observation is called for. The preceding discussion will have shown that, in many respects, I find the changes that Habermas has imposed on the classical analyses to be quite correct. I wholeheartedly endorse Habermas's notion that both natural and positive law theories must be superseded by a procedural and communicative redefinition of legal legitimacy grounded in a new understanding of the communicative nature of the rationality of democratic law. I also endorse his critique of the shortcomings of Niklas Luhmann's excessively semantic model of legal rationality (on this point, see below). However, the implications that Habermas draws from the communicative and procedural dimensions of legal rationality in our "disillusioned" societies already require certain modifications. I shall formulate three proposed modifications that will serve at the same time as an introduction to the more fundamental criticisms that, in my opinion, are called for by the procedural conception of law developed by Habermas. We surely must assess the legitimacy of the law in relation to the rights of democratic participation that underpin the "ethics of communication" in the political and legal fields. As a consequence of this fact, the law has the task of guaranteeing the respect due to subjective fundamental individual rights; these function in a very real sense as conditions of the participatory structure of public communication. But such a formulation will inevitably be ambiguous. In effect, it leaves unanswered the question of the meaning of these fundamental rights, along with the related question of what the appropriate procedures would be for determining their meaning. It is at this level that Habermas's theory lays itself open to the criticism that, much like Ronald Dworkin's theory, it simply assumes the distinction between rights and policies.

The same ambiguity reappears in the question of the separation of powers model of governmental structure. Habermas seeks to provide justification for it by two different routes: first, by reference to a sociological theory of the social integration of modern societies, and second, on the basis of the pragmatics of discourse (this is Habermas's pragmatic distinction between the discourse of justification and the discourse of application). However, these two explanatory "foundations" for the doctrine of separation of powers do not both play quite the same role, and, contrary to Habermas's view, a more adequate approach to the pragmatics of discourse than his would oblige us not to confirm the principle of separation of powers but rather to question modernity's naive faith in it. The model of participatory democracy called for by a communicative approach to law and politics inevitably requires that judges and the political branches of government be subject to "legislative and constitutional" norms that express the "will of the people." But who today, in any case, would argue against this principle?

Recent debates are not so much about the need for the principle as about the way in which it is applied, about what it is to mean in actual practice. Many aspects of the contemporary crisis of the welfare state call for a redefinition of the way the separation of powers doctrine is implemented. Just as we are witnessing a crisis of political representation that has most particularly called into question the exercise of the "will of the people," we are also observing a corresponding questioning of the modes by which the administrative function is exercised—for example, in regard to the necessary regulation of the marketplace—as well as the modes by which the judiciary function is exercised. By simply reproducing in his theory the traditional model of the separation of powers, framing it as he does precisely through the pragmatic distinction between justification and application, Habermas fails to address the contemporary challenge of the necessary realignment of the relations among governmental powers and, beyond this, of a profound reorganization of the relationship between civil society and the state.

Finally, this ambiguity is also evident in the connection Habermas makes between the "communicative legitimacy" of modern law and the characteristics that have come to distinguish the modern state. Although this point is more fully developed in the *Theory of Communicative Action,* the same position is found throughout the argument Habermas developed in his earlier essay, "Facticity and Validity." The organization of market and administrative systems in relation to a guarantee of individual rights, the recognition of conditions for political participation through universal suffrage, and the rights of political and social associations (such as trade unions), and so on, have, as Habermas observes, allowed for the deployment of state structures that permit the progressive establishment, through political and social struggles, of conditions for the defense of individual rights against the potentially abusive powers of the market and administrative systems. Habermas does recognize that we have entered on a fourth phase of the extension of the role of law linked to the development of the welfare state, but this *Verrechtlichung* (juridification) no longer means the protection of the "lifeworld" against the unwarranted intrusions of the "system"; quite the contrary, this process is now precisely the mark of the system's unjustified colonization of the life-world.

For Habermas, the challenge of the present moment is not so much a matter of validating the new forms of law's intervention into the life-world, such as the new roles granted to the courts in the fields of family law and education law. Rather, one could say that such interventions simply reflect the distinguishing traits of the modern state. Therefore if, from the standpoint of Habermas's procedural conception of law, we note shortcomings, these are to be regarded as primarily a matter of hindrances to society's opportunities to participate more actively in the public cultural debate that presides over the adoption of legal norms. It is this observation that provides the central motivation for Habermas's vision of the "proceduralization" of law. And this is why I consider his vision too limited, because its narrow scope does not give us a procedural way to call into question the inherent organizational structures of the state, or the specifically legal mechanisms for controlling the "subsystems of strategic action" of the market and the administrative apparatus. I shall have occasion to expand on this criticism below.

For all that the revitalization of the public space advocated by Habermas appears indispensable, it is nevertheless insufficient. A further stage in the construction of the model of deliberative or participatory democracy is required. Habermas's failure to understand this fact is no doubt due to the inadequacy of his conception of the rationality of language, but it is also due, more directly, to the inadequacy of his conception of law, and more specifically, to the inadequacy of his conception of the judiciary (his "theory of adjudication"), which is founded on a distinction between application and justification, a distinction at the heart of the modern interpretation of the principle of the separation of powers.

Let us consider, first of all, why the decision to take account of pragmatic undecidability compels us to qualify considerably the celebrated distinction between the discourse of the justification of a norm and the discourse of its application. I will then be able to examine more easily the criticisms that Habermas puts forward, quite wrongly in my opinion, against the views of leading constitutional theorists in Germany and against the American communitarian position as it is expressed in Frank Michelman's republicanism.

Habermas's theory of legal judgment (his "theory of adjudication") relies entirely on a procedural version of Dworkin's coherence theory, which is founded on the pragmatic distinction between justification and application. The judge is there not to determine the most valid norms but rather to determine the most appropriate solutions for the particular case that he must decide on the basis of the norms (the rules and principles) of the legal system. This task of selecting the applicable norm most appropriate to the individual case implies therefore that it be based only on the valid normative resources internal to the system, and this is the sense in which the judge's position differs from that of the legislator.

However, this task forces the judge to rule on conflicts that are liable to arise between or among the various norms that may be simultaneously applicable to the case at issue. Any conflict of this kind must be settled by recourse to the *idée regulatrice* of the coherence of the legal system (Dworkin's notion of "integrity"). This task of determining the most appropriate solution from the standpoint of the system's coherence[16] must not be thought of, as Dworkin thinks of it, as deriving solely from the intellectual resources of an idealized judge (Dworkin's "Hercules") but must derive from pragmatic constraints that distinguish the discourse of application from the discourse of justification.

The discourse of application is pragmatically constrained by the fact that the judge must reason on the basis of norms that are presumed to be valid; these norms structure the discursive framework within which he must operate. The discourse of application is constrained by the nature of the arguments that can be invoked; only valid rules from within the system may be called on to support the claims of those engaged in a discourse of application.

The sort of analysis put forward by Habermas must be much qualified, if not completely inverted. In effect, recognizing the undecidability of language obliges us to suppose that, left to its own resources, a reasoned debate over norms will lead ultimately to an inability to differentiate between an act of application and an act of justification, in much the same way that communicative discourse is never able to guarantee its own success. If the success of a speech act can never rest on anything more determinate than the use of substitutive mechanisms, the same thing goes for the act of applying a norm. It is not the pragmatic constraints attached to the discursive process itself which enable the act of application to maintain its specificity but simply the fact of having to resort to conventional substitutional mechanisms. This is linked to the fact that coherence cannot be presumed to be achieved even in the purely idealized framework of an ideal speech situation, any more than can the validity aimed at in what is called the discourse

16. This is what is at issue in the discourse of application; it is the condition whose satisfaction had to be left open by the discourse of justification, wherein it could not be presupposed in other than a counterfactual fashion. This condition resides in the fact that one must interpret an acknowledged norm in such a way that it be coherent in each situation with all of the other valid norms. One cannot thematize the satisfaction of this condition within a discourse of justification, for it only becomes relevant when we must justify a single imperative in a particular situation. KLAUS GÜNTHER, JUSTIFICATION ET APPLICATION UNIVERSALISTES DE LA NORME EN DROIT ET EN MORALE, ARCHIVES DE PHILOSOPHIE DU DROIT, 292 (Herve Pourtois trans., 1992).

of justification.[17] There is no unique meaning even at an ideal level, just as there is no unique validity or unique coherence even in the idealized normative system presupposed by any normative discussion (either of justification or of application).

The current status of the law in our advanced democratic societies makes this logical trait explicit. In many disputes, the conventional points of reference, by means of which judges' reasoning practices could formerly flow into the predetermined molds of valid norms, are becoming increasingly blurred and are opening up the judges' discourse to the same undecidability as that which characterizes the legislators' discourse of justification. Both discourses are increasingly shown to be structured by the same logical models, a fact that poses new problems that the paradigm of procedural law must ultimately address, at least in some measure, and that Habermas's model evidently cannot address because it cannot even perceive these newly posed problems.

This in effect is one profound implication of the broad trend inspired by what in America was called the civil rights movement. As never before, since the fifties and sixties (the trend got under way somewhat later in Europe), judges are put in the position of applying legislative or regulatory norms only if these prove to be in accord with "fundamental individual rights," with these rights being progressively interpreted in a more and more profound, and thus increasingly indeterminate, manner.

We must note that the legal ideology of rights has rightly been criticized, especially in the United States, for its pretension to semantic determinability. This critique of rights, despite the fact that its formulation has often been conceptually weak and intemperately phrased, has at least had the merit of revealing the profound effects of the ongoing transformation of the judges' task ushered in by the civil rights movement. What increasingly followed from the "rights revolution" was a realization of the fundamental undecidability of any judicial reasoning. The undecidability of the discourse of justification has insinuated itself into the discourse of application.

In Europe, the rights revolution was translated into the more classical mechanism of the emergence of constitutional controls, but also and even more important it has led to the impetus for direct applicability of the European Convention on Human Rights within the legal systems of the states that have ratified it.

In what way, then, have these new norms altered the position of the judges? Of course, one could say that these principle-norms are valid norms of positive law, and that as such the pragmatic constraints brought to light

17. Of course, neither Habermas nor Gunther believes that such an ideal speech situation could actually exist. It is a notion that functions simply as an idealization that is always already presupposed in discourse.

by Habermas and Günther to characterize the discourse of application are in no way imperiled, quite the contrary. This observation is undoubtedly correct. But it is also insufficient since it does not indicate what has changed.

With the introduction of these principles arises potential competition with all the other norms of the legal system, but a quite special sort of competition since one can never depart from these principles. To put it in Günther's words, these principles are prima facie applicable to all types of situations on which judges must rule.

Underlying all of the principles that protect fundamental human rights is the principle of equality. It is reflected in all the others. Its significance is that discrimination is acceptable only insofar as it is justified, that is to say, to the extent that it is in proportion to the goal sought, that it is "reasonable." As recent developments in European jurisprudence concerning the principle of equality demonstrate, the "legal" significance of this principle is expressed by the principle of proportionality.

Dworkin, for example, has shown that the application of any principle is never undertaken on an "all or nothing" basis. Its application is always a matter of circumstance. Its "weight" varies as a function of the circumstances and of the relative weights of the other, equally applicable, principles. This, according to Dworkin, is what differentiates principles from rules.[18] The applicability of the principle of equality, on the other hand, is "absolute" in the sense that if it comes into conflict with a rule, either at the stage of examining its validity or at the stage of its application to a particular case, it must always prevail. This "absolute" nature of the principle in no way signifies a restoration of a classical "natural law" theory that has long been made obsolete by the demonstration of the aporia that bedevil any semantic theory of reason. Semantic indeterminacy is inescapable, but what is more noteworthy is the effect the principle of equality has on the pragmatic constraints of normative discourse, and on the distinction between the discourse of justification and the discourse of application, which Habermas and Klaus Günther counterpose to semantic indeterminacy. My thesis is that with the introduction of the principle of equality into the very center of our normative arrangements, this distinction loses its relevance. Why? The application of this principle of equality implies that each norm and each situation be evaluated in the light of the principle of proportionality, to assess the extent to which the solution advocated, either at the general or at the individual level, introduces unjustified discrimination, that is to say, does not conflict with the recognition of a fundamental individual right.

18. However, this observation has been disputed, notably by A. Aarnio who has shown that this relational property holds also for "rules." A. Aarnio, *Taking Rights Seriously*, IVR Colloquium, at Edinborough, 1990.

The form of reasoning linked to overseeing compliance with this special sort of principle, the principle of equality, reveals a blurring of this pragmatic distinction (justification-application); the question of the validity of the norm comes to overlap with the question of its application. The quite particular nature of the principle of equality "clouds the issue." Who cannot see that, in effect, to subject a particular norm to the proportionality test is an operation of the same intellectual nature as asking whether a specific application of this norm is consistent with the equality principle? Furthermore, the fact that both operations, justification and application, depend on the same reference norm already testifies to this logical identity. In both cases, it is a matter of assessing the reasonableness of a particular normative solution in order ultimately to determine its adequacy and its appropriateness for the task of protecting the interests discriminated against, and its proportionality to the objective to be achieved. This is a dimension that Habermas and Günther fail to perceive because they have relied on classical models of normative reasoning without taking into account the special sort of legal reasoning that has arisen under the influence of the new role of the principle of equality. The eventual conflict with the principle of equality is just the same at the level of the disagreements over validity and over application, and ultimately, the conflict is always resolved in favor of the "overarching" principle of equality.

This conception of the nature of the principle of equality is the polar opposite of the classical natural law understanding. The introduction of this principle consists precisely in *potentially* submitting our societies' legal interactions to the logical consequences of an element of idealization that has acknowledged an irreducible pragmatic undecidability. In this sense again, it is necessary to go beyond the simple regulatory effect of the notions of coherence or integrity suggested by Habermas and Dworkin. This leads us, as we have seen, to a situation where the discourses of justification and application overlap. In other words, because the question of validity is subject to the test of proportionality (is the discrimination that the norm leads to reasonable as measured by its proportionality to the goal sought after?), it is affected by such a precariousness that in return the discourse of application no longer has the "determinability" that formerly distinguished it from the discourse of validity. This is a reflexive effect of the overlap between the discourse of validity and the discourse of application. This reflexivity is itself tied to the reflexivity between the principle of equality and individual rights. As we have seen, individual rights are the outcome of the application of the test of proportionality to the question of what forms of legal discrimination are reasonable or acceptable.

Those familiar with the literature of the philosophy of law will recognize that it is at this level that my analysis distinguishes itself from the model of Hans Kelsen, or at least from Kelsen's earlier work. It is this early schema of Kelsen's that strongly colors Habermas's views, in particular, where he dissociates validity from interpretation and where he distinguishes two dimensions of the meaning of every legal norm. With regard to the principle of equality, a third conception of signification emerges which gives the principle its inherent precariousness. The validity of a norm is deployed in a logically undecidable mode, in the sense discussed above.

As in the case of speech act communication, undecidability does not necessarily block actual determination of meaning. The success of linguistic communication can rest only on conventional substitutes, and the same goes for the discourse of legal judgment. In the face of the undecidability of legal discourse, conventional mechanisms must be implemented in order to allow for decidability. These mechanisms cannot conjure away undecidability, but they can counter its effects. Two observations follow from these facts.

First, this enables us to see the extent to which Habermas's schema must be reversed. His claimed pragmatic distinction between application and justification and therefore his imagined "pragmatic determinability" constraints on the discourse of the judge are no more than illusory if we intend for them to refer, as Habermas does, to the level of the analysis of linguistic communication itself. This deficiency in his analysis of the discourse of the judge is simply a consequence of his ongoing adherence to the Kantian paradigm of the wager for reason, as we have seen above.

At the concrete level of contemporary legal practice, Habermas's failure to grasp the logical nature of legal discourse is not without consequences.

What is typical of our present situation is that in certain domains of social relations, the way our courts handle conflicts has been rearticulated so as to introduce into the very center of concern the precariousness that arises from the communicative nature of these relations while at the same time diminishing the security of conventional reference points. Under the effect of the practices affected by the principle of equality and by the proportionality test that results from the current interpretation of this principle, the judge's role has grown considerably in certain domains. This growth has been quite striking in Europe, but the same extension and transformation of court activity have also affected certain American disputes. The crisis of the welfare state and the extension of the role of law and of the courts must be considered in this light.

In effect, what this undecidability implies is that where we give it free rein, it inevitably leads to recourse to the decision-making power of the judiciary. Granted, such judicial decisions are expressed as the result of a reasoned debate, but undecidability takes a form that obliges us to qualify the decisive effects we attribute to pragmatic constraints. The indeterminacy that strikes the semantic level also besets the pragmatic level. The more the law develops itself in light of its communicative nature, the more the precariousness of the judge's role is revealed. What we gain by attempting to submit the social norm to the constraints that derive from its communicative structure—the principle of equality—we may well lose to the very undecidability that is at the heart of communicative discourse itself.

Undoubtedly, even in these disputes that are linked to the development of a discourse of rights, and that are therefore always riddled by indeterminacy, the process is not for all that necessarily arbitrary. The process remains always subject to conventionally settled reference points and to the constraints on argumentation resulting from the validity claims that are always implicit in every discourse (*cf. supra*). Yet it remains the case that this does not eliminate what the hermeneuticist calls, with reference to Aristotle, the dimension of *phronesis* in legal judgment.[19] And as Michael Walzer has correctly pointed out with regard to the American constitutional judge, this fact raises questions of its own. The emerging procedural paradigm of law must incorporate them.

Are there not some indications in current practice of how to face these issues? We can surely not eliminate the dimension of *phronesis* in the role of the contemporary judge. Yet proceduralization must entail not only the procedural transformation of the public space constitutive of the democratic adoption of norms and of the discourse of "justification" in Habermas's sense but also the procedural transformation of the discourse of application in disputes where the precariousness that results from the undecidable nature of communicative logic is revealed at the very heart of the law itself. This procedural transformation of the function of application implies a partial redefinition of the judge's role in these cases. Classically, the traditional descriptions of the principle of separation of powers and its "dogmatic" reference points reduced the decision-making character of the judge's role. Today, as these reference points become blurred at the same time as the inherently normative demands of a mode of regulation that respects the communicative constraint is deployed, these dogmatic reference points become blurred, leaving a sometimes disproportionate power to those in charge of overseeing these normative constraints. A restructuring is called for, and any real proceduralization of law must show us how to meet this demand.

Such a true proceduralization must first take the course of alternative modes of conflict resolution that involve the parties in the direct resolution of their conflict by using a variable "articulation" of the judge.

This procedural transformation can be observed in both Europe and the United States most notably in the areas of family and criminal law. But it is in the areas of administrative law and economic regulation that the search

---

19. In this sense, my position resembles that of Paul Ricoeur. *See* PAUL RICOEUR, SOI-MÊME COMME UN AUTRE (1990).

for novel modalities is both the most urgent and the most intriguing. One way is to modify the decision-making processes themselves so as to permit all interested parties to participate in the decision process, that is to say, all parties who can claim to be potentially affected by the discrimination that will inevitably result from the decision. This certainly implies a relative "legalization" or "juridification" of the very process of decision-making and a transformation of the classical modes of public oversight, especially of economic activity.

In such a conception, the judge's task would be less the task of defining by himself the content of the law and more that of seeing that the argumentative constraints, clearly always interpretable, be respected by the decision-making process. Of course, such a conception neither escapes substantial questions nor can be assured of avoiding capture by interest groups, as American jurisprudence has witnessed in the perverse effects of the "fairness doctrine" in media regulation cases. But is this double imperfection not the inevitable sign of the undecidability of language? And does this procedural perspective not offer at least the advantage, by virtue of its non-idealization, of incorporating into the institutional mechanism a possible reflexive recovery from its inevitable failures? For this model permits in this way a different temporal structure; there is no assured progress toward some final fulfillment. But proceduralization has only a constraining effect on the element of idealization, which serves to render all equilibria unstable in favor of a new equilibrium driven by a new search for justification.

These last observations have already raised the question of the proceduralization of law. Before we examine this question further, however, and before we consider the critiques that must be directed at the interpretation proposed by Habermas, two final comments must be made regarding the question of the judge. These remarks concern more directly the issue of the constitutional judge and the twofold criticism that Habermas makes against German constitutional doctrine and American "republicanism."

Contrary to the view developed by the German constitutional judiciary, Habermas believes that the notion of "balancing of interests" fails to describe adequately the nature of the constitutional judge's task, even where the judge is called on to ensure that the legislature respects constitutional freedoms, as these are interpreted in the extensive fashion required by the evolution of law under the welfare state. Habermas believes that the balancing of interests vision of the judge's task confuses the communicative rationality specific to the judge's discourse with strategic rationality; he maintains that the judge, even within the framework of "objective disputes," does not have to determine, as the legislator does, the best means to realize an objective, but rather has to supervise the application of rights defined by the constitution. In other words, he fails to grasp once again the pragmatic distinction between a discourse of "justification" and a discourse of "application."

This discussion indicates why, in my view, Habermas's critique misunderstands the reality of the contemporary constitutional judge's task. The extension of the judge's responsibility to fundamental liberties and ultimately for the principle of equality that, as we have seen, underlies these fundamental rights technically calls for the judge to apply the proportionality test. It is this test that leads to the operation often called a "balancing of interests." Furthermore, I believe that Habermas's misunderstanding of these facts is linked to his symptomatic misappreciation of the true nature of the concept of individual rights.

I willingly acknowledge that I share Habermas's critique of the utilitarian model and of its tendency to reduce rights to interests. In any case, is this critique not a logical consequence of the element of idealization that structures all linguistic action? Therefore, at this level, even if I conceptualize the nature of this element of idealization differently from Habermas's notion of it, I can only endorse wholeheartedly the general critique that he (along with Dworkin) directs at utilitarianism.

Yet this single critique does not put an end to the discourse of rights. This critique of rights has served as the point of departure for the legitimate criticism that the "identity politics" positions in the United States have directed at the 1960s rights movements. Contrary to what Habermas believes, his vision of a distinction between application and justification does not adequately explain the distinction between rights and interests, nor does it suffice for an adequate critique of the "balancing of interests" description of the role of the judge.

The concept of interests must be understood here as linked to the fact of the undecidability of equality even at an ideal level, and therefore as linked to the fundamental instability of all adjudication between competing rights. An individual right can only be established in relation to the rights of others, and therefore remains tied to the undecidability that permeates all communicative action.[20] Finally, let us note that it is difficult to account for numerous recent developments in positive law jurisprudence without acknowledging this dimension of the "balancing of interests" model. How can Habermas explain not only certain constitutional decisions or certain decisions of the European Convention on Human Rights but also the development of marginal control of administrative activities, or even the kinds of reasoning we see in cases where the judge has subjected

20. Here once again we witness the effects of the fact that Habermas bases his theory on a model of communication based entirely on an analysis of the presuppositions of the role of the speaker. His notion of individual rights is conceived on the basis of the same model.

the legal decision of whether to send a company into bankruptcy to an analysis of the effects of the decision on the company's workers or on the social and economic conditions of the region?[21]

The preceding observations also oblige us to modify or even to disagree with the criticisms that Habermas makes against the American communitarian vision as expressed, for example, in Frank Michelman's "constitutional republicanism." I will not elaborate on this point any further except to recall that taking into account the undecidability of language obliges us not to distinguish as sharply as Habermas does between compromise and consensus, or between ethics and morality, or between private and universal interests. Once again, this is not a matter of criticizing the presence of an element within discourse. Rather, it is a matter of reconstructing the precise "logical" structure of discourse while incorporating within it our recognition of the undecidability that is inescapable even at the ideal level.

As a point of departure for this more correct understanding, as I have attempted to show, we can begin by trying to grasp the fundamental message that communitarians such as Michael Walzer or, in his own way, Frank Michelman have sought to articulate—that all universals are in fact inevitably "particularized." Of course, this formulation remains infelicitous because either, on the one hand, it risks misunderstanding the idealization of language or, on the other, it risks making a false accusation against Habermas who does acknowledge the irreducibly particular nature of the universal.

I believe that the new articulation I am attempting here from the perspective of the undecidability of the ideal will help us to understand better the logical relation between the universal and the particular while also helping us to locate the overidealized elements in Habermas's theory, and to see how therefore we ought to reinterpret the necessary wager for reason. At the same time, it allows us to validate what Walzer has recently termed the two forms of universalism: covering-law universalism and reiterative universalism.[22] Moreover, it is precisely this tension internal to ethics that gives meaning to the requirement put forward by Michelman that the law and the judges see their roles as based on ensuring respect for the procedural demands of a properly understood logic of communicative action. This implies, in my view, the forging of a social bond in light of the undecidability of language and of the normative constraints that embody the idealization inherent in every speech act. It is this project that underlies

21. For an excellent analysis of these developments in Belgian law, see P. MARTENS, L'irresistible ascension du principe de proportionnalité, MELANGES J. VELU 61ff. (1993).

22. Michael Walzer, Les Deux Universalismes, ESPRIT, Dec. 1992, at 114ff. Originally published in English in 11 THE TANNER LECTURES ON HUMAN VALUES 513 (S. McMurrin ed., 1990).

the developments that, however inadequate they may be, have for some time now been taking shape within our legal systems. They mark the emergence of a new paradigm of law that I call, along with Luhmann and Habermas (although in a sense quite different from theirs), the paradigm of procedural law.

III. FOR A NEW APPROACH TO
THE PROCEDURALIZATION OF LAW

I have attempted to show in the preceding discussion that Habermas's conception of language and of the element of idealization that informs it, as well as his conception of the judicial judgment on which he bases it, must be revised. Because he remains riveted to a Kantian conception of the "wager for reason," Habermas misses the pragmatic undecidability that characterizes even the ideal horizon of every speech act.

This undecidability is the reflection in the legal world of the irreducible instability of dissipative structures whose presence in the bosom of the objective world has been unveiled by contemporary research in physics. If there is a metaphor adequate to represent these new implications for the law, it is neither H. L. A. Hart's chess game nor Dworkin's chain novel, but rather the gambling metaphor that Prigogine and Stengers employ to express, in part, the implications of the dissipative structures of physical reality.

There is no doubt that the revitalization of Kant's vision of the public space that Habermas advocates would be most welcome. However, this leaves the necessary transformations of the decision-making mechanisms of law and of the state insufficiently thought through. What is at issue here is Habermas's distinction between the system and the life-world, although this problem also recalls the various other overly dogmatic distinctions that we have already encountered in our discussion of Habermas's theory: the distinctions between compromise and consensus, between strategic and communicative action, between universal and particular interests, between individual rights and private interests, and between application and justification. In order simply to outline the weakness of his system/life-world distinction, it will be useful to situate Habermas's conception of the proceduralization of law in relation to the conception put forward by Niklas Luhmann. On the basis of what differentiates them, I will be able to outline more easily a third conception of this new procedural paradigm of law that will allow us to go beyond the paradigms of liberal formalist legal theory and of the welfare state.

The solution that Habermas offers us implies the rejection of two solutions that he considers to be extreme and philosophically mistaken; these are the neoconservative solution and the systems theory solution. The first of these, which follows from Hannah Arendt's vision of a resurrection of the Greek ideal of democracy, would result in returning politics and law to a simpler model of a civil society and of a generalized public space and would simply dissolve the organization of the market and of the modern state as we know them, as spheres of activity regulated systematically. This theory of direct democracy comes to a dead end, Habermas notes, at the fact that the achievements of modern social rationalization are irreversible, that the autonomous organization of the subsystems of the market and the state are the only forms able to meet the challenges of the complexification of contemporary industrial societies.

On the other hand, Habermas considers Luhmann's systems-theory solution to be just as mistaken as Arendt's vision of direct democracy. Luhmann's theory leads to a failure to grasp the true potential of the self-reflexive actions of society on itself and of the regulation of the political sphere by means of normative claims grounded in the logic of the form of action that aims at mutual comprehension, the form of action that structures the life-world. Each of these theses puts forward a one-sided interpretation of the complex process initiated by modernity.

Neoconservatives underestimate the claims to universality that underlie the potentialities of the rationalization process. Systems theorists, because they remain glued to a purely semantic conception of reason and because they misunderstand the self-reflexive resources that accompany a pragmatic approach to linguistic action, prevent themselves from taking into account the concept of practical reason and, by the same token, also prevent themselves from grasping the importance of normative discourse in political activity.

It is a matter then of attempting to articulate a concept of political reason that acknowledges the force of the normative claims linked to the communicative action constitutive of the life-world just as much as the necessities of systemic regulation linked to the growing complexity of contemporary societies. Habermas's solution does not seek to transform the decision-making process within the subsystems of rational action in relation to some goal but instead to ensure the framing of the life-world, to develop a public space at the center of the life-world, and to invigorate the political debate within civil society.

This vision adds up, one might say, to a "culturalist"[23] conception of the proceduralization of law and of democracy which comes to an impasse with the question of the much-needed transformation of decision-making mechanisms. His vision of democratic culture is linked to the self-deploy-

23. This expression is taken from Habermas's own description, in *La souveraineté populare comme procedure. Un concept normatif d'espace publique*, 7 LIGNES 56 (Mark Hunyadi trans., 1989). Originally published in German in an abridged version in MERKUR, June 1989.

ment of a public space at the center of civil society, and it is by this self-deployment of public space that we are supposed to be able to limit the unwanted intrusion of the systemic regulatory mechanisms of the state and the market into the domain of action reserved to the life-world.

What then of the interpretation of the proceduralization of law that Luhmann offers us? In the first place, Luhmann puts forward a sociological interpretation of the critique of Descartes's *cogito*. Consciousness has no direct access to itself, and we must therefore abandon every metaphysical pretense that reason could deploy itself reflexively so as to grasp its own nature. And, by extension, every reflexive attempt by a subject, or even by a society, to grasp itself is necessarily caught in a similar paradox. As we shall see, this fact does not imply a total absence of reflexivity; but it does rule out any notion of a substantial medium—either the individual subject or the society—that could carry out such a turning upon itself.

According to Luhmann, what follows from this is an altered interpretation of the modern process of rationalization. We can speak therefore, as Habermas phrases it, of "modernity, an incomplete project." But for Luhmann, this incompleteness does not hold at all the same meaning it does for Habermas. It designates rather the lack of rationalization that he finds manifested just as much in the model of liberal legal formalism as in the project of the welfare state. In effect, liberal legal formalism, no less than the instrumentalization of law that accompanies the welfare state, remains bound to the metaphysical assumption that a society is able to grasp itself. It is the society in its entirety that—through the law and the state—gives to itself the instruments of rational action. This move effectively presupposes the possibility that a society could have a global knowledge of itself—even if such a knowledge must always be imperfect in actuality. The possibility of a global self-reflectiveness of a consciousness or of a society entails a view of the process of modern rationalization very different from Habermas's. In any case, the process of society's functional differentiation into subsystems attains a much more extreme form. Society differentiates itself into a set of progressively more autonomous subsystems, and to imagine that one could unify them or totalize them from the standpoint of a center or from an external viewpoint is pure illusion. In this way, for example, the state loses its central position; it is no more than one among the other subsystems such as the economic sphere, the educational sphere, and so forth. Each subsystem is autonomous and functions according to its own normative principles. Each system is defined by its "normative closure."

In this vision, the law has a special and surprising status. In one sense, like every other subsystem, the law is autonomous and is governed by a specific normative code defined by the binary distinction between legal and illegal. But Luhmann, and Gunther Teubner after him, cannot ignore the fact of the omnipresence of the law. Neither external nor central, the law is nonetheless considered the site of the diffraction of the respective self-regulations of the various subsystems. Certainly, it does not represent a central authority; it is not the instrument of the state for ensuring the steering of the whole of society. But it has to inscribe within itself the recognition of the self-regulation of each of the subsystems by the subsystem itself. In other words, the theory of the sources of law must inscribe in its very center the acknowledged possibility of a deployment of "communicative" processes or of different procedures that we must stimulate within each of the subsystems. It is also by means of these processes and procedures that the different actors, both individual and collective, in each of the subsystems must organize the procedures of exchange by which they will constitute the regulation, the undetermined self-regulation of each of the subsystems. Teubner, who has given more consideration than anyone else to the necessary transformation of law that follows from Luhmann's model of a theory of social systems, has shown this ongoing redefinition of the role of law and of the theory of the sources of law in an effort to recognize a "legal pluralism."[24] Proceduralization takes on another meaning here. According to Teubner, it is not a question of knowing whether the rationalization of our societies is threatening the normative claims of a practical reason that calls for universality; each subsystem is capable of regulating itself, according to its own norms, its own code, and has no need to support its normative claims on some external principle. From this point of view, they are self-referential. In this context, the meaning of the proceduralization of the law is twofold: on the one hand, the law must organize as best it can the procedures internal to each of the subsystems in order to permit their self-regulation; on the other hand, it must organize procedures to harmonize the relations among these different systems.

The debate over the proceduralization of law that I have just sketched out has much to teach us. It is in fact its failings—its blind spots—that I will use as a point of departure in proposing a redefinition of the proceduralization of law and democracy. First of all, Habermas's vision appears torn between idealization and resignation. Idealization, because the mere reinforcement of argumentative procedures at the center of civil society seems to me impotent to counter the effects of the relations of force that structure the socioeconomic field. It is doubtful that the mere virtues of argumentation in the midst of a public space can counterbalance the perverse effects of the colonization of the life-world, such as the commercialization of culture and the bureaucratization of important aspects of private life.

24. *See* GUNTHER TEUBNER, *Autopoiesis and Steering: How Politics Profit from the Normative Surplus of Capital, in* AUTOPOIESIS AND CON&GURATION THEORY: NEW APPROACHES TO SOCIETAL STEERING 127–41 (J. Roeland In t'Veld et al. eds., 1992).

Still more grave is the fact that this autonomy of systems keeps us from seeing how their systemic closure has consequences for the very organization of markets, with the effects of irrationality and social exclusion that we know too well. It is not by eliminating the idea of representation in order to put in its place, as the Habermasians propose to do, a mediatized public space that we will enable opinions formed through free discussion to be translated into effective political decisions.

Furthermore, Habermas's rigid dichotomy between system and life-world brings with it a certain sense of resignation in the face of the insurmountable character of systemic regulation. If one simply accepts the processes of systemic regulation, supposing them to be inevitable, one is then left only able to imagine an exogenous form of action based in an autonomous public space that is isomorphic to the life-world. As Thomas McCarthy[25] has helped us to understand, Habermas is perhaps not sufficiently immune to the seductions of systems theory to be able to conceptualize innovative processes of decision making within the very heart of the institutional space of the market and of the state.

But Luhmann's solution is no more satisfactory than Habermas's, and the reason for the inadequacy of Luhmann's theory is the mirror opposite of that of Habermas. By not taking into account the role of the normative claims that accompany speech acts, the distinction between efficiency and rightness/soundness becomes unintelligible. For Luhmann, everything seems to happen as though the ethical conception aimed at by referring to rightness had only a purely rhetorical or ideological value in the legal and economic spheres.

Luhmann's system thus functions on the basis of an error that is the mirror inverse of Habermas's. By radically challenging the perspective of consensual universalization aimed at by the ethics of communication, Luhmann in his own way fails to understand undecidability in that he substitutes for it a regulatory mechanism that functions in a determining fashion, to adopt a Kantian expression.[26]

25. See THOMAS MCCARTHY, *Complexity and Democracy, or the Seducements of Systems Theory, in* COMMUNICATIVE ACTION (Axel Honneth & Hans Jonas eds., 1991).

26. This effectively is what Pierre Livet, although he is writing about game theory, has shown us. Livet's central argument is that the theory of strategic action seeks to resolve the problem of the conventions that govern our exchanges as soon as these pass through the medium of language and to convey requirements through a logical level that corresponds to a hypothesis quite different from rule application. To put it more concretely, and turning for the remainder to Livet's article, game theory fundamentally misunderstands the conflicts of interpretation to which the rules that must govern our behavior are susceptible; this is because game theory in a sense presupposes a univocal rule at the very basis of the definition of our rational behavior, the rule of maximizing individual interests. In the same fashion, I would say that game theory presupposes a normative closure that keeps any problems in the determination of rationality from being drawn to a different interpretation, to a conflict of inter-

The "cultural" approach to proceduralization that Habermas proposes is linked to an excessively idealized vision of reason. This cultural approach also remains riveted to a strictly systemic conception of the functioning of the regulatory modes in the subsystems of the market and the administration, and to a classically republican (in the French sense) vision of the government of laws. The conception of legal judgment developed by Habermas keeps him from being able to consider any but the classical categories of the separation and organization of powers in the state or of the decision-making mechanisms that are at the base of our classical theory of democracy. A similar blindness afflicts Luhmann's model; because he remains fettered to a purely positivist conception of reason and legal judgment, he misses the normative constraints that ought to modify his exclusively functionalist reading of social rationality. Of course, our intention is not to overestimate the role of the judge in the institutional changes that are to be promoted. Such an approach as is sometimes maintained today remains too simplistic.

It is on the basis of perceptible trends and developments currently under way that we can attempt to sketch out a more relevant conception of the necessary proceduralization of law and democracy. These trends and developments seem to me to be unfolding on three levels that are articulated with one another: the first is the multiplication of the sites of communicative exchange in the midst of different zones of power—the market, economic regulation, education; the second is the necessary taking into account of the decision-making dimension that goes along with any regulatory activity; and finally, there is the level of the judicial power to oversee the normative constraints that distinguish proceduralized decision-making processes.

The coming challenge will consist first of all in reflecting on novel institutional mechanisms to ensure a closer interpretation of civil society with the spheres of the state and of the subsystem of economic activity. This is effectively a matter of multiplying the opportunities for the various groups representative of civil society to participate in the decision-making process under the constraints of reasoned argumentation. These mechanisms of dialogue and this ongoing proceduralization of the decision-making

---

pretations to which the norm itself could be susceptible, or simply to the determination of an eventual false application of a rule supposed to be normatively defined and determined. Now, because of the undecidability of the conditions of satisfaction of speech acts, the problems with which we are confronted by language use are those that concern the multivocal interpretations of the rules themselves. From the point of view of a social theory, this implies that the current description of the functioning of our society, principally in the spheres of power and money, remains a description of regulatory codes that entails a normative closure and makes a good deal of the irreducible indeterminacy of any normative code.

mechanisms were already to some extent a constitutive dimension of the welfare state.

What we have been observing in recent years, in the United States most of all, is a constant obligation and mounting manifestation of strategic and dogmatic maneuvers aimed at instrumentalizing these processes of participation in favor of particular groups. But it should be evident that the denunciations of the strategic attempts to corrupt these participatory processes presuppose the same paradigm of a procedural reason riddled by an insurmountable undecidability. There can be no doubt therefore that contrary to the often overly naive belief in the simple virtues of reasoned argumentation, it does not fail to expose the particular representations that unmistakably strive to "instrumentalize" the fairness of the debate.

Pragmatic constraints do not ensure a "determinability" that counters semantic indeterminacy. In this sense once again, the recent American "identity politics" movement is right to criticize the false idealizations of the Kantian paradigm that underlay the 1960s rights movements. We must bring together the wager for reason and pragmatic undecidability. In this sense, the movement to permanently call into question is not linked to the infinite trajectory toward an ideal goal. The process is that of an unstable equilibrium because each new equilibrium re-creates of itself the conditions of its own inadequacy, much as in the play of dissipative structures and unstable systems brought to light in recent research in physics. The new democratic challenge is to rethink the techniques of social regulation in light of this sort of reinterpretation of the wager for reason. Whatever may be the liberal reidealizations and the inevitable instrumentalizations by particular groups of which the proceduralization of public activity that has been greatly developed in the United States has been the object for more than twenty years, the undertaking of which this process is the symptom is adequate. We must certainly rethink its methods and its requirements in terms both semantic and procedural (one cannot make pragmatics autonomous of semantics, as Habermas wishes to do), but this perpetual calling into question of the new corruptions and new inequalities engendered or masked by the "existing procedures" can only be carried out in the name of the paradigm whose conceptualization we are trying to construct here. This also shows that it does not belong to theoretical thought to overcome these limits; the choice of procedural constraints and of semantic requirements concerning individual and collective rights is always contextualized and is in constant redefinition because the equilibria are never other than unstable, and thus cannot help creating the conditions for their own undoing.

This extension of the sites of communicative exchange already shows the second field where proceduralization is going on. Proceduralized communicative exchanges are not sufficient to ensure social self-regulation. Because of the indeterminacy of judgment, the debates may be indeterminate. Decision-making mechanisms are therefore required. But these must be articulated as much as possible with the requirements of an open and reasoned debate. For all their limits and their failings, the proceduralization of administrative activities during the 1970s has constituted an interesting experiment from this point of view. What is interesting in this experiment is not only the constraint imposed on the decision-making mechanisms by the requirements of a reasoned debate but also the seeking—still too limited and yet to be perfected—to frame/situate the administrative authorities having decision-making responsibility within the interested contexts, certainly professional contexts, but also within those contexts open to different sensibilities of the public space inherent to civil society. These experiments and their inadequacies must not lead to a retreat as we see called for by the recent "deregulatory" movements, but rather to a deepening as a function of the goals defined here.

It is in regard to these two former points that it is necessary to progressively reformulate the function of the law and of the judge. This redefinition of the role of the judge is to be developed on two levels. As to the first level, the preceding discussion already suggests that it is not a matter of reinvesting the function of the judge with the right to define by himself the requirements of regulation, but rather of charging the judge with the primary mission of overseeing the normative and procedural constraints linked to the communicative nature, as it has been defined here, of the decision-making mechanisms specific to the "subsystems" of the market and the administration. In this sense, this power of oversight granted to the judge is itself proceduralized, at the same time as there is a need to extend the classical conceptions of the judicial review of legality to which European judges too often remain subject.

There is a second field in which the role of the judge must be redefined. It appears in effect that this conception of proceduralization presupposes, by virtue of its normative conditions, the bringing to light of a certain domain of unavailability—the principle of equality. I will not go over again here the quite special status that we must accord to this "unavailability," colored as it is by the undecidability of speech acts (see the discussion *supra*, on the undecidability of legal judgment caused by the application of the proportionality test that is constitutive of the principle of equality). We see in this way how contemporary law is investing one new legal forum or another with the power to see that acts in the political domain comply with the principle of equality conceived as a test of proportionality. This fact potentially introduces into the heart of the law the germ of an ongoing questioning of the diverse forms of dogmatism that never cease to sprout there.

At this level also, American law is of striking interest. The evolution of public law litigation over the last two decades has given the judiciary a new possibility for controlling the legality of public policy. What is even more interesting is that the growing power accorded to the judge in overseeing the application of public policy decisions (in domains such as education, housing, and corrections policy) in light of the fundamental values of liberty and equality has led the judge himself to proceduralize his own decision-making processes. In effect, once the judge has ascertained the illegality of some public policy in regard to the principles of liberty and equality, he himself gives to the concerned parties the task of finding a negotiated settlement that satisfies these fundamental principles. This is not the place to assess the extent to which this process is fundamentally altering the classical categories of our procedural law. It is enough to note that a new equilibrium is emerging which brings together political, economic, and administrative decision-making mechanisms with the process of ensuring respect for the requirements of reasoned debate. Notwithstanding the illusions and strategic manipulations that these public law litigation mechanisms have led to, the path that these mechanisms has opened is most interesting because of the transformation and reorganization of the roles of the judge and of the litigating parties that it is bringing about.

This ongoing reorganization of the institutional spaces of the legal system may permit us to better integrate the requirements of a deidealized ethics of communication while recognizing the rationality of the functional mechanisms of a complex and differentiated society; it may help us to inscribe within our new regulatory mechanisms both the pragmatic constraints of reasoned argumentation and the consequences of the indeterminacy of ends; finally, it may allow an alliance between efficiency and rightness/soundness. If we construct a theory of proceduralization that maintains the links between pragmatics and semantics, and between the idealization of language and pragmatic undecidability, we will be able to get beyond the inadequacies of the Kantian theory of democracy that, because of its formalism, is always at risk of reintroducing a remainder of dogmatism into justifications of normative activity. Similarly, if we refuse to endorse the positivist theories that claim to express the theoretical essence of the social system, we will be able to undertake forms of legal and political reorganization that reflect the radical indeterminacy of reason, and to give a more fruitful interpretation of the paradoxes of modernity diagnosed by Weber and taken up in different ways by Habermas and Luhmann. The law and the judge will each have a place in this task, but each of them will need to be rethought and restructured in certain of their modes of functioning.

FOUR

Can Rights, Democracy, and Justice Be Reconciled through Discourse Theory?

Reflections on Habermas's Proceduralist Paradigm of Law

*Michel Rosenfeld**

INTRODUCTION

There are different images or paradigms of law which correspond to different conceptions of justice and different sources of legitimacy. Moreover, in
the context of complex, pluralistic contemporary societies, the relationship
between law, justice, and legitimacy has become acutely problematic as competing conceptions of the good cast legal relationships as relationships
among strangers,[1] and as justice according to law[2] seems irretrievably split
from justice against or beyond law.[3] In the face of these difficulties, one
could simply abandon the quest for justice beyond law and settle for a combination of democracy and legal positivism which would reduce political
legitimacy to majority rule and confine the role of law to the stabilization
of expectations among legal subjects. However, if fearful of tyrannical majorities and dissatisfied with the prospect of predictable but unjust laws, one
could opt for justice beyond law and embrace human rights as a shield
against the abuses of legislative majorities and the inequities of positive law.

*Professor of Law, Benjamin N. Cardozo School of Law.
1. *Cf.* MAX WEBER, ECONOMY AND SOCIETY 637 (Guenther Roth & Claus Wittich eds.,
1968) (greater differentiation characteristic of modern legal systems was prompted by the
advent of the market which brought strangers together to exchange goods and which had to
be regulated by universal laws transcending the biases of intracommunal norms).

2. "Justice according to law is achieved when each person is treated in conformity with
his or her legal entitlement." Michel Rosenfeld, *Autopoiesis and Justice*, 13 CARDOZO L. REV.
1681 (1992) (footnote omitted).

3. "Justice against law, on the other hand, is the justice that makes it plausible to claim
that a law is unjust (even if it is scrupulously applied in strict compliance with the entitlements
which the law establishes)." *Id.*

In short, in a contemporary pluralist society, law's legitimacy seems to require sacrificing either democracy or justice.[4]

Being relegated to either democracy or justice is bound to be frustrating, in as much as majoritarian rule cannot be purged of all arbitrariness and justice cannot shed all intracommunal roots to rise above the reach of partial communities.[5] There is, however, an apparent way out of the vicious circle circumscribed by arbitrary democracy and parochial justice. That way out is through proceduralism, or, more precisely, through the kind of proceduralism that is capable of yielding what John Rawls calls "pure procedural justice."[6] It bears emphasizing that most kinds of proceduralism will not do. After all, democratic lawmaking can be viewed as a form of proceduralism based on universal suffrage and majority rule. Nonetheless, it is conceivable that there could be some kind of proceduralism capable of overcoming the residual arbitrariness of democratic lawmaking while, at the same time, maintaining a neutral stance toward the diverse and often conflicting conceptions of the good found throughout the polity.

Habermas's proceduralist paradigm of law has all the makings of a most attractive candidate for the purpose of establishing the legitimacy of law through pure procedural justice. Indeed, Habermas's proceduralist approach based on communicative action deals with the residual arbitrariness of democracy by relying on dialogical consensus as the source of law's legitimacy. On the other hand, Habermas's proceduralism provides funda-

---

4. Recent debates in American constitutional law offer a salient example of the split between democracy and justice. Some have advocated restrictive interpretations of constitutional rights, for fear of unduly trampling on the will of legislative majorities, while others have not hesitated to promote enlarging the scope of antimajoritarian constitutional rights in the name of "fundamental justice" and "basic fairness." Compare, e.g., the majority, concurring, and dissenting opinions in cases such as Planned Parenthood of Southeastern Pa. v. Casey, 112 S. Ct. 2791 (1992); Roe v. Wade, 410 U.S. 113 (1973); and Griswold v. Connecticut, 381 U.S. 479 (1965).

5. Justice beyond law cannot achieve complete impartiality toward all strangers in the relevant class of legal subjects. Therefore, it must, at least in part, rely on a vision of the good that has intracommunal roots, thereby favoring members of the relevant intracommunal group over the remaining legal subjects. Thus, even the most basic and fundamental human rights embodied in numerous international covenants have been criticized as being somewhat parochial or culturally biased. *See generally* Burns H. Weston, *Human Rights, in* HUMAN RIGHTS IN THE WORLD COMMUNITY: ISSUES AND ACTION (Richard P. Claude & Burns H. Weston eds., 1989) (focusing on western liberal origins of modern human rights conceptions); *see also* WILL KYMLICKA, MULTICULTURAL CITIZENSHIP 4 (1995) ("Traditional human right standards are simply unable to resolve some of the most important and controversial questions relating to cultural minorities.").

6. According to Rawls, pure procedural justice is achieved when any outcome is justly provided because a fair procedure was properly followed. JOHN RAWLS, A THEORY OF JUSTICE 86 (1971).

mental rights a legal grounding that seemingly obviates any need to justify such rights in terms of any conception of the good not equally shared by all the members of the polity. Moreover, not only does Habermas's proceduralist approach to law offer a way to resolve the conflict between democracy and justice, it also aims at establishing an internal connection between popular sovereignty and human rights, thus providing a normative underpinning for a legal regime that is poised to satisfy both democracy and justice.

In the last analysis, the value of proceduralism and the possibility of achieving pure procedural justice depend on the background assumptions and the material conditions surrounding the insertion and deployment of the relevant procedural devices and practices. Consistent with this, I will argue that Habermas's proceduralist paradigm of law ultimately fails to generate pure procedural justice and that it falls short of furnishing a comprehensive resolution of the conflict between democracy and justice. Habermas appears to have taken proceduralism as far as it can go, and through his discourse theory has made great progress over the proceduralism that has emerged from the works of his major predecessors, namely, Hobbes, Kant, and Rawls. But, as I shall endeavor to indicate in what follows, even Habermas's more nuanced and versatile proceduralism ultimately confronts the need to embrace contestable substantive normative assumptions in order to contribute to the resolution of conflicts that divide the members of the polity.

In order to be in a better position to provide a principled assessment of Habermas's proceduralism, I shall first attempt to put it in context. Accordingly, in Part I, I briefly examine some of the most salient general features of proceduralism as a means to establish its normative legitimacy. In Part II, I concentrate on the background assumptions, material conditions, and tasks which give shape to Habermas's proceduralism and I provide a critical assessment of certain problems it raises. In Part III, I take a close look at a type of feminist objection which seems to go to the heart of Habermas's discourse-theoretical justification of law. Finally, in Part IV, I conclude that Habermas's discourse-theoretical approach to law, while incapable of generating pure procedural justice, nonetheless can play an important constructive role in determining the normative legitimacy of contemporary law.

I.

Procedural justice—of which pure procedural justice is a limiting case—is a necessary component of any complex system for dispensing justice. Procedural justice, moreover, has an essentially twofold role in a contemporary constitutional legal system: first, to insure the just application of substantive norms belonging to the realms of distributive, corrective, or retributive justice; and second, to protect the worth and dignity of persons whose legal entitlement and obligations are subject to determination or modification by instrumentalities of the state. While these two roles of procedural justice are often intertwined in practice, they remain conceptually distinct. Thus, for example, in the context of the United States's adversarial criminal law system, the defendant's right to counsel and right to cross-examine witnesses can be viewed in two ways. These rights can be seen as both an important tool in the pursuit of the truth—which is essential to the fair application of the substantive norms embodied in the relevant criminal statues—and as a means of recognizing the defendant's inherent dignity by guaranteeing his or her right of participation in a proceeding that may result in a drastic change in his or her legal status. Conceptually, however, procedural justice as a means of application is generally parasitic on the substantive norms which it is designed to implement. Accordingly, the adversary system's suitability as a vehicle of procedural justice depends on whether it provides a reliable means to ascertain the guilt or innocence of the accused. Providing such a means is essential to the implementation of the relevant substantive norms of justice embodied in the criminal code. In contrast, procedural justice as a means to vindicate the dignity of the accused is largely independent from, though it cannot squarely frustrate the application of, the above mentioned relevant substantive norms. Consistent with this reasoning, even when the evidence against a criminal defendant is so overwhelming that guilt is obvious beyond any reasonable doubt, the defendant is still entitled to have "his day in court."[7]

Accordingly, procedural justice simultaneously depends on and transcends particular substantive norms of justice.[8] It does not follow from that, however, that by virtue of transcending a particular substantive norm, or a particular set of substantive norms, procedural justice transcends all substantive norms. In fact, even when procedural justice vindicates human dignity, it depends on substantive norms. However, the norms on which procedural justice depends, in that instance, operate at a higher level of

7. Furthermore, to the extent that its ability to ferret out the truth is what makes the American adversary system of criminal justice procedurally just as a means of applying relevant substantive norms of retributive justice, some of its key features as a guarantor of human dignity—such as the Fifth Amendment's privilege against self-incrimination, which allows the criminal defendant not to testify against him or herself—seem somewhat at odds with its role as a procedural vehicle for the application of substantive justice.

8. Actually, the dependence between procedural justice and substantive norms of distributive, corrective, or retributive justice is mutual rather than one sided. Indeed, if a substantive norm is not capable of being applied in a procedurally just manner, it is altogether not suitable as a legitimate legal norm, although it may still qualify as a legitimate moral norm.

abstraction than the particular substantive norms sought to be applied in a just manner. Furthermore, because it is likely that there would be a greater consensus regarding the substantive norms operating at higher levels of abstraction (compared to the less abstract substantive norms sought to be applied in a just manner), the more abstract norms may appear to be universal or beyond conflicting conceptions of the good. In other words, from the perspective of the level of abstraction at which the conflict of particular substantive norms unfolds, the more abstract norms may be perceived as remaining beyond dispute.

To illustrate this last point, let us consider the following example. Suppose that a state guarantees a certain minimum standard of living to every citizen; everyone who can prove that he or she cannot reach this standard through his or her own means is entitled to receive public assistance. To implement this policy, the state erects a welfare administration charged with the responsibilities of processing applications for public assistance, determining whether to award public assistance to particular applicants, and determining whether to terminate such assistance upon a finding that a particular recipient no longer needs it. Suppose, further, that the state's constitution requires that each citizen be given an opportunity to be heard before the revocation of any statutory entitlement.[9] To assess the administrative procedures designed to carry out the state's public assistance program, reference must be made to the following two norms: each citizen has a right to a state-guaranteed minimum standard of living; and every citizen is entitled to be treated with dignity and respect—which in this case requires that he or she be afforded an opportunity to be heard before the termination of public assistance payments. Although both of these norms are substantive and contestable, the first, which is more concrete, is much more likely to generate controversy than the second. Thus, whereas libertarians, utilitarians, and egalitarians would undoubtedly all endorse the second norm, they would most certainly disagree concerning the legitimacy of the first norm, with the libertarians strongly objecting against welfare rights.[10] Also, from within the trenches of the conflict over welfare rights, the equal dignity norm may be perceived as universally valid or at least settled beyond dispute.

The importance of procedural justice for modern legal systems and the importance of its structure enabling it to fulfill the twofold role identified above are no accident. Given modern law's strong tendency to cast relationships among legal subjects as relationships between strangers, it is hardly surprising that matters of procedure should be brought to the fore-

9. *Cf.* Goldberg v. Kelly, 397 U.S. 254 (1970) (Due Process Clause of the Fourteenth Amendment requires a hearing prior to the termination of welfare payments).

10. *See, e.g.,* ROBERT NOZICK, ANARCHY, STATE, AND UTOPIA (1974).

front often predominating over matters of substance.[11] Perhaps less obvious, but equally important, is the fact that this flight to procedure can never be completely successful, since matters of substance persist although they are often either concealed or displaced. A particularly important example of how substantive norms can be concealed by procedural ones emerges through a closer look at pure procedural justice.

Rawls suggests gambling as an example of pure procedural justice. In his own words, "If a number of persons engage in a series of fair bets, the distribution of cash after the last bet is fair, or at least not unfair, whatever this distribution is."[12] In other words, *any* distribution resulting from a series of fair bets is just, so long as the bets remain fair. If there is no tampering with the betting procedure, such as there would be in the case of cheating, then the outcome of the betting is purely procedurally just (or purely procedurally not unjust). Moreover, since gambling is a means to distribute or redistribute money or goods, gambling which consists exclusively of a series of fair bets produces, in a purely procedural manner, outcomes which further, or at least do not contradict, the requirements of distributive justice.

If we look more closely at the proposition "any distribution resulting from a series of fair bets is just," we can discern two different plausible interpretations: one narrowly focused on gambling as a procedure, the other more broadly focused on gambling as a distributive device. Under the narrow interpretation, fair gambling, in contrast to unfair gambling, is just to the extent that all participants in fair gambling obtain everything which they are entitled to expect, namely an equal opportunity[13] (in the sense of an equal probability) to become the winner. From the broader perspective, however, fair gambling can only be just—or, much more likely, not unjust—if certain material conditions and certain normative assumptions are present. Thus, if fair gambling only involves individuals who risk small amounts of discretionary income, in the context of a normative setting where random allocations of discretionary income would not contravene prevailing norms of distributive justice, then any outcome of fair gambling is not unjust. If, on the other hand, fair gambling were to involve large sums of money, including what for some gamblers would be considered sums nec-

11. An extreme example of the uses of procedural issues to mask conflicts between parties with widely divergent conceptions of the good is provided by the protracted discussions concerning the shape of the negotiating table at the onset of certain peace talks. *See, e.g.,* Thomas L. Friedman, *Third Round of Mideast Talks Closes with Scant Progress,* N.Y. TIMES, Jan. 17, 1992, at A1; Jackson Diehl & David Hoffman, *Participants Gather for Mideast Peace Talks,* WASH. POST, Oct. 29, 1991, at A16.

12. RAWLS, *supra* note 6, at 86.

13. *See* MICHEL ROSENFELD, AFFIRMATIVE ACTION AND JUSTICE: A PHILOSOPHICAL AND CONSTITUTIONAL INQUIRY 42 (1991).

essary for purposes of their subsistence, and if the gambling were to take place in a setting in which, according to prevailing substantive norms of distributive justice, redistributions of income that cause any one to fall below the subsistence level are deemed to be unjust, then even such fair gambling would clearly be (distributively) unjust.

As the example of gambling indicates, pure procedural justice depends on substantive norms of justice as much as the other forms of procedural justice. Pure procedural justice differs only in that under the confluence of certain material conditions and certain substantive norms of justice, application of a given procedure is bound to produce a just (not unjust) outcome or one of many equally just (not unjust) outcomes. Moreover, the perception that pure procedural justice remains independent from substantive norms of justice is made possible by a twofold abstraction. First, the legal subjects who avail themselves of the relevant procedure are abstracted from (in the sense of being lifted out of) the life-world of their daily existence. Second, the relevant procedure is abstracted from the concrete material conditions and particular substantive norms on which it depends for its ultimate justification. The second abstraction would be performed through lifting the relevant procedure from its broader legitimating factual and normative context, and then focusing on this procedure so narrowly as to leave its factual and normative setting out of the resulting picture.

The processes of abstraction present in both procedural and purely procedural justice, while operating somewhat differently, are ultimately relied upon to perform largely similar tasks. On the one hand, abstraction is supposed to sufficiently detach legal subjects from the totality of their concrete trappings in order to place the spotlight on similarities among such subjects, while downplaying the differences that set them apart. Accordingly, in the example of gambling, the individuals involved are considered in relation to their placing bets and not in terms of their differing wealth, education, social class, or family status. Similarly, in the context of the economic marketplace or of contract as a legitimate tool of procedural justice, individuals are considered in their capacities as producer, buyer, seller, or consumer rather than as men or women, rich or poor, or members of an ethnic majority or minority.

In addition to lifting legal subjects out of their concrete sociopolitical circumstances, abstraction serves to minimize or to conceal reliance on contestable substantive norms when attempting to settle conflicts among legal subjects. Moreover, these two different tasks performed by abstraction are not independent from one another, but rather, are closely connected. As already mentioned, the principal normative function of law in complex modern societies is to provide for just intersubjective dealings among legal subjects who relate to each other as strangers. And, as between strangers, justice would seem to require, above all, that all those involved be treated as equals and that the customs, normative beliefs, and ethical commitments of some not be favored over those of others. Also, because one is most likely to perceive a stranger in terms of the ways he or she differs from the members of one's own group, justice among strangers seems to require conceptualizing the realm of intersubjective transactions at a level of abstraction that optimizes awareness of what strangers have in common.

Where legal subjects relate to each other as strangers, procedural justice becomes extremely important and promotes a brand of equality that clusters around similarities. Genuine equality, however, requires taking into account relevant differences as well as relevant similarities.[14] Accordingly, procedural justice seems prone to overemphasize similarities, while underemphasizing differences. Because of this, from the standpoint of achieving global justice, every move in the direction of the greater abstraction required by procedural justice should be paired with a move in the opposite direction in order to prevent the eradication of relevant differences. This latter move, moreover, may either be set in motion automatically, in the context of pure procedural justice operating under propitious material conditions and normative assumptions, or it may be triggered by the application of substantive norms that counter the flight toward abstraction promoted by procedural justice. In short, the task of justice is to account for and reconcile relevant identities and relevant differences. Viewing law as a medium, the above proposition means that the formal equality derived from law, which conforms to procedural justice, must be reconciled with the substantive equality that properly incorporates differences. Furthermore, substantive equality can be promoted through the content of legal norms.

Before turning to an examination of Habermas's proceduralist paradigm, in light of the preceding observations, there are two further points about proceduralism in general which must be briefly mentioned. First, it does not necessarily follow that although proceduralism cannot do away with the need to embrace substantive norms, pure procedural justice is impossible. Clearly, proceduralism cannot rise above substantive norms or appeal to universally valid substantive norms. However, this does not preclude reliance on contestable substantive norms to the extent that such norms must be implicitly or explicitly embraced by all those confronted with the necessity of interacting with others, as legal subjects having to relate to each other as equals and as strangers. In other words, proceduralism may be acceptable in the context of contestable substantive norms. This is true provided that the latter norms cannot be legitimately contested by

14. Inequality results as much from treating those who are different as inferior as it does from imposing treatment as equals onto those whose relevant differences have been disregarded or suppressed. *See id.* at 222–24.

those who come under the sweep of the background assumptions and material conditions underlying the proceduralism under consideration.

Second, a distinction must be drawn between what may be called "primary proceduralism" and what may be referred to as "derivative proceduralism." Under primary proceduralism, deployment of the relevant procedure is both indispensable to and determinative of any outcome that may be considered legitimate. However, under derivative proceduralism, outcomes are ultimately determined and legitimated by something more fundamental than, or logically antecedent to, the relevant procedure. Consequently, the relevant procedure is relegated to an auxiliary or essentially rhetorical role. As an illustration, one can cite the difference between "pure" or "primary" social contract theory and derivative social contract theory:

> Pure social contract theory posits that the ultimate justification of all legitimate social and political institutions lies in the mutual consent of the individuals affected by such institutions. . . . Derivative . . . social contract theories, on the other hand, recognize the social contract device, but do not rely at the deepest level on mutual consent as the source of the legitimacy of social and political institutions.[15]

Consistent with this distinction, Hobbes is an exponent of pure social contract theory, whereas Locke is an exponent of derivative social contract theory.[16] In Locke's theory, the ultimate source of legitimacy is not the social contract itself, but rather the natural right to property. This right to property both prompts the passage from the state of nature to civil society and delimits the scope and function of the social contract.[17]

More generally, pure procedural justice requires primary proceduralism and is ultimately inconsistent with derivative proceduralism. Therefore, derivative proceduralism is not genuine proceduralism but rather substantive theory in procedural garb.

II.

Habermas's proceduralism, rooted in his discourse theory, emerges against the background of Hobbesian as well as Rawlsian contractarianism. Hobbesian contractarianism satisfies the requirements of primary proceduralism yet remains morally arbitrary; Rawlsian contractarianism incorporates the

---

15. Michel Rosenfeld, *Contract and Justice: The Relation Between Classical Contract Law and Social Contract Theory*, 70 IOWA L. REV. 769, 857 (1985).

16. *See id.*

17. *See id.* at 857–58.

standpoint of Kantian morality, but proves ultimately to belong to the realm of derivative proceduralism.[18] In Hobbesian contractarianism, the contractual device both shapes and legitimates the contract of association, which marks the passage from the state of nature to civil society.[19] The contractual device, moreover, performs a critical intersubjective task both by mediating between the conflicting wills of individual contractors and yielding a common will, which differs from every individual will involved, yet is nothing but the product of a voluntary compromise among all the contractors.[20]

Also, in the context of Hobbesian contractarianism, the state of affairs resulting from implementation of the contract may comport with the requirements of pure procedural justice, provided certain material conditions and normative assumptions are satisfied. Those conditions and assumptions are the ones that underlie Adam Smith's conception of a market society in which the "invisible hand" of competition transforms the clash of private interests into a realization of the public interest.[21] In the context of the kind of atomistic competition envisaged by Adam Smith, contract serves to transform the products emanating from the arbitrary wills of individuals into building blocks for the emergence of the public interest.

Absent atomistic market competition, and upon rejection of the Smithian conception of the relationship between the pursuit of private self-interest and promotion of the public interest, contract alone cannot serve to bridge the gap between private and public interest. Accordingly, contract loses its ability to produce pure procedural (distributive) justice. Furthermore, while still a medium for mediation of conflicting wills, contract no longer serves as a means to transcend the arbitrary wills of individual contractors. Finally, in the context of atomistic competition, each contractor presumably has an equal opportunity to influence the shaping of the common will through joint and mutual contract, whereas in the absence of

---

18. *See* JÜRGEN HABERMAS, BETWEEN FACTS AND NORMS: CONTRIBUTIONS TO A DISCOURSE THEORY OF LAW AND DEMOCRACY 449–50 (William Rehg trans., 1996).

19. For a more detailed discussion of Hobbes's social contract theory, see Rosenfeld, *supra* note 15, at 849–50, 852–55, 858–59.

20. In a paradigmatic contract between a buyer who wishes to obtain a coveted good as cheaply as possible, and a seller who wishes to sell that good as expensively as possible, the contract price will be set at a level that is higher than what the buyer wishes, but lower than that wished for by the seller. Moreover, the contract price has to be such that neither the buyer nor the seller prefers to walk away from the contract rather than entering into it. Thus, the conflict between the will of the buyer and that of the seller is settled upon agreement on a contract price, which becomes the joint (intersubjective) will of buyer and seller but which transcends each of their (initial) individual wills.

21. For a more extended discussion of the relationship between Adam Smith's conception of a market society and the achievement of pure procedural justice through the implementation of contracts, see Rosenfeld, *supra* note 15, at 873–77.

rough material equality among contractors, the superior bargaining power of some contractors allows them to have significantly greater influence than others on the configuration of the intersubjective will produced through contract.[22] In short, cut loose from its Smithian moorings, Hobbesian contractarianism in the end is both morally arbitrary as well as partial toward some of the contractors.

Rawlsian contractarianism proposes to resolve both of the defects which plague its Hobbesian counterpart. To overcome moral arbitrariness, Rawls infuses his social contractors with Kantian moral universalism. Whereas Hobbesian contractors are motivated to enter into the social contract to secure indispensable social cooperation on terms most favorable to the furtherance of their own arbitrary will, Rawlsian contractors seek to establish principles of justice upon which they could all equally agree.[23] Moreover, to avoid the pitfalls caused by differences in power among contractors and by partiality, Rawls places his hypothetical contractors behind a "veil of ignorance." This is designed to make it possible for contractors to agree upon principles of justice without taking into account either their social position or their conception of the good.[24]

The veil of ignorance secures equality by allowing strangers to ascend to a higher level of abstraction. At this level they can discover the core of their common identity, unhampered by the power struggles and the clashing differences of their daily existence. Based on that new-found equality predicated on their common identity, strangers, through reciprocal recognition, can discover fair principles of justice to govern all of their intersubjective dealings. However, Rawls's use of the contract device at a higher level of abstraction comes at too high a cost. Indeed, in the course of establishing abstract equality behind the veil of ignorance, Rawls has sacrificed difference, has reduced the social contract from a dialogical to a monological device, and has unwittingly paved the way for the predominance of some

22. Whereas it is obvious that the mere *fact* of contracting tends to lose its legitimating role in the context of a legal contract between two contractors with widely different bargaining power, it is not immediately apparent that an analogous change takes place in the context of the social contract. Upon reflection, however, the analogy seems to hold to the extent that once the "invisible hand" premise is dropped, all the different conceptions of the good are not likely to fare equally well when subjected to the social contract device. Thus, for instance, communitarian and feminist conceptions of the good are much less compatible with the ideology of contract than are individualistic and atomistic conceptions. *See, e.g.,* CAROL PATEMAN, THE SEXUAL CONTRACT 2, 108 (1988) (social contract establishes a "fraternal patriarchy" through which men rule over women). Accordingly, if differences had to be settled through a contractual agreement, atomistic individualists would have a built-in advantage over communitarians or feminists.

23. *See* RAWLS, *supra* note 6, at 11–12.

24. *See id.* at 11.

perspectives which cannot be justified as being superior to those against which they compete.[25]

Rawls's abstract equality behind the veil of ignorance is objectionable to the extent that it drastically downplays difference in its search for a solid common core of identity. Genuine equality requires taking into account relevant differences as well as relevant similarities. Rawls's contractors have been deprived of the means to perceive diversity, and are thus unable to factor relevant differences into their elaboration of fair principles of justice. Differences are also essential to the proper functioning of the institution of contract, as only contractors with different needs, desires, motivations, and resources are likely to seek out one another to negotiate a contractual exchange. Ultimately, Rawls's contractors behind the veil of ignorance are reduced to the position of mere abstract egos.[26] And since abstract egos are interchangeable, as identically constituted and uniform in perspective, in-dividual conclusions would not differ from those reached in concert concerning legitimate principles of justice. Under these circumstances, the contract device seems altogether superfluous, rendering Rawls's principles of justice monological rather than dialogical,[27] and his brand of contrac-tarianism derivatively proceduralist at best.

The most serious defect of the Rawlsian process of abstraction is that it ultimately makes it possible, under the guise of remaining neutral among different perspectives, for some perspectives to gain the upper hand over others. This results from the very means of abstraction that Rawls sets into motion in order to transform the totality of everyday individuals embedded in their particular sociopolitical norms, institutions, customs, and practices into a collection of pure abstract egos acting as social contractors behind a veil of ignorance. Looking closely at this process of abstraction, a distinc-tion can be drawn between physical differences and differences in perspec-tive. For example, there is a difference between racial identity as a function

25. For an extended discussion of these shortcomings of Rawls's contractarianism, see ROSENFELD, *supra* note 13, at 233–37.

26. [Under] Rawls'[s] original position . . . common principles emerge only af-ter all differences in life plans and in natural and social assets have been set aside. Under these circumstances, common principles are reached, not from a diversity of perspectives that incorporates the multitude of existing dif-ferences, but from the mere abstract identity that equalizes all individual per-spectives after having neutralized all the possible sources of individual differ-ences.

Id. at 234–35.

27. This analysis is consistent with Habermas's assessment of Rawls's theory. *See* JÜRGEN HABERMAS, MORAL CONSCIOUSNESS AND COMMUNICATIVE ACTION 66 (Christian Lenhardt & Shierry W. Nicholsen trans., 1990).

of skin pigmentation and racial identity as the product of a distinct historical and cultural-based perspective. Now, we can accept that the veil of ignorance conceals differences based on skin pigmentation just as we can
readily imagine a society that is not comprised of differences in skin color.
However, if historical events such as slavery and racial apartheid have created distinct perspectives, which by and large correspond to differences in
skin color, then how can we go beyond these differences in perspective
while discarding differences in skin pigmentation? If there is a universal perspective that transcends all particular perspectives, proceduralism
would be entirely superfluous or merely trivial. Absent such a universal perspective, however, the abstract egos behind the veil of ignorance would have
to adopt either a racial minority or a racial majority perspective in order to
arrive at any common principles sufficient to sustain fair principles of justice. Under these circumstances, a racially influenced perspective becomes
a material condition that is bound to have an impact on the selection of
principles of justice, yet it remains concealed behind the erasure of differences relating to skin pigmentation.[28]

Habermas's discourse-theoretical proceduralism provides the means to
overcome the particular limitations of both Hobbesian and Rawlsian contractarianism. By relying on communicative action—action oriented toward reaching understanding[29]—as a means to generate consensus, Habermas provides a procedural approach that makes for a clear demarcation
between the *generation* of intersubjective norms and their *use* to one's own
advantage. Consistent with this demarcation, and as a consequence of excluding "strategic action"[30] from the process designed to lead to the consensual adoption of intersubjective norms, Habermas provides a way to
surmount the arbitrariness and lack of impartiality inherent in Hobbesian
contractarianism. Indeed, contract is, above all, the institution of choice
to channel peaceful and orderly interaction among strategically oriented
social actors. Accordingly, the use of contract to generate intersubjective

---

28. For a more extended discussion of the role of race in shaping different perspectives
in the context of American society, as well as the relation between such perspectives and norms
of justice, see ROSENFELD, *supra* note 13, at ch. 9.

29. For a comprehensive discussion of communicative action, see 1 JÜRGEN HABERMAS,
THE THEORY OF COMMUNICATIVE ACTION (Thomas McCarthy trans., 1984) [hereinafter 1
HABERMAS, THE THEORY OF COMMUNICATIVE ACTION], and 2 JÜRGEN HABERMAS, THE THE-
ORY OF COMMUNICATIVE ACTION (Thomas McCarthy trans., 1987).

30. According to Habermas, in strategic action, "the actors are interested solely in the
success, i.e., the *consequences* or *outcomes* of their actions, [and] they will try to reach their objectives by influencing their opponent's definition of the situation, and thus his decisions or
motives, through external means by using weapons or goods, threats or enticements." HABER-
MAS, *supra* note 27, at 133.

norms seems destined to subordinate the perspective of the rulemaker to that of the strategic actor who wishes to press his advantage as far as the rules permit. However, from the standpoint of communicative action, where the focus is on reaching a consensus, both arbitrary will and the strategic actors' thirst for success seem sufficiently isolated and neutralized to move beyond the constraints inherent in Hobbesian contractarianism.

Communicative action also provides the means to overcome the two principal defects of Rawlsian contractarianism—namely its inability to properly account for differences and its unintentional privileging of certain perspectives over others. Not only is everyone supposed to participate in Habermas's discursive procedure for generating and validating intersubjective norms, but there is no veil of ignorance and everyone is free to introduce any matter of concern for discussion. Accordingly, differences are not eliminated *ex ante*, but are taken into full account; the ultimate decision as to which differences to count as relevant to be reached by consensus after full and uninhibited discussion. Moreover, Habermas's dialogical approach, unlike Rawls's contractarianism, is not reductive when it comes to taking different perspectives into account. Indeed, not only does Habermas envisage taking all different perspectives into account, but he insists that his discursive procedure calls for the complete reversibility of the perspectives of all participants in communicative action.[31] In other words, Habermas's proceduralism requires, as a prerequisite to reaching a legitimate consensus, that conflicts presented for discursive resolution be considered by all participants from each and every perspective involved.

Having thus set the procedural path free from unwarranted Hobbesian and Rawlsian constraints, Habermas proposes his proceduralist paradigm. According to this paradigm, the legitimacy of law is to be gauged from the standpoint of a collectivity of strangers who mutually recognize one another as equals and jointly engage in communicative action to establish a legal order to which they could all accord their unconstrained acquiescence. By means of communicative action, a reconstructive process is established through which the relevant group of strangers need only accept as legitimate those laws which they would all agree both to enact as autonomous legislators and to follow as law abiding subjects.

In accordance with this proceduralism, legal subjects can construct a perspective that enables them to view themselves simultaneously as the authors and the addressees of law. From that perspective, moreover, they may jointly determine which laws would be acceptable to them in their capacities as both authors and addressees. And, consistent with this proceduralism based on communicative action, democracy and rights not only

31. *See id.* at 122.

can be reconciled but also apprehended as internally connected and mutually dependent.[32] Indeed, absent the safeguards built in through communicative action, democracy and rights remain at loggerheads since the only guarantee against oppression by legislative majorities would come from antimajoritarian rights limiting the scope of legitimate democratic lawmaking. However, from the standpoint of communicative action, the same rights, which those in the minority would otherwise grasp as shields against the majority, would loom as part of the same bundle of rights and freedoms which enables each member of the legal community to become integrated with every other member of that community.

In addition to reconciling rights and democracy from the standpoint of communicative action, Habermas's proceduralist paradigm of law also offers innovative means to pursue the purely procedural achievement of justice. Indeed, as Habermas indicates, the principal task of the strangers who relate to each other as equal consociates under law is to reconcile the requirements of legal equality with those of factual equality.[33] In other words, through communicative action, legal actors are supposed to reach agreement among themselves as to which factual similarities and differences ought to be taken into account by the law. As we have seen, Hobbesian contractarianism shortchanges the demands of justice to the extent that its proceduralism favors recognition of the identities and differences dear to the most powerful. Likewise, Rawlsian contractarianism also proves inadequate because, among other things, its removal of certain differences *ex ante* renders it only derivatively procedural. Finally, substantive resolutions of the problem of justice necessitate recourse to justice beyond law, which compels favoring certain conceptions of the good over others. In light of these alternatives, Habermas's procedural proposal seems particularly attractive for at least two important reasons: first, it allows all identities and differences to be considered while weeding out strategic uses of them; and second, it requires subjecting all of the identities and differences to every one of the perspectives represented by participants in communicative action. Accordingly, Habermas's proceduralism promises to reconcile legal and factual equality in a way that not only accounts for all existing identities and differences, but that also takes into consideration the importance of

32. As Habermas states,

> a legal order *is* legitimate to the extent that it equally secures the co-original private and political autonomy of its citizens; at the same time, however, it *owes* its legitimacy to the forms of communication in which civic autonomy alone can express and prove itself. This is the key to a proceduralist understanding of law.
>
> Jürgen Habermas, *Paradigms of Law*, 17 CARDOZO L. REV. 771, 777 (1996).

33. *See id.* at 778–79.

every asserted identity and difference for each of the different perspectives represented in communicative action.

The reconciliation of legal and factual equality is a paramount task for postmetaphysical justice. As Habermas notes, however, the two post-metaphysical legal paradigms—namely the liberal-bourgeois paradigm and the social-welfare paradigm (which he seeks to replace with his proce-duralist paradigm)—have not satisfactorily dealt with the nexus between legal and factual equality.[34] The liberal-bourgeois paradigm reduces jus-tice to the equal distribution of rights, thus basically ignoring factual equal-ity.[35] The social-welfare paradigm, on the other hand, seeks to remedy this deficiency by zeroing in on the eradication of factual inequality, and in so doing reduces justice to distributive justice.[36] As a consequence of this, in order to achieve factual equality, the dignity and autonomy of those who must be clients of the welfare state become substantially undermined.[37]

The material conditions underlying the emergence of Habermas's pro-ceduralist paradigm of law thus include both the successive existences and failures of the liberal-bourgeois and social-welfare paradigms. The liberal-bourgeois paradigm relies primarily on a formal conception of equality that clearly places identity above differences.[38] The social-welfare paradigm, in contrast, fosters a material conception of equality that places differences and the need to account for differences in the forefront, leaving equality as identity in the background.

From the broader perspective of the struggle for equality, originating in the repudiation of the feudal order, one can observe an intertwining dia-lectic between identity and difference as well as between equality and in-equality. A brief look into this dialectic is warranted at this point in order to place the struggle to reconcile legal and factual equality, and the three paradigms of law discussed thus far, in a broader context. This should make for a more thorough picture of the background and normative assumptions and of the material conditions surrounding Habermas's proceduralist para-digm of law.

In the struggle against feudal hierarchy, equality as identity achieved predominance, as clearly evinced in the American Declaration of Indepen-dence's famous phrase, "All men are created equal." Moreover, the emer-

---

34. *See id.* at 776–80.
35. *See id.*
36. *See id.*
37. *See id.*
38. In other words, in the liberal-bourgeois paradigm, rights are distributed equally to everyone since every individual is considered identical to every other individual as a being who is inherently entitled to have rights. But if (material) differences among individuals tend to be downplayed, inequalities in the capacity to exercise rights will be disregarded.

gence of equality as identity being a rallying point for eighteenth century bourgeois revolutionaries is set against the feudal order's association of difference with hierarchical relations between superiors and inferiors. In other words, in this particular setting, equality goes hand in hand with identity whereas inequality is coupled with difference. Consistent with this view, the pursuit of equality as identity is to promote the establishment of equal dignity of citizens regardless of status or birth.

There are, however, other contexts in which equality as identity can be used as a weapon against treating all members of society as equals.[39] This occurs when equality has to be purchased at the price of giving up cherished differences; for example, when equal membership in a polity is conditioned on the adoption of an official religion which may require repudiating or suppressing one's own religious preferences. More generally, in terms of the dynamics between identity, difference, equality, and inequality, whether equality as identity ultimately contributes to, or frustrates, treating every member of society as an equal depends on whether equality as identity is pursued in a setting that is best characterized by the metaphor of the master and the slave or by that of the colonizer and the colonized. Indeed, the master treats the slave as inferior because he is different, whereas the colonizer offers the colonized equal treatment provided that the latter give up his own language, culture, and religion and adopt those of the colonizer.[40] Accordingly, in a master-slave setting, equality as identity is a weapon of liberation whereas in a colonizer-colonized setting, it is a weapon of domination.[41]

The dialectic between equality as identity and equality as difference unfolds in the context of the struggle for equality against the backdrop of commitment to prescriptive equality—that is, accepting, as a normative proposition, that all persons are inherently equal autonomous moral agents. Moreover, a discrepancy exists between the ideal of prescriptive equality, which requires a reconciliation of legal and factual equality ac-

---

39. Following Dworkin's distinction, equal treatment—that is, giving to each the same thing—must be contrasted with treating persons as equals—that is, as possessors of the same inherent worth and dignity. *See* RONALD DWORKIN, TAKING RIGHTS SERIOUSLY 227 (1977).

40. For a more extended discussion of these issues, see ROSENFELD, *supra* note 13, at 222–24.

41. A clear example of this contrast is furnished by the constitutional treatment of racial differences in the United States. At the time when racial apartheid was constitutionally sanctioned, the slogan "the constitution is colorblind" was a weapon used against the denial of equal dignity to African-Americans. *See* Plessy v. Ferguson, 163 U.S. 537, 552 (1896) (Harlan, J., dissenting). In the context of modern day claims to entitlement of affirmative action, as a remedy against the lingering effects of past discrimination, however, "the constitution is colorblind" has become the rallying point for those who refuse to redress continuing inequities against African-Americans. *See, e.g.,* Paul C. Roberts, *The Rise of the New Inequality,* WALL ST. J., Dec. 6, 1995, at A20.

counting for all relevant identities and differences, and the conception of equality embraced by active combatants in the struggle for equality. As long as the full realization of the ideal of prescriptive equality remains elusive, combatants struggling for equality seem bound to embrace positions more tilted toward identity or difference, according to whether they wage their fight against particular inequalities grafted upon particular differences or, on the contrary, against inequalities maintained through exploitation of certain identities. In as much as the tilt required to combat inequality unduly sweeps ideally relevant identities or differences, the struggle for equality forces its protagonists to temporally forgo the acknowledgment of certain identities or differences that ultimately must figure in any legitimate reconciliation between legal and factual equality. Finally, the dialectic between identity and difference assuredly compensates for deviations that tilt too far toward identity or difference, without ever reconciling the path of the struggle for equality with the one carved by the ideal of prescriptive equality.

Regardless of whether questions of justice can ultimately be determined independently from questions concerning conceptions of the good, from the standpoint of those engaged in the struggle for equality, *how much* equality there should be and *for whom* is always embedded within the limited horizon of a concrete conception of the good. To the extent that the struggle for equality is likely to involve more than two protagonists, a protagonist's tilt toward identity or difference in dealing with one antagonist may come back to haunt that protagonist when confronting another antagonist. Thus, for example, from the perspective of the generation that carried out the American Revolution and adopted the Constitution, their tilt toward identity, reflected in the phrase "all men are created equal," was undoubtedly useful in the struggle against Britain's monarchy. That same tilt, however, proves to be a nuisance if not a downright obstacle in the context of establishing a constitutional democracy that recognizes the institution of slavery as lawful.[42] This example is admittedly extreme in that the perspective embraced by America's founding generation leads to a blatant contradiction, unless one is prepared to proceed as if slaves were less than human.[43] Even in more mundane cases, however, there is likely to be a ten-

---

42. It is noteworthy that the United States Constitution of 1787 implicitly recognizes the legal validity of slavery. *See, e.g.,* U.S. CONST. art. I, §§ 2, 9. Neither does the Constitution contain equality rights, thus remaining at odds with the 1776 Declaration of Independence. It would not be until after the Civil War that the Constitution would be amended to repudiate slavery, and establish equality rights. U.S. CONST. amends. XII, XIV. For a thorough and enlightening discussion of these issues, see David A. J. Richards, *Revolution and Constitutionalism in America,* 14 CARDOZO L. REV. 577 (1993).

43. Shamefully, this is what the United States Supreme Court did in its infamous *Dred Scott* decision. Dred Scott v. Sandford, 60 U.S. (19 How.) 393 (1857).

sion, if not a contradiction, between the tilt one is forced to assume in one's struggle for equality and the optimal amount of interplay between legal and factual equality consistent with one's perspective grounded in one's own conception of the good. In sum, considering that the struggle for equality is waged from multiple perspectives and against many differently positioned antagonists, the dialectic between equality and inequality generates tilts, either in the direction of identity or difference, which require correction. Overly sweeping claims are also generated, which require adjustment to become better (without ever becoming fully) reconciled with the comprehensive perspective from which they are made. Thus, the interplay between identity and difference must be treated as though it were a dynamic process affecting both the configuration and the scope of equality at any given time and place.

Consistent with the preceding analysis, from the standpoint of every perspective shaped by a particular conception of the good (which is compatible at the highest levels of abstraction with prescriptive equality), the reconciliation between legal and factual equality must satisfy two distinct and, at least to some degree, incompatible requirements. First, such reconciliation should satisfy the optimal relationship between identity and difference within the conception of the good espoused by the relevant perspective. Secondly, such reconciliation should level the playing field between the existing tilts and excesses that result from the ongoing struggle for equality among representatives of different perspectives. If the desired balance is not achieved, the optimal mix between identity and difference could not properly be set in motion in order to become effective. On the other hand, achievement of the desired balance requires reliance on certain identities and differences that are bound to upset, or at least postpone, the implementation of the optimal mix.

The three paradigms of law discussed by Habermas can now be put in context, both in terms of the dynamic struggle for equality, and in terms of competing perspectives on equality and justice. In terms of the struggle for equality, there is a dynamic progression from the tilt toward identity of the liberal-bourgeois paradigm, to the tilt toward difference of the social-welfare paradigm, and finally to the attempt to incorporate, reconcile, and balance the virtues of liberal identity and social-welfare difference within the proceduralist paradigm proposed by Habermas. Therefore, as against the two paradigms which it seeks to replace, Habermas's proceduralist paradigm appears to have significantly levelled the field on which the battle for the optimal reconciliation of legal and factual equality must be fought. This, however, does not necessarily imply that Habermas's paradigm levels the field sufficiently as between the competing perspectives it encompasses, or that it can yield any reconciliation of legal and factual equality that would be acceptable to all the encompassed perspectives.

Focusing on the issue of the perspectives encompassed within Habermas's proceduralist paradigm, three important questions arise. First, does Habermas's proceduralist paradigm, by the very nature of communicative action, effectively exclude certain perspectives? Second, does the proceduralist paradigm provide a workable means of achieving a genuine consensus among the competing perspectives it encompasses regarding the optimal mix of identities and differences, in relation to the legitimate reconciliation of legal and factual equality? And, third, does the proceduralist paradigm provide an adequate means of leveling the field on which the perspectives it encompasses compete for justice and equality? Phrased somewhat differently, these three questions can be restated as: (1) *which* perspectives can expect justice under Habermas's proceduralism?; (2) can such proceduralism produce justice *among* different perspectives?; and (3) can such proceduralism yield equal justice as gauged from *within* each of the encompassed perspectives?

Consistent with Habermas, in answering the first question it is clear that some perspectives are effectively excluded from the discursive resolution of questions concerning justice. Thus, all perspectives that could be broadly characterized as metaphysical perspectives—including those framed by religious dogma and ideology—would effectively be excluded or, more precisely, would effectively exclude themselves from any dialogical process designed to resolve issues of justice. To be sure, this is not problematic for Habermas's proceduralist paradigm since he makes it clear that his paradigm is designed for postmetaphysical conflicts over justice. The exclusion of metaphysical perspectives is noteworthy. It underscores that communicative action is not neutral as between all conceptions of the good, even if in the final analysis it remained neutral among the different conceptions of the good that are not incompatible with it.

Communicative action effectively excludes not only metaphysical perspectives but also nonmetaphysical ones that reject adherence to prescriptive equality. Indeed, there seems to be little point, from the standpoint of nonmetaphysical perspective adherents (who maintain that some are inherently superior), to submit their views concerning justice for discussion with those whom they do not consider as equals. Even if convincing the unworthy is not deemed futile, communicative action by its very structure would still remain manifestly unfavorable toward blatantly inegalitarian ideologies that altogether reject prescriptive equality. In short, it remains to be seen whether Habermas's proceduralism is neutral as between the perspectives it encompasses. However, the exclusion consistent with Habermas's proceduralism of metaphysical and nonmetaphysical hierarchical perspectives indicates that it is ultimately tied to certain substantive normative assumptions, albeit negative ones.

The answer to the second question—namely, whether communicative action can carve out a common ground for justice encompassing all of its perspectives—depends on the nature of the procedural devices involved in communicative action as well as on the existence of material conditions making it plausible for the reversal of perspectives (undertaken by actors engaged in communicative action) to generate fruitful consensuses or compromises. As conceived by Habermas, communicative action requires each participant to have an equal opportunity to present claims for consideration and a universal commitment to be swayed only by the force of the better argument.[44] Thus, the only legitimate normative regulations under Habermas's proceduralist paradigm would be those which have been assented to by all the participants in rational discourses who might be affected.[45] Moreover, in the context of legal as opposed to moral norms, Habermas stipulates that assent could be based on bargaining and compromise as well as on consensus.[46] Finally—and an important advance over Rawlsian contractarianism—the needs, wants, and interests of participants in communicative action are not taken by Habermas to be immutable; rather they are subject to evolution and transformation pursuant to dialogical exchanges. Because communicative action, as conceived by Habermas, can contribute to the formation of opinions and wills,[47] it is not simply relegated to finding overlapping interests; it is also equipped to harmonize interests through dialogical transformation.

In view of the characteristics of Habermas's proceduralism, there are at least three significant impediments to the goal of achieving an accord on justice among representatives of the diverse perspectives engaged in communicative action. First, the reconciliation of perspectives might ultimately prove to be a purely contingent matter. In that case, Habermas's proceduralism would prove inadequate because under many plausible circumstances it would fail to lead to any legitimate reconciliation of legal and factual equality.

One way to avoid this latter possibility is by emphasizing the requirement of rationality. Indeed, if rationality is called for by communicative action in the selection of ends, in dealing with the means toward one's ends, and in dealing with conflicts that exist among persons who pursue different ends, then attaining an accord on justice may no longer be contingent. But that leads to the second problem. If the requirement of rationality is strong enough to foreclose the contingency of an accord, then that accord is dependent on the operative norm of rationality rather than on dialogical reci-

---

44. For a comprehensive discussion of communicative action, see 1 HABERMAS, THE THEORY OF COMMUNICATIVE ACTION, *supra* note 29, at 273–337.
45. *See* HABERMAS, *supra* note 18, at 459–60.
46. *See id.* at 460.
47. *See id.* at 461–62.

procity. Consequently, Habermas's proceduralism would become essentially derivative.

Relying upon bargaining and compromise, as well as on consensus coupled with emphasis on the transformability of needs, provides an alternative way to minimize the chance that the proceduralist paradigm will fail to yield an accord. This last alternative, however, leads to the third problem. If the pressure to reach an accord is intense, then bargaining and compromising—even if they remain free of strategic action—may favor certain perspectives over others (as contrasted with certain individuals over others). If that were the case, Habermas's proceduralism would fail to remain neutral as between the perspectives which it encompasses (much like Hobbesian contractarianism proved unable to remain neutral as between all contractors).

The preceding observations fail to identify any definitive answer to the second question. However, they raise significant doubts whether Habermas's proceduralism alone, unsupported by substantive norms, can reliably lead to an accord on justice among different perspectives without favoring some of those perspectives.

The last of the three questions—namely, can the proceduralist paradigm level the field on which competing perspectives vie for justice—as with the second, cannot presently be given anything nearing a definitive answer. To the extent that proceduralism's search for an accord on justice leads to the favoring of some perspectives, the third question would seem to require a negative answer. However, assuming an accord could be reached without having to favor any of the relevant perspectives, the success of Habermas's proceduralism to level the playing field would appear to depend on whether the requisite leveling could be achieved through dialogue, or whether it calls for predialogical or extradialogical adjustments. To further clarify these matters, I now turn to an important feminist objection to Habermas's proceduralism.

III.

The feminist challenge to Habermas's proceduralism is particularly serious since it is launched from a perspective that is neither metaphysical nor hierarchical in nature. Moreover, the feminist challenge attacks Habermas's proceduralism on at least two different levels. On one level feminists can argue, even assuming communicative action remains neutral between feminist and male-oriented perspectives,[48] the respective needs, wants, and in-

---

48. It is important to remember that what distinguishes feminist perspectives from male-oriented ones are primarily gender-related differences. These differences are largely sociocultural constructs rather than differences merely based on sex. Furthermore, while feminist

terests of each are given such disparate interpretations that it is not realistic to expect any general agreement on how to reconcile legal and factual equality. On another level, feminists can argue that discursive proceduralism cannot level the playing field which has traditionally heavily tilted toward male-oriented perspectives. Additionally, feminists could press the more radical claim that by its very structure communicative action favors male-oriented perspectives over feminist ones. Consequently, no purely dialogical determination of the relation between legal and factual equality could ever prove genuinely acceptable to feminists.

Habermas agrees with the feminists that both the liberal-bourgeois and the social-welfare paradigms evince biases against women.[49] However, he disagrees with the feminists when it comes to the proceduralist paradigm. Essentially, Habermas's response to the feminist challenge is that since gender differences are constructed and not pre-established, conflicts between feminist and male-oriented views should be amenable to dialogical resolution just as other interperspectival conflicts.[50]

To determine whether Habermas's proceduralism can successfully overcome the feminist challenge, it is first necessary to take a closer look at some of that challenge's principal characteristics. Moreover, since there is by no means unanimity among feminists, I shall take a reconstructive approach and combine various elements that have figured in feminist critiques, while advancing the most effective good faith feminist challenge possible. Also, as gender-related issues may vary among cultures, I will only refer to gender-related issues as they arise in the United States.

The feminist challenge in the United States is premised upon a constitutional, legal, cultural, and social tradition that has repeatedly used and/ or constructed differences between men and women to the detriment of the latter, in order to perpetuate a male-dominated society. In that society, with its male-oriented institutions, the best women can hope for is that gender differences will not be used against them. In other words, women's only realistic escape from being subordinated has required them to settle as being colonized[51] in a male run colony. From the standpoint of the relationship between legal and factual equality, women have generally experienced two different regimes during the course of American history. Initially, the relationship between legal and factual equality unfolded in a

---

perspectives may more likely be embraced by women than by men, certain men are genuinely feminists just as certain women side with antifeminists.

49. *See* Habermas, *supra* note 32, at 781–82.
50. *See id.* at 783–84; *see also supra* pp. 796–98.
51. See the distinction between master/slave and colonizer/colonized relationships, *supra* notes 40–41 and accompanying text.

setting tilted toward difference, with differences being, for the most part, weighted against women.[52] More recently, the tilt has shifted toward identity, but women still have been significantly disadvantaged, in as much as identity has essentially meant conformity with male identity.[53]

It is against this background of exploited differences and coerced identities that feminists may construct a comprehensive perspective, with a vision of the good based upon a recasting of identities and differences in ways that are likely to be liberating and enriching for women. Inspired by Carol Gilligan's vision, feminists might construct a conception of the good stressing intimacy, attachment, interdependence, care, concern, responsibility, and self-sacrifice.[54] Such a feminist conception of the good would sharply contrast with its typical male-oriented counterpart, emphasizing separation, competition, and achievement.[55]

Now, let us suppose that representatives of the above-sketched feminist perspective (to whom I shall refer as "the feminists") confront representatives of the typical male-oriented perspective (to whom I shall refer as "the masculinists"), and that they jointly endeavor to reach a dialogical consensus on a mutually acceptable reconciliation of legal and factual equality. Let us suppose, further, that from the outset the feminists stipulate that they concede that the proceduralist paradigm is neutral as between masculinist and feminist perspectives. Under these circumstances, the feminists will start the confrontation by recounting the history of sex discrimination and will argue for the adoption of legal norms that would enhance care, responsibility, and meeting the needs of concrete others.[56] The masculinists, on the other hand, while acknowledging past inequities, will propose legal

---

52. *See, e.g.,* Bradwell v. Illinois, 83 U.S. (16 Wall.) 130 (1873) (state refusal to allow women to practice law held constitutional on grounds that a woman's proper role was that of a wife and mother).

53. *See* Martha Minow, *Justice Engendered,* 101 HARV. L. REV. 10 (1987) (arguing that Supreme Court adjudication on sexual discrimination and pregnancy has posited men's experience as the "norm" against which women are measured).

54. *See* CAROL GILLIGAN, IN A DIFFERENT VOICE: PSYCHOLOGICAL THEORY AND WOMEN'S DEVELOPMENT 12, 73–74, 132 (1982). Gilligan is concerned with morals, not law. Her views, however, have influenced feminist legal theorists. *See e.g.,* Ellen C. DuBois et al., *Feminist Discourse, Moral Values, and the Law—A Conversation,* 34 BUFF. L. REV. 11 (1985). For a critique of Gilligan by a feminist legal theorist, see Jeanne L. Schroeder, *Feminism Historicized: Medieval Misogynist Stereotypes in Contemporary Feminist Jurisprudence,* 75 IOWA L. REV. 1135, 1141 n.12 (1990).

55. Habermas has rejected the validity of Gilligan's challenge relating to issues in the theory of moral development. *See* HABERMAS, *supra* note 27, at 175–84. That controversy, however, has no direct bearing on the use of Gilligan's work to outline the contours of a plausible feminist conception of the good.

56. *Cf.* GILLIGAN, *supra* note 54, at 11 (contrasting men's tendency to focus on "the generalized other" with women's draw toward the "particular other").

norms emphasizing autonomy and fair competition which would preclude gender-based discrimination.

Assuming that no legal norm capable of equally satisfying the masculinists and the feminists were to emerge at that point, our protagonists could proceed to engage in a reversal of perspectives. This would allow them not only to achieve greater empathy toward their antagonists' plight, but also to become aware of the relative importance of each particular claim from within the comprehensive perspective it originated. Awareness of the relative importance of conflicting claims within their respective perspectives might prove quite helpful—it would be rational to sacrifice a claim of lesser importance within one's own perspective to accommodate a claim that within another perspective is much more important. Such a sacrifice would be rational (in the sense of rationality of means rather than rationality of ends) considering the potential for reciprocal gestures that would ultimately inure to the benefit of all those involved.

Now, let us assume that after ranking all wants and interests and abandoning the pursuit of those which rank lower in the hierarchy, in order to facilitate the realization of those which rank higher, the masculinists and the feminists still have not been able to settle on equally acceptable legal norms. At that point, it is possible that each would try to convince the other to change their needs and wants. Thus the feminists would argue that competition is not everything and greater connectedness could enrich the lives of the masculinists. The masculinists would try to impress upon the feminists that competition is not as bad as they think, particularly if it is scrupulously rid of all vestiges of gender discrimination.

At that point in the dialogue, it is possible that a consensus regarding legal norms might be reached. But it is equally possible that a consensus on equally acceptable legal norms might never be reached. The inability of reaching a consensus would not occur because of any strategic behavior, but simply because the honestly held divergent conceptions of the good, even after accounting for all the concessions and adjustments mentioned above, would remain too far apart.

Thus far I have assumed that the feminists do not challenge the proposition that the proceduralist paradigm is neutral as between the feminist and the masculinist perspectives. There are, however, several plausible reasons which would lend support to such a challenge. Furthermore, the feminists could bring either a moderate or a radical challenge against the proposition regarding proceduralist neutrality.

For the moderate challenge, feminists would argue that the procedural guarantees afforded by dialogical proceduralism are insufficient to level the playing field since public discourse has historically been heavily tilted toward masculinist perspectives, as have the liberal-bourgeois paradigms and the social-welfare paradigms and most existing legal norms. Given that masculinist views are so entrenched in the ideology and the institutional structures of the polity, to have an equal opportunity to present one's claims and to attempt to transform existing needs, wants, and interests, seems fairly unlikely to balance the conflicting positions. This is true not because of any strategic conduct by the masculinists, but rather because they are so deeply set in their ways.

Even assuming its validity, the moderate challenge may not be fatal to proceduralism, since even deeply entrenched positions could change over time. However, time is not a trivial matter when it comes to legitimating legal norms. If meaningful changes in opinion- and will-formation can be expected to take several generations, then exclusive reliance on dialogical proceduralism would seem undesirable and inadequate.

Much more threatening to discursive proceduralism is the radical feminist challenge. That challenge takes as its first point of argument Gilligan's view that men's ethics are oriented toward rights, equality, and fairness, while women's are oriented toward responsibilities, equity, and the recognition of differences in need among concrete others.[57] Suppose the masculinists and the feminists incorporate, as part of their conceptions of the good, the views that Gilligan ascribes respectively to men and to women. Feminists could then launch the following attack. By its very structure—which is designed to lead to justice, equality, and rights—the proceduralist paradigm is inherently biased in favor of masculinist perspectives, against feminist perspectives. Ironically, because it provides for a reversal of perspectives, the proceduralist paradigm does not exclude expression of the needs, interests, or desires of feminists and even allows for masculinist empathy toward feminist claims. But those virtues are eventually nullified, in that, by its very nature, the proceduralist paradigm channels all intersubjective conflicts toward resolutions that must comport with justice, equality, and rights. Although the proceduralist paradigm gives the impression of treating feminists as full partners in the dialogical process, the very structure of that process forces feminists to suppress their most fundamental differences in order to obtain a measure of recognition that does not seriously threaten the hegemony of masculinist perspectives. In short, the proceduralist paradigm makes it possible for an individual feminist claim to be given priority over a competing masculinist claim, but it forecloses something much more fundamental from a feminist perspective—the replacement of "the hierarchy of rights with a web of relationships."[58]

In defense of the legitimacy of the proceduralist paradigm, it could be argued that if the radical feminist challenge proves anything, it proves too much. Because its targets include justice, equality, and rights as such,

57. *See id.* at 164.
58. *Id.* at 57.

rather than any particular conception of them, the radical feminist challenge implies that law itself cannot possibly be justified as a medium for legitimate intersubjective interaction. Therefore, the radical feminist challenge would ultimately lead to a social universe devoid of law, in which feminists would either forcibly convert those who would oppose the implementation of their conception of the good, or their antagonists would go their own separate way.

Feminists, however, could argue that their radical challenge does not necessarily have the dire implications mentioned above. Viewed more closely, the radical feminist challenge is not against law itself, but against a paradigm of law which is buttressed by a particular conception of law and rights. Following this line of reasoning, a brief focus on Habermas's conception of rights reveals that while he is open as to the content of legal rights, he clearly embraces a "static" rather than a "dynamic" conception of law as a medium of intersubjective interaction.[59] In Habermas's view, legal rights (as opposed to moral rights) are above all entitlements, which are logically prior to the duties they trigger.[60] Therefore, such rights carve out boundaries which tend to separate the rightholder from those who must assume a duty as a consequence of his or her entitlement. In the context of a dynamic jurisprudence such as the common law, however, because of the presence of greater flexibility, open-endedness, and indeterminacy, rights and duties become the product of interaction among legal actors; thus, they are always susceptible to further perfection through cooperation.[61]

With the distinction between static and dynamic jurisprudences in mind, the feminists can argue that their radical challenge does not demand the abolition of law, justice, equality, and rights—it calls only for the replacement of the proceduralist paradigm and its static conception of rights with an alternative paradigm creating a dynamic conception of rights. This alternative paradigm would alter the importance of justice, equality, and

59. *See* Arthur J. Jacobson, *The Idolatry of Rules: Writing Law According to Moses, With Reference to Other Jurisprudences*, 11 CARDOZO L. REV. 1079, 1125 (1990); *see also* Arthur J. Jacobson, *Hegel's Legal Plenum*, 10 CARDOZO L. REV. 877, 889–90 (1989) [hereinafter Jacobson, *Hegel*]. For present purposes, the key distinction between these two jurisprudences is that dynamic jurisprudences are open-ended and primarily concerned with the realization and development of legal personality. Static jurisprudences are primarily concerned with instituting legal order and, accordingly, draw sharp lines between legal relationships and other intersubjective relationships which remain essentially beyond the reach of law.

60. In Habermas's own words, "[w]hereas in morality an inherent symmetry exists between rights and duties, legal *duties* only result as consequences of the protection of *entitlements*, which are conceptually prior." HABERMAS, *supra* note 18, at 451.

61. *Cf.* Jacobson, *Hegel*, *supra* note 59, at 890–91 (in the common law system persons cannot interact without generating rights and duties, yet cannot know what those rights and duties are until after they have interacted).

rights, by balancing them against normative standards designed to enhance promotion of the "web of relationships." Moreover, any alternative paradigm of law designed to be consistent with the radical feminist challenge could neither be exclusively dialogical nor merely procedural. It would have to press substantive feminist norms against masculinist objections, thus having to rely on predialogical or extradialogical sources of legitimacy.

Proponents of legal proceduralism may object to any alternative feminist paradigm which would countenance the imposition of feminist norms over masculinist objections arguing the paradigm would be arbitrary or inconsistent with a commitment to prescriptive equality. Feminists however could counter, arguing that their proposed alternative paradigm would neither be arbitrary nor in violation of the dictates of prescriptive equality. Focusing on the dialectics between identity and difference, and between equality and inequality, feminists could claim that progress toward an optimal reconciliation of legal and factual equality has always been achieved through a series of thrusts that overshoot their intended target, thereby tilting legal paradigms toward certain conceptions of the good to the detriment of other conceptions. This state of affairs requires compensation which necessitates generating a tilt toward the opposite direction. Therefore, the feminist alternative paradigm, with all its bias, is a logical moment in the ongoing struggle to reach an optimal reconciliation of legal and factual equality. Consequently, such an alternative feminist paradigm is neither arbitrary nor contrary to prescriptive equality.

Based on the above examination of the feminist objection to Habermas's proceduralist paradigm of law, it is now possible to give a more complete answer to the two questions left open at the end of the Part II. First, unaided by additional substantive norms, legal proceduralism cannot be expected to produce justice among different perspectives within its domain. Second, proceduralism alone fails to yield equal justice as gauged from *within* each of the encompassed perspectives.

IV.

Considering that pluralism implies a lack of agreement regarding substantive norms, it would seem to be the most promising ally of pure procedural justice. Ideally, proceduralism should save pluralism from the embarrassment of having to choose among the various competing conceptions of the good it encompasses. However, pluralism and pure procedural justice are ultimately incompatible. Conversely, whereas a community that shares the same substantive norms may seem to have no use for mere procedural justice, pure procedural justice can assume a legitimate role in the context of shared substantive norms, as indicated by the gambling example discussed earlier.[62] If these observations are correct, then Habermas's legal proceduralism may be vindicated to the extent that it is confined to contexts regulated by shared substantive norms. Moreover, while such vindication may fall quite short of pluralist expectations, it is by no means trivial.

Before looking into the relationship between pluralism and pure procedural justice, a distinction concerning pluralism must be briefly addressed. Pluralism may either be methodological or comprehensive. Methodological pluralism can be characterized as a tool designed to prevent any substantive conception of the good from achieving a dominant position in the public sphere. Comprehensive pluralism, on the other hand, is a full-fledged substantive perspective encompassing a particular conception of the good which requires the inclusion and protection of different substantive perspectives that can be accommodated peacefully within the polity. The distinction between these two kinds of pluralism raises the following question: Since comprehensive pluralism relies on shared substantive norms, is it not then compatible with pure procedural justice? As we shall see, the answer to this question is eventually negative, even though comprehensive pluralism reserves an important but limited role for proceduralism.

To get a better understanding of the relationship between pluralism and proceduralism, it is useful to refer back to the image of transcommunal market relationships among strangers.[63] At first, one can assume that the market where strangers came to exchange goods was an important yet occasional focus for intersubjective dealings. Under these circumstances, the market required transcommunal laws to regulate dealings among strangers and to stabilize the latter's expectations. Aside from the occasional forays into the market, intersubjective dealings also took place intracommunally, where they were regulated primarily by common religious and ethical norms or by laws conforming to such norms. Given that everyone returned to his or her own community except for limited market exchanges, it makes sense that the legal norms regulating market transactions would be procedural in nature. Although one cannot properly speak of pluralism in this scenario, it would be fair to speak of a proceduralism bound by a plurality of distinct communities.

At the next stage, one can imagine that the market has become more important, and that all the bordering communities sending people to the market will associate into a loose confederation. In this situation, pluralism and proceduralism co-exist, but their respective spheres of operation remain completely separated from one another.

62. *See supra* pp. 796–98.
63. *See supra* notes 20–27 and accompanying text. For a more extended discussion, see Rosenfeld, *supra* note 2, at 1689–94.

As the market encroaches ever more on communal life, however, proce-duralism and pluralism enter a collision course. On the one hand, the market increasingly expands onto the terrain formerly reserved for commu-nal ethical and religious life, forcing substantive communal norms to spill over into the sphere of market interactions for lack of another suitable out-let. On the other hand, since markets are not perfect, the more perva-sive market relations become, the greater the need to bring in substan-tive norms in order to channel market transactions toward the common good.

To the extent that market self-regulation is no longer satisfactory, proce-duralism must give way or become subordinated to substantive norms. Methodological pluralism may be used in an effort to prevent proponents of certain conceptions of the good from subjugating proponents of other conceptions, but it is merely a limited tool with restricted potential. Com-prehensive pluralism, on the other hand, provides a full-fledged perspec-tive and therefore deserves a closer look.

The ideal underlying comprehensive pluralism is to create a society in which all conceptions of the good are equally encompassed, but in which none is dominant (or superior). However, this ideal cannot possibly be re-alized. It is obvious that the entire pluralist project will collapse unless com-prehensive pluralism itself is given priority over the remaining conceptions of the good. Therefore, to survive, the project of comprehensive pluralism must split and proceed at two distinct levels. Furthermore, this split must take place in two logically, though not necessarily temporally, different mo-ments. In the first moment, comprehensive pluralism must be detached from other perspectives in order to ascend to the requisite position of pri-macy. Yet to survive, pluralism cannot remain detached because it is ulti-mately parasitic on other perspectives. Indeed, if all other conceptions of the good were to disappear, pluralism would become meaningless. Accord-ingly, a second moment must follow.

In the second moment, pluralism must be reconnected with the perspec-tives from which it had been detached. However, the reconnection must allow pluralism to retain its primacy while allowing the other perspectives to remain equal among themselves. To be viable, pluralist norms must oc-cupy the place of a second order of norms, while the norms which emanate from other substantive conceptions of the good would operate as first order norms.

If the equal subordination of all first order norms to the second order norms of pluralism were possible, then comprehensive pluralism could in principle go hand-in-hand with proceduralism. However, this is not possible since equal subordination requires detachment as well as reintegration. In-deed, detachment of pluralism as a second order norm is realized through a process of negation that is embraced by all comprehensive pluralists and deals equally with all first order norms. Hence, in its negative work, comprehensive pluralism could rely on purely procedural devices.

However, with respect to the positive task of reintegrating subordinated first order norms, neither equality nor unanimity can be achieved by comprehensive pluralism. Because, when it comes to reintegrating into a comprehensive pluralist framework, some first order norms—such as those of crusading religions—will prove altogether incompatible with pluralism and therefore have to be suppressed. Other first order norms—such as those of noncrusading religions—will have to be displaced but they will not have to be suppressed. For example, while such norms will be expelled from public places, they will be given a protected place in the private sphere.

Even among those first order norms which should be granted full reintegration into the comprehensive pluralist polity, some will fare better than others. This seems inevitable since the second order norms operating alone cannot determine the configuration of a pluralist society's legal and political institutions. Since all fully admitted first order norms are not likely to coalesce into a harmonious whole, institutional norms and practices are bound to rely more heavily on some than on others.

In sum, comprehensive pluralism is a dynamic system that depends on the concurrent work of a thrust and counterthrust which is propelled by the permanent tension generated by the friction between its negative and positive work. In such a setting, proceduralism has an important negative role to play—it can be vital in pluralism's struggle against the permanent entrenchment of any particular set of first order norms that it encompasses. However, proceduralism can also play a limited, but nonetheless crucial, role on the positive front. By exposing particular inequities through its leveling mechanisms and by revealing concealed inequities through the reversal of perspectives (in the case of Habermas's dialogical proceduralism), proceduralism can channel pluralism's need for contested first order norms toward more encompassing, widely shared, and less oppressive alternatives. Although this would not solve the problem of reconciling legal and factual equality, it might significantly alleviate existing inequities.

To be sure, this seems to be a far cry from what Habermas seems to expect from his proceduralist paradigm of law. All the same, while Habermas may not have reconciled democracy, rights, and justice through proceduralism, he has certainly shown us creative and fruitful new ways to approach these elusive subjects, and has afforded us new means to sharpen our grasp of them.

PART TWO

The Place of Legal Theory in Habermas's Thought

FIVE

Legitimacy and Diversity

Dialectical Reflections on Analytical Distinctions

Thomas McCarthy*†

Jürgen Habermas's discourse theory of democracy has repeatedly been criticized for placing too much emphasis on consensus and not enough on conflict. He wants, it seems, to defend a discourse-theoretical version of the "general will" as the key to democratic legitimacy, whatever the cost. The costs are usually reckoned in terms of the theory's tenuous relation to the hurly-burly of democratic practice, where disagreement is the rule and unanimity is in short supply. Many of these criticisms miss their target, for they are often based on superficial readings and serious misunderstandings. But enough of them hit the mark to indicate that there are real problems here. My own view is that the problems can be addressed without surrendering the discourse approach to democratic deliberation. But adjustments need to be made.

In general, Habermas has more wholeheartedly accommodated conflicts of interests in his model than he has conflicts of values, ways of life, worldviews, and the like. Before 1988, the latter issues were scarcely discussed in his political-theoretical works. Since then, however, he has continuously elaborated upon notions of "ethical-political" culture, identity, and discourse. In the beginning, those elaborations simply left agreement at the center and disagreement in the margins. In more recent years, considerations of diversity, pluralism, multiculturalism, and multinationalism have figured importantly in his discussions of democratic theory and practice. Yet they still have not dislodged rational agreement from the center of his model.

In what follows, I want to take up a line of argument that I introduced

*John Shaffer Professor of Philosophy, Northwestern University.
†The translations in this Article are generally those of the author.

in an earlier essay.[1] I will not discuss Habermas's justification of the discourse theory of democracy, but only whether the theory deals adequately with persistent disagreements rooted in social, cultural, and ideological diversity. Once again, I will focus on legislation (rather than adjudication or administration) and ask if the model of democratic decision making he recommends is a "realistic" normative ideal for democratic practice. And again, rather than advancing views that compete with those of Habermas, I shall try to identify and expand upon tensions in his own ideas. Because his views on law and politics have undergone significant development over the years—creating the problem of aiming objections at a moving target—I have found it convenient to discuss them more or less chronologically. Part I of this Article deals with the account of legitimacy after his discourse theoretical turn in the early 1970s, but before his introduction of a specifically "ethical" mode of discourse in 1988. Part II analyzes that shift and its amplification in the years before the appearance of *Faktizität und Geltung* in 1992.[2] This *magnum opus* of legal and political theory is then examined in Part III. Finally, Part IV considers some important developments in essays that have appeared since. The implications of all this for the discourse-theoretical concept of legitimacy are drawn out in the conclusion, where I will argue that the idea of "the consent of the governed" should not be given so cognitive a conceptualization as Habermas gives it.

I.

After Habermas set forth the basic ideas of his theory of communication early in the 1970s, his discussions of democratic legitimacy were a continuous development of a few central themes.[3] Actually, those themes had first

1. *See* THOMAS McCARTHY, *Practical Discourse: On the Relation of Morality to Politics, in* IDEALS AND ILLUSIONS: ON RECONSTRUCTION AND DECONSTRUCTION IN CONTEMPORARY CRITICAL THEORY 181–99 (1991) [hereinafter *Practical Discourse*].

2. JÜRGEN HABERMAS, FAKTIZITÄT UND GELTUNG: BEITRÄGE ZUR DISKURSTHEORIE DES RECHTS UND DES DEMOKRATISCHEN RECHTSSTAATS (1992) (all translations are those of the author).

3. *See* JÜRGEN HABERMAS, LEGITIMATION CRISIS 95–143 (Thomas McCarthy trans., 1975) [hereinafter HABERMAS, LEGITIMATION CRISIS]; JÜRGEN HABERMAS, *Legitimation Problems in the Modern State, in* COMMUNICATION AND THE EVOLUTION OF SOCIETY 178 (Thomas McCarthy, trans., 1979) [hereinafter HABERMAS, COMMUNICATION AND THE EVOLUTION OF SOCIETY]; 2 JÜRGEN HABERMAS, THE THEORY OF COMMUNICATIVE ACTION (Thomas McCarthy trans., 1984) [hereinafter 2 HABERMAS, THEORY OF COMMUNICATIVE ACTION]; Jürgen Habermas, *Wie ist Legitimität durch Legalität möglich?*, 20 KRITISCHE JUSTIZ 1 (1987) [hereinafter Habermas, *Legitimität durch Legalität möglich*]; Jürgen Habermas, *Law and Morality, in* 8 THE TANNER LECTURES ON HUMAN VALUES 217 (Sterling M. McMurrin ed., Kenneth Baynes trans., 1988) [hereinafter Habermas, *Law and Morality*]. I will cite English translations where available, but I will alter them where required by consistency or accuracy, without making special note of the fact.

been introduced in 1962, in *The Structural Transformation of the Public Sphere*,[4] but the theory of communication supplied the means needed to develop them precisely and in detail. The conception of legitimacy in question was formulated in direct opposition to legal positivist attempts to reduce it to the legality of formal procedures. Against them, Habermas argued that the outcomes of legal procedures could claim legitimacy only if the legal order itself was recognized as legitimate. That is to say, it was the justification of the legal-political system as a whole—a justification that was, for democratic systems, based on appeals to human rights and popular sovereignty—that conferred legitimacy on decisions arrived at via procedures conformable to it. This meant, as Habermas put it, that "the paths of legimation grow longer" as law becomes positive: indirect, "procedural" legitimacy relieves decision-making processes from the "justification problems that pervade traditional law in its entirety."[5] There no longer need be a *direct* moral justification for each and every law; *indirect* justification appealing to recognized procedures of enactment often suffices, at least in the first instance.

At the same time, however, Habermas did not want to say that *only* constitutional fundamentals are susceptible of direct justification. In his view, the validity claims of legal norms generally rest on grounds that can and should be tested in public debate:

> [W]e cannot explain the validity claim of norms without recourse to rationally motivated agreement. . . . The appropriate model is the communication community [*Kommunikations-gemeinschaft*] of those affected, who as participants in a practical discourse test the validity claims of norms. . . . The normative validity claim is itself cognitive in the sense of the supposition (however counterfactual) that it could be discursively redeemed—that is, grounded in a consensus of the participants through argumentation.[6]

On this account, it seems, each and every law requires direct justification; its claim to legitimacy must be tested in rational public discourse to determine whether it expresses what "*all* [could] want," a "common interest" that could be communicatively shared.[7] Any legal norm that is not, or could not be, "based on rational consensus" is "based on force," with one exception: fair compromises arrived at under conditions of a balance of power, which are said to be "indirectly justifiable."[8]

There is an evident tension between these two strands of Habermas's

---

4. Jürgen Habermas, The Structural Transformation of the Public Sphere: An Inquiry into a Category of Bourgeois Society (Thomas Burger & Frederick Lawrence trans., 1989); *see also* Habermas and the Public Sphere (Craig Calhoun ed., 1992).

5. 2 Habermas, Theory of Communicative Action, *supra* note 3, at 178.

6. Habermas, Legitimation Crisis, *supra* note 3, at 105.

7. *Id.* at 108.

8. *Id.* at 111.

earlier account of legitimacy, a tension which, as we shall see, has not been entirely resolved even in his most recent work. A law that claims legitimacy as the *formally* correct outcome of procedures that are themselves recognized as legitimate is not *ipso facto* a law that expresses what all could *substantively* want, even if everyone agrees to its formal correctness. Not only negotiated compromises are a problem here. Any procedure that relies on anything less than substantive rational consensus to arrive at decisions will leave a gap between (formal) procedural legitimacy and (substantive) rational acceptability. One obvious way of closing the gap would be to make legitimate procedures *themselves* depend on rational discourse and reasoned agreement, and that is, in fact, what Habermas does. In the modern period, he writes, "the level of justification has become reflexive. The procedures and presuppositions of justification are themselves now the legitimating grounds on which the validity of legitimation is based. The idea of an agreement that comes to pass among all parties, as free and equal, determines the procedural types of legitimacy. . . ."[9] Ideally, then, democratic constitutions should establish procedures and conditions under which "rational opinion-formation" and "rational will-formation" are likely to occur, that is, under which the formal correctness of legal-political decisions warrants the presumption that they express a general interest to which all could rationally agree. In this way, legitimacy, procedural correctness, rational acceptability, and the general interest are conceptually interlinked—with the significant advantage that the emphasis of legal positivism on legitimation through formal procedure can be accommodated without surrendering the internal relation of law to right.

What makes this possible, according to Habermas, is the formalization of both law and morality in the modern period, as they became increasingly oriented to the core value of impartiality.

> If, in societies of our type, legitimacy is supposed to be possible on the basis of legality, then the belief in legitimacy, deprived of an unquestioned religious or metaphysical backing, must somehow be based on the rational properties of law. . . . We can find the rational core—in a moral-practical sense— of legal procedures only by analyzing how the idea of impartiality in the justified choice and application of binding rules can establish a constructive connection between the existing body of law, legislation, and adjudication. This idea of impartiality forms the core of practical reason. . . . [I]t was developed in theories of morality and justice that laid down procedures for how someone could decide practical questions from the moral point of view.[10]

With this, the rational acceptability of legal norms is tied to their impartiality: general assent can reasonably be expected from free and equal per-

9. HABERMAS, COMMUNICATION AND THE EVOLUTION OF SOCIETY, *supra* note 3, at 185.
10. Habermas, *Law and Morality, supra* note 3, at 241.

sons only for norms that give equal consideration to all. Accordingly, Habermas's "discourse theory of justice" assesses legal-political systems by the degree to which impartiality, and hence practical rationality, is built into their processes of public "opinion- and will-formation." That standard applies as well to the conditions under which political compromises are negotiated; the impartiality of practical reason is expressed not only in agreements reached discursively, but also in compromises arrived at fairly.[11]

The theoretical power of this model of democratic legitimacy derives from its conceptual interweaving of core concepts from normally competing approaches. Its staying power depends on how well those disparate strands hold together. One potential trouble spot is precisely the key connection between procedural correctness and rational acceptability. Even assuming that the procedures in questions are sufficiently ideal, is it reasonable to expect formally correct outcomes to meet with the rationally motivated agreement of everyone involved? In one sense, if we assume that all have rationally agreed to the procedures as fair and impartial, the answer is "yes." In another sense, if we mean that each participant would judge every outcome to be substantively the best, the answer is "no." The distinction between direct and indirect justification remains a feature of the model itself: while constitutional fundamentals and basic procedures must be susceptible to direct justification on grounds that are rationally acceptable to all, specific outcomes need not. And this, of course, accords with our experience of actually existing democracies. General acceptance of basic structures and processes may translate into a general consent of the governed to properly arrive at decisions even when, as is usual, there are those who substantively dissent from them. The clearest indication of this is found in a decision-making procedure central to all constitutional democracies: majority rule. It is clearly designed not to produce substantive consensus, but rather to deal with substantive disagreement; that is, to render decisions possible *even in the face of* persistent disagreements.

Habermas's earlier discussions of democratic legitimacy deal with unresolved disagreements largely by setting negotiation and compromise alongside deliberation and consensus as an acceptable procedure. However, his model of bargaining under a balance of power among strategically acting parties is tailored to conflicts of *interest* and their resolution. It is not at all clear that it could accommodate a type of disagreement that begins to loom larger in his more recent work: disagreements in *value* commitments and judgments, especially when rooted in social, cultural, and ideological differences. The essential elements of the problem are already present in his earlier account of values and evaluative language.

---

11. *See* Habermas, *Legitimität durch Legalitätmöglich, supra* note 3, at 12.

In *The Theory of Communicative Action*,[12] Habermas reminds us that we have access to our needs, wants, inclinations, desires, interests, feelings, and the like only under culturally shared interpretations employing value expressions. Such expressions

> serve to make a predilection understandable . . . and at the same time to justify it, in the sense of making it plausible by appeal to general standards of evaluation that are widespread at least in our own culture. Evaluative expressions, or standards of value, have justificatory force when they characterize a need in such a way that addressees can, in the framework of a common cultural heritage, recognize in these interpretations their own needs.[13]

But if needs and other predilections are, as interpreted, internally related to standards of value whose "justificatory force" is culturally variable, the chance of achieving general consensus on the common good in pluralistic societies is significantly affected. Evaluative perspectives will inevitably inform our conceptions of what is good, not only for ourselves, but also for the communities of which we are members. On what grounds, then, could we expect free and equal citizens with different and often incompatible value commitments to be able to regularly achieve consensus on what is in the common good? To put this point another way, since for Habermas questions of justice have to be posed in terms of what is equally *good* for all, value disagreements will often translate into disagreements about what is right or just.[14] This problem is further aggravated by the fact that individuals are often unwilling to treat values like interests and bargain with them, as contemporary disagreements concerning euthanasia, abortion, pornography, animal rights, and capital punishment illustrate. In such cases, we typically resort to other decision-making procedures, such as voting and majority rule. If these procedures are carried out in ways recognized as legitimate by all parties to the dispute, the outcomes may likewise be recognized as democratically legitimate. But then there is no longer any reason to characterize the results as "reasonable agreements" rather than "reasonable disagreements." The outcomes members accept as formally correct are not *ipso facto* rationally justified in their eyes, if that means justified solely by the force of the better argument, that is, by the cogency of the substan-

---

12. 2 HABERMAS, THEORY OF COMMUNICATIVE ACTION, *supra* note 3.

13. *Id.* at 92. See also *id.* at 42, where Habermas grants that general agreement on values is not always possible, since "values can be made plausible only within the context of a particular form of life." In his view, value standards can be rationally criticized, but the forms critique may take are themselves contextually sensitive in important ways. For further information on this topic, see my discussion of *Practical Discourse, supra* note 1.

14. Essentially the same argument can be made with respect to his conceptualizations of justice in terms of the "common" or "general" interest, and of impartiality in terms of what is "equally in the interest of all." *See id.*

tive reasons offered on the different sides of the issues. For, as Habermas himself has acknowledged, cogency or "justificatory force" can vary with evaluative perspective.

II.

In a remarkable set of essays written in 1988, Habermas began to elaborate upon an aspect of rational will-formation reducible neither to the impartial consideration of everyone's interests nor to the fair negotiation of compromises: specifically "ethical" deliberation.[15] Starting with individual will-formation, he followed Kant in distinguishing the types of practical reasoning appropriate to questions about what is practically expedient, ethically prudent, and morally right. Calculations of rational choice are tailored to the pursuit of particular purposes in the light of given preferences. When serious questions of value arise, there is a need for ethical deliberation on who one is and who one wants to be. Questions of what is right or just, finally, call for the adoption of the moral point of view. And like Kant, Habermas regards matters of this last type, rather than specifically ethical matters, to be the proper domain of moral theory. This is not to say that ethical deliberation is irrational or that it exhibits no general structures of its own, but only that the "disenchantment" of the world has opened the question "How should I (or one) live?" to the pluralism and individualism of modern life. To suppose that the questions of the good life dealt with by classical ethics could be given universally valid answers is no longer plausible. Efforts at self-understanding and self-realization, rooted as they are in particular life histories and forms of life, do not admit of having a general theory; and deliberations on the good life, moving as they do within the

---

15. *See* JÜRGEN HABERMAS, *On the Pragmatic, the Ethical, and the Moral Employments of Practical Reasons, in* JUSTIFICATION AND APPLICATION: REMARKS ON DISCOURSE ETHICS 1 (Ciaran Cronin trans., 1993) [hereinafter HABERMAS, REMARKS ON DISCOURSE ETHICS]. This is a lightly revised version of the Howison Lecture delivered at Berkeley, under a different title, in the fall of 1988; Jürgen Habermas, *Towards A Communication-Concept of Rational Collective Will-Formation: A Thought Experiment,* 2 RATIO JURIS 144 (1989) [hereinafter Habermas, *Collective Will-Formation*]. This is a lightly revised version of a lecture delivered under a different title at Northwestern University in the fall of 1988. JÜRGEN HABERMAS, *Individuation Through Socialization: On George Herbert Mead's Theory of Subjectivity, in* POSTMETAPHYSICAL THINKINGS: PHILOSOPHICAL ESSAYS 149 (William M. Hohengarten trans., 1992) (1988). Jürgen Habermas, *Volkssouveränität als Verfahren: Ein normativer Begriff von Öffentlichkeit,* 6 MERKUR 465 (1989) (reprint of a lecture presented in 1988) [hereinafter Habermas, *Volkssouveränität als Verfahren*]. It was upon the original versions of these four essays and a draft of the first few sections of REMARKS ON DISCOURSE ETHICS, *supra,* at 19–111, that I based my objections to Habermas's account of the relations between morality, ethics, and politics in *Practical Discourse, supra* note 1, which is a revised version of a paper delivered at a conference on Habermas and the Public Sphere in the fall of 1989.

horizons of particular life-worlds and traditions, do not yield universal pre-scriptions.

The general structure of ethical deliberation, as Habermas understands it, is a combination of Aristotelian and Kierkegaardian elements. Serious value decisions involve us in considerations of the good life. Without the support of a metaphysically-based anthropology or an unbroken cultural tradition, questions of the good life shade over into questions of self-under-standing and personal identity. In Habermas's terms, "ethical-existential discourse" on the good life is tied to one's "striving for self-realization and thus to [one's] resoluteness" in living an "authentic" life.[16] The "self-clarification" it achieves arises in the context of a particular life history and remains embedded in it. At the same time, it requires a *critical* appropria-tion of one's life history, such that "one's own past can be accepted in the light of existing possibilities of action as the developmental history of the person one would like to be and continue to be in the future."[17] Heidegger's figure of "thrown projection" nicely captures this dual character of ethical-existential reflection on who one is and wants to be.

Habermas repeatedly warns against the conceptualizing of collective will-formation as if it were individual will-formation writ large. But in his 1988 discussions of ethical-political deliberation he comes close to doing just that in one important respect: the plurivocity of the "we" in public reflection on who we are and who we want to be is not sufficiently thematized. The seeds of the problem lie in the way he conceptualizes individual ethical reflection. By giving it an existential turn, he backgrounds, so to speak, the interper-sonal dimension of ethics while foregrounding the aspect of authentic self-realization. Accordingly, the contrast with moral deliberation gets drawn precisely in terms of morality's concern with the regulation of interpersonal conflicts and its consequent need for a horizon that transcends the telos of an individual's own life.[18] Whatever the pros and cons of schematizing in-dividual will-formation in this way, it makes the transition to collective will-formation all the riskier.[19] The structure of deliberation on questions of

---

16. HABERMAS, REMARKS ON DISCOURSE ETHICS, *supra* note 15, at 9.

17. *Id.* at 12.

18. "[E]thical questions point in a different direction from moral questions: the regula-tion of interpersonal conflicts of action resulting from opposed interests is not yet an issue." *Id.* at 6. At the same time, however, he grants that the maxims in which an "agent's character and way of life are mirrored" lie on a "plane in which ethics and morality intersect because they can be judged alternately from ethical and moral points of view." *Id.* at 7. I will stress below that the same holds for laws.

19. Habermas had already advanced an "existential" model of collective will-formation in his Sonning Prize acceptance speech in 1987. JÜRGEN HABERMAS, *Historical Consciousness and Post-Traditional Identity: The Federal Republic's Orientation to the West, in* THE NEW CONSER-VATISM: CULTURAL CRITICISM AND THE HISTORIANS' DEBATE 249–67 (Shierry W. Nicholsen ed. & trans., 1989).

moral rightness may plausibly be argued to remain essentially the same even with the shift from "I" to "we." By contrast, "self"-clarification about who "we" are and want to be, "self"-understanding in connection with questions of collective identity, and ethical-political discourse about the good life for "us" and about "our" basic values become less like the individual case as the "we" in question grows more heterogeneous. Or to put it in the other way around, the collective case looks more like the individual case as the "we" in question becomes more homogeneous, that is, the more the assumption of a shared history, experience, culture, tradition, and identity are in fact warranted.

In the 1988 papers, the problems that cultural diversity raised for collective identity and political consensus do not come sharply into focus. When collective identity is thematized, it is typically in the singular, with plurality appearing only at the individual level. Thus, ethical-political discussions are said to have as their goal "the clarification of a *collective identity* that must leave room for the pursuit of diverse *individual life projects.*"[20] Specifically political conflicts of value are discussed only fleetingly and typically only in connection with the selection of goals rather than with the resolution of conflict as such.[21] Ethical-political deliberation is said to aim at an "authentic collective self-understanding" and the formation of an "authentic common will."[22] Disputes concerning strong evaluation are to be resolved in just such hermeneutic processes of self-clarification.[23] The operative assumption seems to be that discourses of this type would, at least under ideal conditions, lead to rational consensus, and thus that in this respect they are like discourses about truth claims.

This assumption is clearly at work in Habermas's discussion of majority rule in *Volkssouveränität als Verfahren.* There he cites approvingly the views of Julius Fröbel who sought theoretically to combine "truth-oriented opinion-formation" with "majoritarian will-formation."[24] The validity or legitimacy of laws requires that they be rationally acceptable to *all* who are bound by them, but democratic legislatures typically operate with *majority* rule. To resolve this tension, Fröbel interprets majority rule as the "conditional agreement" of a minority which, while continuing to regard its *opinion* as correct, renounces its *will* in favor of the majority, until such time as it can rationally convince a majority that its views are correct. The open, critical, ongoing nature of the process of discursive opinion-formation ensures that, in the

20. HABERMAS, REMARKS ON DISCOURSE ETHICS, *supra* note 15, at 16 (emphasis added).

21. Thus, in Habermas, *Collective Will-Formation, supra* note 15, the problem of social coordination is divided into tasks of goal attainment and conflict resolution, and the ethical clarification of collective identity is linked with the former.

22. *Id.* at 151.

23. *See id.* at 153.

24. Habermas, *Volkssouveränität als Verfahren, supra* note 15, at 467.

long run at least, erroneous views will give way to correct ones.[25] Of course, this interpretation assumes that there is *a* single correct view in such matters. Without that assumption, the purely fallibilistic reading of existing disgreements as essentially temporary would be in competition with a reading that viewed them as possibly persistent.

In "Practical Discourse," I tried to make a case for the latter reading. Appealing to the sorts of considerations concerning conflicts of value discussed above, I argued that Habermas had to make room for irresolvable differences and reasonable disagreements in his conception of rational opinion- and will-formation. "The success of Habermas's universalization principle in getting from multifarious 'I want' to a unified 'we will' depends on finding 'universally accepted needs.' . . . [But] this may not be possible when there are fundamental divergences in value orientations."[26] I suggested that the tension between the ideal of rationally motivated consensus and the reality of multiple value perspectives might be reduced by moving in the direction Rawls had marked out with his idea of an overlapping consensus.

> Reflective participants will be aware of the "particularity" of general and comprehensive moral views, of their rootedness in particular traditions, practices, and experiences. If they are fallibilists and if they consider the basic political institutions and procedures of their society to be just, they may well regard collective decisions arising from them as legitimate and hence as "deserving of recognition" even when they disagree.[27]

Habermas responded to this argument as follows: when public discussion, rather than leading to rationally motivated consensus on general interests and shared values, instead sharpens disagreements by revealing particular interests to be nongeneralizable or particular values to be neither generalizable nor consensually orderable, we can still seek agreement at higher levels of abstraction.[28] But that response invites the question of whether the level of abstraction at which pluralistic societies can reasonably hope to secure general agreement amidst the play of social, cultural, and ideological differences might not, after all, be similar to the one occupied by Rawls's "political conception." Habermas correctly regards this as an empirical matter:

> [T]he sphere of questions that can be answered rationally from the moral point of view shrinks in the course of development toward multiculturalism within particular societies and toward a world society at the international

25. *See id.* at 468.
26. *Practical Discourse, supra* note 1, at 191–92. Habermas seems to have understood this as an argument for a more communitarian view, but it was meant to push in just the opposite direction.
27. *Id.* at 198.
28. *See* HABERMAS, REMARKS ON DISCOURSE ETHICS, *supra* note 15, at 88–91.

level. But finding a solution to these few more sharply focused questions becomes all the more critical to coexistence, and even survival, in a more populous world. It remains an empirical question how far the sphere of strictly generalizable interests extends. Only if it could be shown in principle that moral discourses *must prove unfruitful*, despite the growing consensus concerning human rights and democracy . . . would the deontological endeavor to uncouple questions of justice from context-dependent questions of the good life have failed.[29]

I would, however, distribute the burden of proof here somewhat differently. Only if it could be shown that such discourses *must prove fruitful*, at least in the long run and under ideal conditions, could legitimacy be tied *directly* to reasoned agreement. But if the assumption of universal rational acceptability *need* not extend further than the basic rights and principles of the democratic constitutional state—which, recall, Habermas interprets in procedural terms—we would be left with a two-level model of legitimation in which efforts to achieve discursive consensus on substantive legal and political issues *could* prove unfruitful.

That Habermas was, in fact, moving closer to Rawls on this point became clearer in an essay written in 1990, "Citizenship and National Identity."[30] There he argues that *political* integration in a multicultural society or multinational federation presupposes only a common *political* culture:

[A] political culture in the seedbed of which constitutional principles are rooted by no means has to be based on all citizens sharing the same language or the same ethnic and cultural origins. Rather, the political culture must serve as the common denominator for a constitutional patriotism which simultaneously sharpens an awareness of the multiplicity and integrity of the different forms of life which coexist in a multicultural society. In a future Federal Republic of European States, the same legal principles would also have to be interpreted from the vantage point of different national tradition and histories. One's own national tradition will, in each case, have to . . . be connected with the overlapping consensus of a common, supranationally shared political culture of the European Community.[31]

In modern societies, he noted, the growing differentiation of political integration—centered around ideas of citizenship—from cultural integration more generally has made it possible for political cultures rooted in

29. *Id.* at 91 (emphasis added).

30. Jürgen Habermas, *Citizenship and National Identity: Some Reflections on the Future of Europe*, 12 PRAXIS INT'L 1 (1992).

31. *Id.* at 7. This paragraph reads somewhat differently in the version published as an appendix to FAKTIZITÄT UND GELTUNG, *supra* note 2, at 632–60; but that version too invokes the Rawlsian metaphor of "overlapping" (*überlappen*). *Id.* at 659. Essentially the same approach was already suggested in the 1987 Sonning Prize speech in which Habermas advanced the idea of a "constitutional patriotism."

constitutional traditions to develop and to coexist with wide cultural differences in other spheres. Consequently, the appropriate model of deliberative democracy "no longer hinges on the assumption of macro-subjects like the 'people' of 'the' community"[32]—nor, I would add, on the assumption of a unified "we" as the subject of *ethical*-political discourse—for "[t]he identity of a political community . . . depends primarily upon the constitutional principles rooted in a political culture and not upon an ethical-cultural form of life as a whole."[33] Given Habermas's procedural interpretation of constitutional principles, it seems to follow that general agreement on legal-political procedures may coexist with irresolvable disagreements on matters of ethical substance, particularly if we recall that he distinguishes ethical questions from strictly moral questions on just such grounds. While it makes sense to assume that there is one correct answer to the latter, this assumption is out of place in ethical disputes. Speaking of abortion, for example, he writes:

> [I]nsofar as what is at issue is in fact a moral matter in the strict sense, we must proceed on the assumption that in the long run it could be decided one way or the other on the basis of good reasons. However, *a fortiori* the possibility cannot be excluded that abortion is a problem that cannot be resolved from the moral point of view at all. . . . [I]t might transpire that descriptions of the problem of abortion are always inextricably interwoven with individual self-descriptions of persons and groups, and thus with their identities and life projects. Where an internal connection of this sort exists, the question must be formulated differently, specifically, in ethical terms. Then it would be answered differently, depending on context, tradition, and ideals of life. It follows, therefore, that the moral question, properly speaking, would first arise at the more general level of the legitimate ordering of coexisting forms of life. Then the question would be how the integrity and coexistence of ways of life and worldviews that generate different ethical conceptions of abortion can be secured under conditions of equal rights.[34]

Now, if what Habermas says here about abortion were to hold for a great many other issues that democratic legislatures typically have to deal with in multicultural societies, we would need an account of democratic public life that was decidedly less centered on rational consensus than is his. Democratic deliberation would *normally* be shot through with ethical dis-

---

32. Habermas, *supra* note 30, at 11.
33. *Id.* at 17.
34. HABERMAS, REMARKS ON DISCOURSE ETHICS, *supra* note 15, at 59–60. This example makes clear that it is, at best, misleading for Habermas to draw the distinction between morality and ethics in terms of a distinction between obligations and goods or between norms and goals. There are ethical norms and obligations too. That approach is suggested, I think, by his existentialist understanding of ethics, which has the effect of relegating ethical life (*Sittlichkeit*) to the background of ethical decision.

putes that could not be resolved consensually at the level at which they arose. Moreover, those disagreements might well carry over to more general questions concerning "the legitimate ordering of coexisting forms of life."

According to Habermas, ethical disputes differ from moral arguments in their degree of contextuality. The former are "always already embedded in the traditional context of hitherto accepted, identity-constituting forms of life."[35] By contrast,

> the moral point of view, however, requires that maxims and contested interests be generalized, which compels participants to *transcend* the social and historical context of their particular form of life and particular community and adopt the perspectives of *all* those possibly affected. This exercise of abstraction explodes the culture-specific lifeworld horizon within which processes of ethical self-understanding take place.[36]

It requires that participants detach themselves from the interpretive perspectives of their particular groups and try to reason as members of "a socially and spatiotemporally unlimited communication community,"[37] that is, that they try to "appeal to reasons that could convince anyone irrespective of time or place."[38] I am not concerned here with assessing this characterization of specifically moral discourse, but I do want to argue that discourses of this description play much less of a role in democratic public life than assigned them by Habermas. The problem is his tendency to regard *questions of legal and political justice* as *moral* questions, and thence to conclude that they must be debated primarily from the point of view of strict universalizability—that is, not as ethical questions of what is good "for us" but as moral questions of what is equally good "for all." Our discussion of such formulas earlier in this section suggests that we have to go beyond this either/or and try to capture the dialectical interdependence *in practice* of these *analytically* distinguishable aspects. If what has to be decided from the standpoint of justice is whether a proposed law, policy, or program is equally good for everyone it affects, then, in practice, discussion will normally concern what is equally good for *all of us,* where the scope of the "us," however indeterminate, does not range across all social spaces and historical times. It refers, rather, to the particular members of a particular society, at a particular time and place, in particular circumstances, and with a diversity of particular interpretive and evaluative perspectives. Of course, reaching some sort of agreement across that diversity will require a degree of abstraction, but it will normally not be the degree of abstraction required for strictly moral norms meant to obligate all human beings. Quite the con-

35. *Id.* at 105.
36. *Id.* at 24.
37. *Id.* at 51.
38. *Id.* at 52.

trary: political discussion will have to take particulars of time, place, circumstances, identities, values, and so on into account in seeking to arrive at decisions that are *just,* that is, *equally good for all of us affected by them.* And, as I argued above, this means that even political discussions about matters of justice will typically encounter disagreements stemming from divergent conceptions of the good. Hence, even when there is widespread agreement at the level of basic principles and procedures, there may well be persistent disagreements at all more substantive levels of discussion.[39] And the generally accepted political processes designed to deal with such disagreements—for example, majority rule—may well produce outcomes that violate some members' deeply held ethical beliefs about the meaning and value of life. Those members may be said to cooperate "willingly" with those outcomes only in the indirect sense that they had a fair chance to convince a majority of what they believed was right, but failed, and will now abide by the rules. They have not simply succumbed to the force of the better argument; nor need they anticipate that what they consider to be the better argument will some day convince all. As reflexive participants, they know that even ideally rational discourse may not lead to substantive consensus concerning what is in the best interest of all of "us," if the "we" is as socially, culturally, and psychologically diverse as it is. Of course, they can still live together peaceably, if they continue to agree on what are fair procedures for dealing with irresolvable differences. But the outcomes of such procedures will not always be directly justifiable in everyone's eyes.

III.

In *Faktizität und Geltung* Habermas elaborates upon the dialectic of the general and the particular that informs democratic deliberation. The legitimacy of law is again tied to decision-making procedures which warrant a presumption that procedurally correct outcomes are likely to be rationally acceptable outcomes. Rational acceptability is tied, in turn, to impartiality, particularly as expressed in the material or substantive equality of law (*Rechtsinhaltsgleichheit*). Finally, equality of consideration and treatment *under law* is tied to equal rights of participation *in the making of law.* Thus, the full circle again connects legitimacy to rational acceptability via impartial procedures geared to the equality of the subjects and objects of law. And again, it is essential to this conception of political legitimacy that the deliberative and decision-making procedures in question be guided by the discourse principle: "Just those action norms are valid to which all those pos-

39. I shall argue in Parts III and IV, *infra,* that ethically-based disagreement may extend to the interpretation and application of basic rights and principles as well.

sibly affected could agree as participants in rational discourses."[40] But now Habermas expands upon the differences between moral and political discourse. Democratic deliberation is geared to the self-organization of *particular* communities in *particular* historical circumstances.[41] Thus, unlike moral norms, which claim to express what all human beings could rationally will, legal norms express the rational will of members of some determinate society, their shared form of life and collective identity, their interest positions and pragmatically chosen ends. Especially in the pursuit of collective goals and in the preservation of common goods, the spectrum of reasons relevant to rational opinion- and will-formation of this sort extends significantly beyond considerations of universal justice. It includes ethical-political and pragmatic reasons, whose cogency is context-dependent.

> A collective self-understanding can only be authentic within the horizon of an existing form of life; the choice of strategies can be rational only in view of posited ends; a compromise can be fair only in relation to given interest positions. The corresponding reasons count as valid relative to the historical, culturally shaped identity of the legal community, and hence relative to the value-orientations, goals, and interest positions of its members.[42]

Thus, in the legal-political domain, there is an inexpungable "facticity," intrinsic even to rational collective will-formation: the legitimacy of law is relative to the "de facto substrate of a legal community's will."[43] As a result, "the moment of construction," that is, of active shaping and design, "emerges more strongly" than it does in morality. And while we may anticipate achieving "rationally motivated agreement" (*Einverständnis*) about the moral duties we *have*, we may reasonably expect only "rationally motivated arrangements" (*Vereinbarungen*) as regards which legal obligations we should voluntarily *take on*.[44] Ideally, the multidimensional deliberations con-

---

40. HABERMAS, *supra* note 2, at 138.

41. *See id.* at 187.

42. *Id.* at 193.

43. *Id.* He adds that many of the reasons figuring in legal-political discourse "hold only relative to fortuitous contexts." *Id.* at 195.

44. *See id.* at 194. It is difficult to capture in English all the nuances of the different words that Habermas uses to render the various types of agreement arrived at through various types of communication. In *Faktizität und Geltung*, he connects *Einverständnis* to discourse and rationally motivated conviction concerning questions of truth and of moral rightness, *Vereinbarung* to negotiation and compromise, and *Konsens* to collective self-understanding, though he is not entirely consistent in this usage. *See id.* at 223. The critical point for my argument is that rationally motivated *Einverständnis* requires that all parties accept an outcome *for the same reasons*, whereas a *Vereinbarung* may be accepted by different parties for different reasons, and a *Konsens* may come about through an *übereinstimmung* (concurrence, consonance, or perhaps even overlap) among the value orientations of different parties. *See id.* at 204.

nected with democratic decision making should strive not only for discursive agreement on questions of justice and negotiated compromise on questions of interest, but also for hermeneutic consensus (*Konsens*) on questions of collective self-understanding. It is this last element that interests us here, and what Habermas has to say about it in *Faktizität und Geltung* takes him still closer to Rawls's conception of an overlapping consensus on political values.

On the one hand, Habermas repeatedly takes note of the pluralism, difference, and conflict of value orientations characteristic of contemporary public life. On the other hand, he usually writes in the singular about "the" form of life, self-understanding, and collective identity of a legal-political community, and he consistently depicts ethical-political discourse as aiming at consensus on such matters. The apparent discrepancy seems to reflect a view, as much suggested as developed, concerning different modes or levels of discourse about values. At one level, value orientations are regarded as informing preferences and goals, and differences therewith are considered to be susceptible of negotiation and compromise. Habermas repeatedly groups conflicts of value *in this sense* with conflicts of interest and assigns both to procedures for arriving at negotiated settlements of various kinds. At another level, however, he regards "strong evaluations" as embedded in forms of life and as constitutive of collective identities. Disagreement at this specifically ethical level are unsuitable for compromise.[45] Rather, they have to be taken up in critical-hermeneutic discourses aimed at discovering or constructing "deeper consonances" (*übereinstimmungen*) in a shared form of life.[46]

> Sometimes contested interest positions and value orientations are so interwoven with a community's intersubjectively shared form of life that serious value decisions touch on an unclarified self-understanding. . . . How we make the traditions and life-forms into which we are born our own by selectively developing them determines who we recognize ourselves as in these cultural heritages—who we are and would like to be as citizens. Serious value decisions arise from and change with the political-cultural self-understanding of a historical community. Clarification of this self-understanding is achieved through a hermeneutics that critically appropriates our heritages and thereby serves the intersubjective confirmation of authentic orientations in life and convictions about values. . . . [T]he outcome turns on arguments that are based on an explication of the self-understanding of our historically transmitted form of life and that weigh value decisions in that context with a view to an authentic conduct of life—a goal that is absolute for us.[47]

45. *See id.* at 218.
46. *See id.* at 204.
47. *Id.* at 198.

The modifiers "as citizens" and "political-cultural" signal a Rawls-like view that the type of ethical agreement critical to deliberation in the democratic constitutional state is ethical-political consensus on our collective legal-political identity and on our basic legal-political values. The differences from Rawls, it seems to me, stem from the different theoretical status Habermas assigns to ethical-political self-understanding. Unlike Rawls's reflective equilibrium, Habermas's hermeneutic self-clarification does not function as the basic level of justification in his theory of justice. Rather, it is theoretically subordinate to his derivation of an "abstract system of basic rights" through an analysis of the presuppositions of democratic self-determination. Particular constitutional traditions may then be viewed as embodiments of this abstract system in concrete polities with concrete cultural heritages. Another difference follows from this: the "reasonable comprehensive doctrines" that belong to Habermas's version of an "overlapping consensus" are reasonable in more than a local sense. The "burdens of reason" they accept are presuppositions of communicative reason at more reflective levels of development. Thus Habermas's version of ethical-political discourse aimed at achieving consensus on shared political values rests not merely on a hermeneutic basis, as does Rawls's reflective equilibrium, but on a communication-theoretical basis *as well.*

Because we only ever have access to the abstract system of basic rights as "refracted" through particular constitutional traditions, hermeneutic processes of self-clarification remain indispensable. But the interpretive perspectives that figure these processes are not delivered up without remainder to the vagaries of history and culture. They can and should be informed by the results of cultural and societal rationalization, particularly by the development and institutionalization of communicative rationality, not only in science and technology but also, and especially, in law and morality. Then we would expect ethical-political discourse to converge on those embedded political values that express our collective identity as citizens of a—*this*—democratic constitutional state and heirs to a—*this*—democratic constitutional tradition. This means that the "overlap" in the overlapping consensus of reasonable comprehensive views would be neither entirely fortuitous nor merely a *modus vivendi.* Moreover, in contrast to Rawls's conception, its contents would not be agreed to for different reasons from different cultural perspectives. The sorts of reasons having to do with the very conditions of possibility of communicative reason, the rule of law, and democratic self-determination would be available to all participants from all "reasonable"—used now in Habermas's developmental-logical sense—perspectives.[48]

48. This could be why he seems to prefer *übereinstimmen* to *überlappen;* it has a stronger connotation of concurrence or coincidence in views.

In the present context, I will not be discussing Habermas's theoretical derivation of a system of basic rights claiming universal (i.e., transcultural) validity,[49] for even if we grant him that, there is ample room for interpretive and evaluative disagreement at every less abstract level of discussion—as Habermas himself acknowledges in scattered remarks, some of which I will now briefly note.

To begin with, "the" system of basic rights does not exist in a state of transcendental purity, but only in the interpretations of it embodied in actually existing democratic constitutional traditions.[50] As these interpretations are multiple, various, and context-dependent, the definite article is warranted only if the different traditions concur (*übereinstimmen*) sufficiently to permit an abstract reconstruction of the performative presuppositions underlying democratic political autonomy generally.[51] As is evident from the debates accompanying the births of actual democratic constitutions, there is a significant basis for reasonable disagreement from the very start. Moreover, "every constitution is a project that can endure only as an ongoing interpretation continuously carried forward at all levels of lawmaking."[52] Our own constitutional tradition shows that this "ongoing interpretation" is no less subject to reasonable contestation for having more or less explicit, already established interpretations as common points of reference. Furthermore, not only the correct interpretation but also the proper balancing of different components of existing systems of rights will be subject to reasonable dispute. Even the interpretation of such core elements of procedural impartiality as equal consideration and equal treatment is "in principle contestable," as is evidenced by disagreements concerning *the relevant respects* in which citizens are to be considered and treated as equal— which matters, for instance, are to be regarded as "public" concerns and which as "private."[53] At various points in his treatise, Habermas also ac-

49. See HABERMAS, *supra* note 2, at 151–65.
50. See *id.* at 163.

> If the system of rights explicates the conditions under which citizens can unite in an association of free and equal legal consociates, then the political culture of a population expresses how they intuitively understand the system of rights in the historical context of their form of life. The principles of the constitutional state can become the driving force for the dynamic project of actualizing an association of free and equal persons only when they are contextualized in the history of a nation of citizens in such a way that they connect with these citizens' motives and fundamental beliefs.
>
> *Id.* at 226.

51. See *id.* at 163.
52. *Id.*
53. The criteria for equal treatment . . . are by no means indifferent to where the boundaries are drawn between the scopes of private and public autonomy. One might understand the historical opposition between social-welfare and liberal

knowledges the essential contestability of collective self-understandings generally and of gender identities in particular,[54] of the broad views of society and diagnoses of the times that inform legislation, adjudication, and administration,[55] and even of the social-scientific knowledge that figures in "pragmatic" discourses.[56]

Given this interpretive and evaluative contestability of legal-political validity claims, it might seem surprising that Habermas should nevertheless insist on the importance of *supposing* that there are right answers to legal-political questions. Because of the importance he attaches to *rational* opinion- and will-formation, not just any deliberative procedures will do; only those procedures likely to produce *grounded decisions* with a presumption of rational acceptability satisfy his conception of legitimacy. Such a desideratum can be accomplished, he maintains, only through discursive practices that operate on the assumption precisely of there being right answers to such questions. Dropping this assumption, it seems, would mean delivering practical deliberation up to "we believe and want/you believe and want" oppositions that could be settled only by force or compromise, whereas he considers questions of justice and of basic political-cultural values to be susceptible of *Einverständnis* and *Konsens*.[57] This is perhaps also why he reiterates in *Faktizität und Geltung* the account of majority rule discussed earlier:

> Majority rule retains an internal relation to the search for truth such that the decision reached by the majority only represents a caesura in an ongoing discussion, recording, so to speak, the interim results of a discursive opinion-forming process. . . . For only then can its contents be viewed as the rationally motivated but fallible results of institutional pressures for a decision.[58]

Is the search for truth about "the" objective world an appropriate analogue of the search for justice in "our" social world? Habermas's inclination to believe that it is arises, I think, from (A) a failure to consistently view ethical and moral questions as *only analytically distinguishable aspects* of legal-

---

paradigms of law also as dispute concerning these boundaries and thus concerning the criteria for equal treatment. . . . It has to be decided from case to case whether and in which respects de facto equality is required for legal equality.

Id. at 500. As a result, the criteria are "essentially contestable" (*grundsätzlich strittigen*).

54. *See id.* at 514.

55. *See id.* at 522.

56. "As soon as expert knowledge is brought to bear upon politically relevant steering problems, its unavoidably normative permeation becomes noticeable and sets off polarizing controversies among the experts themselves." *Id.* at 426.

57. *See id.* at 223.

58. *Id.* at 220.

political problems, aspects *that are thoroughly interdependent in practice,* and (B) a tendency to view the ethical aspect as more consenual and less conflictual than it actually is.

A.

Habermas explicitly characterizes pragmatic, ethical, and moral discourses as thematizing different *aspects* of legal-political problems from different *perspectives or standpoints,* which are reflected in the different *questions* asked and the different *logics* of the forms of communication engaged in.[59] But their analytical differentiation is developed more thoroughly and consistently than is their de facto interdependence. For instance, in the "process model" of argumentation that he sets out, the different modes of discourse are presented as different stages of argumentation dealing with different issues rather than as interconnected thematizations of different aspects of the same issue.[60] And though Habermas does repeatedly stress the interweaving among different forms of discourse and compromise in rational political will-formation, he tends to represent it as a concatenation of separate discourses rather than as an interplay of *in principle* inseparable—because perspectively one-sided and therefore incomplete—thematizations. Taking the aspect analogy seriously would mean, as Habermas put it in *The Theory of Communicative Action* when discussing lifeworld and system perspectives on society, constantly translating back and forth among the different perspectives on a problem.[61] The lack of such reintegration in *Faktizität und Geltung* is most obvious in his treatment of ethical and moral discourse. Rather than developing the dialectic of the right and the good involved in any discussion of what is equally good for all of us, he treats these aspects and their thematizations in sharp separation:

> Unlike the case of ethical-political questions, in moral discussions the circle of those possibly affected is not even limited to members of one's own collectivity. The moral point of view under which policies and laws are subjected to a sensitive universalization test . . . transcends the boundaries of every con-

---

59. *See, e.g., id.* at 197.

60. *See id.* at 201; *see also* JÜRGEN HABERMAS, BETWEEN FACTS AND NORMS: CONTRIBUTIONS TO A DISCOURSE THEORY OF LAW AND DEMOCRACY 8 (William Rehg trans., 1996). In footnote 3 of the "Nachwort" to the fourth German edition of *Faktizität und Geltung,* he regrets this mode of presentation and emphasizes that he has in mind "aspects" that can be separated "only analytically." *Id.* I am arguing that the problem runs much deeper than a single slip up, that the aspectual character of his distinctions is repeatedly ignored.

61. *See Complexity and Democracy: The Seducements of Systems Theory, in* McCARTHY, *supra* note 1, at 152–80. There, I argued that Habermas was also inconsistent in deploying that analytical distinction. For his response, see Jürgen Habermas, *A Reply, in* COMMUNICATIVE ACTION: ESSAYS ON JÜRGEN HABERMAS'S THE THEORY OF COMMUNICATIVE ACTION 214 (Axel Honneth & Hans Joas eds., Jeremy Gaines & Doris L. Jones trans., 1991).

crete legal community, giving one some distance from the ethnocentrism of one's immediate surroundings.[62]

But, in deliberating upon particular laws and policies, we are normally considering norms intended to bind not all of humanity, but only members of our "own collectivity," that is, just the community whose identity and values are at issue in ethical-political self-clarification. Consequently, discussing *legal norms under the aspect of justice* is not the same as discussing moral norms from a strictly universal, wholly decontextualized, moral point of view. Conflating the two gives rise to passages like the following:

> By their structure laws are determined by the question about which norms citizens want to adopt to regulate their life together. To be sure, discourse aimed at achieving self-understanding . . . about the kind of society they want to live in is also an important component of politics. But, as we have seen, these questions are subordinate to moral questions. . . . The making of norms is primarily a justice issue and is gauged by principles that state what is equally good for all. Unlike ethical questions, questions of justice are not related from the outset to a specific collectivity and its form of life.[63]

But "which norms citizens want to adopt to regulate their life together" is indeed "related from the outset to a specific collectivity and its form of life." For legal norms are not meant to be context-transcendently valid in the same way as moral norms; though they must be in accord with the latter, they must also give expression to "the particular wills of members of a determinate legal community" and to their "intersubjectively shared form of life."[64] Consequently the "justice issue" of what is "equally good for all" is not separable from and superordinate to "self-understanding about the kind of society we want to live in": they are two, interdependent aspects of the same problem, namely, "which *norms* citizens want to adopt to regulate *their life together.*" What we need here is a model of practical discourse in which the thematization of any single aspect can take place only against a *background* of implicit assumptions about other aspects, which can themselves be contested and thematized at anytime. Thus, *in practice* political deliberation is not so much an interweaving of separate discourses as a multifaceted communication process that allows for fluid transitions among questions and arguments of different sorts.

B.

Habermas acknowledges that the collective goals to be pursued and the common goods to be preserved are articulated and chosen in the light of

---

62. HABERMAS, *supra* note 2, at 225.
63. *Id.* at 343.
64. *Id.* at 188.

strong evaluations embedded in shared forms of life, that hermeneutic self-understanding is itself embedded in the forms of life it thematizes, and thus that there is an ineliminable element of context-dependence in ethical-political reflection and the value commitments it grounds. Ethical-political reasons "have a relative validity that depends on the context," for a "collective self-understanding can only be authentic within the horizon of an existing form of life."[65] Thus, the hope for consensus on such matters rests on the degree to which the relevant contexts—historical, cultural, and social—are or could be shared. Habermas criticizes liberalism for making democratic deliberation relative to conflicts of "prepolitical" preferences and interests; at the same time, he criticizes communitarianism for making it relative to—indeed the reflective form of—a shared *Sittlichkeit* or ethical life. He insists that democratic deliberation should itself be open to thematizing and thus to transforming the interests and values participants bring to discussion. It should allow them "to discuss value orientations and interpretations of needs and wants, and hence even the prepolitical understandings of [themselves] and the world, and then change these in an insightful way."[66] Habermas does not adequately consider, however, that these insightful changes (or, for that matter, insightful reaffirmations) may not all converge on the same value orientations, need interpretations, self-understandings, and worldviews. As we have seen, he supposes, like Rawls, that in a well-ordered democratic constitutional state there will be sufficient concurrence (*übereinstimmung*), at least on basic *political* principles and collective *political* identity, to provide a framework for dealing with the ethical differences that otherwise persist. But this is a very abstract and general level of agreement; it does not amount to a shared substantial *Sittlichkeit*, for the latter "does not sit well with the conditions of cultural and social pluralism."[67]

As a result, under such conditions, "compromises make up the bulk"[68] of political decision-making processes, for "goals are often driven by interests and value orientations that are by no means constitutive for the identity of the total community"[69] and thus that cannot be reconciled in ethical-political discourse. To the degree that there is consensus on values other than the basic political ones, we have to do with the shared values specific to a culture. They too figure prominently in political discussions—as a source of reasons with special cogency for *this* legal-political community, and as

65. *Id.* at 193.
66. *Id.* at 331.
67. *Id.* at 340.
68. *Id.* at 344.
69. *Id.*

standards against which compromises can be measured, since compromises "must not violate a culture's agreed upon basic values."[70]

But it is not just legal-political communities as a whole that regard their basic values in this way. No group wants to see its basic values violated by political decisions. So once again we confront the sorts of ethical disagreements which, though easily definable in Habermas's categories, are assigned no great systematic importance in his concept of legitimacy. And once again they raise problems of a special kind. Because the scope of ethical agreement that is *required* in any well-ordered democratic society encompasses only the deliberative decision-making procedures at the heart of its constitutional tradition, it can coexist with deep ethical disagreements in other respects. In that case, procedurally correct efforts at rationally motivated agreement may well founder on differences in value orientations, need interpretations, self-understandings, worldviews, and the like. And if those differences are basic to the identities of the groups or individuals involved, they may well regard any compromise that violates them as bad, wrong, and rationally unacceptable for substantive reasons convincing to them. If, in the end, they nevertheless accept a formally correct outcome of the political process as legitimate, it will *only* be because of its formal correctness.[71]

Habermas requires that citizens of a deliberative democracy be reflective participants. Reflective participants will be aware of the possibility of this sort of persistent disagreement. They will agree to disagree and find ways to live together nonviolently despite their differences. Majority rule after public discussion is one such way. But, how should reflective participants now understand it? As we saw, Habermas proposes that they regard it as an interim report on the provisional state of an ongoing discussion seeking the one right answer to a practical-political question but interrupted by institutional pressures for a decision. He takes a similar tack in his analysis of legal argumentation in the judiciary.[72] Oddly enough, that discussion also supplies most of the elements we would need to formulate an account of majority rule different from his. He attempts there to combine the participants' "regulative ideal" of "a single right decision" with reflective awareness of "the fallibility of any actual decision-making" by way of "a strong concept of procedural rationality."[73]

His argument runs as follows: Whether the reasons supporting a legal

70. *Id.*

71. This is the sort of "acceptance" one expects today for rulings on abortion, animal rights, pornography, euthanasia, and the like.

72. *See* HABERMAS, *supra* note 2, at 277.

73. *Id.*

norm's rational acceptability are good reasons can only be determined pragmatically, in discourse itself; but that determination is never final, for "there is no 'natural' end to the chain of possible substantive reasons."[74] Rather, "we end argumentation only when, against the horizon of unproblematic background assumptions, reasons solidify into a coherent whole to the extent that an uncoerced agreement (*Einverständnis*) on the acceptability of the disputed claim comes about."[75] Thus, any such result remains "something provisional, a coherent order of reasons constituted for the time being and exposed to ongoing critique."[76] At the same time, however,

> the idea of an unending process of argumentation striving toward a limit requires that we specify the conditions under which this process has a directional character and which, at least in the long run, make the cumulative progress of a learning process possible. . . . The rationality gap between the individual substantive reasons set out in fundamentally incomplete sequences of argument that generate plausibility at best, on the one hand, and the unconditionality of the claim to the "single right" decision, on the other hand, is closed *idealiter* by the argumentative procedure of the cooperative search for truth.[77]

The intention guiding this procedure is that of "gaining the assent (*Zustimmung*) of a universal audience" without resorting to any force, but to the rationally motivating force of the best reasons, a force that manifests itself only in the actual give and take of an argumentation process in which all of the relevant voices gain a hearing.[78] Habermas notes that in legal discourse the relevant audience is not universal in the strict sense, but "limited to the boundaries of the legal community," and thus the forceless force of the best argument manifests itself "only within the context of an already shared concrete form of life."[79] This idea accords with what was said earlier about the context-dependency of ethical-political argumentation.

It is not difficult to see how these pieces might be reassembled into an alternative account of majority rule in the legislative sphere once we factor in the idea of a "reasonable pluralism." Then the force of particular ethical-political reasons would be expected to exert itself more strongly on some groups and individuals than on others, even as discourse continued. If life-histories and forms of life differed significantly, so too would the "horizons of background assumptions" against which "coherent orders of reasons" took shape. In that case, the de facto end of argumentation would not ex-

74. *Id.*
75. *Id.* at 278.
76. *Id.*
77. *Id.*
78. *See id.* at 281 n.56.
79. *Id.*

press a provisional agreement on the acceptability of a disputed claim, but the provisional outcome of a procedure intended to produce decisions even when there is no such agreement to be had. The for-the-time-being character of any such decision would refer not to the ideal limit point of a directional learning process in which a universal audience was engaged, but to the ongoing effort by minorities to rationally persuade enough of the majority of the greater plausibility of their views to effect a change in the decision. Insofar as ethical-political questions are concerned, then, the appropriate model does not seem to be "a cooperative search for truth"[80] intended to "gain the assent of a universal audience."[81] And the appropriate regulative ideal does not seem to be that of the "single right decision."[82] Deliberative procedures designed to deal with such questions could not, then, be understood as closing the "rationality gap" between actual provisional plausibility and ideal unconditional validity. Rather, they would aim to enhance, as far as possible, the practically-rational character of the decisions that have to be made, while keeping open the possibility of ongoing contestation and eventual change. The rationality gap between "is" and "ought" would be an essentially open invitation to rational criticism and rational persuasion.

Habermas attributes a dual meaning to "the discourse principle": it has "the cognitive sense of grounding a presumption of rational acceptability"; it also has "the practical sense of establishing relations of mutual understanding that are free of violence."[83] In view of the context-dependency of ethical-political discourse and the dialectical interdependence of questions of political right with ethical-political questions, the practical sense must be given greater weight in his account of democratic politics than it has been in the past. Under conditions of posttraditional pluralism and individualism, proposed solutions to the practical problems of living together nonviolently and organizing our common life cooperatively cannot generally be expected to meet with universal agreement. Reasonable people will disagree about such matters, but we can expect that they will nevertheless play by the rules and consent to procedurally correct outcomes as legitimate. In a deliberative democracy, the procedures in question will seek to institutionalize the public use of reason. But the cogency of ethical-political reasons is not independent of context, audience, occasion, and the like; they may be assessed quite differently at different locations in sociocultural space and sociohistorical time. Institutionalized discourse procedures do not change that. Reasonable participants with different value orientations,

80. *Id.* at 279.
81. *Id.* at 277.
82. *Id.*
83. *Id.* at 187.

need interpretations, self-understandings, and worldviews need not always assign the same weight to the same considerations, either before *or* after argumentation. They will, of course, try to persuade others of the force of the reasons they consider best, and try to understand and appreciate the reasons others have for holding the position they do. But that need not lead to a consensual weighing of competing orders of reasons. This is particularly true when the reasons in question are initially unfamiliar because they issue from challenges to established value orientations, self- and world-understandings, and the like—for instance, when they are part of the "struggle for recognition" of subordinated or marginalized groups[84]—but it is also true of the more routine disagreements that stem from socially, culturally, and biographically rooted differences. Reasonable participants will try to speak to (some of) these differences when rationally persuading others to support laws and policies they believe to be in the general interest. They will seek to accommodate (some of) them in the arrangements they propose. And they will learn to live with (all of) them in a nonviolent manner.

IV.

In a recent essay, "Struggles for Recognition in the Democratic Constitutional State," Habermas again comes close to the position I have been advocating, but he ends once again by stressing the consensual aspects of democratic opinion- and will-formation.[85] The topic of the essay lends itself to a focus on interpretive and evaluative differences and hence to a thematization of disagreements that cannot be reduced to conflicts of interest. With emancipatory movements in mind, Habermas turns his attention to "collective actors [who] dispute collective goals and the distribution of collective goods [and] oppose one another in political arenas."[86] He notes that established law has to be reinterpreted continually in light of changing needs, and that this may involve "collective actors . . . defend[ing] themselves against a disregard for their dignity" and articulating "collective experiences of violated integrity."[87] He then goes on to argue that his conception of an abstract system of basic rights with various constitutional realizations is able to accommodate such struggles for recognition. The following are the points most important for our purposes, with some intermittent commentary.

84. *See* AXEL HONNETH, THE STRUGGLE FOR RECOGNITION (1995).
85. *See* Jürgen Habermas, *Struggles for Recognition in Constitutional States,* 1 EUR. J. PHIL. 128 (1993) (this is an English translation of the German original written in early 1993).
86. *Id.* at 128.
87. *Id.*

A.

As the history of feminism illustrates, struggles for recognition often have to do with "elementary levels of a society's cultural self-understanding,"[88] with traditional patterns of interpretation—for instance, stereotypes of gender identity, gender-specific roles, or gender-dependent differences—and with established interpretations of needs.[89] This means that the impartiality or "ethical neutrality of the legal and political order" may also be called into question.[90]

B.

Unlike moral norms, legal norms refer to interactions within specific societies. They are "traced back to the decisions by local legislatures," obtained "within a geographically delimited territory," and "appl[ied] to socially bounded collectiv[ities] of citizens."[91] As a result,

> every legal system is also the expression of a particular lifeform and not merely a reflection of the universalist features of basic rights. Legislation must certainly be comprehensible as an actualization of the system of rights, and policy as an elaboration of it. But the more concrete the subject matter, the more the acceptability of corresponding legal regulations *also* express the self-understanding of a collectivity and its form of life.[92]

This clearly suggests a dialectical model of legitimacy: legitimate law is *at once* a realization of universal rights and an expression of particular self-understandings and forms of life. As concrete, law *must* be both at once. Hence its acceptability or legitimacy can be thematized under both aspects: the right and the good. Whether laws and policies are *equally* good for all of us (affected) and whether they are equally *good* for all of us (affected), are the sorts of questions liberation movements typically raise.

C.

The "unavoidable ethical permeation of every legal community and every democratic process of realizing basic rights" and the cultural-political struggles to which this may give rise need not exclude legal and political consensus, so long as public discourse is able to arrive at "a common conception of the good" and of an "authentic form of life."[93]

88. *Id.* at 133.
89. *See id.*
90. Habermas notes the different scopes of debates figuring in liberation movements of women, ethnic and cultural minorities, nations, and postcolonial societies.
91. Habermas, *supra* note 85, at 138.
92. *Id.*
93. *Id.* at 139.

But on what grounds may we assume that this will always be possible? Is it realistic, under conditions of heightened pluralism and individualism, to expect that discourses of self-understanding will lead in the long run to consensus among participants concerning

> how they want to understand themselves as citizens of a certain republic, as inhabitants of a certain region, as heirs of a certain culture, which traditions they want to continue or break off, how they want to deal with their historical fate, with one another, with nature, and so on?[94]

D.

Habermas stresses the following: ideally, in a democratic constitutional state public opinion- and will-formation is "oriented to the idea of realizing rights."[95] The unavoidable contextualization of this idea in any actual democracy is guided by the task of "continu[ing] the pursuit of an already-established constitutional project"[96] to which "later generations have implicitly or, as immigrants, even explicitly subscribed."[97]

In this connection, Habermas again invokes his Rawls-like distinction between political integration and sociocultural integration. "The ethical integration of groups and subcultures, each with its own collective identity, has to be decoupled from the level of a more abstract political integration that encompasses all citizens of the state."[98] The idea of "decoupling" seems to make this a "real" rather than merely an "analytic" distinction: citizens of a multicultural democratic state have to be able *in fact* to distance themselves from their own particular subcultures and orient themselves to a common political culture when discussing public issues in the public sphere. This common culture is "rooted in an interpretation of constitutional principles"—which, as we have seen, "itself cannot be ethically neutral."[99]

But, it is not clear why we should expect political culture in a pluralistic society to comprise a common interpretation rather than a conflict of interpretations. Acknowledging this, Habermas locates political integration at an even more abstract level: "[p]erhaps it would be better to speak in terms of a common horizon of interpretation within which the citizens of a republic will debate their political self-understanding in connection with actual issues."[100] But how can we know when a conflict of interpretations is

94. *Id.*
95. *Id.*
96. *Id.*
97. *Id.*
98. *Id.* at 144 (footnote omitted).
99. *Id.*
100. *Id.*

situated within a common interpretive horizon? In an established constitutional tradition, part of the answer will be: when debate turns on "the best interpretation of *the same* basic rights and principles," which are "the fixed points of reference for any constitutional patriotism."[101]

I shall leave to one side the question of what "the same" might mean in this formulation.

E.

The common political culture, centered in an "ethically permeated" horizon of interpretation of constitutional principles, must maintain the "neutrality of the legal order" vis-à-vis the multiplicity of forms of cultural integration at subpolitical levels.[102] It can do this only if the horizon of interpretation in question is procedural in emphasis, for substantive consensus on values is not to be expected in complex, multicultural societies, but only "consensus on the procedures for the legitimate embodiment of law and exercise of power. . . . The universalism of legal principles is reflected in a procedural consensus which, of course, has to be embedded in the context of this or that historically determinate political culture, in the form, so to speak, of a constitutional patriotism."[103]

It seems clear, however, that just as different political cultures might advance different interpretations of the "same" abstract system of rights, different ethical subcultures might defend different interpretations of the "same" constitutionally embodied system of rights.

F.

As every concrete legal order is ethically permeated, its ethical neutrality cannot be a matter of abstracting from conceptions of the good altogether. It means, rather, that democratic constitutional states may incorporate into their legal orders only conceptions of the good that all citizens already share or can come to agree upon in political discourse. They may not, however, officially privilege one form of life at the expense of others.[104]

This raises a question about decision-making mechanisms, like majority rule, designed to deal with the large proportion of political issues with which unanimity is not to be had. Since those issues and the decisions regarding them will also have their ethical-political dimensions, the laws passed by majorities might seem inevitably to privilege, on the whole, domi-

101. *Id.*
102. *See id.*
103. *Id.* at 145.
104. *See id.* at 140.

nant over subordinate cultures. If that were the case, ethical neutrality of legal-political outcomes in multicultural societies would be an inherently unattainable goal and perhaps even an illusory ideal.

Habermas introduces a line of thought here that reduces the tension: ideally, democratic procedures should themselves be fashioned so as to respect the integrity not only of individuals, but also of the different lifeworlds and traditions that sustain their different identities, for one cannot protect the former without protecting the latter.[105] This consideration is not based on a presumption of the equal value or worth of all cultures, but on the interdependence of *de facto* and *de jure* equality. The right of legal persons to equal consideration and treatment cannot be assured without protecting in some measure "those intersubjectively shared contexts of experience and life in which they have been socialized and formed their identities."[106] Though the right of citizens to equal respect extends to such identity-forming lifeworld contexts, it does not warrant the "administrative preservation of [cultural] species."[107] Traditions are

> normally reproduced by virtue of the fact that they *convince* those whom they take hold of and whose personality-structures they shape, that is to say, they motivate the latter productively to appropriate and continue them. All the constitutional state can do is make possible this hermeneutic accomplishment of the cultural reproduction of lifeworlds. A guarantee of survival would necessarily rob members of the very freedom *to say yes or no* that is required today to make a cultural heritage one's own and to preserve it. Under conditions of a culture that has become reflexive, only those traditions and forms of life can be maintained which their members experience as binding, even though they expose themselves to critical examination by members and leave succeeding generations the *option* of learning from other traditions or converting and setting out for other shores. . . . Even a dominant culture that does not see itself threatened maintains its vitality only through unrestricted revisionism, through trying out alternatives to the status quo or integrating impulses from the outside—even to the point of breaking with its own traditions.[108]

Thus, the equal right to coexistence of diverse cultures refers to the right of citizens to inhabit and continue their cultures without suffering injury for doing so, but also to their right to criticize and transform them, to be indifferent to and break away from them. In multicultural and rapidly changing societies, traditions and forms of life survive only if they can draw the power for self-transformation from criticisms within and encounters without.

105. *See id.* at 141.
106. *Id.*
107. *Id.* at 142.
108. *Id.*

G.

Fundamentalist efforts to seal off particular life-worlds and promote ultra-stability are incompatible with the democratic constitutional state when they practice public intolerance and fail to respect what Rawls calls "the burdens of reason (or judgment)" in the public sphere. Such dogmatisms remove themselves from a "modern attitude become reflexive" inasmuch as "they leave no space for reflection on their relationship to other world-views with which they share the same universe of discourse and against whose competing validity claims they can be upheld only with reasons. They leave no space for 'reasonable disagreement.' "[109]

Thus, like Rawls, Habermas conceives of public deliberation in multicultural democracies as ideally involving only "not-unreasonable comprehensive doctrines" with "a reflexive attitude that does not merely allow for a modus vivendi" but permits "a civilized disputing of convictions."[110] Only such worldviews make possible the decoupling of ethical and political integration on which multicultural democracies have to rely.

> The equal right to coexistence of lifeforms requires the reciprocal recognition of different cultural memberships: each person must also be recognized as a member of communities that are integrated around different conceptions of the good. The ethical integration of groups and subcultures with their own collective identities must, then, be decoupled from the level of the more abstract political integration that encompasses all citizens in equal measure.[111]

We are not very far from the position I defended in "Practical Discourse." But in a further response to that essay, written at about the same time as "Struggles for Recognition in the Democratic Constitutional State," Habermas was once again at pains to distinguish his position from mine.[112] The sticking point, it appears, is still the emphasis I place on persistent ethical-political disagreements as an indelible feature of democratic public life and on the implications I draw for the concept of democratic legitimacy. The brief rejoinder that follows will serve to bring together the results of the present discussion by reformulating, in discourse-theoretical terms, the idea of (reasonably) agreeing to disagree (reasonably).

Most of the issues between us surface in the following passage.

> [McCarthy] apparently doubts the premise that the legitimacy of laws and policies must rest *in the end* on reasons that, it is claimed, all citizens could

109. *Id.* at 143–44.
110. *Id.* at 143.
111. *Id.* at 144.
112. This is a not yet published "Replik" to critical discussions of Habermas's work. Jürgen Habermas, *Replik*, Rev. INTERNATIONALE DE PHIL. (forthcoming 1996) (on file with author).

recognize or share. . . . This idea stands or falls with *the primacy of the right over the good.* The standpoint of impartiality from which we can judge what is equally in the interest of all has to be institutionalizable in democratic procedures in a neutral manner, that is, *independently of any specific, context-dependent conception of the good.* . . . McCarthy, however, defends the view that we cannot agree on a just procedure—one that ensures neutrality—without *prior* agreement on a common conception of the good, and that attaining such basic ethical agreement *must* founder on the fact of social and ideological pluralism.[113]

I want to make the following points concerning the words and phrases in italics.

1. The phrase "in the end" apparently refers to the fact that, even on Habermas's account, not all decision-making procedures appeal *directly* to universally acceptable reasons. Thus, compromises agreed to by the parties for their own, different, strategic reasons rest only *indirectly* on reasons "all citizens could recognize," namely on those justifying the procedure in question as fair. We have gone over this ground before. The only points I want to make here are, first, that Habermas should be more consistent in drawing, employing, and *terminologically observing* the important distinction between direct and indirect justification, and second, that *he will have to extend it to cover persistent ethical disagreements* as well as conflicts of interest. The key to direct justification is the appeal to substantive reasons that all citizens can reasonably be expected to accept as good reasons; that is, directly justified outcomes are accepted by all for the same procedural *and* substantive reasons. Indirectly justified results of directly justified procedures, by contrast, are accepted by different parties for the same procedural reasons but different substantive ones. Something like this may happen, I am arguing, in the democratic resolution of ethical-political disputes. If so, Habermas will have to adopt a more deeply proceduralist position.

Habermas's proceduralism ties legitimacy to impartiality, and the latter to rational discourse and fair compromise. Because the different types of discourse—pragmatic, ethical, and moral—are in his view all geared to achieving some form of rational agreement on the correct resolution of an issue under discussion, legitimacy through procedure gets tied to legitimacy through rational acceptability; the formally correct outcomes of discursive procedures carry a presumption of substantive rational acceptability as well. But if ethical-political disagreements were not in principle always susceptible of one right answer, their procedural resolutions would, like compromises, not always be acceptable, even ideally, to all parties for the same substantive reasons. They would sometimes be rationally accept-

113. *Id.* at 8 (emphasis added).

able to some members only indirectly, that is, as procedurally correct. It would be misleading in this case to use one term—"rational acceptability"—to refer to two different sources of legitimacy without signaling the difference.

2.   Talk of the "primacy"—or even the "absolute precedence"[114]—of the right over the good can also be misleading if their dialectical interdependence is not signaled just as clearly and consistently. As we have seen, on Habermas's own account, the right and the good are two pervasive *aspects* under which any concrete law, policy, or program may be discussed. The combination of the two is evident in the familiar formulas he uses to express legitimacy: the common *good*, the general *interest*, equally *good* for all, and so forth. Accordingly, we need an account of how discussion under one aspect is internally related to discussion under the other. In any case, the "primacy" or "precedence" of the right could not be "absolute," if that meant being wholly independent of conceptions of the good; it could only refer to the *relative* priority of deliberation from the justice perspective over deliberation from other perspectives. Questions of equal consideration, equal treatment, and the like cannot in the end be divorced from ethical-political considerations.

Taking this tack would further require that Habermas give Taylor and others their due when they insist that justice is a good which, like other goods, is integral to our conceptions of the good life; but he could still insist against them that it is also importantly unlike other goods and superordinate to them in specifiable ways—at least if one wants to allow for a democratic plurality of conceptions of the good.

3.   For the same reasons, the standpoint of impartiality cannot be institutionalized "independently of any specific, context-dependent conception of the good." Rather, "neutrality" has to be interpreted in relation to the cultures and self-understandings of historically determinate collectivities. Habermas himself admits as much when he allows that "every legal system is also the expression of a particular lifeform," and that the "procedural consensus" at the core of "political integration" is rooted in a horizon of interpretation of constitutional principles which is itself "ethically permeated."[115] It is only relative to the plurality of "groups and sub-cultures, each with its own collective identity,"[116] that legal-political procedures can plausibly aspire to neutrality. As Habermas puts it, "what is equally in the interest of all should not be measured against criteria that are only apparently

114. Habermas, *supra* note 85, at 138.
115. *Id.*
116. *Id.* at 144.

universal but actually privilege what is best for a certain group."[117] However, as he made clear in his discussion of equality generally and women's equality particularly, even criteria that are neutral with respect to *disputed* conceptions of the good will reflect some *shared* conception of the good. There is no such thing as absolute ethical neutrality. This also applies to the "neutrality of grounds or reasons" that Habermas invokes against my arguments.[118] He has himself allowed that the setting of collective goals is an ethically embedded process and that the force of ethical-political reasons depends on context, background, form of life, experience, and the like. Consistently with that, he can speak of the neutrality of grounds only in the same sense as Rawls, whom he in fact cites at this point, namely as neutrality *relative* to a shared political culture.

4. According to this dialectical approach, we should not think of ethical-political agreement as temporally "prior" (or subsequent) to agreement on legal-political procedures, but as *a moment of it*. Hence, actual discourses about which laws or policies are right under given or foreseeable cirumstances will, as I argued earlier, "not admit of closure" with respect to discourse about the goods, values, and identities of those involved; and thus "we cannot agree on what is just without achieving some measure of agreement on what is good"—not prior to discussing what is just, but as *part of* discussing it.[119] This, I think, must be Habermas's own considered position.[120] He is not thereby thrown back upon a communitarian approach, or even upon the sort of priority that Rawls cedes to hermeneutics in the method of reflective equilibrium. For in the discourse model, even basic political values may be challenged, subjected to critical interrogation, and transformed through public discussion—as regularly happens, in fact, in the debates that ongoingly accompany the historical "projects" of actualizing constitutional principles in ever-changing circumstances, including changes in the ethical-cultural composition of the legal-political community. Habermas does not, I think, really disagree with this, but he does very much want to avoid having skepticism about the possibility of ethical-political consensus undercut the orientation to reasoned agreement on which he bases his conception of legitimacy.

5. My position has never been that efforts to achieve ethical-political consensus in pluralistic societies "must" fail, but rather that they *may* fail. Between the extremes of maintaining that we can always achieve rational

---

117. Habermas, *supra* note 112, at 8.
118. *See id.* at 9.
119. *Practical Discourse, supra* note 1, at 185, 192.
120. *See* Habermas, *supra* note 85, at 139.

consensus and that we can never do so, lies the view that sometimes we can and sometimes we cannot. Habermas seems to think that my argument turns on denying the very possibility of reasonable agreement in political matters under conditions of social, cultural, and ideological pluralism, when in fact it is meant to affirm the very possibility of reasonable disagreement in such circumstances. Both are possible; neither is necessary. In particular, I have stressed that efforts to achieve consensus in discourse *may* fail owing to basic differences in collective identities and fundamental values, differences that need not dissolve under discussion but may emerge all the more clearly.

To argue that reasonable people *may* ultimately disagree about the meaning and value of life and that this *may* lead to reasonable public disagreements that persist through discourse, it is not necessary to maintain that citizens in a pluralistic society "have no common language, or at least no sufficiently common evaluative vocabulary" in which to carry out their public discussions.[121] The problem is not merely one of mutual comprehension—though that is often enough a serious problem—but one of rational agreement. For the latter, the parties must not only understand each other's reasons but assess their cogency in more or less the same way. And for that to happen it is not enough that "the everyday hermeneutics of mass communication is a melting pot in which subcultural value orientations interpenetrate each other" and give rise to a common public language.[122] This may empirically be the case to a greater or lesser extent. But we can still disagree with those we understand—when, for instance, we give different weights to the same reasons. And that is a conceptual point.

CONCLUSION

Habermas acknowledges that the "unavoidable ethical permeation" of law and politics means that every "actualization of the abstract system of basic rights" will *also* be an expression of a particular way of life, and that this ethical-political aspect will figure into the acceptability of concrete laws and policies. He also allows that "struggles for recognition" may involve ethical-political disputes that range across "the value register of society as a whole" and challenge the impartiality of established laws and procedures. Despite

121. *See* HABERMAS, *supra* note 2, at 9. *But see Practical Discourse, supra* note 1, at 185–87 (my ideas concerning the interpretation of needs, to which Habermas is referring, are part of a longer train of thought meant to identify a variety of sources of reasonable ethical disagreement—not unlike what Rawls calls the "burdens of judgment"—such as differences in value standards and in interpretive and evaluative standpoints, different ideas of the good life, varying contexts of action and experience, sociocultural variations in the cogency of different types of reasons, and divergences in forms of life generally).

122. Habermas, *supra* note 112, at 10.

this acknowledgement of the all-pervasive and essentially contestable ethical dimension of political problems, however, Habermas retains a conception of legitimacy that allows no alternative to open or concealed violence but "consensus arrived at in discourses and in procedurally regulated negotiations."[123] The *prima facie* tension between these two views is resolved for him, it seems, by his belief that what citizens *must* presuppose as participants in rational discourse, they *can* also maintain as observers of society and politics—namely, "the possibility in principle" of "agreeing on democratic procedures that ensure impartiality and [of gaining] intersubjective recognition for the presumption of rationality that procedurally correct outcomes claim for themselves."[124] Against this I have argued that as observers, and thus as reflective participants, citizens must *also* recognize the possibility in principle of reasonable disagreements. *Both* are in principle possible—reasonable disagreement as well as reasonable agreement—and there is no way of determining *a priori* which is in fact which. In each particular instance, that can be determined only *a posteriori*, (and only provisionally) by engaging in discourse and succeeding or failing to come to an agreement.

When efforts to achieve consensus on some public matter do run up against basic ethical-political disagreements and yet legislation regarding it is called for, Habermas suggests a negotiated compromise. He allows, in fact, that in complex, pluralistic societies, *most* political processes will involve bargaining of some sort. And in line with mainstream theory, he understands bargaining as a form of strategic interaction which includes the use of promises and threats that are based on the parties' access to power and resources outside the bargaining situation. Fair compromise must, then, be framed by regulations that somehow ensure an appropriate balance of power among the bargaining parties, regulations that could themselves be agreed to by all parties as participants in practical discourse. But many intractable ethical-political disputes cannot be settled by such means. Disagreements about who we are and who we want to be, about the common good, and about fundamental values are often not susceptible to compromise of this sort. They may be regarded by participants as matters of principle or questions of integrity. Moreover, unlike conflicts of particular interests, they may concern what is "really" in the general interest, and the contending parties may act not as strategic utility maximizers, but, rather, as community-minded consociates. It is important to keep in mind that values inform not only preferences and interests, but judgments of good and bad, and thus of right and wrong, as well. Not only basic values such as respect and dignity have, as Habermas acknowledges, a deontological

123. *Id.* at 11.
124. *Id.*

sense; there is an element of this in any strong evaluation. And that makes disagreements over *public values* less susceptible of compromise than conflicts of *private interest*.

If general consensus is not attainable and strategic bargaining is not acceptable to all, we have to resort to other democratic decision-making mechanisms—in legislative contexts, particularly to majority rule. Habermas seeks to resolve the tension this creates in his model of legitimacy by interpreting majority votes as provisional reports on the state of ongoing discursive processes that could, it must be supposed, lead in the long run to general consensus. But observant participants will be aware that the disagreements in question may as well prove to persist throughout discourse— that is, to be irresolvable, yet reasonable, disagreements. Of course, they have to judge which is which in the not-so-long run; but there may be good, mutually comprehensible grounds for concluding that the opposed parties simply have different views of the meaning and value of life—views that are rooted in different forms of life and historical experiences—and that they could not agree *ethically* without ceasing to be who they are. But then majority rule cannot be understood as Habermas understands it, nor can its general acceptability as a legitimate democratic procedure be grounded as he grounds it. His account of deliberative democracy needs some reworking at this important point.

In the *first* place, Habermas will have to adopt a more strictly proceduralist view which accords legitimacy to formally correct outcomes even when they are not presumed to be, in substance, rationally acceptable to all citizens, just because they involve basic ethical differences. Members may be said "rationally" to accept outcomes with which they substantively disagree only in an attenuated, indirect sense: they abide by the rules they accept as fair even when things do not go their way.[125] Rational acceptance does *not* here have the *cognitive* sense of succumbing to the force of the better argument. However, this modification is not incompatible with the privileged place that Habermas accords to institutionalized discourse, for it is only in and through discourse that ethical differences can be articulated and tested, and can prove to be discursively irresolvable. The rationalizing effect on the quality of public decisions of institutionalizing procedures aimed at producing reasoned agreements is not obliterated by the recognition that consensus is not always attainable, even under ideal conditions and in the long run.

In the *second* place, Habermas will have to reconsider whether there might not be reasonable, nonviolent alternatives to discursive agreement, hermeneutic consensus, and negotiated compromise, other than majority

125. This proceduralist sense of legitimacy is what I was trying to suggest with alternative "b" in *Practical Discourse, supra* note 1, at 197.

rule and similar mechanisms. One such alternative is suggested by his own emphasis, in connection with problems of multiculturalism and multinationalism, on the significance for democratic public life of tolerance, recognition, respect, consideration, and the like. The sorts of arrangements this brings to mind would be more a matter of *mutual accommodation* than of strategic compromise or substantive consensus.[126] One might think of the element of practical reason involved here in terms of Kant's second formulation of the categorical imperative rather than the first, that is, as based on mutual respect for and consideration of the humanity of others—even of others with whom one cannot join in the sort of universal agreement on substantive issues of justice envisioned by the first formulation. It would also be an important and interesting task to explore the logic of the *ethical-political dialogue* that could produce such mutual accommodation and to elaborate its differences from the logics both of truth-oriented discourse and of strategic, self-interested, bargaining.

Taking this tack is, I think, of critical importance for the further elaboration of Habermas's discourse approach to deliberative democracy. Basing democratic institutions, procedures, and practice on the supposition that reasonable agreements on legal-political questions are possible in principle is, as he says, indispensable: there is no substitute for the effect that has on the quality of decision-making processes. On the other hand, the structures and processes of democratic public life should also reflect an awareness that unresolvable yet reasonable disagreements are also possible in principle, and in complex, pluralistic societies may even be likely in fact. To deal reasonably with persistent ethical-political differences we have to rely upon cultural resources and institutional arrangements different from those suited to domains in which there is only one right answer to every well-formulated question. While the natural sciences, for instance, may institutionalize procedures aimed at eventually eliminating all but the one right answer, and while their cultures may instill in practitioners the qualities required to promote this competitive struggle for survival of the fittest views, that is not what we want from political institutions and political cultures when it comes to different forms of life and conceptions of the good. Practical rationality in the face of diversity is as much a matter of recognizing, respecting, and accommodating differences as one of transcending them. Arrangements shaped by the former concern are no less practically rational than those shaped by the latter, and just political arrangements will normally be shaped by both, as well as by negotiation and compromise.

We might be tempted now to extend the ideas of "negotiation" and "compromise" to cover procedures and arrangements that result from respect-

126. This idea of mutual accommodation is what I was trying to get at with alternative "a" in *id.* at 196.

ful mutual consideration as well as from interested utility calculation. But that would conceal the important differences between the two cases. It seems best, then, to acknowledge and analyze independently a type of ethical-political dialogue aimed not at negotiated compromise, not at substantive agreement, and not at ethical-political consensus, but at forms of mutual accommodation that leave space for reasonable disagreements. We can imagine cultures that nourish the corresponding values and virtues, and practices that are predicated not on the assumption of one right answer but on respect for, and a desire to accommodate, ineliminable difference. We can imagine them because we already rely upon them in areas of our lives where it is important for us to maintain harmonious, cooperative, and mutually supportive relations with people with whom we do not always agree, whom we cannot always convince or be convinced by, and whom we do not want simply to outsmart. In multicultural democracies, they will inevitably play a larger role in political life as well.

PART THREE

Law's Proceduralization

The Communicative Model, Systems, and Order

SIX

Quod Omnes Tangit

Remarks on Jürgen Habermas's Legal Theory

Niklas Luhmann*†

I.

Quod omnes tangit, omnibus tractari et approbari debet.[1] The Middle Ages found this rule in Roman law. It had to do with the circumstance of a plurality of legal guardians over the same ward. In the typical case, one guardian's approval was legally sufficient authorization in legal transactions. Since every other rule had seriously damaged business dealings, the business partner's confidence had to be protected. On the other hand, this consideration—that one guardian's approval is legally sufficient authorization for an emancipation—could not have led to a fully realized emancipation of a ward. Nor could it have led to the elimination of the guardianship of all the guardians. For the relations between the guardians the rule was: what concerns everyone (*quod omnes tangit*) requires their agreement.

This seems to have been a reasonable rule. Pursuant to traditional Roman law, case decision making of this kind would, however, be concluded with general reasonings or mnemonics (*Parömien*). This was done in accordance with an ever continuing oral tradition of teaching that supported itself with written texts, yet referred to rules of signs (*Merkregeln*) that made it easier to remember the rules themselves. The teaching needs of the newly erected universities of the Middle Ages and the need to systematize the newly emergent legal culture involuntarily extracted such significant rules from the texts. One compared similar passages, brought the concrete cases back to the texts, and generalized, thus satisfying entirely different needs

---

*Professor of Sociology, Bielefeld University.
†Translated by Mike Robert Horenstein.
1. The literal translation of this phrase is "all those affected should be heard and agree."

of the times through legal doctrine. What was especially new under the title "universitas" was corporation law (*ausgebildetes Körperschaftsrecht*), which included the church, as well as other corporations. The corporation, as distinguished from the dominating family households, was an inner organizational framework that could supply a legal clarification to disputes. In this way, *quod omnes tangit* became a maxim of corporation law that would then always be cited by the better descended (*melior*) or more reasonably argued (*sanior*) party, when members of sufficient social prominence want to announce and accomplish their participation.[2] The political consequences remain assessable. One recalls the conflicts that brought about the Magna Charta or the controversy surrounding the Council movement in the Catholic Church.

The case of the majority of guardians is long forgotten. Today the regulation of representation lacks any indication of social stratification in the quality of the *melior et sanior pars* already given before every dispute. Despite this, *quod omnes tangit* today appears absolutely valid. One says the Owl of Minerva begins its flight at twilight. But how high can she fly?

In other words, how much farther can the rationality of juristic argumentation distance itself from those aids to insight (*Einsichtshilfen*) than it had in its cases? And if one just lets the owl *quod omnes tangit* fly, why not another owl?

With the certainty that his concept of the lifeworld offers him, Habermas, continuing from this point, asserts that not only is a precept such as *quod omnes tangit* valid today, but that it should, with adequate modifications, be extended to maxims of legal rationality. Naturally, it is not possible for all those concerned (including the unborn generations) to be heard and agree. Therefore, the decision cannot be made in a legitimate way. But when this is not possible, one should at least try to pursue the results as though it were possible. These are, however, broad leaps from the Roman tutela to the medieval universitas, to the modern representative constitution and from there to the discourse theory. Does reason withstand this, or does it fall by the wayside?

II.

Our question is, therefore, how does the participation formula encompass *all those involved*? How, despite everything, can its plausibility be preserved? Certainly not in a practicable way because the involvement turns on the decision, thus the involvement cannot be identified in advance of the discourse. Even if this argument did not apply, all those involved would by no

---

2. *See* HAROLD J. BERMAN, RECHT UND REVOLUTION: DIE BILDUNG DER WESTLICHEN RECHTSTRADITION 336 n.54 (1991) (discussing changed context of *quod omnes tangit*).

means accept an invitation to the discourse. To order them to do so would contradict the well considered principles of discourse theory. The problem, therefore, has to be reconstructed so that questions of this kind do not arise in the first place.

Since Habermas does not locate the problem on the level of actually occurring communications, he avoids this possible approach. Instead, he employs a theory of how the reasonable coordination of action can take place if assured of the freely rendered agreement of all involved. This postulate, however, should not be dismissed out of hand as utopian and empirically unrealizable. While one could convincingly do so, such a dismissal could cause one to lose sight of important considerations which justify this conception's topical importance, as well as its concealed affinity with parallel developments in the theory of self-referential systems.

Habermas distinguishes his language-theoretical approach from the subject-theoretical concept of practical intelligence at the level of theoretical self-imaging, and in the context of a general rationality program. This involves a series of important but negative provisional judgments. One must (1) abstain from assuming a transcendental fore-coordination between all thinking subjects. In so doing, the sense of Kant's distinction between the empirical and transcendental disappears. In turn, this further brings into question the basis for assuming that all subjects can in one or another (empirical) way, think or want the same. In this case, coordination ceases to arise out of the facts of consciousness, available to every subject through self-reflection. Rather, it initially arises as the result of a linguistic communication, placed under special conditions. This means that (2) this linguistic discourse is no longer, in the manner of natural law, bound to cognitive or normative conditions which originally arose. This linguistic discourse instead decides itself on its own substantial premises. This self-binding effect (*Selbstbindungseffekt*) arises out of the peculiarities of the use of language. Finally, one must also (3) abstain from assuming contingent moral principles[3] or an ethical law. In addition, such presuppositions are available in the discourse and can only, if at all, be made understandable in a form determined by the discourse.

These assumptions deserve full endorsement, irrespective of any problems in realizing such actual discourse. They amount to an option for a system producing its own uncertainty. Whoever adopts such an option cuts

---

3. Habermas himself does not always operate consistently here. For example, when he engages in direct moral condemnations of the criminal attacks made by youths on asylum-seekers and other foreigners, he thereby tacitly replaces a demo-cratic with a demo-critical perspective. While one agrees wholeheartedly with him, it is a disaster for his theory. Strictly speaking, those who feel themselves affected by delays in the procedures for granting asylum should be invited to the discourses.

all ties to the past and puts himself, and all those involved in the discussion, at the mercy of an unknown future. The uncertainty of the future is the only real invariable of the discourse theory. All procedural measures serve to support these premises much in the same way as they do in court processes or election proceedings of political democracies. The decision has to be regarded as open until it has been made. It is precisely because of this, that the postulates accepted by the discourse theory have been derived from the model of legally regulated procedure.

By intensifying (*Zuspitzung*) in this way, the discourse theory is completely in tune with the times. From a different perspective, the independent production of uncertainty has been understood as characteristic of "postmodern" legal theory.[4] A language theory, which emphasizes that all linguistic statements can assume a yes or no form, and can therefore be linguistically well understood and refused, must come to the same conclusion. The decision theory plays a part, in that it emphasizes that the decision does not arise out of the "choosables," but is rather an original beginning of sequences (*ein originärer Anfang von Sequenzen*) which, in turn, can consist of decisions.[5] The raging value dictates prevailing on the level of party programmes and in the judicial administration of the (German) Federal Constitutional Court have the same effect, because they leave the decision of value conflicts—which all involve deciding value conflicts—to the weight accorded each individual case. All value lists are waiting lists and, as such, condemn those who are seeking justice to waiting for a judge who never appears. There are indeed decisions, but the decision maker, who had constructed the alternative, disappears in the decisions as an excluded ("neutral") third; as an absentee, who remains unconsidered; as an anonymous symbol of the unknown future, which first has to be produced in a communication designed to do so. And last, but not least, in systems theory, it is a question of the same basic circumstances, hidden in concepts such as self-reference, operative closure, autopoiesis, cognitive constructivism, symmetry breaking, nonlinearities, paradoxes and dis-paradoxings (*Entparadoxierungen*), and many others.

With such a heterogenous population theory one cannot be content with attesting to its modernity, however striking this is as a common characteristic. To insist on this commonality is indeed important and could serve to warn adherents here and abroad against misunderstandings. The bleak-

---

4. *See* KARL-HEINZ LADEUR, POSTMODERNE RECHTSTHEORIE: SELBSTREFERENZ—SELBSTORGANISATION—PROZEDURALISIERUNG (1992). Whether the expression "postmodern" is well chosen can, in this context, be left unanswered.

5. *See* G. L. S. SHACKLE, *Imagination, formalism, and choice, in* TIME, UNCERTAINTY AND DISEQUILIBRIUM: EXPLORATIONS OF AUSTRIAN THEMES 19–31 (Mario J. Rizzo ed., 1979) (contrasts the usual claims to objectivity by economic theory stylized as radical subjectivism and therefore relegated to an outside position in the economic sciences).

ness of the banishment to an uncertain future can only, with difficulty, be warmed up by resorting to the coziness of traditional terminology (i.e., democracy, rationality, understanding, consensus, even *Lebenswelt*). The haphazard nature of minor political reprimands is also illuminating. The real test remains the theoretical architecture—the question: how it is done.

III.

For the foundation of the theory of legal discourse discussed here, it is decisive that Habermas sets aside the customary distinction used in the law itself between facts and norms, instead employing his own concept-titles: facticity and validity. Is this likewise a distinction? At any rate, it is not a straight-forward opposition, such as that between facts and norms, in which the edges of the distinction fit together in the sense that they mutually exclude each other. Nor is it a dialectical contradiction, destined to be eliminated by an initially excluded third. However, if it is not any of these things, then what is it?

Habermas contents himself by describing the unity of this distinction as a strained relationship (*Spannungsverhältnis*). While this is not much more than a formula for perplexity, it becomes fascinating (*spannend*) when he describes the self-transcending of the discourses. They are not simply operations, but are what they are and effect what they effect. By reason of the use of language, they transcend themselves. The relevant, valid conditions which have to be accepted in order to make this possible are described by Habermas as idealizations and also as contrafactual assumptions.

This is, at first sight, self-evident. Psychologically individualized and thereby somewhat unruly subjects must be able to assume that they are referring to the same things, despite what might be going on inside of them in terms of mixed experiences. Habermas relies in this respect on language theory. But the same also applies to perception. Even geese must do so when they run cackling through the gate.[6] More important for the overall construction of the theory is the fact that at this point Habermas concentrates on the social dimension and *time stands still*. The idealizations continue to be used in the sequences of communicative actions, as if they were always the same. Formulated in Derrida's terminology, it is a question of *répétition*, not of *itérabilité*. But in reality the overall situation alters—*différence!*—and precisely in linguistic communication from moment to moment. Something said becomes past; that which lies further away thereby

---

6. Humerto Maturana offers a theory that also considers this, taking language as merely behavioral coordination. *See* HUMERTO MATURANA, ERKENNEN: DIE ORGANISATION UND VERKÖRPERUNG VON WIRKLICHKEIT: AUSGEWÄHLTE ARBEITEN ZUR BIOLOGISCHEN EPISTEMOLOGIE (German trans. Braunschweig 1982).

moves closer; one regrets and can only mend; one notes too late what one should have said. The weight and appearance of the idealizations necessary for communication alter all the time. Every identity—each and every one—is produced by a *selective* evaluation of past event-complexes and in its selectivity is continually reconstructed. In other words, identities *condense,* and in ever new situations they are *reaffirmed* and must be correspondingly *generalized.* This can happen fluidly and is a prerequisite for continuous coordination of action. In some instances, Habermas comes very close to this temporal dissolution of idealizations,[7] but in the end still does not perceive that the specifically juridical argumentation is essentially concerned with precisely this issue: fitting ever new cases into a normative structure and thereby reproducing or modifying that structure.[8]

Another disencumbering practice (*Lockerungsübung*) begins with the contrafactual validity mode of normative expectations. Habermas presupposes, and it cannot be disputed, that one can in fact expect contrafactually. While this is also thanks to language, is it not somewhat curious? One can in fact expect, and may continue to expect when the expectation not only has not been fulfilled, but rather disappointed. This is so, not only hypothetically, but also in concrete cases: "You should not have done that!" But why not, when she did it?

Obviously what underlies this is a doubling of reality, such as in other fields, for example, in the pattern game/seriousness, sign/signified (that is, language), immanence/transcendence (religion), fiction/real world (art), average expectations/individual cases (inductive conclusions/statistics). Thanks to such duplications there is a real world and an imaginary world or, more precisely, a real reality and an equally real imagination. In all these cases the duplication serves to make the hardness of the real reality bearable, in religion, for example, as fate, in art as banality. But in the duplication mode this happens in very different ways. The differentiation could have something to do with evolution and with the differentiation of systems. But in this case what is the specific view of reality of the normative

---

7. *See, e.g.,* JÜRGEN HABERMAS, FAKTIZITÄT UND GELTUNG: BEITRÄGE ZUR DISKURSTHEORIE DES RECHTS UND DES DEMOKRATISCHEN RECHTSSTAATS 37 (1992) (on the "Janus face" of validity claims).

8. This method of reasoning can be observed, with few distinctions, in both continental European law and in common law. However, it is more clearly explained in literature discussing the common law. *See, e.g.,* Edward H. Levi, *An Introduction to Legal Reasoning,* 15 CHI. L. REV. 501, 501–74 (1948); Neil MacCormick, *Why Cases Have Rationes and What These Are, in* PRECEDENT IN LAW 155–82 (Laurence Goldstein ed., 1987). Josef Esser once lamented that legal philosophers care more for reasoning than argumentation, "without taking-up legal fieldwork and stock-taking for long." *See* JOSEF ESSER, JURISTISCHES ARGUMENTIEREN IM WANDEL DES RECHTSFINDUNGSKONZEPTS UNSERES JAHRHUNDERTS 12 (1979).

duplication of reality (if one compares them with religion, art, play, statistics, etc.)? Habermas quite rightly recognizes a problem with those validity claims which exceed facticity.[9]

But although he sees it and stresses it, he does not long contemplate that this transgression of facticity actually occurs. But if amazement is already beginning to set in with the problem of the duplication of reality, one is tempted to ask, what constitutes the unity of the distinction between the reality of the factual and the reality of the contrafactual. In so doing, one would then run into the paradox of the sameness of that which had been distinguished. All the certainties which had been constructed also served to solve the paradox. Reason saw the primary function of consciousness and communication as providing firm, distinguishable identities in veiling this and in providing secret agreement with the relevant existing social relations.

Habermas argues consistently. He is concerned with the legitimation of the need for legitimation. For this purpose, he is content with relying on the results of linguistic research. But these results are actually not as solidly founded as it might appear. At any rate, they do furnish a very foreshortened view of the possibilities. It is not a matter of questioning or disproving this gain in insight. But the readiness with which Habermas takes it for granted exacts a price in the theoretical superstructure built upon it.

IV.

"Archaeological" excavations of the kind with which we have concerned ourselves thus far relate to the field in which Habermas attempts to develop his theory, but they do not take theoretical ambition itself into account. They do not proceed in a theoretically immanent way and are not based on a supposedly "better" theory as a basis for criticism. We have only tried to break down premises, in order to spread uncertainty. This is not a matter of the perennially possible skepticism, which can only be employed destructively, rather, it concerns the thematization of time and of observer para-

---

9. *See* HABERMAS, *supra* note 7, at 396. In a noteworthy passage, Habermas himself speaks of idealizations as a "methodical fiction, which should bring to light the unavoidable inertial factors of social complexity, that is, the reverse of communicative socialization" or of idealizations as a contrast to a world "that is *differently* organized." *Id.* at 395 (emphasis added). This directly corresponds with the consideration formulated in the text above, that an imaginary duplication of reality not only allows the play of the imagination to be enjoyed, but also allows the contrasting hardness of reality to be noticed. But Habermas allows this only for an ideal model of communicative socialization and thinks he can escape this by taking into account the facticity of law and politics. But this would only apply if Habermas abstained in this area from idealizing conditions for legitimation.

doxes which can, in their turn, rely on elaborate question-formulations. One could mention names like Jacques Derrida or George Spencer Brown, but what does such digging, such temporalising and re-paradoxising, achieve?

In order to pursue this, let us return to the *quod omnes tangit* problem. All those affected by legal decisions should be heard and engaged in legal discourses until they agree in a reasonable way, or if they do not agree, they should be evaluated as unreasonable. This final division of humanity, into those that include or exclude through reason, may in itself be a vision of horror, where one can rationally (paradoxically) only vote for irrationality. But for the moment this "Last Judgment" is not our problem. The important preliminary question for the legal system is: how can one get that far in a juridically unobjectionable way.

In a critical discussion of the old liberal subjective rights and of the newer dogmatic of subjective rights, Habermas warns that the problem of communicative agreement about validity claims is not adequately considered. The legitimacy of the law cannot therefore be supported by a declaration of freedom in the form of subjective rights.[10] That is certainly correct, but the question then becomes, how it could be done differently, in a way that would work in technical legal terms. After all, subjective rights do not just guarantee freedom, they also limit legally relevant involvement (i.e., limitation of access to the processes of the legal system). If this barrier were to fall, anyone could turn up and request that the court establish rational social integration.

Habermas naturally knows that a discourse with all involved is not possible in any legal process. He therefore does not demand that one should postpone the decision until the last person affected has been born, grownup, and heard. As a result, the key formula states: "Those norms for action are valid, to which all potentially affected persons could agree as participants in a rational discourse."[11] Every concept of this maxim is carefully explained with the exception of the word "could," through which Habermas hides the problem. This is a matter of a modal concept, which, in addition, is formulated in the conjunctive. Ever since Kant, one knows that in such cases the statement must be specified by giving the conditions for the possibility. That, however, remains unsaid. The master and the invisible hand will not be replaced. But who determines, and how does he do so, what *could* find rational agreement? How does this decisive operation, on which everything in the postmetaphysical age depends, become juridified? As a result, it also remains unclear, on all levels of the argument, how the conjunctive becomes an indicative, how the potential becomes a reality,

10. *See id.* at 117.
11. *Id.* at 138.

or, for example, how power "comes forth" out of the freely discussing civil society, which does not of course exist.[12]

Habermas sees the problem, or he would not formulate it in such a carefully thought out manner. It is apparent that he anticipates criticism in stressing that the discourse principle cannot be applied directly to the legal process.[13] In calling for a process that would run under conditions suited to reach decisions and one to which all those affected could agree, Habermas also seeks an escape route. But with this the problem arises again, in the form of a double modality—a "would-could" (*kÖnnten-kÖnnten*). Since not all those affected can be involved in the legal process—the conditions, which specify this impossibility, are obvious—Habermas, astonishingly enough, puts his faith in the legal process. In an ongoing discussion, he speaks of the "proceduralizing" of substantial legal problems.[14] In regulating the process, there should be a guarantee that the parties consent to a communication in a spirit of agreement. Or at least: there should be a guarantee that the communication proceeds under the assumption that this could occur. However, this is nothing but a legal fiction since an agreement cannot really be brought about and conflicts can only be resolved by a judge in a court case and, where legislation is concerned, only on the basis of majorities. Thus in the end the suppressed paradox, previously rendered invisible, emerges in the context of another distinction. The distinction between legality and legitimacy is copied into legality and is expressed as a legal fiction. Legitimacy is legality in a form determined by this distinction.

Through various "*suppléments*"—according to Derrida—this can be repacked and in a second attempt be de-paradoxised again. In the first place, in every process, not only the natural veil of ignorance,[15] but also the uncertainty of the outcome produced by the process itself has an effect. This

---

12. *See, e.g., id.* at 216.

13. *See id.* at 195. But if this is true, then the "mediation" is nothing more than a division according to types of the same principle under concretely formulated conditions.

14. Determining to what extent this is a legacy of Max Weber requires more careful examination. In following Weber, it is common to distinguish between formal and substantial rationality. *See, e.g.,* PATRICK S. ATIYAH & ROBERT S. SUMMERS, FORM AND SUBSTANCE IN ANGLO-AMERICAN LAW: A COMPARATIVE STUDY OF LEGAL REASONING, LEGAL THEORY, AND LEGAL INSTITUTIONS (1987). Here it is a question, reformulated in system-theory terms; of key considerations of juristic argumentation; of the distinction between self-reference and external reference. It is notable, that this important distinction makes no difference to the hopes bound up with "proceduralizing." This may be caused by insufficient familiarity with juristic practice. However, it remains unclear how one is to imagine that substantial problems (in practice: conflicts of legally-recognized interests) could be solved in the form of procedural arrangements.

15. *See also* JOHN RAWLS, EINE THEORIE DER GERECHTIGKEIT 159 (1975). *But cf.* ARISTOTLE, RHETORIC I (offering the same argument generalizing *qua* ignorance of the future in favor of the legislator).

promotes not only the recognition of general viewpoints for a decision, but also the more or less illusionary hope of winning something through involvement.[16] Habermas himself would certainly reject this interpretation much in the same way as he has rejected corresponding proposals.[17] However, it would be well worth considering what one would gain or lose if dominance were replaced by uncertainty. In this scenario, the possibility of making the ruler see reason, for example, would be lost.

The fact that Habermas does not really make use of the argument with time and future might have something to do with the fact that he prefers a different solution to the legality/legitimacy paradox. He solves the problem by externalising in the direction of political democracy. This results in a very traditional emphasis on legislation, thereby underestimating judicial lawmaking. Such an emphasis makes Habermas appear to be a late adherent of the Merkl/Kelsen theory of the step-like structure of legal order. In an agreement-oriented administration of justice, argument objectives have the advantage of giving the legislator, in contrast with the judge, the option of nondecision. Without agreement, there is no decision. Unlike the legislator, this escape route is blocked for a judge. He is subject to the ban on a refusal of justice. Traditionally this has been justified by the idea of being bound by the law; a justification which simultaneously chained and relieved the judge. But today the prevailing notion in both common law and in continental European legal orders is that this is, at best, a half-truth. Furthermore, for a sociologist it is noteworthy that most legal disagreements are decided not on questions of norm interpretation, but on factual and evidentiary questions.

V.

There is an attitude, best described as "idealization of the absent," that lies at the basis of the discourse theory.[18] This attitude lends discourse theory its seemingly irresistible Utopian charm. And Utopia—the place, which is nowhere—is itself indeed one of the most famous paradoxes. Politically, this amounts to a sociolytic therapy recommendation which has been purged of all tragedy. For this, Habermas deploys the concept of morality, by which it is simultaneously indicated that this is good. The law is allotted an appli-

16. How one can incidentally acquaint oneself with an emancipation achieved by the acquisition of procedural rules of competence (*Geschäftsordnungskompetenzen*), remains an enigma to anyone who did not experience and survive the student rebellion of the Sixties.

17. See, for example, the proposal of NIKLAS LUHMANN, LEGITIMATION DURCH VERFAHREN (2d ed. 1983).

18. *See* W. Edgar Gregory, *The Idealization of the Absent,* 50 AM. J. SOC. 53, 53–54 (1944) (discussing a study of the homeland feelings of soldiers occupied with war).

cation of this form, which is not deducible from it, but modified by more concrete conditions. Furthermore, the law retains a relationship to morality, which is insufficient for justifications, but is thoroughly harmonious.

If jurists do call on moral principles, this occurs more frequently in emergency situations (hard cases) and in instances where jurists hope to justify their decisions. Moreover, jurists will hardly be able to recognize or reconstruct their decision-making process. And it is this, more than anything else, that merits serious objection. In legal matters, there are many persuasive arguments and constructive viewpoints favoring the particular resolution of cases. However, since there are good arguments on both sides, opposite decisions are equally justified. This merits the question: how can discourse theory, wherein argumentation occupies such a central position, be so off-base in terms of the peculiarities of the juristic faculties?[19]

This is apparently the result of the low calibre (*Kleinformatigkeit*) of successful juristic argument. In order to equip arguments with decisive force, jurists need two cooperating contexts: cases and texts. On the one hand, the peculiarity of the case enlivens the quest to understand the text. While on the other hand, situations first appear as cases only in light of particular legal texts. Texts and cases are highly selective limitations of communication set free in the legal system by the process of differentiation. In fact, Habermas speaks in this very sense of released communication which seeks support in the law. In one respect, the room for maneuvering is widened by separating these two preconditions since this involves a circular, constitutional relationship. In another respect, it is provided with new limitation possibilities, wherein that which has found recognition as a convincing argument then firmly establishes itself. Thus, it is a complicated relationship involving the escalation of complexity through the reduction of complexity.

This strictly localized nature of juridical rationality is, for the most part, not adequately recognized even in the doctrinal methods of legal teaching. A good argument cannot and should not be understood as the correct application of the correct method. Moreover, courts guard against adopting declarations of method in stating the reasons for their decisions primarily because such statements influence the direction of further decisions.[20]

---

19. Habermas addresses this point noting that the quality of a "good reason" only reveals itself inside an "argument game." *See* HABERMAS, *supra* note 7, at 249. However, he views this as representing a "rationality gap" which he attempts to close through idealizing and universalizing the arguments. *See id.* The logical question which remains is: does this improve the soundness of the reasons, or does it simply serve as a theoretical requirement in the context of an observation of secondary importance?

20. For a discussion of a method typology developed by a work group, see D. NEIL MACCORMICK & ROBERT S. SUMMERS, INTERPRETING STATUTES: A COMPARATIVE STUDY (1991). In a discussion of this book, judges have used case examples to demonstrate the fact

Methods, however, must be available, and how they are used is determined by the aims of the argument developed from the case and the text.

If it is true that the thorough differentiation of a social legal system—or, as Habermas puts it, the dissolution of the sacred unity of facticity and validity—has led to the releasing and explosive multiplication of the system's internal communication possibilities, then this finding need not surprise us. Under these conditions, how else is the legal practice to deal with concrete communications producing sentence after sentence? Moreover, one also finds in the economic system, under the appropriate working conditions of the money economy, a similar state of affairs. The collapse of socialist planning showed that economic rationality is only possible on the basis of balances particular to enterprises and special markets, limited by substitution obstacles; or on the basis of budgets and hard-to-shift preferences. Or, in other words, only in a small scale, local form relative to the size of the system. That may be unsatisfactory and may diminish considerably all hopes of a "market economy." But economic theory is also beginning to recognize this and, to some extent, is beginning to switch from equilibrium models to information processing problems.[21]

This consideration need not hinder one in developing concepts for system rationality. For example, one could describe as rational a system which succeeds in internally removing the difference between system and environment which it continually reproduces; a society, for instance, which had problems with neither ecological conditions nor individuals, because everything had already been taken into consideration. But this is, like every case involving the "re-entry" of a distinction into that which has been distinguished by it,[22] a clear case of paradox. One could take this as the starting point for an endless list of desiderata for a human or ecologically-oriented social ethic. But, in the final analysis, the imaginary space of such a conception is due to a duplication of reality, and its concrete effect can only be to make the hardness of the real reality noticeable. Only much more limited claims are capable of operation respectively. But the possibilities existing here could be much better utilized. At any rate, faced with excessive claims on the one side and resignation on the other, one should avoid disavowing the attainable.

---

that, in practice, arguments are not made with categories since that would be meaningful for a typologizing reconstruction of juristic method. *See id.*

21. Similar conclusions have been reached in the area of academic sociology where it has been found that scientific rationality is also only possible in a communicatively convincing form under local conditions. *See* Karin K. Cetina, *Zur Unterkomplexität der Differenzierungstheorie: Empirische Anfragen an die Systemtheorie,* 21 ZEITSCHRIFT FÜR SOZIOLOGIE 406, 406–19 (1992) (discussing the "social studies of science").

22. *See* GEORGE SPENCER BROWN, LAWS OF FORM (1979).

The decision in the case of the majority of guardians appears to have been quite reasonable. Whether one can say that for the *parömie* derived from it *Quod omnes tangit . . .* , is not in the same degree certain.

VI.

The question remains whether such analyses of the legitimation possibilities of the democratic constitutional state still belong in a tradition describing itself as "critical theory." A verdict on this naturally depends on how far one wishes to extend the concept of the "critical." Habermas uses the theory of discourses open to agreement, in order to reformulate classical notions of liberal theory. It is a question of the free and equal access of all to processes which are so structured that they can represent a reasonable experience— whether this be agreement or understanding based on compromise (freedom and equality, once more). Neither fundamental reforms nor revolution are the aim. The critical factor only arises out of an idealizing of the desiderata: in reality they are, as Habermas repeatedly stresses, always only attained "approximately." The critical point is precisely this: one could improve the process in the stated direction. This corresponds with the ideas of German idealism and also with the critical concept of romantic poetry. What is lacking, however unfortunately, is any trace of irony, and thus any distance from the project.

But in quite a different critical tradition, it became evident that by making freedom and equality absolute, i.e., by the world of political ideas of the middle classes, something was also excluded. This was not only applicable to the anticipated inclusion of the opposite in the concepts themselves; unequal results despite equal starting conditions, or restrictions of liberty as conditions for reasonable freedom. Instead, in the form of an insistence on these rights there lay another, dark, unlighted side which manifested itself in the form of an insistence on these rights—a different reality, which could not participate in the positivity of such a society. Today this need not be understood in terms of a class analysis, which was based, in large part, on a copy of the factory organization of the nineteenth century. But the question regarding "freedom and equality," the other side of the formula, is as current today as ever before. If all can occupy themselves in a free and equal way, there appears to be no more exclusion—no more legal slavery, no more structurally determined speechlessness, no system effects by which many are excluded from work and income. Such exclusion effects, which critics have repeatedly referred to utilizing an ideological criticism, exist on a huge scale and are impossible to overlook. Wherever one wishes to look for the causes (among other things naturally in demographic growth), they appear to go back to the realization of freedom and equality. One need only consider that these principles are reliant on a self-selection of participants and were equally attractive for all as if on the basis of a deeply embedded anthropology. But, where are the many who simply do not want; who cannot want; who suffer from depression; who assess their prospects negatively; who want to be left alone; who have to struggle for their physical survival to such a degree that there is no time or energy left for anything else. This reflects a criticism of the reverse side of the conceptualized value, whether viewed as a therapeutic problem or as one of foreign aid. Those that have witnessed the favelas of a South American metropolis, or are aware of the many lonely people who live in their communities, will quickly come to a different conclusion.

The sensible thinkers who discuss these matters may be dismayed, may devise remedies, and may, beyond relief efforts, reach a reasonable consensus. But reason is also only a form with another side. It excludes the undiscerning and the irrational or, at any rate, that which from their perspective must be so understood. But is it not possible that those people are excluded, in whose name the staging of rationality was undertaken? The hardline social critics will demand a revolution and attempt to bring one about. But today that already belongs to an obsolete tradition, since one knows that there is no other society and there will be no other besides that in which every change of structure must take place. In the final analysis, the dialectical way out is blocked, including a reflection of the dialectic of enlightenment. For when one in principle thinks postmetaphysically like Habermas, one also thinks postdialectically. There is no unity, in which the opposites can be reconciled. There are only the distinctions themselves in one or another form.

It is possible to take account of the autonomy of the social system by introducing the negation of the system into the system itself (just as the avant-garde has done with the negation of art in art). For this purpose, political thought offers the traditional form of Utopia. These days this is easily misunderstood as a kind of idea painting. But Utopias are paradoxes in the strict sense. They culminate in the statement: the positive is the negative—displayed in form differences, that can change without the paradox disappearing. This figure could fit a consistently postmetaphysical system of thought. But discourse theory lacks a sense of tragic choices and irony.

VII.

The foregoing remarks have been largely critical, both with respect to critical gestures and critical theory. But, the intellectual integrity and radicalness with which Habermas tackles a fundamental problem of modern society deserves recognition. Even if in the end one cannot include oneself among those who, subject to the scarcely manageable conditions of a discourse about the discourse theory, could finally agree. It still deserves recognition that a theoretical idea is executed here and therefore its possibilities and consequences can be reviewed.

The starting point is: modern society can no longer externalize its own problems "metaphysically" or "religiously." It must find the solution inside itself. In other words, it must rely on its own operations and be able to relate these back reflexively. This corresponds with other circumstances, likewise observable, involving the centralisation of theoretical efforts on operations whereby structures are produced and reproduced, temporarily validated and devalidated. One finds this in the operative constructivism of epistemological, aesthetic, and therapeutic provenance, in the semiotic of reference-free sign use (such as Roland Barthes), and in the theory of autopoietic systems. Against this background, Habermas takes a decided stand against justifying the law in terms of natural law and classic rational law, and against offering a moral justification. One also would not reach a different verdict on this question from a system-theoretical position. However, if this is what they have in common, then what is the difference? What exactly is Habermas's special interest?

My impression is that what makes Habermas's efforts distinctive are that they are anchored in, and hold fast to, a normative concept of rationality. If one no longer understands this in terms of the world of ideas, but must relate it to actually realizable operations, the theory finds itself forced to become concrete. For if it is a matter of norms, it must also be shown which operations could be judged as nonconformist or deviant, and by which operations this is to be achieved. Thus, to be concrete, where do the sociolytic discourses that remain provincial with respect to the future and the universe[23] take place in a communicatively operating society?

That such communications *could* take place, is not a satisfactory answer. If the theme "facticity and validity" is to retain its meaning, they must, at some point, also take place in fact. Habermas names a series of occasions on which such a "metaphorical event"[24] could assume a concrete form—"as informal opinion forming before the political public," as political involvement inside and outside the parties, as participation in general elections, and in the consultation and decision making of parliamentary bodies, etc.[25]

---

23. *See* HABERMAS, *supra* note 7, at 158. This formulation, it is true, refers only to the monopoly on violence, but it applies to every occurring communication which always happens somewhere in its own presence.

24. *Id.* at 166.

25. *See id.* at 170.

Apparently Habermas himself shrinks before such naiveté, although he has begun to judge the mass media more favorably than before.[26] Those who actually participate have at their disposal an ample measure of contradictory experiences. Therefore, there is also a fall back position. National sovereignty, which in discourse-theoretical terms substantiates itself, "withdraws into the equally subjectless communication cycles of fora and corporations."[27] But their institutional connection remains unclear. How are the participants chosen and what enables them to represent opinions, to which others, or even all parties, "could agree"? The current groundswell in empathy, which balances an equally strong tendency towards ethnic, national, racial, and religious narrow mindedness, could lead one to suspect that, here, Habermas is thinking of a circle. This circle can eloquently express its concern over the predicament of victims, whether they are starving or environmentally damaged, socially or racially oppressed, career-disadvantaged women, or victims of violence or neglect. This is supported by the fact that Habermas accepts, as the rule, "the advocation of moral (i.e., the highest priority) substantiating discourses."[28] The point here is not to deny the gravity of such problems. On the contrary, the problems are on such a scale that, by comparison, the reference to discourses could be taken as a mockery.

I am not certain that an insistence on a normative understanding of rationality, given the state of the world at the end of this century, has to end in such an unsatisfactory way. But if this is the case, there would be a lot to be said for giving up the idea and instead, in the tradition of Marx,[29] studying society as it is and works in order to discover possible variations, which could perhaps lead to less painful conditions. Could!

---

26. *See* JÜRGEN HABERMAS, STRUKTURWANDEL DER ÖFFENTLICHKEIT: UNTERSUCHUNGEN ZU EINER KATEGORIE DER BÜRGERLICHEN GESELLSCHAFT (1990).

27. HABERMAS, *supra* note 7, at 170. Habermas's repetitive use of the phrase "subjectless communication" demonstrates that this is not just an occasional error in formulation. *See id.* at 362, 365. However, it must be asked, whether every communication is not subjectless and, if not, how this difference arises.

28. *Id.* at 224.

29. *See id.* at 66. This is what Habermas has expressed.

SEVEN

De Collisione Discursuum

Communicative Rationalities in Law, Morality, and Politics

Gunther Teubner*†

I.

At the end of the seventeenth century, Johan Nikolaus Hert, a German legal scholar of Roman private law, wrote the treatise *De Collisione Legum.* He was dealing with one of the most disturbing experiences in his epoch of the emerging nation states—the experience that on earth there was more than one law, more than one justice.[1] Hert stood in stark contrast to his more famous French contemporary, the brilliant Blaise Pascal, who reacted to the same problem with critique, deconstruction, and irony: "A funny justice that ends at a river! Truth on this side of the Pyrenees, error on that."[2] Invoking systematic construction and elaborate casuistry, Hert was the first and only German to date to make a serious and thorough attempt to resolve nagging questions of conflict of laws.[3] To work out collision rules was the solution. Hert complexified the so-called statutist method according to which collision rules determined jurisdiction by analyzing the nature of the statutes involved. Developing a complex rule system for the collision of laws, Hert felt compelled to distinguish the incredible amount of sixty-three different casuistic constellations in order to fight Pascal's paradox. For this scholarly exercise he became famous, and rightly so. But his immortality in legal circles is based on the desperate sigh which he hove while draw-

*Professor, London School of Economics.
†The translations in this Article are those of the author.
1. *See* GERHARD KEGEL, INTERNATIONALES PRIVATRECHT VI § 3 (C. H. Beck ed., 7th ed. 1995).
2. BLAISE PASCAL, PENSÉES 151 (1964).
3. For details, see HERRMANN, JOHAN NIKOLAUS HERT UND DIE DEUTSCHE STATUTEN-LEHRE (1963).

ing his tortured distinctions: *"quam sudent doctores."* How the doctors are sweating!

De Collisione Discursuum, the collision of discourses, is a variation on this theme which makes modern and postmodern doctors sweat. It is no more the fragmentation of universal justice in different national laws that haunts us, but the fragmentation of universal rationality into a disturbing multiplicity of discourses. And today, we are faced with a similar alternative of a deconstructive and a reconstructive answer: Blaise Pascal or Johan Nikolaus Hert? Funny rationality that ends at the boundary of discourse? Or a tormented casuistry of collision rules for interdiscursivity?

Jürgen Habermas's earlier work,[4] as he himself concedes, could still be understood as constructing one and only one communicative rationality which integrated discursivity and morality.[5] If, in a plurality of social situations, we raise the question of validity of norms, we enter into a discourse which, under certain procedural conditions and under the guide of the universalization principle, leads us to a consensus about valid norms which we can call rational. Various institutionalized patterns of practical argumentation, like the procedures of legal or political deliberation, are certainly historically contingent. However, their bewildering multitude can be measured against the one ideal of rational discourse which serves as a regulative idea and a standard of critique.[6] In a somewhat different interpretation of Habermas's theory, legal argumentation could be seen as a "special case" of a rational discourse on practical questions which develops its own peculiarities. But the hierarchical relation between general discourse and legal discourse makes sure that there is one—and only one—communicative rationality.[7]

Now, in *Faktizität und Geltung,* Habermas makes a decisive move towards a plurality of discourses—and their concomitant rationalities.[8] Modern plurality, he argues, does not result one-dimensionally from social differentiation as theorists in the Durkheim tradition would have it. Habermas re-

4. *See, e.g.,* JÜRGEN HABERMAS, LEGITIMATIONSPROBLEME IM SPÄTKAPITALISMUS [LEGITIMATION CRISIS] (1973); JÜRGEN HABERMAS, ZUR REKONSTRUKTION DES HISTORISCHEN MATERIALISMUS [COMMUNICATION AND THE EVOLUTION OF SOCIETY] (1976) [hereinafter HABERMAS, REKONSTRUKTION].

5. *See id.*

6. *See* HABERMAS, REKONSTRUKTION, *supra* note 4, at 265.

7. *See* ROBERT ALEXY, THEORIE DER JURISTISCHEN ARGUMENTATION: DIE THEORIE DES RATIONALEN DISKURSES ALS THEORIE DER JURISTISCHEN BEGRÜNDUNG 261 (1978).

8. JÜRGEN HABERMAS, FAKTIZITÄT UND GELTUNG: BEITRÄGE ZUR DISKURSTHEORIE DES RECHTS UND DES DEMOCRATISCHEN RECHTSSTAATS 140 (1992). For the English translation, see JÜRGEN HABERMAS, BETWEEN FACTS AND NORMS: CONTRIBUTION TO A DISCOURSE THEORY OF LAW AND DEMOCRACY (William Rehg trans., 1996).

constructs several historical processes of differentiation in which various communicative practices emerge with highly peculiar procedures, logics of argumentation, and internal rationalities.[9] Not only do different system rationalities appear, but the lifeworld itself becomes autonomous as against functional systems (politics, economy). Moreover, the lifeworld in its turn differentiates internally into diverse spheres—personality, culture, and societal community. Finally, culture develops into several autonomous fields of knowledge, each of them following a specific *Eigenlogik*.[10]

This complex reconstruction enables Habermas to separate autonomous argumentative practices along different dimensions, among others morality from legality,[11] morality from ethics,[12] law from politics, and discourse from negotiation.[13] At the very end, Habermas observes the interplay of five distinct "types of discourse and negotiation."[14] Moral discourses specialize around the principle of universalization; ethical discourses aim at individual and collective identity; pragmatical discourses relate purposes to means and set priorities among collective goals; legal discourses care for the internal consistency of legal rules; and negotiations develop a culture of fair compromise between nongeneralizable interests.

With this move toward discursive plurality, Habermas does not merely render his theory analytically richer and moves it closer to institutional realities. In addition, he systematically brings together two separate intellectual traditions, so that they considerably profit from each other: social differentiation and fragmentation of discourses. Sociologists have observed that modern society has become divided into several social systems and autonomous spheres of rationality. Philosophers have observed language to become fragmented in different language games, logics of argumentation, and apparently incommensurable discourses. Habermas's theory integrates these two traditions and relates them to each other in the interplay of external and internal, in the "double perspective" of functional analysis and rational reconstruction.[15]

But there is a decisive difference. Theories of systemic and discursive plurality tend to stress separation, incommensurability, and nonreconcilable difference. As for interdiscursivity, if these theories recognize it at all, they observe mainly closure and indifference, perhaps structural coupling, at best a certain elective affinity. The most radical position toward the col-

9. *See id.* at 77.
10. *See id.* at 107, 124–35.
11. *See id.* at 135–38, 286–91.
12. *See id.* at 127, 188.
13. *See id.* at 192.
14. *See id.* at 196–207.
15. *See id.* at 57–60.

lision of discourses can be found in Lyotard's "victimology," which is comparable to Pascal's "funny justice" in the conflict of laws. For Lyotard, discourses are hermetically closed; if they "meet" they can only do "injustice" to each other; one discourse is the other discourse's "victim."[16]

Habermas's insistence on practical reason and communicative power makes him opt for the opposite: for unity, not for difference; for integration of discursive plurality, not for their sheer fragmentation. Therefore, discursive plurality, taken seriously, creates a much more dramatic challenge for Habermas's theory that relies ultimately on discursive reason and does not content itself playing around with social differentiation or with linguistic diversity. After the move to pluridiscursivity, the success of Habermas's theory now depends on a plausible solution to the collision of discourses. If Habermas's "proceduralization" of reason is supposed to make sense it needs now to be developed in a double direction: rational procedures for various discourses and rational meta-procedures for interdiscursivity. If practical reason were not to disintegrate into a Pascalian "funny rationality" of discourses, then we are today again in the situation of Johan Nikolaus Hert. Complex rules of collision need to be worked out, tortured distinctions have to be made, even if the doctors are sweating. But here, Rudolf Wiethölter,[17] an erudite scholar in both legal theory and conflict of laws, warns us, predicting not only sweat, but sweat, blood, and tears in the desperate search for a meta-discourse that resolves the conflict of discourses. He calls it a *"Rechtsgottesgericht"*: Where is the forum, who sets the standards, which are the procedures?

II.

Habermas is well aware of the collision problem.[18] His answer in *Faktizität und Geltung:* No hierarchy of discourses—especially no superiority of morality over legality—but discursive compatibility! For the conflicts between pragmatic discourses, procedurally regulated negotiations, ethical-political discourses, and moral and legal discourses, he concludes: the universal concern demanded by the discourse principle finds its guarantee in the compatibility of all discursive programs with what can also be morally justified.[19]

16. Jean-François Lyotard, Le Différend [The Differend: Phrases in Dispute] 21, 42, 43 (1983).

17. Rudolf Wiethölter, *Zum Fortbildungsrecht der (richterlichen) Rechtsfortbildung: Fragen eines lesenden Recht-Fertigungslehrers*, 3 Kritische Vierteljahreszeitschrift für Gesetzgebung und Rechtswissenschaft 1, 22 (1988).

18. *See* Habermas, *supra* note 8, at 141.

19. *See id.* at 206.

On several other occasions, Habermas insists on "complementarity,"[20] "double perspective,"[21] "congruence,"[22] "noncontradiction," "mediation," and "commensurability."[23] These are all variations of the same theme: If we have to take seriously the diversity and the autonomy of discourses, then the unity of practical reason needs to be replaced by discursive compatibility. But, obviously, with compatibility Habermas does not offer a solution. At best, he formulates a problem.

What does compatibility of discourses mean? I have distinguished at least five versions of discursive compatibility—all of which can be traced in Habermas's book.

A. Indifference?

Habermas refers to Kant's famous formulation that law needs to be indifferent to devils and angels.[24] The results of legal reasoning should be indifferent to the motives and reasons of moral angels and rational choice devils. In general, this could mean that discourses are free in developing their idiosyncratic argumentation, and need not care about external consistency with reasons of other argumentation practices if ever their results fit together.

B. Smallest Common Denominator?

Some of Habermas's formulations seem to point in the direction of the famous "ethical minimum" of the law, especially when he demands that law should be compatible with morality, and should not contradict moral reasoning.[25]

C. Ad-hoc Conciliation?

The idea of an "application discourse" apparently points in this direction.[26] The conflict of moral principles, ethical identities, political values, and legal rules cannot be resolved *in abstracto*. Rather, it is the richness of the concrete case-constellation, the "situational reference" that allows one to identify "adequate" criteria for their mutual delineation.[27]

---

20. *Id.* at 137, 145.
21. *Id.* at 107.
22. *Id.* at 128.
23. *Id.* at 206.
24. *See id.* at 144.
25. *See id.* at 193.
26. *See id.* at 266; *see also* KLAUS GÜNTHER, DER SINN FÜR ANGEMESSENHEIT: ANWENDUNGSDISKURSE IN MORAL UND RECHT (1988).
27. *See* HABERMAS, *supra* note 8, at 267.

D. Mutually Exclusive Jurisdictions?

Discourses would claim exclusive areas of competence within the boundaries of their symbolic territories and would mutually respect their sovereignty.[28]

E. Moral-Legal Superdiscourse?

Although the discourse principle is too abstract to resolve practical questions, at least on the meta-level it can develop procedures and criteria able to be universalized to resolve conflicts of jurisdiction between moral, legal, and political discourses.[29]

Although Habermas experiments with all of these different versions of compatibility, his sympathies are with a combination of versions D and E, with a philosophical superdiscourse that delineates exclusive areas of jurisdiction. Discourse theory has the legislative competence to enact collision rules. The method is similar to the above-mentioned old statutists, Bologna's famous conflict-of-law school that distinguished criteria of jurisdiction according to a correspondence of the nature of the *statuta* and the cases involved: *statuta realia, statuta personalia, statuta mixta.*[30] In his "process model" of colliding discourses, Habermas distinguishes various areas of jurisdiction according to the nature of the discourse and the nature of the "issue" involved. "Various types of discourses and forms of negotiation," he asserts, "correspond to the logic of these issues."[31] Thus, the logic of issues determines discursive jurisdiction in five areas: pragmatic, ethical, moral and legal discourses, and procedures of fair negotiation. He systematically defines the nature of these discursive *statuta:* purpose/means relation, collective identity, universalization principle, normative coherence, and fair compromise. He even begins to elaborate a complex casuistry which attributes concrete issues of political life to abstract logics of discourses: abortion and social policies are under the jurisdiction of the moral discourse; in contrast, protection of animals and urban policies are under the jurisdiction of the ethical discourse, and so on.[32] This is where we begin to sweat. The distinctions become tortured. Greetings from Johan Nikolaus Hert!

But at this point we feel a certain hesitation in Habermas's thinking. After having dethroned the moral superdiscourse in favor of a *"Gleichursprünglichkeit,"* an original equality, of relative discourses, Habermas hesi-

28. *See id.* at 196–207.
29. *See id.* at 201–07.
30. *See* KEGEL, *supra* note 1, at III § 3.
31. HABERMAS, *supra* note 8, at 196.
32. *See id.* at 204.

tates to subsequently crown the philosophical discourse king which would now be hailed to possess the competence of competences. Habermas himself does not seem to believe in the distinguishing power of his rules of discursive jurisdiction. After all, moral and legal questions refer certainly to the same problems. In the vocabulary of a collision doctrine, we would call this the "transdiscursive" character of most concrete political issues that does not allow us to plausibly identify a *sedes materiae* in a one-to-one correlation of issue to discourse. And it is not by chance that Habermas stops short of speculating about how to identify concrete institutions in which separate spheres of discursive jurisdiction are exclusively represented.[33] Only tentatively he searches for a certain temporal institutionalization of these differences in a "process model"[34] which, however, he hastens to relativize again by introducing manifold feedback-relations between different phases.[35] And when it comes to existing institutions of political legislation and legal adjudication, the five discourse types remain there in an undifferentiated mix.[36] What seems possible, at best, is to reconcile them ad hoc.

Thus, facing the conflict of discourses, Habermas is oscillating between two positions: leaving it to the heterarchy of relative discourses versus erecting the hierarchy of a superdiscourse. He is confronted with a somewhat uncomfortable alternative. Either practical reason is limited to only one of the five partial aspects—moral justice, collective identity, choice of collective goals and means, fair compromise, and legal consistency—whose interrelation remains unclear. Or there is a superdiscourse which has the legislative capacity to set rules in case the discourses collide.

III.

Perhaps there is something wrong with the clear-cut alternative of heterarchy versus hierarchy, relative discourse versus superdiscourse. Can legal history teach us here a lesson in its century-old and down-to-earth experience with conflict of laws? Indeed, the doctrine of conflict-law did develop a third position between heterarchy and hierarchy which is worthwhile to be looked at more closely. The turning point was the territorial differentiation of European society in autonomous nation-states. Before this point, Bologna's statutists were successfully governing conflicts between local jurisdictions and a universal *jus commune*. However, the more national laws were gaining in autonomy, historicity, and uniqueness, the less convinc-

33. *See id.* at 207.
34. *Id.* at 201–07.
35. *See id.* at 207.
36. *See id.* at 191.

ing became an international *jus commune* of collision rules which maintained the unity of law—at least at a meta-level—deciding about national jurisdictions. With the nation-state and its claim for sovereignty, territorial domination and exclusive jurisdiction, a strange entangling of the norm-hierarchy occurred among particular substantive rules and universal collision rules. The ground-level became indistinguishable from the meta-level, but, paradoxically, remained distinguishable at the same time. What happened was a historical process in which even international collision rules became nationalized. As a clear *contradictio in adiectu,* international private law became national in its character. Instead of one international private law that decided jurisdictional conflicts, there emerged a national multitude of international private laws. Every nation-state developed autonomously its own, idiosyncratic law of conflict between legal orders. Funny justice: The party to a legal conflict became judge in her own cause!

Many international lawyers deplore this "tangled hierarchy"[37] and attribute the (con)fusion of levels to the weakness or the non-existence of a global legal order. For them, lack of globality is the reason why we do not have a truly international law of conflict which, institutionally, would keep rules and meta-rules apart. I think there is a deeper reason for the strange asymmetry. I find it in Habermas's concept of "*Gleichursprünglichkeit*," in the original equality or equal originality of discourses, and, in our case, of laws of nations. If the *diversitas legum* is no longer seen as emanating from the unity of divine or natural law, in any case, from one *jus commune,* if national laws are seen as separate chains of legal distinctions each having its own irreversible history, each stemming from an obscure national filiation, each provided with a myth of origin, then universally applicable collision rules do violate the unique "spirit" of each of these autonomous laws. If the unique characteristics of a cultural identity defines the idiosyncracies of a national law, then such law must also have the power to define the perception of its outside world from its unique perspective. National laws claim the right to a domestic construction of foreign law, literally, to its incorporation in the body of the *lex fori.* Ago gives an especially purist version of this view claiming that collision rules do not deal with the question "Should we apply foreign or domestic law?"[38] Rather, national meta-rules produce themselves national substantive law by using outside rules as material and reconstructing them anew in the context of domestic law: "*l'ordre juridique*

---

37. *See* DOUGLAS R. HOFSTADTER, GÖDEL, ESCHER, BACH: AN ETERNAL GOLDEN BRAID (1979); *see also* Douglas R. Hofstadter, *Nomic: A Self-Modifying Game Based on Reflexivity in Law,* in METAMAGICAL THEMES: QUESTING FOR THE ESSENCE OF MIND AND PATTERN 70–86 (Douglas R. Hofstadter ed., 1985).

38. KEGEL, *supra* note 1, at X § 3.

est toujours nécessairement exclusif dans le sens qu'ils exclut le caractère juridique de tout cequi ne rentre pas en lui-même" (the legal order is always necessarily exclusive in the sense that it excludes the legal character of everything that does not enter into itself).

In more abstract terms, the strange paradox of self-justice in the conflict of domestic and foreign law—the peculiar asymmetry of a law that decides its own conflicts with other laws, and thus violates flagrantly the principle of impartiality—can be reformulated with the concept of re-entry. Once an original distinction has been drawn, it reproduces itself in a subsequent chain of distinctions which builds on the original distinction (legal/illegal). The chain distinguishes itself from the outside world through its very re-productive operations (legal operations/rest of the world). It integrates it-self with the outside world neither by reaching into the world outside its own distinctions nor by appealing to a higher authority (be it of divine or natural law, be it of the doctors of Bologna). Rather, it repeats in itself the difference between two symbolic spaces by distinguishing between its self-perceived identity and a constructed outside world (domestic/foreign law). This is re-entry: a chain of distinctions reformulates its difference to the outside world in the language of its own distinctions (national rules on international collisions). It cannot connect itself to other chains of distinc-tions except by re-entry, by a reconstruction of these other chains in its own terms. The main effect of this re-entry: If, for an outside observer there was incommensurability of different sorts of distinctions, after the re-entry, there is comparability and compatibility. An internal meta-level can be con-structed that transforms the former external heterarchy into an internal hierarchy (substantive rules versus meta-rules of rule collision).

If Habermas takes his idea of discursive *Gleichurspründ-lichkeit* seriously, then "re-entry" seems to offer itself as a formal model of how to deal with interdiscursivity. Due to *Gleichursprüng-lichkeit,* none of the partial dis-courses—neither morals, ethics, law, nor philosophy—is a natural candi-date for a superdiscourse. Otherwise, we would have to admit, all of these original equals actually are superdiscourses. The moral discourse reformu-lates the conflict of different discourses in terms of generalizable interests, the ethical discourse reformulates in terms of individual and collective identity, the legal discourse reformulates in terms of treating norm-case-relations equally or nonequally, and so forth. Each of these discourses has an internal dynamics that propels its chain of distinctions not only for sub-stantive questions, but also for questions of discourse collisions. Discourse collisions search in vain for one central meta-discourse. There is only a plu-rality of decentralized meta-discourses that reformulate collisions in their own idiosyncratic language. After all, Lyotard seems not so wrong with his assertion that in the conflict of discourse no *litige* takes place, but rather a *différend:* By reconstructing foreign rationalities in its own domestic language, each discourse necessarily does "injustice" to the inner essence of the others.

"Justice" would then take on a specific meaning. Under modern conditions, it would not be rendered meaningless, as Kelsen asserted. Nor would justice be identical with the partial and highly specialized rationality of the moral discourse, applying nothing but the stern and rigorous universalization principle, as Habermas suggests today. Rather, justice would have to be reformulated as a relational concept. However, at the same time, this justice is non-hierarchical and asymmetric. Justice relates discursive identity and discursive otherness not from "above," but from the unique perspective each discourse has to the rest of the world of discourses. Legal justice then becomes a matter of degree, not a binary choice. Justice can be realized to the degree as a concrete historical legal discourse is simultaneously able, externally, to incorporate the rationalities of other discourses and, internally, to observe its own requirements of legal consistency. Denoting the richness of the idiosyncratic world construction of the legal discourse, legal justice would be universal and particular at the same time. This is more than "adequate complexity" of the legal system that looks exclusively to the question of how, under the condition of extreme social differentiation, internal legal consistency can still be achieved.[39] Justice will be realized to the degree a concrete legal order is able to respond at the same time to an additional question. Not only to what degree does law do justice to its own requirement of legal equality, but also to what degree does law do justice to the *Eigenlogik* of other discourses. This results in a third question: If law increasingly gives justice to outside discourses, is it capable of changing the internal criteria of coherence accordingly? And Michael Walzer's *Spheres of Justice* would take on a different meaning. Not only would a multitude of specific social and professional contexts develop a multitude of specialized moralities. But specialized argumentation practices would reflect discourse specific norms in their relation to norm projections of other spheres of life.

IV.

If "re-entry" is the third position that marks the difference to Habermas's treatment of interdiscursivity, what are the consequences for legal argumentation? Does the distinction make a difference when moral, ethical, pragmatic, and interest-oriented arguments actually enter the legal discourse? My answer in a nutshell: "enslavement." Indeed, Habermas rightly

---

39. *See* NIKLAS LUHMANN, AUSDIFFERENZIERUNG DES RECHTS: BEITRÄGE ZUR RECHTS-SOZIOLOGIE UND RECHTSTHEORIE (1981); NIKLAS LUHMANN, RECHTSSYSTEM UND RECHTSDOG-MATIK STUTTGART (1974).

stresses the point that despite the profound differentiation of morality and legality, moral and ethical arguments do reappear frequently, and legitimately, in legal reasoning. And he overcomes the obvious contradiction between autonomy and reappearance by the metaphor of "translation." Moral contents, Habermas argues, do not enter law as such; they are "translated" into the "legal code," whatever this means.[40] Thus, he can reject pure legalism *à la* Windscheid, the (in)famous German pandectist who maintained that political, moral, and economic arguments were irrelevant to the "lawyer as such," as being hopelessly out of step with argumentative reality.

In his turn, Habermas constructs legal decision making as a process model in which pragmatic, ethical, moral, and interest-oriented arguments are freely interchanged; only at the end does the result need to go through the filter of legal argument: a test of coherence with established legal norms, especially constitutional norms. This ultimately makes judicial review necessary in which the new programs are examined for their ability to fit into the existing legal system.

Similarly, in the application discourse of judicial adjudication, Habermas identifies a plurality of pragmatic, ethical, moral, and interest-oriented arguments which again are disciplined by the legal requirement of "conditions of decisional consistency."[41] Legal consistency appears in both cases as a screening method that filters out some of the solutions that have been found in the free interplay of discourse types and negotiations. In the collision of discourses, it is an excluding device that rules out certain extravagant results.

To my mind, Habermas underestimates in both cases the "legal proprium." Legal consistency is not only a filtering device. It is the very productive mechanism that opens the gates for a whole cascade of distinctions. "Treat equal cases equally and unequal cases unequally" should not be seen as the *Grundnorm,* the static basic norm but the *Grundverfahren,* the dynamic basic procedure of the legal discourse that opens a self-propelling process of a chain of distinctions. It deals not only with the problem of normative coherence, as Habermas suggests—if and how a consented rule fits into a system of rules. Rather, it triggers a generative mechanism, a "historical machine" as von Foerster would say,[42] when it asks the *question directrice* if a new case should be treated "alike or not alike" to a historically given relation between rules and cases. And in this context, it is not so much "stare decisis" which is of interest, the binding effect of precedents, of treating equal cases equally. Rather it is "distinguishing" and "overruling," treat-

40. *See* HABERMAS, *supra* note 8, at 250.
41. *Id.* at 268.
42. *See* HEINZ VON FOERSTER, OBSERVING SYSTEMS 201 (1981).

ing unequal cases unequally, that unleashes law forces.[43] It is legal unequality that opens a definite conceptual framework for the infinite search for alternative rules and facts, principles and values, and that produces innovations which in their turn reproduce for the next chain of cases the dialectics of "alike or not alike."

And it is this historical machine that legal discourse, on its own territory, uses to "enslave" other discourses. Relentlessly searching for criteria of equal/unequal, the legal discourse freely borrows ideas, rules, and principles from other discourses, exploits moral, ethical, pragmatic, and strategic arguments, but subdues them to the very basic procedure of determining legal equality/inequality. There is no free interplay of arguments, but rather the stern discipline of a legal search procedure that defines, on the basis of its historical configuration, which aspects are relevant and which not, which arguments are admitted and which not, how priorities have to be set, and how conflicting perspectives have to be resolved. For moral philosophers, it is one of the most frustrating experiences when their eloquent suada is brusquely interrupted by a lawyer's argument: "Legally, this is irrelevant." And this interruption is not merely due to arbitrary *auctoritas* of the judge, but equally to the *ratio* of legal doctrine and procedure. It is the present state of the law—*die gegenwärtige Rechtslage*—in its historical evolution that decides about production, admission, and the foundation of unequality. Disposition about unequality is the privilege of the law in the interplay of discourses; the dynamic realization of the "legal proprium" which dictates also the legitimate/nonlegitimate use of nonlegal arguments.

This enslavement of foreign arguments under the basic procedure of law expresses, I submit, a different aspect of the proceduralization idea. Habermas tends to reserve the idea of "proceduralization" for the very general procedural requirements of an ideal discourse on practical questions. Legal procedures, he contends, do not interfere with the "inner logic of argumentation."[44] But is this really true? "Treating new cases alike/not alike" is a procedure that determines the scope and quality of admitted arguments, the sequence of equality tests, and the criteria of what equality in this context means. As a basic procedure for the legal discourse, it interferes deeply with the inner logic of argument, be it legal argument or the legal assimilation of moral, ethical, or pragmatical arguments. It would have as its counterparts other autonomous discourses—the "universalization procedure" of morality in its Kantian, Rawlsian, or Habermasian version, or an "identity search procedure" in ethical discourses, or the utility calculus of "rational choice"—which in their turn typically proceduralize argumentation and

43. *See* NIKLAS LUHMANN, DAS RECHT DER GESELLSCHAFT 110–17 (1993).
44. *See* HABERMAS, *supra* note 8, at 288.

incorporate, but thereby enslave foreign arguments, among them legal concepts, rules, and principles.

V.

But how should such a mundane enterprise like the law be able in its tormented casuistry to "incorporate" the vast multitude of high-culture discourses such as morality, ethics, and pragmatics on the one side and powerful economic and political arguments on the other? Why should the legal discourse be able to make highly diverse aspects compatible, a feat that a philosophical superdiscourse was not supposed to be able to accomplish? Let us have a closer look—with empathy and compassion—at the victims of this semantic slavery. "Alike or not alike—that is the question" which attracts other discourses to law. Once selectively admitted, they suffer a peculiar transformation. Moral maxims, ethical self-realization, pragmatic recommendations, and policy requirements—to use Habermas's very typology—lose their specific identity. They all reappear now in the guise of sheer legal norms, rights, and duties, principles, and values—simple components of the legal discourse. Habermas uses the metaphor "translation" to analyze this transubstantiation of morality into law.[45] As long as the differences of languages is maintained, the immigration of moral contents into law does not signify any immediate moralization of law.[46]

Indeed, it signifies the very opposite, a juridification of morality with the result of leveling out discursive differences. Originally, there were incommensurable rationalities directed into different dimensions of meaning. Now their legal enslavement makes them commensurable, comparable, and decidable—only within the boundaries of law, of course. Here, we find the reason for the shameless eclecticism of law that treats moral maxims and economic policies equally as "values" among which the law can establish priorities according to prior legislative or judicial decisions. Here, we find the reason why high culture is inevitably trivialized whenever lawyers begin to incorporate it in their briefs, as German lawyers tend to say self-critically: *zu kleiner Münze verrechtlicht* (juridified into small coins).

With high sensitivity Habermas analyzes this transformation from moral rules into legal rules: moral contents are translated into the legal code and are endowed with a different mode of validity.[47] This leads him to an informative typology of differentially "moralized" legal norms. However, he seems to underestimate the simplifying effect of this translation when he,

45. *See id.* at 250–53.
46. *See id.* at 253.
47. *See id.* at 252.

in his polemics against Alexy's theory of balancing goods, insists that within legal practice, the difference between deontological principles and teleological values needs to be respected. In my view, this is a paradigmatic case. It shows how the legal discourse deals with fundamental differences between other discourses. Certainly, Habermas is right:

> Norms and values are different, first in their reference to obligatory versus teleological action; second, in their binary versus gradual coding of their validity claims; third in their absolute versus relative oligatoriness; and fourth in the criteria which are applied to the coherence of rule systems or value systems.[48]

There are many legal theorists who would support this distinction and base whole systems of legal theory on it (deontological versus consequentialist theories). Legal practitioners, however, show no interest at all to respect these distinctions; they are determined to resolve collision issues and to transform them into a decidable form. Thus, the argumentative practice of law decides about collisions of discursive logics by leveling out their fundamental differences. For lawyers, their method of *Abwägung* (balancing) has exactly the same structure, be it balancing between principles, between values, or even between interests. They identify them in terms of the case at hand; they determine the degree to which they collide, they evaluate them as legitimate, they weigh them against each other and find the criteria for this weighing in legislative and judicial decisions. Worse, the trivialization of different logics enables them to treat incommensurable things alike and balance—*horribile dictu*—principles, values, and interests against each other. Pears and apples! Justitia is blind!

Maybe Habermas effectively points to the limits of solving discursive collisions by legal trivialization. Maybe he signals an overload of the traditional way in which discourse collisions are translated first into one-dimensional conflicts between legal norms, principles, and values, and then decided via legal doctrine and the hierarchy of courts. This should make us sensitive to other ways—less hierarchical and doctrinal, yet more decentral and processual—in which law deals with the collision of different worlds of meaning.

VI.

Fight fire with fire! Increasingly, law's response to the fundamental collision of discourses seems to be to fight fragmentation by fragmentation! This is the opposite strategy to mapping external conflicts within the uniting con-

---

48. *Id.* at 311.

ceptual framework of one and only one legal doctrine and relying on the hierarchical unity of the court system to decide doctrinal conflicts.

Now, instead of relying on the unity of law, there are tendencies to translate external discourse collisions into internal conflicts between specialized legal fields. And, in their turn, substantive legal fields find again an asymmetrical, self-referential way of resolving their conflicts. We could call this a "double re-entry." The distinction between different discourses reappears first in legal assimilation of other discourses and reappears a second time in the asymmetric collision rules in the conflict between different legal fields.

Internal differentiation of law can be seen as a response to the fragmentation of society in various systems and discourses. As is well known, internal differentiation of law has long since moved beyond the traditional broad distinctions between public law, private law, and criminal law. For example, the fragmentation of private law into a multitude of special fields (*Sonderprivatrechte*) has destroyed the conceptual-dogmatic unity of private law.[49] What is important for our context of discursive plurality, is that this internal differentiation lead to a close symbiosis between discursive domains outside the law and special fields within the law. Joerges puts responsibility on "the prevailing conditions in the social domain concerned which entail the specific differentiation of private law and lead to the fragmentation of the private law doctrine and legislation."[50] And this internally differentiated law looks more and more like a Russian doll that contains in itself ever smaller dolls. Even key areas within private law, such as tort law, can no longer be integrated by means of unified normative principles. The "compartmentalization of the classic 'general' law of tort into a law of specialized torts," for example, seems an irreversible state of affairs, to which the law reacts by providing differentiated "solutions for specific interests and social fields."[51] Nowadays, legal doctrine develops different theories of tort for different social fields, and this is no accident.[52] The practice of the courts has destroyed the old unity of law guaranteed by doctrine and has replaced it by a multiplicity of fragmented legal territories that live in close contact with their neighboring territories in other social practices.

---

49. *See* CHRISTIAN JOERGES, VERBRAUCHERSCHULTZ ALS RECHTSPROBLEM: EINE UNTERSUCHUNG ZUM STAND DER THEORIE UND ZU DEN ENTWICKLUNGSPERSPEKTIVEN DES VERBRAUCHERRECHTS (1981); Christian Joerges, *Quality Regulation in Consumer Good Markets: Theoretical Concepts and Practical Examples, in* CONTRACT AND ORGANIZATION: LEGAL ANALYSIS IN THE LIGHT OF ECONOMIC AND SOCIAL THEORY 142–63 (T. C. Daintith & Gunther Teubner eds., 1986).

50. Christian Joerges, *Die Überarbeitung des BGB-Schuldrechts, die Sonderprivatrechte und die Unbestimmtheit des Rechts,* 20 KRITISCHE JUSTIZ 166, 166–82 (1987).

51. GERT BRÜGGEMEIER, DELIKTSRECHT: EIN HAND-UND LEHRBUCH 82–89 (1986).

52. *See id.* at 313–463.

Demands for restoring the "unity of the legal order" are, of course, merely rhetorical in character, or are used tactically when the occasion arises.[53] Attempts to establish a conceptual or axiological unity through legal dogmatics are doomed to failure.[54] This is as true for private law as it is for the law in general.

How to deal with these internal conflicts that represent larger discursive collisions is still an open question. The idea of the "relative autonomy of legal fields"[55] seems to be both realistic and normatively acceptable. Explicitly, this idea uses concepts developed in the international private law for the collision of legal fields. Prominent among them figures the conflict-of-law principle of *ordre public*. *Ordre public* excludes the domestic application of foreign law in case that foreign law violates fundamental legal principles of domestic law. In its application to intralegal collisions, the starting principle is that doctrinally and procedurally specialized legal fields are essentially independent, and are only subject to limitations in situations where *ordre public* happens to be relevant. Each legal field will develop its own doctrinal structures according to the demands of the social practice involved, but in cases where problems of *ordre public* arise, the particular legal field would have to respect the fundamental principles and policies of the other legal fields. It would have to incorporate them into its own autonomous doctrine as a limitation on its activities. This seems to be a realistic way of reformulating the old idea of the unity of the legal order. In modern legal systems characterized by a high degree of internal differentiation, a close integration is no longer possible, neither through concepts and values nor through the court hierarchy. This is the revenge of the slaves! Certainly, they are enslaved by legal trivialization. But they still have the power to destroy the doctrinal unity of law from the inside. They compel the legal discourse to give up the goal of legal unity. Instead, what can be achieved, at best, is only a measure of compatibility between the doctrines of autonomous legal fields and the mutual reflexive adoption of their fundamental principle.

---

53. *See, e.g.,* HORST JAKOBS, WISSENSCHAFT UND GESETZGEBUNG IM BÜRGERLICHEN RECHT (1983); Ernst Wolf, *Kein Abschied vom BGB,* 15 ZEITSCHRIFT FÜR RECHTSPOLITIK 1–6 (1982).

54. *See* Wolfgang Zöllner, *Zivilrechtswissenschaft und Zivilrecht im ausgehenden,* 188 ARCHIV FÜR DIE ZIVILISISCHE PRAXIS 86, 100 (1988).

55. *See, e.g.,* RAINER WALZ, STEUERGERECHTIGKEIT UND RECHTSANWENDUNG: GRUNDLINIEN EINER RELATIV AUTONOMEN STEUERRECHTSDOGMATIK (1980); Rudolf Wiethölter, *Materialization and Proceduralization in Modern Law, in* DILEMMAS OF LAW IN THE WELFARE STATE 221–49 (Gunther Teubner ed., 1985); Rudolf Wiethölter, *Social Science Models in Economic Law, in* CONTRACT AND ORGANIZATION: LEGAL ANALYSIS IN THE LIGHT OF ECONOMIC AND SOCIAL THEORY 52–67 (T. Daintith & Gunther Teubner eds., 1986); Rudolf Wiethölter, *Proceduralization of the Category of Law, in* CRITICAL LEGAL THOUGHT: AN AMERICAN-GERMAN DEBATE 501–10 (C. Joerges & D. Trubek eds., 1989).

VII.

Let me try a final analogy. Frequently, private international law decides against domestic law and opts for the application of foreign law. Such an "externalization" happens when the case at hand seems to have a "closer relation" to the foreign legal order than to the domestic one. In the conflict of discourses, there is an equivalent to this externalization. The legal discourse resolves the collision by externalizing certain normative questions from its domain and delegating them to other normative practices. *Boni mores* and *bona fides* are the classical examples of resolving a discursive collision by referring it to morality, whatever this meant to be. More modern examples are references to "reasonable man," "public policy," "commercial practices," and "professional standards." Here is a remarkable difference from what we had called "enslavement." There, the law did simulate other argumentative practices by reconceptualizing them in terms of legal norms, principles, and values. Here, the law delegates its norm-creating task to other on-going argumentative practices. And it reads the result of such practices and then tries to assimilate them into legal rules. To be sure, the law plays quite an active role in this assimilation. But the fact remains that it is the ongoing argumentative practice outside the law that has an upper hand in determining the normative result.

How should we interpret this externalization? We might say that the collision of discourses is resolved by a mutual influencing of two argumentative practices that actually take place. In this case, two discourses are simultaneously reading and misreading their results. And in this process, certain *eigenvalues* emerge that have proven themselves in the practice of two discourses. These *eigenvalues* have greater plausibility and greater stability than the above mentioned results of legal trivialization or internal differentiation.

To conclude, I ask why employ these somewhat counter-intuitive tendencies toward asymmetry, re-entry, internal differentiation, and re-externalization? Why opting against a superdiscourse, against unity of law, against central court hierarchy? My tentative answer is: historicity. It is the accumulated experience of institutionalized argumentative practices that is rich enough to develop concrete criteria of relevance, to determine the sequence of distinctions, and to suggest topics of evaluation in order to cope with the disquieting reality of conflicting discourses.

EIGHT

Law and Order

Arthur J. Jacobson *

Every jurisprudence offers a distinctive image of order. Any order—whether of action, logic, or material—describes the ongoing operation of a set of principles or criteria. Principles define an order as the cause of an operation; criteria define it as the effect of other operations. The operation of a set of principles or criteria constituting an order allows observers effectively to distinguish that order from other orders or from no order at all.

An order is static when it is possible for observers to describe operation of the set of principles or criteria constituting the order at a single moment, without reference to past or future. It is dynamic when observers cannot describe operation of the set at a single moment, but must refer to past or future to describe the operation completely.[1]

The jurisprudence in Jürgen Habermas's *Between Facts and Norms*[2] suggests an image of order—indeed, more than one. Habermas, like most legal theorists and all practicing legal systems, draws images of order from both static and dynamic jurisprudence. These two main classes of jurisprudence are distinguished by, among other characteristics, their static and dynamic images of order.

---

*Max Freund Professor of Litigation & Advocacy, Benjamin N. Cardozo School of Law.

1. Note that stasis is not inconsistent with change. A static order may look different at time T^2 than at time T^1. Stasis requires only that an order be completely describable in any arbitrarily chosen present, T^1 or T^2. In other words, change in the appearance of a static order registers as change according to the set of ordering principles or criteria. Not only may static orders change, they may also muster greater or lesser resistance to change.

2. JÜRGEN HABERMAS, BETWEEN FACTS AND NORMS: CONTRIBUTIONS TO A DISCOURSE THEORY OF LAW AND DEMOCRACY (William Rehg trans., 1996).

I. STATIC AND DYNAMIC JURISPRUDENCE

Static jurisprudence insists on maintaining a correlation between rights and duties. Dynamic jurisprudence, on the other hand, breaks the correlation of rights with duties one way or the other. A jurisprudence is correlation-maintaining when for every right held by one person another person must bear the mirror-image duty, and for every duty held by one person another must hold the mirror-image right. A jurisprudence is correlation-breaking when it does away with either rights or duties, or when it insists on disrupting any correlation between rights and duties that might get established. Duty-based and rights-based jurisprudence break correlations the first way, doing away with, respectively, right and duty; common law breaks correlations the second way, by defining law as just the application of law in single cases. Static jurisprudence assigns the task of creating and maintaining correlations to a correlating agency, which is typically (but not always) the state. It is state-oriented jurisprudence. Dynamic jurisprudence rejects the role of a correlating agency. It is state-avoiding jurisprudence.

The defining difference between static and dynamic jurisprudence—one maintains correlations of rights with duties, the other does not—suggests a series of further differences. Four of these differences define the main institutions of legal systems which run along static or dynamic lines.[3]

First, static jurisprudence always distinguishes enforcement of law from legislation. Dynamic jurisprudence never makes this distinction. One static jurisprudence, legal naturalism, describes legal action entirely as enforcement. Legislation in this jurisprudence is an extraordinary event. The other static jurisprudence, legal positivism, restricts legal action to legislation. Enforcement ought to be invisible in this jurisprudence. Either persons follow the commands of the legislature automatically (self-enforcement), or, failing that, judges follow the commands, so that punishment, as Bentham says, falls like a stone.

Second, the source of law in static jurisprudence is always outside the legal system. In the naturalist form of static jurisprudence the source of law is nature, and law is the rational perception of nature by a qualified observer. In the positivist form of static jurisprudence the source of law is an authoritative procedure, and law is whatever those who get hold of the procedure mark as law using the procedure. How one gets hold of the procedure differs from system to system. The most rigorous positivism, such as

---

3. Static and dynamic jurisprudence differ on a host of other issues, which I have described elsewhere. *See* Arthur Jacobson, *Hegel's Legal Plenum*, 10 CARDOZO L. REV. 877 (1989); Arthur Jacobson, *The Idolatry of Rules: Writing Law According to Moses, With Reference to Other Jurisprudences*, 11 CARDOZO L. REV. 1079 (1990); Arthur Jacobson, *The Idea of a Legal Unconscious*, 13 CARDOZO L. REV. 1473 (1992).

Habermas's, gives control of the procedure to a political sphere, differentiated as such from the legal system, the economy, and religion or culture. The source of law in dynamic jurisprudence is always inside the legal system. Specifically, it is the legal person, in one of the three ways dynamic jurisprudence has of describing persons: as passionately right-seeking creatures in rights-based jurisprudence; as striving to emulate the virtues of a perfect legal commander in duty-based jurisprudence; and as driven by legal uncertainty to define and redefine reciprocal rights and duties in common law.

Third, norms in static jurisprudence are static in that it is possible to know a norm completely at a single moment and to follow a norm without changing it. In dynamic jurisprudence it is impossible to know a norm all at once or to follow a norm without changing it. Dynamic jurisprudence thus requires constant alteration of the legal manifold as a basic incident of legality.

Fourth, law does not fill the entire normative universe in static jurisprudence. Some corners of the normative universe are legally empty. Norms from legally empty corners are thus available in static jurisprudence, as custom or morality, to supplement or criticize norms rationally perceived as law by a qualified observer or marked as law by the authoritative procedure. The normative universe in dynamic jurisprudence, by contrast, is constantly filling with legal material. There are no legally empty corners. No social process outside the legal system supplies a vantage point from which to supplement or criticize legal action.

II. ORDERS IN JURISPRUDENCE

Because its norms never fill the universe, static jurisprudence always creates two orders—one of principles internal to the legal system, another of criteria external to it. The criteria define one version or another of social integration—lawfulness as a result, not a cause, of operations.[4] Each static jurisprudence, positivism and naturalism, suggests its own criterion for integration, which reflects, in turn, the principle animating that legal system's internal order.

In positivism, both the principle animating the legal system's internal order and the criterion animating its external order derive from mechanism. The mechanical principle is, first, the procedure for marking norms as law. This principle then carries over into the character of norms, which must be rigid and clear in order for enforcement to proceed automatically, as it must in positivism. Finally, a mechanical criterion defines integration

---

4. "Modern law," writes Habermas, "steps in to fill the functional gaps in social orders whose integrative capacities are overtaxed." HABERMAS, *supra* note 2, at 42.

within a very narrow compass as the consonance of social action with positivist norms. Positivism is, in principle, indifferent to the source of that consonance, whether it be habit, the threat of force, religious conviction, or whatever. Positivism is also indifferent to orders or the absence of orders beyond the narrow territory marked out by its norms.

In naturalism, the principle animating the legal system's internal order differs in form, but not in substance, from the criterion animating its external order. The principle of the legal system's internal order is self-maintenance of a legal manifold by reproduction of the manifold in the perceptions of qualified observers. The criterion for the legal system's external order defines integration as actual production of the manifold in the ordinary activities of "healthy" legal persons. Health thus replaces and reflects the perception of norms by qualified observers. Unlike positivism, however, naturalism cannot be indifferent to the source of integration. The principle of the legal system's internal order requires self-maintenance of the manifold, hence a guarantee of the legal health of persons not qualified to act as observers. Accordingly, qualified observers must also "cure" unhealthy persons, or kill them when they cannot be cured.

Because the legal systems established by dynamic jurisprudence fill the normative universe, dynamic orders are orders of principle only, not criteria. That is to say, dynamic jurisprudence strives to rework all social interaction according to the ordering principles of the jurisprudence, and neither tolerates nor recognizes orders external to the jurisprudence. Strictly speaking, therefore, a social system in which dynamic jurisprudence is dominant has no criterion of integration. Since there is no perspective outside the legal system in such a system, it would not strictly be true to say that the order inculcated by dynamic jurisprudence is disruption or social disintegration. Nevertheless, when dynamic jurisprudence works alongside static jurisprudence in a practicing legal system (as it practically must), then the achievement of order in dynamic terms registers as a potential for disorder in static terms.

It is an absolute requirement of dynamic jurisprudence that some domain of social interaction successfully resist reworking, or some new unworked domain appear as the unintended consequence of a successful reworking of other domains. Failing fresh supplies of unworked domains, the order of dynamic jurisprudence collapses—it cannot be unless it is in motion. The only way to guarantee that dynamic jurisprudence never finishes reworking social interactions is to confine the orders created by dynamic principles to potential, not actual, orders.

An order is actual when the order causes operation of the set of principles defining the order. "Cause" must be taken here in its literal, Cartesian meaning. Thus, the mechanical order of positivism is actual because the mechanism forces both correct operation of the procedure to mark norms as law and lawful behavior according to the norms. The biological order of naturalism is actual because healthy persons produce the legal manifold in their behavior and qualified observers reproduce it in perceptions and by curing or killing unhealthy persons.

An order is potential when the order does not cause operation of the set of principles defining the order in the Cartesian manner. For a non-Cartesian account of the relationship between operations and order, let us turn to the work of a physicist, the late David Bohm, who has described a physical model of non-Cartesian order—the "implicate order."[5]

The aim of Bohm's novel account of order is to reconcile the basic orders implied in relativity theory and in quantum theory, which have otherwise been in complete contradiction: "Thus relativity requires strict continuity, strict causality and strict locality in the order of the movement of particles and fields. . . . [I]n essence quantum mechanics implies the opposite."[6] Writing with Hiley, Bohm notes that the basic orders of relativity and quantum mechanics have in common a quality of "unbroken wholeness":

> To see what this means, let us first consider relativity. As is well known the concept of a permanently existent particle is not consistent with this theory. But rather it is the point event in space-time that is the basic concept. In principle all structures have to be understood as forms in a generalised [sic] field which is a function of all the space-time points. . . .
>
> The notion of unbroken wholeness is, however, still of limited applicability in the theory of relativity, because the basic concept is that of a point event which is distinct and separate from all other point events. In quantum theory however there is a much more thoroughgoing kind of unbroken wholeness. Thus even in the conventional interpretations, one talks of indivisible quantum processes that link different systems in an unanalysable way. . . . But in our [Bohm's and Hiley's] interpretation there is also the fact that because the quantum potential represents active information, there is a nonlocal connection which can, in principle, make even distant objects into a single system which has an objective quality of unbroken wholeness.[7]

Bohm and Hiley propose the idea of "implicate order" to reflect the character of "unbroken wholeness" that the basic orders of relativity and quantum mechanics have in common:

---

5. *See generally* DAVID BOHM & BASIL J. HILEY, THE UNDIVIDED UNIVERSE: AN ONTOLOGICAL INTERPRETATION OF QUANTUM THEORY 351 (1993).

6. *Id.* at 351.

7. *Id.* at 352. "The basic idea of active information," they say, "is that a form having very little energy enters into and directs a much greater energy. The activity of the latter is in this way given a form similar to that of the smaller energy." *Id.* at 35. As an example of active information Bohm and Hiley ask us to consider a radio wave whose form carries a signal. The

We begin by noting that the ordinary Cartesian order applying to separate points, finds one of its strongest supports in the function of a lens. What a lens does is to produce an approximate correspondence of points on an object to points on its image. The perception of this correspondence strongly brings our attention to the separate points. But as is well known, there is a new instrument used for making images called the hologram which does not do this. Rather each region of the hologram makes possible an image of the whole object. When we put all these regions together, we still obtain an image of the whole object, but one that is more sharply defined, as well as containing more points of view.

The hologram does not look like the object at all, but gives rise to an image only when it is suitably illuminated. The hologram seems, on cursory inspection, to have no significant order in it, and yet there must somehow be in it an order that determines the order of points that will appear in the image when it is illuminated. We may call this order implicit, but the basic root of the word implicit means "enfolded." So in some sense, the whole object is enfolded in each part of the hologram rather than being in point-to-point correspondence. We may therefore say that each part of the hologram contains an enfolded order essentially similar to that of the object and yet obviously different in form.

As we develop this idea, we shall see that this notion of enfoldment is not merely a metaphor, but that it has to be taken fairly literally. To emphasise [sic] this point, we shall therefore say that the order in the hologram is *implicate*. The order in the object, as well as in the image, will then be unfolded and we shall call it *explicate*. The process, in this case wave movement, in which this order is conveyed from the object to the hologram will be called *enfoldment* or *implication*. The process in which the order in the hologram becomes manifest to the viewer in an image will be called *unfoldment* or *explication.*[8]

Bohm and Hiley see implicate order at work in the constant unfoldment and enfoldment of classical reality from and back to the quantum wave function. The quantum wave function is a potential, or implicate order, which becomes actual, or explicate, through active information.[9]

---

sound we hear does not come directly from the wave, but from the batteries powering the radio,

> which provide an essentially *un*formed energy that can be given form (i.e. in-formed) by the pattern carried by the radio wave. . . . The information in the radio wave is *potentially* active everywhere, but it is actually active, only where and when it can give form to the electrical energy which, in this case, is in the radio.
>
> *Id.* at 35–36.

8. *Id.* at 353–54.

9. Their "ontological" description of the relationship between the quantum wave function and the reality described by ordinary classical physics is meant to replace Bohr's "Copenhagen

A similar notion may work as well to describe the potential orders of dynamic jurisprudence. Instead of "causing" operation of the set of principles constituting the order, the orders of dynamic jurisprudence constantly unfold and enfold operation of the principles. Indeed, the order of rights-based jurisprudence dynamically *en*folds operation of the principles of right, while the order of duty-based jurisprudence dynamically *un*folds operation of the principles of duty. The order of common law both *en*folds and *un*folds operation of the principle that law is just the application of law to single cases.

Consider, first, rights-based jurisprudence. This jurisprudence breaks the correlation between rights and duties by suppressing or ignoring duty to the extent possible. Practitioners of this jurisprudence are constantly engaged in a passionate effort to satisfy their drive for recognition. They do so by mutually recognizing mirror-image rights. Operation of the principle of mutual recognition constantly expands the number of rights, the number of persons recognizing rights, and the institutional expressions of mutual recognition. Consequently, the order of rights-based jurisprudence opportunistically enfolds into the single, stable ground of mutual right ever larger territories of legal material.

Consider, next, duty-based jurisprudence. This jurisprudence breaks the correlation by eliminating right altogether. The dynamism flows from the quest of persons to emulate the personality of the perfect legal person. Operation of the principle of emulation unfolds both the content and number of actual duties. Actual duties constantly unfold from the single, stable ground of the personality of the legal commander for two reasons. First, the principle of emulation requires partnership with the ideal legal commander in the creation of actual duties. Without the experience of creating duties, the legal person would miss that part of the ideal commander's legal experience. Second, the object of emulation is the personality of the legal commander. This personality is concrete and historical, not the abstract,

---

interpretation" of the relationship. In the Copenhagen interpretation, the quantum wave function represents a statistical distribution of attributes of particles and fields. *See id.* at 17. Measurement of an attribute "collapses the wave function" in Von Neumann's interpretation of quantum theory, so that the measurement gives a single, nonstatistical value of the attribute in Newtonian space-time. *See id.* at 20. These interpretations thus make us place a "cut" between two orders of nature: a quantum reality, which is statistical and non-local, and the classical reality established by measurement. But we have no reasonable way of placing the cut, of distinguishing measurement from any other physical event. Bohm and Hiley do away with the distinction between quantum reality and measurement. All reality is quantum reality. The quantum wave function is a real wave (De Broglie's "pilot wave"), encoding active information. We experience quantum reality as classical reality when quantum waves interfere to create patterns less "subtle" than the pattern of each quantum wave taken individually. These less subtle patterns are the particles and fields of ordinary classical physics. *See id.* at 176–80.

ahistorical personality of the Kantian person (though Kant does have a version of the jurisprudence of duty). The personality emulated by practitioners of duty-based jurisprudence is thus engaged in constant unfolding, like any concrete, historical personality. Hence, to emulate the personality of the legal commander, persons must constantly transform what is, in this jurisprudence, the central component of personality—its duties.

Common law breaks the correlation of rights with duties in both directions in order to produce a succession of correlations, according to the principle that law is just the application of law in single cases. Here dynamism flows from the incessant activities of legal persons to assemble, then disassemble, then reassemble correlations. Operation of the principle of application both unfolds fresh law in the next case in the stream of applications, and enfolds into the next case all prior applications. The applications in the stream need not, and generally will not, reach the point where a judge writes an opinion deciding a dispute. Rather, the stream of applications includes applications in disputes settled short of litigation to final judgment or appeal, as well as applications without dispute, in which persons simply engage in planning, guided by prior applications.

The orders of these three forms of dynamic jurisprudence are potential, not actual, orders. The interest of persons in a jurisprudence of right is recognition, hence mutual recognition of rights. A person may or may not be interested in using rights thus recognized. Whether a person uses a right or not is far less important in this jurisprudence than the legal dignity the person gets from recognition per se. If a person encounters resistance using a right, the jurisprudence of right does not leap to impose a duty on the person offering resistance. Rather, the offended person withdraws recognition of the same right from the offender. That is the preferred sanction in rights-based jurisprudence. As soon as the consciousness of a person switches from mutual recognition of right to following a duty, the order of the jurisprudence of right becomes actual, and the jurisprudence fails.

Similarly, the interest of persons in a jurisprudence of duty is perfection according to the model of a legal commander. Persons do their duty because they wish to attain that perfection, not because they must. The only sanction they suffer is the one inherent in imperfection, the self-loathing or communal ostracism that accompanies failure in this jurisprudence. As soon as the person follows a duty because the legal commander has ordered it, the order of the jurisprudence of duty becomes actual and here too, the jurisprudence fails.

Finally, the interest of persons in common law is reducing legal uncertainty by collaborating in a stream of applications. Persons wrestle rights and duties into correlation in the course of an application because they wish to reduce legal uncertainty. They violate the common law principle of order either by treating prior applications as fixing without doubt the rights and duties of a current application, or by treating a current application as fixing without doubt the rights and duties of some future application. In either case the potential order of common law becomes actual, and the jurisprudence fails.

Bohm's implicate order may not be entirely suitable as a model for the potential orders of dynamic jurisprudence, because Bohm's aim is to replace the statistical, mysterious elements of quantum mechanics with a deterministic theory consistent with the basic order of classical physics. The major difference between the order of classical physics and Bohm's implicate order is that the implicate order is an order of the quantum wave function, not particles or fields. Nevertheless, like the order of classical physics, the implicate order is fully deterministic. It certainly seems paradoxical to be using a deterministic model of order for dynamic jurisprudence. Even so, Bohm's overall judgment is that his worldview is "neither absolutely deterministic nor absolutely indeterministic."[10] Unlike the order of classical physics, we shall never be able to know all the active information encoded in quantum waves completely. Our instruments are simply too gross. They can detect only the relatively stable patterns that unfold from the interference of many quantum waves. The quantum waves encode much more active information than our instruments will ever be able to measure. Quantum reality is "subtle"; the classical reality we measure is not.[11] Hence, for all practical purposes, the statistical, mysterious interpretations of quantum reality are correct. They are just not ontologically true.

Why not just use the order suggested in the statistical, mysterious interpretations of quantum reality that Bohm seeks to replace with implicate order? After all, the order proposed in those interpretations squares nicely with the order of Legal Realism, where legal reality is fundamentally statistical until and unless an official takes action.[12] Why is Bohm's implicate order a superior model for the potential orders of dynamic jurisprudence?

Bohm's model is superior, because the orders of dynamic jurisprudence show a duality, just like the duality of implicate and explicate order. Duty-based jurisprudence assumes a single, unchanging ground from which we draw all actual duties. Nevertheless, like Bohm's implicate order, the ground of duty is never completely knowable. Hence, it appears constantly to be changing as we work with the legal commander to learn our duties. Similarly, rights-based jurisprudence assumes a potential for limitless recognizability as the root of all actual rights that we achieve together in struggles for actual recognition. Each of these forms of dynamic jurisprudence sup-

---

10. *Id.* at 324.

11. *See supra* note 9 and accompanying text.

12. Thus Legal Realism needs a "cut," just like the one Von Neumann proposed for dividing quantum from measured reality. *See supra* note 9 and accompanying text.

poses a stable limit, at once circumscribing and calling forth actual rights or duties, just as Bohm's implicate order supposes a stable wave function underlying and generating all classical reality.

Common law does not propose a stable limit this way. Unlike rights-based and duty-based jurisprudence, it does not suppose an unchanging ground from which we get either actual rights or actual duties. The ground from which fresh correlations spring—the stream of prior applications—changes with each application and is redetermined in each application. Thus, the legal manifold in common law is constantly in motion, in fact as well as in appearance. Common law lacks a stable ground, because it both unfolds and enfolds its ordering principle in each application. Rights-based and duty-based jurisprudence do one or the other. As a consequence, they both depend on sustaining an actual order of rights or duties against a potential order. The order in common law is always only potential. Thus, the ground from which correlations spring and into which they are absorbed resembles the quantum wave function of Bohm's implicate order. The potential order of common law is rich with far more active information than anyone can know. The active information constantly informs a myriad of applications spread over space and time, but we shall never know the active information in common law's ground altogether.

Just as the interference of quantum waves creates "relatively autonomous" patterns that register as the particles and fields of the classical world, the streams of applications in common law also create relatively stable patterns that register as rules, typical applications of rules, or practices. In Bohm's account, the "autonomy arises wherever the quantum potential can be neglected so that the classical world can be treated on its own as if it were independently existent."[13] Whether the quantum potential is sufficiently small to produce classical results is a product of the mathematics in the interaction of the wave functions. What determines relative stability in the potential order of common law?

We do not know. Let me suggest one last image of order that may be helpful in thinking about relative stability in a common law system. Stuart Kauffman has proposed a "bold hypothesis" that unifies the theory of natural selection in evolution with recent theories of spontaneous organization: "Living systems exist in the solid regime near the edge of chaos, and natural selection achieves and sustains such a poised state."[14] "Such poised systems," he argues,

> are . . . highly evolvable. They can adapt by accumulation of successive useful variations precisely because damage does not propagate widely. Useful altera-

13. BOHM & HILEY, *supra* note 5, at 177.
14. STUART A. KAUFFMAN, THE ORIGINS OF ORDER: SELF-ORGANIZATION AND SELECTION IN EVOLUTION 232 (1993).

tions in the behavior of one functionally isolated island can accumulate with useful alternations in another island. Furthermore, evolvability is high in networks near the order-chaos boundary because here many mutations cause minor changes and some mutations cause major changes. In a changing environment, this range of responses provides adaptive buffering: If the abiotic or coevolutionary world changes dramatically, large useful changes due to single mutations can be found rapidly; if the world changes only slightly, minor useful changes in behavior lie to hand.[15]

Common law's streams of applications may also "exist in the solid regime near the edge of chaos," and it may be that a selection of rules, typical applications of rules and practices "achieves and sustains such a poised state." If the relatively stable patterns of common law are selected according to Kauffman's "bold hypothesis," then a jurisprudence emphasizing the common law principle of order would have an adaptive advantage in buffering the economic, political, and cultural conflicts of a complex society.

III. HABERMAS'S ORDERS

Habermas starts from the position of positivism, that law is whatever is marked as law by an authoritative procedure. Hence, from the internal perspective of the legal system he regards order, at least initially, as mechanism, and from the external perspective of the social system he regards order as social integration. The issue in positivism is always the source of the authoritative procedure. The positivist procedure can never bootstrap itself, derive itself from its own procedure or from a super-procedure, which then in turn must be derived, and so forth. Some positivists, such as Lon Fuller and H. L. A. Hart, have a naturalist account of the source of the procedure, in which the procedure is what a qualified observer perceives upon reflection. Others attempt to ground the procedure in a jurisprudence of right, in which the procedure is a product of the effort of persons to satisfy the drive for recognition. This is one position held by Habermas, and in different ways, Dworkin and Hobbes.[16] Still others ground the procedure in a jurisprudence of duty, in which the procedure aids the quest of persons to attain the personality of a perfect legal person. This is the position of Bentham.[17] No theorist of the stature of these has attempted to ground the positivist procedure in common law, where the procedure would be just the application of the procedure, perhaps because this is impossible.

The jurisprudence of right in which Habermas attempts to ground his

15. *Id.*
16. *See generally* RONALD DWORKIN, TAKING RIGHTS SERIOUSLY (1977).
17. *See* THOMAS HOBBES, LEVIATHAN ch. 14 (Michael Oakeshott ed., 1962) (1651).

positivist procedure is truncated and diminished in comparison with the jurisprudence of right deployed by Hobbes.

Hobbes starts his *Leviathan*[18] with a legal state of nature in which legal persons experience a plenitude of right. Every man has a right to everything, which is to say that no justificatory statement is unavailable to anyone, in any situation. The role of the contract of commonwealth is to cut back sharply on statements available for justification. Hobbes moves from the legal state of nature, where the jurisprudence of right holds, to the commonwealth, where positivism holds, by a naturalist self-reproduction of positivist procedure through the reflections of a qualified observer. This figure—a move from a jurisprudence of right to positivist procedure through naturalist articulation of the procedure—is extremely common in jurisprudence, and was invented by Hobbes.

It is of supreme importance to Hobbes that the legal state of nature, the jurisprudence of right, be absolutely irretrievable for persons in the positivist commonwealth. Hobbes understood vividly both the need for a jurisprudence of right in order to prepare persons for citizenship in the commonwealth of law and the potential of rights for disruption of the commonwealth. The strategy throughout the *Leviathan* is to suppose an initial position dominated by the jurisprudence of right at every level—the levels of language, personality, and science—and then to erase the initial position through a variety of mechanisms—the Tower of Babel in the case of language; reorientation of the personality towards authority; and replacement of absolute by conditional knowledge. Nevertheless, it is equally important to Hobbes that the trace of the initial position be preserved in the condition of commonwealth in order to sustain the efficacy of the positivist procedure and the administration of laws pursuant to it.

Hobbes's notion of right is compromised, however, by the limited role Hobbes accords the jurisprudence of right in his *Leviathan*. Rights are instruments for satisfying passions, principally the passion for power, but no citizen of Hobbes's legal commonwealth has a passionate attachment to rights for their own sake. A pure jurisprudence of right, shorn of all static elements, was first the achievement of Hegel. The legal person in *Hegel's Philosophy of Right*[19] passionately desires rights in order to achieve recognition from other persons. Hegel's legal person could no more live without rights than without sex, shelter, or food. The *Philosophy of Right* traces the quest of the passionately right-seeking creature for recognition, through reciprocity in property relations, contract, crime, and so forth. The quest, which begins with the erotic drive of the legal person for recognition, ends in a state of war. Hegel thus presents the conquest of institutions by pas-

18. *Id.*
19. HEGEL'S PHILOSOPHY OF RIGHT (T. M. Knox trans., Oxford Univ. Press 1967) (1952).

sionately right-seeking creatures, postponing death by eroticizing institutions.

Habermas does not repeat Hobbes's figure—from jurisprudence of right to positivism through naturalism. Habermas goes directly to positivism from the jurisprudence of right. He does not use Hobbes's naturalist device of walling off the jurisprudence of right from the legal commonwealth in order to contain the disruptive potential of rights. Nonetheless, without Hegel's eroticization of institutions and his frankly grasping the beneficial domestic effects of the external state of war, Habermas must find a different way of containing the disruptive potential of rights than Hobbes's figure.

Habermas accomplishes the task of containing rights by two devices. First, he defines rights as spheres of choice protected by the state. This is no different than the stunted rights of Hobbes's commonwealth: Persons may play in the empty corners of the legal universe. The erotic significance of rights—the passionate connection of the person to rights, the ceaseless quest of persons for ever more recognition leading finally to war—is, as for Hobbes, entirely missing. Rights are instruments for living the good life, not the good life in themselves. Second, Habermas confronts persons exercising rights "with the normative expectation of an orientation to the common good,"[20] drawn from the prior participation of persons in the discursive democratic procedure in which the rights being exercised were formulated in the first place. Habermas thus subordinates rights to the processes of a fully differentiated public sphere. Habermas takes back with one hand what he gives with the other. The state tells persons they have rights, but asks them to exercise the rights with a good conscience. This rather spoils the fun of the empty corners, and certainly detaches rights from any suggestion of eroticism. It is the legal equivalent of permitting persons to make love only for the purpose of conceiving children.

If all that were at stake in Habermas's method of containing rights were Eros, then I suppose we should have to give Eros up in favor of a cold, but necessary civic virtue. But this is not all that is at stake. A passionate connection to rights serves a function for modern society as important as integration. Rights must disrupt, destabilize, and disintegrate whatever consensus citizens may reach in modern society, as a supreme instrument for maintaining social and political conditions of toleration. The keystone of modern society is toleration. It is not, as for Habermas and Weber, the appearance of an independent judiciary for guaranteeing a set of even ideal procedures. Without the potential for law to disrupt its own arrangements, even those reached communicatively and open to revision in an ideal communicative procedure, toleration is impossible. Toleration always requires disruption to be present in legal arrangements, especially when they are

20. HABERMAS, *supra* note 2, at 83–84.

arrived at through a communicative consensus. The more attractive or fair the consensus, the more aid individual persons need in order to disrupt it.

The work of enlightenment is never done, and law too, in the disruptive potential of rights, is enlightened. The attempt to suppress justifications simply because decisions must be made in order to achieve integration can never entirely succeed. The notion that losing justifications, however unattractive, may be suppressed is entirely pernicious. It deprives losers of recognition and invites the return of the repressed. It is faithless to the reality that the universe of justifications is always full and ineradicable. The difficulty of social life is that there is too much justice in the world, not too little. If law does not disrupt as well as integrate, it forfeits the chance to provide decisions with legitimation.

Finally, what is unsaid in law is even more important than what is said. Dynamic jurisprudence recognizes this fact in that it grasps and exploits the potential of a legal unconscious. No law can entirely express the values that lie behind it, and laws always express a conflict of values. Law is born in strife and lives in strife. Law never says what will be, but what the field shall be for further battles.

PART FOUR

Law's Reconstruction, Justification, and Application

NINE

Habermas and the Counterfactual Imagination

Michael K. Power*†

INTRODUCTION

The epistemological problem of critical theories is easy to state but hard to resolve. On the one hand, if the theories are too descriptive and draw their conceptual resources from the ideas and institutions which currently exist, they lose their critical force. While they may provide elaborate reconstructions of the structure of social practices, they remain internal to these practices, part of a field of knowledge in which, at worst, theory is merely a form of public relations. On the other hand, if they articulate forms of critique that are entirely external to the systems of knowledge and practice that exist, then they threaten to become elitist and dependent on "transcendental" support, hence lacking any basis in the experience of the subjects for whom the theory is articulated in the first place.

In short, the problem for critical theories is one of self-grounding that requires the norms which inform critique to somehow be observed, albeit in distorted form, within actual social and economic practices. Max Horkheimer and Theodor W. Adorno's critical theories, in contrast to "traditional" theories, draw their intellectual resources from the reality of more or less suppressed forms of conflict. The way facts appear as facts, both in theories and in wider fields of practice, is the object of critique. It is this sense of the hidden social conflict, informing the production of both reality

*Professor of Accounting, The London School of Economics and Political Science. The author is grateful for the helpful comments of Peter Miller, Tim Murphy, and Hugh Willmott.

†The translations in this Article are those of the author.

and traditional theories of reality, that gives to critical theories their "immanent," internal status while also saving them from mere description.[1]

Without doubt, Jürgen Habermas has raised the epistemological stakes of critical theories. In contrast to a perhaps more pessimistic conception of critique as negation, Habermas has in various ways sought to articulate the normative potential embedded in forms of public life and practices, such as law, that play a central role in public life. This commitment required a reworking of the self-grounding status of critical theories, a reworking that is visible in its most explicit form in *Knowledge and Human Interests*,[2] and has resurfaced in various forms since then.[3] For all the twists and linguistic turns that Habermas's work has taken over the years, the problem of self-grounding is a more or less continuous preoccupation.

The purpose of this Article is to consider this preoccupation in the light of Habermas's ideas in *Faktizität und Geltung*.[4] Although the cast in 1992 is different from that of 1968 (Karl Marx and Sigmund Freud have given way to John Rawls and Ronald Dworkin), there is a continuity that links Habermas's early and later works. My label for this continuity is the "counterfactual imagination"[5] whose unity is the product of two principal components: "reconstructive-transcendental" and "critical-reflective." The former argues for the counterfactual conditions of possibility of knowledge practices, while the latter seeks to anchor these conditions within an understanding of actual social and institutional structures.

---

1. Of course, the fact of conflict has always been highly contested by opponents of critical theory. In turn, critical theory is always vulnerable to despair in the face of the "totalizing" society where conflict is repressed. Hence, for both critical theorists and their critics, the epistemological status and visibility of conflict has always been a problem.

2. JÜRGEN HABERMAS, KNOWLEDGE AND HUMAN INTERESTS (Jeremy J. Shapiro trans., 1971).

3. *See* Jürgen Habermas, *A Postscript to "Knowledge and Human Interests,"* 3 PHIL. SOC. SCI. 157 (1973).

4. JÜRGEN HABERMAS, FAKTIZITÄT UND GELTUNG: BEITRÄGE ZUR DISKURSTHEORIE DES RECHTS UND DES DEMOKRATISCHEN RECHTSSTAATS (1992). Page references within this Article are to this German edition. For the English translation, see JÜRGEN HABERMAS, BETWEEN FACTS AND NORMS: CONTRIBUTIONS TO A DISCOURSE THEORY OF LAW AND DEMOCRACY (William Rehg trans., 1996).

5. The concept of a "counterfactual imagination," which I use to illuminate the structure of Habermas's philosophical thinking, clearly bears a familiar resemblance to the ideas in MARTIN JAY, THE DIALECTICAL IMAGINATION: A HISTORY OF THE FRANKFURT SCHOOL AND THE INSTITUTE OF SOCIAL RESEARCH, 1923–1950 (1973). However, Jay's notion of the dialectical imagination, applied as it is to an older generation of critical theorists, is concerned with characterizing the tension between the possible ineffectiveness of social critique on the one hand, and its potential cooptation on the other. *See id.* at 15. The "counterfactual imagination," as I use it, is more epistemological in orientation. I also apologize to analytic philosophers for whom the concept of counterfactuality has a different meaning which attempts to characterize the "lawlikeness" of the propositions we accept as laws.

In *Knowledge and Human Interests,* this two-fold structure seems to take the following form: Charles Peirce and Wilhelm Dilthey provide a basis for reconstructing the deep interest structure that constitutes two fields of knowledge, natural science and human science. The elaboration of interests as neo-Kantian conditions of the possibility of knowledge is paradigmatic of "reconstructive-transcendental" thinking. However, according to Habermas, another theme is also visible in both of these cases. This theme is made more fully visible in the case of Marx and Freud for whom, in different ways, neo-Kantian arguments must be subsumed within broader processes of self-formation and reflection oriented towards enlightenment.

The epistemological problem here is clear. Neo-Kantian reconstruction remains at the level of "traditional" theorizing (despite the use of the word "critical") unless it can be related to strategies of enlightenment, the critical-reflective component in which possibilities for the acceptance of the validity of critical theory are possible. For critical theorists, reconstructive-transcendental arguments and critical-reflective strategies are intertwined and mutually constitutive. For analytic philosophers, they are suspiciously circular because they seem to presuppose the very things they are intended to demonstrate.

In *Knowledge and Human Interests,* Habermas attempts to hold together these two components of critical theory. The reconstructive-transcendental component, standing alone, is invalid as an argument. It must be integrated into contexts of critical-reflection to establish its validity in actual forms of acceptance. Nothing less is at stake here than an attempt to hold together universalistic and contextualistic bases for the validity of critical theory. Whereas Adorno was more or less content with a "critical-reflective" contextualist form of negative thinking alone, Habermas has been committed to recovering the "context-transcending" conditions that make immanent critique possible.

To distinguish in this way between reconstructive-transcendental and critical-reflective components of Habermas's approach to critical theory is not an attempt to save Habermas or critical theorizing at all costs. Rather, it is an attempt to elaborate the deep structure of critical theorizing so that the nature of its problems and the forms of objections to it are more clearly understood. In *Faktizität und Geltung,* Habermas expresses the distinction between the two elements in Rawlsian terms: the difference between, on the one hand, theory construction and, on the other, the reflexive conditions under which such a theory might gain acceptability by virtue of being "contingently embedded."[6]

6. HABERMAS, *supra* note 4, at 86. Habermas states:

The more Rawls believes he can only support the theory of justice itself locally, with culturally molded intuitions that none "of us" can reasonably reject, the less

This reading of Rawls precisely reflects the deep structure of Habermas's counterfactual imagination in which philosophical argument and concrete life-projects coincide. The reconstructive-transcendental component can be likened to a "forward" argument that establishes the deep conditions of the possibility of "orderly" social practice. The critical-reflective component resembles a "backward" argument that seeks to "anchor" these theoretical conditions within concrete forms of social life. However, the image of a "reflective equilibrium" between these two components also suggests Habermas's increasing distance from the terms of reference of the older members of the Frankfurt School.

In *Faktizität und Geltung,* Habermas attempts to work out a reconstructive theory of law in which sociological ("external") and jurisprudential ("internal") theories are accommodated and reinterpreted as "moments" of a more general theory.[7] At the heart of this project he is concerned with explicating the close conceptual relation between "facticity," understood as the way the facts of positive law appear as facts, and "validity," understood as the communicative basis by which the facticity can be grounded and justified. This analysis addresses the implicit communicative foundations of both positivistic jurisprudence and systems theory. According to Habermas, traditional dualisms between the sociological and the legal, the positive and the normative, and the external and the internal, are overcome at the level of discourse in which conceptual-pragmatic relations are established. In short, Habermas attempts to demonstrate that the communicative presuppositions of varied legal discourses establish that certain ideal conditions of validity redemption are necessary conditions of any legal positivity.

It should be clear that, in a neo-Marxist sense, there is not much left of critical theory in this project. In this Article the focus is on the general issue

---

clear the boundary becomes between, on the one hand, the business of grounding principles of justice philosophically and, on the other, a concrete legal community's enterprise of reaching a political self-understanding about the normative basis of their living together.

Id. at 82.

7. The distinction between "external" and "internal" intellectual perspectives on a practice is undoubtedly a problematic point of departure for Habermas's proposed reconciliation. One approach to the distinction is suggested by ANDREW ABBOTT, THE SYSTEM OF PROFESSIONS: AN ESSAY ON THE DIVISION OF EXPERT LABOR (1988). From Abbott's point of view, the distinction cannot be made in absolute terms, but only in terms of relative positions in the system of professional knowledge. This would give Habermas the points of continuity that he needs between the internal and external modes of theorizing as a basis for his discourse-theoretic reworking of their relation. Thus, sociological theorizing exists at the periphery of the professional knowledge system of law. However, there is nothing necessary about this; such locations are fluid.

of an epistemological structure that posits a counterfactual construct at its very center. However, this has implications for the "end of critical theory" which I shall address in due course. In the next section I consider the first of the two components, or "moments," of Habermas's counterfactual imagination—his reconstructive-transcendental arguments. Three further subcomponents become visible and are considered in subsequent sections. This discussion unfolds toward an analysis of the second "moment" of the counterfactual imagination: the reflexive basis by which the theory is to embed itself in concrete institutional processes, processes by which the theoretical edifice is "validated" as immanent and in which the counterfactual conditions of communicative rationality can paradoxically realize themselves.

At the center of this critical-reflective component lies the vulnerable and problematic process of "realizing" the counterfactual. For critical theories, the conditions of possibility made visible at the reconstructive-transcendental stage are in limbo until they can be validated by reference to concrete practices. The more critical the theory, the more these practices will be oriented toward social change; critical theorizing is connected to practice in such a way that social change and theoretical validity are mutually supporting.

In the development of Habermas's thinking, the critical reflective component has been modified such that in *Faktizität und Geltung*, the neoliberal model of reflective equilibrium replaces strategies of enlightenment. I argue that the unity of Habermas's counterfactual imagination is preserved at the price of becoming less critical. Indeed, there is a certain tragic inevitability that once the problem of the self-grounding is posed, critical theory necessarily compromises itself in one of two directions: either it retains its critical force at the expense of grounding itself, or it softens the terms of critique in order to preserve the possibility of self-grounding. In *Faktizität und Geltung*, Habermas has chosen the latter path.

I. FACTICITY AND COUNTERFACTICITY

In seeking to make sense of Habermas's counterfactual imagination in terms of two moments, the reconstructive-transcendental and the critical-reflective, pragmatism presents an immediate obstacle. For example, perhaps similar to Adorno, thinkers such as Richard Rorty are dismissive of reconstructive-transcendental claims and argue that they are a redundant element of "critical" theories aimed at changing the conditions of social life: "I do not think that demonstrations of 'internal incoherence' or of 'presuppositional relationships' ever do much to disabuse us of bad old ideas or institutions. Disabusing gets done, instead, by offering us sparkling new ideas, or utopian visions of glorious new institutions."[8] However, Rorty is too busy traversing the "escalator" of Western philosophy to attend to the very practices that pragmatism reveres. The concept of a counterfactual imagination expresses a modality of thinking that is *internal* to practices, and confronts the paradox that we can often only make sense of such practices in terms of counterfactual constructs or fictions that are "context-transcending."

I argue that the reconstructive-transcendental moment of the counterfactual imagination is an *internal* feature of the rich redescriptions that Rorty and others favor. Indeed, the pragmatist's fear of meta-narratives is so great that it gives rise to the bizarre effect that, in the name of practice, we are disallowed from attending to the more abstract structures and relations that sustain practice. Accordingly, the concept of the counterfactual imagination, as it is used to reconstruct Habermas's philosophical project below, also represents a protest against the pragmatist's paradoxical "hollowing out" of the practical.

The question of what makes the factual universe of social practices factual does not arise for pragmatists, but is at the heart of the counterfactual imagination. Though the "nongivenness" of empirical facts is a common theme to a broad range of post-empiricist thinking, the idea that factuality is sustained and constituted not by deeper or more fundamental levels of other facts but by "counterfacts," or fictions, is distinctive and problematic. It is the idea that material practices are constituted paradoxically by certain fictions that provide the conditions of possibility of their operations and of their manner of making facts visible. We can only "make sense" of certain practices on the basis of assuming an operative role for deeply embedded fictional norms.[9] These fictions are foundations from within, without any heavyweight metaphysical support.

In *Faktizität und Geltung*, Habermas's "heroes," or at least his points of sympathetic departure, can be characterized by counterfactual constructs that express a "foundational intuition." In the context of *Faktizität und Geltung*, the reconstructive interpretations of Rawls and Dworkin are good examples. Both are characterized by Habermas as motivated to provide a "deep theory"—i.e., "our best account of present practice." Both appeal to

---

8. Richard Rorty, *Is Derrida a Transcendental Philosopher?*, in Essays on Heidegger and Others 121 (Richard Rorty ed., 1991).

9. Lawyers are well acquainted with the constitutive role of fictions in legal reasoning processes, but the point is generalized to the economic domain. For example, accounting practice is constituted by economic fictions such as "value" and "profit" that can never be unambiguously realized but that serve a regulative function.

counterfactual constructs, the original position, and Hercules's positions, respectively, in order to do this. Both raise the question of the embeddedness of the theory as a condition of its validity. According to Habermas, both must be reformed by reference to the theory of communication.

For pragmatists such as Rorty, Habermas's "constructivist" impulses, and those of his heroes, are tainted by a Neo-Kantian foundationalism. Yet, there is an important difference between attempts to put knowledge practices on *firm foundations,* and attempts to construct a *deep theory* that provides an understanding of what "holds practices together" as stable projects. The latter cannot automatically be associated with a discredited philosophical project solely on the basis of resemblances in vocabulary.[10] What is at stake here is the plausibility of a constitutive role for counterfactual constructs. Critics of Habermas's concept of an "ideal," and therefore counterfactual speech situation, usually argue for the impossibility of the "teleology without metaphysics" that it represents, and its indefinite postponement of emancipation. Even theorists who accept that facts are not simply "given" have more difficulty with the idea that they are deeply constituted by counterfactual constructs. Fictional and empiricist sensibilities seem incompatible.

If the epistemic status of counterfactual constructs, such as the ideal speech situation or an original position, is a considerable problem from certain empiricist points of view, then equally, such constructs cannot simply be dismissed or "falsified" as if they failed to acknowledge the empirical "complexity" of the world. Their status is neither purely logical nor empirical, since they are embedded in strategies for their own realization or, more accurately, for making it possible to describe them as realized. Paradoxically, the ideal speech situation is claimed to be both necessary (in a reconstructive-transcendental sense) and as yet unrealized (in a critical-reflective sense). For Habermas, this idealization is "unavoidable" if we are to make sense of ourselves as engaged in communicative practices. From this point of view, we cannot have a self-sustaining notion of positivized communicative practices without reference to a counterfactual fiction that is internal to the realities inscribed by those practices.

10. In any case, the neo-Kantian philosophical project has been caricatured by Rorty. Elsewhere I provide a more extensive critique of the antifoundationalist pragmatizing consensus. The core of this critique is a rereading of Kantianism in which the thing-in-itself, far from being an unknowable entity, is interpreted as a limiting concept that is constitutive of objectivity. Accordingly, Rorty's division of philosophical territory between neo-Kantianism and hermeneutics is overdrawn. *See* Michael K. Power, *Buchdahl and Rorty on Kant and the History of Philosophy, in* METAPHYSICS AND PHILOSOPHY OF SCIENCE IN THE SEVENTEENTH AND EIGHTEENTH CENTURIES: ESSAYS IN HONOUR OF GERD BUCHDAHL 265 (Roger S. Woolhouse ed., 1988).

Habermas's theory of communicative action "absorbs the tension between facticity and validity into its fundamental concepts"[11] and posits the
"fragile ground [of] context transcending validity claims"[12] as the counterfactual basis for truths that become positivized, routinized, and insulated
from possible criticism. Habermas is engaged in the immanent critique of
a self-sufficient "facticity" such that it is always "projected" into questions
of validity. What counts as a practice-relative fact is constituted, in some
way, by reference to a counterfactual construct that, for Habermas, provides the conditions of possibility for the practices under which such facts
can be criticized and stabilized.

It must be asked whether there is any more to this idea of a constitutive
role of counterfactual fictions than some ultimate philosophical commitment or faith. To answer this, I address three forms in which the reconstructive-transcendental moment of the counterfactual imagination expresses itself: a style, an argument form, and a philosophical archetype.
The style is the vocabulary of the "as if." The argument is the transcendental argument form. The philosophical archetype is that of the regulative
idea.

II. THE VOCABULARY OF THE "AS IF"

The counterfactual imagination is characterized by a distinctive vocabulary.
In the context of *Faktizität und Geltung,* this vocabulary consists of expressions such as "points beyond," "becoming," "anticipation," "overshoots the
given," "limit positing idealising conceptions,"[13] and many others. This language has its origins in the philosophy of idealism but extends beyond it
in the form of a vocabulary of the "as if," which is both metaphysically more
modest than idealism and also more problematic.[14] For Habermas, these
expressions constitute an unconscious and insistent resource, the heritage
of German idealism and its fidgety lack of respect for the present.

An important feature of this language is the dynamic of its core metaphors and the sense of motion and *telos* implied by certain key words.[15] And
yet, at the very same time that this movement is conveyed, any sense of
actual evolution or teleology is negated. Accordingly, the language is char-

11. HABERMAS, *supra* note 4, at 22.
12. *Id.*
13. *Id.* at 24.
14. *Cf.* H. VAIHINGER, THE PHILOSOPHY OF 'AS IF': A SYSTEM OF THE THEORETICAL, PRAC-
TICAL AND RELIGIOUS FICTIONS OF MANKIND (C. K. Ogden trans., 2d ed. 1935).
15. The importance of the verb *"werden"* in German is perhaps indicative of this. The
English verb "to become" does not have the same resonances.

acterized by a tension between the problematic facticity of facts and a counterfactuality that explicitly fictionalizes itself. Limit concepts are therefore invoked, not so much to characterize an achievable state of affairs (i.e., utopia), but to express a fictional directionality that "makes sense of" the procedural structures of current practices and, in the case of *Faktizität und Geltung*, recovers the normativity of juridified law. The counterfactual fiction of ideal speech *defines* the normative boundaries of specific knowledge systems, such as law and accounting, and hence also the boundary between the lifeworld as the source of normative authority and its differentiated subsystems.

Such a language imposes considerable stress upon our either/or sensibilities.[16] At the level of this "as if" logic, it is necessary to read the universalist claims of Habermas's theory of communication in terms of a metaphorical movement from the local to the universal, a movement that is never complete and that approaches universality only as a limitation of the local. Hence, the universality of ideal speech is not simply posited by Habermas, but rather "unfolds" as an internal condition of the local that points beyond itself only "problematically" in Kant's sense.

Rorty argues that ideal speech is a "wheel which plays no part in the mechanism of social criticism"[17] largely because of its "universalistic" status.[18] But the universality of ideal speech is consistent with an "internal realism," in which reality is conceived less as a problematic external referent and more as a *limit* to theoretical discourse.[19] Habermas states that reality "contains a reference to something independent of us and thus, in this sense, [is] transcendent."[20] However, this is always "transcendence from within." The implication is that the "real," which is posited by internal realism, is effectively an ideal reference point, the elusive but nevertheless constitutive *telos* of empirical inquiry.

The "vocabulary of the 'as if' " expresses a hybrid discourse in which moments of pragmatism and idealism are reworked. It thereby creates a conceptual field that attempts to resist reductionist tendencies. Simply pointing to a certain language or style, however, is an insufficient explication of Habermas's counterfactual imagination. It is also necessary to consider the nature of the argument structure that is at work in this language.

16. *Cf.* RICHARD J. BERNSTEIN, BEYOND OBJECTIVISM AND RELATIVISM: SCIENCE, HERMENEUTICS, AND PRAXIS (1983).

17. Richard Rorty, *Habermas and Lyotard on Post-Modernity*, 4 PRAXIS INT'L 32, 35 (1984).

18. *Id.* at 34–35.

19. *Cf.* HILARY PUTNAM, REASON, TRUTH AND HISTORY (1981).

20. HABERMAS, *supra* note 4, at 30.

III. TRANSCENDENTAL ARGUMENTS[21]

The reconstructive-transcendental component of Habermas's counterfactual imagination has a distinctive "transcendental" argument structure that attempts to elaborate the necessary communicative conditions of practices. Given the existence of a practice, which is always relative to the ways of describing it, it can be asked: what are its conditions of possibility? For the Kant of the *Critique of Pure Reason*,[22] the "practice" in question was "experience in general," and the conditions of possibility were the categories of the Understanding and the forms of Intuition—spatiality and temporality. For Habermas, the practice in question is communication and the condition of possibility in question is a counterfactual situation of ideal communication in which actors are motivated solely by the force of the better argument. The argument can be formalized as follows:

1. C
2. C only if IS
3. Therefore IS

C is the assumption that we have communication oriented towards understanding; IS describes the conditions of an ideal speech situation. Habermas has never been fully explicit about the form of the argument. Consequently, a number of commentators have attempted to reconstruct it in terms similar to those given above.[23]

To characterize Habermas's recent position in terms of a "transcendental argument" is potentially misleading, given the close association between that term and the Kantian project.[24] Analytic philosophers retain the label "transcendental" for an argument type which, though not dependent upon an idealist metaphysical framework, nevertheless seems to share a logical structure with Kant's transcendental idealism. Habermas's transcendental argument is weak, in this metaphysical sense, in so far as it is displaced from the context of the "philosophy of consciousness." But this metaphysical modesty disguises ambitions that are also strong.

From an analytic point of view, transcendental arguments fail for two reasons: because C can be argued to be something we do not have to accept

---

21. This section is an abridged version of a more extensive discussion. *See* Michael Power, *Habermas and Transcendental Arguments: A Reappraisal*, 23 PHIL. SOC. SCI. 26 (1993).

22. IMMANUEL KANT, CRITIQUE OF PURE REASON (Norman K. Smith trans., 1961) (1781).

23. *See* John B. Thompson, *Universal Pragmatics, in* HABERMAS: CRITICAL DEBATES 116 (John B. Thompson & David Held eds., 1982); Dmitri N. Shalin, *Critical Theory and the Pragmatist Challenge*, 98 AM. J. SOC. 237 (1992).

24. Habermas describes his early philosophical position as "quasi-transcendental," an expression he abandons in favor of the language of rational reconstruction. However, the substantive differences between these ideas are not so great and both can be linked to what I call the "counterfactual imagination."

and because, even if C were true, stage 2 above is invalid. But, as I have argued elsewhere, a transcendental argument is not merely a formal argument that proceeds from a *given* practice, C, and argues for what must be presupposed by it, i.e., IS. Habermas's transcendental arguments are not just descriptive metaphysics in Strawson's sense. The transcendental argument is an intellectual process by which the description of that practice, C, is (re-)negotiated.[25] Thus, the counterfactual supposition of an ideal speech situation is part of an argument in which the factuality of C is contested and in which the counterfactual becomes a normative basis for redescribing such practice.

This gives a certain hermeneutic flavor to the strategy that the more linear idea of an argument does not capture. It also shows how the first premise C of the transcendental argument is, in the language of classical critical theorizing, a site of potential struggle for the social conditions under which the truth of that premise could be accepted. Its empirical falsity does not mean it is rejected out of hand but that, within the critical-reflective component of Habermas's theory, its truth is contested. Even the classical examples of transcendental arguments are not simply conditions of possibility arguments, but rather, derive their force by virtue of redescribing and negating previously held positions. For example, Kant's critical turn takes place as a reaction to the Leibnizian preoccupations of his youth and many of the transcendental argument structures in the *Critique of Pure Reason* have Leibniz firmly in their sights.

In other words, Habermas's transcendental argument continues the spirit of *immanent critique,* particularly where it demonstrates that the claims of an opponent (or hero) can be reconstructed in terms such that they must presuppose the theory they reject.[26] Habermas's transcendental arguments must be seen in terms of a "depth hermeneutic" or "metacritique" in which incumbent conceptions of communication must be transformed at the same time that their counterfactual conditions of possibility are made visible.

Habermas's argument strategy is strong because he attempts to capture the conceptual space in which practices understand and represent them-

25. *See generally* Power, *supra* note 21.

26. This strategy is particularly evident in JÜRGEN HABERMAS, THE PHILOSOPHICAL DISCOURSE OF MODERNITY: TWELVE LECTURES (Frederick Lawrence trans., 1987). In *Faktizität und Geltung,* Habermas has at least two such subarguments. Against Teubner's systems theoretic account of law, he argues that the concept of a "legal code" is only possible on the presupposition of structures of intuitive understanding. Against Dworkin, he argues that the idea of a Herculean interpreter can only be founded in terms of a possible communication community. Thus, all roads lead back to the theory of communication via a network of transcendental arguments that seek to disclose the communicative conditions of possibility for the target position.

selves, such as jurisprudence in the case of law. Habermas is engaged in a "critical redescription" in which the transcendental and the pragmatic cannot be sharply distinguished. The truth of the first premise of the transcendental argument provides the point of internal linkage between the reconstructive-transcendental and critical-reflective components of the counterfactual imagination. For Habermas, the former cannot "work" purely at the level of argument and the latter cannot "work" purely at the level of criticism. They are locked together in a contingent, concrete project of recovering the self-authorship of social arrangements.

According to Habermas, the theory of communicative action "detranscendentalizes the intelligible world only in order that the idealizing force of context transcending anticipations . . . might settle in the unavoidable pragmatic presuppositions of speech acts."[27] It is open to his critics simply to deny the existence of such context transcending anticipations and it must be conceded that the explicit nature of Habermas's transcendental arguments is often difficult to discern, coming as it does in a variety of forms. One particular difficulty is that Habermas often uses the term "must" in a reconstructive-transcendental (presuppositional) sense rather than a "prescriptive" sense; this is likely to bewilder the unsympathetic reader. For example, when he says that "interacting participants must consider themselves mutually accountable,"[28] either sense could be invoked. But the whole strategy derives its force from obscuring the distinction between the transcendental and the prescriptive. They are two moments of a unified critical strategy.

This more or less explicit transcendental argument structure is the basis for distinguishing Habermas's position from mere moralizing and utopianism because it attempts to anchor the normativity of mutual recognition, as a speech partner, as a condition of possibility for all practices which depend on communication.[29] Transcendental arguments do not operate at the level of moral prescription directly, but they ground such prescriptions that would otherwise remain merely external. Transcendental arguments always "fail" as purely logical arguments, and hence, they can never be deductive. However, their point is not formal deductivity, but a mode of critical redescription in which presuppositional and normative structures coincide.

---

27. HABERMAS, *supra* note 4, at 35.
28. *Id.*
29. This point is not fully appreciated by sympathetic critics such as Raymond Geuss, who distinguishes sharply between an acceptable "contextualism" and an unacceptable "transcendentalism" as the basis for critical theory. Such a dualism fails to do justice to Habermas's *internal* transcendentalism. *See* RAYMOND GEUSS, THE IDEA OF A CRITICAL THEORY: HABERMAS AND THE FRANKFURT SCHOOL 67 (1981).

IV. REGULATIVE IDEAS

Thus far, I have addressed a language and an argument structure that is characteristic of the counterfactual imagination. Both of these elements depend upon the construct of the regulative idea and cannot make sense without it. In this respect, it is the Kant of the *Transcendental Dialectic* (which is the second part of the *Critique of Pure Reason*) that is the enduring theoretical heritage in Habermas's thought. In his appended discussion of *The Regulative Employment of the Ideas of Pure Reason*,[30] Kant engages in a de-transcendentalization strategy of his own. In a dazzling philosophical move, he reinterprets certain "ideas of reason" (God, soul, and totality) which give rise to antinomies when understood substantively ("dogmatically"). These problematic metaphysical notions are given a procedural status by Kant, a philosophical strategy that has, at least, two important effects.

First, regulative ideas that are substantively incompatible (antinomic) become procedurally compatible. Thus, mechanistic and teleological world views are compatible as procedural ideals but not as substantive accounts of the world. Second, the transcendental argument strategy becomes weaker in the sense that regulative ideas are no longer the conditions of possibility of "experience in general," but rather, of practices. This is both more plausible and more difficult. It is more plausible because the argument is no longer burdened by the need to demonstrate *necessary* conditions of *all* experience. It is more difficult because we can always be left with the question: Why is this particular regulative idea a necessary condition for making sense of the normative stability of this practice?

In the face of such skepticism there are two options. The first option is to further elaborate the argument that such practices (e.g., science, law, accounting) could not make sense internally except on the presupposition of certain guiding regulative principles that counterfactually anticipate an ideal speech situation. This would be to develop the reconstructive-transcendental side of the argument. The second option is to invoke the critical-reflective strand of the counterfactual imagination. If the first premise of a transcendental argument is not descriptive, but rather provides a critical-redescription of a practice, then the "validity" of this redescription must in some way be coupled to actual or potential institutional processes of will-formation in which that redescription could be accepted. This is somewhat similar to making a philosophical skeptic reflect upon his or her status as a citizen.

The conditions of an ideal speech situation are regulative ideas in Kant's sense. This is not to say that an ideal speech situation could ever be realized or experienced. Commentators who have explained that participants in

30. KANT, *supra* note 22, at 532.

ideal speech would have nothing to say to each other miss Kant's profound point about regulative ideas. Regulative ideas do not constitute possible objects of experience, but are presupposed in the procedures and practices. The paradox of regulative ideas, like the ideal speech situation, must be faced head on; their fictionality is a necessary condition of their role in constituting practices. It is precisely *because* communication would be unnecessary in an ideal speech situation that it is valid as a regulative idea. For Habermas, ideal speech is a limit concept of all communicative practice and one that can be made operative or real only in a critical sense. Although it indirectly influences the legitimacy of practices and their procedures, rather than being a directly realizable state of affairs, the paradox of the regulative idea of an ideal speech situation remains. How can it be both operative and fictional?

V. FACTUALIZING THE COUNTERFACTUAL

Habermas argues that the tension between facticity and validity does not correspond to that between reality and norm. As I have remarked above, the weak transcendentality of the counterfactual supposition cannot amount to moral normativity and it is no argument against Habermas that the norms embedded in counterfactual idealizations are not empirically instantiated. This, after all, is what makes them counterfactual. And yet, the ideality of the ideal speech situation remains problematic. Habermas talks in a seemingly paradoxical manner when he argues that the IS is not realizable and yet it is at risk; social integration operates with "permanently endangered counterfactual suppositions."[31] But how can a counterfactual construct be endangered?

Here we appear to have two difficulties with the concept of ideal speech and its regulative status: its anemic normativity and its unrealizability. One response to these difficulties is simply to reject the concept. But, from a more sympathetic point of view, these difficulties can only be resolved by reference to the distinction between the reconstructive-transcendental and critical-reflective registers of Habermas's thinking. Thus, the presuppositional "must" of a transcendental argument belongs to the former, and is not yet a practical prescriptive strategy. The idea of an ideal speech situation is that of a "decentered complex of pervasive, transcendentally enabling configurative conditions, but it is not a subjective capacity that would tell actors what they ought to do."[32] Hence, at the reconstructive-transcendental level, communicative theory is not an "immediately instructive nor-

31. HABERMAS, *supra* note 4, at 37.
32. *Id.* at 18.

mative theory, but a guide for reconstructing the network of opinion building."[33] In this sense, the unconditionality of context-transcending validity claims is not empirically realizable and can only be understood as a limit to contingent projects.

When we turn to consider the critical-reflective form of Habermas's thinking, where conditions of will-formation and institutional potentials for the possibility of validity redemption are at stake, then the realizability of a public sphere that is "guided" by reconstructions is a relevant preoccupation—"[t]hese idealizations inhabiting language itself acquire, in addition, an action-theoretic meaning if the illocutionary binding/bonding forces of speech acts are enlisted for the coordination of the action plans of different actors."[34] It is only at this level that the "counterfactual suppositions of actors who orient their action to validity claims also acquire immediate relevance for the construction and preservation of social order."[35] It is undoubtedly an empirical question whether there is any "striving" for such an order. But this empirical question must itself be treated with caution and, in terms of Habermas's project in *Faktizität und Geltung,* can only be understood by reference to a critical-reflective basis for theory acceptance. We do not find recognizable *arguments* so much as *strategies* for factualizing the counterfactual in which what counts as empirical is necessarily contested.

We lose sight of the meta-critical unity of Habermas's position if, following Rorty's pragmatism, we attempt to set the critical-reflective moment entirely free from the reconstructive-transcendental.[36] The temptation to allow critique to drift in a sea of conversation is great where reconstructive-transcendental strategies can be made to appear redundant. This pragmatist temptation can only be overcome by recognizing the "productive tension" between the reconstructive component, which argues for the counterfactual validity basis of the factual, and the reflective component, which addresses the factual conditions for the realization and acceptance of the counterfactual.

Only this interpretation of two complimentary modalities, or levels of Habermas's thinking, puts us in a position to understand his claim that:

> To the extent to which it suggests a concrete form of life, even the expression "the ideal speech situation" is misleading. What can be outlined are the necessary but general conditions for the communicative practice of everyday life

33. *Id.* at 19.
34. *Id.* at 33.
35. *Id.*
36. For a more explicitly Hegelian interpretation of this meta-critical unity, see GARBIS KORTIAN, METACRITIQUE: THE PHILOSOPHICAL ARGUMENT OF JÜRGEN HABERMAS (John Raffan trans., 1980).

and for a procedure of discursive will-formation that would put participants in a position to realize concrete possibilities.[37]

These necessary but general conditions can themselves only be validated by strategies that seek to factualize their counterfactual status, a kind of theoretical bootstrapping. At this level, Habermas's counterfactual imagination engages the institutional arrangements where the tension between facticity and validity has been "leveled out" ("juridified") in favor of the former.

Habermas's objective in *Faktizität und Geltung* is to restore this tension, and his position differs in emphasis, though not in basic conception, from the Rawlsian idea of "reflective equilibrium." As I stated above, the distinction between the reconstructive-transcendental and the critical-reflective that has been used to interpret Habermas's position is one that Habermas reads in Rawls. Thus, Habermas's rejection of Rorty's "contextualistic appropriation" of Rawls is also a form of self-defense:

> Rorty pulls together the two stages of argument distinguished by Rawls and confuses the reconstructive character that reflective equilibrium has in the context of justification with the sense of illuminating existence or of ethical self-understanding that the theory of justice takes on if it proves suitable for shedding light on its own context of origin.[38]

In *Faktizität und Geltung,* an important strand of the project of "shedding light on the context of origin" (echoes of Horkheimer) is to rethink the counterfactual preconditions of positive law as a mechanism by which communicative action is unburdened on the one hand, but is not compromised on the other. The avoidance of compromise is articulated as the "factualization" of counterfactual conditions under which the positivity of law is acceptable as the product of rational authors. The institutional possibilities for preserving these conditions only make sense on the basis of the deeper reconstructive-transcendental project. These possibilities are realized, however, in terms of Habermas's theory of the constitutional state, whereby law is a crucial medium through which a lifeworld based "communicative power" is translated into "administrative power." In this way, Habermas confronts the problem of reconciling the *de facto* restrictive role of legal rules with integrative and liberty-preserving mechanisms that can, in turn, only be traced to possibilities for intersubjective recognition and the redemption of validity claims.

Habermas conceives of the mediating function of law in procedural terms, terms in which the rights of citizens, primarily as a set of "communicative" liberties, are central. This seems to follow consistently from the broad characterization of ideal speech as entailing "equal opportunity" to

37. HABERMAS, *supra* note 4, at 69.
38. *Id.* at 85.

engage in speech acts. Corresponding to this role for law, administrative action systems function only in a derivative sense and embody pragmatic discourses that extend "only to the construction of possible programs and the estimation of their consequences."[39] Administrative technologies are articulated by Habermas primarily in terms of operationalizing communicatively preformed strategies which are mediated and organized by law. The constitutional state simply regulates the "conversion of communicative power into administrative power" for the purpose of "steering" various subsystems.

A certain emphasis is apparent here that necessarily follows from Habermas's engagement with the problems of democratic constitutionalism and its implications for administrative action systems. Such systems execute and concretize the law subject to internal methods of self-surveillance, a materialization process which is the preoccupation of sociolegal studies of executive discretion in the context of policy implementation. This constitutional emphasis embodies a very specific focus upon the procedural rationality of administrative processes and a formal-ethical reading of the concept of "steering." This reading is a natural consequence of the debates within which Habermas elaborates his theory of law. In short, Habermas's project of "factualizing the counterfactual," the critical-reflective strand, in *Faktizität und Geltung* has a *specific* institutional focus: constitutional legality.

In terms of the two components of critical theorizing, there are gains and losses from this focus. Critical theory has always suffered from a self-consciousness about its status as mere argument and from a certain remoteness from the practices on the far side of discourse. In other words, despite the use of a certain "activist" form of language, critical theory has always been dogged by the relative weakness of its critical-reflective component, and hence, of the facticity of its self-grounding. As Habermas has developed and refined the reconstructive-transcendental element of his thinking in the form of a theory of communicative action, his status as a critical theorist in its classic sense has become more problematic.

In *Faktizität und Geltung*, Habermas provides a solution to these difficulties, but there is a cost, a cost that has its mirror image in his early work. In *Knowledge and Human Interests*, the psychoanalytic model enabled arguments and strategy to be tightly coupled in therapy. The unity of critical theory was sustained, but the critical-reflective component was regarded as heroic and implausible as a basis for concrete strategies of enlightenment. Subsequently, Habermas refined the concept of reflection, abandoned the language of transcendentality, and dropped the psychoanalytic model. In the communicative turn following *Knowledge and Human Interests*, the reconstructive-transcendental component is developed and the problem of

39. *Id.* at 203.

engagement with practices, by which the theory could anchor itself, is less prominent.

In *Faktizität und Geltung*, Habermas finds in the image of legal practice the link that is needed between the two components to pull his theory of communicative action back from the brink of mere abstraction. Reconstructive-transcendental arguments and critical-reflective strategies can be tightly coupled here because law, for Habermas, is itself fundamentally about arguments, a communicative practice par excellence. Accordingly, legal practice provides Habermas with the basis for putting together the two components of the counterfactual imagination. The price to be paid, in direct contrast to *Knowledge and Human Interests*, is a loss of critical edge. Habermas reads legal practice through the lens of neoliberal jurisprudence.

Law undoubtedly plays a special role for Habermas's theoretical system. It is a practice that can be made to fit the terms of the theory of communicative action; it is the material correlate of the theory. In contrast to legal pluralists, such as Gunther Teubner,[40] Habermas conceives of law as more than just one system among others; it embodies privileged connectivities with lifeworld sources of "communicative power." The law steers systems on behalf of the lifeworld.

The irony of all this should be clear: in *Faktizität und Geltung* Habermas rescues the unity of critical theory at the expense of abandoning its critical status. The unity of metacritique in *Knowledge and Human Interests* has been replaced by the unity of reflective equilibrium. Indeed, there is a certain tragic inevitability that a self-reflective critical theory will undermine itself. The moment that critical theory locates its ultimate validity in forms of acceptance, it becomes a hostage to the world unless it can moderate its critical claims.

CONCLUSIONS

According to Habermas, political theory is an incessant iterative process, "tossed to and fro between facticity and validity,"[41] in which a "point of reference in reality" provides limits to what is theoretically reasonable.[42] In *Faktizität und Geltung*, Habermas is more conservative about these limits than in the earlier work which connects him to an older generation of critical theorists; the facticity of positive law carries a weight for him that it would not for others. But the apparently conservative nature of *Faktizität*

---

40. *See* Gunther Teubner, *The Two Faces of Janus: Rethinking Legal Pluralism*, 13 CARDOZO L. REV. 1443 (1992).

41. HABERMAS, *supra* note 4, at 21.

42. *Id.* at 53.

und Geltung is complex. Rather than a shift in taste or values, it is a product of the internal dynamics of a counterfactual imagination that, having pursued the reconstructive-transcendental theory of communication to its limits, necessarily returns to critical-reflective preoccupations which ground it in concrete practices. In *Knowledge and Human Interests,* facticity (positivism) gave way to validity (reflection). In *Faktizität und Geltung,* Habermas recognizes that validity must also return to facticity to ground itself. But instead of positive science, he returns to positive law.

It is therefore Habermas himself who has been "tossed to and fro" (*Hin und hergerissen*) between his reconstruction of the validity basis of communication and the need to connect this to the facticity of practices. This is an inevitable dynamic that defines the problem of self-grounding for critical theories. *Faktizität und Geltung* is the present resting place for this dynamic and law plays a unique role for Habermas in resolving the tension.

This Article embodies the hermeneutic arrogance of claiming to know an author better than himself. However, in the distinction between reconstructive-transcendental and critical-reflective themes, I believe that the engine room of Habermas's philosophical vision can be clarified. Only in these terms can both the empirical vulnerability of Habermas's theory be determined and "real" debates with opponents be constructed. I have argued supportively here for the coherence of the reconstructive-transcendental moment. In the end, it expresses a commitment to "alternative vocabularies" that goes deeper than pragmatist tastes for the practices in which we happen to engage. Pragmatists will argue that this notion of "depth" is simply a smokescreen for another contingent practice. But only the counterfactual imagination is seriously concerned with both the contingent *and* the noncontingent dimensions of practice in the form of the fictions that are necessary to make sense of first order practical commitments. Pragmatists may be too busy celebrating the diversity of practices to look closely enough at the varied moments of ideality that constitute their limits.

Faktizität und Geltung will no doubt be read as the final abandonment of critical theory. Further, Habermas's conception of law and its mediating role is likely to be regarded as naively ideal. Free from the burden of self-grounding, pragmatists and political radicals alike will find it easy to be critical. But in attempting to reveal the inner structure of Habermas's project, I have attempted to show how certain compromises and dilutions might be an inevitable product of the project and of the counterfactual imagination that drives it.

TEN

Jürgen Habermas's Theory of Legal Discourse

Robert Alexy*

Jürgen Habermas's discourse theory of law attempts to show that the ideal contents of the discourse principle can be realized within the institutional frame of a legal system. The result is a theory of the democratic constitutional state whose basic idea is the association and self-determination of free and equal consociates under the law.[1] This theory is far more than a mere application of discourse theory to the law. Discourse theory, on the one hand, demands the institutionalization of a legal system for reasons internal to the theory.[2] On the other hand, the positive law remains dependent on discourse theory in order to equate legality with legitimacy. Thus, ideal and reality are connected.

On the way to a discourse theory of the law one encounters essentially all the problems of legal philosophy and theory, constitutional theory, and political philosophy. This can only be so because an adequate theory of the law can only be successful as a comprehensive theory of the legal system. It is not possible to present Habermas's system in full here, nor is it possible to comment critically on all its aspects. I shall therefore consider the basic ideas of discourse theory as given and concentrate on the question of whether Habermas's theory of legal discourse is adequate as a theory of the rationality of adjudication.

---

*Professor of Public Law and Legal Philosophy, Christian Albrechts University, Kiel, Germany.

1. *See* JÜRGEN HABERMAS, BETWEEN FACTS AND NORMS: CONTRIBUTIONS TO A DISCOURSE THEORY OF LAW AND DEMOCRACY 176, 387 (William Rehg trans., 1996).

2. *See id.* at 223.

I. FACTICITY AND VALIDITY

The governing topic of Habermas's theory of law is the tension between facticity and validity. In legal discourse, this tension manifests itself "as a tension between the principle of legal certainty and the claim to a legitimate application of law, that is, to render correct or right decisions."[3] In short, the tension is between "the certainty of law and its rightness."[4] A theory of legal discourse intending to do justice to the "claim to legitimacy"[5] therefore must answer the question how legal decisions can be both true to past institutional decisions and "rationally grounded in the matter at issue."[6] Habermas's answer concentrates on the concepts of coherence, principle, the application discourse, appropriateness, the paradigm, and legal discourse.

II. COHERENCE

The concept of coherence has always fascinated jurists and legal theorists. It promises a bond both to the positive law and to rationality. Authority and rationality seem to be able to walk together in any system.

Despite this apparent harmony, Habermas's attitude towards coherence is ambiguous. On the one hand, Habermas takes up Dworkin's idea of an "ideally justified coherence of the legal system,"[7] while on the other hand he criticizes the "coherence theory of law" because of its indeterminacy.[8] Habermas bases his criticism on Klaus Günther's theory of the application discourse. According to this theory, the weight of the relevant rules, principles, and policies can only be determined when deciding individual cases.[9] By doing this, the system degenerates to a catalogue of topoi, and loses the power to guarantee legal certainty.

One has to agree with Habermas in that a coherence theory of the law alone cannot solve the problem of the rational application of the law. Just as much as rules are unable to apply themselves, a system cannot itself create the right answer. For this, persons and procedures are necessary. Habermas is, however, also right in still keeping up the idea of coherence, for coherence is an elementary postulate of rationality. However, the role of coherence remains vague.

3. *Id.* at 197.
4. *Id.* at 199.
5. *Id.* at 198.
6. *Id.*
7. *Id.* at 219; *see also id.* at 192, 198, 260.
8. *Id.* at 219.
9. *See id.*

III. PRINCIPLES

Coherence properly rests between the historical-institutional and the rational-correct. Its means for employment is systemic argumentation. The most important part of systemic argumentation is the argumentation of principles—a concept that plays an important part in Habermas's thinking. Still, his theory of principles causes far more questions than can be dealt with here. I therefore want to limit myself to two points: the deontological status of principles and whether legal principles can be regarded as commands for optimization.

Habermas explains the concept of principle by distinguishing it from that of value. Principles are to have a deontological meaning, while values are to have a teleological one.[10] This distinction, which epitomizes the classical dichotomy between the right and the good, must be agreed with. Problematical, however, is Habermas's claim that "[t]he 'oughtness' of binding norms has the absolute sense of an unconditioned and universal obligation; what 'one ought to do' claims to be equally good for all."[11] In contrast,

> [t]he attractiveness of intersubjectively shared values has the relative estimation of goods that has become well-established or been adopted in cultures and forms of life: serious value choices or higher-order preferences tell us what is good for us (or for me) overall and in the long run.[12]

If one takes this literally, principles are the issues of moral discourses and values the issues of ethical ones.[13] But this causes problems in the case of legal principles. Habermas emphasizes that legal questions differ from moral ones. He claims that legal norms "[i]n general . . . do not say what is equally good for all human beings; they regulate the life context of the citizens of a concrete legal community."[14] Therefore, the discourses of justification and application within the law had to open themselves up towards pragmatic and ethical arguments.[15] That, however, excludes a definition lacking further qualification of *legal* principles as norms with absolute binding character[16] in the universalistic sense explained above, because that would finally turn them into *moral* norms.

Habermas acknowledges the problem. He tries to solve the basic rights problem by pointing out that the basic rights concretize a discourse-theoretically—and therefore universalistically—justifiable system of rights. This

---

10. *See id.* at 255.

11. *Id.*

12. *Id.*

13. *See* JÜRGEN HABERMAS, *Vom pragmatischen, ethischen und moralischen Gebrauch der praktischen Vernunft, in* ERLÄUTERUNGEN ZUR DISKURSETHIK 100, 101 (1991).

14. HABERMAS, *supra* note 1, at 153.

15. *See id.* at 154.

16. *See id.* at 255.

fact is intended to grant them "strict *priority*" over "policy goals and value orientations of the legislator."[17]

However, not all principles, and especially not all norms of a legal system are, like the elementary basic rights, necessary from a point of view of a universalistic morality, not allowing the legal system to take on any content that contradicts them.[18] Still, all legal principles and norms have a deontological character. From this, it follows that the deontological character does not include the absolute character. Legal norms have a deontological status even if the legislator enacted them for pragmatic or ethical reasons. The basic rights' "strict priority," as far as it exists, is substantiated morally, rather than by the logic of norms.

Severing the deontological meaning of principles from an absolute character leads to the question of whether they can be regarded as optimization commands while keeping their deontological character. Habermas seems to exclude this for conceptual reasons because he identifies the construction of principles as optimization commands with their incorporation in a cost-benefit analysis.[19] With a view to normative aspects, he fears that the conceptualization of principles as optimization commands could lead to their arbitrary restriction in favor of collective goods such as "[t]he 'functional capacity' of the armed forces or the judicial system."[20]

The conceptualization of the principles as optimization commands does indeed lead to the incorporation of criteria of economic rationality into the law, which is the precise purpose of this conceptualization. Those criteria epitomize the principle of proportionality in German constitutional law, which says that an interference with basic rights may only happen under three conditions. It must, first of all, be *suitable* for reaching its intended goal. Second, it must be *necessary* for reaching the goal—that is, there must be no softer, less interfering means. Third, it must be *proportional in the narrower sense*, meaning the reasons justifying the interference must weigh the heavier, the more intensive the interference. Habermas concedes that "not every right will win out over every collective good in the justifications of concrete decisions," while stressing that "a right will not prevail only when the priority of a collective good over a corresponding norm can itself be justified in the light of higher norms or principles."[21] "In the final analysis, only rights can be a trump in the argumentation game."[22] Whether the latter is true can only be judged on the basis of the logical relationship

17. *Id.* at 256.
18. This fact, with respect to legal norms, is caused by the understanding that legal norms must not contradict moral norms. *See id.* at 155, 282.
19. *See id.* at 260.
20. *Id.* at 259.
21. *Id.*
22. *Id.*

between individual rights and collective goods.[23] These complicated considerations are not necessary here, because the thesis of optimization is true even if the legal discourse in its last instance is a pure rights discourse. No matter whether an individual right is restricted in favor of collective goods or of other persons' individual rights, the restriction is necessarily prohibited and violates the right unless it is suitable, necessary, and proportional in the narrower sense. Only those who deny this can deny the thesis of optimization, for the principle of proportionality, with its three subrules, implies the thesis of optimization, and vice versa.[24]

The objection remains that the rights lose their character as Dworkinian trumps and, accordingly, their greater justificatory force, and that consequently "the fire wall erected in legal discourse by a deontological understanding of legal norms and principles collapses."[25] The danger of an undue restriction of individual rights in favor of collective goods does, indeed, exist. However, it should not be banned by a generalized priority of the deontological over the teleological—which in law is ambiguous and cannot be strictly kept anyway—but rather by substantially justified definitive and prima facie priorities of individual rights over collective goods.[26] Anything else could only be valid if there were better solutions to the problem of the collision of principles. According to Habermas, the concept of the application discourse, which is ruled by the idea of appropriateness, is supposed to be the key to such a better solution.

IV. DISCOURSE OF APPLICATION, APPROPRIATENESS, AND PARADIGMS

According to Habermas, discourses of application are not concerned with the validity of norms, but only with the correct decision of an individual case. The decision of an individual case is said to be correct if it is based on the appropriate norm. In order to find out whether a norm is appropriate in a given situation it is said to be necessary, as well as sufficient, to judge it with a view to all the situation's aspects and all potentially alternative norms.[27] "[T]he justification of a singular judgment must be based on the set of all appropriate normative reasons that happen to be relevant for the case at hand in view of a complete interpretation of the situation."[28]

23. *See generally* Robert Alexy, *Individual Rights and Collective Goods, in* RIGHTS 163 (Carlos Nino ed., 1992).

24. *See* ROBERT ALEXY, THEORIE DER GRUNDRECHTE 100 (1985).

25. HABERMAS, *supra* note 1, at 258–59.

26. *See generally* Alexy, *supra* note 23, at 176.

27. *See* KLAUS GÜNTHER, DER SINN FÜR ANGEMESSENHEIT: ANWENDUNGSDISKURSE IN MORAL UND RECHT 257 (1988).

28. HABERMAS, *supra* note 1, at 218.

The idea of the discourse of application is at the same time correct, empty, and easy to misunderstand.[29] It is *correct* as far as it expresses the old hermeneutic demand for the consideration of all aspects. This demand is an elementary postulate of rationality. It is *empty*, because it does not say which aspects are to be considered in what way. Habermas comes near this attitude when he says that the demand "that one exhaustively reviews an entire system of valid norms in the course of considering all the relevant circumstances of the case at hand . . . as a rule, overtax[es] even a professional adjudication."[30] Habermas believes that indeterminacy could be reduced by employing the help of a "paradigmatic legal understanding."[31] He concedes, however, that this, too, is no perfect solution due to the competition of different paradigms.[32] To this one could add that paradigms like those of a liberal, social, or procedural understanding of the law are highly abstract. In many cases they are not sufficient for determining a definite decision. They can at most substantiate prima facie priorities between principles. Like the concept of coherence, the concept of appropriateness is therefore too vague to solve the problem of the rational legal decision.

Finally, the idea of the discourse of application is *easy to misunderstand*, because it houses the danger of a nonuniversalist practice of decision making. This danger becomes acute if the administration of justice is regarded exclusively as an application discourse and thus separated from discourses of justification. Habermas claims that "[t]he public interest in the harmonization or consistency of law highlights a concise move in the logic of adjudication."[33] A harmonization or unification of the law in the sense of a universalist practice of decision making is only possible if, in deciding individual cases, rules are formed which can win the power of precedence. These rules, however, have the character of relatively concrete norms and therefore can—and must—be substantiated. Thus, every application discourse includes a discourse of justification.

V. THE LEGAL DISCOURSE

The short look we have taken at the concepts of coherence, principle, the discourse of application, appropriateness, and the paradigm has shown that the problem of the rationality of adjudication cannot be solved with their help alone. The solution can only lie in a theory of legal discourse. This

29. *See generally* Robert Alexy, *Justification and Application of Norms*, RATIO JURIS, July 1993, at 157.

30. HABERMAS, *supra* note 1, at 220.

31. *Id.*

32. *See id.* at 221.

33. *Id.* at 237.

theory has three tasks. First, it must determine the relationship between the certainty of law and its rightness. Second, it must unfold the unsaturated potentials of rationality embedded in the concepts of coherence, principle, appropriateness, and the paradigm. Third, it has to incorporate the argumentative and the institutional procedure of the application of the law into a theory of the democratic constitutional state. Those three tasks determine the character of legal discourse, and only this shall be of interest here.

Habermas opposes the thesis that legal discourse is a special case of general practical discourse.[34] Whether the special case thesis is correct or not depends on what one means by "general practical discourse." Habermas argues against the attitude "that legal discourses should be conceived as a subset of moral argumentation,"[35] that is, against the thesis that legal discourse is a special case of *moral discourse.*[36] This thesis is indeed wrong, because legal discourse is open not only for moral, but also for ethical and pragmatic reasons.[37] The special case thesis therefore can only be correct if one understands "general practical discourse" as meaning a practical discourse in which moral, ethical, and pragmatic questions and reasons are connected. The formulation of this concept of practical discourse is both sensible and necessary, because between the three kinds of reasons there exists not only a relationship of supplementation[38] but also of permeation.[39] If one presupposes this concept of general practical discourse, the special case thesis is correct. Legal discourse is a special case of general practical discourse characterized by institutional bonds. Those are expressed by linguistic, genetic, and systemic arguments.[40] These arguments, which can be called "institutional," are supplemented, permeated, and controlled by general practical arguments which again can be regarded as "substantial."

Anything else would only be true if the moral, ethical, and pragmatic arguments necessary in legal discourse in some way lost their general character by being employed there, and took up a specifically legal nature. Habermas's thesis that legal discourses "*refer from the outset* to democratically enacted law and . . . not only refer to legal norms but, together with their

---

34. *See id.* at 230–37.

35. *Id.* at 230.

36. The concept of moral discourse is used here in the sense defined by Habermas. HABERMAS, *supra* note 13, at 113.

37. *See* HABERMAS, *supra* note 1, at 155–56, 230, 283.

38. *See* HABERMAS, *supra* note 13, at 110.

39. That there is a relationship of permeation can be demonstrated by the fact that the choice between a liberal or a libertarian conception of justice depends essentially on how one conceives oneself and the community in which one lives.

40. *See* Robert Alexy, *Interpretazione giuridica, in* 5 ENCICLOPEDIA DELLE SCIENZE SOCIALI (1996) (on file with author).

institutionalized forms of communication, are themselves *imbedded* in the legal system" seems to come near this.[41] It contradicts, however, the thesis also defended by Habermas, which says that "legal discourse cannot operate self-sufficiently inside a hermetically sealed universe of existing norms but must rather remain open to arguments from other sources."[42] The correct solution is probably that the general practical arguments used in legal discourse remain what they are: general practical arguments. On the other hand, the legal discourse as a whole expresses the "*specifically limited . . . meaning*"[43] of the law[44] and its "more-complex validity dimension."[45] The special case thesis aims at both aspects. Thus it shows the unity of practical reason which is—or can be—realized in the law.

41. HABERMAS, *supra* note 1, at 234.

42. *Id.* at 230. This thesis, however, is not quite unambiguous, because Habermas adds that the arguments from other sources "[i]n particular" consist of "pragmatic, ethical, and moral reasons brought to bear in the legislative process and bundled together in the legitimacy claim of legal norms." *Id.* The choice of the words "in particular" shows that Habermas does not believe that all pragmatic, ethical, and moral reasons considered in legal discourse are already contained in the legislator's intention and in the legal norms. But apart from this, with the quoted formulation he comes quite near the problematic idea that in the end almost anything is contained in the legislator's intention and the legal system anyway.

43. *Id.* at 534 n.33.

44. *See id.* at 154–56.

45. *Id.* at 233.

ELEVEN

Communicative Freedom, Communicative Power, and Jurisgenesis

*Klaus Günther**

One of the doubts raised against discourse theory by many critics concerns the place of the individual. Liberals especially fear that the individual gets involved in a system of obligations which is derived from certain pragmatical presuppositions of communication and which forces the individual to participate in discourses whenever he or she pursues his or her own happiness in society. But Jacques Derrida too, who could scarcely be called a "liberal" in the traditional sense, characterizes those presuppositions of communication which entail an obligation for the speaker and the hearer as "violence."[1] For these critics, it must now be a surprise to read in Jürgen Habermas's book that the individual possesses negative rights,[2] especially a right to privacy, which entitles him or her even to refrain from all those obligations which are linked with communication. "Legally granted liberties entitle one to *drop out* of communicative action, to refuse illocutionary obligations; they ground a privacy freed from the burden of reciprocally acknowledged and mutually expected communicative freedoms."[3] This does not mean, however, that Habermas follows the traditional line of argumentation, which derives a conception of negative liberties from their opposition to the executive power of the state. The concept of "communicative

---

*Dr. iur. Assistant Professor, Johann Wolfgang Goethe-University Law School, Frankfurt am Main; 1995–1996 Fellow, Wissenschaftskolleg (Institute for Advanced Study), Berlin.

Thanks to John Farrell for his help with the argument and with the English language. I am responsible for all remaining mistakes and obscurities.

1. *See* Jacques Derrida, *The Politics of Friendship*, 85 J. PHIL. 634 (1988).

2. *See* JÜRGEN HABERMAS, BETWEEN FACTS AND NORMS: CONTRIBUTIONS TO A DISCOURSE THEORY OF LAW AND DEMOCRACY 120 (William Rehg trans., 1996).

3. *Id.*

freedom" holds a strong position and is mentioned quite often in the other parts of the book,[4] but without further explanation.

Habermas later links this concept with Hannah Arendt's concept of communicative power.[5] When the members of a community use their communicative freedom, they can generate communicative power. Habermas writes:

> [D]iscursively produced and intersubjectively shared beliefs have . . . a *motivating* force. Even if this remains limited to the weakly motivating force of good reasons, . . . the public use of communicative freedom also appears as a generator of power potentials. . . . By mobilizing citizens' communicative freedom for the formation of political beliefs that in turn influence the production of legitimate law, illocutionary obligations . . . build up into a potential that holders of administrative power should not ignore.[6]

The concept of communicative power explains how reasons become factual. By being accepted on the basis of communicative freedom, reasons acquire a motivational force. This thesis needs further elaboration, and this will require the rational reconstruction of communicative freedom. It should then become evident that communicative power is a motivational resource for the obedience of norms, and thus presents itself as an alternative to coercion and violence.

Habermas discusses the legal enforcement of obedience of a rule only in relation to moral motivation generated by good reasons which are acceptable to everybody. With the concept of communicative power, the deliberative procedure becomes a generator of motivation on its own, one which is independent of moral motivation on the one hand and coercion on the other. The deliberative process is, according to Habermas's formulation, internally structured by ethical, moral, political, and pragmatic reasons.[7] Externally, it is comprised of democratic procedures within a legal form. Communicative power is dependent on reasons, but independent of the specific kind of reasons; it only links up with the properties of the procedure which generates those reasons. These properties enable the participants to advance and question reasons and counterreasons for the cluster of validity claims which is always connected with political issues. Under this condition alone, the factual acceptance of a validity claim can acquire motivational force.

Although communicative power seems to be the strongest kind of power, since it motivates people to act on the basis of rational insight and commu-

4. *See, e.g., id.* at 132.
5. *See id.* at 147–50.
6. *Id.* at 147.
7. *See id.* at 82–131.

nicative freedom, it is also the weakest in another sense. Because of its de-pendence on rational motivation, communicative power is endangered by the following kinds of threats: reasonably justified dissent, dissent based on reasons which do not convince a majority, and unjustified and stronger countermotives. It was a republican utopia to believe that countermotives could be overridden by the public spirit of the city and its members. Even if republicans accept that people can be bad, evil can be limited by coun-termotives which get their strength from communicative power. The evil in mankind is powerful only in those cases where communities fall apart and people separate and disperse.[8] But even in this case, republicans need a medium which stabilizes communicative power—that is, legal rules, consti-tutions, and institutions. And sometimes they even need to coerce those people who insist on their unjustified countermotives. The liberal concept of law, which is more interested in the coercive force of the law and its justification than in its integrating aspects, seems to be more realistic. Nev-ertheless, the relationship between communicative power and law needs further elaboration.

The following discussion seeks to demonstrate that these concepts are more fundamental to Habermas's conception of a system of rights than he himself seems to think. My remarks are intended less as a critique than as a comment on Habermas's own argument. I want to make some sugges-tions as to how the relation between communicative freedom and individ-ual liberty (often called negative liberty) has to be conceived,[9] and how communicative freedom is related to communicative power.[10] Finally, I want to draw some conclusions for a discursive theory of law.[11]

I. COMMUNICATIVE FREEDOM

Let me begin by quoting some definitional remarks on the meaning of "communicative freedom." "Communicative freedom exists only between actors who, adopting a performative attitude, want to reach an understand-ing with one another about something. . . ."[12] I understand communicative freedom as the possibility—mutually presupposed by participants engaged in the effort to reach an understanding—of responding to the utterances of one's counterpart and to the concomitantly raised validity claims.[13]

The concept of communicative freedom is different from "negative" and

8. See generally HANNAH ARENDT, ON REVOLUTION (1963).
9. See infra part I.
10. See infra parts II & III.
11. See infra part IV.
12. HABERMAS, supra note 2, at 119.
13. See id.

"positive" liberty, and from "freedom of action" or "freedom of the will." It refers to one of the most obvious aspects of "freedom": the possibility to say "no." This possibility is also included in the traditional definition of "freedom of action" as the awareness of an actor that he or she could have done otherwise, if he or she had had the will to do so. The possibility to say "no" is constitutive for the possibility of alternatives, and for the actor's awareness that he or she could decide between taking an affirmative position toward a plan of action.[14] Taking an affirmative position then means taking a negative position toward the counterreasons which could be mobilized against the action plan. Thus, the actor's will can be interpreted as the result of a double negativity, that is, as the negation of the possibility of a negation of her intention.[15] Then, it seems that this structure of double negativity is the central feature of communicative freedom. But why "communicative"?

Speaking of a "negative position" toward subjective inclinations, social forces, or objective obstacles is only metaphorical. In fact, a negative position refers to linguistic entities, such as propositions and speech acts. The negation of a proposition is a logical operation, but one can say "yes" or "no" only to a proposition which is embedded in a pragmatic context; propositions expressed in a speech act include an order, a request, an invitation, or an imperative, as well as an assertion, a declaration, and a wish or an intention. This interdependence between the negative position and the pragmatic properties of a speech act leads to the presumption that the double negativity should be explained in terms of illocutionary relationships between speaker and hearer. It is not the logical operation of negation, but the hearer's refusal to accept the speaker's utterance, which is fundamental to communicative freedom. When a hearer says "no" to such a speech act, she refuses to accept the validity claim which is raised for the speech act and its propositional content. The possibility to say "no" is the freedom to take a position toward the validity claim of a speech act.[16]

Obviously, a speaker often has several means to make the hearer accept

---

14. This is accepted even by radical subjectivist approaches to the notion of "freedom." *See, e.g.,* GALEN STRAWSON, FREEDOM AND BELIEF (1986).

15. *See* ERNST TUGENDHAT, VORLESUNGEN ZUR EINFÜHRUNG IN DIE SPRACHANALYTISCHE PHILOSOPHIE 110 (1976).

16. According to Immanuel Kant, the "negative attitude" is of greatest importance to the application of the first of the three maxims of common human understanding: "to think for oneself," or *Selbstdenken;* the other two being "to think from the standpoint of every one else," or *erweiterte Denkunsart,* and "always to think consistently," or *konsequente Denkungsart. See* IMMANUEL KANT, THE CRITIQUE OF JUDGMENT 152 n.1 (James C. Meredith trans., 1952). To think for oneself, without prejudice, requires actively doubting any knowledge which seems to be pregiven and natural. As such, Kant considered the "negative attitude" to be the constitutive intellectual attitude of enlightenment. *See id.*

a validity claim by the latter's taking an affirmative position, like deception, force, threat, rhetorical means, etc. On the other hand, the hearer might have different motives for taking an affirmative (or negative) position, like fear of sanctions or disadvantages. There is only one possibility where the freedom to take a position is reciprocally attributed by speaker and hearer. This is the case when the speaker is willing to give reasons for the validity claim, and when the hearer herself is willing to give reasons for her taking a negative position. Reasons are directly related to the freedom to take a position. Only by saying "no" does the proposition expressed by the speaker acquire the pragmatic feature of an "assertion," that is, become a proposition which is embedded in the pragmatic context of a speech act for which the speaker raises a validity claim. The hearer can decide not to react at all and to withdraw from communication or to change her attitude and to treat the reaction as a symptom which she merely observes from an external point of view. But if she decides to react by taking a position, she ascribes certain features to the expression and to the speaker, and she accepts the obligation to give reasons for her doubts. When the speaker raises a validity claim, she announces that she anticipates doubts and negations and that she is therefore willing to give reasons for the proposition. She situates her assertion within the space of possible "yes" or "no" reactions. As a consequence, the acceptance of a validity claim can now be interpreted on the basis of communicative freedom as the negation of doubts. If the hearer takes a negative position on the speaker's utterance, and the speaker decides to justify the validity claim which she raised for her utterance, she has to give counter-counterreasons against the hearer's counterreasons. The hearer's conviction of the validity of the speaker's utterance, then, is the result of a dialectical episode in which doubts are invalidated by reasons.

The freedom to take a position, as it is explained above, is only possible within a space of mutual obligations. To say "yes" or "no" sincerely, always means to accept the obligations inherent in the interplay of validity claims, doubts, and counterreasons. But the explanation of "communicative freedom" would not be sufficient if it did not entail the freedom to withdraw from communication as such, that is, to "step out" of the mutual illocutionary obligations. Without this third possibility to choose "exit" instead of "voice" or "loyalty," communicative freedom would not be a kind of freedom at all. The decision to communicate must be free. It is constitutive for the freedom of the speaker to raise a validity claim as well as for the hearer's freedom to take a positive or negative position. Any coercion would violate the sincerity condition of the illocutionary success of a speech act. Thus, "communicative freedom" always presupposes "negative liberty" on a very fundamental level. But it is a different question to ask how negative liberty is related to communicative freedom after speaker and hearer have accepted mutual illocutionary obligations. I shall come back to this problem[17] after the explanation of the relationship between communicative freedom and communicative power.

Communicative freedom forms part of every kind of argumentation, be it on truth claims, rightness claims, or on the sincerity of a subjective expression. The reciprocal attribution of the freedom to take a position belongs to the illocutionary obligations of an exchange of speech acts. In most of these cases, communicative freedom is not explicitly thematized by speaker and hearer; it is in the background of communication. The situation changes when human action is concerned. Here, communicative freedom comes to the fore. This has to do with a certain property possessed by the illocutionary obligations of speech acts. Communicative freedom does not just entail the obligation to give reasons for a validity claim and to argue for one's counterreasons in the case of doubt. When the hearer accepts a validity claim on the basis of communicative freedom because she is convinced that her counterreasons cannot be defended against the speaker's counter-counterreasons, her acceptance also entails an obligation for the sequel of interaction. With her factual acceptance, the hearer binds herself in the presence of the speaker to take the propositional content of the accepted speech act into account in her following actions. This illocutionary obligation is also based on the same communicative freedom as the acceptance of the validity claim. It is the bridge to motivation. In general, this illocutionary obligation is central to the theory of communicative action.

According to the theory of communicative action, the observance of illocutionary obligations by the speaker and the hearer has consequences for their future interaction. Habermas speaks of "obligations relevant to the sequel of interaction," or "*interaktiousyfolgenrelevante Verbindlichkeiten.*"[18] If the hearer takes an affirmative position on a validity claim which was raised by the speaker for her speech act, this has consequences for his future actions. Certainly, these consequences are only relevant if speaker and hearer try to coordinate their action plans by the mutual acceptance of validity claims. To that extent, they use the illocutionary forces of communication for the purposes of coordinating their action plans. This feature distinguishes communicative action from other types of teleological action. But the illocutionary mechanism functions as an action-coordinating mechanism only if it obliges the speaker and the hearer to change their roles and to become actors.

In the special case of action norms, these illocutionary obligations become especially relevant, because the propositional content of the speech

---

17. *See infra* part IV.

18. 1 Jürgen Habermas, The Theory of Communicative Action 296 (Thomas McCarthy trans., 1984).

act refers directly to human action, so that the acceptance of a regulative speech act entails the illocutionary obligation to do what is required in order to satisfy the valid norm. And one can expect that the dialectical episode of reasons and counterreasons will be continued in the episode of motives and countermotives. Hence, communicative freedom links with freedom of action and autonomous motivation. And it is this link which makes communicative power so powerful. But one can also foresee that this tentative explanation of the idea of communicative freedom will make the relationship to "negative liberty" even more dramatic.

My thesis is that taking an affirmative position on a validity claim generates this illocutionary obligation which links reasons to motives. When the hearer takes an affirmative position, she is obliged to adopt the reasons justifying the validity claim as her own reasons, and as her own reasons for action. Taking an affirmative position is the turning point at which the speaker and the hearer legitimately expect of one another that each act according to the reasons. As a consequence, the illocutionary obligation serves as a bridge between reasons and motives. This thesis needs to be elaborated further.

II. THE MOTIVATIONAL MEANING OF THE ILLOCUTIONARY

The illocutionary force of reasons for action motives can be analyzed in three dimensions: the subjective, the intersubjective, and the relationship between the two. In the subjective dimension, the motivational force of reasons consists of the invalidation of countermotives. In the intersubjective dimension, mutually accepted reasons generate a shared expectation of action and a "singular action community." In the third dimension, the illocutionary obligation entails a special relationship between the actor and the community, which consists in the ascription of a special status to the actor: she becomes the accountable subject of the expected action, the one who is held responsible and treated as the author of her action. To be sure, these elements cannot be regarded as sufficient conditions for the causation of motives.

A. The Subjective

1. Ego, along with alter, has accepted a validity claim because of reasons which both share, and thus, has no convincing counterreasons which would justify taking a negative position toward the validity claim, and, consequently, would justify the corresponding countermotives. The shared conviction of ego and alter, that there are no counterreasons for countermotives, is a negative element in the motivational force of reasons. Obviously, this is true only for a *ceteris paribus* clause. In the next moment, ego and/or alter can discover new counterreasons which justify countermotives. As long as this is not the case, the negative force of reasons holds: neither alter nor ego is able to trace back any countermotives to a position whose reasons were not invalidated. On the other hand, the conviction that there are no countermotives which can be justified by counterreasons does not mean that there are no countermotives at all. De facto, in most cases, countermotives do exist. They can be stronger than the motives which are justified by reasons. From this it follows that the motivational force of reasons is very weak. It lasts only as long as there are no counterreasons for countermotives, and as long as the existing countermotives are weaker. Nevertheless, existing countermotives can be changed and weakened by reasons, and this would be impossible if reasons had no motivational force at all.

2.   The rationally motivated acceptance of a validity claim includes the illocutionary obligation to act according to the valid proposition. Something has to be done (or omitted) in order to fulfill the obligation. What has to be done is something which counts as the realization of the valid proposition. A singular action[19] has to take place, one which is done by a singular actor in a singular situation. If the valid proposition is not fulfilled by a singular action, the illocutionary obligation is violated and the shared expectation will be disappointed. Two different kinds of nonfulfillment can be distinguished. The first one concerns the cognitive aspect, that is, those cases where the valid proposition is incorrectly applied to the concrete situation.[20] The second one is of more interest here. It concerns the motivational aspect, that is, those cases where the valid proposition is not fulfilled, because what is required to fulfill it in a concrete situation is not done at all (not even incorrectly).

B. The Intersubjective

1.   Reasons which have been defended against doubts and thus have justified the acceptance of a validity claim also justify a shared expectation of an action for those who have accepted the validity claim. This expectation refers to the motive for a singular action which counts as the fulfillment of the valid proposition. Alter may now expect that ego will have the corresponding action motive—and so does ego in relation to herself. Ego accepted a validity claim which was raised by alter, because of reasons which convinced ego to reject her doubts. To the extent that these reasons con-

19. "Action" here always means an action or an omittance.
20. For the case of moral and legal norms, see KLAUS GÜNTHER, THE SENSE OF APPROPRIATENESS: APPLICATION DISCOURSES IN MORALITY AND LAW (John Farrell trans., 1993); WILLIAM REHG, INSIGHT AND SOLIDARITY: A STUDY IN THE DISCOURSE ETHICS OF JÜRGEN HABERMAS 179–250 (1994).

vinced ego, she shares them with alter. Consequently, insofar as the expectation of ego's action motive is based on these shared reasons, the expectation of an action motive is also shared. It gains a kind of objectivity. Ego is now able to adopt a third person's point of view on her own motivational complex, and this point of view represents a legitimate expectation of an action. And alter may also expect that ego will have this expectation of herself. The possibility of such a shared expectation constitutes the social horizon within which an actor is able to form her motives in accordance with reasons. This is even true in the case of ethical deliberation: What constitutes my good life is represented by ethical reasons which are valid according to the requirements of ethical deliberation. When I accept an ethical reason, then I have to do what is good for me, and if I acted according to my countermotives, I would not act in accordance with my true self.

2. As a representative of a shared expectation of action, ego is also a representative member of something like a "singular action community." This community shares only one conviction and its members mutually expect of each other the corresponding singular action. Ego's reasons for acting are thus always reasons for the members of this community. The existence of this community is highly precarious, because it is only constituted around this one conviction which was formed in the deliberative process of raising doubts against and providing defenses for validity claims. Consequently, this community is terminated when a member uses her communicative freedom and doubts the shared conviction using new and convincing counterarguments. Then the shared expectation of action loses its legitimacy, and the community necessarily falls apart. In the case of unjustified countermotives, the shared expectation of action keeps its legitimacy, and the community continues to exist. But if the agent acts according to her unjustified stronger countermotives, she loses her membership and excludes herself from the "singular action community."

C. The Relationship Between the Subjective and the Intersubjective

1. When alter and ego have a mutually shared expectation of ego's singular action, and when ego takes the perspective of a representative member of the "singular action community" toward herself, she has a special status in her relationship to the community. Ego is responsible to the community for a singular action which counts as an appropriate realization of the valid proposition. The shared expectation of the singular action community, on the one hand, and the responsibility of a singular actor to act, on the other, are two complementary aspects of the illocutionary meaning of the acceptance of a validity claim. Because ego is a member of the "singular action community" too, she is also responsible to herself. A conse-

quence of ego's responsibility is her accountability to the community in cases of violation of the illocutionary obligation. Obviously, accountability is already included in communicative freedom; the freedom to say "yes" or "no" implies the mutual ascription of the capability to orient oneself according to validity claims. The feature of accountability is now extended to actions in general. My acceptance of a validity claim makes me accountable to the members of the "singular action community" for my acting against the propositional content of the shared conviction.

With regard to my motivation, I am subject to a change in my status.[21] I am no longer treated as a bundle of beliefs, desires, and other motives which determine my behavior. As a member who is responsible to the community for my acting according to the legitimately shared expectation, I may not simply obey my countermotives and leave the "single action community." If I acted according to my countermotives, then I would be asked for my reasons and I would have to answer these questions for the other members who legitimately share the expectation. Being responsible means that my actions will be judged from the point of view of the shared expectation by the other members of the community—as well as by myself, who accepted the valid proposition and the illocutionary obligation inherent in the acceptance. And I have to give justifications (e.g., that I had a convincing counterreason to violate the shared expectation), or I have to provide an excuse which suspends or diminishes my responsibility (e.g., that I was coerced into violating the shared expectation; that I could not recognize that it was the shared expectation which I violated in this concrete situation; that there were stronger countermotives which are acceptable).

2.   The mutual attribution of responsibility would be impossible if there were nobody to whom it could appropriately be attributed. The illocutionary meaning of the rationally motivated acceptance of a validity claim must therefore include something more than an obligation and the corresponding responsibility. In the context of "obligation," the actor is required to obey a self-imposed imperative by overriding her countermotives. But then, the motivational force of reasons would be simply another kind of coercion—although it differs from coercion in general by its quality of being self-imposed. The performative power of reasons includes more than this "negative" aspect of weakening the strength of countermotives. It also gives something "positive" to the actor. The illocutionary meaning of the acceptance of a validity claim does also entail something like an illocutionary enfranchisement or empowerment of a singular actor to act. Ego is recognized by alter as someone who can make a beginning, who can initiate something.

21. For the semantical converse relation between "competence" and "liability," see, with reference to W. N. Hohfeld, ROBERT ALEXY, THEORIE DER GRUNDRECHTE 219 (1985).

With the acceptance of the mutual illocutionary obligation to act according to the valid proposition, we authorize each other to place one another at the beginning of an action. According to the tradition of metaphysics, the actor is recognized by the singular action community as a *causa sui* and *causa libera*, the traditional notions of freedom. In less metaphysical terms, the actor is recognized as the single author of her succeeding actions. To say it in a tautological fashion with reference to the etymological relation between *"auctor"* and *"auctoritas"*: We authorize each other to assume the position of authorship of our actions. To become the author of an action means more than being an actor. To be an actor means to possess a set of physiological and psychical capabilities and dispositions which are required for the formation of intentions (goals), and for the realization of operations (e.g., to raise one's arm), and because of which the actor can be observed as a cause of an event. But this is also true for someone who is causally determined by any kind of motives. To consider an actor to be also the author of her actions means something different. A singular action counts as her action only if it is done by exercising an individual power to act (*Handlungsmacht*) or agency. To be sure, this kind of power always includes psychological and physiological capabilities and dispositions, but its character as initiating a change in the world by itself is attributed to the actor by those with whom she shares an expectation of action, and because she shares it with them. Then, instead of being a reacting bundle of motives, ego becomes an actor in the very meaning of the term. She now interprets her motives in such a way that she is the origin of them. Only under this condition does it make sense to say that she could have weakened her countermotives, and that she could have avoided violating the shared expectation. The members of the community can now say to her, and she can say to herself, that she can do it, that she could really become the origin of actions. The illocutionary meaning of the acceptance of a validity claim has an enabling character; it opens up a space in which we can mutually recognize our motivational complex as a power to act which every single member can exercise by him- or herself. Being recognized as the origin of her own action motives, she can in fact become the origin of her own action motives; she can in fact exercise the power to act which was attributed to her. She can become the real author of her actions and can internalize the role of an actor who is author, thereby ascertaining her authorship. The attribution of agency thus becomes a genuine source of motivation which enables the actor to weaken her countermotives. It serves as a transformer of reasons into motives for action.

A consequence of the recognition as an author in this sense (and not only as a cause of an event) is that those who attribute the power to act to the actor take a certain attitude toward her. To recognize her as the author of her actions then means to disregard all other possible external and internal (psychic) causes and circumstances which might have influenced the event which is considered the author's action. The meaning of this recognition that the actor as author is an idealization which is internal to the community and is built into the acceptance of the illocutionary obligation. The members of the community expect that it is she who will do it, even if they know that internal and external circumstances always influence behavior more or less intensely. As an idealization, it presupposes that it will be only she, and nobody and nothing else, who does it—no demons, no fate, not the social milieu, nor psychic tension. To the extent that the shared expectation is legitimate and the actor is held responsible for her action, the members of the community take the participant's or the internal point of view, and not the observer's. From this point of view, internal and external circumstances are not relevant as long as the shared expectation is legitimate and nobody raises doubts about the actor's responsibility. The same is true for the actor: only when she takes the participant's point of view toward herself can she realize that it is she who is expected to act, and not her neighbor or anybody else; that she cannot refer to the circumstances or to fate. And she can only maintain the participant's point of view if she really acts. If she does not, she will be asked for justifications or excuses, or her behavior will be treated from an observer's point of view as a symptom for something else (e.g., the dominating influence of a psychic defect).

The argument that the actor is recognized as the *causa sui* of her actions does not imply any ontological thesis about freedom of the will. The decisive feature is the communicative constitution of the role of an actor who is author. A line can be drawn from the illocutionary meaning of taking an affirmative position toward a validity claim to the concepts of responsibility and accountability, and to the attribution of an individual power to act. From ego's perspective, she realizes her agency by responding to the expectation she shares with alter. To put it bluntly, the experience of freedom has primarily to do with fulfilling or disappointing expectations, with fulfilling and breaking promises, and not so much with successful or unsuccessful interventions in the external world as a means of reaching a goal. By responding with an action to the illocutionary meaning (either by fulfilling or violating the shared expectation), we acquire a sense of freedom, and not so much by the experience of changing something in the external world.

The communicative constitution of the idealized role of the actor as an author does not mean that the singular actor is merely derived from the community, acting as if she were a puppet. There are at least two different barriers which prevent the illocutionary community from overriding the individual. The first one is the individual's right to take a negative position toward a validity claim. As long as the hearer is not convinced by counterreasons, the validity claim is not accepted and the illocutionary meaning of the acceptance cannot unfold its obligating and empowering effects on the actor. The communicative recognition of an actor as author presupposes communicative freedom. Without any right to say "no," the subsequent action does not count as an action of an author who is responsible and who can be held accountable for her behavior. On the other hand, the hearer's acceptance of a validity claim alone launches the illocutionary obligation with all the consequences mentioned above. If the acceptance can be interpreted as the hearer's rationally motivated conviction that her counterreasons against the validity claim were invalidated by counter-counter-reasons, then we may say that the actor gets her power to act from the procedure in which her counterreasons were invalidated.

The second barrier which prevents the community from treating the actor as if she were a puppet is the gap between reasons and motives. If reasons were immediately transformed into sufficient action motives, the acceptance of a validity claim would trigger a simple mechanism only, one which ends with an action. It would not, however, result in illocutionary obligations and empowerments for actors who interpret themselves as the origin of their action motives, who have to make up their mind, who have to weaken countermotives, and who have to perform a singular action on their own. These consequences of the acceptance of a validity claim only make sense against the background of existing countermotives which have to be weakened by the responsible actor. The requirement of a factual acceptance of a validity claim corresponds to the factual decision of an actor. Otherwise, the shared expectation of a singular action could not be distinguished from collective repression, and the singular action community would simply exercise some group-dynamic power over its members. The attribution of responsibility and accountability could not then be distinguished from a disciplinary power which conditions the individual in a manner Foucault associated with the functioning of modern institutions.

III. COMMUNICATIVE POWER

Up to now, I have only explained the generic features of the illocutionary meaning of the acceptance of a validity claim with reference to subsequent actions and interactions. It must be true for any kind of validity claim and any kind of reason; for truth claims as well as for ethical, political, and moral claims. The motivational force of reasons, as it is realized through illocutionary obligations and empowerments, is the same in every case. Differences exist in the content of reasons. The manner in which the acceptance of a truth claim constitutes an illocutionary obligation for subsequent interaction differs from the manner in which the motivational force of reasons for accepting moral, ethical, or political claims unfolds. The acceptance of a truth claim entails an illocutionary obligation to take a certain description of the objective world into account while drafting and executing an action plan. It enables the actor, the moment she engages in action, to trust a state of affairs as represented in a true description of the situation and its consequences. The acceptance of a truth claim empowers ego and alter to rely on a true description of their environment; in a pragmatistic sense, it constitutes a "habit" of acting.

The illocutionary consequences of accepting normative claims (moral, ethical, political) are different. Here, the obligation and empowerment are not secondary effects of the acceptance; rather, the illocutionary force primarily produces an effect which is relevant to subsequent actions. Norms are generalized expectations of behavior which are counterfactually stabilized. If somebody accepts the validity claim of a norm, it means that the "*conditions of satisfaction*—formulated to begin with in semantic terms—are interpreted in terms of obligations relevant to the sequel of interaction."[22] The norm's relevance to subsequent action is already part of the semantic content of the norm, whereas the binding force of the norm's relevance to subsequent interaction is an illocutionary consequence of the acceptance of its validity claim. In this case, the actor's acceptance of the validity claim *uno acto* entails the acceptance of the obligation to have the motive to obey the norm, that is, to act and to operate in such a way that the norm is fulfilled.

Morally motivated action is a special case. Here, the illocutionary obligation to transform reasons into motives refers to those reasons, and only to those reasons, which could be accepted by everybody as participants in a moral discourse. Consequently, Kant defined moral action as acting because of duty, that is, with respect to the moral law. This is obviously not true for ethical or political norms.

The decisive element in the constitution of illocutionary obligations and empowerments relevant to subsequent actions is the factual acceptance of the validity claim. Unless a validity claim is factually accepted—in a procedure which enables participants to exercise communicative freedom—the motivating force of reasons for action motives cannot be realized. It needs the mediating agency of factual acceptance for the unfolding of illocutionary obligations and empowerment. The potential of illocutionary forces becomes a power only if factual acceptance is brought about. Nevertheless, the simple fact of the acceptance of a validity claim does not suffice for the constitution of power as long as it is ego alone who accepts a validity claim raised by alter. What has to be added is a factual social dimension.

Communicative power is a reflexive identification and confirmation of those who have factually accepted a validity claim. The social space which

22. 1 HABERMAS, *supra* note 18, at 299.

came into being with the factual acceptance and with its illocutionary obligations relevant to subsequent interactions is now cognitively reidentified and volitively reconfirmed. By this reflexive move, the individual acquires a reflexive relationship to the first person plural—to a we who is in agreement about convictions relevant to actions. Communicative power is not simply inherent in the fact that some people accept a validity claim and share the corresponding conviction. Communicative power comes from the further fact that every individual legitimately believes that he or she belongs to a "singular action community," and that he or she wants to belong to that community. The shared conviction is not only a social fact which can be observed from an external point of view. It is constitutive for this social fact that the participants believe that we share a conviction. This belief is a notional, not a relational element of the conviction; it is a part of its meaning.

By reflexive identification and confirmation, the illocutionary community is transformed into a social community which consists of all those participants who factually accepted a validity claim and who have a knowledge of there being a community. The infinite space which is open to the members of the illocutionary community who legitimately share an expectation of action is now reduced to a finite social community which is open to the members who know from each other that they factually accepted the validity claim. They can expect that we (i.e., every single member of us) will act according to the valid proposition. This is the decisive feature of communicative power, as Hannah Arendt has described it several times: to act in concert.[23] Thus, communicative power is a motivational resource for a community, and a medium for the allocation of powers to act.

As my explanation of communicative power has already indicated, it is one of the strongest kinds of power on the one hand, but also one of the weakest, on the other. There are at least three different threats to the continuity of communicative power; some are internal, some are external to it. First, communicative power is threatened from within by every dissent based on justified counterreasons. All the elements that constitute communicative power—that is, the invalidation of counterreasons which justify countermotives, the shared expectation, the singular action community, the attribution of responsibility, and the power to act—subsist as long as the reasons invalidate the counterreasons. As soon as new counterreasons invalidate reasons, communicative power linked to the factual acceptance of a validity claim ends immediately. This kind of a "risk of disagreement"[24] is inherent in communicative power; it is one of its constitutive elements.

---

23. *See* HANNAH ARENDT, ON VIOLENCE 52 (1970) [hereinafter ARENDT, ON VIOLENCE]; *see also* HANNAH ARENDT, THE HUMAN CONDITION 200 (1958).

24. HABERMAS, *supra* note 2, at 21.

Communicative power depends on communicative freedom. Communicative freedom produces illocutionary obligations relevant to subsequent interaction—and it again puts them into question. The negative position which is taken by the hearer opens the horizon of reasons with which the speaker can convince the hearer to invalidate her doubts and negations. And by this procedure, the speaker can motivate the hearer to accept the validity claim and the illocutionary obligation to act according to the valid proposition. But the negative position can also justify countermotives against the originally shared expectation. The social community of those who factually accepted a validity claim again opens into the infinite space of anonymous illocutionary forces.

The second threat is of a similar kind. It consists of a rationally motivated dissent. It happens when some participants are convinced by reasons to accept a validity claim, whereas others are not. In this case, communicative power comes into being only among those who factually accepted the validity claim—but it also has consequences for those who reasonably refuse to accept it. They are concerned by the actions which follow from the illocutionary obligation of those participants who accepted the validity claim. If they are in a minority, they could be forced to submit to the communicative power exercised by the majority.

The third kind of threat is external to communicative power. Communicative power is weak when the actor has stronger countermotives. As long as these countermotives are not justified by counterreasons that could invalidate those reasons which sustain the validity claim, they simply prevent communicative power from being generated. It is an external threat, because unjustified and stronger countermotives cannot invalidate reasons and cannot destroy the validity of the normative proposition. It even leaves the illocutionary obligation intact. It only disappoints the shared expectation, which is based on the illocutionary obligation, because the action that was expected does not take place. An actor who acts according to her stronger countermotives not only disrupts the coordination of action, but she also withdraws from the illocutionary bonds established by speaker and hearer when they enter the procedure of giving and rejecting reasons. When she accepts a validity claim and violates the illocutionary obligation to act according to the valid proposition, she will be held responsible and she has to give justifications or excuses.

How can communicative power be maintained against these different types of threat? The defense has to be appropriate to the kind of risk. Unjustified countermotives cannot be defeated in the same way as a justified dissent that leads to justified countermotives. In the first case, an illocutionary obligation has to be executed against stronger countermotives. This seems to be possible only by counter-countermotives which are still stronger than the countermotives—that is, some kind of coercion. In the other case, communicative power has to institutionalize itself. Institutions which maintain communicative power are needed even if counterreasons justify countermotives. Not any counterreason which justifies countermotives should lead to a breakdown of illocutionary obligations to act in concert. Therefore, communicative power is applied to itself—the We, made up of those who factually accepted a validity claim and reidentified and reconfirmed themselves as a singular action community, can itself become a political community. Then, the reidentification and the reconfirmation of a singular action community is interpreted as the foundation of constitutional rules, procedures, and institutions which enable its members to reproduce communicative power through and within an institutional framework. The factual acceptance of the institutional framework generates the illocutionary obligation for the members of the political community to act according to the constitutional rules, and to reiterate the communicative power through every single issue about which they argue within the institutional framework. Rational dissent within the institutional framework does not destroy the communicative power inherent in the factual acceptance of the institutional framework itself.

IV. THE LAW: A PATTERN OF LINKS AND INTERRUPTIONS BETWEEN REASONS AND MOTIVES

Obviously, the two strategies that are to cope with the threats to communicative power can undermine communicative power itself. Coercion as a medium for overriding countermotives decouples the internal illocutionary link between communicative freedom and action motives. This would deny the functioning of communicative power as a motivational resource, because the actor who is coerced to act cannot trace back her action motive to illocutionary empowerment. The second strategy to maintain communicative power, the institutionalization of a political community, is in danger of turning the actor into a virtuous citizen who is required to support the constitution actively even if her dissent is reasonable. This is obvious in the case of minorities: should they renounce their counterreasons, accept the reasons of the majority, and transform these reasons into their motives? What if they are still convinced of their counterreasons? This would ask for either conversion or hypocrisy.

The law serves as a medium which can solve both problems at the same time. It can do so because it is a complex pattern of links and interruptions between reasons and motives. To conclude, I would like to illustrate the relationships between law and communicative power with respect to both elements of the illocutionary link between reasons and motives: (1) the "negative" or obligatory aspect, and (2) the "positive" or empowering aspect.

A. The "Negative" or Obligatory Aspect

Legal norms drive a wedge between the freedom to take a position and the obligation to adopt a reason as one's own reason for action. They open an artificial gap which makes subjective freedom or negative liberty necessary. Legal norms do not entail the obligation that they be adopted as one's own reasons for future actions; they are not connected with the legitimate expectation to become a motive for the actor, as are those action norms that are reciprocally accepted by speaker and hearer on the basis of an affirmative position. Instead, legal norms become relevant to the sequel of interaction by virtue of their link with coercive force. Because of this link, legal norms lose contact with illocutionary obligations. Coercive force cannot produce action motives as an affirmative position can, a position that was taken on the basis of reciprocally attributed communicative freedom. For this reason, legal norms do not care about the source of the motives for their observance. A motive to follow a legal norm which was generated by taking an affirmative position on its validity claim is as good as a motive generated by fear of sanctions or by the calculation of advantages. Consequently, as a legal person everybody is allowed to get his or her action motives from wherever he or she likes; nobody is obliged to adopt only those reasons as his or her own reasons for action which he or she accepted by taking an affirmative position on a validity claim. What action motives he or she has is up to the individual—as long as he or she does not violate the legal norms. This is the meaning of the right to negative liberty or individual freedom. A legal person is no longer obliged, with respect to legal norms, to trace her action motives back to an affirmative position taken on a validity claim and on the basis of communicative freedom. Therefore, a legal person may "step out" of the obligations of communicative action and renounce the right to take an affirmative or a negative position at all.

On the other hand, legal norms and the corresponding negative rights, although they are neutral with respect to the motives of their observance, may not exclude or destroy the possibility of being followed by reasons which were adopted because of an affirmative position. Otherwise, legal norms would abolish communicative freedom. But how can the idea of communicative freedom be preserved with regard to legal norms and negative rights? According to the discourse principle, communicative freedom presupposes that everybody can accept an action norm on the basis of taking an affirmative position on a validity claim. Concerning legal norms, this presupposition cannot be realized without violating the neutrality of these norms with regard to the motives for their acceptance and their observance. This dilemma can only be solved by transforming the right to take a free position on a norm into a legal right to participate in a democratic political process of public will-formation and legislation. As a consequence of this transformation, the right to take a free position changes its character.

On the one hand, as a legal right, it includes the right to negative liberty. Political rights must not oblige their holders to take a position in the political process of legislation. They may use their right to political participation, or they may, as Habermas says, "step out" and withdraw from the political sphere, without being excluded from it, meaning without losing their political rights and their status as a citizen. This is the only way in which communicative freedom can be preserved with regard to legal norms and rights. On the other hand, as a legal right which refers to a public, democratic procedure of will-formation and legislation, it allows for those citizens who participate in the procedure to produce communicative power as a motivational resource for obedience to the resulting legal norms. But this kind of communicative power differs from the one discussed earlier.[25] It does not depend on the factual acceptance of those reasons which are brought forward for a legal norm—although democratic legislation does not deny or reject this relation between reasons and motives in those rare cases when a citizen really is rationally motivated to accept a legal norm and to obey it. Instead, the source of communicative power lies in the acceptance of the procedure which guarantees every citizen the right to exercise communicative freedom equally. If a legal norm is a result of such a procedure, the acceptance of the procedure can produce a motive to obey this legal norm—even for those who are not convinced of the norm's validity because they can reasonably reject the reasons.[26]

This shift from the acceptance of a norm to the acceptance of the procedure is also the key to the solution of the minority problem. It, too, begins with an interruption of the link between reasons and motives. A minority is only obliged to obey the majority's law if, at the same time, there is a procedure which guarantees everybody the right to argue for his or her counterreasons. Only under this condition do minorities have a chance to change the majority's mind and to convince it of their counterreasons' acceptability. As a consequence, legal norms may not claim that their validity

25. *See supra* part III.
26. To be sure, this shift in the reference of communicative power from norm to procedure does not totally remove the gap between reasons and motives, and it does not oblige the citizens to support the legal order because of their acceptance of the procedure. It leaves open the possibility to obey the norm on the basis of motives which are *independent* of the acceptance or rejection of the procedure. I can reject the procedure but obey the norm because I fear the sanctions for violation. The shift from norm to procedure explains only how the motivational resource of communicative power in a democratic society is still possible even if the link between reasons and motives with regard to the acceptance of single legal norms is interrupted.

entails the obligation to obey them because of the reasons which support their validity. Those who refuse to accept these reasons are obliged to obey the law because of the democratic procedure, and because they have the right to change the law through participation in and under the conditions of that procedure. The obligation to obey the norm is shifted from the acceptance of the norm's validity claim to the acceptance of the procedure. This shift allows for the neutrality of the legal norm toward the citizen's action motives. But the right to political participation is a *conditio sine qua non* of the legitimacy of this gap between reasons and motives.[27]

B. The "Positive" or Empowering Aspect

Another consequence concerns the "positive side" of the illocutionary link between reasons and motives, that is, the attribution of a power to act. On the one hand, it is one of the essentials of communicative power in a political community not only to generate illocutionary obligations to act, such as an imperative which has to be obeyed or legally enforced, but also to produce a genuine motivational resource, one which gives a power to act to the people. On the other hand, the decoupling of reasons and motives, which is a consequence of the coercive properties of the law, seems to destroy exactly this kind of motivation. It separates the people from each other and takes away their power to act in concert. The solution lies in the bifurcation of the power to act. In a political community that decides to submit to legal rules which its members give to themselves within public, democratic procedures, the power to act is divided in itself. It is shaped as a public power to act, on the one hand, and a private power to act, on the other.

Public or political rights and private rights correspond to this division. The public power to act is preserved by public procedures and the equal right of the citizens to participate in these procedures by exercising their communicative freedom and generating communicative power. As a consequence, citizens are politically responsible for their law; it is up to them to exercise their communicative power in order to change the rules.[28] While using their equal right to communicative freedom in order to argue for and against legal rules, citizens recognize each other as being politically competent, even if they strongly dispute one another's arguments. Finally, the public power to act is the legitimating source for the limited authori-

---

27. Obviously, this argument is similar to Alexis de Tocqueville's argument in his book, *Democracy in America. See* 1 ALEXIS DE TOCQUEVILLE, ÜBER DIE DEMOKRATIE IN AMERIKA 360 (Hans Zbinden trans., 1962).

28. *See* ARENDT, ON VIOLENCE, *supra* note 23, at 38–39 (Arendt's analysis of diminished political responsibility in a bureaucracy as the opposite of democracy).

zation of an administrative power for the execution of the law and of political decisions in concrete cases.[29]

The private power to act is preserved by the artificial construction of a legal person. Within her legal domain, the legal person may exercise her own private will as long as she does not violate the equal legal domain of others. She is also legally competent to change her legal relationships according to the law, for example, to make a contract or to give up property. As a consequence, she is legally responsible to obey the law, and she is legally held accountable as the author of her actions if she violates the law. When she is held accountable for violation of the law, she is not obliged to trace back her motives to those reasons which she could have accepted as a participant in public discourse, that is, when she exercised her communicative freedom. Her status as a legal person is independent of her status as a citizen. Her legal competence to exercise her private power to act subsists in the absence of public power. Similarly, she is legally responsible in the absence of any legitimate expectation of a "single action community," an expectation generated by a factual acceptance of a validity claim. However, her status as a legal person who is legally competent and responsible is, again, indirectly linked with her status as a citizen who shares in public power. The legal competence to exercise one's private power to act, together with the complementary legal responsibility for actions, originates from the communicative power inherent in the original decision of the members of a political community to constitute itself as a legal community.

The communicative power inherent in this decision never appears in a pure fashion. From the beginning, communicative power is bifurcated. People who use their illocutionary forces to constitute a legal community *uno actu* appear as legal persons who have political and private rights. This is why, according to Habermas, communicative power is linked from the beginning to the system of rights.[30] Thus, communicative power is preserved as a productive and reproductive motivational resource for a constitutional democracy.

---

29. *See* HABERMAS, *supra* note 2, at 148.
30. *See id.* at 151.

PART FIVE

Law, Ethics, and Democracy

TWELVE

Against Subordination

Morality, Discourse, and Decision in the Legal Theory of Jürgen Habermas

*William Rehg**

This reflection explores the manner in which Jürgen Habermas's *Between Facts and Norms* establishes a relationship between law (or legal procedures) and an idealized conception of rational practical discourse.[1] Part I of this Article spells out a problem that arises if one subordinates law to such idealizations of practical reason; here I will argue that the subordination of law to morality is part of a larger problem that one does not escape simply by analyzing law in the broader terms of discursive justification in general. Part II pursues further the question of whether Habermas's legal theory escapes this difficulty, turning next to his account of the democratic institutionalization of discourse and its relation to the legal form as a system of rights. Part III responds to the more subtle subordination that persists in Habermas's account of rights and closes by suggesting that legitimate decision making involves not only discourse but a form of procedural fairness that Habermas's discourse-theoretic analysis tends to neglect.

I.

One can approach the relevant problem by first asking the question: How is the law related to morality? In articles prior to his book-length study, *Between Facts and Norms,* Habermas argued that the legitimacy of law arose

*I am grateful to James Bohman, Thomas McCarthy, and R. Randall Rainey for reading and commenting on earlier versions of this Article.

1. JÜRGEN HABERMAS, BETWEEN FACTS AND NORMS: CONTRIBUTIONS TO A DISCOURSE THEORY OF LAW AND DEMOCRACY (William Rehg trans., 1996). The German text appears in JÜRGEN HABERMAS, FAKTIZITÄT UND GELTUNG: BEITRÄGE ZUR DISKURSTHEORIE DES RECHTS UND DES DEMOKRATISCHEN RECHTSSTAATS (1992).

from the way in which moral-practical rationality and institutionalized legal procedures "interpenetrated" one another.[2] This moral aspect of the law was itself explained in procedural terms, so that Habermas could speak of the law as involving two kinds of procedural rationality, a moral-practical one and a legal one. The procedural rationality appropriate to morality found its fullest expression in a notion of impartiality expressed by a principle of universalization: for a norm of action to be *morally* valid, it must be capable of gaining the assent of all those subject to it—after they have considered the various effects that the norm's general observance would have on each person's interests and needs. Moral validity, then, is defined by an idealized procedure of perspective taking in which each person affected by the issue or conflict in need of regulation examines the issue and its proposed normative solution from the standpoint of *every other* affected person.[3] Of course, real conflict resolutions rarely if ever arrive at such an idealized unanimous rational agreement on a norm. Hence the need for the other half of Habermas's "interpenetration" equation, namely legal procedures that guarantee clear results within limited time frames.[4] Given the difficulty in reaching rational consensus in real conflict situations, definite legal procedures for reaching unambiguous and binding decisions become a necessary complement to moral discourse. However, some of Habermas's earlier formulations could tempt one to take yet a further step and tacitly *subordinate* law to morality—the egalitarian metaphor of "interpenetrating" or "interlocking" procedures notwithstanding. That is, one easily could be tempted to see legal outcomes as legitimate precisely insofar as the institutionalized legal procedure approximated features of the universal perspective taking enshrined in the idealized moral procedure.[5] To be sure, in other formulations Habermas clearly acknowledged the complexity of le-

2.   Legitimacy is possible on the basis of legality insofar as the procedures for the production and application of legal norms are also conducted reasonably, in the moral-practical sense of procedural rationality. The legitimacy of legality is due to the interlocking of two types of procedures, namely, of legal processes with processes of moral argumentation that obey a procedural rationality of their own.
                JÜRGEN HABERMAS, *LAW AND MORALITY, IN 8*
                THE TANNER LECTURES ON HUMAN VALUES 217, 230
                (Sterling M. McMurrin ed., 1988).

        3.   Thus Habermas's moral theory is based on a dialogical version of Kant's Categorical Imperative. *See* JÜRGEN HABERMAS, *Discourse Ethics: Notes on a Program of Philosophical Justification, in* MORAL CONSCIOUSNESS AND COMMUNICATIVE ACTION 43–115 (Christian Lenhardt & Shierry W. Nicholsen trans., 1990); *see also* THOMAS MCCARTHY, THE CRITICAL THEORY OF JÜRGEN HABERMAS ch. 4 (1978); WILLIAM REHG, INSIGHT AND SOLIDARITY: A STUDY IN THE DISCOURSE ETHICS OF JÜRGEN HABERMAS pt. 1 (1994).

        4.   Habermas, *supra* note 2, at 230, 244, 246–57.

        5.   For example, in *Law and Morality,* Habermas writes: "Legality can produce legitimacy *only to the extent* that the legal order reflexively responds to the need for justification that origi-

gal legitimacy: idealized procedures of moral argumentation account for only a part of legitimacy.[6] Yet the temptation is an instructive one, for it shows how easily the metaphor of interpenetration can slide into a form of subordination bearing strong traces of the "Platonic legacy" that Habermas detects in Kant's analysis of law, i.e., the idea that law measures its validity against standards given by an ideal realm, in Kant's case a moral one.[7]

What is wrong with moralizing law the way that Kant did? For the purposes of this discussion, the key difficulty lies in its oversimplification. Subordinating law to morality does not do justice to the complexity of the considerations and arguments informing the legitimacy of modern law. In the wake of the differentiation processes brought on by modern societal rationalization, legitimate legal decisions must be attuned not only to moral considerations; they must also attend to possible technical-pragmatic questions about the selection of effective means and strategies for dealing with a given problem; they must be acceptable in the light of the community's authentic self-understanding—what Habermas now calls an "ethical-political" issue; and they must see to the fairness of any elements of compromise between competing particular interests.[8] An account of legitimacy that does not reflect this complexity is questionable from both normative and sociological standpoints. Moreover, it will only add to the difficulties involved in explaining legitimacy in a manner that does justice to both private

---

nates from the positivization of law and responds in such a manner that legal discourses are institutionalized in ways made pervious to moral argumentation." *Id.* at 243–44 (emphasis added).

6. "Political power exercised in the form of positive law that is in need of justification owes its legitimacy . . . —at least in part—to the implicit moral content of the formal properties of law." *Id.* at 241–42. This ambiguity in Habermas's earlier writings has also been noted in BERNHARD PETERS, RATIONALITÄT, RECHT UND GESELLSCHAFT 130–31 (1991).

7. *See* HABERMAS, *supra* note 1, at 105–07.

8. These distinctions reflect Habermas's discourse-theoretic categorization of the different forms of practical reasoning. *See id.* at 158–60. Moral discourse, in the strict sense, deals with justice questions; in a moral discourse participants strive to reach agreement on how to regulate interpersonal relations according to "generalizable interests," i.e., in a way that everyone can accept from the standpoint of fairness or respect for persons. This form of practical discourse contrasts not only with technical (or pragmatic) discourse but also with ethical-political discourse and bargaining. Ethical-political discourse is concerned with a polity's good, i.e., with determining the collective goals and policies the group ought to pursue, given its traditions, values, and ideals. Bargaining becomes necessary when a conflict of particular interests cannot be resolved by appeal either to a generalizable interest or to shared values. In that case a peaceful resolution requires the parties to seek a compromise, the fairness of which depends on the parties having roughly equal bargaining power. In Habermas's view, an adequate analysis of legal and political discourses requires attention to each of these discursive dimensions. *See id.* at 103–07, 151–68.

autonomy and public sovereignty, to the individual's negative liberties, and the polity's collective capacity to organize and govern itself by laws.[9]

In *Between Facts and Norms* Habermas defines the law-morality relation in a way that attempts to avoid such a subordination. In the context of his earlier formulations, the key move might be described as follows: the two interlocking procedures of morality and law *both* institute a more abstract *impartialist discursive rationality* expressed by the "discourse principle" ("*D*"). Earlier, Habermas had presented this as the leading principle of his moral theory; now he repositions *D* so that it overarches both law and morality in a manner prejudicial to neither. In the context of moral judgment formation, *D* takes the more specific shape of the universalization principle discussed above; in the context of the institutionalized action systems of law, it assumes the shape of a "democratic principle" that unfolds as a system of basic rights. The way now seems open to account for the specific character of legal rationality and legitimacy that involves more than copying moral idealizations.

This repositioning of *D* allows Habermas to situate legal validity in relation to the whole range of discursive rationalities and bargaining processes. That is, the full complexity of legitimacy can emerge more clearly than it did in the earlier formulations. As expressed in the democratic principle, the legitimacy of law depends on legal procedures that institutionalize, not only the logic of argumentation corresponding to moral universalization, but also the argumentational logics corresponding to the technical-pragmatic choice of means and strategies, ethical-political decisions about policies and goals, and compromises between particular interests.[10]

However, if repositioning *D* simply means connecting legal legitimacy with a more complex set of discursive idealizations, then a further problem associated with the subordination motif persists. To get at this problem, recall Habermas's formulation of *D:* "Just those action norms are valid to which all possibly affected persons could agree as participants in rational discourses."[11] This is a general principle of rational justification containing at least two idealizations.[12] The first is that all the parties affected by a decision must agree before the decision may be deemed valid. The second, less obvious but nonetheless present, is that such agreement must come about on the basis of insight into the better argument, i.e., through partici-

---

9. For Habermas's sociological account of modern differentiation, see *id.* at 94–99, 105–07; for his normative critique of subordination as oversimplifying, see *id.* at 229–34. The problem of striking a balance between private and public autonomy runs through all of Chapter 3, but see in particular *id.* at 83–84, 92–94, 99–104, 121–22.

10. *See id.* at 108, 155–56.

11. *Id.* at 107.

12. *See id.* at 107, 108–09.

pation "in rational discourses."[13] True, one must bear in mind here the different types of decisions and discourses. Moral issues, for example, require the agreement of all persons, whereas questions of policy and collective goals require the agreement of a concrete community.[14] In both cases, however, the logic of the respective argumentation process aims at complete agreement in the relevant circle of addressees. The problem here is this: the idea of rational unanimity only goes part way toward explaining the legitimacy of legal procedures. This idea still abstracts considerably from the specifically *institutional* complexity of legal-political decision making: the broader discursive idealizations of *D* do not tell us much more about where to set the institutional limits necessary to reach clear decisions under time constraints than does the idealized moral procedure. As Bernhard Peters has put it, an idealized procedural rationality is too indeterminate to define decision-making institutions appropriate to the concrete limitations of space and time, limitations that deny us the leisure to discuss a disputed issue until perfect unanimity is achieved.[15]

Discursive idealizations seem most useful for telling us why participants consider a particular outcome more or less legitimate—for example, why they consider a decision made on the basis of a relatively lengthy and open debate and issuing in a three-fourths majority more legitimate than a decision that barely passes after a hasty deliberation. But one cannot move directly from the ideal discursive procedure to concrete prescriptions for institutionalized decision-making procedures. One cannot conclude from this example that an *institutional requirement* of a three-fourths majority is more rational—and hence engenders greater legitimacy—than the requirement of a simple majority.[16] The general problem is that legal procedures not only create the space for discourse; they also *curtail* the demanding discursive requirements on validity. Might not this very curtailment specific to legal decision making reveal further conditions of legitimacy beyond those captured by ideas of rational discourse? If so, then the idea of impartial justification, even in its more complex form, only partly explains the specific legitimacy of democratic institutions and their forms of

---

13. *Id.* at 163–64.

14. *See id.* at 123–24.

15. *See* PETERS, *supra* note 6, at 246–50.

16. For an overview of the complexities attending majority rule, see ROBERT A. DAHL, DEMOCRACY AND ITS CRITICS 135–52 (1989). The problem here parallels difficulties in moving from an ideal of equality to voting procedures. *See, e.g.,* CHARLES R. BEITZ, POLITICAL EQUALITY: AN ESSAY IN DEMOCRATIC THEORY chs. 1–4 (1989); Peter Jones, *Political Equality and Majority Rule, in* THE NATURE OF POLITICAL THEORY 155 (David Miller & Larry Siedentop eds., 1983).

decision making. Herein lies the deeper significance of Habermas's demo-cratic principle, which I will take up in greater detail in the next section.

II.

Part of the difficulty in the above reflections lies in the nature of idealiza-tions themselves. They are not—even in principle—empirically realizable *descriptions* of a possible consensus situation, but rather *suppositions* that the participants in discourse must make if they are to consider a consensus at all rational.[17] Hence, even to talk of democratic procedures as "approxima-tions" to rational unanimity can be misleading. Still, there is a valid core to the concern with subordination; the fundamental difficulty seems to lie in construing legitimacy solely by reference to discursive idealizations. If these alone define the legitimacy of a procedure, then any institutional requirements that curtail the demands of rational discourse simply have the negative role of limiting an ideal—they simply reveal our inability to achieve fully rational discourse. Some kind of subordination, however subtle, is difficult to avoid in such a construction. This raises the question of whether, and, if so, how, this specifically institutional dimension *positively* contributes to legitimacy, i.e., in a manner not fully explicable in terms of the discursive idealizations that define rational unanimity. If it does, then we should be able to identify a component of legitimacy that somehow has to do with institutionalization as such, in a manner that is not reducible to discourse. More precisely, we should be able to distinguish, for given legal (or political) procedures, an aspect of the procedures that does not increase the amount and quality of discourse, yet is nonetheless important for legiti-macy. As we shall see, what Habermas calls the "legal medium" or "legal form" is, for present purposes, roughly equivalent to this specifically insti-tutional component.[18]

In view of such difficulties it is significant that Habermas looks to the *democratic principle* as the immediate source of legitimate lawmaking. This principle presupposes the discursive rationality given in *D* and tells us how to institutionalize it as a "rational political opinion- and will-formation."[19] It thus represents a definition of legitimacy grounded in *both* discursive idealizations and the specific requirements of legal institutionalization. As

17. *See* HABERMAS, *supra* note 1, at 323; *see also* JÜRGEN HABERMAS, JUSTIFICATION AND APPLICATION: REMARKS ON DISCOURSE ETHICS 54–57 (Ciarin Cronin trans., 1993).

18. See HABERMAS, *supra* note 1, at 113–18, on Habermas's sociological interpretation of the legal form; *see also id.* at 178–79. To avoid a source of possible confusion, note that Haber-mas has dropped his earlier distinction between "law as institution" and "law as medium." *See id.* at 561 n.48.

19. *Id.* at 110.

Habermas puts it, the democratic principle results from the combination of the discourse principle and the legal form. He defines the democratic principle as follows:

> [T]he principle of democracy should establish a procedure of legitimate law-making. Specifically, the democratic principle states that only those statutes may claim legitimacy that can meet with the assent (*Zustimmung*) of all citizens in a discursive process of legislation that in turn has been legally constituted. In other words, this principle explains the performative meaning of the practice of self-determination on the part of legal consociates who recognize one another as free and equal members of an association they have joined voluntarily.[20]

Although this definition still refers to the discursive ideal of full consensus, a point I will come back to, it also links legitimacy to the mutual recognition of free and equal legal subjects. The constitution of such subjects—which is precisely the contribution of the "legal form" to legitimacy—cannot be reduced to discourse. To see how the legal form has a positive role to play in the legitimacy of law, then, we must examine the system of rights that define the legal subject.

The democratic principle can take institutional shape only in the system of rights necessary if citizens are to be both addressees and authors of laws that "legitimately regulate their living together."[21] More specifically, the "application of the discourse principle to the medium of law as such" issues in a set of rights guaranteeing the private autonomy of the addressees of law, while the requirement that the addressees also be authors of law generates rights of political participation and thus the public autonomy of citizens.[22]

This suggests that we can pinpoint a specifically institutional contribution to legitimacy at the level of the negative liberties defining private autonomy, for it is here that the discourse principle and the "legal medium as such" come together. In fact, private autonomy involves three general types of rights, according to Habermas. The first are those negative liberties that guarantee spheres of individual autonomous action. The second comprises rights of membership in a political community. The third are those rights of legal recourse that allow individuals to sue for the first two types of rights.[23] According to Habermas's account, a constitutional state must interpret and elaborate more specific rights and laws that fall within these three categories. The three categories themselves are not identical with any specific set of particular rights; these categories are rather abstractions that require historical-political elaboration. By way of illustration, one can note

20. *Id.* at 110.
21. *Id.* at 118, 121.
22. *Id.* at 122.
23. *See id.* at 123–26.

that rights to personal dignity, life, liberty, bodily integrity, etc., interpret the first category. The category of membership rights includes the various laws and rights that define the status of members in a legal community. Here Habermas includes prohibitions against extradition, rights of political asylum, and so on. Finally, the third category finds expression in due process rights: the prohibition against retroactive punishment, etc.[24]

Rights such as these are central to modern law. As constitutive of the legal form, they define spheres of action in which individuals can confidently pursue their private ends free of others' interference and without having to justify their choices in discourse.[25] Through such individual rights, then, law is able to secure realms of action in which persons are relieved of the need to reach consensus through discourse: in contrast to forms of social coordination that require participants to reach an agreement based on each one's insight, coordination based on law requires only external compliance. In this sense, individual rights are not mere instruments of discourse. However, they have a legitimating function only insofar as they guarantee *equal* individual liberties to citizens, and this equality is not a necessary feature of the legal form itself. According to Habermas, "only by bringing in the discourse principle can one show that *each person* is owed a right to . . . *equal* liberties."[26] So if we are looking to such rights for the specifically institutional side of legitimacy, then we will not find it apart from discourse—even if the rights defining private autonomy are themselves neither reducible to discourse nor mere instruments for the sake of discourse.

Habermas's intuitive argument here is this: if discourse is to be institutionalized, then the legal form itself must assume a certain structure, even before any legal-political discourses have begun. That is, legal subjects must be defined as free and equal members of a legal community. For discourse presupposes that its participants are autonomous individuals, and only a legal code structured in terms of individual rights that secure such autonomy can antecedently designate even potential participants for real discourses—however participation happens to be further defined in terms of voting rights, representation, and so on. As Habermas puts it, "the establishment of the legal code as such already implies liberty rights that beget the status of legal persons and guarantee their integrity." These rights are "necessary enabling conditions" for the exercise of political autonomy.[27] The attempt

24. *See id.* at 125–26.
25. *See id.* at 115–19, 125.
26. *Id.* at 123.
27. *Id.* at 128. Note that Habermas has not yet brought state power into the picture; although a legal system cannot stabilize itself (and thus cannot stabilize expectations) without the backing of a coercive state power, the system of basic rights is conceptually prior to this in Habermas's reconstruction. *See id.* at 122–23, 132–33.

to institutionalize discourse thus puts certain constraints on the legal medium in which such institutionalization can occur—constraints found in the three types of rights that establish private autonomy.

What concerns me here is not so much how one might defend the claim that private autonomy is a necessary precondition for deliberative democracy.[28] Rather, I am primarily interested in how Habermas understands the specific contribution made by such rights of liberty in the legitimization of the democratic process. Even if he does not directly derive negative liberties from discursive ideals, he nonetheless maintains that the legitimating properties of such rights flow from their indirect relation to discourse. Specifically, rights establishing private autonomy have a role in democratic legitimation only as connected with political discourse. Only by virtue of rights of political participation, which empower privately autonomous citizens to engage in collective self-governance, can legal subjects reflexively interpret and elaborate their civil rights, thereby becoming authors as well as addressees of law.[29]

This means, in sum, that private and public autonomy mutually presuppose one another in an explanation of legitimacy.[30] Hence the legal form, in the specific shape of equal individual liberty, does indeed play a positive role in democratic legitimation. However, it is revealing that, in the marriage of the discourse principle and the legal form, only the latter is really affected—namely, it is forced to adopt a specific shape. The discourse principle, on the other hand, melds into the democratic principle without alteration, inasmuch as the unanimity requirement remains intact in the democratic principle. This is somewhat odd, given that democratic decision making is normally defined in terms of majority rule rather than unanimity. The discourse principle thus plays the dominant role in explaining legitimacy, which suggests that the subordination motif still persists in Habermas's account of rights despite the positive role played by the legal form. Although Habermas does not follow Kant's moralistic explanation of equal liberties,[31] he does explain the liberties in relation to the institutionalization of a discourse that measures its success against an idealized unanimity—whence the continuing subordination to this demanding standard in the democratic principle.[32]

Perhaps this more subtle subordination of law to idealized discourse does not have the problematic connotations burdening Kant's legal theory. Its

28. For further discussion of the relation between negative liberty and democratic process, see Albrecht Wellmer, *Models of Freedom in the Modern World*, 21 PHIL. F. 227 (1989–90).

29. *See* HABERMAS, *supra* note 1, at 126–27.

30. *See id.* at 408.

31. *See id.* at 105–06; *see also id.* at 84, 92–94, 99–104, 120.

32. For a critique of unanimity models of legitimacy, see Bernard Manin, *On Legitimacy and Political Deliberation*, 15 POL. THEORY 338 (Elly Stein & Jane Mansbridge trans., 1987).

presence is certainly understandable, given that Habermas primarily wants to emphasize the necessity of discourse for legitimate lawmaking.[33] The interpenetration of law and discourse has another side, however. If law and politics are first and foremost *decision-making* institutions, then deliberation and discourse represent just one dimension. Besides the need to bring the discourse principle into law, one must also bring fair and binding *decisions* into discourse. With its unanimity requirement, the democratic principle can hardly tell us how to decide controverted issues. Consequently, there is a level of institutionalization that the democratic principle does not reach. More specifically, in the final section I will suggest that the fairness considerations operative at this decision-making level are not fully captured by an ideal of impartial justification.

III.

In no way do I dispute Habermas's intuition that legal institutions and procedures are meant to provide the space for processes of argumentation obeying an idealized logic of their own. This orientation to discourse may well be the more important factor in the legitimacy of law. To this extent, law and politics represent forms of institutionalized discourse. What I want to get at here, though, is precisely the modifier of discourse in this equation, i.e., "institutionalized." Real procedures can foster discourse only up to a certain point, after which a decision is required. The question, then, is whether the decision making itself can be fair in ways that are not expressed in Habermas's concepts of discourse or compromise.

We find a clue to the character of this decision-making rationality in chance procedures. We can fix terms with a simple example.[34] Suppose two children, coming across a marble more or less simultaneously, begin to argue over who saw the marble first and thus has a rightful claim to it. Each

33. For example, the point of "a genuinely proceduralist understanding of democracy . . . is this: the democratic procedure is institutionalized in discourses and bargaining processes by employing forms of communication that promise that all outcomes reached in conformity with the procedure are reasonable." HABERMAS, *supra* note 1, at 304. In fairness to Habermas, at certain points he does approach the point I want to make; *see, e.g., id.* app. I, §§ 2, 4 ("Popular Sovereignty as Procedure": discussing majority rule and the distinction between informal discourse and constitutionally structured decision making).

34. I take this example from WEYMA LÜBBE, LEGITIMITÄT KRAFT LEGALITÄT: SINNVERSTEHEN UND INSTITUTIONENANALYSE BEI MAX WEBER UND SEINEN KRITIKERN 118–22 (1991). For more realistic scenarios, see the discussion of child custody battles in JON ELSTER, SOLOMONIC JUDGEMENTS: STUDIES IN THE LIMITATIONS OF RATIONALITY ch. 3 (1989). Elster argues at length for the possibility of using random methods for deciding child custody cases. His point is that discursive procedures entail disadvantages for the child that possibly offset the gains in information and a more complete consideration of arguments.

believes it has a *just* claim to the marble and *argues* for its claim, so that the issue at least arises as a moral question involving argumentation. In the event that neither side can convince the other, however, it is rational for the children to agree on a procedure such as tossing a coin in order to settle their dispute (assuming they want to maintain good relations). This decision procedure itself does not seem to be explicable in terms either of discourse or of single right answers. In a moral discourse of justification, reaching consensus involves a corrigible claim that future considerations of the same issue will not overturn the original consensus. By contrast, the coin toss—which is arguably a *fair* procedure—does not pretend to arrive at an outcome that future coin tosses would confirm, as though the first toss produced a "right" or "just" result. At the same time, we are not dealing with a compromise precisely as Habermas defines it: on the one hand, one side will lose and the other will win; on the other hand, it may turn out subsequent to the toss that further information—new arguments—comes to light that suddenly makes it clear to both parties who really deserves the marble. In principle, the issue remains a question of justice.[35]

I do not mean to equate legal procedures with coin tosses, though lotteries have been, and are still used, in law and politics.[36] Rather, I choose this example only because it brings out—in an extreme form—the difference between discourse and decision making. That is, the decision procedure itself, which appears fair, has in this case only a minimal relation to the requirements of rational discourse. Other legal-political decision-making procedures such as majority rule or court procedures admittedly enjoy a closer relation to discourse. Nonetheless, an analogous difference still persists between pursuing a discourse until each and every participant arrives at the same insight, and a stipulated procedure that calls for a vote, or an authoritative judicial decision, after each party or its representative has had an equal chance to present its case. The coin toss is only an extreme example of the stipulated point where a real procedure cuts off rational discussion and demands a decision.

There is an easy and quick reply to the above observation: the procedure by which a decision is reached will be fair only if it is *itself* the subject of a kind of metadiscourse, so to speak, in which participants rationally discuss the best way to reach a decision in the case at issue. In this sense, even

---

35. Habermas distinguishes bargaining processes (which aim at compromises) from justice issues in terms of the kind of interests at stake: the former involve the clash of merely particular interests, whereas the latter involve potentially generalizable interests able to ground a solution that is cognitively "right." Compromises can at most be "fair" insofar as they are based on an equal balance of power. *See* HABERMAS, *supra* note 1, at 161–67.

36. *See* ELSTER, *supra* note 34, at 62–67.

chance procedures have an indirect relation to discourse—a point Habermas already makes in regard to compromises.[37] As shown by discussions of both chance procedures and majority rule, such metadiscourses involve complex considerations. In considering a chance procedure, participants would, however, at least ask themselves whether tossing a coin could systematically disadvantage one of them. Presumably, the parties would accept such a procedure only if it gives each an equal chance at winning. While this is not the only consideration, the coin toss does manage to "safeguard the important values of equal treatment and equal opportunity."[38] Metadiscourses on majority rule or on forms of authoritative decision making in a civic polity are, no doubt, even more complex. Indeed they would focus on how well the respective procedural stipulations increase the chances that the outcome at least enjoys a supposition of coinciding with the outcome a rational discourse would reach, given sufficient time. But here, too, ideas centering on equal treatment and opportunity constitute some of the most important justifications.[39]

What "equality" means here is a complicated question, and my remarks on it in this Article will have to be brief. The broader point, in any case, is that more needs to be said about legitimacy than the quick reply above. The difference between discourse and decision making, and the role of equality in the latter, opens the door to a more complex account of democratic legitimacy under pluralist conditions. Even if decision-making procedures should be discussed in metadiscourses, once a procedure is institutionally established its intrinsically equalitarian features can operate as an immediate criterion of legitimacy *alongside* its discursive features. In the space remaining I can only roughly suggest some possible implications of this.[40]

Note first that utilizing a metadiscourse does not eradicate the distinct

---

37. *See* HABERMAS, *supra* note 1, at 166–67. This implies that Habermas might be able to assimilate the point I am making by expanding his notion of compromise. To do this he would have to acknowledge that a kind of compromise infects justice issues themselves—i.e., issues one would expect to have correct, discernible answers—were only the time and knowledge available to pursue these answers. Elster, in fact, does consider chance procedures as a kind of compromise. *See* ELSTER, *supra* note 34, at 99.

38. Elster's discussion shows that questions of substantive justice, the values and costs of deliberation, other rights of the participants, and other issues, would also arise in such a metadiscourse. *See* ELSTER, *supra* note 34, at 170–71.

39. *See, e.g.,* DAHL, *supra* note 16, at 108–11; *see also* Thomas Christiano, *Social Choice and Democracy, in* THE IDEA OF DEMOCRACY 173 (David Copp et al. eds., 1993).

40. For general overviews of issues associated with the various notions of equality, see, for example, 9 EQUALITY (American Society for Political and Legal Philosophy, J. Roland Pennock & John W. Chapman eds., 1967); DOUGLAS RAE ET AL., EQUALITIES (1981); for a discussion of the specific issues at stake in democratic decision making, Beitz's *Political Equality* is excellent. BEITZ, *supra* note 16.

character of the decision procedure itself. By agreeing to use a coin toss, for example, participants bind themselves to a procedure they can accept as fair from the standpoint of equality, but whose outcome does not necessarily coincide with what would be impartially justified in a sufficiently pursued rational discourse. If this reveals something about all legal-political procedures, then one can, in general, distinguish the intrinsic fairness of such procedures—whether a coin toss gives each side equal chances for winning, or whether each participant has had an equal chance to present its arguments and cast its vote—from the degree to which they approximate the requirements of rational discourse. The result of a coin toss, a vote, or a judicial proceeding, even if fairly structured, does not necessarily coincide with the ideally just result that a discourse would arrive at given sufficient time. As long as all those affected are symmetrically situated in relation to the decision, however, we are normally inclined—at least at first glance—to call the procedure "fair" even though it does not meet the demanding cognitive requirements set by idealized logics of argumentation.[41]

The difference between impartial discourse and fair decision making emerges from the fact that, at any given point in most real discourses, the "better argument," deserving unanimous assent, is not clear. Reasonable persons can reasonably disagree, even if, in the long run, only one answer will prove right. Thus at any given point in time, the rational or just solution to a legal or political issue is indeterminate or uncertain.[42] In this situation, legal procedures can provide at least two things at once on the way to a timely decision: (1) they make room for "discourse," thereby increasing the chances that the defeasibly better argument will sway at least a majority or a legal authority (depending on the kind of procedure); and (2) they give each party to the dispute an "equal opportunity" to affect the outcome.[43] Here equal opportunity is not exactly the same as the equality required by discursive idealizations. The latter posits an equal right to take part in the formation of a shared conviction, so that each individual can equally assent

41. This distinction between procedural fairness and a just decision is already found in BRIAN BARRY, POLITICAL ARGUMENT ch. 6 (1965). The distinction also underlies a recent criticism of Habermas similar to the one I am making here. See David Ingram, The Limits and Possibilities of Discourse Ethics in Democratic Theory, 21 POL. THEORY 294 (1993).

42. This point was made early-on by the American Legal Realists. See KARL N. LLEWELLYN, THE COMMON LAW TRADITION: DECIDING APPEALS (1960). John Elster offers an extended set of arguments for this point, especially in regard to the estimation of future consequences of policy decisions and political and social reforms. See ELSTER, supra note 34; see also JOHN RAWLS, POLITICAL LIBERALISM 54–58 (1993) (discussion of the "burdens of judgment"); Thomas McCarthy, Legitimacy and Diversity: Dialectical Reflections on Analytical Distinctions, 17 CARDOZO L. REV. 1083 (1996).

43. One might also add here that the fallible character of rational discourse requires that, if possible, decisions be open to review and revision. Note too that the manner in which, or even whether, equal opportunity is present may depend on the type of procedure.

to the substantive outcome on the basis of personal insight into its correctness. In real discourse, however, there may not be a shared conviction at the end of the day, though there may be a vote in which each person casts one ballot. This latter form of equality, which governs decision making proper, is typically defined as "equal power over outcomes" (i.e., an equal chance to influence the outcome).[44] However, the notion of power is subject to serious ambiguities connected with contingencies of group composition and context.[45] Hence, an adequate elaboration of equal opportunity in decision making should refer, not just to influence on outcome, but also to an idea of solidaristic inclusion built on equal respect for each citizen. From this standpoint, what matters is that the terms of participation in a procedure "should convey a communal acknowledgment of equal individual worth."[46]

If this assertion is on track, then fair proceduralization exhibits a solidaristic, volitional aspect of law. This aspect of legal procedure could partly explain compliance by parties who continue to disagree with the justice of a given substantive outcome. That is, inasmuch as a procedure expresses a recognition of one's equal status as a citizen regardless of how insightful one's judgment on a given issue, participation in the procedure can reinforce group solidarity, at least to some degree. This, in turn, could foster compliance with unfavorable outcomes. At the least, it could make losing parties more reluctant to break laws or to refuse to cooperate with legal-political programs enacted over their dissent.[47] This is not to say that critique and civil protest are impossible, but only to point out that such actions may involve solidarity costs in addition to the costs of facing legal sanctions.[48] In any case, one would have a source of compliance that involves more than sanctioned coercion but is not yet the rationally motivated compliance based on insight into the normative validity of a law.

In centering legitimacy so exclusively on the discourse principle, Habermas risks neglecting the intrinsic procedural fairness in law and its potential contribution to solidarity and compliance. Moreover, if such fairness can be considered a factor in legitimacy, then it allows one to define, at least analytically, exactly how idealized discourses and fair legal procedures in-

---

44. *See* BEITZ, *supra* note 16, at 4.

45. *See id.* at 4–17; *see also* Jones, *supra* note 16, at 163–72.

46. BEITZ, *supra* note 16, at 110. Ronald Dworkin seems to have a similar idea in mind when he discusses the "fundamental right [of citizens] to equal concern and respect." RONALD DWORKIN, TAKING RIGHTS SERIOUSLY 266, 278 (1977).

47. *See* ELSTER, *supra* note 34, at 203. For the "group value" theory of procedural-fairness effects suggested by this account, see E. ALLAN LIND & TOM R. TYLER, THE SOCIAL PSYCHOLOGY OF PROCEDURAL JUSTICE 230–40 (1988).

48. Habermas considers the latter costs an important part of civil disobedience. *See* JÜRGEN HABERMAS, *Ziviler Ungehorsam—Testfall für den demokratischen Rechtsstaat, in* DIE NEUE UNÜBERSICHTLICHKEIT: KLEINE POLITISCHE SCHRIFTEN V 90 (1985).

terpenetrate in such a way that both discursive rationality and the legal form contribute to the legitimacy of law. Inasmuch as the issues at stake in legal-political discourse have pragmatic, moral, and ethical components, their discussion is subject to the idealized requirements of rational argumentation processes. To this extent, legal-political discourses are set up to allow such argumentation to take place in order to foster the participants' insightful judgment on the matter at hand. But rational judgment formation is not enough: exactly where and how a given legal procedure structures and ultimately cuts off discourse for the sake of a definite decision is subject to the parity requirements of fair proceduralization. To this extent, legal-political decision making is geared to reach binding decisions in a manner that maintains solidarity through the mutual recognition of the equal worth of both winners and losers.

This suggests that an adequate explanation of the legitimacy of law must include both moments. A suitable formulation of the democratic principle, therefore, must be neutral to the distinction between rational justification and fair decision making. This means the democratic principle cannot be formulated in terms of unanimity—the discourse principle cannot acquire institutional form without being fundamentally affected. As it stands, Habermas's democratic principle reflects an overemphasis on discourse. How to correct this problem raises further questions, of course, which cannot be addressed here. But the solidaristic aspect of procedural fairness suggests that a good start would involve further examining the law from the standpoint of solidarity in decision processes and group cohesion. If the brief remarks in this reflection are on the mark, then the modern rule of law presupposes something like a rational solidarity having both discursive and volitional sides. While not denying this duality, Habermas has primarily developed the discursive aspects of law and politics—indeed, he has elaborated the importance and ramifications of discourse to a remarkable degree. Given the growing challenges that pluralist democracies face today, his contribution deserves an interdisciplinary follow-up of equal proportions.

THIRTEEN

Short-Circuit

A Critique of Habermas's Understanding of Law, Politics, and Economic Life

*William E. Forbath**

This work by Jürgen Habermas asks important questions and refuses easy answers. Is democracy conceivable in today's advanced societies? If so, what understandings of law and constitutionalism might best support it?

In addressing these questions, Habermas has read deeply in contemporary American constitutional scholarship but his thinking seems untouched by an earlier moment in American legal thought: the breakthroughs of Legal Realism, and, specifically, Realism's account of the relations between state and society, and law and the economy. This essay suggests that the insights of Realists and kindred thinkers among economists, historians, and social theorists—about the nature of market and property relations, about the role of law and politics in constituting economic life, and, above all, about the variousness of plausible institutional arrangements—give the lie to key assumptions Habermas makes about economic life.

Habermas hews to a sophisticated, contemporary version of the view that the economy is a self-regulating system, which must be sealed off from the intrusions of the polity or else be derailed. He adopts this view from systems theory, and embraces it, perhaps, because it seems a sober alternative to the romantic illusions of Marxists and many radical democrats regarding economic affairs and the dismal failures of the socialist economies of the former Soviet Union and Eastern Europe. But the view Habermas has adopted has its own illusions, and its illusions weaken his important contribution to democratic and constitutional theory.

Habermas has conceived his constitutional machinery so that governmental power must be generated "from below," by an active citizenry. No

*Professor of Law, University of California, Los Angeles.

other source will do. Yet, I will argue, Habermas's rigidly dichotomous understanding of "politics" versus "economics," and "politics" versus "administration," leads him to ban democratic processes and participation from aspects of governance that might engage ordinary citizens in the ongoing fashion his machinery demands. Moreover, Habermas's ban clashes with his own awareness that insulating public administration and economic life and decision making from democratic "interference" readily leads to a demobilized, passive citizenry.

Thus, Habermas finds himself in the grip of contradictions. Sensing that his machinery is bound to stall, Habermas violates his own injunctions. He sternly excludes the unruly norms and practices of democracy from the economic realm; then, at critical points, he smuggles them back in. The result is a deeply ambiguous and ambivalent account of the relationship between democratic principles, practices, and public spheres on the one hand, and the realms of the economy and public administration on the other. Yet these are the very worlds that law, in Habermas's view, must bridge, the very relations law must structure and meditate.

I.

Habermas believes that the object of constitutional government is to create and sustain the institutional conditions for what the "republicans" in contemporary American constitutional scholarship call deliberative democracy, or what Habermas calls "democratic opinion- and will-formation."[1] He embraces not only enhanced deliberative processes but a robust, substantive conception of political equality, broad participation by a free and equal citizenry, and an expanded domain for democratic governance.

However, Habermas parts company with the republicans and joins forces with their foes, the "interest group liberals," in rejecting what he regards as the republicans' nostalgia for the polis—their deluded notion that "a regenerated citizenry can, in the forms of a decentralized self-governance, (once again) appropriate bureaucratically alienated state power."[2] Likewise, he rejects the characteristic radical republican's (and radical democrat's) conviction that political democracy requires that democratic principles play a significant part in the workplace and broader economy.

Instead, Habermas holds that contemporary society is far too complex, far too "functionally differentiated," for such views to wash. The "steering mechanisms" and "objective purposiveness" of the economy and the administrative state properly stand apart from democratic processes or

1. JÜRGEN HABERMAS, BETWEEN FACTS AND NORMS: CONTRIBUTIONS TO A DISCOURSE THEORY OF LAW AND DEMOCRACY 298 (William Rehg trans., 1996).
2. *Id.* at 297.

LAW, ETHICS, AND DEMOCRACY

controls. But whereas the liberals hold out relatively weak normative and practical expectations regarding the citizenry's democratic will-formation, for Habermas, this remains the engine of the constitutional state. Keeping the engine running seems implausible without forms of democratic, citizenly involvement in economic and administrative affairs that run afoul of Habermas's boundaries between polity and economy, and polity and administration. As a consequence, a deep ambivalence runs through this work, one that impedes it from helping to answer the very questions, one imagines, Habermas hopes to illuminate: what forms of representative democracy, public administration, and secondary associations do we need today?

II.

In characterizing this ambivalence, allow me, as an American historian by training, to introduce two Habermases; one who echoes the great Federalist, Alexander Hamilton, the other who resembles the obscure, but recently much-celebrated William Manning, a Massachusetts farmer and profound democratic critic of the Federalists' outlook and handiwork.[3]

I begin with the Hamiltonian Habermas, and with Hamilton's famous answer to the argument that the new Constitution—with its tacit, but, for both Hamilton and his critics, unmistakable inauguration of judicial review—trammeled the principle of popular sovereignty.[4] Not a bit, Hamilton replied. What was afoot was not a limit on the democratic impulse but an expression of it. The Constitution is both the founding and also the self-limiting act of the sovereign people, who thereby have willed constitutional limits upon themselves and their own legislators.

Henceforth, it is not for the people's representatives to interpret those constitutional limits; that would render them "superior to the people themselves." No, the courts, the legal elite, would interpret and enforce those limits in the name of the people's sovereign will, enshrined in the constitutional text.

There was grandeur and insight in this high Federalist rendering of the idea of popularly enacted precommitments. There also was deceit, because, of course, limiting the democratic impulse of the ordinary citizenry was very much at the heart of Hamilton's enterprise. Having acted in their sovereign capacity by ratifying the new Constitution, the citizenry,

3. See generally THE KEY OF LIBERTY: THE LIFE AND DEMOCRATIC WRITINGS OF WILLIAM MANNING, "A LABORER," 1747–1814 (Michael Merrill & Sean Wilentz eds., 1993); see also CHRISTOPHER L. TOMLINS, LAW, LABOR, AND IDEOLOGY IN THE EARLY AMERICAN REPUBLIC 1–8 (1993).
4. See THE FEDERALIST No. 78 (Alexander Hamilton) (Issac Kramnick ed., 1987).

in Hamilton's view, were to be encouraged, by various constitutional and other means, to leave the business of government to their betters.

It is in his way of reconciling and entwining the citizenry's "democratic action" with the "system of rights" as constitutional limits that Habermas first echoes Hamilton. The citizenry makes an "originary use" of its capacity for democratic action in a way that limits future actions, in the name of popular sovereignty.[5]

The question arises, however: what sustains the democratic legitimacy of this scheme once the founding moment of constitution making passes? Habermas has a ready answer, and one that seemingly puts him at a great distance from Hamilton's deep mistrust of popular political action. For Habermas, the original use of civic automony for democratic constitution making must aim to secure the conditions for ongoing civic autonomy. Moreover, for him, the "paradoxical emergence of legitimacy from legality" is assured only insofar as the legal order is constituted as a "circular process that continuously feeds back" into the arena of citizenly engagement and debate.

Thus, for Habermas legitimate lawmaking is always simultaneously a process of generating communicative power.[6] "Strictly speaking," he explains, communicative power "springs from the interactions among legally institutionalized will-formation [i.e., procedures of elections and legislative decision making] and culturally mobilized publics"[7] in widely diversified public spheres.[8] Thus forged, law is "the medium through which communicative power is translated into administrative power."[9] But this does not end the role of communicative power in the process. The administrative system itself must somehow be "tied to the lawmaking communicative power" so that administrative power cannot reproduce itself, but "only be permitted to regenerate [itself] from the conversion of communicative power."[10] This requirement aims at insulating the administrative system from "illegitimate interventions of social power, (i.e., of the factual strength of privileged interests to assert themselves)."[11]

For Habermas, then, not only lawmaking but goverance in its ongoing, administrative aspect must draw its energy and authority from the citizenly generation of communicative power. This bold vision would seem to call

5. *See* HABERMAS, *supra* note 1, at 128.
6. *See id.* at 147–52, on the "*interpenetration of discursive law-making and communicative power-formation.*" *Id.* at 151.
7. *Id.* at 301.
8. *See id.* at 365.
9. *Id.* at 150.
10. *Id.*
11. *Id.*

for a vast increase in the amount of "communicative power" presently flowing through this or any other contemporary democracy. As Habermas points out, communicative power is generated only "from below," only from mobilized citizenries. Thus, his vision seems to demand a substantial renovation of our existing public spheres, and the creation of many new spaces and institutional forms for citizenly engagement in the processes of lawmaking and governance.

Habermas derives the key concept of "communicative power" from Hannah Arendt.[12] He first elaborated the concept in a 1977 essay entitled, *Hannah Arendt's Communications Concept of Power.*[13] There Habermas sketches the significance of Arendt's concept in relation to other understandings of power; he also highlights some shortcomings of Arendt's own formulation of the idea.

Arendt insisted on rescuing the public sphere from the intrusion of social and economic affairs. Social welfare and economic life, in her view, were realms of technical problems with technical solutions, and their intrusion in the polity necessarily frustrated every attempt at a politically active public realm. In response, Habermas assailed Arendt's "rigid dichotomies" between "freedom and welfare," and between "political-practical activity and production"; he chided her for engendering a politics "cleansed" of social and economic issues, an "institutionalization of public liberty which is independent of the organization of public wealth."[14]

Yet, on one reading of this and other recent work by Habermas, he has done something similar to Arendt—with unhappy consequences for the business of generating communicative power. I have in mind Habermas's familiar scheme of the lifeworld and the world of systems. The lifeworld is the site of the public sphere, while the systems-world is comprised of the economy and the administrative state. Habermas is at pains to enjoin any intervention from the former into the latter. Such intervention, or "meddling," would only interfere with the systems' self-steering mechanisms, the market dynamics of the economy, and the "power code" of the administrative state.[15]

Far from advocating modes of democratic participation in economic or administrative affairs, Habermas speaks defensively—in terms of guarding the lifeworld and, with it, the public sphere from colonization by the systems. He advocates the creation of "sensors" to detect intrusions on the

12. *See* HANNAH ARENDT, THE HUMAN CONDITION (1958).
13. Jürgen Habermas, *Hannah Arendt's Communications Concept of Power,* 44 SOC. RES. 3 (1977) [hereinafter *Hannah Arendt's Communications*].
14. *Id.* at 15.
15. HABERMAS, *supra* note 1, at 150.

systems' part; and continuing the electronics metaphor, he depicts law as a "step-up transformer" to concentrate and carry to the systems the "weak impulses" of the communicative activity of the public sphere.

At least to someone from Los Angeles, "sensors" evokes the eerie world of complex alarm systems, and this anxious metaphor seems to capture an important strand of Habermas's thought, as does the sharp anxiety about citizens' meddling with the putative hard-wiring or "power codes" and "steering media" of the economic and administrative systems.

Although the metaphors differ, these sentiments supply a second echo of Alexander Hamilton, who was nothing if not adamant about keeping the *demos* away from regulating commerce or meddling in state administration. He too saw nothing but dangerous regression if the citizenry were allowed to get their hands on the delicate machinery of commerce and government.

However, Habermas's constitutional vision, unlike Hamilton's, aims at mobilizing the democratic energies of citizens rather than neutralizing them. Yet, his theory seems to cordon off many of the key arenas that might enlist those energies. It is hard to imagine a flourishing Habermasian republic if decisions about the allocation of social resources, the administration of public agencies, as well as the everyday world of work and exchange remain organized in ways that would not only differ from the constitution's principles, but also would promise to limit their influence and subvert his operation.[16]

III.

Habermas recognizes that mobilized, engaged publics "find a basis in the associations of a civil society."[17] Not surprisingly, he insists on keeping these secondary associations separate and distinct "from both state and economy alike."[18] Unfortunately, this preoccupation with separation, mediation, and boundaries leads him to overlook much of what we know about the conditions in which such associations actually work in the manner Habermas envisions: countering the power of concentrated interests and privileged elites by enabling broader-based groups of ordinary people to deliberate and act in a citizenly fashion.

Obviously, secondary associations fail in this task when they are mere creatures of the state, like the labor organizations of communist and fascist

---

16. *See* ROBERT A. DAHL, A PREFACE TO ECONOMIC DEMOCRACY (1985); CAROLE PATEMAN, PARTICIPATION AND DEMOCRATIC THEORY (1970); Philip Green, *Considerations on the Democratic Division of Labor,* 12 POL. & SOC'Y 445 (1983).

17. HABERMAS, *supra* note 1, at 301.

18. *Id.*

regimes; or mere creatures of dominant economic institutions, like many company unions of American corporations in the 1920s. But Habermas is wrong in assuming that simple autonomy is sufficient.

Such associations work when their members experience themselves acting not only democratically but also efficaciously. Efficacy is essential for two reasons. First, to paraphrase Oscar Wilde on the topic of socialism, most people are not predisposed to long meetings devoted to mutual deliberation. However, if the actions that spring from deliberation bear some fruit, if they significantly affect the governance of the realm of life that brings the association's members together, then the associations are vastly more likely to endure over time, enlisting the energies and educating the desires of their constituents. Second, without such efficacy, the associations will not only fail to sustain the kinds of "publics" Habermas envisions, but the "interpenetration" of communicative power-generation, on one hand, and lawmaking and administration, on the other, would be a sham. Citizenly involvement would be window dressing rather than foundational to the business of government.

What then are the conditions for such efficacy? In addition to a substantial degree of autonomy from state or private elite-domination, such associations seem rarely to flourish without some institutional role in the deliberation and bargaining that attend law and policy making, and/or in the ongoing interpretation and implementation of laws and policies.[19] Frequently, forging and sustaining such a role requires affirmative state intervention and support, often in the form of legal mandates. Thus, the association must contend with potentially conflicting imperatives; it needs both state support and autonomy from state domination. Moreover, the broader, more diffuse, or more subjugated the constituencies and potential "publics," the more pressing the need for state support—the more likely it is that the associations are, in some significant measure, artifacts of state action.[20]

As such, the associations are hopelessly tainted from Habermas's perspective. Neither in genesis nor in operation are they "quite distinct from both state and economy."[21] But this impurity may stem from the rigid dichotomies of Habermas's theory rather than deficiencies in the associations.

---

19. See generally Joshua Cohen & Joel Rogers, Secondary Associations and Democratic Governance, 20 POL. & SOC'Y 393 (1992). For a comparative study touching on these issues, see William E. Forbath, Courts, Constitutions, and Labor Politics in England and America: A Study of the Constitutive Power of Law, 16 LAW & SOC. INQUIRY 1 (1991).

20. See Cohen & Rogers, supra note 19; Forbath, supra note 19.

21. HABERMAS, supra note 1, at 301.

IV.

From Habermas's perspective, the communicative and practical political activities of citizens have no proper place in the economic or administrative systems. To counter Habermas, it will not do to simply point out that without a decent purchase on those systems the citizenly associations he prizes would wither. And it will not do simply to point out that Habermas's systems-theoretic perspective has introduced into his thinking the same "rigid dichotomies" for which he chided Arendt. It will not do because these objections are bootless if the economic and administrative systems are hardwired in fact, as they are in Habermas's theory. If the Hamiltonian Habermas is right, then warning sensors and transmitters of weak impulses are the best we can hope for.

But the economic order is neither hard-wired nor "self-regulating" in the manner Habermas assumes.[22] That is the burden of a diverse body of learning that ranges from the work of institutional economists like Albert Hirschman and Geoffrey Hodgson,[23] to sociologists and social theorists like Amitai Etzioni[24] on one hand and Charles Sabel[25] and Roberto Unger[26] on

22. Limitations of space will prevent me from pursuing a parallel line of argument with respect to the adminstrative or bureaucratic order of the state. There is, however, a well-known literature making the case. *See, e.g.,* JOEL F. HANDLER, DOWN FROM BUREAUCRACY (1996); JOEL F. HANDLER, LAW AND THE SEARCH FOR COMMUNITY (1990); JANE J. MANSBRIDGE, BEYOND ADVERSARY DEMOCRACY (1980).

23. *See* ALBERT O. HIRSCHMAN, RIVAL VIEWS OF MARKET SOCIETY AND OTHER RECENT ESSAYS (1986); GEOFFREY HODGSON, ECONOMICS AND INSTITUTIONS: A MANIFESTO FOR A MODERN INSTITUTIONAL ECONOMICS (1988); Albert O. Hirschman, *Against Parsimony: Three Easy Ways of Complicating Some Categories of Economic Discourse,* 74 AM. ECON. REV. 89 (1984); *see also* Mark Granovetter, *Economic Action and Social Structure: The Problem of Embeddedness,* 91 AM. J. SOC. 481 (1985).

24. *See* AMITAI ETZIONI, THE MORAL DIMENSION: TOWARD A NEW ECONOMICS (1988); *see also* FRED BLOCK, POSTINDUSTRIAL POSSIBILITIES: A CRITIQUE OF ECONOMIC DISCOURSE (1990) [hereinafter BLOCK, POSTINDUSTRIAL POSSIBILITIES]; FRED BLOCK, REVISING STATE THEORY: ESSAYS IN POLITICS AND POSTINDUSTRIALISM (1987); CLAUS OFFE, DISORGANIZED CAPITALISM: CONTEMPORARY TRANSFORMATIONS OF WORK AND POLITICS (1985).

25. *See* MICHAEL J. PIORE & CHARLES F. SABEL, THE SECOND INDUSTRIAL DIVIDE: POSSIBILITIES FOR PROSPERITY (1984); CHARLES F. SABEL & JONATHAN ZEITLIN, WORLDS OF POSSIBILITY: FLEXIBILITY AND MASS PRODUCTION IN WESTERN INDUSTRIALIZATION (1996) [hereinafter SABEL & ZEITLIN, WORLDS OF POSSIBILITY]; CHARLES F. SABEL, WORK AND POLITICS: THE DIVISION OF LABOR IN INDUSTRY (1982) [hereinafter SABEL, WORK AND POLITICS]; Charles F. Sabel & Jonathan Zeitlin, *Historical Alternatives to Mass Production: Politics, Markets and Technology in Nineteenth-Century Industrialization,* 108 PAST & PRESENT 133 (1985).

26. *See generally* ROBERTO M. UNGER, FALSE NECESSITY: ANTI-NECESSITARIAN SOCIAL THEORY IN THE SERVICE OF RADICAL DEMOCRACY, (1987) [hereinafter UNGER, FALSE NECESSITY]; ROBERTO M. UNGER, PLASTICITY INTO POWER: COMPARATIVE HISTORICAL STUDIES ON THE INSTITUTIONAL CONDITIONS OF ECONOMIC AND MILITARY SUCCESS (1987).

the other, as well as to legal theorists in the Realist tradition. Most familiar to Habermas's readers in American law schools are the many classic arguments by Realists and their heirs in Critical Legal Studies that "there is no such thing as the free market" or a self-regulating market order. All markets, in this account, are political artifacts, based on and constituted by highly plastic cultural norms and legal rules. If the outcomes of encounters and clashes among market actors and all of their various efforts at competition and cooperation appear determined from somewhere else—by a "system logic" which largely constrains choices and dictates winners and losers—that is both true and untrue.

It is true, because entrenched institutional and imaginative contexts do constrain ordinary actions and everyday conflicts in the market as elsewhere, notwithstanding the plasticity of the norms and rules that regulate them. It is untrue, because the contexts are never immune from revision; alternative institutional and imaginative orderings are always present in the margins of conventional doctrines and conventional forms of work, enterprise, and commerce.[27] Moreover, the constraints are messy; no "system logic" determines when routine conflicts and conundrums—over, for example, the application of a given rule or norm—engender transformative opportunities.

At one level this Realist perspective is old news to Habermas as much as anyone else. Yet, with the systems theorists as well as neoclassical economists, Habermas seems to assume something like this: it is true that any market system presupposes a set of property rules or entitlements defining ownership and contract rules defining the ground rules for bargaining; still, the legal concepts of property and contractual exchange are reasonably well-defined and uncontroversial. Therefore, conceding that all markets are structured by legal rules comprising a regulatory regime, nevertheless, there exists only a certain well-bounded range of such possible "regulatory" regimes that fulfill the underlying criteria of autonomy and efficiency for which the opposition between market versus governmental ordering of economic life is a convenient, if somewhat misleading, shorthand. Within this range fall economic systems that we call market systems; outside fall those that are run according to other criteria, spurning efficiency in favor of, for example, worker democracy or state planning.

This more elaborate version of the idea of a self-regulating market system seems to be the one to which Habermas subscribes. And it is this version that today's Neo-Realists, critical legal scholars like Duncan Kennedy and Karl Klare, as well as kindred social theorists like Sabel, Unger, and Block,

---

27. *See* UNGER, FALSE NECESSITY, *supra* note 26; *see also* Duncan Kennedy, *Form and Substance in Private Law Adjudication*, 89 HARV. L. REV. 1685 (1976).

have assailed.[28] One burden of their work has been to suggest that conservatives, liberals, and radicals alike have failed to appreciate the extent to which market and property relations can be radically reorganized without sacrificing freedom or efficiency.

Radicals, for their part, have been preoccupied with the ways that inherited institutional arrangements of economic life produce hierarchies and inequalities. Confusing these arrangements with "markets" and "private property" as such, radicals have reached for distant and vague solutions that inspire well-deserved skepticism—and that leave intact the idea (shared by conservatives and liberals) that the Soviet-style socialist-bureaucratic or the various worker-ownership models are the only real alternatives radicals have to offer to the established economic regimes. I suspect that this kind of thinking, on the part of fellow leftists, has contributed to Habermas's embrace of the systems-theory outlook regarding the economy.

The Neo-Realists have followed a different path. First, they have shown in painstaking detail that far from being reasonably self-defining, the legal concepts of property and contract leave open a great variety of possible sets of rights and ground rules, each with distinctive distributive consequences. One may believe that markets, as decentralized arenas of exchange and coordination, are indispensable to freedom and efficiency, and still one must choose among an indefinitely wide range of alternative sets of rules and rights, and of alternative arrangements for decentralized production and exchange. Which of them are most autonomy enhancing, or most conducive to democracy, or most likely to promote economic growth? These are empirical questions that cannot be answered by the mere analysis of the concepts of a market economy or a private order.

Of course, it is not only in choosing among alternate sets of background bargaining rules and ownership rights that substantive value choices and questions of practical judgment arise. The genius of the Realists and their heirs has been in demonstrating that such choices inevitably arise in interpreting and applying a particular right or rule to a particular case. Critical legal scholars have shown, again and again, the ways that routine conflicts over the meaning and application of particular rules within a given institutional context are potentially linked to more radical conflicts about the context and array of rights and rules (and relationships and practices) comprising it. For these reasons, insulating the economic order from democratic decision making means excluding a world of political choices from the very processes that Habermas insists should govern such choices.

Of course, expanding the freedom to experiment with the institutional arrangements for production and exchange seems to require subjecting

28. *See* BLOCK, POSTINDUSTRIAL POSSIBILITIES, *supra* note 24, at 48.

capital allocation to more explicit collective deliberation and control. This seems potentially disastrous, for it threatens to undo the principle of market decentralization, which, I have claimed, Habermas and the Neo-Realists share in common. But there are many ways to achieve accountability of capital without abandoning market decentralization, and many institutional forms that accountability and market relations can assume.[29]

Thus, historians and political economists working in this anti-necessitarian vein have demonstrated that the particular institutional forms which capital accumulation and allocation have assumed are not the upshot of any developmental logic inherent in the extension of markets or the creation of new technologies. Rather, they emerged out of a series of practical political contests among contending groups with competing visions of the nation's industrial development, groups with very different, but often equally plausible—and more or less democratic—accounts of the appropriate institutional ordering of its markets in goods, labor, and capital.[30]

Further, contemporary neo-Realists have shown that beginning with an overarching commitment to efficiency and individual and group self-determination, it is illogical to favor "market autonomy" in the abstract. There is, for example, as Klare and others have shown, no necessary conflict between the principles of efficiency and free bargaining on one hand, and, on the other, such democratizing experiments as vigorous, egalitarian reconstruction of labor-market institutions aimed at enhancing workplace participation and diminishing the contrast between task-defining and task-executing jobs, which turns the workplace into a permanent countermodel to the exercise of democratic citizenship.[31]

These arguments by legal scholars find support in comparative studies

29. *See generally* MARKETS AND DEMOCRACY: PARTICIPATION, ACCOUNTABILITY AND EFFICIENCY (Samuel Bowles et al. eds., 1993); A FOURTH WAY?: PRIVATIZATION, PROPERTY, AND THE EMERGENCE OF NEW MARKER ECONOMIES (Gregory S. Alexander & Grażyna Skapska eds., 1994); PATHWAYS TO INDUSTRIALIZATION AND REGIONAL DEVELOPMENT (Michael Storper & Allen Scott eds., 1992); *see also* DAVID HELD, DEMOCRACY AND THE GLOBAL ORDERS FROM THE MODERN STATE TO COSMOPOLITAN GOVERNANCE 239–66 (1995); BLOCK, POSTINDUSTRIAL POSSIBILITIES, *supra* note 24, at 155–218; UNGER, FALSE NECESSITY, *supra* note 26, at 480–535.

30. *See, e.g.,* SABEL & ZEITLIN, WORLDS OF POSSIBILITY, *supra* note 25; MARK J. ROE, STRONG MANAGERS, WEAK OWNERS: THE POLITICAL ROOTS OF AMERICAN CORPORATE FINANCE (1996); GERALD BERK, ALTERNATE TRACKS: THE CONSTITUTION OF AMERICAN INDUSTRIAL ORDER, 1865–1917 (1994); PHILIP SCRANTON, FIGURED TAPESTRY: PRODUCTION, MARKETS, AND POWER IN PHILADELPHIA TEXTILES, 1885–1941 (1989); William Forbath, The "Curse of Bigness" Revisited: The Anti-Monopoly Alternative to Corporate Capitalism (unpublished manuscript on file with the *Cardozo Law Review*).

31. *See* Mark Barenberg, *Democracy and Domination in the Law of Workplace Cooperation: From Bureaucratic to Flexible Production,* 94 COLUM. L. REV. 753 (1994); Alan Hyde, *In Defense of Employee Ownership,* 67 CHI.-KENT L. REV. 159 (1991); Karl E. Klare, *Workplace Democracy & Market Reconstruction: An Agenda for Legal Reform,* 38 CATH. U. L. REV. 1 (1988).

that reveal the actual diversity of past and present forms of workplace and industrial organization.[32] Both the theorists and the empirical scholarship have gone some distance toward showing that the possible forms and arrangements of economic life are simply not constrained by the "logic" of markets or of technical development in the fashion that Habermas assumes. The variety of possible forms, the room for democratization, and ongoing contest and revision, are much greater than he allows.

V.

At this point, another reading of Habermas beckons. Less clearly outlined than the systems-theoretic/Hamiltonian version, Habermas as William Manning flickers into view. Manning, as I mentioned, was a Massachusetts farmer and representative radical of the early Republic—a local tribune of a constitutional order in which legislatures retained greater powers and the "people," acting in their capacity as citizens, could have had a larger part in making decisions, shaping the course of commerce and economic development as part of government and not simply as individual buyers and sellers.

By "Habermas as Manning" I mean to point to ideas and suggestions of Habermas's that seem thoroughly at odds with his own general framework. These ideas flaunt the boundaries between polity, economy, and administration, in favor of a more pragmatic and pluralist understanding of these relationships. Here, we will find that democratic principles and practices quietly invade the economic and administrative realms, and authority over spheres of social and economic life is more variously and democratically organized than the general framework allows.

Perhaps most striking is a passage from chapter seven,[33] which contains one of the book's few references to social class and the obstacles which class inequalities pose to political equality.[34] Immediately before the passage in question, Habermas has laid out certain key distinctions between different aspects of the public sphere. He distinguishes between the "procedurally regulated" public spheres of parliamentary and lawmaking bodies, and the "informal" or "general" public sphere, "unregulated . . . [and] borne by the general public of citizens."[35] It is the latter sphere and the associational life animating it that supply the opinions out of which democratically constituted "opinion- and will-formation" must proceed. However, Habermas ob-

---

32. *See, e.g.,* SABEL, WORK AND POLITICS, *supra* note 25; SABEL & ZEITLIN, WORLDS OF POSSIBILITY, *supra* note 25; PIORE & SABEL, *supra* note 25.
33. *See* HABERMAS, *supra* note 1, at 307–08.
34. *See id.*
35. *Id.* at 307.

serves that this sphere is vulnerable to "the repressive and exclusionary effects of unequally distributed social power . . . and [the] systematically distorted communication"[36] that unequal social power inevitably produces. Therefore, he goes on, the general public sphere must rest on a society "that has emerged from the confines of class and thrown off the millennia-old shackles of social stratification and exploitation."[37] Otherwise, the public sphere and "equal rights of citizenship" will lack a "societal basis."[38]

Indeed! Having primly roped off the economy from the unruly norms and practices of democratic citizenship, Habermas seems to have smuggled these norms and practices back in with this eloquent but delphic remark. But who knows? It is odd for a thinker as systematic as Habermas to introduce without explanation or elaboration a notion as complex and contested as that of the classless society, particularly when the notion is deemed a necessary condition for the form of politics and lawmaking the entire book seeks to delineate.

What might Habermas mean by a society "that has emerged from the confines of class" and "social stratification"? Since this imagined society is invoked as a needed basis for equal citizenship, it is possible he has in mind something like Thomas H. Marshall's influential notion that "social rights" to housing, health care, education, and a decent subsistence—in other words, a full-blown welfare state—is necessary to "complete" or actualize the status of citizenship that is only incompletely forged by equal civil and political rights. Marshall recognized that securing these "social rights" would not abolish all social and economic inequalities. However, he held that not all inequalities deprive individuals of full membership in the political community. To be impoverished and ill-educated is to lack equal standing in the polity; to earn less than the next person is not.

If this is what Habermas has in mind when he speaks of unfettering citizenship from the confines of a class-bound society, then his injunction against democratizing the economy or the administrative state apparatus may remain relatively intact. But he will have purchased this intactness at the cost of ignoring a whole world of arguments and evidence, with which he is quite familiar,[39] to the effect that welfare provision under the auspices of state bureaucracies produces dependency and clientelism, leading to a second-class, rather than equal citizenship. Introducing democratic and

36. *Id.* at 307–08.
37. *Id.* at 308.
38. *Id.*
39. *See generally* JÜRGEN HABERMAS, LEGITIMATION CRISIS (Thomas McCarthy trans., 1975); Jürgen Habermas, *The New Obscurity: The Crisis of the Welfare State and the Exhaustion of Utopian Energies,* 12 PHIL. & SOC. CRITICISM 1 (1986).

participatory norms and practices into welfare administration is a frequently championed remedy.

But that remedy would violate Habermas's injunction. In any case, it is hard to imagine that Habermas's language—"casting off millennia-old shackles"—is meant to evoke nothing more epoch-making than a generous welfare state, as desirable as such a state might be.

It is also hard to imagine that, as distant as Habermas is from classical Marxism, he would stray so far as to divorce the idea of class from questions of power over work, industry, and the accumulation and deployment of capital. A more robust notion of class seems implicit in the link Habermas makes between class-bound society and those asymmetries of social power that enable some social groups (presumably those with great advantages in the control of strategic resources) to distort the free flow of communication in the public sphere. But if that is true, then Habermas surely has succeeded in quietly smuggling democratic norms and practices into the heart of the economic order.

There is more substantial textual evidence to support this smuggling charge than the delphic reference to classlessness. I have in mind the discussion of bargaining that occurs in chapter four.[40]

Bargaining is one of the forms of communication for which Habermas has prescribed procedural protocols. No less than with moral and political debate, the terms of bargaining must observe their distinct protocols if the republic is to lay claim to a rationally forged political will. Bargaining norms, in other words, have constitutional salience.

The norms are stringent. They require regulation sufficient to ensure that "all the relevant interests are given equal consideration and all parties are furnished with equal power."[41] Regulation must insure against, inter alia, outcomes in which "exploited parties . . . contribute more to the cooperative effort than they gain from it."[42]

On what terrains are these norms of inclusiveness and equal bargaining power meant to operate? It is possible to read chapter four's discussion of bargaining to suggest that the norms must apply wherever the terms of market and property relations are hammered out. Certainly, Habermas seems to envision a multiplicity of such arenas of regulated bargaining outside the public political sphere.

But if that is the case then I am unwarranted in chiding Habermas for seeking to rest the world of work and exchange on principles hostile to those of the democratic constitution. To the contrary, Habermas seems to

40. *See* HABERMAS, *supra* note 1, at ch. 4.
41. *Id.* at 177.
42. *Id.* at 166.

have gone some way toward identifying the distinctive procedural or discursive protocols necessary to rest that world on principles harmonious with his constitutional vision.

On the other hand, however, if this reading is right, then the conservative Hamiltonian Habermas has every reason to rise up and demand: *What has become of my sober injunction against political interventions from the lifeworld into the self-steering system of the economy? There is no limit to the principle of equal bargaining power short of pervasive public-political meddling in economic relations!*

In the end, the character of Habermas's constitutional vision will remain clouded until he sets out the relationship between politics and economic life in terms other than the various electronics metaphors he finds so congenial, and I so disturbing. They disturb because they stand for an unjustifiably limited and confining conception of that relationship. They are dispiriting too, because they convey so well how recent experience has short-circuited critical thinking, even on the part of this great critical theorist.

More than once during this conference Habermas commented on the question of economic democracy as though the failure of socialism and the success of the American economy defined the limits of the possible. This familiar outlook probably helped prompt Habermas's embrace of systems theory's sophisticated brand of dogmatic liberal political economy.

Perhaps Habermas has read the wrong American law professors. He may have gained something from the quarrels between liberal and republican constitutional theorists. But, the Realists have more salient insights to share.

FOURTEEN

The Retrieval of the Democratic Ethos

Richard J. Bernstein*

For over thirty years I have been a sympathetic although critical reader of Habermas. Initially, I was struck by his nuanced insight into the American pragmatic tradition and his appropriation of the radical democratic ethos of the pragmatic movement. I felt then, and still believe, that Habermas has a more profound and subtle understanding of what is best and most enduring in pragmatism—especially in the thought of Peirce, Dewey, and Mead—than many of my American colleagues. I was also attracted to Habermas for other reasons. He is a dialectical thinker who has the courage to buck fashionable trends—who refuses to get on the bandwagon that celebrates difference, fragmentation, alterity, and singularity, *and* that damns rationality, universality, intersubjectivity, and normative validity. Although frequently caricatured by his opponents, Habermas has never flinched from defending what he takes to be valid in the Enlightenment legacy—the striving for human autonomy and emancipation from all forms of oppression. He has never been cowered by the shrill rhetoric that condemns all forms of humanism. He has resisted the sneer of cynicism that sees only undifferentiated manipulative power everywhere. It would be difficult to name another twentieth century thinker who has taken the idea and practice of public debate and dialogue more seriously. Habermas is constantly engaging his critics—seeking to learn from them, defending his convictions, and modifying and abandoning claims when challenged by good reasons.

Habermas has entitled his new book *Faktizität und Geltung*,[1] but this

---

*Graduate Faculty, New School for Social Research.

1. JÜRGEN HABERMAS, FAKTIZITÄT UND GELTUNG: BEITRÄGE ZUR DISKURSTHEORIE DES RECHTS UND DES DEMOKRATISCHEN RECHTSSTAATS (1992). The English translation of this

might also serve as an appropriate title for his entire corpus. Throughout his career, Habermas has sought to do justice to the poles of facticity and normative validity and to the tensions that exist between these poles. In his more "sociological" mode, he seeks to provide a comprehensive understanding and analysis of the facticity of modern societies in their full complexity. But he has also consistently argued that an adequate account of the development of modern societies *must* do justice to the implicit and explicit claims to legitimacy and normative validity. He has argued—as he does so persuasively in his present book—that no normative theory (whether of democracy, law, morality, or ethics) is adequate unless it can be related to, and integrated with, the sheer facticity of everyday social life.

Finally, but not least importantly, Habermas (like John Dewey) has been an exemplar of the responsibly engaged intellectual. Although he has always insisted upon a rigorous distinction between theoretical research and practical interventions, he has taken strong political stands on a variety of issues related to his democratic convictions. He has been a persistent and relentless critic of those who seek to tone down, modify, suppress, or forget the full horrors and irrationality of the Nazi era.

For these, and many other reasons, I have always found his writings stimulating and thought-provoking. But I must confess that there has also been a growing uneasiness as I have followed the development of his theory of communicative action and rationality, his discourse theory of morality and ethics, and now his discourse theory of law and democracy. Habermas makes use of a complex set of controversial, interrelated, and idealized conceptual distinctions: e.g., the good and the right; procedural and substantial; justification and application; pragmatic, ethical-political, and moral argumentation. The *use* that he makes of these distinctions has become increasingly rigid and stark. Rather than serving to clarify relevant issues, *some* of these hard and fast distinctions actually obscure more than they illuminate. It is the reification of distinctions that are, and ought to be, fluid, open, and flexible that troubles me.

Before I explain and justify my critical reservations, I want to clarify two points so that the purpose of my critical remarks is not misunderstood. (1) I certainly am not objecting to the need to introduce conceptual distinctions in Habermas's discourse theory. Every theory requires the introduction and use of such distinctions. (2) I am not objecting to the fact that Habermas's central conceptual distinctions do not always correspond with the ways in which we speak in everyday contexts or even the way in which

work is JÜRGEN HABERMAS, BETWEEN FACTS AND NORMS: CONTRIBUTIONS TO A DISCOURSE THEORY OF LAW AND DEMOCRACY (William Rehg trans., 1996). Page references within this Article are to this English translation.

other theorists have drawn similar distinctions. For example, I do not believe that any previous thinker has drawn the distinction between moral and ethical-political argumentation in the *precise* way in which Habermas draws this distinction. But there is nothing objectionable about such a stipulative characterization. Expressions such as "moral" and "ethical-political" are terms of art, conceptual idealizations that Habermas introduces to elaborate his discourse theory. My objections will focus on the specific *use* that Habermas makes of these distinctions.

Given the pragmatic and fallibilistic proclivities that I share with Habermas, I do not think there is any "wholesale" way of showing what is dubious about his idealized conceptual distinctions. One must work through them, exposing specific difficulties. This is what I intend to do with two closely related sets of distinctions that stand at the very center of his discourse theory: the distinction between procedural and substantial, and the distinctions among pragmatic, moral, and ethical-political employments of practical reason.

In order to focus my critical examination, I want to state boldly what most troubles me about Habermas's discourse theory of law and democracy: (1) The more Habermas insists upon the "purity" of his discourse theory—i.e., that it is free from any taint or contamination by substantial-ethical commitments—the more formal and empty (in the pejorative sense) it becomes. The theory *fails* to do the work that Habermas claims for it: to provide a rational basis for justifying a theory of deliberative procedural democracy. (2) To the extent that Habermas's discourse theory is rationally persuasive, it is because he implicitly, and sometimes almost explicitly, builds substantial-ethical commitments into his theory. Habermas's discourse theory of law and democracy *presupposes*—to use Habermas's language—a postmetaphysical universal *Sittlichkeit*.

Habermas, as I read him, presents himself as performing the first task—that is, elaborating a discourse theory that does not make any substantial-ethical presuppositions. He sharply distinguishes his theory from those "communitarian" and "republican" theories of democracy that do make substantial-ethical commitments. Despite Habermas's own self-understanding (or rather, self-*mis*understanding!) of his project, I shall argue that what he is doing is closer to the second alternative. He has elaborated a discourse theory that relies on, and presupposes, substantial-ethical considerations. Now, from Habermas's perspective (when he is being most insistent about the "purity" of his theory), if he were "guilty" of making substantial-ethical presuppositions, he would be "guilty" of the fallacy of "vicious" circularity. For such a theory cannot, and should not, presuppose what it sets out to justify. But this is misleading because not all forms of circularity are "vicious." The circularity characteristic of Habermas's discourse theory is analogous to a hermeneutical or interpretive circularity. There is no adequate discourse theory of democratic procedure that avoids presupposing a democratic ethos—an ethos that conditions and affects *how* discussion, debate, and argumentation are *practiced.* Such a democratic substantive ethos does not by itself determine specific norms, values, and decisions. It is procedural precisely because it leaves plenty of space open for substantive disagreement. I am making an even stronger claim. There *cannot* be any discourse theory that does the work that Habermas claims for it *unless* it presupposes the existence of determinate ethical dispositions and virtues. In short, if Habermas were more thoroughly faithful to the pragmatic insight that all social and political theory involves ethical presuppositions and commitments, he would embrace the second alternative, and give up his anxieties about being caught in a vicious circle.

I begin my argument in what may seem to be an oblique manner, but one which will quickly take us to the heart of the matter. At a crucial stage of Habermas's analysis, when he discusses the "core of a genuinely proceduralist understanding of democracy," he writes:

> The point of such an understanding is this: the democratic procedure is institutionalized in discourses and bargaining processes by employing forms of communication that promise that all outcomes reached in conformity with the procedure are reasonable. No one has worked out this view more energetically than John Dewey: "Majority rule, just as majority rule, is as foolish as its critics charge it with being. But it never is *merely* majority rule. . . . 'The means by which a majority comes to be a majority is the more important thing': antecedent debates, modifications of views to meet the opinions of minorities. . . . The essential need, in other words, is the improvement of the methods and conditions of debate, discussion and persuasion."[2]

Habermas's citation and endorsement of this passage from Dewey's *The Public and Its Problems*[3] raises several central issues. It helps to locate a crucial ambiguity in Habermas's understanding of what is "procedural" and how it is distinguished from what is "substantive."

Majority rule—when regulations are specified concerning who is qualified to vote, what counts as a vote, how much of a majority is required—is a procedure that is frequently, but not always, adapted for democratic decision making. Here there is a relatively clear and straightforward sense in which majority rule is a procedure. Majority rule, by itself, does not determine the content or substance of what is decided by majority rule. We might call this a minimalist sense of procedure. But Dewey (and Habermas) thinks that to focus exclusively on majority rule—abstracted from its context—is "foolish." Dewey (and Habermas) is most concerned with "[t]he

---

2. *Id.* at 304 (footnote omitted).
3. JOHN DEWEY, THE PUBLIC AND ITS PROBLEMS (Samuel J. Tildon trans., 1954).

means by which a majority comes to be a majority,"[4] that is, with the public debate, discussion, and persuasion that precede and influence this voting practice. We can, of course, call this complex process procedural—where the actual voting is embedded in this process as a final stage—because, even after the most responsible and enlightened discussion, it is still an open question as to which substantive decisions will be made by majority rule. It is here that the crucial ambiguity arises, for this is a very different sense of procedure. Such a procedure involves substantial-ethical commitments. When Dewey speaks about "debate, discussion and persuasion,"[5] he is *not* simply referring to formal rules of communication, rather his major concern is with the ethos of such debate. For democratic debate, ideally, requires a *willingness* to listen to and *evaluate* the opinions of one's opponents, *respecting* the views of minorities, advancing arguments *in good faith* to support one's convictions, and having the *courage* to change one's mind when confronted with new evidence or better arguments. There is an ethos involved in the *practice* of democratic debate. If such an ethos is violated or disregarded, then debate can become hollow and meaningless. We might even say that the practice of debate in a democratic polity requires the democratic transformation and appropriation of classic virtues: practical wisdom, justice, courage, and moderation. Democratic versions of these virtues are required for engaging in democratic debate.

Dewey wrote *The Public and Its Problems,* in part, because he believed that the sense of community needed for the flourishing of a democratic ethos was in danger of disappearing or being distorted. This is what he meant by the telling phrase, "The Eclipse of the Public."[6] Although Habermas basically agrees with Dewey, he sometimes writes as if we do not need to make any explicit reference to such an ethos in justifying democratic practices. We need only to appeal to the formal-pragmatic conditions of communication. But even Habermas's references to good reasons and "the force of the better argument"[7] presupposes such an ethos where participants debate and agree with each other in good faith. Without such an ethos, democracy is always in danger of becoming a mere sham—a set of mere "formal" procedures without any substantial-ethical content—without much democratic content.[8]

4. HABERMAS, *supra* note 1, at 304.
5. *Id.* (quoting John Dewey).
6. DEWEY, *supra* note 2, at 110–42.
7. 1 JÜRGEN HABERMAS, THE THEORY OF COMMUNICATIVE ACTION 24 (Thomas McCarthy trans., 1984).
8. Habermas does, at times, distinguish what is "substantial-ethical" from the formal procedures of ethical discourses, although I do not think he ever uses the term "procedural-ethical." But even this distinction still obscures the fact that there is a crucial sense in which the

I can highlight my point from a slightly different perspective. We can, of course, interpret debate, discussion, and persuasion in the same minimalist sense that we interpret majority rule. For example, in many constitutional states there are formal rules specifying the requirement that debate must take place before voting on the passage of a bill. These formal requirements do not specify anything about the quality, integrity, or character of the debate. All too frequently in "actually existing democracies," these so-called debates are little more than an occasion for cynical monological speeches. They are not the place in which "real" politics takes place. The worst scoundrels can manipulate "democratic" procedures for their own strategic purposes. Following such procedures is no guarantee that democracy—in its normative sense—is being practiced. On the contrary, they may be symptoms of the debasement of democratic practices.

Sometimes, Habermas comes very close to admitting that "the core of a genuinely proceduralist understanding of democracy"[9] presupposes a democratic ethos. More frequently, however, he appears to deny this, and suggests that a discourse-theoretical understanding of democracy is superior to its alternatives precisely because it doesn't make any presuppositions about the democratic virtues of citizens. This strand in Habermas comes out most sharply when he is criticizing what he calls the "communitarian" and "republican" defenders of democracy such as Frank Michelman.[10]

In Chapter Six, "Judiciary and Legislation: On the Role of Legitimacy of Constitutional Adjudication,"[11] Habermas discusses the views of several legal theorists concerning the process of judicial review. Habermas contrasts "liberal" and "republican" conceptions of the citizen, law, and constitutional review in order to show how his discourse theory incorporates what is best in these opposing positions, and at the same time avoids their respective pitfalls. Nevertheless, Habermas acknowledges that his approach is closer to the type of "republicanism" represented by Michelman. I do not want to examine all of Habermas's criticisms of "republicanism," but I do want to focus on his criticisms of the ethical presuppositions of republicanism—as Habermas understands them.

Habermas writes, with reference to both Michelman and Cass Sunstein:

> Interestingly enough, though, republicanism does not present itself as an advocate for judicial self-restraint, contrary to what its radical-democratic inspiration might lead one to expect. Rather, it pleads for judicial activism insofar

---

procedures of democratic debate involve substantial-ethical commitments and the exercise of democratic virtues. *See infra* note 20.

9. HABERMAS, *supra* note 1, at 304.
10. *See id.* at 267–74.
11. *Id.*

as constitutional adjudication is supposed to compensate for the gap separating the republican ideal from constitutional reality. As long as deliberative politics is rejuvenated in the spirit of Aristotelian politics, this idea depends on the virtues of citizens oriented to the common good. And this expectation of virtue pushes the democratic process, as it actually proceeds in welfare-state mass democracies, into the pallid light of an instrumentally distorted politics, a "fallen" politics.[12]

Again, Habermas objects to the "exceptionalistic description" of "authentic" democracy by republicans where it is assumed that "[o]nly virtuous citizens can do politics in the right way."[13] Habermas emphatically states why he believes that a discourse-theoretic interpretation is superior to "republicanism."

An interpretation along the lines of discourse theory, by contrast, insists on the fact that democratic will-formation does not draw its legitimating force from the prior convergence of settled ethical convictions. Rather, the source of legitimacy includes, on the one hand, the communicative presuppositions that allow the better arguments to come in to play in various forms of deliberation and, on the other, procedures that secure fair bargaining conditions. Discourse theory breaks with an ethical conception of civic autonomy, and thus it does not have to reserve the mode of deliberate politics to exceptional conditions.[14]

Habermas comes close to caricaturing Michelman's sophisticated understanding of constitutional adjudication and democratic politics. We can discern what worries Habermas, and also what seems to blind him. Republican theories tend to favor small republics and to be skeptical about mass democracies. They have emphasized the strenuous civic virtues required of citizens and their active willingness to participate in agonistic politics. From Habermas's perspective, if we confront the facticity of modern mass democratic societies, it is intellectually irresponsible and elitist to focus on the idealized virtues of a small polity where all citizens can be expected to participate. Furthermore, any adequate procedural democratic theory for contemporary societies cannot simply assume that all citizens will be like the Founding Fathers of the United States—exemplifying distinctive republican virtues. Decision making in a democratic state is not to be modeled on the exceptional circumstances that arise in those crisis situations which lead to the founding of a constitution.

These are important and legitimate concerns, but they should not blind one—as I think they sometimes blind Habermas—from appreciating that this strong sense of republican virtue is not to be confused with the demo-

12. *Id.* at 277.
13. *Id.* at 278.
14. *Id.* at 278–79.

cratic ethos required to participate in a procedural deliberative democratic politics. In this limited but important sense one *can* affirm that "only virtuous citizens can do politics in the right way." Even when a democratic ethos is betrayed—as it so often is in "really existing democracies"—we can still recognize its normative power.

One might think that Habermas would agree with the following statement by Michelman, which sounds very much like Habermas himself:

> Persuasive arguments and discussions seem inconceivable without conscious reference by those involved to their mutual and reciprocal awareness of being co-participants not just at this one debate, but in a more encompassing common life, bearing the imprint of a common past, within and from which the arguments and claims arise and draw their meaning.[15]

Habermas *does* object to this formulation, primarily because of Michelman's references to a "common life" and a "common past." Habermas immediately comments: "Of course, the ethical particularism chracteristic of an unproblematic background consensus does not sit well with the conditions of cultural and societal pluralism that distinguish modern societies."[16]

Habermas thinks that the advantage of discourse theory, especially in contrast to "republican" theories, is that it doesn't have to make *any* presuppositions about the civic virtues of the citizens of a democratic community. Thus he tells us: "According to discourse theory, the success of deliberative politics depends not on a collectively acting citizenry but on the institutionalization of the corresponding procedures and conditions of communication, as well as on the interplay of institutionalized deliberative processes with informally developed public opinions."[17]

But what does this really mean? What is the contrast that Habermas is drawing between "a collectively acting citizenry" and "the institutionalization of corresponding procedures and conditions of communication"? Think for a moment how such procedures are institutionalized. They are not abstract disembodied procedures, but must be concretely embodied in the everyday *practices* of social agents. Participating in a democratic debate is not merely a technical skill nor is it simply following the "formal pragmatic" rules of communication. It is a fragile, complex social practice. This practice itself cannot be adequately understood unless one appreciates what Alasdair MacIntyre calls the "internal goods" of such a practice. Constitutive of such a democratic practice is the exercise of the relevant democratic *virtues*. Here I am employing MacIntyre's "partial and tentative definition

15. *Id.* at 279 (quoting Frank I. Michelman, *Law's Republic*, 97 YALE L.J. 1513 (1988)) (citation omitted).
16. *Id.*
17. *Id.* at 298.

of a virtue." "A virtue is an acquired human quality the possession and exercise of which tends to enable us to achieve those goods which are internal to practices and the lack of which effectively prevents us from achieving any such goods."[18]

Habermas is most forceful and persuasive when he comes close to acknowledging that what he "really" means by "the institutionalization of the corresponding procedures and conditions of communication" is the institutionalization of those practices and the corresponding virtues required to engage in reciprocal, symmetrical communication and discourse. I am tempted to call this the "good" Habermas. The "bad" Habermas is the one who leads us into thinking that discourse theory based on the discourse principle does not make *any* substantial-ethical commitments.[19]

Just as, I think, that Habermas has a tendency to conflate senses of "procedural," he also conflates different senses of "substantial" or "substantial-ethical." Habermas does not distinguish between (using Rawls's expression) a "thin" conception of substantial-ethical convictions and a "thick" conception of such convictions. When Habermas objects to those theories of democracy based upon substantial-ethical presuppositions, his main targets of attack are those theories that seem to presuppose the existence of a community whose members already share a *fully* determinate set of values and preferences—values which are constitutive of their identity as mem-

---

18. ALASDAIR MACINTYRE, AFTER VIRTUE: A STUDY IN MORAL THEORY 178 (2d ed. 1984). MacIntyre gives a perspicacious analysis of social practices in which he makes a distinction between two kinds of goods: those that are internal to a practice—that is, standards of excellence which are to be achieved or approximated in order to engage in the practice—and those that are external to the practice—the types of goods we hope to achieve by engaging in the practice but which are not intrinsic to the practice. If I play chess or ice skate, there are standards of excellence (internal goods) which I must strive to achieve to engage in these practices. However, I can also play chess or ice skate for the sake of fame or money (external goods). One can still criticize MacIntyre's substantive theory of virtue while accepting his characterization of a social practice and his "tentative" definition of a virtue. For my criticisms of MacIntyre, see RICHARD J. BERNSTEIN, *Nietzsche or Aristotle?: Reflections on Alasdair MacIntyre's After Virtue, in* PHILOSOPHICAL PROFILES 115 (1986) [hereinafter PHILOSOPHICAL PROFILES].

19. The discourse principle is: "Just those action norms are valid to which all possibly affected persons could agree as participants in rational discourses." HABERMAS, *supra* note 1, at 107. This discourse principle which is so fundamental for Habermas seems to presuppose that (ideally) "participants in rational discourses" are contemporaries. But the action norms which we take to be valid frequently affect those who *do not* and *cannot* participate in "rational discourses," for example, future unborn generations. It has never been clear to me how Habermas's discourse principle applies to a future unborn humanity or how Habermas deals with the types of issues that are so prominent in Hans Joas's theory of responsibility *for* the future. Does the acceptance of the discourse principle mean that we can *never* know whether they would be accepted by those who are as yet unborn but who may be affected by our action norms—sometimes in disastrous ways? It is too facile and misleading to suggest that we must rely on an imaginative thought experiment in order to decide whether unborn potential participants would accept *our* action norms.

bers of the community. This "thick" understanding of shared substantial-ethical commitments can lead to the type of parochial ethnocentrism that Habermas rightly wants to avoid. Nevertheless, this "thick" or "strong" understanding of substantial-ethical commitments must *not* be confused or identified with the "thin"—but crucial—substantial-ethical dispositions and virtues required for engaging in democratic procedural practices.[20]

Earlier, I suggested that the type of circularity involved in a developed discourse theory of democracy is not a "vicious" circularity, but rather is analogous to hermeneutical circularity. Such a democratic theory does presuppose a democratic ethos (*Sittlichkeit*), that affects the ways in which the practices of debate, discussion, and persuasion are conducted. Such an ethos may itself be influenced and modified by democratic practices; there is nothing vicious about this circularity. On the contrary, it is the way in which "really existing democracies" may be transformed to come closer to more "ideal" democracies. In this sense, democracy is what Dewey said it was—"a way of life"—a way of life that is intrinsically ethical "in its foundations, its methods, and its ends."[21]

Still, we may ask why is Habermas so insistent on the "purity" of discourse theory? Why is he so nervous about any suggestion that discourse theory may involve "substantial-ethical" commitments? Why does he draw the misleading contrast between "substantial-ethical" convictions and "communicative presuppositions" when he claims:

> [a]n interpretation along the lines of discourse theory, by contrast, insists on the fact that democratic will-formation does not draw its legitimating force from the prior convergence of settled ethical convictions. Rather, the source of legitimacy includes, on the one hand, the communicative presuppositions that allow the better arguments to come to play in various forms of deliberation.[22]

I have already indicated the reasons for Habermas's concern, and for his insistence on this distinction. He wants to avoid "vicious circularity" where we presuppose what we set out to justify. He wants to avoid the "bad" sort of ethnocentrism or Eurocentrism where one is "simply" affirming the norms and values shared by a common tradition. He wants to avoid the pitfalls of

20. The contrast between "thin" and "thick" substantial-ethical commitments must not be understood as a hidden evaluative contrast. By "thin," I mean those virtues and substantial-ethical convictions required for engaging in democratic debate, discussion, and persuasion. Exercising such virtues does not by itself determine the substantial-ethical content of one's everyday life. Any adequate theory of democracy must do justice to the substantial-ethical conflicts (even irreconcilable conflicts) that can occur within a democratic polity.

21. For a discussion of Dewey's understanding of democracy, see *John Dewey on Democracy: The Task Before Us*, in PHILOSOPHICAL PROFILES, *supra* note 18, at 260.

22. HABERMAS, *supra* note 1, at 278.

the type of republicanism that cannot deal with the facticity of modern pluralistic democratic societies. He wants to root out the "moralism" and the "purity of heart" of those who seek to place exclusive weight on the virtue of individual citizens. After the French Revolution—and especially after Hegel's devastating portrait in the *Phenomenology of Spirit*[23]—we know all too well the dangers of a "republic of virtue."

These are legitimate concerns, but they do not show that discourse theory is devoid of ethical substance. What is initially so paradoxical about Habermas's position is that, on the one hand, he forcefully argues that any adequate theory of law and democracy must be *normative*. He argues that positivist or empiricist theories of democracy that seek to exclude any reference to obligatory norms get entangled in "performative contradictions." On the other hand, he tells us, over and over again, that the "communicative presuppositions" of discourse do not presuppose or depend upon "substantial-ethical convictions." To unravel this apparent paradox we must probe the distinctive meaning of "ethics" and the sharp way in which Habermas distinguishes it from "morals." We need to explore the meaning and soundness of this important distinction which shapes his entire discourse theory.

Habermas typically makes a tripartite distinction among the pragmatic, the ethical, and the moral employments of practical reason—all of which are required for a fully developed discourse theory of law and democracy.[24] These are the three non-reducible employments of practical reason—reason concerned with action, or more specifically, reason directed to "justifying choices among alternative available courses of action"[25]: "Pragmatic" in this context is used in a narrow sense to approximate what Max Weber called *Zweckrationalität*[26]: purposive-rational argumentation. This is what Habermas has characterized as strategic and/or instrumental rationality. The paradigms of "pragmatic" argumentation are means-ends rationality and the varieties of "rational choice" decision theories. I want to set aside a consideration of "pragmatic" argumentation, not because it is unimportant, but because it is not directly relevant for understanding the distinction that Habermas draws between "the ethical" and "the moral." It *is* important, however—indeed, vital for understanding Habermas's discourse theory—to emphasize that practical reason is *not* identical with, or reducible to, the "pragmatic" employment of practical reason. The very possibility of a dis-

23. GEORG W. F. HEGEL, PHENOMENOLGY OF SPIRIT (A. Miller trans., 1977) (1807).

24. One of the clearest formulations of the tripartite distinction is to be found in Habermas's essay, "On the Pragmatic, the Ethical, and Moral Employments of Practical Reason." JÜRGEN HABERMAS, JUSTIFICATION AND APPLICATION: REMARKS ON DISCOURSE ETHICS 1 (Ciaran Cronin trans., 1993) [hereinafter JUSTIFICATION AND APPLICATION].

25. *Id.* at 8.

26. MAX WEBER, ECONOMY AND SOCIETY 24 (Guenther Roth & Claus Wittich eds., 1978).

course theory depends on showing that there is "more" to practical reason than "rational choice" or pragmatic argumentation.[27]

Earlier, I noted that "ethical" and "moral" are terms of art for Habermas. He introduces and stipulates a sharp distinction between them. But precisely how does Habermas understand this distinction—and why is it so basic for his discourse theory?

Ethical discourses are concerned with the life history of an individual or a group. They seek to answer the question: "what is good for me?" or "what is good for my group (my class, people, nation, etc.)?" Such discourses are intended "to justify important value decisions and to gain assurance concerning [one's] identity."[28] Furthermore, these discourses must be "comprehensible in intersubjective terms."

> The individual attains reflective distance from his own life history only within the horizon of forms of life that he shares with others and that themselves constitute the context for different individual life projects. Those who belong to a shared lifeworld are potential participants who can assume the catalyzing role of impartial critics in processes of self-clarification.[29]

According to Habermas, when I ask (and argue about) what it means to be a Jew, an African-American, a Serbian nationalist, etc., I am primarily engaged in raising ethical questions—questions about the ethos, values, and good for my people, or about my ethical-existential "place" among my people. Given this understanding of "ethics," we can understand why Habermas says such discourses are always grounded in contingent historical contexts; refer to traditions that I share with others; are essentially teleological; and are concerned with questions of what is good for me or my group.

Even in ethical discourse, we can make a distinction between substance and procedure.

> [A]s long as such an ethics makes substantial statements, its premises remain confined to the context in which particular historical or even personal interpretations of the self and the world arose. As soon as it is sufficiently formal, however, its substance at best consists in elucidating the procedure of ethical discourses aimed at reaching self-understanding.[30]

---

27. Just as Habermas is critical of those "empiricists" who identify practical reason with pragmatic argumentation, he is critical of Kant (and Kantians) who identify practical reason exclusively with moral argumentation. He also rejects the Aristotelian approach that identifies practical reason with ethical argumentation. Habermas's broad understanding of practical reason is intended to encompass and to do justice to these three different employments of practical reason.

28. JUSTIFICATION AND APPLICATION, *supra* note 24, at 11.

29. *Id.*

30. HABERMAS, *supra* note 1, at 64.

Moral-practical discourses must be sharply distinguished from *ethical*-practical discourses. The former are deontological, not teleological. They are concerned with issues of justice and right, not with good and value. They have, at once, a much more limited range than ethical questions, but unlike ethical discourses they are not limited to specific historical contexts. Moral-practical discourses are not particularistic—limited to a particular historical group. They are genuinely universal and concern the equal respect and rights of *all* human beings. We can read Habermas as providing a series of crucial "footnotes" to Kant because most of the major contrasts he introduces between ethics and morals can be traced back to Kant.[31] His major departure[32] from Kant is the dialogical or communicative turn his thinking takes away from Kant's monological conception of practical reason. Habermas is a "communicative Kantian."

Habermas tells us that his discourse theory "takes its orientation for an intersubjective interpretation of the categorical imperative from Hegel's theory of recognition but without incurring the cost of historical *dissolution* of morality in ethical life."[33] This last phrase "a historical dissolution of morality in ethical life" is crucial because Habermas objects to the way in which Hegel, and Hegelians, distinguish *Moralität* and *Sittlichkeit*. According to Habermas, Hegel *does* dissolve morality into a universal, substantive *Sittlichkeit*. This dissolution is what the *Aufhebung* of *Moralität* by *Sittlichkeit* entails. (This is surely a contestable claim about Hegel.)

But Habermas's way of distinguishing ethics and morals is distinctive, for he departs from both Kant and Hegel. In his historical excursus in Chapter 3, Habermas tells us:

> The modern ideas of *self-realization* and *self-determination* signaled not only different issues but two different kinds of discourse tailored to the logics of *ethical* and *moral* questions. The respective logics peculiar to these two types of questions were in turn manifested in philosophical developments that began in the late eighteenth century.[34]

So according to Habermas, it is only in modern times—beginning in the late eighteenth century—that the systematic distinction between ethics and morals arises. With the emergence of a plurality of value systems in modern times, ethics—which is limited to "individual life histories and . . . intersubjectively shared traditions and forms of life"[35]—can never satisfy the *demand* for universal justification. In the modern period

---

31. Kant, however, does not draw the distinction between morals and ethics in the way that Habermas does.

32. Habermas also rejects the Kantian distinction between phenomena and noumena.

33. JUSTIFICATION AND APPLICATION, *supra* note 24, at 1.

34. HABERMAS, *supra* note 1, at 95.

35. *Id.* at 96.

there has been a growing need for justification, which, under the conditions of postmetaphysical thinking, can be met only by *moral discourses*. The latter aim at the impartial evaluation of action conflicts. In contrast to ethical deliberations, which are oriented to the telos of my/our own good (or not misspent) life, moral deliberations require a perspective freed of all egocentrism or ethnocentrism. Under the moral viewpoint of equal respect for each person and equal consideration for the interests of all, the henceforth sharply focused normative claims of legitimately regulated interpersonal relationships are sucked into a whirlpool of problematization.[36]

Given the above understanding of the idealized, sharply delimited [*scharf geschnitten*] distinction between moral discourse and ethical discourse, we gain a much better understanding of why Habermas resists the suggestion that his discourse theory makes any substantial-ethical presuppositions. For if discourse theory were dependent on a substantive ethos, then this would mean that it could never achieve the type of universality required to justify a universal moral point of view. Rather, a discourse theory that is based upon an ethos (even a democratic procedural ethos), would willy-nilly be ethnocentric.

Habermas has never claimed that a discourse theory of law and democracy can be generated by appealing to the formal-pragmatic conditions of communication. He strongly objects to this type of *a priori* normative theorizing.[37] A fully developed discourse theory of law and democracy must take account of legal, moral, ethical, and pragmatic argumentation. Habermas is emphatic that discourse theory by itself does not generate determinate action norms or values. These emerge only within the context of historical forms of life. The purpose of a discourse theory is *not* to generate norms and values, but to test them and to clarify the procedures involved in rationally assessing norms and values. But a discourse theory of law and democracy does presuppose a sharp and rigorous distinction between moral and ethical, as well as pragmatic, discourses.

Now the basic question arises: why should we accept this sharp, idealized distinction between ethics and morals? Or to use Habermas's idiom, are there good reasons for accepting this distinction—even granting that it is intended to be an idealization? I do not think so. Indeed, I think there are good reasons for *rejecting* it as a hard and fast conceptual distinction.

Of course, there is something right and sound in what Habermas is claiming. Historically and systematically, we can acknowledge that there are many legitimate vital ethical issues that are limited to my own life history

---

36. *Id.* at 97.

37. He sometimes suggests that his colleague Karl-Otto Apel is "guilty" of this type of transcendental or *a priori* theorizing.

or that of my group. When I struggle with the issues of my responsibilities, either as an American committed to a belief in radical deliberative democracy or as a Jew struggling with the significance of the Holocaust, I am not confronting questions that are applicable or relevant to *all* human beings.

One of the reasons why ethical issues—in Habermas's sense—have become so pressing in our times is because groups—racial, sexual, national, cultural, etc.—have been thrust together in novel ways giving rise to all sorts of tensions and conflicts. And with the growing awareness of one's social identity and differences, ethical questions concerning who I am and we are, become more urgent. Habermas himself agrees that one of the great failures of the modern Enlightenment tradition has been its neglect of the legitimacy of genuinely local and particularistic ethical questions.

This is where Habermas's terms of art—"ethics" and "morals"—reach a breaking point. Consider "actually existing" ethical traditions. Embedded in their historical contingency are *universal* demands and obligations. If I identify myself with the Jewish people, I am not limited in my ethical reflections to questions of shared intersubjective values with my fellow Jews. It would make a mockery of this tradition if I did not recognize that I have obligations and responsibilities that transcend my fellow Jews and are relevant to *all* human beings. The "validity" of a commandment like "Thou shalt not kill" is not limited to the people with whom I share intersubjective values. If I identify myself as an American and take pride in the heritage of the Founding Fathers, I do not, or rather, ought not, interpret the claim that "all men are created equal," as applying only to Americans. I can recognize that we can no longer be satisfied with the limited interpretations of this substantial-ethical claim. It is a fiction—and indeed a violently distortive fiction—to suggest that ethical discourse is limited to discourse *about* particular historical groups—that ethical discourse *qua* ethics never has a genuinely universal scope. It is a fiction to suggest that there are, or ever were, two separate types of discourse—ethics and morals, with two independent logics. Such a dichotomy falsifies both ethics and morals—utilizing Habermas's terms of art. Problems do not come to us labeled "ethical" or "moral"; to sort problems into these pigeon holes tends to distort living ethical *and* moral discourse.

Consider the following passage where the arbitrariness and tensions of Habermas's sharp distinction are exhibited:

> In ethical-existential discourses, reason and the will condition one another reciprocally, though the latter remains embedded in the life-historical context thematized. Participants in processes of self-clarification cannot distance themselves from the life histories and forms of life in which they actually

find themselves. Moral-practical discourses, by contrast, require a break with all of the unquestioned truths of an established, concrete ethical life, in addition to distancing oneself from the contexts of life with which one's identity is inextricably interwoven.[38]

My first response to the claims made in this passage is that they are simply false! More judiciously, however, I would say that they are extremely misleading. What is the basis for saying that "participants in processes of self-clarification *cannot* distance themselves from the life histories and forms of life in which they actually find themselves."[39] This may be true for bigots and fanatics, but as reflective individuals we do this all the time. If I take my own life history as a Jew or as an American—or as many of the other ways in which I identify myself and my life histories—I certainly do not restrict myself to questions concerning my fellow Jews, Americans, etc. I want also to understand my responsibilities and obligations to those who are not members of the identified group. It is precisely because I can distance myself from my life history that I can engage in the critical reflection of what it means to be an American, a Jew, a New Yorker, etc. It is completely artificial and arbitrary to suggest that when I ask more universal questions I am shifting to a different type of discourse with a different logic of argumentation. Habermas seems to be guilty of what Karl Popper once called—in a different context—"the myth of the framework," the myth that "we are prisoners caught in the framework of our theories; our expectations; our past experiences; our language."[40] For Habermas seems to suggest that from an ethical perspective we are prisoners locked into our historically contingent forms of life. But no serious substantial-ethical tradition or form of life is closed and limited in this way.

It is just as misleading to claim that "moral-practical discourses by contrast require a *break* with all of the unquestioned truths of an established, concrete ethical life."[41] To speak of "unquestioned truths" in this way is to caricature "concrete ethical life." For ethical life, especially in modern times, consists of doubts, questions, and reflective debates and conflicts. If Habermas had said that "in concrete ethical life" we can distinguish more particularistic and more universal concerns, one could hardly disagree with him. At times he comes close to saying this when he asserts that "[m]oral-practical discourse represents the ideal extension of each individual com-

---

38. JUSTIFICATION AND APPLICATION, *supra* note 24, at 12.
39. *Id.* (emphasis added).
40. For a discussion of the "Myth of the Framework," see RICHARD J. BERNSTEIN, BEYOND OBJECTIVISM AND RELATIVISM: SCIENCE, HERMENEUTICS AND PRAXIS 84 (1983) (quoting Karl Popper) (footnote omitted).
41. JUSTIFICATION AND APPLICATION, *supra* note 24, at 12 (emphasis added).

munication community from within. In this forum, only those norms proposed that express a common interest of all affected can win justified assent."[42] But even this statement is ambiguous. It can be interpreted in either
a moderate or an extreme fashion. The more judicious interpretation
would be that "moral-practical" refers to the universal questions applicable
to all human beings that are raised within concrete ethical life histories and
discourses. The more extreme, or misleading, interpretation is that "moral-
practical" refers to what is not and *cannot* be raised within the context of
concrete ethical life histories and discourses. It requires an entirely different logic of argumentation. This is why a "break" is required in order to
sharply distinguish genuinely moral-practical questions from ethical-practi-
cal questions.

The artificiality of Habermas's rigid distinction between ethical and
moral discourse is also reflected in the rigid distinction he draws between
values and norms.

> Principles or higher-level norms, in the light of which other norms can be
> justified, have a deontological sense, whereas values are teleological. Valid
> norms of action obligate their addressees equally and without exception to
> satisfy generalized behavioral expectations, whereas values are to be under-
> stood as intersubjectively shared preferences. Shared values express the pref-
> erability of goods that, in specific collectivities, are considered worth striving
> for and can be acquired or realized through goal-directed action. Norms of
> action appear with a binary validity claim and are either valid or invalid; we
> can respond to normative sentences, as we can to assertoric sentences, only
> by taking a "yes" or "no" position or by withholding judgment. . . .
>
> Norms and values therefore differ, first, in their references to obligatory
> rule-following versus teleological action; second, in the binary versus gradu-
> ated coding of their validity claims; third, in their absolute versus rela-
> tive bindingness; and fourth, in the coherence criteria that systems of
> norms and systems of values must respectively satisfy. The fact that norms
> and values differ in these logical properties yields significant differences
> for their application as well. . . . In the light of norms, I can decide what ac-
> tion is commanded; within the horizon of values, which behavior is recom-
> mended.[43]

There is nothing intrinsically objectionable in making a rigorous distinction
between norms and values. Considering the careless tendency to lump together questions concerning norms and values, this is an important and
useful distinction. But consider what is implied in the way in which Habermas employs this distinction. Although he draws the above distinction in

42. *Id.* at 12 (footnote omitted).
43. HABERMAS, *supra* note 1, at 255–56.

the context of a discussion of legal principles and norms, it is moral discourse as deontological that is primarily concerned with the justification of norms while ethical discourse as teleological is concerned with the assessment of goods and values. The reason why I say this is "violently distortive" is related to Habermas's own insistence on doing justice to the facticity of our concrete everyday social practices. For the concrete ethical traditions with which we identify ourselves are *not* limited to teleological assessment of values and goods. They are also concerned with our obligations and the norms that have an "ought"-validity. To suggest that ethical life and ethical discourse *must* always be context-dependent, and are limited to assessment of values that we share with other members of the groups with which we identify, is to do violence to the ethical traditions, contexts, and life histories within which we live our lives.

I return explicitly to the question of a democratic ethos. If we give up Habermas's rigid distinction between moral and ethical discourse, if we recognize that at best this rigid dichotomy points to what is actually a continuum in our concrete "ethical-moral" practices, then Habermas's anxiety about the purity of a discourse theory no longer has any basis. We can recognize that a discourse theory of procedural democracy relies upon and presupposes a democratic ethos—a democratic *Sittlichkeit*. There is no reason to think that such a theory is "viciously" circular or parochial; that such a theory cannot be genuinely universal. We can recognize that there is a perfectly valid sense in which democracy is dependent on the virtues of its citizens, that democracy is—in Dewey's words—"a moral way of life" without thinking this enmeshes us in some sort of self-defeating contextualism. We need no longer pretend that the formal-pragmatic conditions of communication are sufficient to justify a discourse theory. In a genuinely pragmatic sense, we can recognize that we rationally support our belief in a *substantial-ethical procedural* democratic theory. It is not oxymoronic to speak of a "substantial-ethical procedural democracy." It is rather a way of emphasizing that a theory of deliberative procedural democracy presupposes a democratic ethos.

Many years ago, even before Habermas fully articulated his discourse theory, I argued that there was a "deep unresolved conflict" between the transcendental and pragmatic tendencies in his thinking.[44] The conflict is still unresolved. Habermas's hankering after a purified discourse theory which is not tainted by any substantial-ethical commitments is still evidence of the "transcendental" lure for a proper *grounding*. The formal-pragmatic conditions of communication play a role analogous to Kant's transcendental conditions for the possibility of experience. But Habermas, despite this

44. *See* RICHARD J. BERNSTEIN, THE RESTRUCTURING OF SOCIAL AND POLITICAL THEORY 219–25 (1976).

transcendental legacy, is much more persuasive and effective when he allows his pragmatic insights to prevail. The time has come for Habermas to acknowledge what the pragmatists—especially Dewey and Mead—emphasized long ago: there is no democracy—in *theory* or in *practice*—without a *democratic ethos*.

PART SIX

Liberalism, Republicanism, and Constitutionalism

FIFTEEN

Family Quarrel

Frank I. Michelman*

In Chapter 6 of *Between Facts and Norms,* Jürgen Habermas examines what he calls the republican conception of lawmaking.[1] He draws this conception, which he also styles "communitarian," partly from writings of this author[2] that have in turn been much inspired by the works of Professor Habermas.[3]

Habermas treats the "republican"[4] conception critically, or perhaps it would be better to say dialectically; his own preferred discourse-theoretic paradigm of law, developed over the dialectical course of the entire book, here takes the step of parting itself from another conception with which it recognizes some family ties. Both republicanism and the favored paradigm

*Robert Walmsley University Professor, Harvard University.

1. JÜRGEN HABERMAS, BETWEEN FACTS AND NORMS: CONTRIBUTIONS TO A DISCOURSE THEORY OF LAW AND DEMOCRACY 238–86 (William Rehg trans., 1996).

2. *See* Frank I. Michelman, *Conceptions of Democracy in American Constitutional Argument: Voting Rights,* 41 FLA. L. REV. 443 (1989); Frank I. Michelman, *Conceptions of Democracy in American Constitutional Argument: The Case of Pornography Regulation,* 56 TENN. L. REV. 291 (1989); Frank Michelman, *Law's Republic,* 97 YALE L.J. 1493 (1988) [hereinafter Michelman, *Law's Republic*]; Frank I. Michelman, *The Supreme Court, 1985 Term—Foreword: Traces of Self-Government,* 100 HARV. L. REV. 4 (1986) [hereinafter Michelman, *Traces*].

3. *See* Michelman, *Law's Republic, supra* note 2, at 1526–28; Michelman, *Traces, supra* note 2, at 31–32; Stephen M. Feldman, *The Persistence of Power and the Struggle for Dialogic Standards in Postmodern Constitutional Jurisprudence: Michelman, Habermas, and Civic Republicanism,* 81 GEO. L.J. 2243 (1993).

4. It is a fair question whether "republican" really is an apt name for the conception here at issue. *See, e.g.,* Miriam Galston, *Taking Aristotle Seriously: Republican-Oriented Legal Theory and the Moral Foundation of Deliberative Democracy,* 82 CAL. L. REV. 331, 333–35 nn.13–15 (1994). It is, at any rate, the name that Habermas understandably uses. So "republican" (without the scare-quotes) hereafter simply means the conception that Habermas presents and criticizes in the terms I describe below.

adopt what Habermas calls a "deliberative concept of democracy."[5] Each is a distinctly rationalist and a distinctly proceduralist conception; each is normatively freighted.[6] According to Habermas, the two conceptions part company over the question of how far and in what respects legal discourses are bound to the cultural contingencies of forms of life in historically specific societies. For both the Habermasian and the republican conceptions, the very idea of discursive justification of norms presupposes intersubjectivity, or what Habermas calls "symmetrical relations of mutual recognition."[7] At issue is republicanism's perceived insistence on binding the very idea of discursive justification of legal content not just to intersubjectivity, but to intersubjectivity concretized in joint awareness of a shared ethical-cultural consciousness. Republicanism, Habermas says, goes wrong by extending to the "originary" justification of laws (as distinguished from secondary discursive processes of applying laws to cases) its insistence on a "necessary connection between the deliberative concept of democracy and the reference to a concrete, substantively integrated ethical community."[8]

It is Professor Habermas's perception of this specific difference between republicanism and the discourse paradigm that I want to consider here. First, I look at Habermas's intriguing diagnostic account of just where and how republicanism went wrong. I find this account open to serious question. This finding leads to a further inquiry into how much difference there really is between the two conceptions. Finally, allowing *arguendo* that there is in at least one respect a significant difference, I argue in defense of the republican side of the divide.

I.

The activity of a constitutional court might be strictly secondary (that is, an activity of following), or it might be originary as well. On the strictly secondary view of it, judicial constitutional review is an activity of regulating politics by supervisory application of an antecedently given doctrine of right. Typically, the regulative doctrine is held to deserve its primacy over the politics it regulates by virtue of two factors somehow combined: rightness, and enactment by a legitimate constituent power. The rightness factor may be conceived in a variety of ways. In one conception, rightness means suitability to serve as a set of constitutive rules for politics conceived as strategic; the regulative doctrine is right insofar as it constitutes a fair and

5. HABERMAS, *supra* note 1, at 280.
6. *See generally* Pierre Schlag, *Normativity and the Politics of Form,* 139 U. PA. L. REV. 801 (1991).
7. HABERMAS, *supra* note 1, at 251.
8. *Id.* at 258, 280.

efficient competitive game. In another—Habermasian—conception, rightness means the regulative doctrine's conformity to rationally reconstructible preconditions for politics conceived as a mutualistic communicative activity oriented to understanding and agreement.[9]

An originary view of constitutional court activity is one that sees the judges as somehow participant in the constituent power, as diviners and enacters of the regulative doctrine rather than as just its appliers or interpreters. Habermas construes republicanism to grant an originary role to judges and furthermore to justify this grant in a special way. Republicanism, says Habermas, justifies originary judicial activity as an emergency service required by the "fallen" state of democratic politics[10]; "fallen," that is, by comparison with a counterfactually idealized popular constituent power. The constitutional court serves in default of the popular constituent power, public-spirited and vigilant, that ought to be present but is not.

Habermas apparently finds in this substitutive-originary view of the constitutional court two kinds of bad tendencies, both nicely conveyed by his charge against the "fallen politics" idea that it hands over sovereignty to a judicial regent.[11] The first bad tendency is spiritual. Although he does not quite say it, Habermas seems to find here a case of alienated politics, a demoralized displacement of self-government to a not-here, not-now by people regarding it as actually impossible here and now for them. The other bad tendency is institutional, toward a kind of retrograde de-separation of powers. Habermas finds that the "fallen politics" justification for judicial activism tends toward ironing out all sense of a working distinction between enactment and application of basic law. It tends further toward vesting in the judiciary a totalizing "*jurisdictio,*"[12] and thus toward defeating the hardwon political prudence—"the precautionary *interruption* of an otherwise self-referentially closed circle of legitimation"[13]—that we call the separation of powers. (In fact, Habermas sees republicanism collapsing the "fire wall"[14] between lawmaking and law-applying from the other end, too; not just by admitting the judiciary to originary "discourses of justification" (of laws),[15]

9. *See, e.g., id.* at 226–28.

10. *See id.* at 277, 281.

11. *See id.* at 278.

12. "[T]he notion of 'jurisdictio' has the premodern sense of a political authority supported by suprapositive law, to which the ruler is entitled in his adjunct role of supreme judge. Hence, the term connotes an authority that *preceded* the constitutional separation between making and applying law." *Id.* at 249.

13. *Id.* at 262.

14. *Id.* at 258–59.

15. *But see id.* at 439 (recognizing that in practice the devolution upon the judiciary of a "gray area between legislation and adjudication" requires that "juristic discourses of application ... be visibly supplemented ... by elements taken from discourses of justification").

but by inviting originary lawmakers into substantial-ethical reflections that properly belong only to "discourses of application."[16])

I do not contest the reality of these tendencies. They are potentially to be found wherever judicial review is found—in part because (as I argue in Part III) no clear demarcation can possibly be maintained, in a working constitutional regime devoted to a rule of law, between originary discourses of justification and secondary discourses of application. It is unclear how the risk of these bad tendencies might be in any way unique to republicanism. Habermas seems to indicate that it is, though, when he traces their occurrence in republicanism to republican thought's alleged overcommitment to substantial-ethical community. It is this diagnosis that I question.

The diagnosis issues from a somewhat complex reconstruction of republican thought, which we shall need to unpack. In this reconstruction, a logical first step is to identify an immediate cause for republicanism's turn to judicial regency. As this immediate cause, Habermas picks out republicanism's demand for civically virtuous motivation as a condition of validity for enacted laws—a demand reflected in republicanism's highly idealized view of the popular political events that (republicanism says) must once have occurred in the course of legislating valid basic law for the country. In this view, only a genuinely public-spirited popular political practice, directed by all participants to the common good, can ever be normatively adequate to the production of valid laws. Habermas calls "exceptionalistic" this republicanly idealized view of "doing politics right," assigned as it is to a past perhaps not ever to be repeated. Habermas says that it is this "exceptionalistic description" of how "political practice . . . really ought to be" that issues in the call for "a pedagogical guardian or regent; the latter [that is, the court] must exercise its regency" because, in republican thought, the proper sovereign—the people—in actuality "prefers to keep to the private realm" instead of "fulfill[ing] its duties" in the "political public sphere."[17]

According to Habermas, then, the immediate cause of republican submissiveness to government by judiciary is an excessively idealizing stance toward normatively adequate popular politics. But Habermas further suggests that this stance itself has an identifiable cause. He writes: "The exceptionalist image of what politics should be is suggested by a republican tradition that binds the citizens' political practice to the ethos of an already-

---

16. "[P]arliament and constitutional court . . . converge in their development of law. The former is demoted from originary lawmaking to the provision of concrete specifications, the latter is promoted from interpretative application of law to its creative concrete, specification." *Id.* at 249 (quoting ERNST-WOLFGANG BÖCKENFÖRDE, *Grundrechte als Grundsatznormen: Zur gegenwärtigen Lage der Grundrechtsdogmatik, in* STAAT, VERFASSUNG, DEMOKRATIE: STUDIEN ZUR VERFASSUNGSTHEORIE UND ZUM VERFASSUNGSRECHT 189–91 (1991)). For further discussion on this matter, see *infra* part III.

17. *Id.* at 278.

integrated community."[18] By these words, Habermas gives us to understand that republicanism's excessive demand for civic virtue as a condition of a normatively adequate legislative process, a demand that is said by Habermas to issue *in* acceptance of judicial regency, itself issues *from* republican insistence on the necessarily ethical-consensual character of every genuinely persuasive originary legislative discourse.

The intimation of a causal nexus here, between republican attachment to substantial-ethical community and republican submission to government by judiciary, is crucial to Habermas's claim that overattachment to community is a fundamental flaw in republicanism. However, the causal nexus is obscure. What exactly is it supposed to be? Habermas unfortunately does not spell out a complete answer.

From Habermas's text we can gather the following as his partial reconstruction of the republican train of ideas.[19] *First,* legislative validity requires conformity of the laws to a general will. *Second,* a general will is discoverable only through the agreement of citizens approaching politics in the proper public-spirited frame of mind (thus, "only virtuous citizens can do politics the right way"). *Third,* such civically virtuous political motivation requires cultural support—it has to be "secured in advance by a substantial consensus" of dispositions. What Habermas does not ever precisely say, though, is exactly how such a train of ideas, anchored in ethical community, would "give rise" in republican thought to the excessively idealizing and demanding ("exceptionalistic") stance toward normatively adequate politics that Habermas says is the immediate cause of republican submission to judicial regency. It is up to us, then, to try to complete the argument.

The most readily apparent completion is this: it seems there must always be located *somewhere* (within a "paradigmatic understanding of law and democracy"[20]) a power of revision—correction, adjustment, elaboration, ex-

---

18. *Id.*

19. Here, for reference, is a full quotation of the crucial passage:

> [I]t is the *exceptionalistic description* of political practice—how it really ought to be—that suggests the necessity for a pedagogical guardian or regent; the latter must exercise its regency only as long as the sovereign prefers to keep to the private realm rather than occupy the place he has inherited, the political public sphere, and appropriately fulfill its duties. The exceptionalist image of what politics should be is suggested by a republican tradition that binds the citizens' political practice to the ethos of an already integrated community. Only virtuous citizens can do politics the right way. This *expectation of virtue* already led Rousseau to split off the citizen, who is oriented to the common good, from the private man who would be overburdened by such ethical-political demands. The unanimity of the political legislature was supposed to be secured in advance by a substantial consensus not so much of minds as of hearts.
>
> *Id.* at 278.

20. *Id.* at 384 (emphasis omitted).

tension—of a country's basic laws. In the republican view, basic law revision properly belongs to a constituent power that is popularly based and civically motivated. But suppose that republicanism also finds that no such civically motivated, popular communicative power is any longer producible in our post-Edenic world. (This is what Habermas means by republicanism's "exceptionalistic description of political practice—how it really ought to be.") Then (Habermas evidently thinks) republicanism is ripe for judicial regency. This is how republicanism's proneness to judicial regency is supposed to result from its "exceptionalistic" stance toward true politics and true constituent power.

Now let us look more closely at what is supposed to account for the exceptionalistic stance. Plainly, the exceptionalistic stance must reflect republican disbelief in the availability here and now of some prerequisite of proper constituent power. *What* prequisite? Obviously, civically virtuous motivation. Now we can begin to see what Habermas must mean by writing that republicanism falls into exceptionalism, and thence into judicial regency, *because* it binds normatively adequate politics to substantial ethical consensus. He must mean that this happens because republicanism, *having already determined or presupposed that "a substantial-[ethical] consensus" of dispositions is prerequisite to the civic motivation required for valid constitutional legislation by a popular constituent power,* now discovers that in modern liberal society the requisite substantial-ethical dispositional consensus is not available. Enter, then, the judiciary *faute de mieux.* It is those who demand of normatively adequate politics a counterfactual (and counterliberal) level of solidary civic virtue who turn to judicial saviors upon coming face to face with the shortage of such virtue abroad in liberal societies.

There is a difficulty in this diagnosis. Professor Habermas appropriately pictures republicanism as, at heart, ideally a doctrine of participatory democracy.[21] Although republicanism may justify electoral and representative institutions as an inevitable compromise with practical considerations, the turn to such institutions represents for republicanism (in Habermas's depiction) a direct loss in primary political values.[22] It seems on reflection, however, that such a radical-democratic leaning would make little sense for anyone whose ideal vision of politics relied on a presupposition of thick ethical bonds to enable discovery of a general will through political communication. For suppose you were imagining, for the moment, that there really was some such thick ethical substance out there, capable of binding

---

21. *See id.* at 267–74.
22. Contrast Madisonian and other (relatively) optimistic public choice approaches, for which electoral mediation of democracy promises a direct gain in the validity and legitimacy of law. *See, e.g.,* THE FEDERALIST Nos. 10, 51 (James Madison).

together the great bulk of the citizens. Why, then, would you also think that only the full body of citizens, as opposed to a sizeable body of elected parliamentary proxies, would be able to get things right politically? Why wouldn't you be at least as likely to think that an elected (and there-fore presumably mainstreamed) sample—specialists, in fact, in the arts of politics—would be at least as responsive as the full population to any existent, heavy-duty, population-encompassing ethical substance as there might be?

Now switch the case. Suppose you see—*contentedly* see—your society's condition as precisely not one of "substantial consensus" of dispositions, but rather one of deep visionary plurality. You think, let's suppose, that in your society there is little prospect for a substantial consensus on the concrete content of institutionalized subjective rights (property rights, say, or auton-omy rights). You do not, however, exclude every last kind and degree of conscious commonality. You don't exclude a consciously shared grasp of a principle of abstract right, arising from a shared "intersubjective [sense] of . . . symmetrical relations of mutual recognition" by individuals of each other as "subjects who are both free and equal."[23] Such a possibility you cannot exclude—as Jürgen Habermas has well taught—if you want to pre-serve, in the face of the pluralistic facts of your society, the possibility of ra-tional democratic will-formation and hence (in a discourse-theoretic view) of the moment of validity in law.[24]

Given such a modern pluralist understanding of political conditions, would it not be utterly clear why republicanism must take the position that only all the citizens, and not any mainstreamed elected subset, can do poli-tics right, in the specific sense of imparting by their discursive procedure the moment of validity to enacted law? The radical-democratic impulse that Habermas detects in republicanism springs most naturally from a lib-eral-pluralist view of our actual condition. It does not nearly so plausibly have its cause or source in perceptions of thick community or affectionate hopes for the same. It is precisely when one acceptingly sees society char-acterized by ethical plurality, not unity, that one also thinks that nothing but all-inclusive discourses of justification can possibly impart validity to enacted law.[25] In short, the republican idealization of popular politics, the politics of the whole citizenry at large, precisely ought not to be blamed on any attachment to the idea of thick, substantive consensus. But then neither can we explain in that way whatever republican support there may be for an originary role for judges in constitutional adjudication.

23. HABERMAS, *supra* note 1, at 251.

24. "Under postmetaphysical conditions, the only legitimate law is one that emerges from the discursive opinion- and will-formation of equally enfranchised citizens." *Id.* at 408.

25. *See id.* at 409–27.

II.

In the republican view of which Habermas speaks, validation of a country's basic law, as an act or process of self-government by all, ideally depends on a process of argumentation leading—without coercion, manipulation, or constraint by anything but reasons freely found to be good—to a conclusion by all affected persons that they have "what they ought for their own sakes to regard as good reasons" for accepting the law as valid.[26] It has been the contention of this republicanism that the persuasive character of such a process of argumentation would have to depend on "the normative efficacy of some context that is everyone's," some "past that is constitutively present in and for every self as language, culture, worldview, and political memory."[27] Such efficacy would require "conscious reference by those involved to their mutual and reciprocal awareness of being co-participants not just in this one debate, but in a more encompassing common life, bearing the imprint of a common past, within and from which the arguments and claims arise and draw their meaning."[28]

How far does this text demand to be read (as Habermas reads it) as locking republican constitutional-legislative discourse onto constant reference to a "concrete, substantively integrated" community? The answer depends on what exactly is meant by "concrete, substantively integrated community." If that descriptor covers every kind and degree of a people's sense of sharing in a somewhat particular historical and cultural situation, then this republicanism plainly denies that constitutional discourse can ever, at any point, escape reference to a concrete, substantively integrated community. If not, then perhaps not.

Professor Habermas has written: "Universalist moralities are dependent on forms of life that are rationalized in that they make possible the prudent application of universal moral insights. . . . Only those forms of life that meet universalist moralities halfway in this sense fulfill the conditions necessary to reverse the abstractive achievements of decontextualization and demotivation."[29] Now, "form of life" here evidently names a class of contingent empirical facts—roughly speaking, a class of cultural facts. According to Habermas, some facts in this class—some instantiations of the class—do,

26. *See* Michelman, *Law's Republic, supra* note 2, at 1512; *see also* Frank I. Michelman, *Kollectiv, Gemeinschaft und das Liberale Denken, in* VERFASSUNGEN: AUF DER SUCHE NACH DER GRECHTEN GESELLSCHAFT (Günter Frankenberg ed., 1994).

27. Michelman, *Law's Republic, supra* note 2, at 1513.

28. *Id.* (citation omitted).

29. JÜRGEN HABERMAS, *Discourse Ethics: Notes on a Program of Philosophical Justification, in* MORAL CONSCIOUSNESS AND COMMUNICATIVE ACTION 43, 109 (Christian Lenhardt & Shierry W. Nicholsen trans., 1990); *see also* Jürgen Habermas, *Morality and Ethical Life: Does Hegel's Critique of Kant Apply to Discourse Ethics?, in* MORAL CONSCIOUSNESS AND COMMUNICATIVE ACTION, *supra,* at 195, 207–08 [hereinafter *Morality and Ethical Life*].

and some do not, satisfy a certain prerequisite for the flourishing of universalist moralities. Each class member (form of life) that meets the prerequisite does so by virtue of some distinct bias of perception or impulse of sensibility—some empirically conditioned resource of "meaning"[30]—that is native to the form of life and sensibly compelling upon its inhabitants. But Habermas also rejects any essential dependence of normative justificational discourses on "concrete, substantively integrated community." It seems, therefore, that not every kind and degree of cultural distinction or bias discoverable in a form of life can count, for Habermas, as "concrete, substantively integrated community." Specifically, this description must exclude whatever minimum cultural content is required for the support of a universalist morality, which for Habermas means "liberal patterns of political culture and socialization" that render a form of life receptive to rationalization of social interactions.[31]

Can we say anything more about this content? From a discourse-theoretic standpoint, we may at least additionally deduce this: the requisite content—not found (Habermas must mean) in every form of life—must be congenial to a certain kind of insight or perception. The form of life must be conducive to nourishing in the population a consciousness of intersubjectivity, a consciously shared awareness of "symmetrical relations of mutual recognition" by individuals of each other as subjects "both free and equal." For it is conscious reciprocity of this kind that gives rise to the principle of abstract right whose elaborated form is a universalist morality. So it would seem to be a condition of a population's capacity for persuasive moral-justificational discourse that the population reflectively share at least this much awareness of intersubjectivity. Thus we may conclude that neither this much awareness nor this much intersubjectivity takes us over the line into "concrete, substantively integrated community."

We see that if a form of life is to meet the universalist morality halfway, it must do so (how else could it possibly?) by virtue of some persuasively compelling, proto-legal, intersubjective meaning.[32] This meaning corresponds to communicative-ethical sensibility. It proceeds from that "intersubjective sense," of which Habermas speaks, "of . . . symmetrical relations of mutual recognition" by subjects of each other as free and equal. Institutionally developed, this content becomes the law required for securing "the internal connection between private and civic autonomy."[33] Habermas writes:

---

30. *See* HABERMAS, *supra* note 1, at 358–59.

31. *Id.; see also id.* at 410–12.

32. Habermas speaks of "intersubjective relationships constituting the common civic practice of citizens." *Id.* at 245.

33. *Id.* at 407–08, 410, 414–15.

A well-secured private autonomy helps "secure the conditions" of public autonomy just as much as, conversely, the appropriate exercise of public autonomy helps "secure the conditions" of private autonomy. This mutual dependency, or circular reinforcement, is manifested in the genesis of valid law. This is because legitimate law reproduces itself only in the forms of a constitutionally regulated circulation of power, which should be nourished by the communications of an unsubverted public sphere rooted in the core private spheres of an undisturbed lifeworld via the networks of civil society. . . . A legal order *is* legitimate to the extent that it equally secures the co-original private and public autonomy of its citizens; at the same time, however, it *owes* its legitimacy to the forms of communication in which alone this autonomy can express and prove itself. . . . This is the key to a proceduralist understanding of law.[34]

According to the discourse-theoretic reading of the system of rights, positive law . . . must split up the autonomy of legal persons into the complementary relation between private and public autonomy, so that the addressees of enacted law can at the same time understand themselves as authors of lawmaking. . . . [E]nfranchised citizens must, in exercising their public autonomy, draw the boundaries of private autonomy in such a way that it sufficiently qualifies private persons for their role of citizens. This is because communication in a public sphere that recruits private persons from civil society depends on the spontaneous inputs from a lifeworld whose core private domains are intact.[35]

[T]he *discourse theory of law* conceives constitutional democracy as institutionalizing—by way of legitimate law (and hence by also guaranteeing private autonomy)—the procedures and communicative presuppositions for a discursive opinion—and will-formation that in turn makes possible (the exercise of political autonomy and) legitimate lawmaking.[36]

Now compare the republican view:

Republicanism has been . . . the strain in constitutional thought that has been sensitive to both the dependence of good politics on social and economic conditions capable of sustaining "an informed and active citizenry that

34. *Id.* at 404–09.

35. *Id.* at 417; *see also id.* at 418 (quoting Ulrich K. Preuss, *Verfassungstheoretische überlegungen zur normativen Begründung des Wohlfahrtsstaats, in* SICHERHEIT UND FREIHEIT: ZUR ETHIK DES WOHLFAHRTSSTAATS 106, 125 (Christoph Sachße & H. Tristram Engelhardt eds., (1990)):

> [D]emocratic society as a whole depends on the citizens' decisions having a certain quality. . . . For this reason society also has an interest in the good quality of enfranchised citizens: specifically, it has an interest in their being informed, in their capacity to reflect and to consider the consequences of their politically relevant decisions, in their will to formulate and assert their interests in view of the interests of their fellow citizens as well as future generations. In short, it has an interest in their "communicative competence."

36. *Id.* at 437.

would not permit its government either to exploit or dominate one part of
society or to become its instrument," and the dependence of such conditions,
in turn, on the legal order. These perceptions irresistably motivate a republican attachment to rights [including] rights of speech and of property . . .
[and also stronger] privacy rights . . . than [perhaps] many contemporary liberals would welcome.[37]

If "a government of laws" stands—as surely it does—for the institutionalized
discipline that would render legislative politics trustworthy, then "law" in the
"government of laws" formula must stand in a circular relation with politics
as both outcome and input, both product and prior condition. . . . [R]epub-
lican thought is no less committed to the idea of the people acting politically
as the sole course of law and guarantor of rights, than it is to the idea of law,
including rights, as the precondition of good politics. Republican thought
thus demands some way of understanding how laws and rights can be both
the free creations of citizens and, at the same time, the normative givens that
constitute and underwrite a political process capable of creating constitutive
law.[38]

This comparison of texts suggests a possibility that Habermas does not
mention: that there could be, so to speak, a *sittlichkeit* of communicative
ethics. Perhaps the same cultural content of a form of life that is required
to "meet universalist moralities halfway" could also satisfy the republicanly
perceived need for reference, in constitutional-legal discourses both origi-
nary-justificational and secondary-applicational, to a shared sense of common life and history.

III.

Suppose that this turns out for some reason to be not a possibility worth
entertaining. Then there would indeed be a manifest difference between

37. Michelman, *Law's Republic, supra* note 2, at 1504–05 (citations omitted); *see also* Frank
Michelman, *Private Personal But Not Split: Radin Versus Rorty,* 63 S. CAL. L. REV. 1783, 1790
(1990) (arguing that "defense of epistemic democracy against the repressive . . . effects of the
bias of idioms" requires respect for "relative privacies . . . of sense and sensibility, knowledge
and spirit, personhood and self-possession").

38. Michelman, *Law's Republic, supra* note 2, at 1501, 1505; *see also* Michelman, *Traces,*
supra note 2, at 43 ("Deliberative political reason, it seems, must end by enunciating something—law—that ought to constrain the deliberation itself"). *Cf.* HABERMAS, *supra* note 1, at
428 (quoting Klaus Günther, *Der Wandel der Staatsaufgaben und die Krise des regulativen Rechts,*
in WACHSENDE STAATSAUFGABEN—SINKENDE STEUERUNGSFÄHIGKEIT DES RECHTS 57 (Dieter
Grimm ed., (1990)):

> [L]aw must not be completely reduced to politics if the internal tension between
> facticity and validity, and hence the normativity of law, is not to be extinguished:
> "Law becomes an instrument of politics, yet at the same time [it] stipulates the
> procedural conditions under which politics may have law at its disposition."

republicanism and the discourse paradigm. Let us now try to specify what the difference would be.

It is one thing to grant (as Habermas does) that universalist moralities depend for recognition and support on congenial forms of life. It would be quite another thing to concede (as Habermas emphatically does not) that moral argumentation, argumentation in search of resolutions that are "equally good for all," must not always *reach back* to awareness of a communicative reciprocity, and along with that reciprocity a principle of right, whose essential character it is to be prior to—abstracted from—all sociocultural particularity. The question, though, is whether republicanism has denied this. I am not aware that it has.

To be sure, republicanism has been insistent that the persuasive character of a law-determining dialogic exchange must also depend *from the outset* on "the normative efficacy" of some concrete historical and cultural "context" that all participants share; persuasive justification of laws depends on a shared sense of "co-participation in an encompassing common past, within and from which the arguments draw their meaning."[39] But to say in this way that originary discourses of legislative justification must always proceed on ground that is already ethical is not to deny that they also must always proceed within a horizon of universalist morality, *sub specie aeternitatis*. It is, however, to disagree with the claim of Habermas that questions of justice are always at their "outset" detached from "specific collectiv[es] and [their forms] of life."[40]

There, then, is the exact point of disagreement between Habermas and republicanism. The quarrel is over republicanism's affirmance of the always already substantial-ethical character of originary-justificatory discourse. Now, this quarrel does not occur in an open hyperspace of pure practical reason. It occurs on the always already institutionalized field of constitutional practice. At issue is practical reasoning in the determinations of constitutional law. Constitutional law is institutional stuff from the word go. In the republican view as rendered by Habermas, constitutional law is a political practice of staged discursive distillation, out of the stew of "substantial ethical life," of relatively abstract liberal terms of association under law.[41] In a discourse-theoretic account, constitutional law is a reverse move-

39. *See supra* text accompanying note 28.
40. HABERMAS, *supra* note 1, at 282.
41. On the republican view, . . . "[p]olitics" is conceived as the reflexive form of substantial ethical life—as the medium in which the members of . . . communities become aware of their dependence on one another and, acting with full deliberation, further shape and develop existing relations of reciprocal recognition into an association of free and equal citizens.

Id. at 269.

ment: a practice of staged discursive precipitation of substantially-ethically inflected institutional rights out of a universal ether of abstract right.[42] But (so says republicanism), it is true either way that the discourse can never free itself of substantial-ethical references. For suppose we start, as the discourse-theoretic paradigm would have it, with a liminally abstract principle of right (that mere "intersubjective sense," again, of symmetrical recognition between free and equal subjects). Then there is nowhere to go from there—nowhere to go from where we start—except by steps that cannot be taken without reference to institutional-practical questions of concrete definition in context. When *law* is the agenda, the questions of concrete definition in context are, inescapably, always already pending.[43]

Habermas congratulates Kant for having "dissociated" moral justification from "application and implementation of moral insights."[44] But the dissociation is analytical, not empirical-practical. In pure discourse-theoretic analytics, agreement to having laws is secured in the first instance, at an "originary" or legislative level, through relatively universalistic discourses of justification. Discourses of application—of relatively concrete definition—are analytically distinct and posterior. However, the practical-institutional logic of constitutionalism precludes anything like a strict working dissociation of justification from application. Constitutionalism requires enactment *at the originary level* of what are called *laws,* because constitutionalism *means* a rule of law, a government of laws. "Laws" correspondingly means resolutions that can *rule,* which is to say the laws can effectively govern the actions of secondary appliers. Required, in other words, are originary resolutions that not only are nondiscriminatorily general but also *already carry significations sufficiently concrete to bind and constrain their addressees,* judges emphatically included. What a constitutionalist originary justificational discourse must justify, then, is always a resolution already concrete enough to constrain, decisively enough to satisfy that hard-won prudence of separated powers, a *post*-originary legal discourse of ap-

---

42. Compare this view with Ronald Dworkin's distinction between "background" and "institutional" rights, and also with John Rawls's analytic movement from a highly abstract "original position," through "constitutional" and "legislative" stages, to a "judicial" stage. *See* Ronald Dworkin, Taking Rights Seriously 185–204 (1977); John Rawls, A Theory of Justice 195–201 (1971).

43. Habermas writes:

> [A]s soon as the constitution is conceived as a demanding process of realizing rights, the task of historically situating this project arises. But in that case . . . the involved actors must form an idea of how the normative content of the democratic state can be effectively and fully exploited within the horizon of existing social structures and perceived developmental tendencies.
>
> Habermas, *supra* note 1, at 395.

44. *Morality and Ethical Life, supra* note 29, at 206.

plication. For resolutions of that character, republicanism maintains, persuasive justification is inconceivable without reference to an ethical context.

In the United States today, for example, constitutional law strongly protects freedom to utter racist hate speech.[45] In Canada, it does not.[46] Consider two alternative argument-theoretic accounts of this situation:

1. The same (universal) constitutional law of freedom, resting on the same (universal) discourse of justification, prevails in both countries; doctrinal differences we observe are secondary applicational variances reflecting differing local social facts at the moment.

2. In two countries having somewhat differing social, cultural, and ethical histories, two somewhat variant discourses of originary constitutional-legal justification correspondingly develop over historical time.

Which formulation seems initially likely to have the advantage?

In sum, it is *law* of which we speak. Law is an ineluctably institutional domain. Within the always already institutional domain of law, norms projected by a constituent power have to satisfy simultaneously strong requirements of discursive justifiability and justiciable concreteness. Even if discursive justification in general must in concept transcend all ethical context, justification of that which is already apprehensible as justiciably concrete cannot conceivably do so.

---

45. R.A.V. v. City of St. Paul, 505 U.S. 377, 380, 395–96 (1992) (invalidating as prima facie First Amendment violation the St. Paul, Minnesota Bias-Motivated Crime Ordinance, which prohibited the display of a symbol likely to "arouse[ ] anger, alarm, or resentment in others on the basis of race, color, creed, religion, or gender").

46. R. v. Keegstra, 3 S.C.R. 697 (Can. 1990). Chief Justice Dixon wrote:

[H]ate propaganda [can alter the view of members of society at large, and this alteration] may occur subtly, [without] conscious acceptance of the communicated ideas. Even if the message of hate propaganda is outwardly rejected, there is evidence that its premise of racial ... inferiority may persist in a recipient's mind as an idea that holds some truth.

Id. at 746–48. The Chief Justice relied on sociological observations of this kind as a basis for upholding, as "demonstrably justified in a free and democratic society," a law broadly criminalizing expression that "wilfully promotes hatred against any ... [racial or religious] group." *Id.* In the U.S. First Amendment culture represented by *R.A.V.,* 505 U.S. at 377, we are strongly disposed to regard such broadly couched sociological premises as inherently uncertain, thus voided of capacity to justify such a sweeping, content-specific restriction of speech content.

SIXTEEN

Communicative Power and the Concept of Law

Ulrich K. Preuss*†

I. THE AMBIGUITIES OF POSITIVE LAW

The idea that the law was founded on the self-interest and the will of rational individuals was first developed and proven in the social contract theories of Hobbes, Locke, and Rousseau. These theorists reacted—admittedly, in extremely different ways—to the problem of finding a collective basis in a world which had lost its common religious fundaments and the economic basis of feudal communal life. The European world of the seventeenth century had fallen apart. The universalism of the catholic world had been replaced by a plurality of subjective worldviews championed by individuals, groups, sects, and new social entities. How could one conceive of a collective basis for society, one that would be able to prevent outbreaks of civil war, without imposing a common social and cultural form of life that had lost its cohesive force?

Students of Western philosophy know the Hobbesian, the Lockean, and the Rousseauist answers to this question. Hobbes reduced the members of society to radically individualistic, strategic actors who could not even conceive of social interactions with others based on trust, and who, consequently, would not be able to develop a common understanding of the world. In Hobbes's concept, political power consisted of a sovereign's capacity to keep peace, i.e., to maintain an order in which the individual's right to self-preservation is safeguarded. Under such a system the law is the will and the command of the sovereign. This is the most radical notion of political power and of the law, since it derives all political and legal obliga-

*Professor, ZERP Universitätsallee, Bremen, Germany.
†The translations in this Article are those of the author.

tions from the individual's right to self-preservation, i.e., from the individual's radically subjective worldview.

The Lockean response to the erosion of the feudal-catholic European community is not any less individualistic, since he too derives all political and legal obligations from the natural rights of the individual. But Locke's individuals are able to engage in social relations, to trust each other, and to feel mutual sympathy. They are able to engage in social life even in the state of nature. As a consequence, Locke's concepts of government and law reflect both the individualistic and the social dimensions of the individual's state of nature. The competence and authority of the government are clearly reduced to the protection of the individual's rights that precede any kind of political rule; consequently, the law can never touch upon this sphere of the individual's natural rights. But, in contrast to Hobbes, the law is not reduced to the role of an institutional representation of every individual's quasi monadic right to self-preservation. To Locke, the law is an institutional device that connects the different perspectives of individuals by harmonizing the natural rights that they equally enjoy. The law is an embryonic form of a common understanding in that it effectuates a negative coordination among the individuals. To do that, it presupposes the idea that self-preservation and interest maximization can only be achieved if there is a sphere where individuals can trust each other, i.e., where they do not act strategically, and where the concern for the natural rights of others constitutes a kind of new moral consociation.

In a further twist, Rousseau developed the truly revolutionary idea that it is not the moral quality of natural rights that ultimately justifies and defines the limits of the government and the laws, but, conversely, that it is the individual's participation in the formation of the general will through which individuals impose on themselves the rules under which they are willing to live. This general will constitutes the moral quality of the individuals as members of a political community and, moreover, determines the character of their rights. In Rousseau's *Social Contract*, the individuals do not exchange their natural freedom for the security of civil society; rather, they substitute civil freedom for natural freedom.[1] In civil society, man "acquires . . . moral freedom, which alone makes man master of himself; for to be governed by appetite alone is slavery, while obedience to a law one prescribes to oneself is freedom."[2] Neither the sovereign power nor the law

1. *See* JÜRGEN HABERMAS, FAKTIZITÄT UND GELTUNG BEITRÄGE ZUR DISKURSTHEORIE DES RECHTS UND DES DEMOKRATISCHEN RECHTSSTAATS 6 (1992) [hereinafter FAKTIZITÄT UND GELTUNG]. For the English translation, see JÜRGEN HABERMAS, BETWEEN FACTS AND NORMS: CONTRIBUTIONS TO A DISCOURSE THEORY OF LAW AND DEMOCRACY (William Rehg trans., 1996).

2. FAKTIZITÄT UND GELTUNG, *supra* note 1, at 8.

is understood as restraints or limits to the enjoyment of the natural rights of individuals; instead, they are understood as conditions that enable the individuals to acquire freedom in the first place. In other words, it is the engagement of the individuals in the formation of a common will and of a common worldview that enables them to develop themselves into moral persons and to acquire true individual freedom.

The Hobbesian, the Lockean, and the Rousseauist concepts of political rule and of the law represent three main traditions in modern legal and political reasoning. The first such tradition, the law as a *sovereign command,* is closely associated with the asocial, self-preserving, strategic actors who fight amongst themselves for scarce resources and must be protected from each other by the authoritative will of the sovereign. In the second tradition, the law as a *reasonable mediator* between competing utility-maximizers, the law forms the noncompetitive basis for their competition. In other words, the law delineates the realm in which they must cooperate in order to be unburdened from the pressure to communicate and to cooperate in other areas. Finally, the third tradition is the law as the expression of a *collective identity* from which the individuals derive their legal status in the political community, or, in other words, a concept of law where the formation of a political-legal community by lawmaking is the most distinguished realization of individual freedom.

At that stage of the historical development, the problem that the aforementioned authors had to unravel was to find a theoretical construction capable of justifying political rule without violating the then only available source of justification, the natural freedom of every individual. In a way, all three theorists found powerful political incarnations in the eighteenth and nineteenth century: the American model of the constitutional state has a primarily Lockean origin; the French model of the democratic republic is clearly inspired by Rousseau; and the Prussian-German preconstitutional state of the nineteenth century is similar to the Hobbesian view. Despite important differences in the founding conditions of these three models of the modern constitutional state, there is reason to presume that today they suffer more or less from the structural problems set forth below.

A. The Positivity Problem

Since modern law is predominantly positive law, lawmaking has become the business of specialized agencies—the legislatures according to the different constitutional orders—that have increasingly used lawmaking more as an instrument of social steering and engineering. This has both qualitative and quantitative consequences. Qualitatively, the law is "general" in the sense that it touches the life spheres of all citizens. Further, it no longer reflects a "spirit" of a society or a common knowledge of the society as a whole. Rather, the law has become a tool for managing very different problems in very different social areas. As a consequence, legal problems have become problems that can be understood and resolved only by experts. This has generated a quantitative problem: apart from the consequence that social problems are ever more defined in terms of legal problems, the production of laws has developed a self-referential legal system in which the necessity to maintain the coherence of the system generates ever more legal rules that, in turn, endanger the internal coherence which can be restored only by the production of new rules.

B. The Legitimation Problem

Notwithstanding the historical changes of the notion of law, its concept has always been associated with the idea that it is dignified by a particular quality, whether it be its character as an eternal source of wisdom and justice, its revelatory character, its generality, or its universalism. In democratic societies, it is the democratic genesis of the law that distinguishes them from all other types of political rule. The democratic character of the law harbors the natural law tenet that no political rule is legitimate if it is not grounded on the consent of those subject to it. In all constitutional democracies there is an uninterrupted chain of democratic legitimation, beginning with free, equal, secret, and universal elections, and ending with the promulgation of laws. In all these societies, however, the phenomenon of political alienation of great portions of the population from their political representatives is patent.

The democratic legitimation of the laws is very much diluted by the weakness of the political system itself in attaining legitimation. But this is only one element of the legitimation problem of modern law. The transformation of law into a great bulk of specialized technical regulations for the multitude of social, economic, and technical problems mentioned above has loosened—in fact frequently severed—the connection between the democratic source of the law and its regulative force and function. The law has become one technical instrument among a great number of others that government managers use for the solution of a great number of problems in a functionally differentiated modern society. And, perhaps most importantly, the world of law and the lifeworlds of individuals have been completely separated. The transformation of a problem of individuals into the language of law has properly been described as a soft expropriation of individuals' problems and conflicts—a particularly cruel version of domination.

C. The Efficiency Problem

This problem refers to the often-described occurrence where legal regulation does not achieve the goals that it is supposed to perform, or where it produces undesired side effects that outweigh the intended advantages of the regulation itself. Catchwords such as "over-regulation" and "over-bureaucratization" sufficiently describe this problem. The frequently recommended remedy against this malfunctioning of legal regulation—deregulation—insinuates that the efficiency problem is essentially a problem of over-legalization. However, we have good reason to assume that the category of problems that cannot be handled adequately by law, power, or money is increasing, and that the efficiency problem is the consequence of the incompatibility between problems and problem-solving devices rather than one that can be traced back to an inefficient use of the problem-solving device.

D. The Indeterminacy Problem

The law is supposed to safeguard both justice and certainty, i.e., the predictability of the parameters of individual social action. The positivity problem and the legitimation problem have pointed to some aspects of the failure of the law to fulfill the promise of justice. The indeterminacy problem refers to the fact that legal certainty has become problematic as well. Aphorisms such as "On the high sea and before the courts we are in God's hand," or "There is justice, but there are also the courts," clearly demonstrate that the people's trust in the predictability of court decisions has considerably decreased. Also, the fact that people cannot make use of the law without the professional help of legal experts who themselves struggle over the meaning of not only a particular legal stipulation, but of the law itself, does not reinvigorate the layman's confidence in the virtues of the law.

II. LEGAL NORMATIVITY IN COMPLEX SOCIETIES

Given this list of problems, which is by no means exhaustive, it is not surprising that the disenchantment of the modern world did not exclude the law. The promises of the law were: first and foremost, to subject all social relations to a homogeneous, normative standard; further, to allow individuals not only to live together nonviolently, but also to cooperate and communicate on the basis of every individual's equal freedom; to generate commutative and distributive justice among individuals; to restrain and civilize physical, economic, and social power; and, finally, to enable individuals to determine the conditions of their collective life according to the rational standards of law. All of these promises have remained more or less unfulfilled. It would not be too difficult to show that they could not be fulfilled because the idealistic assumptions of the law did not catch up to the structural properties and requirements of modern societies. It appears that the prevalence of strategic, utility-maximizing actions in almost all social fields has marginalized the areas in which legal regulation depends upon a common understanding of the legal consociates. On the other hand, modern society generates problems whose solution—or at least, whose adequate handling—requires discourses about justice. Such discourse may involve: the relations between different generations, genders, or races; the relations between citizens and aliens; how to use and distribute scarce natural resources; what should be taught in schools and universities; or what portion of its wealth an economically advanced nation should be ready to share with poorer nations.

Since it is rather evident that the answers of the liberal age are no longer responsive, and that the law of the welfarist mass democracy has in many respects proven insufficient as well, we must find a concept of law with a sufficient analytical frame for the simultaneity of strategic, normative, and rights discourses in our societies. In a way, the task is to integrate the relative truths of Hobbes, Locke, and Rousseau into a comprehensive modern theory of law. Such a theory would have to avoid both a submission to the structural failures of law in modern societies, and its purely idealistic negation in an equally stubborn and empty normativism. What it would have to perform and what, I believe, Habermas's "discourse-theoretical" approach to law indeed accomplishes, is an attempt to save the original normative intentions of the concept of law under the conditions of complex societies. While the modern societies seem to have become increasingly impervious to the normative presuppositions of their own legal orders, the example of the postcommunist societies of eastern and central Europe bears sufficient evidence that modern societies are not able to achieve social integration without an institutionalized locus of reflection on their normative fundaments.

I am certainly not going to repeat in my sparse words what has been elaborated so richly in the book of Professor Habermas. Rather, I will restrict myself to comment on one aspect that not only seems particularly interesting to me but is of strategic importance for the whole argument of the book, namely the concept of communicative power and its connection with the concept of law.

III. AN INTERPRETATION OF THE DISCOURSE THEORY OF LAW

Generally speaking, the discourse theory of law gets over the two principal paradigms that legal theory has developed in the last three hundred years: the liberal and the welfarist. The former was mainly concerned with the construction and protection of a realm of an individual free will (*individuelle Willkür*) where each person can pursue his or her personal goals, including personal happiness. In contrast, the latter was basically attentive to the use of the law for the realization of substantive justice. Rights versus policies, limits versus goals, freedom versus equality, enabling law versus protecting law, and similar conceptual oppositions have been used to explicate the distinction between the liberal and the welfarist legal paradigms.

The weaknesses of the liberal paradigm are well known. From a discourse-theoretical angle, the most important fact is that an equal distribution of freedom rights is not a sufficient condition for the generation of a just society. This is because subjective rights to freedom not only include the legal power to define an individual sphere, but also the legal power to keep others off the limits of that sphere. In other words, subjective rights to freedom do not connect the individuals, i.e., they do not convey a common worldview of the right-holders. In the liberal legal paradigm, the indispensable minimal amount of connection between the individuals is created and maintained by the sovereign power of the state. It is the sovereign state power that safeguards not only the physical, but also the economic, social, and cultural preconditions of the individual's sphere of freedom, and which unburdens them from the necessity to form a legal community "from below." In other words, the legal community in which they live is created by and dependent upon political power that, at least in the German tradition, is not *constituted,* but only *limited* by the law, or, for that matter, by the constitution.

Within this liberal understanding, the concept of political power and the concept of law are connected in the following manner: the law is reduced to function as a safeguard for subjective rights and to delimit the subjective legal spheres of the individuals. Thus, it exonerates the individuals from the burden to form a legal community and to develop a common view of collective goals and aspirations. This function is executed by the political power of the state, which in turn is restrained by external limits that are imposed on it by the constitution and the law. In this model, political power is a resource that is not inherently connected with the law; however, it could exist—and indeed, in Germany and in other parts of Europe it did exist—independently of the law. German constitutional history of the nineteenth century consists mainly of the struggle of the liberal bourgeoisie to impose legal constraints on the military-bureaucratic power of the monarchy. Political power and the law had very different, even antagonistic sources. Hence, in the east and central European constitutional states, including Germany, there has always been a more or less visible tension between the two modes of political integration, namely the mode in which the law prevailed, and the mode in which political power prevailed, in the maintenance of the cohesion of the society. In the extreme situation of National Socialism in Germany, the sovereign state power was used as an overall substitute for the law to control the centrifugal forces of a society and to forcefully calm the class conflict.

Given this theoretical tradition, it is not surprising that very often individual rights and popular sovereignty have been regarded as incompatible. In the understanding of many continental jurists, popular sovereignty was merely another ideological justification for the supreme, homogeneous, and undivided power of the state. For example, the character of the French state after the revolution was perceived as hardly different from the absolutist power of the prerevolutionary era; the difference was the difference between monarchical and popular absolutism. In this sense, any kind of sovereign power, whether it be monarchical-absolutist, or democratic, was a threat to the integrity of individual rights. While this position definitively prevailed in Germany, this was not the position of the French doctrine. Be that as it may, political power remained the primary threat to the integrity of subjective rights, and this threat did not decrease by the mere fact that the power had become democratic. Under this doctrine, there is no inherent connection between political power and democracy. This may explain why the instrumental concept of political power was never fundamentally revised after mass democracy was established in Germany in 1919. To the contrary, Weber's, Michel's, Pareto's, and Schumpeter's "realistic" theories of democracy can be read as different attempts to subsume the dynamic, perhaps even anarchic, elements of the democratic principle under the disciplining force and the functional imperatives of the traditional concept of sovereign state power. A statist concept of democracy is still prevalent in Germany, and it is this theoretical tradition that is mainly challenged by Habermas's discourse-theoretical concept of political power.

Before I try to explain the internal structure of this notion of political power and its relation to the law in greater detail, let us have a look at what I have termed the "welfarist" paradigm. This paradigm is not so much concerned with rights as with the goal of substantive justice; it is more concerned with equality than with freedom. The problem with this concept is that the political power is used as a means to reach an end—social justice. This requires a permanent and never-ending activity of the state's interventionist authority whereby the legitimizing source, the idea of social solidarity, is consumed without being renewed because the substantive goal is reached. The "welfare state" needs the state power to perform its redistributive policies, and it needs the votes of the masses in democratic elections to have a democratic legitimation for those policies. However, the welfare state does not need a concept of distributive or social justice or a substantive idea of social solidarity. This is because social justice can be defined—and in fact is defined—in terms of equal distribution of those scarce goods that are deemed necessary for a decent standard of living. Social solidarity is expected to be achieved through administrative power, i.e., by a means that isolates individuals from each other.

Since the administrative state power is ultimately legitimized—although not really redeemed—by the democratic principle of popular sovereignty, here too the rights of the individuals and the principle of popular sovereignty are perceived as hostile to each other. The state produces social solidarity coercively, via administrative power; the administrative power executes the redistributive acts, and the law contains the normative justification. But neither does the administrative power really need the law to achieve its goals, nor does the law really guide the actions of the administrative power. In other words, the welfare-state notion of law is not inherently and necessarily connected with the concept of political power. Rather, political power could exist without any legal mediation and self-mediation. This isolation of the idea of social solidarity from the concept of law and its close association with the concept of political power may be one of the reasons why the processes of social de-solidarization are presently proceeding in all countries of a previously social-democratic political culture, not including the formerly Communist countries of eastern and central Europe.

Not surprisingly, the principal goal of Habermas's notion of political power is to reconnect the concept of political power with that of law, i.e., with freedom and social solidarity. This assumes that the democratic character of political power is conceptually essential and indispensable. Although Habermas does not ignore the notion that modern state power is predominantly administrative power that is necessary for the creation of binding decisions, in his theoretical framework the category of power that is a prerequisite to administrative power is Hannah Arendt's notion of "communicative power." As Habermas notes, such a power can neither be possessed, nor be understood

> as a potential for asserting one's own interests or realizing collective goals, nor as the administrative power to make binding decisions, but rather as an *authorizing* force expressed in the creation of legitimate law and in the founding of institutions. It manifests itself in orders that protect political liberty; . . . in the liberty-founding acts that bring new institutions and laws into existence. It emerges in the purest form in those moments when revolutionaries seize the power lying in the streets.[3]

Communicative power is the power that emerges from the exercise of political autonomy, and hence cannot be separated from the discursive processes of will-formation, i.e., from democracy. Both categories of power do not coexist uncoordinated, or, as was the case with the traditional concept of political power, in a relationship of latent tension. They are linked with each other, and the institutional link between democratic will-formation and administrative power is the law. Habermas views

3. *Id.* at 21–22.

law as the medium through which communicative power is translated into administrative power. For the transformation of communicative power into administrative has the sense of an empowerment within the framework of legal licenses. We can then interpret the idea of modern government by law generally as the requirement that the administrative system which is steered through the power code, be tied to the law-making communicative power and kept free of the effects of social power, i.e., of the de facto strength of privileged interests to assert themselves. Administrative power should not reproduce itself, but should only be permitted to regenerate from the conversion of communicative power.[4]

Under this concept, "human rights and popular sovereignty mutually presuppose one another,"[5] because both use language, i.e., discursive acts, as their primary source of social integration.[6] However, the law does not always emerge as the result of the discursive processes of communicatively acting subjects. It must also meet the functional requirements of a complex society. And even in the sphere of social integration through language, different discourses must be discerned.

The most important distinction is the one between legal and moral discourses. Legal discourses aim at legal norms that pertain to a concrete multitude of individuals in a concrete territory.

> While moral norms are directed to every person, though, legal norms address only the members of the legal community. . . . The equal consideration of all interests means something different in the law than it does in morality. . . . Legal material touches on collective goals and goods in a way that allows questions bearing on the concrete form of life to arise, if not questions of shared identity as well.[7]

Further differentiations are necessary. Although a legal and a moral community are two different phenomena, this by no means excludes the notion that *moral* issues can—and frequently do—become the object of a *legal* discourse. According to this conceptual framework, there is no such thing as a purely legal issue in that the concept of self-referentiality defines the law and legal issues. In Habermas's framework, the law is a particular and rational form through which a political community regulates its affairs. It follows from this that the legal discourse can touch on either *morally* or *ethically* relevant issues, or on *interests* that are not amenable to any kind of generalization or rational discourse.[8] Examples of the former category of issues are not only questions of criminal law, including abortion and crimi-

4. *See id.* at 24.
5. *Id.* at 4.
6. *See id.* at 23.
7. *Id.* at 29.
8. *See id.* at 44.

nal proceedings, but also questions of social policy, tax law, and problems of educational or health policies. In these cases, "discourses are called for that submit the contested interests and value orientations to a universalization test within the framework set by the constitutionally interpreted and elaborated system of rights."[9] As examples for the latter category—ethically relevant issues—Habermas mentions questions concerning: the protection of the environment and animals; traffic control and city planning; immigration policy; and the protection of cultural and ethnic minorities. In general, he mentions questions of political culture. In these cases, "discourses are called for that, pushing through the contested interests and values, engage the participants in a process of self-understanding by which they become reflectively aware of the deeper agreements in a shared form of life."[10] Finally, we must discriminate the issues that can only be handled in bargaining processes. "Bargaining processes are tailored for situations in which social power relations cannot be neutralized in the way rational discourse presupposes."[11] Where value orientations prevail, actors seek consensus, whereas in the fields where interests are predominant, compromises are the adequate and most sought after solutions of conflicts.[12] According to Habermas, consensus convinces all parties in the same way, whereas compromises are accepted by the parties on different grounds.[13] Compromises are only rational if they have been reached under fair conditions. But this does not alter the fact that compromises belong in the realm of strategic action where competing preferences are compatibilized or sometimes reconciled.[14] In this field, more than an aggregate total will cannot be reached.

In these three categories of discourse the constellations of reason and will—the two essential elements of every law—vary in a characteristic manner.[15] The discourse in which will and power prevail is the realm of compromise. In the discourse-theoretical perspective, the discourses about moral and ethical issues are the most important. In the former case, reason is clearly predominant. The results of this discourse are subject to the criterion of universalizability; its *idée directrice* is justice. In the discourse about moral issues we strive for a point of view that can be accepted by all: "[i]n moral discourse the ethnocentric perspective of a determinate collective expand into the comprehensive perspective of an unlimited communication community all the members of which put themselves in each individ-

9. *Id.*
10. *Id.*
11. *Id.* at 45.
12. *See id.* at 11.
13. *See id.* at 44.
14. *See id.* at 61, 64.
15. *See id.* at 42.

ual's situation, worldview and self-understanding, and together practice an ideal role-taking. . . ."[16]

It is much more difficult to discover the proportion of reason and will in the discourses about ethically relevant issues. The *idée directrice* of this discourse is not justice, but authenticity or, for that matter, the identity of a community. Ethical discourses clarify the "question of who we are and who we seriously want to be."[17] While in moral discourses we seek a solution that is "good for all," in ethical-political discourses we seek a common understanding about what is "good for us."[18] Evidently, it is the identity of a concrete community that sets the standard for what is reasonable and what is the purely self-asserting will power of a particular group.

In my view, for the ensuing discussion, the following problems need further clarification:

1. How can we distinguish morally relevant from ethically relevant issues? In what way, for example, does the issue of abortion, a tax law, or the organization of the health system have a different normative quality than, say, a question of environmental protection, city planning, or immigration policy? On what grounds are the results of discourses in the former field subject to the "justice" test, i.e., the test of what is "good for all," when the solutions in the latter area are open to the question of whether they are "good for us." What is the difference in a discourse-theoretical perspective?

2. Given this distinction between justice and authenticity as two different discursive logics, is it possible to follow the two logics simultaneously, depending on the issue? In other words, is it possible to take the universalist and the communitarian view at the same time, or must we assume that they are mutually exclusive?

3. If we accept the contention that moral norms are far more abstract than legal norms and that "as soon as rational collective will-formation aims at concrete legal programs, it must overstep the boundaries of justice discourses and include problems of achieving self-understanding and a balance of interests,"[19] the question arises if in this case moral standards, i.e., standards of universal justice, can be overruled by aspects of authenticity and by pragmatic compromises, or if they must be satisfied at all. If so, under which aspect are the logics of authenticity and of interest compromises relevant?

4. In the traditional framework of the constitutional state, subjective liberties entitle every citizen to step out of communication and to claim the famous right to be left alone. But this is, of course, not possible with respect

16. *Id.* at 40.
17. *Id.* at 64.
18. *Id.* at 38.
19. *Id.* at 29.

to the civil rights that entitle the individuals to participate in the formation of a democratic will. As we have seen, in Habermas's concept the quality of the popular will, the right proportion of reason and will, and hence the legitimacy of the political and administrative power, depend on the quality of the public and democratic discourses. Would it not be consequent to force the individuals to communicate? Do they not owe the community their active participation in the communicative processes? Does this concept not ultimately require a theory of civic duties, perhaps even of civic virtue?

5. In one passage of his book, Habermas speaks of the "danger" that "consists in the fact that compromise procedures get applied to moral or ethical questions, so that these are redefined into strategic questions without anyone noticing or calling attention to this."[20] The question is whether what Habermas describes as a problem should instead be viewed as a solution. Since it is much more difficult to find consensus in value-laden issues and conflicts than in interest conflicts, the transformation of a moral or ethical conflict into an interest conflict is frequently the only alternative to civil war. Hence, the question is whether the discourse-theoretical concept of the modern constitutional state does not imply a "communicative overload" in that it underestimates the peacekeeping and peacemaking function of strategic actions and of interest compromises.

20. *Id.* at 61.

SEVENTEEN

Constitutional Adjudication in Light of Discourse Theory

András Sajó*

INTRODUCTION

In the last one hundred years the empirical consequences of applied rationality have destroyed the last remnants of the trust in reason (*Vernunftvertrauen*). Postmodern law suffers from its own contradictory trends, which may be cured according to social practices indicated by discourse theory. In *Between Facts and Norms,*[1] Jürgen Habermas applies the theoretical scheme of communicative action in a specific argumentation context, namely to legal discourse.

The law of the welfare state suffers from the disparity of its structuring principles. The conflict between democracy and basic rights is at the root of the debate between federalism and republicanism. Either of these principles could and would serve as legitimation for law. However, they exist together and they prevail at each other's expense. According to the democracy principle of law, a statute is legitimized by the legislative process because all citizens (may) have participated in the determination of the law. The application of the principle of democracy entails that the majority principle prevails and that the law expresses the will of the majority (or the general will). The fundamental rights approach, on the other hand, goes back to European liberalism (i.e., free market advocacy). Nineteenth century free market liberalism considers the general or majority will as constrained by individual rights. Law is intended to safeguard these boundaries against arbitrary politics and the despotism of the state. The boundaries and safeguards are established by the constitution.

---

*Professor of Law, Central European University, Budapest.
1. JÜRGEN HABERMAS, BETWEEN FACTS AND NORMS: CONTRIBUTIONS TO A DISCOURSE THEORY OF LAW AND DEMOCRACY (William Rehg trans., 1996).

The conflict of these two trends was aggravated by the development and institutionalization of the welfare state and its services. The constitutional welfare-service state is becoming less and less transparent, and its diffuse and nontransparent nature causes a further defeat of rationality. Law is at jeopardy as a project of reason (*Vernunftprojekt*). If, however, the liquidation of the formal qualities of law and the annihilation of legal foreseeability (legal certainty) continue, this will endanger the steering capacity of law. Therefore, law would be unable to carry out its social integrative function.

Contemporary law shares the postmodern condition, which means that the rationality assumptions of modernity seem to be transcended. Consequently, the rationality of legal discourse, like that of any other social discourse, becomes suspicious and requires confirmation. In Habermas's view, the rationality deficit can be corrected by procedural rationality and *mutatis mutandis* that apply to law. Constitutional adjudication suffers the same tension as the legal system: it is torn apart by welfare-state services that are legitimated only partially by the principle of democracy and the protection of (individual) constitutional rights and freedoms. It remains to be seen whether constitutional adjudication can operate as part of a discourse project. If Habermas is right, then constitutional adjudication, in line with discourse theory assumptions, will become a legitimate and undisputed component of the legal system. It will play a crucial role in making the legal system itself legitimate and functional (*Funktionsfähig*) in the postmodern condition. If constitutional adjudication will operate according to discourse theory expectations, it will contribute to the rehabilitation of the project of modernity by setting limits to the ongoing destruction of legal rationality and the destructive consequences of reason in general.

Discourse theory may supplement the democracy principle and the constitutional rule-of-law system in such a way that enables the transcendence of their conflicting and one-sided functioning. Discourse theory opens up a vista where participatory democracy harbors a rights-based constitutional system. If suppositions of discourse theory are met, the constitutional order will cease to function as a mere legitimation of particular interests that claim to be *the* public good. Without a new rationality developed under discourse theory presuppositions, the present empirical situation will prevail. Empirical or realist sociologists, like Werner Becker, are at ease to point out that the systems of democracy are based on political nonparticipation (e.g., exclusion of and withdrawal by the citizens) and that, therefore, democracy transforms the interests of very narrow social groups into constitutionally recognized, lawful monopolies.[2]

2. *See generally* WERNER BECKER, DIE FREIHEIT, DIE WIR MEINEN: ENTSCHEIDUNG FÜR DIE LIBERALE DEMOKRATIE (1982); *see also* HABERMAS, *supra* note 1, at 287–328.

Habermas is attracted to the fundamental dilemma of constitutional adjudication, namely that the adjudication should give credibility to the principles of legal certainty and rational acceptability at the same time. Following and reinterpreting Ronald Dworkin, he concludes that a constructive practice of legal interpretation is possible and that the question to be answered remains, "how such a constructive practice of interpretation can operate within the bounds of constitutionally separated powers without the judiciary's encroaching on legislative powers (and thereby also undermining the strict binding of administration by law)."[3]

The relations between legislation and the judiciary were determined by the substantive priority of the product of legislation. There is no place for constitutional adjudication and review in traditional theories of separation of powers. The originally harmonious relation of subordination became increasingly problematic due to the activities of constitutional tribunals. Constitutional adjudication is not something taken for granted in the functioning of a traditional rule-of-law system.[4] From a historical perspective, the institutionalization of constitutional adjudication is exceptional, and this is particularly so if it is carried out by a constitutional court.[5] According to the criticisms expressed in traditional "separation theory," constitutional review extended its powers to a domain pertaining to the legislative branch. Theories of democratic legislation share this criticism of constitutional review as being lawmaking by a nonelected body that has no democratic mandate whatsoever and is clearly without legitimacy.

This Article analyzes the (theoretically potential) role of constitutional adjudication in the constitutional system and in the legal system in general. In order to extend the analysis to a sufficiently greater number of experiences, the term *constitutional adjudication* is used to avoid the country-specific connotations associated with judicial review.[6] *Judicial review* in this

---

3. HABERMAS, *supra* note 1, at 238.

4. Carl Schmitt advocated that decisions in matters regarding conflict of competence shall be reserved to the sovereign (the president) and that, therefore, there is no reason to use the form of judicial procedures. *See generally* CARL SCHMITT, DER HÜTER DER VERFASSUNG (1931).

5. Of course, bodies with authority to settle conflicts among state organs did exist from the dark ages, and it was quite common that these bodies acted as if they were administering justice using judicial procedures.

6. The translation of Habermas's *Between Facts and Norms* that I refer to in this Article also uses this term. *Judicial review* in England does not encompass the review of the constitutionality of legislation. *Constitutional review* is too closely related to activities of constitutional courts, although in a number of countries the activity is carried out by noncentralized courts or by centralized courts that function as appellate courts. *See generally* Louis Favoreu, *Constitutional Review in Europe, in* CONSTITUTIONALISM AND RIGHTS: THE INFLUENCE OF THE UNITED STATES CONSTITUTION ABROAD 38 (Louis Henkin & Albert J. Rosenthal eds., 1990); Mauro Cappelletti, *Repudiating Montesquieu? The Expansion and Legitimacy of "Constitutional Justice"*, 35 CATH. U. L. REV. 1 (1985).

Article indicates the review of legal provisions, particularly acts of parliament, by court-like bodies. The review process aims to establish whether the scrutinized provisions (or legal situations) are in conformity with the constitution. This Article is based primarily on experiences of the United States Supreme Court, the German Constitutional Court, and the Hungarian Constitutional Court,[7] but due credit is given to the French Constitutional Council's different kind of experience.[8] The common term for a constitutional court, council, or supreme court will be *tribunal.*

In order to clarify the political nature of the law generated by constitutional adjudication, Part I of this Article reviews lawmaking by constitutional adjudication. Part II addresses accusations that constitutional adjudication is an accomplice of modern law in abandoning modern law's liberal mandate to save basic individual rights and freedoms from state incursion. Part III deals with the nature of discourse in constitutional adjudication. Based on the results of the discourse theory, the contribution of constitutional adjudication is to assure that law serves the project of modernity under circumstances of the postmodern welfare state. It remains to be seen whether constitutional adjudication will contribute to the survival of a rights-based and foreseeable legal system.

European constitutional systems, including Great Britain's, are developing a supranational constitutional dimension through the Luxembourg and Strasbourg courts. This external control of national constitutional adjudication contributes to bringing constitutional review closer to a discourse-theoretical model.

7. The Hungarian experience seems accidental and, indeed, it is mentioned partly because of my familiarity with that court. However, the Hungarian Constitutional Justice Court represents a particularly interesting development, as it allows *anyone* to petition the court for any allegedly unconstitutional law. The court has to admit all petitions. The Hungarian court functions as a fundamental institution of the constitutional state in a social environment where civil society is underdeveloped and therefore the social sources of an independent public opinion are not always available. Political traditions are in many respects authoritarian, and the language of individual rights is underdeveloped. However, the press and the media are similar to those in Western Europe. These circumstances represent very special conditions of a discourse-based constitutional adjudication. It remains to be seen how far the constitutional discourse of the court and that of the constitutional law-oriented political-elites may go under these conditions.

8. Italian, Spanish, Rumanian, Bulgarian, and Austrian experiences were taken into consideration to the extent of their relevance to specific issues. One should also remember that constitutional structures have an important role in shaping the position of the tribunal. Switzerland has a less centralized system than that of the United States. Therefore, the Swiss Federal Appeals Court has a much more restricted jurisdiction than federal courts in the United States, and thus is less actively involved in constitutional interpretation.

A number of democracies have noncourt-based constitutional review systems. In Finland a special commission of Parliament is responsible for checking drafts from the constitutional perspective.

I. CONSTITUTIONAL ADJUDICATION IN THE POLITICAL PROCESS

Perhaps the most common criticism of constitutional adjudication is it creates law under the pretext of review and interpretation. Moreover, constitutional adjudication, allegedly, not only annihilates and rewrites acts of parliament, but also supplements and even amends the constitution.

The origins of constitutional adjudication go back to tribunals of competence, or simply to courts that had to adjudicate matters of conflict via the competence of state organs.[9] This original position was in harmony with the separation of powers doctrine and it was even a logical requirement in the system. Even today, jurisdictional adjudication represents the bulk of the activity of a supreme or constitutional court, particularly in the case of noncentralized review of the control of constitutionality that is couched in terms of competence problems.[10] Of course, much adherence to competence issues does restrict the concept of constitutional control.[11]

One may ask why the form of adjudication and the court system have been chosen to handle these competence strifes. In the case of adjudication by a court, a permanent body of personally independent, nonaccountable, democratically, and politically uncontrolled persons is acting, thus, giving fairness a chance. By definition, courts in a rule-of-law system are believed to act according to law and the constitution. A dispute handled by the administration of justice will be depoliticized, and because of the fairness of the process, the outcome will be more legitimate. Once a state organ is entitled to decide (e.g., has the competence), its law will be formally constitutional. In the case of contemporary constitutional adjudication, the statute (or its reinterpretation or replacement) will become legitimate not

9. Franz W. Jerusalem's position is characteristic of this early, interwar approach. He stated that a constitutional law dispute requires that the unconstitutional conduct breach the competence of a state organ. *See generally* FRANZ W. JERUSALEM, DIE STAATSGERICHTSBARKEIT (1930).

10. The United States Supreme Court also has a strong tendency to discuss problems of rights in terms of competence. This is partly due to language in the Bill of Rights, as it often stipulates freedoms as exemptions from federal and state legislative powers. Privacy rights (i.e., abortion) are to a great extent discussed in terms of federal legislative competence vis-à-vis state powers.

11. At an early stage, the Austrian Constitutional Court expressly refused to review the constitutionality of federal "constitutional" laws, as it believed that it had neither authorization nor standards to apply. 1952 Erkenntnisse und Beschlüsse des Verfassungsgerichtshofes [Vfslg] 2455. (According to the Austrian Constitution, "constitutional laws" shall be passed by a qualified majority. BUNDES-VERFASSUNGSGESETZ [Constitution] [B-VG] art. 44(1)).

The Belgian Arbitrage (Court of Arbitration) was also created as a tribunal of competence. However, relying on an equal protection clause of the Belgian Constitution, its powers were extended to the protection of rights set forth in the equal protection clause. *See generally* ANDRÉ ALEN ET AL., TREATISE ON BELGIAN CONSTITUTIONAL LAW (André Alen ed., 1992).

only, or primarily, as the expression of (correctly formulated) political will, but as directly authorized by the constitution. If constitutional adjudication could have limited itself to this almost unproblematic function, it would have been destined to become the safeguard of, and undisputable evidence of, the constitutional state premised on rights. Of course, after *Marbury v. Madison*[12] this relation became more problematic and centralized constitutional courts had a different mandate. Nevertheless, there was always a tension with respect to the constitutionality of laws even if there was no forum to handle the problem. However, the conflict remained isolated at the level of single courts and was, therefore, politically invisible (politics has little power to perceive peripheral events).

Not only United States judges, but their continental counterparts as well, had to face the problem of applying statutes that appeared to the judges to be unconstitutional. Sometimes these problems were solved in terms of interpretation by the lower courts. Decrees of the executive branch were already subject to judicial review in the nineteenth century, although lower-level judges were asked to suspend procedures and request decisions from appellate (or supreme) courts.[13] The tradition survives in constitutional provisions (of Italy, Germany, Hungary, etc.) requiring ordinary judges to ask for constitutional review.

After the Second World War, European countries that experienced the constitutional system's failure to protect rights, opted for centralized[14] constitutional courts that were directly responsible for the safeguard of fundamental constitutional rights (in addition to the traditional court of competence jurisdictions). The emphasis on rights protection and the wish to constitutionalize politics resulted in *abstract norm control;* where specific political actors were entitled to bring a statute to the court to have its text reviewed without an actual, individual controversy. The resulting actual performance of most of the constitutional courts and supreme courts went beyond the unproblematic and forced open the separation of powers arrangement. It has perpetuated the *potential* of confrontation with the legis-

---

12. 5 U.S. (1 Cranch) 137 (1803).

13. *See generally* GEORG JELLINEK, GESETZ UND VERORDNUNG: STAATSRECHTLICHE UNTERSUCHUNGEN AUF RECHTSGESCHICHTLICHER UND RECHTSVERGLEICHENDER GRUNDLAGE (1964). In some Imperial German States, ordinary courts were entitled to review the legality of regulations. Of course, there was a theoretical difference between constitutional and statutory review.

14. The Spanish solution relies on both the centralized and the loose models. Under the loose or decentralized model, any court may give constitutional redress in cases of actual violations of constitutional rights. The institution of *amparo* allows the Spanish Constitutional Court to grant extraordinary review in such cases.

342   LIBERALISM, REPUBLICANISM, AND CONSTITUTIONALISM

lative power.[15] It is an intrinsic characteristic of rights-protective constitutional review to defy legislative sovereignty.

However, the interventionism of constitutional adjudication is not necessarily as strong as it may seem, based on the aggressiveness of the demand of rights protection. Other features of the adjudication process, including its rules of procedure and the political environment of constitutional adjudication, exercise a balancing effect.

First, the political powers behind the legislative branch do not risk too much by temporarily institutionalizing, within the administration of justice, control over the actual legislative branch. The courts have no power of initiative—a court has to wait until a ripe case or petition comes up.[16] Except when exercising preliminary review, which is still unusual[17] and may not become the rule of constitutional adjudication, tribunals are reacting to past events. Procedure itself takes a long time, and the lapse of time or the force of events that took place under the problematic act forces the tribunals to respect the *status quo*.

One injustice is a tragedy; the occurrence of one hundred thousand cases is a statistic. Like all other political institutions, constitutional tribunals are not ready to deny and liquidate social and political facts that were established since the promulgation of an unconstitutional law, or to disregard social and political mass action.[18] Such a disregard is very costly, sometimes

15. The power of some constitutional courts to give "mandatory" advisory opinions on the meaning of the sections of the constitution is another source of such conflicts.

16. By extending the circle of those who can petition the constitutional tribunal, this restraint lost some of its importance. Of course, there are always enough petitions to allow a tribunal the choice of whatever it would like to deliberate on, giving the tribunal a power that is dangerously close to the power of initiative. However, the Hungarian Constitutional Court may even initiate cases, but because of self-restraint it has never made use of this power.

17. The French Council, and in other respects the *Conseil d'Etat*, exercises such powers. The Hungarian Court is also authorized to exercise preliminary review, but it has vehemently resisted the exercise of such powers despite being, at times, in rather clear violation of the letter of the law. *See generally* Peter Paczolay, *Judicial Review of the Compensation Law in Hungary*, 13 MICH. J. INT'L L. 806 (1992).

18. The French Constitutional Council declared the direct presidential election amendment of the French Constitution constitutional after it was approved by a referendum. In the process of presenting the draft of the referendum, the Council ruled, in a nonbinding opinion, that the procedure was unconstitutional. After the referendum, the Council declared that they no longer had competence. (62–20 DC, *Recueil Dalloz* (1962)). *See* ALEC STONE, THE BIRTH OF JUDICIAL POLITICS IN FRANCE: THE CONSTITUTIONAL COUNCIL IN COMPARATIVE PERSPECTIVE 65–66 (1992).

In 1983 the German Constitutional Court declared constitutional the dissolution of Parliament at the finish of the electoral campaign. Judgment of Feb. 16, 1983, 62 Entscheidungen des Bundesverfassungsgerichts [BVerfGE] 1 (F.R.G.).

In Hungary, the Constitutional Court declared that a decree on school headmasters' ap-

technically impossible, and will generate resistance among those who relied on the law. It is no surprise that although constitutional adjudication is based on the assumption that unconstitutional norms are void *ab initio*, most courts limit voidness to the case adjudicated. For example, the Turkish Constitution expressly states that voidness only begins after the promulgation of the unconstitutionality.[19]

It is much more difficult to explain the exceptional case of judicial politics making. In case of clear, court induced changes in politics, the decisions are argued in the most meticulously legalistic way. *Brown v. Board of Education (Brown II)*[20] is a case in point. Constitutional courts are ready to accept that the integrity of the state has "ontological" precedence over the constitution, as the constitution cannot exist without the precondition of statehood. Such statehood preconditions prevail against the will of other branches as well: legislation respects the priority of state (territorial) integrity needs.[21]

As Häberle put it: "[H]e who has the power of pleading, has the power of interpretation."[22] The circle of those entitled to request abstract review is restricted. Therefore, the constitutional adjudication process is more the continuation of a contemporary separation of powers and that of structural

---

pointments was unconstitutional. However, the appointments were held valid until the day of the promulgation of the decision, enabling the government to replace many schoolmasters who were considered disloyal. 47/1991. (IX. 24. AB).

In *Youngstown Sheet & Tube Co. v. Sawyer,* the Supreme Court decided that the government's seizure should be terminated and the plants returned to private operation. 343 U.S. 579, 585–89 (1952). However, in this case only one object was concerned and there were specific effects to be remedied. In cases concerning Native American lands, the Supreme Court has always been reluctant to apply the standard consequences of illegal mass takings.

19. Act of Nov. 7, 1982, No. 2709, *amended by* Act of May 17, 1987, No. 3361 (Turk.).

20. 349 U.S. 294 (1955).

21. The German Constitutional Court did in fact recognize the unconstitutionality of the Saarland Treaty, which returned the Saar province to Germany after World War II. The treaty was declared valid law: "[W]henever it comes to an international treaty which regulates the political relations of the Federation . . . one cannot overlook those political realities which are created or amended by the treaty." Judgment of May 4, 1955 (Saar Treaty Case), 4 BVerfGE 157, 168–70 (F.R.G.) (my translation). For details, see OTTO BACHOF, DER VERFASSUNGS-RICHTER ZWISCHEN RECHT UND POLITIK (1966); VERFASSUNGSGERICHTSBARKEIT (Peter Häberle ed., 1976) [hereinafter Häberle].

Similar considerations prevailed in the Soviet nationalization case. The German Constitutional Court upheld the German Unification Treaty and the German Democratic Republic-Federal Republic of Germany treaty, which denied restitution of property to those whose property was confiscated by the Soviets before 1949. Allegedly the Soviets insisted that there shall be no restitution during the unification negotiations. The German Constitutional Court found that the unification interest shall prevail against the property clauses of the Basic Law.

22. Häberle, *supra* note 21, at 35 (my translation).

differentiation of the state than a challenge to separation of powers. From the perspective of the recognition of new branches of power or new structural components of the contemporary state, political parties and territorial units are to be recognized as elements of the system of checks and balances. Political parties were recognized by the German Basic Law as participating in forming "the political will of the people."[23] The German Court recognized, in many respects, that the parties are constitutive elements of the state structure (*Parteienstaat*). In accordance with this trend, a number of countries have extended the right to initiate abstract review to parliamentary (party faction) minorities, with the minimum requirement varying between twelve and thirty-three percent of the representatives. In this respect, these minorities are treated on equal footing with state organs. Under the traditional separation of powers doctrine, only state organs were entitled to bring a suit for competence adjudication, although member states of a federation were also entitled to do so. However, the separation of powers doctrine also has a vertical dimension.

Nineteenth century parliamentary politics and legislation were based on discontinuous and unstable deliberations. Once the legislature made a decision, the lawmaking process came to a halt and the models of legal relations were fixed for a long period of time. Growing complexity and the need for continuous adjustment in postmodern society require the replacement of that model. Law is unfinished in the sense of being open-ended and easily amendable. Legislation has become a system of replacement and adjustment. Law is not the symbol of stability, but rather a temporary (even ad hoc) arrangement or compromise. Statutes are neither comprehensive nor self-executory. The complexity and instability of social relations suggest that the administration takes over the regulatory powers of the legislature.

Given these preconditions, the enactment of laws is not the termination of the legislative process: in the best of cases, laws reshape the conditions of the struggles and bargaining that preceded their enactment. Legislation *writ large* does not end with the formal vote-taking in parliament. This approach is not necessarily in contradiction with principles of democracy. As long as the components of the continued process are democratically legitimate, there will be no democratic deficit; of course, the rules of the game of this continued process may be subject to different conditions of democracy. Even the process of constitutional adjudication may meet the criteria of democracy, as long as it is subject to the control of democratic public opinion and some of the participants are the democratically established political actors.

Modern political systems are forced to allow the continuation of the legislative process under the circumstances of the administration of justice.

23. GERMAN BASIC LAW art. 21(1).

The political powers that control legislation and government have to accept that the political majority's solution of the legislative conflict is subject to review following the request of the losing party or, even, injured individuals. Abstract norm control means the continuation of the legislative legal discourse in a social context that has a great potential for publicity. Constitutional adjudication may diminish the internal tensions of the political system through its independent, nonpolitical processes, although possibly at the price of establishing a procedure that is not directly accessible to and controllable by political actors. Moreover, at the end of the adjudicatory procedure these politically less controlled decisions may feed back[24] to new legislation tensions by confronting the legislator with a "constitutional alternative." Once the possibility of continued legislation is established, the legislature is forced to *anticipate* possible reactions of the constitutional tribunal and act within the limits set by the tribunal.[25]

The above concession of politics to constitutional adjudication is due to changes in the field of activity and intensity of the state. The welfare state has extended its activities to new areas of social life, and this involves the extension of law to previously self-steering areas (e.g., the "juridification" of relations).[26] Constitutional adjudication is a paradoxical consequence of this extension of law, or juridification. The extension of law to welfare services implies an instrumental approach to law. The rule-of-law system was based on noninstrumental reason serving the protection of rights. This program required some control over the new instrumentalism, and constitutional adjudication was originally developed as an attempt to protect these rights. To varying degrees, the rule-of-law system could not resist the requirements of the welfare system and has generated new mechanisms of instrumentalism limiting the original rights.

---

24. As a way to channel legislation without embarrassment, the German Court developed a system of admonitory decisions (*Appellentscheidurgen*). The court declares a statute unconstitutional, but applicable (not void), to allow the legislature to take action, often within a specified time. This self-restraint is accompanied by excessive activism because the court tends to give guidelines for new legislation. *See generally* Wiltraut Rupp-von Brünneck, *Germany: The Federal Constitutional Court,* 20 Am. J. Comp. L. 387 (1972).

The Hungarian Court goes beyond this practice by setting legislative deadlines.

25. "Constitutional aspirations . . . rule out some, but not all, choices. Indeed, they fail to rule out indefinitely many choices. The judicial function is to determine which choices are ruled out. The legislative function is to select among the choices not ruled out. . . . " MICHAEL J. PERRY, MORALITY, POLITICS, AND LAW: A BICENTENNIAL ESSAY 170 (1988).

26. The need for politics to be "juridically constituted" is related to the fact that in modern societies it is the legal form based on equal rights that creates conditions of acceptance for a rationally structured society. Aside from legitimacy needs (which means the perspective of the actors resulting in acceptance of the conditions), juridification has further related advantages for the political power. The neutrality of the legal form disguises political one-sidedness.

Habermas describes the original functions of politics in the constitutional state:

> [I]n virtue of its internal relation to law, politics is responsible for problems that concern society as a whole. It must be possible to interpret collectively binding decisions as a realization of rights such that the structures of recognition built into communicative action are transferred, via the medium of law, from the level of simple interactions to the abstract and anonymous relationships among strangers.[27]

In the welfare state, the above effort of politics to achieve juridification becomes highly problematic. The failure of politics to carry out its integrative function in legal terms has negative impacts on the legitimacy and steering capacity of law itself, which may result in a "whirlpool of legitimation deficits and steering deficits."[28] Politics too is at risk:

> The constitutionally regulated circulation of power is nullified if the administrative system becomes independent of communicatively generated power, if the social power of functional systems and large organizations (including the mass media) is converted into illegitimate power, or if the lifeworld resources for spontaneous public communication no longer suffice to guarantee an uncoerced articulation of social interests.[29]

Under these circumstances, one can understand the increased interest of politics to allow constitutional review. Constitutional adjudication responds, at least partly, to the needs of politics. These needs include the need for institutionalization of a self-referential legal system that is independent of political power games. Incapacitated politics is ready to submit itself, to some extent, to neutral external control in order to gain credibility and steering capacity.

Irrespective of the new self-understanding of politics in structuring the state, one cannot acquit constitutional adjudication of the accusation regarding the orthodox violation of the separation of powers doctrine. Some of the systems, namely the Hungarian one, allow individuals to ask for abstract constitutional review. Individuals are nonentities in traditional state theories. The simplest empirical survey will point out that a fair number of decisions consist of actual determinations of the constitutional content of statutes, implying the revision and rewriting of legislation by the tribunals

27. HABERMAS, *supra* note 1, at 385.

28. *Id.* at 386. Habermas points out that in case of weakness of civil society, the development of such deficits is quite likely: the prospects of constitutional adjudication and the rule of law in general are, therefore, particularly dim in the postcommunist societies, notwithstanding the imitation of Western legal forms. *See id.*

29. *Id.*

in the form of interpretation. Certain laws are struck down,[30] and some courts supplement or even amend the constitution itself.

However, politicization of the law through constitutional adjudication remains restrained. This can be illustrated by two of the most dramatic examples of resistance to politics or government by constitutional tribunals on political grounds. The first example involves the United States Supreme Court's challenge to New Deal policies that eventually had to be withdrawn. The second example involves the antisocialist French Constitutional Council refrain from frontally attacking the nationalization law of the socialist government in 1982, limiting its resistance to legally relevant smaller points (which were accepted, and others anticipated, by the government).

In these cases of extreme political conflict, the courts adhered to values of formerly governing political programs and parties that, by the time of the deliberation, had become political minority positions. This adherence meant that the majority of the sitting justices shared political values with the ousted former political party and, more importantly, that their decisions were now binding precedents upholding the basic philosophy of the previous legislature. This is not to say that specific legal policies were declared to be unalterable constitutional solutions. Constitutional tribunals generally allow a broad discretion to legislatures to determine economic and other policies. The majorities within the courts were affiliated with political groups that were not ousted from power and maintained a position in core politics. These groups remained political actors in the sense that they had fair chances to regain political decision-making power according to the rules of parliamentary democracy. These forces of the "semipast" were, in fact, of considerable political significance.

The conservationist constitutional tribunal fights as a "rear guard" against legislation that is narrowly understood. The rear guard's position is based on prior positions of constitutional law developed under previous political regimes. There is nothing special in institutionalizing the power of the past over the present. Laws requiring a qualified majority for amendment, along with the constitution's prohibitive rules of amendment, express the wish for either a larger political community or a consensus against the whims of a temporary majority. Similarly, the fixation of the constitutional tribunal to previous political power sharing enables the (indirect) involvement of political opposition, which has no actual power to affect the legislative bargain in parliament. Constitutional adjudication extends the legis-

---

30. There is no reliable quantitative study of voided statutes that would indicate the percentage of the legislation voided. In Hungary, the court has found, during its first three years of existence, unconstitutional provisions in about twenty percent of the statutes reviewed. Compared to Germany, and even to Italy, this is high.

lative process and, in these circumstances of extension, will represent a restricted position of the opposition.

All of this amounts to partial involvement, in the legislative process, of those political parties that were temporarily excluded from parliamentary legislation. Of course this participation is narrow and limited, yet it enables the views of those political actors who are temporarily excluded from legislation to be taken into consideration. The least that can be avoided is the enacting of legislative deliberations that are irreversible, either legally or because of the accumulating normative weight of social facts developed under the impact of the contested legislation.

As the above examples indicate, the political independence and oppositional activity of the constitutional tribunals are restricted to rear guard actions supporting some of the ideas of temporarily ousted political groups. If a constitutional tribunal goes beyond this limit by advocating views of parties or groups that have no chance to get closer to power, or by advocating constitutional positions that are irrelevant to political power holders (even if these positions are the most faithful to constitutional beliefs of the founding fathers), the tribunal should consider that their decisions may not be observed. The tribunal will lose its legitimacy in consequence of the nonexecution of its decisions and, as a result of this process, the tribunal will, in the end, simply be pushed aside. In 1952, the South African Supreme Court, which was highly regarded as an independent and determined protector of constitutionalism, tried to resist the popularly endorsed apartheid policies of government—such efforts were simply dismissed through constitutional amendment.[31]

Habermas considers legislation a bargaining process that fundamentally differs from moral or ethical discourses. However, legitimate legislation occurs under discourse conditions and, in this respect, belongs to rational discourse. Given the past-oriented mandate of the tribunals, they will generate continued legislative bargaining couched in normative (constitutional) terms, thus moving away from majority legislation toward a broader *social consensus*.

Of course, the move toward a social consensus is limited. The tribunal's discourse allows the involvement of theoretical and actual positions of major political parties that can be revived. This opening is more available to

31. *Harris v. Minister of the Interior,* 2 S. Afr. App. Div. 428 (1952) (Coloured Vote Case). *See generally* Cappelletti, *supra* note 6; Erwin N. Griswold, *The "Coloured Vote Case" in South Africa,* 65 HARV. L. REV. 1361 (1952).

Chief Justice Zorkin's Russian Constitutional Court, at least partly, shared the same fate. In the Russian case, however, one could state that the court was unable to find the right distance from politics. The fate of the Russian court indicates that there are natural boundaries that limit a constitutional court's involvement in politics, and, in addition, a healthy court has its own mechanisms to protect itself from political involvement.

political elites than to the public sphere. The tribunals are not sensitive to emerging political forces that have not had the opportunity to plant their representatives on the bench. On the other hand, given the limited social and political diversity of the justices, the constitutional tribunals are in many respects more open to allowing the public sphere to represent itself than one would expect. Constitutional justices come from elite legal or academic circles that highly esteem academic freedoms. These tribunals are inclined to express the views of certain intellectual elites aside from those of the political elite. Academic elites have a particular interest in maintaining conditions of public discourse. This is the source of the well-known, worldwide constitutional law protections of free speech and privacy.[32] The effort to safeguard free speech contributes to the safeguarding of the public sphere and its communicative power,[33] enabling emerging groups to participate in the public sphere and compete with already well-entrenched political parties.

A further charge against constitutional adjudication voices a complementary objection based on the separation of powers doctrine. In this case, the impairment of administration of justice privileges (instead of the impairment of legislative power) is recalled. According to the charge, if the tribunal is involved to a great extent in legislation, it will become politicized and an accomplice in the process of replacing law with politics ("political law"). Such politicization of the law will endanger the autonomy and distinctiveness of the law, thus causing its delegitimation.

One of the arguments in support of the above politicization thesis relates to the system of appointing constitutional judges. Such appointments are not solely the result of bargains, party politics, and compromises among

32. Robert McCloskey wrote in a classic article that a

> major difficulty with [the formulation that treats free choice in the intellectual and spiritual realms as more deserving of protection than economic liberty] is that there is the smell of the lamp about it: it may reflect the tastes of the judges and dons who advance it, rather than the real preferences of the commonality of mortals. Judges and professors are talkers both by profession and avocation. It is not surprising that they would view freedom of expression as primary to the free play of their personalities. But most men would probably feel that an economic right, such as freedom of occupation, was at least as vital to them as the right to speak their minds. Mark Twain would surely have felt constrained in the most fundamental sense, if his youthful aspiration to be a river-boat pilot had been frustrated by a State-ordained system of nepotism.

> Robert G. McCloskey, *Economic Due Process and the Supreme Court: An Exhumation and Reburial,* 1962 SUP. CT. REV. 34, 46 (citation omitted).

33. Once again, rights-protective intervention in the domain of free speech is highly ambiguous, especially in the case of electronic media. If there is no intervention, public communication and, thus, the mass culture imposed on the social sphere, will be exposed to merciless domination by the mass media. If, however, there are quantitative restrictions (e.g., quotas) or access rules, the media may lose its freedom.

different governmental branches. Sometimes appointments are simply rewards of political (partisan) loyalty. It is rare for legal systems to require only a minority of constitutional judges to come from the judiciary.[34] In Europe, lack of tenure further contributes to lack of independence from political forces.

One should not confuse undeniable politically principled partisanship with loyalty to an actual party formation. Once one accepts that constitutional review is the continuation of the legislative process by other means and under different circumstances, the fact that the constitution is interpreted by people with politically colored value systems will fit the "continuity" hypothesis. The constitutionality of a statute shall be interpreted by continuing with the interpretative assumptions of those political forces that participated in the legislation *writ large*, including the interpretative assumptions of the public sphere.

However, the main charge against constitutional adjudication (i.e., that it involves the politicization of law through constitutional adjudication) is unrelated to personal dependence. Politics in the law means that legal provisions are evaluated according to nonlegal considerations. The constitutional tribunal allegedly creates law following its own politics. This accusation is to some extent counterfactual, as legislation by the courts runs into serious technical obstacles. The courts are entitled to *void* unconstitutional provisions. Even if the courts outline the "constitutional solution" to a regulatory problem, generally the legislature has no obligation to enact laws according to the prescriptions of the constitutional tribunal. Even if the legislature formally complies, or has to comply, with the guidance of the tribunal, it has more than one way to circumvent the tribunal's requirements. In fact, constitutional tribunals have more of a chance to provide lasting and unsupervised determinations of the law by interpreting the law rather than voiding it. In this case, the tribunal, by its interpretative action, keeps the provision within the administration of justice—no other branch will have the opportunity to review its decision. Furthermore, this action, which in practice may mean a complete reshaping of the norm, is completely valid because it is the result of interpretative actions that are entirely legitimate according to the separation of powers doctrine.

"Political argumentation," as used in constitutional adjudication, implies that a tribunal will use political considerations in its deliberation. It will replace a norms/principles-oriented argumentation with a consequentialist one, where the consequences are discussed in political terms. The effects

34. Although this is the case in Italy and Germany. However, under the Turkish Constitution, judicial and other nongovernmental bodies have the power to determine the candidates.

will be measured according to consequences in power sharing, access to power, destabilization, etc. Such a political argumentation is not necessarily couched in terms of party politics, and it is not intended to generate power monopolies. In the case of constitutional adjudication, political argumentation will certainly not serve the tribunal's aspirations for unlimited power. What happens when a constitutional tribunal allows political considerations to prevail is, in fact, that the tribunal allows the other branches of power to act *without* constitutional control. The tribunal yields to create and carry out the politics of the other branches, and in accepting political considerations, it renounces its constitutional mandate to exercise control. This refusal by tribunals to consider their own political views, or at least to increase the level of their control, is the most common manifestation of the politics of constitutional adjudication. Tribunals have developed a whole series of doctrines, rights, and powers to justify this self-restraint[35] (i.e., the political questions doctrine, preferred rights, police powers, and *Funktionsfähigkeit*). As Chief Justice Marshall once wrote: "Let the end be legitimate, let it be within the scope of the constitution, and all means which are appropriate, which are plainly adapted to the end, which are not prohibited, but consistent with the letter and spirit of the constitution, are constitutional."[36]

However, such constitutional "nonchalance" became problematic within the context of the welfare state. In many respects Michael Perry is right: "The real danger is not that the judge will go too far, against government, but that she will not go far enough."[37] Legislation, as a steering program, became less and less capable of regulating increasingly more complex, diffuse, and changing social relations through abstract legal categories. Acts of parliament are increasingly goal setting, relying on the administration to fill the huge, undetermined area according to its own efficiency concepts. Constitutional courts accept the liberty of the legislative branch to use open-ended and indefinite notions, which enables accommodation for changing circumstances, although at the expense of traditional accountability and predictability.[38] "Various symptoms of . . . a *cognitive overburdening* of deliberative politics give credence to the assumption, by now widely

35. For those developed in Germany, see Judgment of July 31, 1973 (Inter-German Basic Treaty Case (II)), 36 BVerfGE 1, 14 (F.R.G.); Judgment of June 18, 1973 (Inter-German Treaty Ratification Case (I)), 35 BVerfGE 257, 262 (F.R.G.).

36. *McCulloch v. Maryland*, 17 U.S. (4 Wheat.) 316, 421 (1819), *reprinted in* LAURENCE H. TRIBE, AMERICAN CONSTITUTIONAL LAW 337 (2d ed. 1988). For similar German opinions, see Judgment of Apr. 13, 1978 (Military Defense Obligation Case), 48 BVerfGE 127, 160 (F.R.G.); Judgment of May 4, 1955 (Saar Treaty Case), 4 BVerfGE 157, 168 (F.R.G.).

37. PERRY, *supra* note 25, at 149.

38. *See, e.g.*, Judgment of Aug. 8, 1978 (Kalkar Case), 49 BVerfGE 89 (F. R. G.).

accepted, that discursive opinion- and will-formation governed by democratic procedures lacks the complexity to take in and digest the *operatively
necessary* knowledge."[39]

The politicization of constitutional adjudication, which is only relative, is
to be interpreted in the above context. What is generally described as politics is, in most of the cases, a desperate attempt to reconstruct law's rationality through procedural means, which is at jeopardy because of administrative practices. Unfortunately, constitutional argumentation, in practice,
cannot liberate itself from the social and intellectual context that overbur-
dens it with nonlegal, political considerations, and it may well be that the
cure will be worse than the disease. In particular, principled reasoning (instead of abiding to rules) is problematic in this respect.

The result is ambiguous. Constitutional adjudication is not ready to exercise full constitutional control over an economy that was left to individual
initiative by liberal constitutionalism. Constitutional adjudication, as mentioned above, tries to take a noncommittal position vis-à-vis welfare service
and economic interventionism. This withdrawal means, in practice, that the
tribunal, in its ventures to extend governmental control over freedoms in
the private sphere,[40] consents with the legislation whenever the services
proposed limit private initiative and choice.

The tribunal's constitutional mandate requires that this complicity be
carried out in the guise of rights protection (of course, not in the guise of
curtailed freedom rights, but in the guise of other, partly new welfare or
traditional rights that, under the new circumstances, provide actual services and require active governmental support). Paradoxically, in this process of noninterference, the constitutional tribunal must, in the name of
equality, simultaneously exercise certain control and guidance over the
vague legislation and over the discretionary realization of the administration's legislative goals.

Respect of the neutral state is another rebuttal of the never clearly defined charge of judicial activism. Activism, of course, exists as an empirical
phenomenon, but it is well contained by the political system primarily due
to organizational constraints. Respect of neutrality is valid to the extent
that it makes constitutional tribunals paradoxically active again. Tribunals
are often ready to strike down laws that breach the principle of neutrality.
Respect of the neutral state means that the tribunal perceives itself as part
of a neutral state. As tribunals conceive themselves as judicial organizations
of the neutral state, state action expressed in the form of statutes will not

---

39. HABERMAS, *supra* note 1, at 320.
40. Note that there is an enormous difference in intensity between constitutional control
over the state-owned (public) and private economy.

be overturned simply because the legislature may have inaccurately predicted the consequences of social or economic policy. As the *Codetermination* and *Kalkar* cases make plain, the court grants a generous margin of "error" to the legislature. It will uphold an ordinary statute unless it clearly violates the principle of proportionality (*Verhältnismässigkeit*), the rule of law (*Rechtsstaatlichkeit*), or some related principle of justice such as legal security, clarity, or predictability.[41]

The courts are rather passive and, in these cases, do not impose their constitutional vision on legislation. The limits to such leniency are to be found in a second meaning of neutrality. The court will become quite active in rejecting legislation that would likely impose upon society a vision of the good life because "so long as some view about the good life remain[ed] disputed, no decision of the state [could] be justified on the basis of its supposed intrinsic superiority or inferiority."[42] Of course, the tribunal must look at the public sphere to determine the existence of such a dispute, although the constitution itself may serve as a reference. The violation of a fundamental right or freedom entails that the government-imposed vision of the good life is disputed. Acting under the guidance of neutrality is not necessarily activism: neutrality will indicate what is a breach of neutrality, but it will not suggest the correct regulatory action. Indeed, there is more than one acceptable action.

II. MATERIAL JUSTICE

At this point one cannot avoid facing the objections to constitutional adjudication voiced by liberal critics and cited by Habermas.[43] Constitutional adjudication seems to have switched constitutions in order to abandon, at least partly, the liberal mandate and act as a neutral guardian of rights. Constitutional tribunals feel compelled to act as enforcers of material jus-

41. DONALD P. KOMMERS, THE CONSTITUTIONAL JURISPRUDENCE OF THE FEDERAL REPUBLIC OF GERMANY 58–59 (1989) (citations omitted).

> The Constitutional Court of Hungary stated that in the exercise of discretionary powers (in matters of tax exemptions) "the legislator is entitled to consider short term economic policy . . . considerations which are not deductible from the Constitution. . . . In his deliberation, although bound within constitutional limits . . . the legislator is primarily determined by nonlegal considerations, and consequently, eventually wrong decisions, which conflict with the interests of society, mak[ing] the legislator prominently politically liable." 61/1992. (XI. 20. AB, ABH).

42. CHARLES E. LARMORE, PATTERNS OF MORAL COMPLEXITY 47 (1987), *quoted in* HABERMAS, *supra* note 1, at 309.

43. *See* HABERMAS, *supra* note 1, at 244. Habermas relies on the criticisms of Ernst-Wolfgang Böckenförde, Erhard Denninger, and Dieter Grimm.

tice, and this results in judicial policy making without a democratic, or even constitutional, mandate.

The constitutional condition of the welfare state would represent a political order that not only provides individual protection of rights, but takes care of the social welfare and social security of its citizens. In the liberal order, private good and public good are neatly separated. The goals and tasks of the state are left for politics and are not subject to constitutional control (except to the extent that the realization of politics encroaches into a protected private domain). This is expressed in German doctrine by the concept of *Abwehrrechte,* or defensive rights. According to the doctrine, the constitutional legal order shall determine the exact borders of state intervention. One can find parallels to this approach in the United States Supreme Court's pre-Depression jurisprudence, which considered that the role of the Constitution is to *contain* the state within limits. Under these assumptions, the legal order's attitude toward the administration is limited to the protection of its citizens against the administration's arbitrariness.

Habermas contrasts these assumptions with the realities of the welfare state (*Sozialstaat*).[44] The legal system of the welfare state is not primarily composed of programs with well-determined conditions; instead it contains political goal-statements. Decision making, according to principles, will function to the detriment of constitutional architectonics. Legal reasoning will be replaced by moral considerations and political opportunity, thus restricting the autonomy of citizens by granting powers to the administration of justice. The fall of human (individual) or citizen autonomy means the collapse of the project of enlightenment. Böckenförde argues that the constitutional court's control and management of welfare-state public administration services results in narrowing the gap between legislative and judicial law development. "In this competitive relation the initiative belongs to legislation, but the priority in hierarchy belongs to the constitutional court."[45] Böckenförde believes that fundamental rights are only rights *against* state power, but that these fundamental rights are not "norm principles" (*Grundsatznorm*) that would have objective validity in all areas of law.[46] In other words, the extension of "objective norm principles" to the whole legal system is endangering private autonomy. The constitutional court is undertaking to do exactly that without democratic or (perhaps) constitutional mandate. The constitutional court liberates the public administration of its chains that were intended to protect individual liberty,

44. *See id.* at 244–45.

45. ERNST-WOLFGANG BÖCKENFÖRDE, *Grundrechte als Grundsatznormen: Zur gegenwärtigen Lage der grundrechtsdogmatik, in* STAAT, VERFASSUNG, DEMOKRATIE 189, 194 (1991) (my translation).

46. *See id.* at 194, *quoted in* HABERMAS, *supra* note 1, at 249.

and it accepts the functioning of a loose welfare administration that operates exclusively by material justice and efficiency considerations and disregards legal rationality. Principled constitutional reasoning did develop, among others, the doctrine (or principle) of third party effect (*Drittwirkung*) which consequently restricted certain fundamental rights, like that of free speech.[47]

The submission of governmental politics to legal supervision may certainly result in the deformation of the traditional legal system. The deformation would include diminished steering capacity and freedoms-protecting capacity of formal legal structures, and it could contribute to another loss of rationality and a defeat for rational discourse. If law is the result of social bargains based on the fair and reasonable expression of different interest considerations, then modern constitutional adjudication is really a threat to law because it develops, at least apparently, outside of legitimate, interpretative, and open legal discourse. In this scenario constitutional adjudication would deprive law of politically relevant general solutions by excluding the public sphere. As a matter of fact, the actual performance of constitutional adjudication is (at least partly) a contribution to the legal control of public administration. Furthermore, the theoretically reconstructed nature of constitutional adjudication will show that it is structured in such a way that allows it to get close enough to discourse theory expectations to enable its capable performance to contribute to the project of modernity in the world of social welfare services.

Following Tribe's reasoning, one may conclude that the result of the United States Supreme Court's judicial review in matters of economic/welfare legislation was the replacement of the original "minimum rationality" requirement of state regulation with an increasingly more demanding test of equal protection.[48] Welfare recipients are entitled to equal treatment, and at least the likelihood of factual differences is needed to rationalize any distinction among them.

Habermas believes that the principles developed by the Supreme Court in this respect would meet discourse theory expectations, and that the purposes served by the Court's judicial review will fit into the traditional rights-

47. However, another judge of the German Constitutional Court, Dieter Grimm, comes to a completely different conclusion. He is disappointed with the possibility that the constitution will be reduced into a *partial order* of the legal system, as it is unable to penetrate into the public administration or to terminate the steering deficit through its control. *See* DIETER GRIMM, DIE ZUKUNFT DER VERFASSUNG 437 (1991), *quoted in* HABERMAS, *supra* note 1, at 390–91.

48. For a similar position of the Hungarian Constitutional Court, see 772/B/1990. AB hat. ABH 1991. 519. 520. The Hungarian Court does not extend its scrutiny to inefficiency of regulations. For a United States Supreme Court opinion upholding economic legislation supported by *any* rational basis, see *United States v. Carolene Prods. Co.*, 304 U.S. 144 (1938).

protective agenda of liberalism. Habermas relies here on a study by Cass Sunstein.[49] Sunstein's suggested goals for law are "the effort to promote deliberation in government, to furnish surrogates for it when it is absent, to limit factionalism and self-interested representation, and to help bring about political equality."[50] These goals would have been denounced by Max Weber as material justice, although they may indeed be needed. If we accept Sunstein's analysis, the Supreme Court would operate with "background norms" (having the function of principles) which surrender the legal system to the Court, for example, when "obsolete statutes are kept consistent with changing developments of law, policy, and fact; . . . the complex systemic effects of regulation are taken into account; and, most generally, . . . irrationality and injustice, measured against the statute's own purposes, are avoided."[51] Habermas, following Denninger, finds similar trends in Germany.

If the above reconstruction of constitutional adjudication is correct, it is a cause for serious concern for liberal values, particularly for the protection of constitutional freedoms. If these freedoms are not protected any more, then the fiasco of modernity is repeated again, and law will become unable to provide human autonomy with its fundamental contribution. This remains a significant danger even if the constitutional court restricts freedoms in order to materialize (promote) other constitutional rights, when in fact one cannot read most of those rights.[52]

In order to better understand the above process of rights being endangered by modern law through constitutional adjudication, a typical case of the activist welfare interpretation will suffice.[53] The German Constitutional Court restricted academic freedom (the autonomy of universities) in a series of decisions. These decisions were based on article 12(1) of the Basic

---

49. *See* HABERMAS, *supra* note 1, at 251–52 (quoting CASS R. SUNSTEIN, AFTER THE RIGHTS REVOLUTION: RECONCEIVING THE REGULATORY STATE 170–71 (1990)). Note, however, that Sunstein's language is *prescriptive*.

50. SUNSTEIN, *supra* note 49, at 171.

51. *Id.*

52. It is particularly disturbing that constitutional tribunals generate their own concept of constitutional order from specific statements of the constitution and use requirements and principles derived from that concept of order to restrict expressed freedoms. Of course, in a number of cases the approach of the tribunals relies to a great extent on social realities, but social reality should not be taken for granted, and there are indeed many possible constructions of reality. In this respect the court is not simply selecting a reality that has to be taken into consideration. Rather, it is imposing one or more constitutional visions of reality on a competing reality.

53. Traditional liberal criticism emphasizes that by enforcing welfare services, law destroys private initiative even if the protection of objective fundamental rights is less stressed in the private sector (and private business sector) than in the example of *publicly* financed higher education.

Law, which provides for the free choice of vocation and education.[54] According to one such decision, the first *Numerus Clausus* case:

> [t]he Federal Constitutional Court has repeatedly declared that basic rights in their capacity as objective norms also establish a value order that represents a fundamental constitutional decision in all areas of the law. Therefore . . . basic rights are not merely defensive rights of the citizen against the state. The more involved a modern state becomes in assuring the social security and cultural advancement of its citizens, the more the complementary demand that participation in governmental services assume the character of a basic right will augment the initial postulate of safeguarding liberty from state intervention.[55]

Placing a basic right (i.e., the freedom to choose an occupation) into practice, primarily in the private sector, is enough to ensure freedom from any coercion. In the situation of choosing a place to pursue a higher education, this right needs an actual ability to be exercised, and therefore the state must provide the services.[56] In this context the German Constitutional Court "has transformed itself into a veritable ministry of education."[57] However, the consequences are ambiguous from the perspective of rights protection. The Constitutional Court is deeply involved in providing material conditions of equality. The same effort, however, did considerably restrict the discretionary powers of governmental administration by subjecting it to judicial review and by constraining legislation to set formal legal criteria in a sphere that was previously left to educational policy. This is inarguably contributing to legal rationalization and the certainty of politics. Politics is juridified, however, at the expense of the quality of law. The institutionalization of constitutional adjudication is subjecting public administration to public legal control. This is a form of self-defense for modern law, which is otherwise on the way to becoming a set of "conditional programs."[58] Without further protection, law "as a system of rights safeguards" will be transformed into a system of securing legal goods (*Rechtsgütersicherheit*) that " 'modifies and dissolves' [the] individual legal protection"[59] of rights.

---

54. It is remarkable that the conflict with the freedom of education (teaching) was not even mentioned by the Court, although the issue arose because the legislation of various *Länder* already disregarded that autonomy by regulating entry into the universities.

55. Judgment of July 18, 1972 (Numerus Clausus Case I), 33 BVerfGE 303, 330–31 (F.R.G.), *translated in* KOMMERS, *supra* note 41, at 298.

56. In subsequent cases, the obligation of the state to provide services or material conditions was interpreted in the context of actual university facility use. The Court allowed the state to create new facilities as long as all needs were met, although the pace of satisfying such needs depended on the state's performance capacity, which was not subject to judicial review.

57. KOMMERS, *supra* note 41, at 303.

58. HABERMAS, *supra* note 1, at 190.

59. *Id.* at 433 (quoting ERHARD DENNINGER, DER GEBANDIGTE LEVIATHAN 33, 35 (1990)).

However, constitutional adjudication does provide further protection. Administrations became subject to judicial review due to constitutional review of the enabling statutes. Under the "due process" concept of the German Constitutional Court, legislation was constrained[60] in order to open up the procedures of bureaucracies to the public. Not denying public participation results in the voiding of the administrative decision by the courts. In exchange for allowing a less law-bound,[61] more goal-than-law oriented administration, a new participatory democracy legitimation is outlined by

60. The legislature is generally reluctant to impose strict control over the administration, and it is ready to allow the administration to develop its efficiency-oriented self-definitions.

61. As mentioned already, constitutional tribunals were traditionally less inclined to review what was considered politics or policy, as long as it did not interfere directly with basic rights. Legislatures insisted on retaining their privilege to authorize the public administration to take certain actions, not necessarily because they really wanted to determine administrative issues, but in order to remain in a position of supremacy and control: without legislative appropriation there was no administrative action possible. This was not taken too seriously in the common law countries. In the United States, under the separation of powers doctrine, the President was not in need of authorization and Congress had to develop the institution of legislative veto to keep some level of control over the administration. Following Alexander Hamilton's interpretation of the executive power, the Supreme Court wrote, in *Myers v. United States:* "The executive power was given in general terms . . . and was limited by direct expressions where limitation was needed. . . . " 272 U.S. 52, 118 (1926). In England, legislative approval of administrative regulation was not important because of, among other factors, the royal prerogative. In France (the Rousseauian tradition), and according to German liberalism (Georg Jellinek), detailed legislative authorizations of delegation were believed to safeguard legislative supremacy.

The emphasis on law's supremacy—the statute is the primary and original source of law, and executive regulations are only intended to implement statutes as expressly authorized by the act—has echoed in post-World War II constitutions. *See, e.g.,* FR. CONST. art. 13 (1946); GERMAN BASIC LAW art. 80(1).

The current trend seems to be reversed. The 1958 French Constitution expressly recognized that the executive has original lawmaking powers (and in these areas denied the powers to parliament). The Basic Law requires that in the case of delegating regulatory powers to the administration, the purpose, contents, and extent of the delegation shall be fixed in the law. In the Emergency Price Control Case, Judgment of Nov. 12, 1958, 8 BVerfGE 274 (F.R.G.), the German Constitutional Court ruled that the purpose of the precision in delegation

is to make encroachments by the state as predictable as possible. . . . A "vague blanket provision" which would permit the executive [branch] to determine in detail the limits of [the individual's] freedom conflicts with the principle that an administrative agency must function according to law.
Further, the principle of separation of powers dictates this result.
Id. at 274, *translated in* KOMMERS, *supra* note 41, at 148 (alterations in original).

In the Kalkar Case, Judgment of Aug. 8, 1978, 49 BVerfGE 89 (F.R.G.), the Court cited the separation of powers doctrine again, but with a different outcome:

A monistic theory of power incorrectly deduced from the principle of democracy, which would confer a monopoly of decision-making power on parlia-

constitutional adjudication.[62] Decisions of the administration are less determined, but it is exactly this low level of determination that allows citizens to participate in the process of decentralized decision making. This enables the preventive protection of their rights. As citizens have the chance to participate in local decision making, they can *prevent* the administration from violating their rights.

In a related way, constitutional adjudication increasingly requires that rules of "transparency" (disclosure) be applied in politics and the public sphere in general. Transparency requirements once again may result in the restriction of basic freedoms, but it might be that judicial review and procedure are sufficient restraints in this respect.[63]

Public participation induced by constitutional adjudication creates a new

---

ment, must not undermine the concrete distribution and balance of political power guaranteed by the Basic Law. . . .

. . . .

. . . The provisions of the statute in question make use of indefinite legal terms such as "reliability" and "necessary knowledge" (*unbestimmte Rechtsbegriffe*) — terms that are not precisely defined.

. . . .

It is within the legislature's discretion to use either undefined legal terms or precise terminology.

Id. at 89, *translated in* KOMMERS, *supra* note 41, at 150–54.

62. This is an emerging trend, or perhaps only a discourse-theoretical potential of constitutional adjudication. The German Constitutional Court expressly denied participatory rights in the first Numerus Clausus case, Judgment of July 18, 1972, 33 BVerfGE 303 (F.R.G.), where the court stated:

We may put aside the question of whether participatory rights [in state benefits] can be partially derived from [the concept that] a social state based on the rule of law takes on a guarantor's obligation to implement the value system of the basic rights. We have determined that the legislator must decide whether and to what extent it will grant participatory rights within the limits of administrative services—even in a modern social welfare state—and the citizen cannot force the legislature to make this decision.

Id. at 303, *translated in* KOMMERS, *supra* note 41, at 298.

In the Judgment of Dec. 20, 1979 (Mülheim-Kärlich Case), 53 BVerfGE 30 (F.R.G.), the court ruled that the use of nuclear energy and the regulation of such use by the administration is a constitutional restriction of the basic right to life, but the court advised that public participation in licensing be established by legislation in order to protect freedoms.

Public participation is slowly gaining importance in the European Community because of mandatory public participation in environmental impact assessment.

63. In *Buckley v. Valeo*, 424 U.S. 1 (1976), the Supreme Court stated that although disclosure rules may discourage political participation in a few cases, overall it will create a more informed public, thereby encouraging participation and increasing the credibility of democracy.

In the Judgment of July 19, 1966 (Party Finance Case I), 20 BVerfGE 56 (F.R.G.), the German Constitutional Court forced the *Bundestag* to legislate on party finance disclosure.

dimension for the public sphere, as well as a new constitutionally protected opportunity for the social control of administrative and political power. The antiparliamentarism of some constitutional tribunals may result in a discourse-friendly republican decentralization. This may not be illegitimate or unconstitutional, as very few constitutions institutionalize an exclusively tripartite system of separation of powers, and democracy doctrines may give full support to such new developments.

III. A PRINCIPLED DISCOURSE

All the above empirical and political science considerations are of preliminary importance from the perspective of discourse theory. For a discourse theory analysis we shall review the argumentation of the tribunals and the communicative features of their operations. The success of the project of modernity would require that constitutional adjudication, as an intellectual operation, be determined by legal rationality, and, conversely, that the discourse at the tribunals shall have a rationalizing impact on contemporary law. The rationality of law is provided by the administration of justice if the decisions are foreseeable and modern law is legitimate if it is based on a rights-protective discourse.

The argumentation in constitutional adjudication is based on the assumption that the operations of the constitutional tribunal refer to the constitution as a whole (the Basic Law's structural unity).[64] The more developed a tribunal's argumentation becomes, the more self-referential it will be. Tribunals are increasingly engaged in determining their own position and role in the political-legal system, and they tend to deal with their relation to their own presuppositions. The typical constitutional tribunal decision is less interested in social consequences or even social values than it is in the correspondence of the decision to the principles that are partly stated in the constitution but, more often, are developed by the tribunal in reference to the constitution that they reshaped.

From the legal certainty perspective, the trouble with constitutional argumentation is that it may rely on principles and not on rules. This differs from an "ordinary" administration of justice, where the courts are expected to *apply rules*, and not principles, to facts. Apparently, constitutional

---

64. This occurred in the first major decision of the German Constitutional Court, Judgment of Oct. 23, 1951 (Southwest State Case), 1 BVerfGE 14 (F.R.G.). The court stated that " '[n]o single constitutional provision may be taken out of its context and interpreted by itself. . . . Every constitutional provision . . . must always be interpreted in such a way as to render it compatible with the fundamental principles of the Constitution and the intentions of its authors.' " *Id.* at 14, *translated in* KOMMERS, *supra* note 41, at 52. The Hungarian Court followed suit in 61/1992 (XI. 20. AB), declaring that the antidiscriminatory clause of the constitution applies to the whole legal system.

adjudication is inclined to transfer even constitutional rules into principles, thereby increasing the degree of freedom of constitutional adjudication. The transition to principles feeds the accusations of uncontrolled judicial activism.

The process is highly problematic not only for a separation theory but even more so for a theory of legal rationality, as it will be less predictable. Principled reasoning, however, is an inevitable feature of constitutional adjudication, particularly of abstract norm control (advisory opinion).

In order to have a balanced view on principled reasoning, one should take into account the difference between ordinary judicial decision making and constitutional adjudication. In the latter case, one should not compare a state of facts and a prescription of a norm (rule), but rather norms should be compared with each other. Argumentation means, in this context, that a hierarchy of norms shall be reconstructed convincingly, and the logical operations are carried out in that hierarchical space. Lack of hierarchy in the case of two conflicting norms of equal rank requires some kind of algorithm to solve the "impasse." Such conflicts develop, for example, when the rule in a statute is in conformity with one of the provisions of the constitution (or is even needed to realize the constitutional provision), but contradicts another provision of the constitution. It is in this context that principles become important, as they allow a certain hierarchization to solve the norm conflict. "Principles are . . . structurally correct, as . . . they attempt to develop objective [*sachlich*] rules of decision."[65]

The reliance on principles is, of course, partly related to the nature of the language of the constitutions. Even if the provisions are self-executory or the constitution is justiciable, the provisions of a constitution remain very abstract and programmatic or declaratory, and they are more general than other norms. Generality and abstraction make constitutional provisions less determinate than statutory rules. The challenge to constitutional adjudication related to principled argumentation is that it should generate a high level of foreseeability and rationality to principle-based decisions, but principles do not yield easily to discipline.

The inclination toward principles, resulting from abstract review, applies even where the tribunal proceeds within the case and controversy context.[66]

65. Horst Ehmke, *Prinzipien der Verfassungsinterpretation, in* Häberle, *supra* note 21, at 304, 308 (my translation).

66. Alexander Bickel contrasts statutes with the decisions of courts. He believes that statutes "deal typically with abstract or dimly foreseen problems. The courts are concerned with the flesh and blood of an actual case." ALEXANDER M. BICKEL, THE LEAST DANGEROUS BRANCH: THE SUPREME COURT AT THE BAR OF POLITICS 72 (1962).

The concern of a supreme court is to save the coherence of the legal system and, in the case of constitutional adjudication, coherence within the constitutional system. It is to some extent irrelevant to discourse, at the level of constitutional adjudication, what would follow

The Supreme Court of the United States proceeds in a way that is very distant from ordinary court procedure: the role of parties' motions and arguments is indirect at best. Within the context of the actual case, the Supreme Court sets norms against norms and refers statutory rules to its own principles.

At this point the meaning of principle has to be narrowed down. There are a great variety of meanings and definitions attributed to principles in constitutional adjudication.

In Robert Alexy's opinion, principles are norms that order that something has to be done, possibly to a great extent, in relation to legal and factual possibilities.[67] In case of a conflict between two norms, a collision law will determine the hierarchy of these principles *under the given circumstances*. Under different circumstances there might be a different hierarchy. The conflict of principles is, therefore, possible. Principles remain valid, only to some extent, if their provision is carried out. It is not possible, however, to have two contradictory rules—either the one or the other is valid.

Even if one disagrees with Alexy's definition, his position clearly indicates what makes principled constitutional decisions disturbing for a traditional juridical interpretation. Constitutional "interpretation" has more creative power than ordinary interpretation. It will determine its own collision laws (which are not made explicit *ex ante*). Constitutional adjudication will set through these collision laws, the context in which the rules shall apply. Moreover, the constitutional tribunal will have the power to develop new principles or to transform what was intended to be a rule by the constitution into a relatively indefinite principle. The result is a lesser degree of predictability compared to the ordinary administration of justice that was used as a standard in theories of separation of power. Legal certainty will suffer because of the unexpected intervention of principles, which act as the *deus ex machina* in a classic French play. The question is, to what extent will the legal and political communities act like the audience at the *Comedie Française* by finding such surprising interventions normal.

---

from the ordinary rules of procedure. Habermas discusses at length the procedural conditions of rational discourse in court procedures ("forensic action"). *See* HABERMAS, *supra* note 1, at 229–33. Of course, it is true that even constitutional adjudication "must remain open to the pragmatic, ethical, and moral reasons," but only within the restricted perspective of constitutional control (e.g., only certain macro social and political pragmatism is acceptable). *Id.* at 230. Conditions of impartiality stemming from communicative conditions are also important, but again partisanship here cannot be interpreted as being biased for or against the legislature. Most of the difficulties in finding elements that hamper rational discourse in forensic action are irrelevant for constitutional adjudication (e.g., that parties are not interested in truth, or that a discourse based on unreasonable statutes cannot serve as a satisfactory reference point in a reasonable discourse).

67. *See* ROBERT ALEXY, THEORIE DER GRUNDRECHTE 75 (1985).

Legal certainty expectations are based on ordinary judicial interpretation. At this point, we have to refer once again to the relation between constitutional decision and its consequences. An ordinary judge is expected to act like a paragraph-dispensing automat, or, as someone guided by secondary norms and applying valid existing rules. However, even this judge is taking into consideration the consequences of his decision, particularly in regard to the parties concerned. The higher the judge is situated, the more he has to reckon with indirect consequences; as his decision may result in a broader application by other courts. Law is somewhat sensitive to these concerns and allows consequentialist corrections within specified limits. In sentencing, for example, the felon's age and health conditions are taken into consideration. More broadly speaking, positive law does recognize equity as a correction of the socially (morally) unacceptable consequences of the strict application of law. Such equitable considerations are not relevant in constitutional adjudication, because the justices are not confronted with the impact of their decision on an actual human being. All judges and constitutional justices are isolated from these consequences and cannot be held directly responsible for them. The constitutional justices are, however, confronted with the consequences of their decision on the legal system and, at least indirectly, on the social relations affected.

Again, specific cognitive, moral, and organizational factors restrict consequentialism. Complexity reduction suggests that the enormous complexity of consequences is simply disregarded. Aside from this cognitive problem, there is an ethical problem. It is ethically questionable to assume responsibility for something for which one cannot be held liable. Finally, a tribunal, as a bureaucratic organization, will try to limit its work load.[68] All three factors result in a defensive, decision-avoiding attitude that employs tactics and excuses such as lack of competence, or ripeness, mootness, or, wherever applicable, the denial of certiorari. Such argumentation, if carried out at all, is carried out in the most legalistic form possible by referring to rules (not principles) of competence.[69] This constitutional denial of justice will result in the acceptance of the status quo and allow facts to develop their normative potentials.

Even where the tribunal undertakes to consider social consequences,[70]

---

68. The German Constitutional Court's civil servants discourage in writing complaints addressed to the Court as a first matter. Only repeated written complaints will be considered.

69. See, for example, in the German *Vorlageverfahren*, the rules to limit referral from lower courts.

70. Consideration of social consequences differs from argumentation based on social facts (practices). Social facts, if used at all, are styled in a legalistic way and brought up (and, consequently, selected and controlled) primarily by the tribunal itself. To follow Alexy's approach, social facts are used to establish those circumstances that were considered necessary to apply the collision law. In a way, this is a past-oriented consequentialism that does not defy

it will do so in a principled discourse. The principles of the discourse are subject to the internal publicity of the constitutional tribunal. The most important constitutionalized consequentialist principle is that of "maintenance of state functioning." This is not, however, any accidental functioning of the government and public order *writ large*, but one that fits into the constitutional system and intends to accomplish it. The authorization to regulate under the "capacity to function" principle has constitutional limits in a rule-of-law system. Of course, the more the public order is at peril, the less constitutional controls are extended, as reflected in emergency regulations.

Not even the emergence of activist and self-restraining principles, that were developed by the tribunal, cause constitutional adjudication to run amok and allow the tribunal to apply its "own constitution." Contrary to what may follow under systematic theoretical considerations and autopoietic theories, constitutional tribunals do not and cannot follow their self-generated programs in a closed system. Although, as mentioned above, consequentialism is limited by external constraints and legitimate argumentation techniques, there remains enough direct and "constitutionalized" openness to consequences (and other nonlegal—i.e., ethical—considerations) to enable law to steer other social spheres. Once again, this openness and the resulting steering capacity may result in the colonization of a lifeworld and the decline and fall of rationality in the postmodern condition.

Of course, whether these controversial developments can, in fact, realize the democratic and rights-protective potentials, and whether this is a trend that will develop into the prevailing mood, depends on, among other things, the nature of constitutional adjudication itself. If constitutional adjudication fits into a web of discourses open to, and for, the public sphere, then the law's potential to continue the modernity project is much better than generally believed. Michael Perry believes that "[c]onstitutional discourse, then, *at its idealized best,* is the moral discourse of the constitutional community."[71] If constitutional adjudication structurally guarantees that its

---

legal certainty (once it is taken for granted that it will be considered), as this is something known or accessible to all other social actors. In the landmark case of *West Coast Hotel Co. v. Parrish,* minimum wage laws were discussed in light of "recent economic experience," and the exploitation of workers to the detriment of their health was described as a normatively (ethically) relevant fact, triggering legitimate legislative action. 300 U.S. 379, 399 (1937), *discussed* in Duncan Kennedy, *Form and Substance in Private Law Adjudication,* 89 HARV. L. REV. 1685, 1755–56 (1976); *see also* TRIBE, *supra* note 36, at 585.

71. PERRY, *supra* note 25, at 158. It remains to be seen to what extent the "idealized best" assumption is valid, particularly if one is not taking for granted neither the existence nor the possibility of a constitutional community.

decisions will be accessible to the public sphere, then the above trends will prove to be nonaccidental.

At first glance, discourse in constitutional adjudication seems to be extremely restricted. Constitutional tribunals are not open to the public sphere. They are not accountable to, and do not care much about, the press, nor do they have to. In the legislative process, the problem and power of the public sphere consists of the *discovery* of problems. The legislature is at least constrained to react to problems selected by the public sphere and public opinion in particular. Congress had to enact the Comprehensive Environmental Response Compensation and Liability Act (CERCLA)[72] in response to the Love Canal scandal, and the German *Bundestag* reacted to Chernobyl with a new radiation law. The legislative *answer* continues to be determined primarily by the interests and beliefs of the participants in the legislative process (broadly conceived).

Constitutional adjudication is structured precisely in a way that allows the tribunal to resist external formulations of problems by the public sphere.[73] The isolation of the constitutional tribunal is, however, less impermeable, as the isolation follows from institutional arrangements. In the case of abstract review it is nearly impossible to deny justice, although there are no time limits. A law pending in a constitutional court creates social and political uncertainty that cannot be professionally tolerated. In courts which work with the case and controversy requirements, it is again nearly impossible to disregard expectations of public opinion by not taking action. Imagine if the Supreme Court had have delayed its decision about the Nixon tapes until the next election! Constitutional adjudication does, at least, take into consideration the *politically mediated* public opinion.

Constitutional adjudication can be initiated either by a restricted circle of constitutional powers and state organs, or, as is the case in the United States, by depending on the judges (a considerable minority of four) to start a procedure. In the latter case, discourse is monopolized by the body itself. Under all these systems, the powers of the public were traditionally nonexistent. Recent developments in Hungary, and to a lesser extent in

---

72. 42 U.S. C. § 9601 (1988).

73. As mentioned earlier, some tribunals resist even questions posed by the other branches in the form of the prohibition of advisory opinions. Perry, in his "idealized best" presentation, emphasizes that "constitutional deliberation is dialogical." However, he notes that this is not limited to the court, as "moral deliberation requires community." PERRY, *supra* note 25, at 157. Therefore, the dialogue extends to the morally pluralistic political community. The justices may be responsive to certain elements of the moral community, but this is not at the level of an actual moral dialogue. In multicultural societies with a plurality of morals, the role of a constitutional tribunal is limited to maintaining the coexistence of the differing groups.

Spain (*amparo*), represent a potential breakthrough. In these countries, citizens may initiate a case that makes a crucial element of the discourse accessible to the public sphere.[74] The procedure at the tribunal is mostly closed or secret, making all talk about procedural fairness moot.

Participants in the discourse (i.e., the justices) are participating on equal footing—conditions of equality and of equal and perfect information are met. The participants have no direct personal interest in the outcome except for a truth interest. External limits and constraints are typically negligible, and, theoretically at least, not even time limits exist.[75] Except in cases of maladministration, judges are not responsible to anyone and are independent. These judges are in the position of institutionalized nonresponsibility.

The situation apparently meets the requirements of an ideal discourse (speech) situation. According to Habermas, a discourse will bring fair and/or rational results if there are no limits on information flow or information handling.[76]

The internal procedures of constitutional tribunals allow considerable formal exchange of views and arguments during deliberation (there are informal rules against informal discussions in some countries).

Based on the decisions and circumstantial evidence, argumentation within the constitutional tribunal is probably strongly self-referential in the sense that the judges refer to their previous positions and to earlier positions of the tribunal. Precedents are treated as facts with normative value, but the "law" is not restricted to those developed by the tribunal itself. During their arguments, the tribunals try to generate answers to issues raised by lower courts during the prior process. Further relevant arguments may come from legal scholarship and dogmatics, although once again preference is given to the tribunal's own secondary rules and interpretative canons. Social facts,[77] and in hard cases even nonlegal normative arguments (i.e., natural law and moral or political philosophy theory), are cited.

There is no audience, but one has reasons to believe that a professional audience (other judges and perhaps scholars) has to be taken into consideration.[78] The primary purpose of the argumentation, however, is to

---

74. Of course, there are emerging defenses against this opening. The decision of whether to take a case is left to the discretion of the Hungarian Constitutional Court, allowing it to reestablish control through the power of selection.

75. The French preliminary review is a remarkable exception.

76. *See* HABERMAS, *supra* note 1, at 296.

77. Exceptional expert opinions and evidence taking are admitted, and the Court may be confronted with social science considerations.

78. German Chief Justice Ernst Benda openly acknowledged the "critical importance" of the "partnership" of the justices with German constitutional scholars. *See* KOMMERS, *supra* note 41, at 66.

get the support (acceptance) of the majority of the justices. The decision, which was created in the isolated discourse, becomes public. The message of constitutional adjudication is primarily intended for the legislature. The message may have far-reaching consequences because of further communication within the legislative and political spheres. As a consequence, a political consensus may be generated within parliament,[79] or the interest bargains and harmonization may continue with the new impetus coming from the constitutional tribunal.[80] Indeed, attempts by a constitutional tribunal to preempt further discourse will result in criticisms of activism.

It varies country by country as well as historically whether the decision itself will disclose elements of the discourse that resulted in its creation. In some of the countries (i.e., Italy and France), only the majority opinion will be known as the court's opinion. In other countries, tradition dictates the use of apodictic decisions. Paradoxically, but quite understandably, the remnants of discourse disagreements (separate dissenting or concurring opinions) diminish the authoritative legitimacy of the decision while enabling further social discourse and promising revision (which may keep the hope of changing arrangements within the legal system). The dissenting opinion is not lost. It has an impact on future decisions and enjoys the status of constitutional argument within the court as well. Justice Holmes wrote American legal history with dissenting opinions that were turned into majority decisions thirty years later.

A system of constitutional adjudication is intended[81] to contribute to the control of the administration since the establishment of such control was partly neglected by legislation. Constitutional adjudication is expected to participate in enabling the public sphere to allow its authorizations and problem choices to prevail in politics.[82] Of course, constitutional adjudication has a very ambiguous position vis-à-vis the public sphere. The jurisprudence of the "active" tribunals is very sensitive to issues of the public sphere, and the lifeworld's spontaneity is protected by rules of privacy. On

79. The consensus is necessary to comply with the decision and enact the required law or to refrain from unconstitutional practices, or, conversely, it may be needed to overrule the Court's decision by qualified majority (as in Romania).

80. *See* Häberle, *supra* note 21, at 25.

81. The emergence of constitutional adjudication is not wholly purposive—the doggish activism of the courts plays a role that is uncontrolled by politics.

82. This [Bernhard Peters's] sociological translation of the discourse theory of democracy implies that binding decisions, to be legitimate, must be steered by communication flows that start at the periphery and pass through the sluices of democratic and constitutional procedures situated at the entrance to the parliamentary complex or the courts (and, if necessary, at the exit of the implementing administration as well).

HABERMAS, *supra* note 1, at 356.

the other hand, the adjudication itself, although very close in many respects to the ideal communicative community, is not transparent for the public sphere, and, at least indirectly, is independent of the authorizations and problem setting of the public sphere and defies its communicative power. Moreover, constitutional adjudication represents the public sphere and a constitutional law embodying the public's choices vis-à-vis politics and legislation that attempts to formally juridify politics. In this respect, constitutional adjudication communicates into law its own values, which are values shared by the public sphere. The constitutional values of the tribunal reflect the outcome of normative and ethical discourses (which did not necessarily take place). To sum up: notwithstanding the social sterility of the discourse, it has the potential to contribute to the social discourse and to act as a safeguard for continued social discourse.[83] As mentioned already, constitutional adjudication is an opportunity for lawmaking to be carried out under the circumstances of rational discourse. Whilst legislation maintains elements of discourse rationality by allowing rational and fair interest bargaining, here in the constitutional argumentation norm rights-oriented discourse may still prevail. Constitutional adjudication, with its sterile discourse, is not the end of a larger legislative social discourse; it is only a stage of modern lawmaking. The tribunal's formulation of norms is very broad and principle-like, and it goes back to the legitimate legislator for reshaping into a rule.

Unfortunately, the mere fact that constitutional adjudication is producing law according to discourse theory expectations may not suffice to guarantee its potential contribution to social discourse. Of course, the openness of constitutional adjudication to legal discourse (where arguments are rights-oriented and argumentative procedures are determined not only by the court but by the legal profession in the form of dogmatics) means openness to *reactive* rationality only. The rationality (in the sense of foreseeability and certainty) of the discourse is certainly restricted compared to other areas of administration of justice because of the "flexibility" implications of the overwhelmingly principled reasoning by the tribunal, which was denounced as undermining freedoms and rights.

Constitutional adjudication's apparent ideal elite discourse situation is undermined by the inevitable empirical fact that all tribunals operate as organizations that make their decisions subject to the limited or bounded rationality of organizations.[84]

---

83. As mentioned earlier, constitutional tribunals have an intellectual bias that favors the safeguard of public opinion's autonomy. This follows from the justices' academic and professional commitment to free speech.

84. *See generally* Herbert A. Simon, *Rational Choice and the Structure of the Environment,* 63 PSYCHOL. REV. 129 (1956). We have seen some of the caseload reducing bureaucratic tech-

CONCLUSION

The analysis of constitutional adjudication indicates that constitutional tribunals dispose of the potential to contribute to legal rationality and to maintain discourse in law and legislation, and this restraint is quintessential to maintaining the discourse that generates rationality. The contribution of constitutional adjudication is particularly important regarding the extension of legislative procedure. Constitutional adjudication brings quality control into legislative production, and also allows and legitimatizes new sources of participation. The performance of constitutional adjudication is controversial in matters of protection of rights and freedoms in two respects. First, it allows restrictions of freedoms and rights for the sake of the material realization and promotion of other rights that are more dependency generated expectations than autonomy rights. Second, it undermines rights by institutionalizing principled arguments to the detriment of clear rules, and so, legal certainty also suffers.

The balance is troubling. Of course, one cannot expect that constitutional adjudication itself will be able to save postmodern society from the fiasco of rational law in a postmodern complexity. However, perhaps postmodernity means that in the long run and in more than a hidden way, reason only serves more violence, oppression, and suffering (reasonably distributed among those who cannot resist it). Perhaps in a similarly cunning way, reason creates institutions and procedures that perform reasonably under postmodern conditions by correcting the autonomy-protective capacity of law when law seems to abandon it for the sake of its steering mission. This may cause transitory legitimation crises, but a mandate for the tribunal to produce limited legislation can be generated by public opinion. Given the social acceptance of the performance of constitutional tribunals, public opinion is indeed rewarding constitutional adjudication for the services it has rendered to maintain the public sphere.

This is the optimistic interpretation of constitutional adjudication. Habermas, as a self-proclaimed optimist in his effort to save the project of modernity, puts his bet on those elements of the legal (and social) sys-

---

niques, and, of course, caseload reduction also has impacts on legal reasoning through routinization, schematic simplification, and shorthand in argumentation. In consequence, elements of a special, self-referential language emerge with notions that are not penetrable by public opinion. Organizational constraints and considerations, as well as internal coalition creation (which is not based on the power of argument but on reciprocity of votes), further undermine the ideal speech situation. These internal constraints may play an important role indeed. To give just one extreme example: the United States Supreme Court is sometimes reluctant to take cases of paramount importance to the public even though public opinion expects some guidance, possibly because the judges fear that due to internal splits in the court, the cure of the new decision will be worse than the disease of the problematic law.

tems that are preserving rationality and that make reason operate. Constitutional adjudication had a significant contribution to modern law. It remains to be seen what will happen to this contribution. It is not necessary that all efforts of reason will turn counterproductive,[85] although it is hard to say whether reason is action at all.

'

---

85. The most spectacular of court induced revolutions, the Supreme Court's decision in *Brown v. Board of Educ.* (Brown II), 349 U.S. 294 (1955), did, in value, change and lead to the diminution of segregation. One of the most troublesome aspects of postmodernity is that one cannot get rid of dark sides. The pessimistic deconstructive interpretation of *Brown* is that either it resulted only in the destruction of certain forms of official segregation in order to replace it with other segregations, or it chose the least efficient way—similar to slavery's abolition, which was morally correct but did not diminish exploitation of the former slaves as the North argued.

EIGHTEEN

The Dynamics of
Constitutional Adjudication

Bernhard Schlink*

I.

Habermas determines the role and legitimacy of constitutional adjudication through three confrontations. First, he confronts both the liberal and the welfare-state paradigms of law, seeing constitutional adjudication move from the former to the latter. Habermas wants this move to arrive at a procedural paradigm of law. Second, he confronts a norm- and a value-oriented understanding of the constitution. Habermas indicates the dangers of the former and the merits of the latter, and attempts to show that principles, understood as norms, should guide constitutional adjudication. Third, he confronts the liberal and the republican views of the political and constitutional process, developing the republican view into a procedural one. Finally, Habermas determines the role and legitimacy of constitutional adjudication—to watch over the democratic process[1] and to "implement[ ] . . . democratic procedure and the deliberative form of political opinion- and will-formation."[2]

II.

This determination of the role and legitimacy of constitutional adjudication is rather far from the reality of constitutional adjudication, and certainly far from that which exists in Germany. There are only a few cases

*Professor of Public Law and Legal Philosophy, Humboldt University, Berlin; Justice of the Constitutional Court of the State of Nordrhein-Westfalen, Germany.
1. Jürgen Habermas, Between Facts and Norms: Contributions to a Discourse Theory of Law and Democracy 280 (William Rehg trans., 1996).
2. *Id.*

that challenge the existing German democratic process. Take as examples the member of parliament who does not belong to a political party and who therefore does not get access to crucial information and facilities[3]; the small faction that is excluded from important parliamentary committees[4]; and the small radical party that is not allowed the use of public assembly rooms that are open to the large, mainstream parties.[5] Beyond these cases, there are few others where the democratic process is being fundamentally challenged. Of course, there are cases that deal with the role of parliament, political parties, or civil service in the political system, as well as those that deal with the electoral process and the formation of political opinion and will.[6] Also closely related to the democratic process are cases on freedom of speech, freedom of the press and broadcasting, and freedom of assembly and association.[7] But the principle that democratic procedure and the deliberative form of political opinion- and will-formation have to be enforced is much too vague, and thus too weak, to serve as a guideline in these cases. Freedom of offensive speech in conflict with individual dignity; freedom of assembly in conflict with public security; ways of organizing public and private broadcasting; or ways of subsidizing certain political parties and activities against the others—these are the problems which arise from the above-mentioned cases. They are not solved or even clarified by the appeal to enforce deliberative democratic procedures.

At one point, this appeal becomes more specific. Habermas suggests that constitutional courts, in reviewing the constitutionality of a statute, should ask not what reasons could justify the statute, but rather what reasons the legislature actually and explicitly set forth, and whether those reasons are in fact sufficient justification. However, the task of the German Federal Constitutional Court (*Bundesverfassungsgericht*) is to establish whether a statute violates the Constitution.[8] If the statute does not violate the Constitution, it does not matter whether the legislature had bad intentions and delibera-

---

3. Judgment of June 13, 1989, 80 Entscheidungen des Bundesverfassungsgericht [BVerfGE] 188, 217–44 (F.R.G.).

4. Judgment of Jan. 14, 1986, 70 BVerfGE 324, 354–66.

5. Judgment of Mar. 28, 1969, 31 Entscheidungen des Bundesverwaltungsgericht [BVerwGE] 368, 368–72 (F.R.G.).

6. *See, e.g.,* Judgment of Apr. 9, 1992, 85 BVerfGE 264, 283–329 (F.R.G.); Judgment of Oct. 31, 1990, 83 BVerfGE 60, 71–81 (F.R.G.); Judgment of Sept. 29, 1990, 82 BVerfGE 322, 337–52 (F.R.G.); Judgment of June 6, 1988, 42 NEUE JURISTISCHE WOCHENSCHRIFT 93 (1989).

7. *See, e.g.,* Judgment of May 19, 1992, 86 BVerfGE 122, 127–32 (F.R.G.); Judgment of Mar. 25, 1992, 86 BVerfGE 1, 9–15 (F.R.G.); Judgment of Oct. 23, 1991, 85 BVerfGE 69, 74–77 (F.R.G.); Judgment of June 26, 1991, 84 BVerfGE 212, 224–32 (F.R.G.); Judgment of Feb. 5, 1991, 83 BVerfGE 238, 295–340 (F.R.G.).

8. GRUNDGESETZ [Constitution] [GG] art. 93 (1)(2), art. 100 (F.R.G.); BUNDESVERFAS-SUNGSGERICHTSGESETZ § 13(6)(11).

tions. Similarly, if there is a violation, the legislature's good intentions and deliberations are irrelevant.

III.

The main workload of the *Bundesverfassungsgericht* is to establish whether fundamental rights have been violated and, if so, how they can be restored.[9] Since most fundamental rights of the German Constitution focus upon rights of freedom—protecting the individual citizen against unwarranted intrusions by the state—the majority of the decisions of the *Bundesverfassungsgericht* deal with the freedoms themselves, state intrusions into these freedoms, and claims by citizens against state intrusions. This role is not something old-fashioned and outdated. It was only recently that the court established the right of the citizen to decide what personal information and data could be collected and used by the state.[10] This right is of paramount importance in today's world of computers. The *Bundesverfassungsgericht* has not limited itself to defending freedoms against state intrusions. It also defends freedoms of one citizen against intrusions by another citizen who claims a state entitlement that allows such intrusion.[11] Furthermore, the court requires government institutions and procedures to be organized in a manner such that the freedoms of all involved can coexist peacefully.[12] It requires the state not only to refrain from intrusions into fundamental rights, but also to support and protect these rights.[13] Finally, the *Bundesverfassungsgericht* has even considered the notion that entitlements to government services may be derived from fundamental freedoms.[14] While it has never actually reached that conclusion, the *Bundesverfassungsgericht* has determined that equality as a fundamental right requires equal distribution of existing government services.[15] This is, of course, a very rough summary of almost forty years of constitutional decision making on fundamental rights. But it may suffice to ask and answer the following questions: In what direction has the *Bundesverfassungsgericht*, which has definitely gone beyond the limits of the traditional liberal understanding of fundamental rights, actually gone? To a welfare-state paradigm of law? Or beyond that, to a proce-

9. GG art. 93(1)(4a); *see also* BUNDESVERFASSUNGSGERICHTSGESETZ § 13(8a); KLAUS SCHLAICH, DAS BUNDESVERFASSUNGSGERICHT 153–62 (2d ed. 1991).
10. Judgment of Dec. 15, 1983, 65 BVerfGE 1, 38–71 (F.R.G.).
11. The leading case is Judgment of Jan. 15, 1958, 7 BVerfGE 198, 203–30 (F.R.G.).
12. The leading case is Judgment of May 29, 1973, 35 BVerfGE 79, 109–70 (F.R.G.).
13. The leading case is Judgment of Feb. 25, 1975, 39 BVerfGE 1 (F.R.G.).
14. Judgment of July 18, 1972, 33 BVerfGE 303, 333 (F.R.G.).
15. *Cf.* Judgment of Oct. 22, 1991, 85 BVerfGE 36, 54 (F.R.G.).

dural paradigm of law? Or rather to a value-oriented understanding of fundamental rights?

IV.

The *Bundesverfassungsgericht*'s value orientation is a myth. It is true that between the 1950s and 1970s the *Bundesverfassungsgericht* discussed fundamental rights as being values and as forming a value system. But it has never meant this in a philosophically ambitious sense, in the sense of the material value ethics developed by Max Scheler or Nicolai Hartmann. Rather, the court meant that fundamental rights are more than both individual freedoms and equality rights in the traditional liberal sense. The court needed an umbrella concept, under which it could develop the impact of fundamental rights upon relationships between citizens as well as upon government institutions and procedures. The court also needed to provide for an active protection of freedom and quality of life, and, tentatively, even for entitlements to government services. But, since the 1970s, it has no longer used the value concept.[16] Rather, it discusses objective norms, objective fundamental decisions, and objective principles to pursue exactly the same goals and obtain exactly the same results.

When I wrote my dissertation on fundamental rights,[17] I was very intrigued by and concerned with the decision in which the *Bundesverfassungsgericht* talked for the first time about fundamental rights being values.[18] When I had the chance to talk to one of the justices who had decided that case, I asked him what they had done, why they had done it, and what they had meant philosophically. He was frank. The court had no philosophical interests or ideas, but rather had needed a new concept. Someone had called for a boycott of a film by a notorious Nazi film maker. A civil court had prohibited this demand and the *Bundesverfassungsgericht* wanted to reverse the prohibition. The court applied, for the first time and without precedent or much preparatory scholarly work, fundamental rights to the relationship between citizens. The concept of fundamental rights as values thus served as the new concept under which the *Bundesverfassungsgericht* could make an unorthodox decision.

However, since the *Bundesverfassungsgericht*'s value orientation is a fiction, Habermas's confrontation of principles as values and principles as norms must also miss the reality of the *Bundesverfassungsgericht*'s constitutional adjudication. Principles as norms are not opposed to principles as

16. The last time the *Bundesverfassungsgericht* gave the value concept a dominant role was in Judgment of May 29, 1973, 35 BVerfGE 79, 114–16 (F.R.G.).

17. BERNHARD SCHLINK, ABWÄGUNG IM VERFASSUNGSRECHT (1976).

18. Judgment of Jan. 15, 1958, 7 BVerfGE 198, 203–07 (F.R.G.).

values. Because principles become legally relevant only when conflicting with other principles, they are on the one hand valid, yet essentially free to be changed for the better, and on the other hand absolutely binding, but relatively successful in resolving a given conflict. This is so because principles in general are coherent and only conflict in specific situations. This flexibility is the reason for the development of principles and the understanding of fundamental rights as principles in constitutional adjudication. And such flexibility allows the *Bundesverfassungsgericht* to introduce its new interpretations of fundamental rights.

The *Bundesverfassungsgericht* has not developed from a norm orientation to a value orientation. Nor has it developed from a liberal to a welfare-state paradigm. This is true because the definition of the welfare state is, constitutionally speaking, still very much open. The impact of fundamental rights for the relationship between citizens, for government institutions and procedures, and for the active protection of freedom and equality, is not welfare state-related, even though admittedly it also may not come easily to a traditional liberal understanding. The entitlement to government services, on the other hand, is welfare state-related. But as yet, this entitlement has been enforced only reluctantly by the *Bundesverfassungsgericht*.

V.

The *Bundesverfassungsgericht* develops neither paradigms nor systems, value-oriented or otherwise. It decides cases. It has far-reaching powers to do so and, as with every powerful institution, a tendency to enjoy and widen its powers to the maximum. Therefore, it develops concepts and theories that are flexible, rather than strictly and narrowly defined, in order to enhance its grip on more cases and problems.

The changes in the interpretation of fundamental rights over the last forty years are owed more to the existence of a constitutional court with far-reaching powers than with theoretical developments. In the 1950s, the constitutional legal community was neither less aware of Germany's having become a welfare state nor less interested in principles than it is today.[19] But it was far less dominated by the *Bundesverfassungsgericht*, which had only just begun its constitutional adjudication.

Since its rise as an academic discipline in the last third of the nineteenth century and continuing up to the middle of the twentieth century, consti-

19. For an in-depth discussion of *Rechtsstaat und Sozialstaat*, see Wolfgang Abendroth, *Zum Begriff des demokratischen und sozialen Rechtsstaats im Grundgesetz der Bundesrepublik Deutschland*, in FESTSCHRIFT FÜR LUDWIG BERGSTRÄSSER 279–300 (Alfred Herrmann ed., 1954), and Ernst Forsthoff, *Begriff and Wesen des sozialen Rechsstaates*, 17 VERÖFFENTLICHUNGEN DER VEREINIGUNG DER DEUTSCHEN STAATSRECHTSLEHRER 8–36 (1954).

tutional law in Germany has been a field of law without a corresponding jurisdiction.[20] Therefore, its concepts and theories could maintain a certain doctrinal purity. Problems and cases that did not fit under existing scholarly concepts and theories could simply be excluded as irrelevant.

This situation had to change when the *Bundesverfassungsgericht,* with its far-reaching powers and the will to use and widen them, was installed. The court did not become interested in concepts and theories, but rather in the narrowly tailored decisions of particular cases—the solutions of actual problems. The most interesting development is not the shift from one paradigm to another, one orientation to another, but rather from a dominance of theories to one of decisions. Additionally, the court has placed emphasis on case law, an evolving trend that is presently under way.

The dynamics of constitutional law in Germany result not from shifts in paradigms and orientations, but rather from the problems with which the *Bundesverfassungsgericht* is confronted—namely, from the cases it decides, the use the court makes of its far-reaching powers, the natural tendency to widen its powers, and the political inclinations of the different justices. We can see the *Bundesverfassungsgericht's* political pendulum swing from one side to the other. Accordingly, we had liberal decisions on freedom of speech in the early 1990s,[21] and a welfare state-oriented interpretation of the constitution's property clause in the 1970s.[22] There is even the possibility that one day the value concept may again be used if it serves some other specific purpose. The course taken depends entirely upon which cases and problems are presented to the court, and upon the justices' political inclinations. The concepts, theories, paradigms, and orientations that constitutional legal scholarship detects and depicts always come after the decision has been rendered. Constitutional legal scholarship works in the wake of the *Bundesverfassungsgericht* rather than ahead of it, following the paths defined by the powerful Court. This scholarship elaborates on the Court's solutions, and compiles and systematizes the Court's decisions.

Constitutional legal scholarship could and should more often take on a critical and even a leading role. However, it fails to do so because, in the field of constitutional law, theory has not yet found its balanced relation to practice nor scholarship its relation to adjudication. Constitutional legal scholarship started, developed, and bloomed without the presence of a con-

20. *See* Bernhard Schlink, *German Constitutional Culture in Transition,* 14 CARDOZO L. REV. 711 (1993).

21. *See, e.g.,* Judgment of Oct. 9, 1991, 85 BVerfGE 23, 30–36 (F.R.G.); Judgment of June 26, 1990, 82 BVerfGE 272, 280–85 (F.R.G.); Judgment of Apr. 19, 1990, 82 BVerfGE 43, 50–54 (F.R.G.).

22. *See, e.g.,* Judgment of Mar. 1, 1979, 50 BVerfGE 290, 322–78 (F.R.G.); Judgment of Feb. 4, 1976, 38 BVerfGE 348, 367–71 (F.R.G.); Judgment of Apr. 23, 1974, 37 BVerfGE 132, 141–49 (F.R.G.).

stitutional court or similar body. And yet today, constitutional legal scholarship is still overwhelmed by the Court's presence, even after its forty-year existence.

VI.

It is obvious that the dynamics resulting from particular cases and decisions, from actual problems and solutions, and especially from the impact that a court and its practices has on a thus far practice-less legal scholarship, will catch the eye of a lawyer more easily than the eye of the philosopher. Beyond that, the philosopher may feel tempted to dismiss the actual dynamics of constitutional adjudication as mere facts which bear no relevance to the critical question of what constitutional judicial review ought to be according to the principles of democracy, constitutional state (*Rechtsstaat*), and separation of powers.

However, the critical question of what constitutional judicial review ought to be can only be sensibly asked in a specific constitutional and historical context. In this specific context, there is no democracy, no constitutional state, and no separation of powers as such. These concepts are only framed by a particular constitution at a certain historical moment. Also, there is no constitutional judicial review independent of a given constitutional and historical context. Criticism that does not operate within this context and that is blind to the actual dynamics of constitutional adjudication thus misses the point.

With different constitutions, different roles ascribed to constitutional adjudication by these constitutions, and different historical and political backgrounds, the discussions that took place in Weimar differed profoundly from those in Bonn, and those in Germany differ from those in the United States. If these discussions are confounded, the conclusion cannot be more specific than "the constitutional court should keep watch over just that system of rights that makes citizens' private and public autonomy equally possible."[23] General statements such as this do not trigger any serious progressions in dealing with actual problems of constitutional adjudication. Furthermore, they neither pose nor solve "the problem of legitimating constitutional judicial review in the context of a theory of democracy."[24]

How much of a legitimation problem remains once we view constitutional adjudication as being established by the constitution? Even those critics cited by Habermas criticize certain decisions, trends, or powers of

23. HABERMAS, *supra* note 1, at 263. The "just" in this sentence makes the statement stronger than it sounds in the original German version, even making it false. What is meant is something between "exactly" and "especially."

24. *Id.* at 264.

the court, but not constitutional adjudication as such. Constitutional adjudication may look problematic according to the constitutional, political, moral, and social views and wishes that one has. For this very fact, it does not have a legitimation problem. The constitution defines its role and grants its own legitimacy. More legitimacy it neither needs nor gets.

PART SEVEN

Habermas Responds to His Critics

NINETEEN

Reply to Symposium Participants, Benjamin N. Cardozo School of Law

Jürgen Habermas*†

INTRODUCTION

Every author owes a debt to his readers. This is especially true when an author presents a wide-ranging and complex investigation that draws the critical attention of outstanding colleagues. I have profited a great deal from my colleagues' thoughtful commentaries, as will be evident from this Reply which is a token of my appreciation.

Due to the constraints of space however, my Reply must be selective. This has nothing to do with the quality of the contributions. There is nothing I can add to Klaus Günther's exemplary analysis of the public use of communicative freedoms as the context in which communicative power emerges.[1] The concept of "communicative freedom" that is used in Chapter 4, Section II of *Between Facts and Norms*[2] grew out of stimulating discussions with Klaus Günther.[3]

The questions raised by Andrew Arato demonstrate a precise knowledge of my theory and a broad agreement with me.[4] These questions require a

*Professor Emeritus, University of Frankfurt, Germany.

†Translated by William Rehg.

1. *See* Klaus Günther, *Communicative Freedom, Communicative Power, and Jurisgenesis*, 17 CARDOZO L. REV. 1035 (1996).

2. JÜRGEN HABERMAS, BETWEEN FACTS AND NORMS: CONTRIBUTIONS TO A DISCOURSE THEORY OF LAW AND DEMOCRACY (William Rehg trans., 1996) [hereinafter HABERMAS, BETWEEN FACTS AND NORMS].

3. For a discussion of the concept of communicative freedom, see Günther, *supra* note 1.

4. *See* Andrew Arato, *Reflexive Law, Civil Society, and Negative Rights*, 17 CARDOZO L. REV. 785 (1996).

deeper, extended analysis that cannot be carried out here. András Sajó has provided a comparative survey of problems of constitutional adjudication.[5] Here I can only take notice of his study, which I have found quite instructive. Bernhard Schlink labels the "value jurisprudence" of the Federal Constitutional Court a "myth"[6]; since I did not invent this interpretation but took it from the numerous writings of prominent scholars and even members of the Court itself, I would rather leave this dispute for legal scholars to settle. There are other reasons for avoiding Peter Goodrich's polemic.[7] In any case, the very nature of a reply requires me to focus more intensively on some contributions than on others. This by no means implies that those arguments and objections have more weight, but only that for me personally they were especially thought-provoking.[8]

I limit myself to seven thematic complexes that allow me to deal with the remaining articles in the following sequence. To begin, in Section One, I take a metacritical position on *how the "right" is embedded in conceptions of the good.* Richard J. Bernstein and Frank Michelman each accentuate this moderate contextualism differently—Bernstein approaching it from a pragmatist perspective inspired by Aristotle,[9] Michelman from a civic-republican perspective.[10] Bringing matters closer to home, in Section Two, Thomas McCarthy sharpens the controversy by asking whether the discourse model—in particular its assumption that each case admits one right answer—does justice to the value conflicts that are typical of multicultural societies.[11] In Section Three, I will examine the perspective of legal scholars

5. *See* András Sajó, *Constitutional Adjudication in Light of Discourse Theory,* 17 CARDOZO. L. REV. 1193 (1996).

6. *See* Bernhard Schlink, *The Dynamics of Constitutional Adjudication,* 17 CARDOZO L. REV. 1231 (1996).

7. Peter Goodrich, *Habermas and The Postal Rule,* 17 CARDOZO L. REV. 1457 (1996). I quit reading Goodrich's essay at the place where, vaguely referring to my *Philosophical Discourse of Modernity,* he accused me of defending modernity "against the irrationalists, the conservatives, the postmodernists, the heretics, the nomads and the outsiders, the Jews." *Id.* at 1458 (footnote omitted); *see also* JÜRGEN HABERMAS, THE PHILOSOPHICAL DISCOURSE OF MODERNITY: TWELVE LECTURES (Frederick T. Lawrence trans., 1987). Anyone who suspects me of antisemitism hardly expects a response; more generally, whoever denounces someone wants to speak about him, not with him.

8. Two essays were not yet available to me when I composed the present reply. William E. Forbath, *Short-Circuit: A Critique of Habermas's Understanding of Law, Politics, and Economic Life,* 17 CARDOZO L. REV. 1441 (1996); Ingeborg Maus, *Liberties and Popular Sovereignty: On Jürgen Habermas's Reconstruction of the System of Rights,* 17 CARDOZO L. REV. 825 (1996).

9. *See* Richard J. Bernstein, *The Retrieval of the Democratic Ethos,* 17 CARDOZO L. REV. 1127 (1996).

10. *See* Frank I. Michelman, *Family Quarrel,* 17 CARDOZO L. REV. 1163 (1996).

11. *See* Thomas McCarthy, *Legitimacy and Diversity: Dialectical Reflections on Analytical Distinctions,* 17 CARDOZO L. REV. 1083 (1996).

by discussing the work of Michel Rosenfeld, who continues the discussion concerning the *priority of procedure over a substantial background understanding.*[12] Rosenfeld concludes by suggesting an alternative that Arthur J. Jacobson then develops into a *dynamic conception of law.*[13]

In Section Four, I deal with William Rehg's question concerning the *relation between discourse and decision,* which leads him into more fundamental issues of theory construction.[14] In addition, Section Four will address Michael Power's discussion of the *role of idealizations,*[15] and Jacques Lenoble's *objections based on a critique of reason* that concerns the entire approach of a theory of communicative action.[16]

Like Lenoble, David Rasmussen,[17] Robert Alexy,[18] and Gunther Teubner[19] give me the occasion, in Section Five, to delve once more into the *logic of application discourses.* In Section Six, I will examine both Ulrich Preuss's[20] and Günter Frankenberg's[21] discussion of the different aspects of the *relation between private and public autonomy,* and Dick Howard's[22] and Gabriel Motzkin's[23] analysis of the *political content* of my legal theory. Finally, in Section Seven, I respond to the *sociological objections* that Mark Gould[24] brings from a left-Parsonian perspective and that Niklas Luhmann[25] raises from the standpoint of systems theory.

---

12. *See* Michel Rosenfeld, *Can Rights, Democracy, and Justice Be Reconciled through Discourse Theory? Reflections on Habermas's Proceduralist Paradigm of Law,* 17 CARDOZO L. REV. 791 (1996).

13. *See* Arthur J. Jacobson, *Law and Order,* 17 CARDOZO L. REV. 919 (1996).

14. *See* William Rehg, *Against Subordination: Morality, Discourse, and Decision in the Legal Theory of Jürgen Habermas,* 17 CARDOZO L. REV. 1147 (1996).

15. *See* Michael K. Power, *Habermas and the Counterfactual Imagination,* 17 CARDOZO L. REV. 1005 (1996).

16. *See* Jacques Lenoble, *Law and Undecidability: A New Vision of the Proceduralization of Law,* 17 CARDOZO L. REV. 935 (1996).

17. *See* David M. Rasmussen, *Jurisprudence and Validity,* 17 CARDOZO L. REV. 1059 (1996).

18. *See* Robert Alexy, *Jürgen Habermas's Theory of Legal Discourse,* 17 CARDOZO L. REV. 1027 (1996).

19. *See* Gunther Teubner, *De Collisione Discursuum: Communicative Rationalities in Law, Morality, and Politics,* 17 CARDOZO L. REV. 901 (1996).

20. *See* Ulrich K. Preuss, *Communicative Power and the Concept of Law,* 17 CARDOZO L. REV. 1179 (1996).

21. *See* Günter Frankenberg, *Why Care?—The Trouble with Social Rights,* 17 CARDOZO L. REV. 1365 (1996).

22. *See* Dick Howard, *Law and Political Culture,* 17 CARDOZO L. REV. 1391 (1996).

23. *See* Gabriel Motzkin, *Habermas's Ideal Paradigm of Law,* 17 CARDOZO L. REV. 1431 (1996).

24. *See* Mark Gould, *Law and Philosophy: Some Consequences for the Law Deriving from the Sociological Reconstruction of Philosophical Theory,* 17 CARDOZO L. REV. 1239 (1996).

25. *See* Niklas Luhmann, *Quod Omnes Tangit: Remarks on Jürgen Habermas's Legal Theory,* 17 CARDOZO L. REV. 883 (1996).

I. THE GOOD AND THE RIGHT
A.

My friend Richard Bernstein is second to none in his acute knowledge of my work. Bernstein follows and interprets my publications with great hermeneutical sensibility,[26] and he convincingly situates them in contemporary discussions.[27] For more than two decades Bernstein and I have been companions in a philosophical exchange that has left its mark on my work. Since our first conversation, Bernstein has continually presented me with good arguments to "detranscendentalize" the Kantian heritage. Again and again, entirely in keeping with the Hegelian spirit of pragmatism, Bernstein sought to dissolve rigid dichotomies. Distinctions have no value in and of themselves, but must prove themselves through the problems they help us solve. Like C. S. Peirce, he asked: What is the difference that makes a difference?[28] Again Bernstein asks this here, though now evidently with growing impatience. Bernstein objects to two things: (i) the neutrality claim of a proceduralism that in fact requires a specific democratic ethos; and (ii) the abstract distinction between moral and ethical issues, which in his opinion is an empty distinction that misses the real problems.[29]

1. In Bernstein's view, specific procedures and communicative presuppositions can ground the presumption that the outcomes of democratic opinion- and will-formation are rational (in the sense of well-informed and impartial) only if the participating citizens are imbued with a "democratic ethos."[30] Citizens must be motivated by civic virtues, i.e., generalized value-orientations that do not yet predetermine anything about *individual norms.*[31] If this thesis is read in its weaker sense, it does not present any objection to my position. A political system based on the rule of law is not self-contained, but *also* depends on "a liberal political culture" and a population accustomed to freedom. Indeed, it depends on "the initiatives of opinion-building associations" and corresponding patterns of socializa-

---

26. *See* Richard J. Bernstein, *Introduction* to HABERMAS AND MODERNITY 1 (Richard J. Bernstein ed., 1985); *see also* RICHARD J. BERNSTEIN, THE RESTRUCTURING OF SOCIAL AND POLITICAL THEORY 171–236 (1976).

27. *See* RICHARD J. BERNSTEIN, BEYOND OBJECTIVISM AND RELATIVISM: SCIENCE, HERMENEUTICS, AND PRAXIS (1983); RICHARD J. BERNSTEIN, THE NEW CONSTELLATION: THE ETHICAL-POLITICAL HORIZONS OF MODERNITY/POSTMODERNITY (1991).

28. Bernstein's hermeneutical generosity occasionally misleads him into blurring differences that one should hold onto. *See, e.g.,* RICHARD J. BERNSTEIN, *What Is the Difference that Makes a Difference? Gadamer, Habermas, and Rorty,* in PHILOSOPHICAL PROFILES: ESSAYS IN A PRAGMATIC MODE 58 (1986).

29. *See* Bernstein, *supra* note 9, at 1129.

30. *See id.* at 1130–31.

31. *See id.*

tion—"deliberative politics is internally connected with contexts of a rationalized lifeworld *that meets it halfway.*"[32] If one also recalls what I said in *The Theory of Communicative Action*[33] regarding the rationalization of lifeworlds, then one can easily understand this accommodating lifeworld context in the sense of a "postconventional *Sittlichkeit*" or a democratic ethos.[34]

As I see it, systematic reasons make it necessary to speak of democratic processes as embedded in a "constitutional patriotism." This requirement arises from the fact that even basic political rights take the form of subjective rights and thus can be interpreted as individual liberties. In modern legal orders, citizens are free to determine how they will exercise their rights of communication and participation. An orientation to the common good may be called for, but it cannot be made into a legal duty. Nevertheless, this orientation is necessary to a certain degree, because democratic legislation draws its legitimating force solely from a process in which citizens *reach an understanding* about the regulation of their common life. Consequently, the emergence of legitimacy from legality ceases to be paradoxical only if the political culture disposes citizens not just to take the self-interested attitude of market participants, but *also* to exercise their political liberties in the service of mutual understanding, i.e., to engage in what Kant called the "public use of reason."

This "also" is what separates the weak reading from the strong, classical republican reading that Bernstein favors. To sharpen his thesis into an *objection*, Bernstein must ultimately place the burden of democratically legitimating law *entirely* on the political virtues of united citizens. By contrast, in explaining the democratic process, discourse theory employs a structuralist argument that relieves citizens of the Rousseauian expectation of virtue— the orientation to the common good only needs to be exacted in small increments insofar as practical reason withdraws from the hearts and heads of collective or individual actors into the procedures and forms of communication of political opinion- and will-formation. In other words, practical reason shifts from the individual level of ethical motivations and insights to the social level of gathering and processing information. This signifies a certain intellectualization. That is, processes of deliberation and decision making must be set up in such a way that discourses and bargaining function like a filter: only those topics and contributions that are supposed "to count" in reaching a decision are permitted to pass through. The false re-

---

32. HABERMAS, BETWEEN FACTS AND NORMS, *supra* note 2, at 302 (emphasis added).

33. 1 JÜRGEN HABERMAS, THE THEORY OF COMMUNICATIVE ACTION (Thomas McCarthy trans., 1984).

34. *See* Albrecht Wellmer, *Bedingungen einer demokratischen Kultur: Zur Debatte zwischen Liberalen und Kommunitaristen, in* GEMEINSCHAFT UND GERECHTIGKEIT 173 (Micha Brumlik & Hauke Brunkhorst eds., 1993).

alism that rejects the meaning of democratic self-determination as inherently "idealistic" can be better countered if we have a normative account that replaces the expectation of virtue with a supposition of rationality.

Consequently, I oppose the republican tradition only insofar as I shift the burden of justifying the effectiveness of practical reason from the mentality of citizens to the deliberative forms of politics. Contrary to what Bernstein believes, however, this proceduralism does not mean that the citizens' practice of self-determination has been normatively neutralized. To be sure, the normative expectation of legitimate lawmaking is primarily linked with the communicative arrangement and not with the competence of the participating actors (even though the procedures and processes are not self-supporting but must be embedded in an open political culture). However, this mode of lawmaking, which is supposed to secure the equal autonomy of all, has a strong normative content. Democratic procedure justifies a presumption of rationality in the sense that it promises neutrality, that is, impartial outcomes: procedural rationality is supposed to guarantee justice in that it provides an impartial regulation of practical questions.

2.   Bernstein has a further misgiving that is directed not so much at the proceduralist conception itself as at the understanding of political justice associated with it. Practical reason embodied in procedures and processes inherently refers to a justice (in both the moral and legal senses) that *points beyond* the concrete ethos of a particular community or the worldview articulated in a particular tradition and form of life. To make this clear, I distinguish between moral questions of justice and ethical questions of self-understanding. When we approach a problem as a moral question, we ask which regulation lies in the equal interest of all (or what is "equally good for all"). However, when dealing with ethical questions, we weigh alternatives from the perspective of individuals or collectivities that are seeking to confirm their identity and that want to know which life they should lead in light of who they are and want to be (or what "is good for me/us on the whole and in the long run"). Each question corresponds to a different perspective or standpoint. Whereas questions of the "good life" are inscribed with the perspectival worldview and self-interpretation of a first-person singular or plural, justice questions can be judged impartially only if equal consideration is given to the worldviews and self-interpretations of *all* participants (hence George Herbert Mead's requirement of an "ideal perspective-taking"). Bernstein does not dispute this analytic distinction as such. Rather, he maintains that having hypostatized it, I fail to use it in a meaningful way, succumbing to the "myth of the framework."[35]

To begin with, I must clear up a misunderstanding. Questions of ethical self-understanding are context-dependent in a different sense than moral questions. This is because ethical questions arise within the horizon of a personal life-history or an intersubjectively shared form of life and can be answered only *by referring* to this *pre-existing* context. Naturally, even in ethical discourses we must adopt a reflective attitude not burdened by the pressures of immediate interests and imperatives to act; we must, to a certain extent, interrupt the naive conduct of life and gain some distance from our own present life context. But *this* distancing from the network of our self-formation cannot (and need not) go as deep as the distancing we undertake in moral reflection where we adopt a hypothetical attitude toward the problematic validity of *individual norms*. It is precisely pragmatism that teaches us that we cannot make an object of our identity and entire lifeworld by the fiat of a "paper doubt."

The sole issue of dispute is whether we can raise and answer moral questions only *within* the horizon of our own ethically articulated, and thus particular, worldview and self-interpretation, or whether we can attempt to *expand* this interpretive horizon by taking the moral point of view, indeed so radically that, to use Gadamer's term, our horizon "fuses" with the horizons of all other persons. On this question of the priority of the right over the good, Bernstein is not entirely clear: "If I take my own life history as a Jew or an American . . . I certainly do not restrict myself to questions concerning my fellow Jews, Americans, etc. I want also to understand my responsibilities and obligations to those who are not members of the identified group."[36] To begin with, this quotation simply states that justice questions *arise* for us as persons with particular self-interpretations and worldviews, and that we *understand* these questions against this horizon. However, whether we can also *adequately answer* the question within the given horizon is not trivial. So long as I want to become clear about my identity as a Jew or a Protestant, American or German, it is neither necessary nor possible to transcend these particular horizons. But questions regarding our moral obligations toward Bosnian refugees or the homeless, and also legal questions such as how to regulate new forms of duress (e.g., spousal abuse), have to do with the legitimacy of expectations and claims that we do not just have toward one another as members, but that we also direct toward strangers, across great geographical, historical, cultural, and social distances. In this case, it is not a matter of what is "good" for us as belonging to a collectivity (distinguished by its own ethos). Rather, it is a matter of what is "right" for *all*, whether all those who belong to the universe of speaking and acting subjects or those of a local, or if necessary, even global legal community. In judging such questions of justice we seek an impartial solution, which must be able to gain the considered assent of all participants (and those affected)

36. *Id.* at 1143.

in a noncoercive dialogue conducted under symmetrical conditions of mutual recognition.

Currently, there are three positions on this question. (1) As long as each idea of justice is inseparably permeated by a particular conception of the good, then even when we judge justice questions we cannot escape the *given* horizon of our own self-interpretation and understanding of the world. In that case, an agreement (*Einverständnis*) between two parties with different backgrounds can come about only through assimilation, insofar as *their* standards are assimilated to *ours*[37] or through conversion, insofar as we surrender *our* standards in favor of *theirs*.[38] (2) However, as soon as we take into consideration the plurality of "modern" worldviews that can be tolerant toward one another because of their inherently universalist potentials, we may count on an overlapping consensus in questions of political justice.[39] Religious freedom provides the prime example. Because a certain expansion of horizons (defined by religions and worldviews that have become reflexive) is presupposed here, a rationally motivated consonance (*Übereinstimmung*) is the *result*. However, this happens only in such a way that the same principled solutions are accepted by each party for respectively *different* reasons. (3) Finally, the manner in which discourse theory introduces the distinction between moral and ethical questions and maintains the priority of justice over the good means that the logic of justice questions becomes dynamic. This demands the progressive expansion of horizons: against the horizon of their respective self-interpretations and worldviews, the different parties refer to a presumptively shared moral point of view that, under the symmetrical conditions of discourse (and mutual learning), requires an ever broader decentering of the different perspectives. G. H. Mead spoke in this regard of the appeal to an ever wider community.[40]

Contemporary discussions on the topic of "multiculturalism" make it clear that distinguishing between moral and ethical questions in the area of political justice is certainly not trivial, but "makes a difference."[41] This is evident in the efforts to find peaceful solutions to ethnic conflicts in Palestine and the Balkans. This was also evident in the Vienna Conference

---

37. *See generally* RICHARD RORTY, OBJECTIVITY, RELATIVISM, AND TRUTH: PHILOSOPHICAL PAPERS (1991); RICHARD RORTY, CONTINGENCY, IRONY, AND SOLIDARITY (1989).

38. *See generally* ALASDAIR MACINTYRE, WHOSE JUSTICE? WHICH RATIONALITY? (1988).

39. *See generally* JOHN RAWLS, POLITICAL LIBERALISM (1993) [hereinafter POLITICAL LIBERALISM]; JOHN RAWLS, A THEORY OF JUSTICE (1971) [hereinafter A THEORY OF JUSTICE].

40. *See* GEORGE H. MEAD, *Fragments on Ethics, in* MIND, SELF, AND SOCIETY: FROM THE STANDPOINT OF A SOCIAL BEHAVIORIST 379 (Charles W. Morris ed., 1962).

41. Jürgen Habermas, *Struggles for Recognition in the Democratic Constitutional State, in* MULTICULTURALISM: EXAMINING THE POLITICS OF RECOGNITION 107 (Amy Gutmann ed. & Shierry W. Nicholson trans., rev. ed. 1994) (Charles Taylor ed., 1992) [hereinafter Habermas, *Struggles for Recognition*].

on Human Rights, where Asian and African participants argued with the representatives of Western societies over the interpretation and application of basic rights that, in themselves, had been accepted.

B.

It is no accident that Frank Michelman is one of the three or four contemporary authors whom I have cited most frequently. Michelman's works have taught me the most about deliberative politics, and through reading them I have been encouraged to apply the discourse principle to law and lawmaking, or "jurisgenesis," as he calls it.[42] As a result of this (definitely nonsymmetrical) dependence there is considerable agreement between our positions. In a family quarrel the differences are often so minimal that one can make them visible only by exaggerating them. Perhaps I have been guilty of such exaggeration in my presentation, which has been motivated more by systematic than by hermeneutical concerns. I am not sure whether Michelman's misgivings result, like those of Bernstein, from what is ultimately a philosophical difference *in re*, or whether they are due to a difference in disciplinary perspectives.

I find the expository arguments in the first section of Michelman's article convincing.[43] My only reservations have to do with a "dialogic" conception of deliberative politics that, when contrasted in an idealizing manner to "instrumental" politics, excludes the large bargaining component (i.e., the balancing of interests through compromise). Michelman's second section presents a more precise version of the concept of postconventional *Sittlichkeit*, which is supposed to form the motivational context for the appropriate exercise of civil rights.[44] Certainly such an "accommodating" political culture always emerges from the context of a national history. But what first makes for a "liberal" political culture, able to create and sustain a shared civic consciousness across all differences of a pluralistic society, is still the common *reference* to universalistic constitutional principles that promise equal rights.

Naturally, a number of constitutional regimes have arisen that are different from one another, even prior to their specific institutional arrangements, in the wording of their founding documents: "Constitutional law is institutional stuff from the word go."[45] However, what makes these regimes into constitutional democracies is the implementation of basic rights, whereby each interpreter assumes that these rights have a universalistic meaning, however much of this meaning is contested among competing

---

42. *See, e.g.*, Frank Michelman, *Law's Republic*, 97 YALE L.J. 1493, 1513 (1988).
43. *See* Michelman, *supra* note 10, at 1164–70.
44. *See id.* at 1170–74.
45. *Id.* at 1175.

horizons of interpretation. "But to say in this way that originary discourses of legislative justification must always proceed on ground that is already ethical is not to deny that they also must always proceed within a horizon of universalist morality, *sub specie aeternitatis.*"[46]

Michelman does not contradict this point when, in his last section, he discusses the ties that link constitutional scholars, and above all judges, to an ethically permeated legal tradition. He illustrates such ties by showing how American and Canadian courts have treated the new crime of "hate speech" differently. Michelman poses two alternative ways of interpreting this difference. I would like to use these to construct a third alternative, which appears to me to be appropriate in such a case: "The same (universal) principle of equal liberties for all, resting on somewhat different variants of discourses of originary constitutional justification, prevails in both countries, which have somewhat different cultural and ethical histories. The doctrinal differences that we observe are secondary applicational variants reflecting (what is probably a combination of) different legal traditions and differing social facts at the moment."[47]

II. NEUTRALIZING VALUE CONFLICTS AND "LIVING WITH DIFFERENCES"

Thomas McCarthy has been a stroke of luck for me—I usually have the impression that he understands my texts better than I do. Each time he criticizes me,[48] he defends views that I later come to acknowledge as our common position. His criticism (especially of Foucault, Rorty, and the deconstructionists)[49] is so astute that I experience some anxiety when he so emphatically contradicts my work in his essay.[50] For two decades, McCarthy has raised hermeneutical doubts about the strong systematic claims of rational reconstruction, especially when it is connected with evolutionary assumptions. Thus, I am surprised not so much by the general thrust of his criticism, which now has a more pronounced pragmatist tinge, as by its antiuniversalistic point. Similar to Bernstein, McCarthy insists that the right

---

46. *Id.*

47. *Compare with id.* at 1177.

48. Very early on, McCarthy drew my attention to problems that affected the structure of my theory as a whole. *See* THOMAS MCCARTHY, THE CRITICAL THEORY OF JÜRGEN HABERMAS (1978); *see also* THOMAS MCCARTHY, *Complexity and Democracy: The Seducements of Systems Theory,* in IDEALS AND ILLUSIONS: ON RECONSTRUCTION AND DECONSTRUCTION IN CONTEMPORARY CRITICAL THEORY 152 (1991) [hereinafter IDEALS AND ILLUSIONS].

49. *See* DAVID C. HOY & THOMAS MCCARTHY, CRITICAL THEORY (1994).

50. *See generally* McCarthy, *supra* note 11. The basic outlines of McCarthy's criticism were already developed in THOMAS MCCARTHY, *Practical Discourse: On the Relation of Morality to Politics,* in IDEALS AND ILLUSIONS, *supra* note 48, at 181 [hereinafter *Practical Discourse*].

and the good dialectically interpenetrate each other: "the 'justice issue' of what is 'equally good for all' is not separable from and superordinate to 'self-understanding about the kind of society we want to live in': they are two, interdependent aspects of the same problem, namely 'which *norms* citizens want to adopt to regulate *their life together.'*"51* As with Bernstein and Michelman, the claim once again is that the analytically distinct perspectives "are indistinguishable in practice."

McCarthy starts with the important observation that in modern societies a gap opens up between, on the one hand, the rapidly growing differences that confront citizens in their daily interactions and, on the other, the expectation imposed on these citizens by an egalitarian legal system to normatively *disregard* these increasingly noticeable differences. The spectrum of differences that must be assimilated by individuals at the level of simple interactions is growing in temporal, social, and substantive terms. In ever shorter time intervals and through ever more fleeting contacts, we must reach an understanding with persons who are, to an increasing extent, strangers (shaped by entirely different sociocultural backgrounds) to increasingly numerous and specialized problems (which are further aggravated by the trust we must place in unknown experts).[52] The individualization of lifestyles and, above all, the ethnically heterogeneous composition of multicultural societies display these abstractive demands in an especially drastic form only because the colliding lifestyles and forms of life—as totalities that constitute identities and penetrate personality structures as a whole—touch off "existential" value conflicts. McCarthy begins with such conflicts between permeating value-orientations because, unlike conflicts of interest, they cannot be settled by compromises over the distribution of recognized compensations.

Since forms of life have a collective character, their equal right to coexist is not *directly* secured by instruments of private law. "Subjective" rights secure liberties whose immediate purpose is to provide a protective belt surrounding the autonomous pursuit of *individual* life plans. The liberal paradigm still assumed that individuals were isolated or spread out to a certain extent. Individuals were supposed to be able to stay far enough apart in realizing their respective conceptions of the good that they would not have to run into and mutually "disturb" one another. As multicultural and highly individualized societies grow more complex, however, the "sections" of social space and historical time that can be occupied and "privatized" by different individuals and members of *different* subcultures are shrinking. Today, the abstract legal person of classical jurisprudence must be replaced

51. McCarthy, *supra* note 11, at 1105.

52. *See* Claus Offe, *Moderne Barbarei: Der Naturzustand im Kleinformat*, 34 J. FÜR SOZIALFORSCHUNG 229 (1994).

with an intersubjective concept: the identity of the individual is interwoven with collective identities. Since legal persons are also individuated only by way of socialization, their integrity cannot be guaranteed without protecting those intersubjectively shared contexts of experience and living in which they have developed their personal identities and in which alone they can stabilize those identities.[53]

After examining two constitutional mechanisms for neutralizing value conflicts, I will take up the various details that strike me as important for clarifying the controversy. Then, I will discuss the alternative that McCarthy proposes. Finally, I will offer some tentative thoughts on a really problematic point—the premise of "one right answer."

A.

Constitutional democracies have a limited repertoire for regulating value conflicts that result from the unavoidable interactions between (the members of) coexisting forms of life that are "alien" to one another in an existentially dissonant way.[54] In the present context, two means of normatively neutralizing differences deserve our attention above all: (i) the guarantee of an equal right of coexistence; and (ii) securing legitimation through procedures.

1. For the first approach, it is essential to distinguish between questions of justice and questions of the good life. This is illustrated by issues like euthanasia or abortion. Let us assume, simply for the sake of argument, that sufficiently discursive public discussions have shown that the contested issue cannot be neutrally framed in relation to worldviews or ideologies because the competing descriptions of the matter in need of regulation are conceptually interwoven with the religiously or ideologically articulated self-understanding of different confessions, interpretive communities, subcultures, and so on. Therefore, we are faced with a value conflict that cannot be resolved either by discourse or by compromise. In this case, in a constitutionally organized pluralistic society, such an *ethically controversial* issue may not be regulated under the ethically permeated description of a self-understanding that, from the perspective of the universe of fellow citizens, is just one among several collective self-interpretations (even if it is that of the majority culture). Rather, it is necessary to seek a neutral regulation that, at the *more abstract* level of the equal right of different ethically integrated communities to coexist, can find the rationally motivated recognition of all parties to the conflict. To accomplish this shift in the level of

53. *See* Habermas, *Struggles for Recognition, supra* note 41, at 122.
54. Following McCarthy's example, I restrict myself to this "multicultural" type of conflict.

abstraction, a *shift in perspective* is required. Each participant must turn away from the *ethical* question of which regulation is respectively "best for us" from "our" point of view. They must, instead, take the *moral* point of view and examine which regulation is "equally good for all" in view of the prior claim to an equal right to coexist.

The difficulty that McCarthy sees connected with this abstraction admittedly calls for qualification. The shift in perspective is intended to make it possible to arrive at a morally acceptable solution—a regulation acceptable to each party for the same reasons—that leaves the *value* conflict unsettled. Such a regulation does not mean that the burdens associated with the regulation are symmetrically distributed. The regulation is "equally good for all" in view of the goal of equally entitled coexistence, not in view of *all* the consequences that can arise in each case. It is not to be excluded—in fact it is rather likely—that a "just" solution entails an unequal distribution of "hardships" for the ethical self-understanding of one or another group. In general, abstraction tends to work in favor of a comparatively "liberal" regulation (which in the case of euthanasia, for example, I personally would find rather unbearable). On the other hand, the normative expectation connected with this—that when necessary we *tolerate* the members of another group whose behavior is ethically reprehensible to "our" view—does not necessarily imply any damage to our integrity: "we" (for instance, as Catholics confronted by a "liberal" abortion law) may continue at an ethical level to abhor the legally permissible practice of others as we have in the past. Instead, what is legally required of us is tolerance for practices that in "our" view are ethically deviant.

Tolerance is the price for living together in an egalitarian legal community, in which groups with different cultural and ethnic backgrounds must get along with one another. If the basis of mutual respect among legal persons is to remain intact, tolerance is necessary. However, the price of "living with" ethical differences of this sort can also be reasonably required by law, insofar as the equal right of different forms of life to coexist is secured. Such an ethically "abstract" legal right provides the standard for regulations that, because they can be accepted by all for the same reasons in view of the goal of coexistence, spare citizens the essentially more painful, integrity-endangering *compromises* in irreconcilable value conflicts.

2. All this presupposes that a conflict actually involves an ethical issue that *as such* immediately precludes a consensual moral solution. As previously assumed, this should have been established in sufficiently discursive public discussions. This foreground dispute becomes especially deadlocked when the shift to a higher level of abstraction favors solutions that require more tolerance from some rather than others. And this raises questions regarding the second means of neutralizing differences—legitimation

through procedure. Even if, as we assumed in the previous scenario, one could agree on the more abstract standard—the equal right to coexist of different communities whose identities are not to be violated—one is no closer to a basis on which the conflict could be solved *in principle*. Even at this level of moral discussion, consensus (*Einverständnis*) is, in fact, rarely reached. As experience has taught, even narrowly defined questions of justice often remain controversial, particularly in a heterogeneous society. And nothing changes in the phenomenology of ongoing controversies when all participants jointly assume (or at least happen to agree in presuming) that moral questions, if framed with sufficient precision, have just one right answer. Therefore, McCarthy persists in asking whether the premise of a single right answer, which may still be plausible from the perspective of participants, might not be merely an illusion. From the observer's perspective, we realize that in normatively controversial political questions an agreement (*Einigung*) will be reached rarely, if at all. Given the undeniable phenomenon of permanent dissensus, why should participants in the democratic process orient themselves toward such a dubious goal as a consensus that is *possible in principle?*

An answer to this central question requires two steps. Specifically, two things must be explained: (i) why the premise of a single right answer is at all necessary; and (ii) how one can, when necessary, reconcile this premise with the overwhelming evidence of persistent dissensus.

The first question is best answered *e contrario*. If we consider the constitutional state to be a legitimate order that in turn makes possible legitimate legislation and other broadly legitimate lawmaking processes (where "legitimacy" is understood in a nonempiricist sense[55]), then we imply that it is possible to reach an understanding over political questions *without resorting to violence*. This is so because "reaching an understanding" (in this broader sense) may be considered as an alternative to the imposition of the stronger interest (based on custom, coercion, superior influence, deception, or seducement) only if the participants (either directly or indirectly) freely accept the results of political discussion (or could accept these results under suitable conditions). "Understanding" refers to consensuses and justified decisions based on the rationally motivated recognition of facts, norms, or values and their corresponding validity claims, or on procedures of discursive opinion- and will-formation (including decision making based on argumentation). But the broader sense of "understanding" also includes negotiated agreements (*Vereinbarungen*) that arise through the free (or presumably voluntary) expression of will by contracting parties and bargaining partners, or that are adopted in accordance with rules of compromise for-

55. *See* HABERMAS, BETWEEN FACTS AND NORMS, *supra* note 2, at 289–95.

mation that have been freely accepted (i.e., recognized as just or fair). What qualifies mutual understanding as an alternative to violence is the fact that the participants ultimately rely on the associative force produced by communicatively confirmed insight and institutionally secured freedom in the expression of will (or by a procedurally regulated combination of "reason" and "will"). They could not rely on this common basis if they could not assume that a constitutionally established network of legitimating communicative processes, on the one hand, and the presumption of rationality associated with these processes and establishments, on the other, were acceptable to all citizens for the same good reasons.

This still permits a republican reading of the "single right answer" premise: the good reasons that citizens have to trust the legitimacy of the constitution and the legitimating force of the democratic process could happen to coincide with a customary local political ethos. In this case, such reasons would not be convincing beyond the boundaries of one's own political community. This interpretation, however, is not open to McCarthy because he excludes an indigenous value consensus for multicultural societies. Rather, he assumes that endemic value conflicts are such that even the incessant debates over the political-ethical self-understanding of the nation as a whole must be regarded by the citizens themselves as insoluble in principle. In contrast to McCarthy, my argument first implies that, given McCarthy's premises, he cannot explain how democratic legitimacy is even possible. If questions of justice cannot transcend the ethical self-understanding of competing forms of life, and if existentially relevant value conflicts and oppositions must penetrate *all* controverted political questions, then in the final analysis we end up with something resembling Carl Schmitt's understanding of politics.[56] If political conflicts are essentially ethical in nature, and thus *as such* do not allow one to expect a rationally motivated solution at the more abstract level of justice, then citizens must assume that for the sphere of politics as a whole it is fruitless to expect anything other than (more or less reasonable) dissensus. Any alternative other than this would mean that citizens could also adopt *a different* perspective, say that of justice, which would take them beyond the perspective of members who are *immediately* engaged in value conflicts. As long as this is not considered a possibility, it remains incomprehensible how political debates shot through with rationally irresolvable value conflicts and dominated by opposing identities should be settled at all except by existential struggle or force imposed from above, or at best by imposed procedures of compromise (that have become

56. *See generally* CARL SCHMITT, THE CONCEPT OF THE POLITICAL (George Schwab trans., 1976); CARL SCHMITT, THE CRISIS OF PARLIAMENTARY DEMOCRACY (Ellen Kennedy trans., 1988).

customary over time). In that case, an empiricist description of the legitimation process is called for—an approach that McCarthy fails to find satisfactory.[57]

Deliberative politics would lose its meaning and constitutional democracy would lose its basis of legitimacy if participants in political discourses do not want to convince and learn from others. Political disputes would forfeit their deliberative character and degenerate into purely strategic struggles for power if participants do not assume—to be sure, fallibilistically, in the awareness that we can always err—that controversial political and legal problems have a correct solution. If they were not oriented toward the *goal* of solving problems by giving reasons, participants would have no idea what they were *looking for.* At the same time, even as participants, we may not naively ignore the empirical evidence. McCarthy is correct to insist that what we *know* from the observer perspective about permanent dissensus must be integrated with what we *assume* as participants seeking to reach an understanding in political deliberations and discussions—the former should not contradict the latter. In practical affairs, decisions must be made despite ongoing dissensus, but they should nonetheless be made in such a way that they can be considered legitimate.

Properly conceived, "legitimation through procedures" satisfies this seemingly paradoxical requirement. Thus far, we have focused our attention on the fact that enacted law must acquire its legitimacy from a discursive opinion- and will-formation. The flip-side of this, however, is just as interesting: the legitimation process itself has a need for legal institutionalization. In virtue of institutionalization, political discourses (and bargaining) are furnished with the formal properties of law. Now, a specific feature of law is that it can legitimately *compel.* Thanks to this peculiarity, time constraints on decision making that are necessary from the *observer perspective* can be introduced via law into democratic processes of deliberation in a way that does not harm the legitimating force of discourses from the *participant perspective.* I have attempted to show elsewhere how deliberation and decision making can be legally institutionalized (and embedded in informal public communications) such that they justify the presumption that outcomes conforming to procedure are rational. The "procedure" of the "democratic process" should be understood in a complex sense. In this process, legally facilitated informal opinion-formation in the political public sphere is channelled into legally institutionalized deliberations (and bargaining), whose outcomes are then combined with legally binding decision procedures.

One of the more important decision procedures is majority rule (appropriately qualified when necessary) because its "procedural rationality," in

57. *See* McCarthy, *supra* note 11, at 1094.

combination with the discursive character of the preceding deliberations, bestows legitimating force on majority decisions. Democratic majority decisions are only caesura in a process of argumentation that has been (temporarily) interrupted under the pressure to decide; the results of this process can be assumed even by the outvoted minority as a basis for a practice binding on all. For acceptance does not mean that the minority accepts the content of the outcome as rational, and thus would have to change their *beliefs*. For the time being, however, the minority can live with the majority opinion as binding on their conduct insofar as the democratic process gives them the possibility of continuing or recommencing the interrupted discussion and shifting the majority by offering (putatively) better arguments. Majority rule owes its legitimating force to what Rawls calls an "imperfect" but "pure" procedural rationality.[58] It is imperfect because the democratic process is established so as to *justify the presumption* of a rational outcome without being able to *guarantee* the outcome *is* right. On the other hand, it is also a case of pure procedural justice, because in the democratic process no criteria of rightness *independent* of the procedure are available; the correctness of decisions depends solely on the fact that the procedure has actually been carried out.[59]

B.

If I am not mistaken, the controversy with McCarthy rests partly on misunderstandings. These primarily have to do with three questions of detail: (i) the distinction between national and subnational levels of ethical integration; (ii) the concept of collective identity, which should be understood as a process; and (iii) the ethical permeation of a country's legal order.

1. Within the framework of a nation-state, we must differentiate between at least two legally relevant levels of ethical integration. The value conflicts we have considered so far arise from the fact that different confessional or interpretive communities, ethnic subcultures, and forms of life coexist inside a nation of enfranchised citizens (assuming they are not separated territorially). Often these subnational conflicts flare up because the historically prevailing ethos of a majority culture dominates legal relations, and thus obstructs equal treatment of (the members of) groups that are ethically integrated at this subpolitical level in a mutually dissonant fashion. In their role as citizens of the same nation-state, however, members of different subcultures are obligated when conflict arises to take into account,

58. *See* A THEORY OF JUSTICE, *supra* note 39, at 85.
59. This does not address the further distinction between the "direct" or substantive justification of the procedure itself and the "indirect" justification of the individual decisions reached by correctly applying the procedure.

through abstract regulations, the prior norm of equal coexistence. As previously explained, such regulations, which protect the precious integrity of each individual in *his or her particular, identity-forming cultural memberships,* can often be obtained only at a social-psychological price. The political-ethical integration at the level of the national community must be distinguished from integration on this subcultural level.

At the national level we find what in the United States is called ."civil religion"—a "constitutional patriotism" that binds all citizens together regardless of their different cultural backgrounds or ethnic heritages. This is a metalegal quantity; that is, this patriotism is based upon the interpretation of recognized, universalistic constitutional principles within the context of a particular national history and tradition. Such a legally unenforceable constitutional loyalty anchored in the citizens' motivations and convictions can be expected only if citizens conceive the constitutional state as an *achievement* of their own history. Constitutional patriotism will be free of the usual aspects of ideology only if the two levels of ethical integration—national and subnational—are kept separate. Normally, this separation must be fought for against the resistance of the majority culture. Only then does a favorable motivational basis emerge as support for the expectations of tolerance entailed by legally maintained differences *between* ethically integrated communities *within* the same nation.[60]

2.   McCarthy reminds us of the structural dissimilarity between the intersubjectively shared self-understanding of a community and the identity of individual persons. I have also continually warned against using ego-identity as a model for the collective identity of a community of citizens.[61] Rather, each is related to the other as its complement. Thus, there is certainly no subject writ large ("a unified we") that emerges from the ethical integration of a political community. However, those belonging to a state are also not simply members of an organization. Rather, they share a political form of life that is articulated in a corresponding self-understanding. Members of a collectivity intuitively know in which respects and in which situations they say—and also expect one another to say—"we." To be sure, in a post-traditional, pluralistic society, and especially in a multicultural so-

60. This also holds *mutatis mutandis* for the neutrality of a political self-understanding that is equally required of all, in contrast to other differences (of gender, social class, age, etc.). The different life circumstances based above all in sex and socioeconomic class are cumulatively associated with cultural and ethnic distinctions.

61. As early as 1974 I made this point in my address upon receiving the Hegel Prize, see JÜRGEN HABERMAS, *Können komplexe Gesellschaften eine vernünftige Identität ausbilden?*, in ZUR REKONSTRUKTION DES HISTORISCHEN MATERIALISMUS 92 (1976). For an abridged English translation, see Jürgen Habermas, *On Social Identity*, TELOS, Spring 1974, at 91.

ciety, the question that explicitly arises on given occasions—how "we" want to understand ourselves as citizens of a particular republic—is essentially contested. Also, with shifting contexts, the discourses of self-understanding remain in flux.

Our identity is not only something we have received; it is at the same time our own project. Certainly, we cannot choose what traditions we have: one tradition has behind it the Founding Fathers and a two-hundred-year-old constitutional tradition; another has the French Revolution; and the Germans have the so-called "War of Liberation" against Napolean, the futile Revolution of 1848, the Wilhelmine Reich, the unsuccessful Weimar Republic, National Socialism and its crimes against humanity, the momentous events of 1989, and so on. It is up to us, however, to determine which traditions we want to perpetuate and which we want to discard.[62] This corresponds to a *process concept* of collective identity. The identity of a nation of enfranchised citizens is not something fixed. Today, it is reflected in those parameters that set the boundaries of the current spectrum of public disputes over the best interpretation of the constitution and over an authentic self-understanding of the constitutive traditions of the political community. As long as established constitutional principles form the common focus of these discourses of self-understanding, which are tailored to the nation's form of life as a whole, competing interpretations sufficiently overlap to secure a consensus (*Einverständnis*)—for the time being—that may be diffuse but is able to sustain the political-ethical integration of citizens. In any case, discussions over particular topics bearing on the nation's shared historical form of life take place against this fluctuating background. As a somewhat trivial example of such a political-ethical question, one might consider a population's willingness to accept more or less serious risks when weighing technological safety standards against their economic costs.

3. McCarthy is rightly skeptical of my attempt to correlate the pragmatic, ethical, and moral aspects with specific classes of legislative matters. Political questions are normally so complex that they must be discussed under all three aspects simultaneously—which are certainly analytically distinguishable.[63] But McCarthy draws false conclusions from the fact that every national, spatiotemporally situated legal order is "permeated" by the ethical self-understanding of a political form of life. For the ethical permeation of law by no means eradicates its universalistic contents.

62. JÜRGEN HABERMAS, *Grenzen des Neohistorismus, in* DIE NACHHOLENDE REVOLUTION 149 (1990) [hereinafter HABERMAS, DIE NACHHOLENDE REVOLUTION].

63. *See* HABERMAS, BETWEEN FACTS AND NORMS, *supra* note 2, at 565 n.3.

Each national constitution represents a historically different way of construing *the same*—theoretically reconstructible—basic rights, and each positive legal order implements *the same* basic rights in a different form of life. But the identity of the meaning of these rights—and the universality of their content—must not be lost in the spectrum of these different interpretations. Established law certainly always applies within the boundaries of a particular legal order, and even a globally implemented international law remains provincial in comparison to the universe. Nonetheless, these legal orders could not claim legitimacy if they were not compatible with universalist moral principles. The claim of the system of rights to represent universal human rights becomes especially relevant wherever the growing interdependencies of today's world make an issue of the controversial selective readings of these rights by different cultures. This contest of interpretations makes sense only on the premise that it is necessary to find a single correct reading that claims to *exhaust* the universalistic content of these rights in the present context. Even inside the framework of a national legal order, the different aspects of justice and self-understanding do not dialectically interpenetrate in a way that would leave us with an irreconcilable conflict between context-dependent conceptions of justice. The universalistic content of basic rights is not restricted by the ethical permeation of the legal order; rather, it thoroughly penetrates nationally specific contexts. It is for this reason that the legal neutralization of value conflicts, which would otherwise fragment the political community, requires that the justice aspect *have a privileged position.*

Questions of justice enjoy normative priority for another reason as well: there are conceptions of the good that sanction authoritarian relationships within the group. In Germany, for example, the rights of young Turkish women must, if necessary, be enforced against the will of fathers who appeal to the prerogatives of their culture of origin. More generally, individual rights must be enforced against collective claims springing from a fundamentalistic or nationalistic self-understanding. For example, I do not believe that governments today may still impose universal conscription (i.e., require specific age groups (of males) to risk their lives for their country). I agree with McCarthy when he says: "legitimate law is *at once* a realization of universal rights and an expression of particular self-understandings and forms of life. As concrete, law *must* be both at once."[64] But I would agree with his concluding sentence only up to a point: "Hence its acceptability or legitimacy can be thematized under both aspects: the right and the good."[65] This is correct under the proviso that in cases of conflict justice arguments

64. McCarthy, *supra* note 11, at 1111–12.
65. *Id.* at 1112.

are Dworkinian "trumps" that win out over considerations arising from the
internal perspective of just one particular form of life.

C.

McCarthy's position on the central question—whether one can justify the
priority of justice over the good—is not entirely clear. From the ethical-
existential perspective of a personal life project, "justice" certainly counts
as one among several values, and hence as a value that must be weighed
against other values that may sometimes outrank it. This is true even when
it is clear that the preferred practice should be compatible with standards
of justice. But within the framework of the shared constitutional life of a
multicultural society, justice questions claim priority. McCarthy admits this
on the one hand, but on the other hand he insists that even here justice
questions "ultimately" cannot be separated from ethical-political questions.
He repeats his earlier statement: " 'we cannot agree on what is just without
achieving some measure of agreement on what is good.' "[66] While this
is true, it is trivial insofar as "prior agreement" only refers to the *functional* requirement that subcultural forms of life sufficiently overlap. Every
political community must rely on the integrating force of a shared political culture if it is not to disintegrate into its segments. This is a sociological proposition. As a philosophical proposition, the sentence allows two interpretations. Either it describes the communitarian position of Charles
Taylor and Alasdair MacIntyre,[67] which holds that all ideas of justice are
conceptually dependent on contexts defined by particular conceptions of
the good.[68] Accordingly, only with a shared ethical basis will we be able to
agree about the concept of justice. Or, the proposition claims that all ex-
planations of an intentionally universalist concept of justice must inevitably
start within the horizon of one's own conception of the good. But here, the
mutual critique of different ways of selectively construing "justice" is still
premised on the underlying assumption that discursive contest can bring
out the universalistic content of the intuitive concept in a way that is, *in
principle*, context-independent.

In any case, McCarthy finds discourse theory unsatisfactory in its explanation of constitutional practices, so he suggests an alternative. This alternative should allow a nonviolent common life based on the recognition of

66. *Id.* at 1119; *Practical Discourse, supra* note 50, at 192.
67. *See* JÜRGEN HABERMAS, JUSTIFICATION AND APPLICATION: REMARKS ON DISCOURSE
ETHICS 69–76, 96–105 (Ciaran Cronin trans., 1993) [hereinafter HABERMAS, JUSTIFICATION
AND APPLICATION].
68. This point is beyond the scope of this Reply, but see LUTZ WINGERT, GEMEINSINN UND
MORAL (1993).

"reasonable disagreements": "Members may be said 'rationally' to accept outcomes with which they substantively disagree only in an attenuated, indirect sense: they abide by the rules they accept as fair even when things do not go their way."[69] However, this alternative seems to boil down to the kind of procedural legitimacy proposed above. That is, it is supposed to guarantee that the conflicts one may reasonably expect in pluralistic societies, i.e., conflicts between the value standards of different communities integrated around their own conceptions of the good, are neutralized: one party should not be allowed to have its way of life at the expense of another's way of life. Only the next sentence allows us to see the difference from the explanation offered by discourse theory: "Rational acceptance does *not* here have the *cognitive* sense of succumbing to the force of the better argument."[70] McCarthy puts tolerance, mutual respect, care, and so forth in place of the expectation that mutual understanding is possible in principle. He does not define this alternative any further. This, I suspect, is due to a certain ambiguity over the cognitive conditions that must be fulfilled for tolerance to be reasonable.

We can agree to the mutual toleration of forms of life and worldviews that represent existential challenges for each other only if we have a basis of shared beliefs for "agreeing to disagree." Now, according to McCarthy's assumptions, shared ethical beliefs and even a shared basis in questions of justice are lacking. But if we do not consider a reasonable agreement to be possible even at this more abstract level, then the only remaining recourses are custom, the violent assertion of interests, and unwilling conformity (compliance). That may temporarily suffice for the precarious balance of a moratorium or a *modus vivendi,* but not for a normatively justified appeal to tolerance. In fact, complex societies increasingly rely upon the legally noncoercible tolerance invoked by McCarthy, and thus upon the willingness to accommodate existentially significant differences and to cooperate with members of dissonant forms of life. At the same time, this requirement (*Ansinnen*) is increasingly experienced at the subjective level as an unreasonable demand (*Zumutung*). From the perspective of a sociological observer, tolerance is a diminishing resource. As a result, the expectation of tolerance itself requires a normative justification to a growing degree. And this justification must satisfy the claim that the legal protections governing the peaceful coexistence and mutual integrity of forms of life are fair—i.e., are rationally acceptable to all sides.[71]

---

69. McCarthy, *supra* note 11, at 1123.

70. *Id.*

71. John Rawls's concept of an "overlapping consensus" is unsatisfactory because it is ultimately a matter of accident whether the different ethical viewpoints of competing worldviews lead to consonance or assent regarding *the core components* of those principles of justice that

D.

The democratic process promises to deliver an "imperfect" but "pure" procedural rationality only on the premise that the participants consider it possible, in principle, to reach exactly one right answer for questions of justice. To this extent, an analogy to disputes over questions of fact arises. We would not conduct such factual disputes by argumentation if we did not assume that, in principle, we are convincing one another of the truth or falsity of a proposition. Of course, the fact that in taking a performative attitude we consider ourselves "capable of truth" does not mean we must have strong expectations of consensus, nor does it mean we could not be mistaken at any time. In science, contradiction and dissent ultimately are institutionalized in the service of a cooperative search for truth. At the same time, we should not take this analogy too far. If we disregard the differences between assertoric and normative validity claims, then we end up with moral realism, that is, with an intellectualist misinterpretation of what practical reason can accomplish. McCarthy is quite right in asking, "Is the search for truth about 'the' objective world an appropriate analogue of the search for justice in 'our' social world?"[72] In view of the assumption of "a single right answer," this is indeed a disturbing question.

Discussions with Friedrich Kambartel on intuitionism in mathematics have led me to weaken the strong thesis that I previously held. The principle of bivalence makes good sense for empirical propositions about things in the objective world. In view of the universe of symbolic objects *that we produce,* however, I now suspect we must deal with a class of propositions that *hic et nunc* are neither true nor false. These propositions become decidable only in the event that we succeed in *constructing* a procedure of justification (similar to a method of proof in mathematics). Turning to the ontological constitution of the social world—which as Giambattista Vico, and later Karl Marx, maintained, we ourselves produce, though not in a fully deliberate manner—it is plausible that the relation between construction and discovery assumed for knowledge of the objective world shifts in favor of the constructive element, that is, abductive imagination. When we are confronted with difficult problems, the correct constructions must "occur" to us.

---

are not supposed to be capable of independent, neutral justification from the moral point of view. When Rawls is understood this way, moreover, it is incomprehensible that his *Theory of Justice* itself can still make a validity claim. Does it claim only to explain the functional contribution that the principles of justice can make to sustaining a stable order? *See* A THEORY OF JUSTICE, *supra* note 39; Jürgen Habermas, *Reconciliation Through the Public Use of Reason: Remarks on John Rawls's Political Liberalism,* 92 J. PHIL. 109 (1995); *see also* John Rawls, *Reply to Habermas,* 92 J. PHIL. 132 (1995).

72. McCarthy, *supra* note 11, at 1103.

Naturally, I do not mean that law and morality are on a par with the domain of mathematical objects and relations. The propositions in the two areas are actually quite different in kind, as one can see from their differing definitions of validity. Something like "analytic truth" (supposing there is such a thing, pace Quine) cannot serve to elucidate "moral rightness" or "legitimacy." Moreover, law and morality refer to the regulation of interpersonal relationships among actors who are, so to speak, anchored in the objective world where they have a *fundamentum in re.* On the other hand, modern orders of "enacted" law are artificially produced or constructed, similar to the way intuitionism assumes the objects of geometry and arithmetic are constructed. So it is not wholly misguided to acknowledge, in this universe as well, that some questions do not yield a univocal right answer as long as the participants have not "succeeded" in arriving at the right "construction." Perhaps we should not assume *a priori* that the principle of bivalence is valid for the normative regulation of social interaction. Indeed, what may be lacking in the particular case is not skill in argument but creativity. Nevertheless, in this sublunary realm in which decisions must be made under time pressure one way or another, we cannot *wait* forever for constructive ideas to arise. If our presumption is correct, then in such normatively hopeless situations we would operate with the (generally valid) premise of "one right answer" merely as a promissory note or bill to be paid at a later date. But even in that case, we would not be able to drop this premise without the democratic process losing both its procedural rationality as well as its legitimating force. Under the conditions of postmetaphysical thinking, however, I see no alternatives to this presumption.

III. FORM AND CONTENT:
THE "DOCTRINAL" CORE OF PROCEDURALISM

A.

Michel Rosenfeld attempts to demonstrate that the proceduralist paradigm of law that I have elaborated is "proceduralist" only in a "derivative," and not in a "genuine," sense.[73] Rosenfeld explains: "derivative proceduralism is not genuine proceduralism but rather substantive theory in procedural garb."[74] As opposed to a theory that does not acknowledge its own substantive presuppositions, Rosenfeld proposes a "comprehensive" (i.e., substantive) pluralism.[75] In contrast to the liberal variety of pluralism, comprehensive pluralism does not appeal to a neutral method for settling value conflicts. However, I would like to direct this accusation back at Rosenfeld:

73. *See generally* Rosenfeld, *supra* note 12.
74. *Id.* at 800.
75. *See id.* at 821.

comprehensive pluralism is not substantive theory but rather procedural-ism in substantive garb. In order to identify the point where this involves more than a dispute over words, I comment first on the concept of "proce-dure," and then explore the problematic of substantive legal equality.

1.   Rosenfeld points to Thomas Hobbes's social contract theory as an example of genuine proceduralism, because it justifies the rules for living together in society through a negotiated agreement that all the participants arrive at by following a procedure[76] (by contrast, John Locke's theory is an example of "derivative" proceduralism, because the natural right to prop-erty provides a substantive criterion for the social contract). In criticism of Hobbes, Rosenfeld maintains quite plausibly that a legal order cannot be legitimated solely on the basis of procedural justice: "proceduralism may be acceptable [only] in the context of contestable substantive norms."[77] This thesis is correct to the extent that it comprehends a narrow concept of procedure. As a matter of fact, the conclusion of the Hobbesian social contract (modeled on private legal contracts) rests solely on the partici-pants' proper declaration of intention. This legal motif was supposed to guarantee both "perfect" and "pure" procedural justice.

Rosenfeld, however, attempts to apply his thesis to other legal proce-dures as well, such as courtroom procedures (or similar hearings) that se-cure a procedural justice that is pure (i.e., independent of substantive cri-teria) but imperfect.[78] As an example, he refers to the client interviews that welfare officials or administrative agencies hold to decide whether to dis-pense social-welfare entitlements.[79] In such cases, carrying out proper pro-cedure secures respect for the client's human dignity. However, the proce-dure itself is in turn subject to a prior, substantive welfare norm that is just or unjust independent of the procedure. If one pursues this example fur-ther back in time, however, one comes upon the democratic procedure of the political legislature that must have adopted this norm. Then one arrives at the question that is really at issue: from where do legal norms—whether they regulate behavior, create powers, or stipulate procedures of legisla-tion, adjudication, administration, and their interaction—ultimately draw their legitimacy: from substantive reasons or procedure? How one under-stands *this* legitimating process determines what role is played by the form/ content distinction in the proceduralist paradigm of law.

My reconstruction of the meaning of a legitimate legal order begins with the original resolution (*Entschluß*) that any arbitrary group of persons must

76. *See id.* at 800.
77. *Id.* at 799.
78. *See id.* at 794.
79. *See id.* at 795.

make if they want to constitute themselves as a legal community of free and equal members. Intending to legitimately regulate their life by means of positive law, they enter into a common practice that allows them to frame a constitution. The performative meaning of this constitution-making practice consists of jointly seeking out and adopting those rights that the participants must mutually recognize as fair or valid (under the aforementioned premises). Thus, this practice depends on two prior conditions: on positive law as the medium of *binding* regulations and on the discourse principle as the guiding thread for *reasonable* deliberation and decision making. The combination and interpenetration of these two formal elements must suffice for establishing processes of producing and applying legitimate law. Under conditions of postmetaphysical thinking, we cannot expect a further-reaching consensus that would include *substantive issues*. This restriction to presuppositions that are *formal in this sense* is tailored for the specifically modern pluralism of worldviews, cultural forms of life, interest positions, and so forth. Naturally, this does not mean that a constitution-making practice of this kind would be free of all normative content. On the contrary, the *performative meaning* of this practice, which is merely *set forth* and explicated in constitutional principles and the system of rights, already contains as a doctrinal core the (Rousseauian-Kantian) idea of the self-legislation of voluntarily associated citizens who are both free and equal. This idea is not "formal" in the sense of being "value free." However, it can be fully developed in the course of constitution-making processes that are not based on the previous choice of substantive values, but rather on democratic procedures. Hence, there is a justified *presumption* that the deontological idea of self-legislation or autonomy is neutral with respect to worldviews, provided that the different interpretations of the self and the world are not fundamentalist but are compatible with the conditions of postmetaphysical thinking (in Rawls's sense of "not unreasonable" comprehensive worldviews[80]).

This distinction between form and content refers in the first place only to a presumptive neutrality of legal principles in relation to the content of worldviews. Its formal nature shows up in the procedural legitimation of lawmaking and enforcement, especially in political opinion- and will-formation (as focused on the legislative process) and in adjudication. Both legislation and adjudication are processes that are regulated by "procedure" in the broader sense. As already mentioned, this complex concept of procedure is not altogether normatively neutral. It is "formal" or neutral in a sense that requires explanation.[81]

In these cases, we are dealing with social decision-making procedures or

80. *See* POLITICAL LIBERALISM, *supra* note 39, at 58–61.

81. In the sweeping explanation that follows, I cannot go into the important differences between legislative, judicial, and administrative procedures.

institutions[82] that bind decisions to the outcome of deliberations by coupling discourses with decision procedures (normally voting mechanisms). Both as a whole and in their structure and temporal sequencing, processes of opinion- and will-formation are legally institutionalized. Three sorts of procedures interpenetrate in this structure. The core is made up of discourses in which arguments are exchanged in answer to empirical and normative or evaluative questions (i.e., to solve problems). These processes of argumentation follow purely cognitive procedures. The beliefs achieved through argument then form the basis of decisions that are in turn governed by decision procedures (usually by majority rule). Both types of process, deliberation and decision making, are then institutionalized in various legal procedures. These procedures regulate, *inter alia*, the composition of lawmaking bodies (as a rule by election or delegation), the distribution of participant roles (e.g., in court procedures), the specification of issues (admissible topics and contributions), the steps in the analysis (e.g., the separate treatment of factual questions and legal questions), the sources of information (e.g., experts, methods of investigation, etc.), and the proper timetables and scheduling of events (e.g., repeated readings, decision deadlines, etc.). In short, legal procedures are supposed to establish discursive processes of deliberation and fair decision making that have binding force.

Insofar as this densely interwoven process is supposed to bear the burden of legitimation, at its heart are discourses that have different logics depending on the type of question to be answered; in parliamentary settings, these discourses are linked with fair (i.e., discursively justified) procedures of compromise. As previously mentioned, though, processes of argumentation only satisfy the conditions of an imperfect procedural rationality—in this case, conditions that are met by following forms of communication and rules that promote a "cooperative search for truth." The institutionalization of (a network of) discourses (and bargaining) must be primarily oriented toward the goal of fulfilling, as much as possible, the universal pragmatic presuppositions of argumentation in general: universal access, an equal right to participate and equality of opportunity in making contributions, the participants' orientation toward reaching understanding, and freedom from structural coercions. Thus, within the substantive, social, and temporal limits on different sorts of decision making, discourses should be established to insure the free movement of topics, proposals, and contributions, information and arguments in a way that best allows the rationally motivating force of the better argument (or of the more convincing contribution on the relevant topic) to come into play.

Here is where the masking of substance by form that Rosenfeld warns us against seems to have its source. That is, one can, with Bernhard Peters,

82. *See* BERNHARD PETERS, RATIONALITÄT, RECHT UND GESELLSCHAFT 227–71 (1991).

doubt that the practice of argumentation may be described as an imperfect but "pure" procedure able to justify the presumption of rational outcomes.[83] In the final analysis, do not the substantive reasons, rather than the "procedure" of a regulated exchange of arguments, prove decisive for a correct outcome? Are not reasons available, independent of the procedure itself, for judging an outcome reached according to procedure—so that we cannot really speak of procedural legitimation? The answer depends on how we think practical questions admit of "truth."

According to noncognitivist positions, argumentation in law and morality can only give a false impression of producing insights, when in fact only preferences and attitudes, emotions and decisions, are possible in those domains. However, it is equally unsatisfactory to hold a moral realism that assumes there are moral facts or natural rights—a normative order existing independently of our constructions. If the correspondence theory of truth is already implausible for descriptive propositions, then we cannot even begin to assume that the rightness of normative propositions involves a correspondence with something given. Nevertheless, we cannot deny that such propositions make a cognitive claim. So the only solution is to conceive "rightness" as rational acceptability under certain idealized conditions. When we consider a normative proposition to be valid, we are claiming that it can be justified in argument. Since "justification" depends both on the practice of justification and on the justifying reasons, this formulation is admittedly ambiguous. What meaning can "proceduralism" have if the outcome of a correctly followed practice of justification can nonetheless be criticized in light of particular substantive reasons? This is Bernhard Peters's question.[84]

In view of the fundamental fallibility of our knowledge, neither of these two elements alone, neither form nor substance taken by itself, suffices. On the one hand, however well structured the practice of justification is, this structure can, at best, make it probable that the exchange of arguments takes in all the relevant, currently available information and reasons and employs the currently most fruitful vocabulary. On the other hand, there are no sources of evidence and evaluative criteria that would be given *prior* to argumentation, that is, that could not, in turn, become problematic and have to be validated through a rationally motivated agreement reached under the conditions of discourse. Because there are no "ultimate" sources of evidence or "definitive" kinds of arguments in practical questions, we must have recourse to the process of argumentation as our "procedure" if we are to explain how it is possible for us to raise and vindicate validity claims that "transcend" the present context.

83. *See id.* at 253, 258.
84. *See id.* at 258–61.

Procedures and reasons, form and content, interpenetrate in such a way that we are convinced that we can defend the propositions that we consider valid with good reasons—in reply to all objections, whenever and by whomever they may be raised. This anticipation of rebutting "every" possible objection contains an idealization that allows one to distinguish the (assertoric or normative) truth of propositions from their "rational acceptability" without stripping validity of the epistemic relation of something that is "valid (*Geltens*) for us." This explains the peculiar ambivalence on which Peters bases his question.[85] On the one hand, substantive reasons are what convince us that an outcome is right; on the other hand, the soundness of these reasons can be *demonstrated* only in real processes of argumentation, namely in defense against every objection that is actually raised.

This holds true for rational discourse in general. The deliberations that are institutionalized in democracies and coupled with deadlines and voting procedures do not guarantee valid outcomes, but rather justify the *presumption* that outcomes are rational. They thereby insure only that decisions reached in conformity with procedure are "rationally acceptable" to citizens. They cannot, of course, guarantee "the truth." Confronted with such a procedure, one can always insist on the difference between a valid outcome and an outcome that is rationally acceptable within an institutional framework. Members of a minority insist on this difference, for example, when they comply with procedurally unobjectionable decisions without changing their opinion. Civil protestors do so when they engage in symbolic protests and when, having exhausted formal legal channels, they resort to illegal actions as a way of appealing to the majority to reconsider an issue that involves basic principles.

2.   Even if he were to accept proceduralism in this sense, Rosenfeld need not withdraw his objection. For questions of justice he rejects context-*transcending* validity claims: "Justice beyond law cannot achieve complete impartiality . . . it must, at least in part, rely on a vision of the good that has intracommunal roots, thereby favoring members of the relevant intracommunal group over the remaining legal subjects."[86] According to this view, it is conceptually impossible for modern legal orders to fulfill their promise of securing equal private and public autonomy for each person. Specifically, the dialectic of legal and factual equality must repeatedly lead to one-sided solutions that, depending on the context, either produce too much equality at the price of *suppressing* relevant "differences" or produce too little equality at the price of *exploiting* those "differences." Nor would the principle of equal treatment be a corrective—whether against the leveling of differ-

85. *See id.*
86. Rosenfeld, *supra* note 12, at 792 n.5.

ences or against illegitimate inequality. According to Rosenfeld, the attempt to realize the idea of equal rights for all cannot escape moving back and forth between the leveling of differences and the withholding of equal treatment. In my opinion, neither the conceptual argument nor the historical example is convincing.

Rosenfeld indeed believes that liberal rights—which were once successfully pitted against early modern inequalities according to the slogan "all men are created equal"—could later also serve as a standard for claiming social rights. However, in new contexts, such as decolonization or the struggle of an ethnic minority against a majority culture, it appears that the same principle of equal treatment that once facilitated emancipation now justifies the pressure toward assimilation and thus the suppression of legitimate differences:

> [T]he master treats the slave as inferior because he is different, whereas the colonizer offers the colonized equal treatment provided that the latter give up his own language, culture, and religion. . . . Accordingly, in a master-slave setting, equality as identity is a weapon of liberation whereas in a colonizer-colonized setting, it is a weapon of domination.[87]

Rosenfeld attempts to use this example to show that identical principles of justice have different meanings inside the framework of different conceptions of the good. To this extent, such principles do not stand on their own. In fact, however, the example shows that the critique of the lack of legal equality in feudal systems or stratified societies and, one might add, the critique of the lack of social equality in *laissez-faire* capitalism are based on precisely *the same* normative criteria as the critique of the lack of consideration for cultural differences under the imperialist pressure of assimilation. At stake in *all* of these cases is the demand to treat equals equally and unequals unequally. In the first case, a feudal society, the equal rights that are claimed refer to legal powers and capacities. In the second case, a class society, they refer to social entitlements that are supposed to provide an equal opportunity to utilize these powers and capacities. And in the third case, a colonized society, they refer to both legal powers and social entitlements, though not primarily with respect to the balance of power and interests achievable with the help of certain recognized types of social compensations (e.g., money, leisure time, education, etc.). Rather, equal rights are claimed with respect to national independence or cultural autonomy, or in the case of multiculturalism, with respect to equal rights of membership for different cultural, ethnic, or religious groups. What is *always* at stake, however, is the claim to the protection of the integrity of legal persons who are guaranteed equal liberties in the sense of a substantive legal

87. *Id.* at 808 (footnote omitted).

equality that is not understood selectively. Citizens are supposed to be guaranteed these liberties not only formally, but also effectively—they are supposed to enjoy equality in the social and cultural *conditions for the genesis* of their private and public autonomy.

In principle, it is no different with feminist postulates of equality. For the sake of argument, Rosenfeld sketches two competing, gender-specific forms of life whose value patterns clash irreconcilably: one side emphasizes intimacy, connections, care, and sacrifice, while the other stresses distance, competition, achievement, and so on.[88] Now, this monolithically stylized opposition between two "visions" of the good life would, in any case, break up into many different competitions between various groups of women and men as soon as the regulation of particular interest positions and value conflicts were at stake. Moreover, in each distinct sphere of life, a different functional imperative would have to be considered. From the perspective of a procedural paradigm of law, these conflicts can be resolved, provided, of course, that the power to define gender-specific experiences and situations is no longer left to delegates or experts. Participants themselves must struggle in public forums for the recognition of suppressed or marginalized need interpretations, so that new circumstances and facts are recognized as relevant matters for legal regulation and new criteria are negotiated by which similar cases can be treated similarly and different cases differently. However, without the underlying principle of equal treatment, every critique and every demand to revise old criteria would, *a fortiori*, not have a leg to stand on.

Finally, Rosenfeld poses the "feminist challenge" even more sharply: he contends that the very medium and structure of law itself is put in question by the demand to replace the hierarchy of rights with a network of interpersonal relationships.[89] To the extent that this demand is merely based on the critique of the possessive-individualist reading of "rights" that has long been dominant, there are good reasons for accepting an intersubjective concept of law. Rights are inherently relational, because they are supposed to establish or reinforce relations of symmetrical recognition. This is also true for private rights, which *one person can bring to bear against another* in cases of conflict; they too originate in a legal order that requires everyone to recognize each as a free and equal legal person and thereby guarantees equal respect for each. This order can be legitimate only insofar as it emerges from a *shared* practice of civic self-determination.

However, if the critique targets the concept of rights itself, then the discussion shifts to another level. Then the opponent must propose either an alternative *to* law, as Marx did in his day, or an alternative concept *of* law. I

88. *See id.* at 816.
89. *See id.* at 818–20.

have no problem with this type of questioning, since I am not proposing a normative justification for law as such. We are not under an *obligation* to regulate our living together by means of positive law. A meaningful discussion can only get underway, though, after the alternatives have been stated with sufficient precision. I consider it sufficient to provide a *functional* explanation for why it is advisable or prudent to prefer orders of positive law (or, in the language of classical contractarianism, why we should leave the state of nature and enter into society). I see no functional equivalent for this way of stabilizing behavioral expectations (i.e., through equally distributed individual rights). The young Marx's romanticist hope that law would "wither away" is not likely to be realized in the complex societies we have today.

The alternative that Rosenfeld suggests at the end of his essay picks up the idea of a "reiterative universalism" and thus still moves within the conceptual framework of a theory of rights. The vague allusion to a "dynamic conception of rights"[90] only indicates the desire for an alternative conception of law.

B.

This alternative becomes clearer in the essay by Arthur J. Jacobson.[91] He begins by contrasting the theory of rights with a theory of duties. If I understand him correctly, the latter is based on a political theology that indicts modern law as the expression of the decline in a binding divine authority—a point also made by Leo Strauss and Carl Schmitt, albeit with quite different consequences. In fact, Hobbes is the first to insist on a positivist concept of law, and the modern principle that everything that is not forbidden by law is permitted. Hobbes thereby destroyed the symmetry between duties and rights in the moral domain, giving priority instead to rights that specify individual liberties or private spheres of free choice. In modern legal orders, legal duties first emerge as the *result* of the reciprocal limitation of such liberties under general laws. Jacobson contrasts this with an Aristotelian (or Thomistic?) conception of divine law that knows only duties—this law obligates addressees to emulate the person of a perfect lord or "ideal legal commander."[92] Finally, he conceives common law as a dialectical mediation between these two types:

> Common law breaks the correlation of rights with duties in both directions in order to produce a succession of correlations, according to the prin-

90. *Id.* at 820.
91. *See generally* Jacobson, *supra* note 13. His critique of my conception of law involves so many misunderstandings that it would be too laborious to go into it here: if I am a "positivist," then Jacobson is a "natural law theorist."
92. *See id.* at 926.

ciple that law is just the application of law in single cases. Here dynamism flows from the incessant activities of legal persons to assemble, then disassemble, then reassemble correlations.[93]

Whereas modern law and divine law, as actually applied, fail to achieve their respective goals—the former is supposed to satisfy a kind of narcissistic need for recognition, and the latter is supposed to satisfy the person's striving for perfection—common law fails at a higher level, so to speak. Here is where the central motivation behind Critical Legal Studies comes into play. In appropriating the insight into the fundamental failure of all divine justice on earth, Critical Legal Studies expects its addressees to accept the indeterminacy of law in a radical sense. Of course, even here judges and clients are continually tempted to fix the law by treating individual decisions as precedents. According to Jacobson, we can, in the spirit of common law, take the individuality of each new case into account only if we accept the fact that the falsely assumed identity of law is dissolved in the flux of decisions that cannot be anticipated. Jacobson states, "law is *just* the application of law to single cases."[94] Thus there emerges the picture of an incomprehensible law fatefully at work in the tumble of decisions that are always original: "[T]he legal manifold in common law is constantly in motion. . . . [It] lacks a stable ground, because it both unfolds and enfolds its ordering principle in each application."[95] If I am not misled, this crypto-theological construction is an attempt to employ the tools of deconstruction to renovate the idea of the German Historical School that a "living" law is expressive of the *Volksgeist*.

I must admit that this alternative concept of law, even if it could be formulated more precisely, strikes me as implausible not only for normative reasons, but for historical and functional reasons as well. It appears normatively implausible because its practical effect is to displace the legitimation of law away from the democratic legislator onto the medieval *"jurisdictio"* of a higher authority that emerges as a competing legislature. Moreover, one must have doubts about the usefulness of a law that, caught up in the aura of a (no longer lamented but) canonized "indeterminacy," renounces, in principle, the *predictability* of judicial decisions and therewith its function of stabilizing behavioral expectations. Finally, it is precisely in private law that we observe an astonishing convergence of legal developments in *all* Western societies. As a result, from a comparative legal standpoint, the common law can hardly claim a special position in comparison to continental codifications.

93. *Id.*
94. *Id.* at 925 (emphasis added).
95. *Id.* at 928.

IV. PROBLEMS OF THEORY CONSTRUCTION

A.

I am grateful to William Rehg for one of the most astute and productive analyses and elaborations of discourse ethics. As the title of Rehg's book *Insight and Solidarity*[96] indicates, he is unsatisfied with a certain intellectualism in this approach. Rehg is convinced that the shared practice of argumentation leads to insights only if the participants can rely upon previously established solidary relationships. On the one hand, the participants will be sufficiently motivated to go out of their way and enter into the discursive process of reaching an understanding only if they all happen to consider "rational cooperation" to be a "good," preferable to other forms of interaction. The decision between the alternatives of rational agreement and a violent dispute (however sublimated) is thus based on a preference that is at least more reliably anchored in *shared* value orientations than in individual interests. On the other hand, Rehg believes that the discourse-ethical approach can be freed of the last vestiges of the philosophy of the subject only when the inevitably incomplete fulfillment of the ideal pragmatic presuppositions of argumentation, which go beyond spatial and temporal contexts, is *compensated* by the participants' "trust" in the regulation of an expanded, transsubjective process of communication carried on above the participants' heads and beyond the limits of actual discussion. Rehg states, "if rational consensus is cooperative even to the degree of requiring a decentered 'cooperative insight,' then it would seem that something like trust must inhabit the heart of rational conviction."[97] Interestingly, Rehg postulates that we have a *prima facie trust* in the procedures we use to bring the demanding presuppositions of argumentation into a nondefeatist harmony with the empirical constraints on the situated local discourses that must be conducted here and now under the pressure of decision making. In Rehg's opinion, the loyalty toward such procedures, which rein in and cut short the process of argumentation, must be based on a Peircean trust in the integrity and cooperative spirit of the wider community.

In his present essay, Rehg once again takes up the theme that the moment of insight requires a complementary moment of prior trust and ethical commitment. His interest now, however, is the relation between discourse and decision in democratic opinion- and will-formation.[98] The legal institutionalization of deliberation intensifies the problem of how can one justify the constraints imposed on discourse by such institutionalization. In

96. WILLIAM REHG, INSIGHT AND SOLIDARITY: A STUDY IN THE DISCOURSE ETHICS OF JÜRGEN HABERMAS (1994).

97. *Id.* at 237.

98. *See generally* Rehg, *supra* note 14.

their negative role as limitations, legal procedures reveal only the inevitable departures from an assumed ideal. Rehg, however, suggests that law, as the medium through which discourse-limiting decision procedures are implemented, makes its *own specific* contribution, independent of discourse, to the legitimation of the whole process.

In fact, in fulfilling its "specific function" of stabilizing behavioral expectations and thereby guaranteeing what is known as "legal certainty," law has at its disposal a legitimating force inherent in the legal form. This ethical minimum of legality is due, moreover, to the structure of actionable individual rights that guarantee, in a morally acceptable way, spheres of private choice that have been morally neutralized. However, Rehg mentions these moments only in passing. He is primarily interested in whether the legitimating force of the democratic process can be traced back solely to the discursive character of deliberations, or whether it does not also stem from the enveloping legal form that ties discourse into decision-making processes.[99] When we speak of the procedural justification "of" law, do we intend only the *genetivus objectivus,* or do we also intend the *genetivus subjectivus?* The contribution that the medium of law as such makes to the legitimating force of the democratic process consists in the fact that law links the "cooperative search for truth" to decision processes via procedures (in the narrower sense of legal procedures), thereby rendering this search a discursive preparation for decision making. Rehg bases his thesis on the following: the procedures that first establish the internal linkage between discourse and decision draw their legitimating force not from the cognitive sources of further discourses in which procedures are justified, but from a volitional source prior to all discourses, i.e., the inclusion of all affected persons in the procedure.[100]

I am not entirely convinced by this. It is true that inclusive participation in procedures fulfills two different functions. On the one hand, inclusive participation in discourse is supposed to ensure that the spectrum of contributions is as broad as possible. On the other hand, a fair participation in the decision-making process is supposed to ensure that the results of deliberations are transferred to decisions as reliably as possible. Votes—in German, *Stimmen,* which literally means "voices"—thus mean two things in the democratic process: judgments and decisions. But this by no means implies that inclusive participation in the decision-making process is subject to a standard of fairness that would stem, not from impartial judgment, but actually from the bonding character of such procedures. This is precisely what Rehg maintains: "an adequate elaboration of equal opportunity in decision making should refer, not just to influence on outcome, but

99. *See id.* at 1155.
100. *See id.* at 1155–57.

also to an idea of solidaristic inclusion built on equal respect for each citizen. . . . Habermas risks neglecting the intrinsic procedural fairness in law and its potential contribution to solidarity and compliance."[101]

To elucidate the intrinsic quality of justice in decision-making procedures, Rehg turns to chance procedures. These are often considered fair, even though they have a purely decisionistic character, insofar as they are not linked with substantive justifications. But must not the fairness of the procedure be justified in relation to the situation in which it is applied? A chance procedure qualifies as a fair procedure only in specific contexts (e.g., lotteries that give each participant an equal chance of winning, the Hobbesian case of unbearable anarchy where any decision is better than none, or in cases of the just distribution of positional goods which must be consumed individually but cannot be divided into as many parts as those seeking them). There are good reasons why political decisions are made democratically and not *by lottery*.

Rehg has his eye on an important phenomenon. In comparison with morality, law has an artificial character, so that we construct a legal order rather than discover it. Although law is supposed to be in harmony with morality, it extends to matters that must be regulated from pragmatic and ethical points of view as well, and thus within the horizon of a given set of goals and an accepted form of life. Furthermore, such matters must also be regulated on the basis of compromises, and hence through the balance of existing interest positions. Thus, goals and value orientations, needs and preferences, which are barred from morality, find their way into law. Because it mirrors the actually existing will of a society, law must be "positive": it must be "posited" or enacted because the elements of mutual understanding interpenetrate with elements that are just chosen or agreed to by negotiation.

Unlike morality, then, the emergence of law could once be conceived in contractarian terms, a view that, though incorrect, is also not *entirely* false. The sheer weight of existing forms of life and interests is already enough to ensure that the volitional moment of decision, in comparison with the cognitive moment of judgment and opinion-formation, has a crucial role in the lawmaking process. This moment is merely reinforced by the practical necessity of institutionalizing deliberative processes in a binding way. For *both* these reasons, legitimate lawmaking requires that decision making, and not simply the discursive structures that justify the presumption that judgments are right, be fairly regulated. But the regulations that were provided for this purpose, which cover the entire gamut from the Constitution down to parliamentary procedures or rules of agenda setting, must be justified. Because this occurs in discourses of justification, I cannot discover in

101. *Id.* at 1161.

the "fairness" of decision rules any intrinsic quality that would reside in legal procedures as such, independent of discourse.

In a certain sense, the "in-principle" equal participation in decision procedures is anticipated by the fact that a constitutional democracy is a construction legitimated by its reference to a practice of constitution making. Unlike morality, which is valid for all subjects capable of speech and action, every constitutional project rests on the datable *original resolve* of a historical group of people (whose composition is, normatively speaking, a matter of accident). One cannot decide on morality; one can at most decide to live more or less morally. But given the artificial character of law, one must make up one's mind to make a constitution. This original choice already implies the mutual recognition of free and equal persons, and thus also the obligation of inclusion that Rehg wants to introduce, along with the concept of solidarity, as a source of legitimation independent of discourse. The performative meaning of a constitution-making practice includes the fact that a spatiotemporally-situated group is *resolved* to constitute itself as a voluntary association of citizens. Since the purpose of this choice is to *legitimately* regulate the common life of the group by means of positive law (which requires justification), the moments that Rehg separates, namely discourse and decision, are unified from the start.

B.

Michael Power is another commentator who understands the author better than the latter does himself.[102] That is, Power establishes systematic links between *Knowledge and Human Interests*[103] and *Between Facts and Norms*[104] that largely escaped my notice. In drawing out these surprising parallels, however, he may have underestimated the shift in perspective that occurred when I replaced the epistemological question with the linguistic question concerning the necessary conditions for the possibility, not of cognition, but of mutual understanding. As a result of this shift, the attempt to reconstruct the know-how of subjects competent to speak and act no doubt came to the forefront and, to a certain extent, pushed aside the analysis of the self-reflection of formative processes. But I doubt that this has led to a weakening of critical energies, let alone to the "end of critical theory."[105]

Power convincingly analyzes the role of idealizations and the depth her-

102. *See generally* Power, *supra* note 15.

103. JÜRGEN HABERMAS, KNOWLEDGE AND HUMAN INTERESTS (Jeremy J. Shapiro trans., 1971).

104. HABERMAS, BETWEEN FACTS AND NORMS, *supra* note 2.

105. Otfried Höffe speaks of a "conversion." *See, e.g*, Otfried Höffe, *Abenddämmerung oder Morgendämmerung? Zu Jürgen Habermas' Diskurstheorien des demokratischen Rechtsstaats*, 12 RECHTSHISTORISCHES J. 57 (1994).

meneutics of weak transcendental arguments.[106] I would, however, outline the linguistic transformation of the Kantian architectonic somewhat differently. In particular, I would interpret differently the pragmatic transformation of Kant's concept of reason as the capacity for world-constitutive ideas. However, when Power analyzes the concept of "counterfactual presuppositions," or more generally the "vocabulary of the 'as if,' " he puts his finger on the nerve of my entire theoretical undertaking.[107] There is still much work to be done in this area.

I have a stronger reservation only against Power's emphasis on the "ideal speech situation."[108] I see a problem here, and not just because we already make counterfactual presuppositions in everyday communication—insofar as participants assume they use linguistic expressions with identical meanings, insofar as they raise context-transcending validity claims, insofar as they reciprocally consider themselves accountable, and so forth. What I find more disturbing is the fact that the expression "ideal speech situation," which I introduced decades ago as a shorthand for the ensemble of universal presuppositions of argumentation, suggests an end state that must be strived for in the sense of a regulative ideal. This entropic state of a definitive consensus, which would make all further communication superfluous, cannot be represented as a meaningful goal because it would engender paradoxes (an ultimate language, a final interpretation, a nonrevisable knowledge, etc.). As I have learned from Albrecht Wellmer's criticism,[109] one must instead conceive the discursive redemption of validity claims (i.e., the claim that the conditions for the validity of a statement are fulfilled) as a metacritical, *ongoing* process of rebutting objections. Here I am attempting to use discourse theory to explain what Hilary Putnam has, in the context of philosophy of science, called "rational acceptability under ideal conditions,"[110] or what Crispin Wright, following Michael Dummett, has called "superassertability."[111] These analyses have emerged from debates about truth that are as lively today as ever.

One idealizes assertability conditions in response to the necessity of distinguishing "truth" or "validity" in general, from rational acceptability. Once the semantic concept of truth is no longer available, the need for that distinction arises from the triadic structure of "something being valid for us" in an epistemic sense. However, I am not simply *stipulating* a normatively loaded concept of discourse. Rather, I maintain that one can demonstrate,

---

106. *See generally* Power, *supra* note 15.

107. *Id.* at 1014.

108. *Id.* at 1012.

109. For a recent argument, see ALBRECHT WELLMER, *Wahrheit, Kontingenz, Moderne, in* ENDSPIELE: DIE UNVERSÖHNLICHE MODERNE: ESSAYS UND VORTÄGE 157 (1993).

110. *See generally* HILARY PUTNAM, REASON, TRUTH AND HISTORY (1981).

111. *See* CRISPIN WRIGHT, TRUTH AND OBJECTIVITY 33–70 (1992).

by way of a presuppositional analysis, that anyone who earnestly takes part in argumentation *unavoidably* accepts certain communicative presuppositions with a counterfactual content. I am guided here by the intuition that in all argumentation the participants presuppose that their communication should meet the following conditions: (i) a rationally unmotivated termination of debate is precluded; (ii) each party has an equal right to an unrestricted access to deliberation and, within deliberation, each has equal and symmetrical opportunities to participate, thereby securing both freedom in the selection of topics and the consideration of all available information and reasons; and (iii) any coercion affecting the discursive process of understanding, either from outside or emerging from within the process itself, other than the force of the "better argument," is excluded, thereby neutralizing all motivations besides that of a cooperative search for truth. If the participants do not presuppose these conditions, then they cannot assume that they *are convincing* one another of something. Hence, the above presuppositions of argumentation cannot be "rejected" in the sense that anyone who denies their explicit propositional content while engaged in argumentation cannot escape a performative self-contradiction.[112] These idealizations do not imply any anticipation of an ideal end state. They only serve to illuminate the difference between, on the one hand, the rational acceptance of a validity (*Geltung*) claim in a given context and, on the other, the validity (*Gültigkeit*) of a statement that would have to be demonstrated in all possible contexts.

Power quite clearly sees that these idealizations, which originate in the social facticity of everyday practice itself, are not intended to save an abstract universalism, but rather to justify, from the resources of existing lifeworld contexts, a "transcendence from within." Power states, "[w]e can only 'make sense' of certain practices on the basis of assuming an operative role for deeply embedded fictional norms. These fictions are foundations from within, without any heavyweight metaphysical support."[113] Although this is preeminently true of the practice of argumentation, it is not exclusive to this practice. Now that Kantian reason has been decisively detranscendentalized, the tension between the supersensible and the empirical has withdrawn into the social facts themselves.

C.

Jacques Lenoble's wide-ranging contribution also takes aim at the foundations of discourse theory.[114] Lenoble's essay is too complex to address his

---

112. *See* Karl-Otto Apel, *Fallibilismus, Konsenstheorie der Wahrheit und Letztbegründung, in* PHILOSOPHIE UND BEGRÜNDUNG 116 (Forum für Philosophie eds., 1987).

113. Power, *supra* note 15, at 1010 (footnote omitted).

114. *See generally* Lenoble, *supra* note 16.

objections in detail. On the whole, I have the impression that Lenoble would like to reduce the formal-pragmatic view of language and the deconstructionist view to a common denominator, thereby reconciling the irreconcilable. On the one hand, Lenoble wants to maintain the basic principle of the formal-pragmatic theory of meaning, according to which we *understand* (*Verstehen*) a linguistic expression if we know how we could use it to help us *reach an agreement* (*verständigen*) with someone about something in the world. On the other hand, despite this internal relation between meaning and validity, Lenoble insists it is fundamentally undecidable whether any attempt to communicate succeeds in its illocutionary aims—participants in communication supposedly cannot *ascertain* whether or not one person accepts the speech-act offer of the other as valid.[115] In reply, I first argue against this undecidability thesis, which is central to everything else, so that I may then defend the distinction between the orientation toward reaching an understanding and the orientation toward success, as well as the corresponding distinction between illocutionary and perlocutionary goals. Finally, I conclude with some remarks on Lenoble's probabilistic ontology.

1. It makes sense to distinguish the following cases: (i) *A* makes an assertion "p," thereby claiming to be able to justify the proposition "p," which is either true or false; (ii) *A* utters the conjecture "that p," and thus has reasons for "p" without immediately claiming to be able to defend "p" against everyone; (iii) *A* utters "p" in a hypothetical attitude, thus temporarily withholding judgment on the truth or falsity of "p"; and (iv) *A* utters "p" as a (mathematical) proposition that is undecidable in the strict sense, such that its undecidability can be demonstrated (in rare cases). The first case is clearly the basis for the remaining cases which parasitically depend on it, for even undecidability must be defined in relation to the alternatives of true and false. Moreover, the assertion of a proposition that can be true or false, correct or incorrect, is the rule in everyday communication.

The speaker's speech-act offer together with the hearer's "yes" or "no" response may be conceived and analyzed as the elementary unit of the analysis. This analysis is undertaken from the perspective of a second person. That is, the speaker's dual aims, to express herself clearly and to reach an agreement with someone about something, are defined from the standpoint of the hearer who is supposed to understand what is said and to accept it as valid, although the hearer can at any time say no. The standard of *understanding* an utterance consists in the conditions for *reaching a possible agreement* about what is said. These conditions are fulfilled when the hearer accepts the validity claim that the speaker raises for her proposition. The

---

115. *See id.* at 951, 954–56.

basis for reaching an agreement is thus the intersubjective recognition of a validity claim that can be criticized by the hearer and that the speaker guarantees—with more or less *prima facie* credibility—to vindicate discursively, should this be necessary. Naturally, it may turn out that this guarantee does not carry much weight. But, given a broad background consensus on lifeworld certainties, even a fragile guarantee often enough serves as a basis for an acceptance that creates obligations relevant to further action. What appears to be rationally acceptable to the hearer does not have to be valid. Everyday communicative action is carried along by the acceptance of *claims* to validity that appear sufficiently rational to the addressees in the given context, and not by the validity of speech acts that prove to be rationally acceptable on closer examination.

Lenoble contests the approach taken in the above analysis (which I have only briefly sketched) when he asserts that the speaker can never decide whether or not her speech-act offer has been earnestly accepted: illocutionary success is undecidable in principle.[116] For example, according to Lenoble a speaker cannot know whether a hearer who agrees to an assertion actually believes the proposition or doubts it, or whether a hearer who carries out a command does so in obedience to the command or for entirely different reasons.[117] Here Lenoble evidently views linguistic communication in terms of a philosophy of the subject according to which communication transpires not in the medium of publicly accessible symbolic expressions but between two mutually opaque minds. Lenoble does not seem to realize that intentionalist provisos are pointless after a rigorously executed linguistic turn. Regardless of what the hearer thinks in doing so, his affirmative response to an assertion or command creates a social fact open to public verification. In the course of further interaction it will also become publicly evident whether or not the addressee violates the obligations he has taken on with his "yes" (i.e., to take into consideration the fact that has been accepted as true; to carry out the commanded action, whatever his motives). As a further example of this, consider a promise that the speaker keeps for reasons different from those she declared in making the promise. Here too, the act of promising creates a new social fact, which is the obligation toward another person; whether this promise was sincerely intended will be shown, in the course of further interaction, solely by the earnest attempt to redeem the promise. The seriousness of the speaker's intention is one of the presuppositions of the use of language oriented toward mutual understanding, but like all presuppositions this one too may turn out to be false. This particular presupposition, which remains implicit in constative and regulative speech acts, first becomes thematically salient in expressive

116. *See id.* at 957–58.
117. *See id.* at 958.

speech acts such as avowals (in which a speaker reveals an experience to which she has privileged access). The explicit claim to sincerity in such speech acts can likewise only be tested indirectly, "in the course of further interaction," that is, it cannot be directly tested in a discourse but only in further behavior consistent with the claim.

In his debate with John Searle, Jacques Derrida introduced various examples to demonstrate the undecidability of communicative success, examples that at first glance seem more plausible. Derrida drew these from the realm of fictional speech as well as from metaphorical and ironic uses of language. For example, if a fire has actually broken out in a theater and one of the actors on stage wants to warn the audience by crying "Fire!," under the ambiguous circumstances of a play he may not be taken seriously even if he adds, "I am speaking quite seriously."[118] This special example illustrates the general fact that the speaker's communicative success requires more than the hearer's understanding of the *literal* meaning of what is said. The interpenetration of linguistic knowledge and empirical knowledge also implies that competent hearers correctly understand an utterance only if they know when a sentence (whose literal meaning is comprehensible) is *appropriately* uttered in a situation. It is only on the basis of such an understanding of the background features of typical situations of usage that hearers can in nontypical cases *infer* speaker's intention and, where it deviates from the literal meaning, can understand the "transferred" or ironic meaning of her utterances.

In using this strategy of analysis, I certainly do not mean to deny the occasional, fleeting, and diffuse aspects of everyday communication in which possibilities for reaching understanding can be realized only transitorily through the polyphonic dissonance of unclear, fragmentary, and ambiguous utterances open to misunderstanding and in need of interpretation. The starting point of this analysis is, however, that through this murky medium the countless contingent plans of nay-saying actors are nevertheless woven into a dense network of more or less smooth interactions. Every transcendental analysis aims to illuminate the conditions of possibility for a specific fact which the analysis takes for granted. Kant started with the fact of Newtonian physics and asked himself how objective experience is at all possible. Formal pragmatics replaces this epistemological question with a linguistic question—how it is possible to reach mutual understanding

---

118. Albrecht Wellmer deals with this example, in connection with Donald Davidson, from a standpoint that is interesting for our purposes. *See* Albrecht Wellmer, Autonomie der Bedeutung und das Principle of Charity aus sprachpragmatischer Sicht (1994) (unpublished manuscript, on file with author). I am also indebted to this manuscript for the distinction between "knowing the literal meaning of a sentence" and "knowing whether it is appropriate to use the sentence in a given situation." *Id.*

through communication. In doing so, formal pragmatics starts with the equally astonishing lifeworld fact of social integration, effected without violence through (largely implicit) processes of mutual understanding. The success of such processes is thus presupposed in an analysis intended to explain how this is possible. In answer to Lenoble's doubt, I believe I may hold on to this presupposition all the more because, for the participants, the success of attempts at mutual understanding is gauged unmistakably by the public "yes" and "no" of the addressees.

2.   From the undecidability of communicative success, Lenoble concludes that one can distinguish neither between the use of language with an intersubjective orientation to mutual understanding and its use with an egocentric orientation to one's own success, nor between illocutionary and perlocutionary goals.[119] The *role of the second person* is decisive for these distinctions. This role must not be ignored if one does not want to assimilate the understanding of linguistic expressions to an observer's formation of hypotheses (*á la* Quine and Davidson), or if one does not want to reduce communication in a natural language to the indirect influence that mutual observers exercise so as "to let the other know" his or her intentions (*á la* Grice or Luhmann). The attitude toward a second person with whom I want to reach an understanding in a shared language about something is intuitively easy to distinguish from the attitude I have in the first person toward an (observed) third person, whom I bring to understand my own opinion or intention insofar as my cleverly calculated behavior allows him or her to draw the right conclusions.

By way of illustration, consider situations that involve an involuntary change in attitude, such as when the doctor in a psychiatric clinic realizes in the course of my conversation with him that I have sought him out, not say as a colleague, but as a patient, at which point he suddenly directs his gaze upon me in a *searching* manner to decipher what I am saying as *symptomatic* of something unsaid. The specific "estrangement" that then occurs in such situations is explained by the involuntary change in the addressee's position: under the objectifying gaze of the observer, I feel myself being removed from the role of second person and placed in the position of someone being observed. I am no longer someone *with* whom the other speaks but have become someone *about* whom others speak. Michel Foucault has impressively investigated how this clinical gaze has crystallized into the institutional core of medical practices[120] and Irving Goffman has developed the phenomenology of this gaze from harmless scenes of every-

119. *See* Lenoble, *supra* note 16, at 960–62.
120. *See* MICHEL FOUCAULT, THE BIRTH OF THE CLINIC: AN ARCHAEOLOGY OF MEDICAL PERCEPTION (A. M. Sheridan Smith trans., 1973).

day life.[121] These experiences have their innocent basis in an ordinary language inscribed with the system of pronouns, and thus inscribed not only with the first and third person pronouns but also with the second person as well.

Because illocutionary success is gauged by assent to a validity claim that the addressee can contradict, the speaker is capable of achieving her aim only in the attitude oriented toward second persons. For given a shared understanding of what is said, the assent to or denial of an uttered proposition is possible only from the perspective of an involved person (or at least of a virtual participant). This is shown in the status of consensus and dissensus, wherein assent and denial terminate: both differ in virtue of their intersubjective character, from the consonance or lack of consonance (ascertainable from the observer perspective) of different opinions. Each person can, by him or herself alone, have an opinion that is *consonant* with others. But a *consensus* can be produced only in common, whereby the commonality of the enterprise is based on the fact that speakers share the same system of interpenetrating and reciprocally interchangeable I-Thou perspectives.

What we call "perlocutionary effects," by contrast, are effects on the addressee brought about through speech acts, whether such effects are internally linked with the meaning of what is said (as in carrying out a command), whether they are dependent upon contextual coincidences (as when one is startled or frightened by some news), or whether they arise through deception (as in cases of manipulation). Perlocutionary effects are elicited by the (intended or unintended) influence on an addressee *without her collaboration*—they happen to her. The speaker who pursues perlocutionary goals orients himself toward the consequences of his utterance—consequences he can accurately predict if, taking the observer perspective, he correctly calculates the effects of his *own* intervention in the world. Illocutionary success, relying as it does on the rationally motivated response of a second person, cannot be *calculated* in this manner. There is a particular class of speech acts that are specifically meant to produce pejorative effects, such as threats, insults, curses, etc. I would classify these speech acts as "perlocutions"—expressions whose standard meaning is no longer determined by the very illocutionary act they consist of but by the intended perlocutionary effects. In general, achieving these effects does not require language in an essential sense: nonlinguistic actions are often functional equivalents for such a use of language oriented not toward mutual understanding as such, but toward the consequences of such actions.

Similarly, strategic interactions differ from practices in which action coordination is effected through the mutual understanding of performa-

121. *See* IRVING GOFFMAN, THE PRESENTATION OF SELF IN EVERYDAY LIFE (1959).

tively-oriented participants, i.e., practices that *essentially* rely upon language.

tively-oriented participants, i.e., practices that *essentially* rely upon language. Strategic interactions follow a pattern of reciprocal influence. Accordingly, strategic actors are oriented solely toward the consequences of decisions they make on the basis of their own preferences. Having taken the objectivating attitude of an observer, strategic actors cannot lay claim to the rationally motivating bonds of illocutionary acts. This distinction between action oriented toward understanding and action oriented toward success is not a theoretical artifact, a point that can easily be intuitively verified through moral feelings. We may feel offended or outraged at another person's violation of a norm, or conversely we may ourselves have a guilty conscience, but only if we assume that a normative background consensus exists and that we behave "correctly" toward one another when we take the performative attitude of actors oriented toward reaching an understanding. In other words, we assume that our behavior can also be justified, if necessary, in the light of this consensus. We are quite aware of the two attitudes we can take to norms: when we obey a norm it is because we recognize it as valid or obligatory and when we merely act in conformity with a norm it is because we want to avoid the consequences of deviant behavior. In the first case, we act for agent-neutral reasons, following from intersubjectively recognized norms (or norms about which we believe we can reach a consensus). In the second case, we act for agent-relative reasons that only count relative to our own goals and preferences. The concepts of law and legal validity (and not just the Kantian versions of these) are based on these distinctions. Thus, I do not see how Lenoble could analyze legal behavior and legitimate orders without making use of such distinctions, or ones equivalent to them.

3.   Lenoble attempts to deconstruct the basic distinctions, whose intuitive plausibility I have just noted, because he assumes this conception is still caught in the classical determinist worldview. Like Jacobson, he appears to be impressed by cosmological speculations that are inspired—at some distance—by research in chaos theory. In any case, Lenoble places the in-principle undecidability of communicative success and the random dynamics of speech events within the framework of a probabilistic ontology. In his view, world events, which are only comprehensible in statistical terms, are more appropriately modeled on the Laplacian dice-thrower than on the Kantian critic who weighs reasons against one another instead of counting off sums of randomly generated numbers. The suspicion is clear: communicative reason postulates too much order in the whirl of signifiers.

Just as one can conceive the turn to the subject (or mentalism) in modern philosophy as an answer to a new experience of contingency, namely the experience of a nature that had become universally contingent, so also the linguistic turn assimilated the irruption of a new kind of historical contingency that first achieved philosophical relevance with the rise of a new historical consciousness in the late eighteenth century. The detranscendentalized consciousness of the knowing subject now had to be situated in historical forms of life and embodied in language and practice. In the process, the world-constitutive spontaneity of the transcendental subject became the world-disclosive function of language. The crucial question for today's rationality debates is whether communicating subjects are from start to finish *imprisoned* in epochal interpretations of the world, discourses, and language games. Or, restated, whether their *entire fate* is at the mercy of the ontological preunderstanding that makes innerworldly learning processes possible or whether, to the contrary, the results of these learning processes can feed back into and revise the very world-interpretive linguistic knowledge itself. If we want to do justice to the transcendental fact of learning then we must indeed reckon with the latter alternative—and with a communicative reason that no longer prejudges the contents of a particular view of the world. This entirely procedural reason operates with context-transcending validity *claims* and with pragmatic *presuppositions* about the world. But the presupposition of an objective world that is the same for all participants in communication only has the formal meaning of an ontologically neutral system of reference. It only implies that we can refer to the same—reidentifiable—entities, even as our descriptions of them change.[122]

V. ON THE LOGIC OF LEGAL DISCOURSES

Lenoble criticizes the concept of communicative reason and the basic assumptions of the theory of communicative action because he sees the "indeterminacy" of law and judicial decision making simply as a reflection of the "undecidability" that supposedly inheres in linguistic practices as such.[123] It is unclear to me how law could fulfill its function of stabilizing behavioral expectations if clients, as well as experts, could not be confident that the law of the land adequately determines *ex ante* which procedures and normative criteria should be used to interpret and decide future cases. Legal certainty requires a certain measure of predictability. Although such certainty should not be absolutized, it does contribute to the legitimacy of the legal order in a manner inherent in the form of law. The themes that Lenoble touches on in this context return with other authors. David Rasmussen defends legal hermeneutics,[124] Robert Alexy argues for his own

---

122. *See* CHRISTINA LAFONT, SPRACHE UND WELTERSCHLIESSUNG: ZUR LINGUISTISCHEN WENDE DER HERMENEUTIK HEIDEGGERS (1994).

123. *See* Lenoble, *supra* note 16, at 978.

124. *See generally* Rasmussen, *supra* note 17.

version of discourse theory,[125] and Gunther Teubner reformulates the old problem of conflicting legal norms.[126]

A.

David Rasmussen approaches my analysis of adjudication and appropriation of legal hermeneutics as a philosopher familiar with the German discussion that began with Edmund Husserl and Martin Heidegger, was continued by Hans-Georg Gadamer, and has been more recently taken up by Karl-Otto Apel. Rasmussen's metacritical reflections bring him to the following thesis: "Habermas's argument claims too much for a theory of rationality. At the same time, while buying into a form of the philosophy of language, it claims too little for language."[127] Against the background of the debates between hermeneutics and transcendental phenomenology, Rasmussen believes that, notwithstanding the linguistic turn, the formal-pragmatic investigation of the universal presuppositions of communication forgets the starting point: that pure consciousness has been detranscendentalized. The mistake, in his view, is the assumption that, after the linguistic turn, one can retain the transcendental style of argumentation—one must instead, along with hermeneutics, renounce all idealizations and entirely surrender the transcendental legacy of a tension between facticity and validity.

It surprises me that Rasmussen does not hesitate to answer negatively the rhetorical question: "Does interpretation require idealization?"[128] Gadamer and Davidson have shown, each in his own way, that the interpretation of linguistic expressions and symbolically prestructured formations in general requires a principle of charity. We must assume that actors are accountable and that their utterances are rational, which is what the theory of communicative action demands.[129] Although idealizations only play a *methodological* role here, they do have a *fundamentum in re*, specifically in the presuppositions of rationality that undergird the very practice of reaching mutual understanding.

I myself have repeatedly emphasized that one may not *directly* connect the practice of rational discourse with the procedure of democratic opinion- and will-formation. Moreover, even a discourse-theoretic understanding of adjudication does not entail a demand to "democratize" the courts. Rather, in postulating that the judiciary should be embedded in an open community of lay interpreters who criticize adjudication, one makes

125. *See generally* Alexy, *supra* note 18.
126. *See generally* Teubner, *supra* note 19.
127. Rasmussen, *supra* note 17, at 1074.
128. *Id.* at 1078.
129. *See* 1 HABERMAS, *supra* note 33, at 102–36.

political demands only with respect to the present evisceration of the separation of powers. The more the judiciary tacitly assumes the role of a competing legislature when developing the law, the more resolutely it must be required to justify itself, not just before an internal public of experts, but also *externally* before the forum of citizens.

B.

It was Robert Alexy's dissertation that encouraged me to extend discourse theory, which was originally developed for morality, to law and the constitutional state.[130] In addition, his *Theorie der Grundrechte*[131] helped me understand the dialectic of legal and factual equality. To be sure, in the latter text Alexy also proposed an interpretation of legal norms that has been criticized by both Klaus Günther and myself.[132] According to Alexy, the deontological understanding of norms can be translated into an equivalent understanding of corresponding value contents. Alexy is quite aware of the difference between these two ways of looking at norms:

> What is prima facie best according to the values model is a prima facie obligation in the principles model, and what is definitively the best according to the values model is a definitive obligation in the principles model. Thus principles and values differ only because the former have a deontological character and the latter, an axiological one.[133]

The dispute, however, concerns the word "only." Alexy states, "[l]aw has to do with what is obligatory. This suggests we should model it on principles. On the other hand, there is no problem . . . in modelling legal argumentation on values instead of principles."[134] Alexy has developed this thesis in the form of an optimizing or weighing model, which includes cost-benefit analyses.

In Alexy's present text, he defends his position with an interesting argument against the rigid distinction between deontological and axiological

---

130. *See* ROBERT ALEXY, THEORIE DER JURISTISCHEN ARGUMENTATION: DIE THEORIE DES RATIONALEN DISKURSES ALS THEORIE DER JURISTISCHEN BEGRÜNDUNG (3d ed. 1990). For an English translation of the first edition, see ROBERT ALEXY, A THEORY OF LEGAL ARGUMENTATION: THE THEORY OF RATIONAL DISCOURSE AS THEORY OF LEGAL JUSTIFICATION (Ruth Adler & Neil MacCormick trans., 1989).

131. *See* ROBERT ALEXY, THEORIE DER GRUNDRECHTE (1985) [hereinafter THEORIE DER GRUNDRECHTE]; *see also* ROBERT ALEXY, BEGRIFF UND GELTUNG DES RECHTS (1992).

132. KLAUS GÜNTHER, THE SENSE OF APPROPRIATENESS: APPLICATION DISCOURSE IN MORALITY AND LAW 268–76 (John Farrell trans., 1993); HABERMAS, BETWEEN FACTS AND NORMS, *supra* note 2, at 253.

133. THEORIE DER GRUNDRECHTE, *supra* note 131, at 133.

134. *Id.*

standards.[135] This distinction, Alexy believes, does not fit legal norms because they regulate comparatively concrete matters and must, therefore, be justified not only from a moral standpoint, but also in view of political goals and ethical values as well.[136] Alexy anticipates my reply that such justification still involves the *relative* priority of arguments from principle over arguments of policy; otherwise the legal form (and the obligatory character of legal norms) would be damaged, because *from its inception* law shares with morality the task of solving interpersonal conflicts and, unlike policies, does not primarily serve to realize collective goals.[137] Alexy is not satisfied with this rejoinder. As he understands it, the deontological or unconditional character of normative validity, which I want to preserve for legal norms, means that such validity extends universally to all subjects capable of speech and action. The rest is easy: in contrast to deontology (as he interprets it), legal norms are binding only for a historical, spatiotemporally bounded community of persons. Therefore, such norms cannot be "deontological."

In response, it should be noted that the expression "deontological" only refers to the binarily coded obligational character of behavioral expectations, in contrast to values, which must be transitively ordered in each case. The code of precepts that distinguish between right and wrong (as analogous to truth and falsity) and the corresponding unconditionality of the normative validity claim connected with such precepts are not affected if one limits the sphere of validity to a particular legal community. Inside this sphere, the law still confronts its addressees with a validity claim that does not allow rights to be "weighed" as though they were "legal values" with different degrees of priority. How we assess our values and decide what is "good for us" and what is "better," at a given time, changes every day. As soon as we reduce the principle of legal equality to merely one good among others, individual rights can be sacrificed at times to collective goals. As a result, we do not see that one right can "yield" to another right, without loss of validity, when the two happen to conflict.

This is more than just a semantic dispute, as shown by the understanding of the principle of proportionality that guides adjudication in cases where rights collide. According to Alexy, the fact that in legal discourse rights play the role of reasons that are "weighed" against each other confirms his view that principles may be treated *like* values. In fact, a statement may be more or less supported by good reasons, but the proposition itself will be either true or false. We assume that the "truth" of true statements is a property

135. See generally Alexy, supra note 18.

136. See id. at 1033–34.

137. See HABERMAS, BETWEEN FACTS AND NORMS, supra note 2, at 427; see also RONALD DWORKIN, TAKING RIGHTS SERIOUSLY (1977).

that "cannot be lost," even though we can judge such statements only by reasons that, should the need arise, *justify* our considering them true. The difference between the principles model and the values model is evident by the fact that only the former preserves the binary code of "legal/illegal" as its point of reference—a court presents the general legal norms from which it derives a singular judgment as reasons that are supposed to justify its ruling on the case. If, however, the justifying norms are viewed as values that have been brought into an ad hoc transitive order for the given occasion, then the judgment is the *result* of a weighing of values. The court's judgment is then *itself* a value judgment that more or less adequately reflects a form of life articulating itself in the framework of a concrete order of values. But this judgment is no longer related to the alternatives of a right or wrong decision. By thus assimilating ought-statements to evaluations, one opens the way to legitimating broad discretionary powers. Normative statements have different grammatical features than do evaluative statements. By insidiously assimilating the first type of statement to the second type, one robs the law of its clear-cut, discursively redeemable claim to normative validity. As a result, the strict requirement to justify decisions also disappears. Positive law should be subject to this requirement because it is armed with sanctions and is allowed to delicately impose penalties upon the autonomy of private persons.

A similar point can be made regarding the assimilation of application discourses to justification discourses.[138] Alexy is quite aware that the questions in each case involve different logics. Discourses of justification aim to justify general legal norms in light of the consequences one might anticipate for typical cases. Discourses of application attempt to justify singular judgments in light of norms that are already accepted as valid. However, Alexy cannot explain certain phenomena, such as the different communicative arrangements governing legislation and adjudication. These varying arrangements result from the different principles and corresponding logics of argumentation that govern the two types of discourse (i.e., universalization in the case of justification and appropriateness in the case of application). For example, the role of the impartial third party that defines the structure of judicial discourses would be out of place in discourses of justification, in which there cannot be any nonparticipants. Moreover, denying the difference between these two types of discourse destroys the rational basis for a functional separation of powers justified by the different possibilities of access to certain kinds of reasons. The reasons the political legislator uses, or could reasonably use, to justify adopted norms are not simply

---

138. I cannot go into the relevant discussions between Robert Alexy and Klaus Günther, but see Klaus Günther, *Critical Remarks on Robert Alexy's "Special Case Thesis,"* 6 RATIO JURIS 143 (1993); Robert Alexy, *Justification and Application of Norms,* 6 RATIO JURIS 157 (1993).

at the disposition of the judiciary and the administration when they apply and implement the norms. This point has a critical meaning when the judiciary and the administration must make decisions that further develop the law, or whenever they must take on disguised legislative tasks, thereby opening themselves to demands for legitimation that are *not* provided for in the traditional separation of powers. (From a legal-political standpoint, this situation creates the need for critical fora for judicial opinions, participation in administration, ombudspersons, etc.)

C.

Gunther Teubner's critique addresses a more fundamental issue.[139] To begin with, he agrees that discourse and bargaining are different forms of deliberation and that discourses differ according to the various forms of argumentation (i.e., pragmatic, ethical, moral, and legal). However, if in the face of this discursive pluralism one does not assume—*à la* Lyotard, for example[140]—that discourses are semantically closed and mutually indifferent, then the further problem that piques Teubner's interest arises. Namely, there must be a way of unifying the different discourses when they collide: "[a]fter the move to pluridiscursivity, the success of Habermas's theory now depends on a plausible solution to the collision of discourses."[141] We require procedures—"rational meta-procedures for interdiscursivity,"[142] as Teubner puts it—that allow us to decide which matters should have priority, or which of the different aspects, under which one can deal with the same matter, is supposed to have priority. Teubner asks me to choose between two alternatives: a heterarchy of discourses, each of which has an equal status, or a hierarchy of discourses capped by a superdiscourse. He thinks that I expect discourse theory to have the role of such a superdiscourse. But this is not the case.

It is true that the clarification of pragmatic, ethical, and moral modes of questioning, and the analysis of the corresponding rules of argumentation and types of discourse, are philosophical undertakings. However, philosophy conducts one discourse, among many others, and explains why there cannot be a superdiscourse. Thus, sociologically speaking, philosophers do not enjoy a more privileged position in public affairs than do other scholars. At most, they can offer themselves as experts for hearings on relevant matters, or enter uninvited as intellectuals. They certainly cannot, however, lay claim to the institutional role of arbiter.

139. *See generally* Teubner, *supra* note 19.
140. *See* JEAN-FRANÇOIS LYOTARD, THE DIFFEREND: PHRASES IN DISPUTE (Georges Van Den Abbeele trans., 1988).
141. Teubner, *supra* note 19, at 904.
142. *Id.*

My reflections on discourse theory lead to the conclusion that modes of questioning are self-selective. The logics of the corresponding discourses map out rational transitions from one discourse to another. A brief illustration should suffice here. To the extent that articulating and weighing policies depends on the selection of purposive-rational means or strategies (on the basis of empirical information), there must be a consensus on sufficiently clear preferences. If the preferences themselves are contested because of a clash of opposing interests, then procedurally fair compromises must be found (while the fairness of the procedure is decided upon in moral discourses). However, if the preferences are not so much contested as they are unclear, then participants must reach an understanding in ethical discourse concerning their form of life and collective identity in order to assure themselves of shared value orientations. If there is an irreconcilable conflict of values instead of a conflict of compromisable interests, then the parties must jointly shift to the more abstract level of moral reasoning and agree upon rules for living together that are in the equal interest of all. That is just one of many examples of interdiscursive relations. What matters here is that these relations are not *dictated* from the perspective of a superdiscourse. Rather, they emerge from the logic of questioning within a *given* discourse, with the result that the good is privileged over the expedient and the just over the good. In cases of collision, moral reasons "trump" ethical reasons and ethical reasons "trump" pragmatic ones because once the respective mode of questioning becomes problematic in its *own* presuppositions, it points out where it is rational to cross its boundaries. The fact that compromises must be in harmony with the basic ethical values acknowledged by a particular group, and that these values in turn must be in harmony with valid moral principles, results from the logic of the modes of questioning and from the interdiscursive connections governed by it.

This "self-selectivity" of modes of questioning can function, however, only if there is no dispute over the selection of questions and the choice of aspects under which a controverted matter should be handled. Thus a "collision of discourses" exists when the participants cannot agree about whether an issue involves, for example, a conflict of compromisable interests or irreconcilable values; or whether it involves an ethical or moral question; or whether it at all concerns something that must be addressed politically and can be regulated legally. Since there is no metadiscourse even for such second-order problems, legally institutionalized procedures must be effective in such cases. For these procedures imply a preselection only insofar as every case that is heard *must* be interpreted in the language of law and decided according to legal standards (so long as this is desired by one of the entitled parties). Legal procedures can regulate cases of colliding discourses because the code of law is too unspecific to detect the "logic" of the issue at hand. There is no legal procedure for *sorting out* issues according to the mode of questioning. This is procedurally useful because it allows decisions to be made under time pressure in each case, and thus in cases of collision as well. There is no doubt that this is unsatisfying from a substantive point of view, because it does not rule out the possibility that conflicting values will sometimes be compromised, that ethical questions will sometimes be decided from the moral point of view, that private affairs will sometimes be unduly politicized, that domains of action will sometimes become unduly juridified, and so forth. These "sorting errors" can be countered only if legal procedures simultaneously facilitate argumentation and leave it intact; that is, they must unleash discourses without interfering with their logic. To the extent that this succeeds, the self-selectivity of modes of questioning and corresponding types of discourse can come into play.[143]

However, this solution certainly does not imply that legal discourse in Teubner's sense could be deployed as a superdiscourse. In advancing this proposal, Teubner relies on two problematic assumptions: (i) that the different discourses that come together in legal discourse are mutually incommensurable; and (ii) that the specific role of legal discourse is to reduce the other discourses to a common denominator, thereby rendering them compatible with one another.[144]

1. Teubner exemplifies what he means by "incommensurability," in a legally unspecified sense, by turning to international private law, which has always had to cope with the problem of how to regulate individual cases in which the legal orders of different nations conflict.[145] To deal with such problems, international private law has developed collision rules that determine whether domestic or foreign private law should apply. But these meta-rules are still framed from the perspective of the different national laws. Hence, the application of such rules only reproduces, at a higher level of reflection, the difference between what is domestic and foreign law *from one's own perspective.* Teubner states, "[d]iscourse collisions search in vain for one central meta-discourse. There is only a plurality of decentralized meta-discourses that reformulate collisions in their own idiosyncratic language."[146] According to this description (*à la* Rudolf Wiethölter), international legal standards, which realizes "the" single international private law only in the plural of the many national legal orders, serve for Teubner as an example for the general problematic of communication between discourses that present foreign worlds to each other. These are not semantically closed in the sense of being *incomprehensible* to each other. But they are

143. *See* HABERMAS, JUSTIFICATION AND APPLICATION, *supra* note 67, at 117.
144. *See* Teubner, *supra* note 19, at 907.
145. *See id.* at 908–09.
146. *Id.* at 910.

governed by different, mutually incompatible rationalities and basic concepts, so that what is right or has priority in one universe is wrong or subordinate in another. This incommensurability of validity standards is the same kind as that found in existential value-conflicts inside a single country, where each of the conflicting communities is integrated by its own conception of the good. For example, each of these communities describes "abortion" according to its own perspective. Accordingly, since there is no shared evaluative perspective, the identity of the very matter in need of regulation disappears. However, for Teubner, the foregoing argument has the unpleasant consequence that his conception of incommensurability tacitly gives "ethical" discourse priority over all other types of discourse. This contradicts the premise that the different discourses are of equal rank, precisely the premise that is first supposed to yield the unavoidable asymmetry of communication between discourses. I will come back to this at the end of the present section.

In fact, the asymmetry that Teubner illustrates with the collision rules of international private law is the counterintuitive result of a theoretical approach still attached to the subject-centered tradition, i.e., the philosophy of consciousness or mentalism. If one starts with systems or discourses that, like transcendental subjects, constitute their "world" according to their own premises, then communication can only be conceived intentionalistically on the basis of mutual observation, such that one observer "induces" the other's own specific operations. This theoretical strategy is counterintuitive because it ignores the fact (and the basic hermeneutical insight) that we cannot reach an agreement with someone about something in the world unless we have mastered the system of personal pronouns and their transformations and know how to produce a symmetry between the *reversible* perspectives of first and second persons within an interaction that can be observed only from the third-person perspective.

By way of addendum, only when one is speaking of the national legal orders of *sovereign* states does international private law illustrate how a legal system must *inevitably* use its own premises to solve conflicts with other legal systems. But it was only during the period between 1648 and 1914 that states were "sovereign," in the sense that they neither submitted to an internationally binding human rights convention nor enacted basic human rights in their own constitutions. Once such provisions are in place, the universalistic content of basic rights makes its mark through private law legislation on all concrete regulations. An effective system of rights, which today applies pressure from both inside and outside a country, certainly does not rule out intercultural controversy over the interpretation of these rights. But such controversy is in turn informative for the *legal battles* that are decided, one way or another, by international courts. One can at least *conceive* such a cosmopolitan legal order without contradiction, which shows that the historical example of collision rules does not provide any evidence for the inevitability of the diagnosed asymmetry, i.e., for a *paradox*.

2.   According to Teubner's conception, the role of a superdiscourse devolves upon law because law relates to all other discourses in the awareness that these constitute incommensurable worlds *for one another*.[147] Therefore, because of their asymmetrical relationships, they must mutually inflict injustice (*unrecht*) on one another—"injustice" in the metaphorical sense of a postmodern theory of incommensurable language-games. The medium of law compensates for this "injustice" by appropriating in its own way, and making mutually compatible, all the discourses that it encounters in its environment. Accordingly, law specializes in rendering what is grammatically incompatible compatible. Naturally, it succeeds in this task only on its own premises, since legal discourse, too, is supposed to display the property of incommensurability. Teubner states, "[j]ustice can be realized to the degree as a concrete historical legal discourse is simultaneously able, externally, to incorporate the rationalities of other discourses and, internally, to observe its own requirements of legal consistency."[148] Legal discourse (and its "inner logic") is distinguished not just by normative coherence, that is, the linking of each new case to the chain of previous decisions, but also by a specific mode of questioning—how like cases can be treated alike and different cases differently. This implies that the appropriated rationalities of alien worlds of discourse are assimilated to law's own standard of equal treatment. Law is the "master" of equality and inequality. This standard underlies the "comparison" of discourses, or the exercise of "compensatory justice" toward discourses that, as incommensurable, can only relate to one another "unjustly" (in Derrida's and Lyotard's aestheticist sense of injustice). By leveling things out in this assimilating manner, Teubner also explains the "shameless eclecticism" of an adjudication whose motto is the "weighing of values"—"be it balancing between principles, between values, or even between interests."[149]

Even if one were to accept Teubner's description of incommensurability and "injustice" (in the higher deconstructionist sense), his conception of law as a compensatory "superdiscourse" would not be convincing for at least two reasons. First, the principle of equal treatment cannot be considered the exclusive property of law because morality validates this same principle. Law and morality obey the same discourse principle and follow the same discursive logics in application and justification. Law is not distinguishable from morality by the abstract question of how interpersonal conflicts

147.   *See id.* at 909–10.
148.   *Id.* at 910.
149.   *Id.* at 914, 915.

should be regulated in the equal interest of all, nor by the rules of argumentation provided by universalization and appropriateness. The specific difference separating law from morality lies not in discourse, but in the fact that discursively justified and applied norms have a legal form, i.e., they are *enacted* politically, *interpreted* in a binding manner, and *enforced* with the threat of state sanctions. The legal form is also bound up with the institutional differentiation between discourses of justification and of application, i.e., the specific pressure to make rules that are precisely formulated, systematically coherent, and consistently applied. These properties of the legal code call for a "translation" of the various arguments—pragmatic, ethical, and moral—and compromises that find their way into the legal system through the deliberations and decisions of the political legislature and that provide a point of reference for the legal discourse of the judiciary.

The foregoing consideration does not imply that the practice of judicial decision making may simply disregard the deontological meaning of legal norms. This is the second reason Teubner's argument fails. If, as Teubner contends, the judiciary could operate with a free hand inside a framework of values, and if it had to reduce principles and policies, norms and values, to a common denominator and "balance" or "weigh" these against one another, then legal discourses would assume the role of paternalistic proxy discourses for a political-ethical self-understanding taken over from the citizens. The practice of the higher courts certainly provides examples for a tacit privileging of a value ethic in relation to law and morality, but this is hardly what Teubner has in mind.

VI. ON THE POLITICAL SUBSTANCE
OF THE PROCEDURAL PARADIGM

A.

I am indebted to Ulrich Preuss for outlining the German tradition of legal thought that provides the background for linking law and communicative power.[150] The liberal tradition generally explains the rule of law in terms of the antagonism between a law that guarantees individual liberties and the governmental power that realizes collective goals. This "authority of the state" (*Staatsgewalt*) is thereby traced back to an autochthonous, "barbaric" origin untouched by law: the capacity to physically overpower all others.[151] In the politically civilized societies of the West, however, this antagonism is not sharpened into a struggle between opposing principles. Rather, it has always been perceived as an opposition that must be balanced out in the

---

150. *See generally* Preuss, *supra* note 20.

151. *See, e.g.*, Charles Larmore, *Die Wurzeln radikaler Demokratie*, 41 DEUTSCHE ZEITSCHRIFT FÜR PHILOSOPHIE 321 (1993).

constitutional state. In Germany, though, it was seen instead as an irresolvable competition between two *mutually exclusive* forms of political integration, one through law and the other through the executive power of the state. The burning question discussed between liberal and conservative constitutional scholars concerned the degree to which the monarchy should be subject to legal curbs. Feared by liberals and celebrated by conservatives, the "substance" of the state embodied in the army, police, and bureaucracy had an aura of essentially irrational overpowering violence (*Gewalt*). Consequently, even the Left could conceive democracy only as an inverted royal sovereignty, set on its feet by turning the monarchy on its head. Democracy remained a statist concept even for its defenders.

Against this background, Marx's idea of the "withering away of the state" becomes understandable as a more radical form of the theory that Friedrich Engels took from Claude Henri Saint-Simon. This is the idea that the "political" domination of human beings over other human beings should be converted into the "rational" management of things. This idea has fascinated me from the start. Through Carl Schmitt and his disciples, the tradition of glorifying the "political element" of the state continued without interruption, even after the end of the National Socialist regime in which such glorification had culminated.[152]

Like Preuss himself, I am indebted to the Marxist-based *counter*-tradition of "contentious" legal scholars, above all to Hermann Heller, Franz Neumann, Otto Kirchheimer, and Wolfgang Abendroth.[153] To be sure, the central idea that Preuss rightly highlights is taken in a different direction by these constitutional theorists: they investigated the democratic "overcoming" (*Aufhebung*) of the authoritarian substance of the state primarily from the anticapitalist standpoint of a transformation of the socioeconomic organization of inequality. By contrast, I have taken an immanent approach to the idea of a "rationalization" of the exercise of administrative power. This led me to reconstruct the normative contents specific to law and constitutional democracy. It is this—and not simply the proximity of one's teachers, which makes it easy to forget what one has learned from them—that probably explains why I did not explicitly go into these sources.[154] Nevertheless, I realize now that it was a mistake not to examine more closely

---

152. *See* JÜRGEN HABERMAS, KULTUR UND KRITIK 355–64 (1973).

153. *See* STREITBARE JURISTEN: EINE ANDERE TRADITION (Kritische Justiz ed., 1988).

154. However, points of connection can be found in the reflections of Jürgen Seifert on the constitution as a forum, which not by accident was dedicated to the memory of A. R. L. Garland. *See* Jürgen Seifert, *Haus oder Forum: Wertsystem oder offene Verfassung, in* STICHWORTE ZUR GEISTIGEN SITUATION DER ZEIT 321 (Jürgen Habermas ed., 1979). This article also provides references to further literature. More recently, see JORG P. MÜLLER, DEMOKRATISCHE GERECHTIGKEIT: EINE STUDY ZUR LEGITIMITÄT POLITISCHER UND RECHTLICHER ORDNUNG (1993).

the tendencies that currently make the democratic process into an instrument by which the majority has the power to exclude sizable minorities. The constellation has changed. Class structures have been replaced by the less conspicuous segmentation of marginalized groups that have become *superfluous,* and by the crumbling of the infrastructure in cities and entire regions. Perhaps this, too, should have consequences at a normative level. These could take the form of veto rights and special minority rights, as well as advocacy agencies for those who, pushed ever further from established public spheres, have increasingly fewer opportunities to better their situation on their own and thus raise their voices. The trend toward weakening party loyalties, and especially the increasing disengagement of voters, demands an unrelenting analysis that would also bring in the normative perspective of an equal opportunity to utilize rights of political participation.

I agree with Preuss that neither the liberal nor the social-welfare paradigm of law has made a serious effort to elucidate the internal relation between law and political power.[155] This task can only be accomplished by a concept of power that dissolves the false dichotomy between law and state power: the power that arises from the citizens' public use of communicative freedoms is intimately related to legitimate lawmaking.

Elsewhere, I have implicitly answered the questions that Preuss poses at the conclusion of his essay.[156] In many cases, the matter to be legally regulated must be simultaneously discussed from pragmatic, ethical, and moral points of view. However, the aspect of justice claims priority over the other aspects. To be legitimate, the politically enacted law of a particular legal community must remain compatible with moral principles. I interpret the complex validity claim of legal norms as, on the one hand, the claim to satisfy strategically asserted particular interests in a manner compatible with the common good and, on the other hand, the claim to uphold justice principles within the horizon of a particular form of life shaped by specific value constellations. The production of communicative power and legitimate law makes it necessary for citizens to lay claim to their democratic rights not just in the manner of individual liberties (i.e., in a self-interested way), but also as entitlements to the public use of communicative freedoms (i.e., with an orientation to the common good). There are sound reasons why they may not be legally compelled to do this. It is certainly necessary, in the sense of being functionally required, that citizens be accustomed to institutions of liberty within a liberal political culture. However, because political indoctrination must be avoided, the empirical question concerning the conditions for a favorable political socialization should not be di-

155. *See* Preuss, *supra* note 20, at 1185.
156. *See id.* at 1191.

rectly translated into the normative demand for values and political virtues. Preuss himself has elsewhere referred to the fact that public virtues can be exacted only "in small increments."

Perhaps this is also what motivates his proposal for converting value conflicts, which *as ethical* are irresolvable, into compromisable conflicts of interest. But this move cannot be justified from a normative standpoint, because the redefinition of values into interests can end up harming identities. An existential life project or a cultural mode of life is articulated in the light of ideals undergirded by "strong evaluations." In many cases, questions of security or health rank ahead of questions of distributive justice or education. In other cases, the reverse is true. But these value relations can be changed only through discourses of self-understanding and not through compromises, for bargaining is meaningful only if the competing claims or interests refer to the same or comparable goods. This is the only way to define, before the parties begin to bargain, what is relevant and open to negotiation (as with Rawls's primary goods, i.e., socially recognized and distributable collective goods such as income, leisure time, social security, and any social benefits that have monetary value). To the extent that compromise formation extends to the defining framework of goods themselves, it must at least be specified, *a priori*, which relevant matters are nonnegotiable, namely the "basic values" that constitute the participants' identity and self-understanding. One cannot, at the political level, exchange love or respect for money nor can one trade one's native language or religious affiliation for employment. Whatever intrudes upon definitions of identity in this way is not subject to compromise. Besides, such encroachments would imply a violation of human dignity and, if nothing else, would be legally inadmissible.

B.

Welfare policies are at the heart of the welfare state and the social-welfare interpretation of law. The guarantee of basic social rights first took the form of compulsory income-based insurance programs for occupational hazards and risks, such as illness, accident, incapacitation, unemployment, and age (though without regard for the burdens of housework and child-rearing that continue to be gender-specific). Since then, these traditional duties of caring have been replaced by bureaucratically administered provisions of basic necessities. As this transformation occurred, the consciousness of belonging to a community that was held together, not simply through abstract legal relationships but also through solidarity, fell by the wayside. Deteriorating relationships of solidarity cannot be regenerated among isolated clients who lay claim to entitlements from welfare bureaucracies.

Günter Frankenberg is interested in the normative side of this process.[157] Frankenberg believes that a correct normative understanding of social rights must precede the correct form of implementation. Thus the question: "Why care?"

Frankenberg considers the *relative* justification of social rights inadequate. According to a relative justification (which I, too, have proposed), basic social rights and other guarantees are supposed to secure the living conditions necessary for an equal opportunity to utilize private liberties and political civil rights, both of which are justified in absolute terms. This strategy of justification, which gives priority to rights immediately granting private and public autonomy, is directed against the effects of welfare paternalism. Citizens must be able to make actual use of their rights for an autonomous conduct of life. Thus, their material conditions of life must make it possible for them, and even encourage them, to exercise their formally guaranteed powers. Frankenberg objects to this conception on two grounds, one of which is stronger than the other.

First, the principle of "helping people help themselves" can work only for persons who are either in full possession of their abilities, will one day achieve the status of maturity (as in the case of children), or can regain their abilities and competencies (as in the case of those who are temporarily ill or disadvantaged).[158] Providing aid for the tormented, the handicapped, and invalids, or caring for the incurably ill, is something different. Such aids obviously have an intrinsic value and cannot be reduced to their function of engendering or restoring autonomy. I do appreciate the moral impulse related to positive duties, but I doubt that it can be directly translated to the political level where a "moral division of labor" is necessary simply for organizational reasons.[159] A feeling of solidarity anchored in the political culture can at best express itself in public support for the corresponding policies and aid programs.

Frankenberg takes the argument in a different direction when he says that the reference to the conditions for the genesis of private and public autonomy leads to a one-sided conception of social rights.[160] These rights are, Frankenberg suspects, in danger of degenerating into instruments for restoring the ability to work or for qualifying people for active citizenship. Only if social rights are justified absolutely, namely as an element of rights of membership, will their meaning for solidary relationships among "members" be preserved. Frankenberg states, "Instead of underprivileging social rights as 'implied' or 'relative' . . . it seems preferable and more plausible

157. *See generally* Frankenberg, *supra* note 21.
158. *See* Frankenberg, *supra* note 21, at 1382–84.
159. *See* Henry Shue, *Mediating Duties*, 98 ETHICS 687 (1988).
160. *See* Frankenberg, *supra* note 21, at 1384–85.

to argue for social rights as self-incurred obligations to limit one's autonomy in order to realize it in society."[161] Frankenberg attempts to counter the dichotomy of private and public autonomy with the social autonomy that each person can realize only in community. This move rests on the intuition that the possessive-individualist understanding of individual rights must be overcome in favor of a solidaristic understanding. From this follows the communitarian conclusion that only a revival of the *ethical* substance of the community can counteract the disintegrating tendencies of the (merely) *legal* system. Frankenberg answers the question "Why care?" with an appeal for more "civic virtue," more "communal spirit," and a stronger "sense of solidarity."[162]

In my opinion, this concept is not only unrealistic, but it is also problematic because it places too little confidence in the integrating force of law and too much confidence in the universalistic potential of the prepolitical bonds of informal communities. Law is the only medium through which a "solidarity with strangers" can be secured in complex societies. Perhaps appraisals like Frankenberg's still reflect the legacy of an early socialism that simultaneously looked forward to an emancipated future and backward into an idealized past. This brand of socialism intended to *raise up* the socially integrative forces of *worn out* guilds, extended families, and close-knit solidary communities and to transform and save them under the changed conditions of industrial society. In any case, Frankenberg believes that social rights cannot be conceived primarily from the moral point of view of *equally enabling* private and public autonomy, i.e., in terms of the equal respect for the dignity of each person. In Frankenberg's view, the real problem is mobilizing a consciousness of solidarity that, inside the boundaries of an ethically integrated community, makes it acceptable to *limit* personal autonomy in favor of other members.

However, this conception of private liberties as a zero-sum game is based on an undialectical opposition between private and public autonomy. By contrast, according to an intersubjective approach, rights are derived from comembership in an association of free and equal consociates under law, and thus draw their legitimacy solely from the reciprocal recognition of equal freedom for everybody. Under this approach, the solidarity familiar from relationships of recognition in simple face-to-face interactions is able to structure the law itself. In a more abstract form, such solidarity *continues to be* a resource from which the democratic self-determination of citizens must be nourished if legitimate law is to result. Legal regulations are legitimate only if they treat equals equally and unequals unequally, and thus effectively secure equal freedom. Legitimate regulations can be expected

161. *Id.* at 1385 (footnotes omitted).
162. *Id.* at 1388.

only if citizens make use of their communicative freedoms together in such a way that all voices have equal opportunities to be heard. Thus, the effective utilization of private and public autonomy (as reciprocally presupposing each other) is at the same time both the condition for the appropriate interpretation and protection of civil rights in changing contexts, and the condition for the further development of the universalistic content of these rights. Because the reproduction of law, normatively speaking, always implies the realization of an association of free and equal citizens in which all the members are bound by equal respect for one another, the circular process of mutually enabling and safeguarding private and public autonomy leaves no space for a *social* autonomy that would require the members' solidarity to result in *some other way* than from citizenship.

C.

Despite their conceptually abstract quality, philosophies of law contain a political and diagnostic content that tends to mirror the context in which they emerged. As is well known, Hegel's philosophy of right was politically explosive, provoking passionate responses from several generations. Despite Dick Howard's flattering allusions,[163] *Between Facts and Norms*[164] does not suggest any comparison with Hegel in this regard. Furthermore, I am pleased by the political diagnoses that Howard[165] and Gabriel Motzkin[166] provide for the project. I often receive a different response. Even if readers do not always see the "end of critical theory" in this project, they frequently think it defuses the critique of capitalism and just gives in to political liberalism.

A world-historical event like the collapse of the Soviet empire certainly requires us to rethink our political positions, but for decades I have continued to defend a radical reformist line.[167] Despite all the changes in my theoretical position,[168] I also understand the discourse theory of law in a radical democratic sense. Howard's analysis of the significance of the lifeworld and civil society in this theory, and his search for an heir to revolution—which he finds in a political culture of unleashed communicative freedoms—meets my intentions. Likewise, Motzkin's description of the politi-

163. *See generally* Howard, *supra* note 22.
164. *See* HABERMAS, BETWEEN FACTS AND NORMS, *supra* note 2.
165. *See generally* Howard, *supra* note 22.
166. *See generally* Motzkin, *supra* note 23.
167. *See* HABERMAS, *Nachholende Revolution und linker Revisionsbedarf, in* HABERMAS, DIE NACHHOLENDE REVOLUTION, *supra* note 62, at 179, 179–204.
168. For my most recent effort to account for these shifts, see Jürgen Habermas, *Further Reflections on the Public Sphere, in* HABERMAS AND THE PUBLIC SPHERE 421 (Craig Calhoun ed. & Thomas Burger trans., 1992).

cal constellation to which I am responding seems correct. His grasp of the internal situation in the enlarged Federal Republic of Germany is quite accurate, even if in Germany one should, from historical and sociological perspectives, speak not so much of right-wing as of "centrist extremism."[169] Motzkin states,

> The defeat of the left means that the center must now serve as the defense of the left, that the threat to liberal democracy now stems again from the right, and that once again the question arises as to the possible basis for a reconciliation between liberalism and socialism. The critical enterprise . . . is not one of dismantling the power structure and replacing it by another, but rather one of buttressing the existing power structure against the threat looming from the right—whether the political, the economic, or the religious right.[170]

VII. THE SOCIOLOGICAL COMMENTARIES: MISUNDERSTANDINGS AND FOOD FOR THOUGHT

When I returned to a university philosophy department after twelve years of research at a social-science institute, it struck me more strongly than ever that philosophers sometimes think they can pass judgment on empirical matters from within their own discipline without even taking notice of complex specialized literature. This mandarin air led me to make a biting remark[171] that Mark Gould now cites against me.[172] However, not only are there philosophers who deal with the empirical realm in a prescientific manner, there are also sociologists who, without giving up the methodological perspective of their own discipline, lay out an entire philosophy—who appear as philosophers in the sociological sheep's clothing, so to speak. In certain rare cases this may express originality, as it undoubtedly does with Niklas Luhmann,[173] but in other cases it manifests a certain naiveté.

A.

Mark Gould lets himself out of his Parsonian shell so little, and at the same time trusts his capacity for judgment so much, that his special expertise

---

169. *See* EXTREMISMUS DER MITTE: VOM RECHTEN VERSTÄNDIS DEUTSCHER NATION (Hans-Martin Lohmann ed., 1994).

170. Motzkin, *supra* note 23, at 1431–32.

171. *See* JÜRGEN HABERMAS, *Morality and Ethical Life: Does Hegel's Critique of Kant Apply to Discourse Ethics?*, *in* MORAL CONSCIOUSNESS AND COMMUNICATIVE ACTION 195, 211 (Christian Lenhardt & Shierry W. Nicholsen trans., 1990).

172. *See* Gould, *supra* note 24, at 1253 n.36.

173. *See generally* NIKLAS LUHMANN, RISK: A SOCIOLOGICAL THEORY (Rhodes Barrett trans., 1993); NIKLAS LUHMANN, A SOCIOLOGICAL THEORY OF LAW (Elizabeth King & Martin Albrow trans., 1985); Luhmann, *supra* note 25.

(which I have highly regarded for a long time) is occasionally conjoined with an astounding hermeneutical insensibility. In any case, he so poorly grasps the pluralist approach of my theory that he confuses practically everything.[174]

If one does not wish to restrict oneself—as would indeed be legitimate—to normative reflections on a theory of justice, to the analysis of relevant basic concepts, or to legal ruminations on the methodology of judicial decision making, then a philosophy of law is no longer available today, as it was in Hegel's day, in one unified system. For this reason, in *Between Facts and Norms,* I first turned to the theory of communicative action as a vantage point from which to develop the general relation between facticity and validity, and to clarify law's socially integrating function. I then contrasted the sociological objectivation of law with the normative perspective of the contractarian tradition. This contrast gave my philosophical analysis a different methodological status inside the framework of a reconstructive social theory which employs a "dual perspective" while fulfilling descriptive requirements. This certainly does not mean that the reconstruction of law, undertaken from the internal perspective of the legal system (in chapters 3 through 6) is leveled out.[175] Rather, this rational reconstruction of rights, the principles of the rule of law, judicial decision making, and its relation to legislation has the status of a normative theory of law. The comparison of law and morality also requires considerations that are philosophical in the narrower sense, while the investigation of legal discourses of application calls for reflections on legal methodology. The perspective then shifts (in chapters 7 and 8) from legal theory to social science.[176] Even these analyses, which are focused on the legitimation process, do not aim at a *sociology of law* and democracy.[177] Rather, the proposed model for the circulation of political power is only meant to make it plausible that the reconstructed normative self-understanding of modern legal orders does not hang in midair. The proposed model should explain how this self-understanding connects with the social reality of highly complex societies. The result of these analyses[178]—and what I consider important in the sociological excursus—provides the backdrop against which the sociological content of the legal paradigm can be assessed (in chapter 9).[179] Like the liberal and social-welfare paradigms, this paradigm is also based on a certain interpretation of society as a whole *from the perspective of the legal system.*

---

174. *See generally* Gould, *supra* note 24.
175. *See* HABERMAS, BETWEEN FACTS AND NORMS, *supra* note 2, at 82–286.
176. *See id.* at 287–386.
177. *See id.*
178. *See id.* at 384–87.
179. *See id.* at 388–446.

To spell out this paradigm, however, it was necessary to return once again to the internal perspective of the legal system and its members. Insofar as the theory as a whole relates to practice, it aims at changing the fallible preunderstanding that provides the horizon in which not only legal experts, but also citizens and their politicians, make their specific contribution to the process of interpreting the Constitution and realizing the system of rights. Gould misreads this democratic conception of the relation between theory and practice because he starts with the instrumental view that sociology should enlighten the judiciary as an agent of social reform.[180] Gould calls for a "jurisprudence rooted in social science,"[181] where sociology receives the role of an action-guiding authority: "[a]ny suggestion that courts implement equitable standards must rest on a preliminary theory of social development that attempts to discover an immanent progression from within our liberal legal structure."[182] Gould does not realize that my proposed philosophy of law is a plea for a new paradigmatic understanding of law. It is not a social theory intended to mobilize judicial activism and contribute to social change.

What I find still more problematic is Gould's insensitivity to the above-mentioned shift in perspective. As a result, he confuses analytic levels, making the same mistake of which he accuses me. Otherwise Gould could not have been tempted to infer my sociological concept of action from the specifications of the "ideal speech situation"—a concept that had its place only in the theory of truth. By this curious route, Gould concludes that I conflate norms with values, values with interest positions, and the orientation to values with preferences. Even worse, I supposedly operate with an atomistic and empiricist concept of social action, I do not distinguish factual constraints on action from normative ones, and I understand moral obligations in utilitarian terms. All artifacts of a biased reading. The single serious difference of opinion at this basic conceptual level results from the fact that I do not share Parson's noncognitivist understanding of morality and value-commitments.[183] Thus, I do not exclude "moral values" from the sphere of what is "reasonable." In this respect, Gould is content with the self-assurance that there is an irreducible, nonrational component of moral principles. Gould also "believes" that the values of "institutionalized individualism" should, too, find their way into the legal system.[184] This is not a question of belief, but rather a question of philosophical argumentation. Gould, however, is not interested in such argumentation.

180. See Gould, *supra* note 24, at 1342–45.
181. *Id.* at 1341.
182. *Id.* at 1340 (footnote omitted).
183. For a further discussion, see 2 HABERMAS, *supra* note 33, at 256–82.
184. See Gould, *supra* note 24, at 1321–22.

The lengthy remarks on the proportionality principle and the prohibition of excessively intrusive means in private law jurisprudence readily fit into the development that I described, with the Weberian phrase, as the "materialization of law." However, the remarks are of no use for the critique of proceduralism, whether one (i) proceeds immanently, by looking to the procedural norm of contractual freedom, or (ii) carries such considerations over to legally institutionalized procedures of argumentation. Nor (iii) can I discover a new criterion in the distinction between "equity" and "equality."

1.   Under the liberal understanding of law, freedom of contract was meant to provide private persons' business transactions with a procedure that guaranteed "pure" procedural justice. The result was considered correct or "right" independent of the contents of the contract as long as the parties adhered to the prescribed form. However, with the growing inequality in socioeconomic power, the fictive character of the "free declaration of intention" (in connection with the freedom to conclude contracts) became increasingly clear. This explains the "materialization" of the formal right of contract. The interpretive maxim of adjudication that Gould highlights—unconscionability—also acquired its present significance in connection with such changes. But Gould falsely interprets this development when he refers to unconscionability in an attempt to show how material "values" of social justice have penetrated formal law and called into question a procedural conception of law.

Instead, the materialization of contract law shows that with changes in the perceived social contexts, specific factual conditions for a nondiscriminatory application of the procedure became objects of public awareness and political regulation. Even under the liberal paradigm of law, the expectation of justice associated with the freedom of contract had been at least implicitly dependent upon the satisfaction of these conditions. Hence the social-welfare revisions can be understood as realizing *the same principle* that also undergirded the liberal paradigm of law—equal distribution of individual liberties. Moreover, the principle of separating form and content does not change if the procedural norm must be changed in such a way that a nondiscriminatory application is possible in a changed social context.

2.   Even if Gould's interpretation were correct, it would not entail any objections to my "proceduralist" understanding of law. For in all essential respects, the type of legally institutionalized deliberative and decision-making procedures on which the proceduralist paradigm is based differs from the model based on contractual freedom. The procedural norm governing contracts is geared solely toward freedom of choice and the securing of pure procedural justice. In contrast, the procedures relevant for the pro-

ceduralist paradigm involve interpenetrating processes: rational discourse is intertwined with bargaining, and legal procedures are intertwined with discursive "procedures" that guarantee only "imperfect" procedural justice. Moreover, the relevant conditions of communication are only supposed to ensure that "available" information and reasons remain free-floating, so as to *facilitate* problem solving *and* learning processes; these conditions cannot themselves generate the substantive input and contributions that communication requires. Gould correctly notes that the principle of treating like cases alike and different cases differently remains empty without an appropriate criterion of comparison. However, this is not a counterargument. Rather, it supports the view that equal individual liberties can be guaranteed only when the persons affected, acting as citizens through the public use of their communicative freedoms, clarify and agree upon the appropriate interpretation of the needs at stake and the relevant criteria for comparing typical life situations. If we want to avoid paternalism, this may not be left solely to the decisions of a judiciary (even one guided by social science). Accordingly, this internal (and reciprocal) relationship between private and public autonomy is not trivial; it is, rather, the normative core of the proceduralist paradigm I propose.

3. Gould attempts to distinguish between "equality" in the sense of abstract legal equality and "equity" in the sense of an equality in the application of law to cases. This issue of terminology would not be interesting if it were not associated with the critique of "formalism" in an allegedly "liberal" conception of law (where "liberal" is used pejoratively). In Gould's view, my theory of application discourses[185] is bound up with an abstract notion of legal equality. Consequently, it cannot satisfy the idea of substantive legal equality, or equity, because it sunders the justification of norms from their application. Gould states, "[t]he meaning of a principle can only be determined in the light of its consequences and thus its 'justifiability' and 'appropriateness' are always intermingled."[186] In contrast to Gould's approach, Klaus Günther has explained in detail how concrete cases assume different roles in the logics of argumentation that govern discourses of justification and application respectively.[187]

In discourses of justification, such cases serve as hypothetical *standard examples* that allow one to work out the possible consequences of a general observance of a norm. In discourses of application, the *individual cases* that have actually arisen require a decision that considers the concrete aspects

185. I am indebted to Klaus Günther for my views on application discourses. *See generally* GÜNTHER, *supra* note 132.
186. Gould, *supra* note 24, at 1351 (footnote omitted).
187. *See generally* GÜNTHER, *supra* note 132.

of the case in all its complexity. Whereas a discourse of justification tests the universalizability of a practice in light of consequences that can be illustrated only in foreseeable typical cases, a discourse of application must explain which prima facie norm is most appropriate to all the relevant features of an actual case of conflict. By "equity" Gould means precisely this equal treatment in the concrete, tailored to the particularity of a given situation. But this application must not refer exclusively to the complex constellation of those who are immediately involved. These persons only have a claim to be treated as equal members of the universe of equally entitled citizens under law, and only the totality of norms constituting the legal community secures this reference to "all others." On the other hand, these norms play a constitutive role only insofar as they have already been acknowledged as valid, and thus before actual cases arise. These norms must "exist" before they are applied to conflicts that have occurred. This relation is also displayed by the forms of communication used in the corresponding processes of deliberation and decision making (whether legislative or judicial): in principle, all those affected must equally (thus without privileges or discrimination) participate (albeit for the most part indirectly) in justification, whereas the application of presumedly justified norms to the individual case is undertaken from the perspective of a third party—as the representative of the general community—such that those who are immediately involved in the conflict are "heard" as they present their contested views of the case.

Gould does not see the central problem that must be solved in such application discourses—the resolution of collisions between norms, and thus the rational decision between prima facie valid candidates that are competing for "appropriateness" in a given case. Instead, Gould has a special situation in mind: cases of socially unequal treatment that can be solved only if implicitly discriminatory work relations, forms of organization, family structures, and so forth, are changed. However, this is generally possible only through the implementation of new legal programs. Thus, these cases primarily concern the political legislature and not the judiciary. Taking the practice of the Supreme Court during the New Deal era as his model, Gould advocates a strategy to channel social reform through sociologically enlightened, activist higher courts. However, this would eventually lead to a judicial paternalism incompatible with the principles of constitutional democracy.

B.

So far my replies have followed, or attempted to follow, the rules of scholarly argumentation: objections and their reconstruction followed by answers. However, Niklas Luhmann, the true philosopher, practices a different style of reflection.[188] With some comments that are light-handed only in appearance, Luhmann bores his way into the whole.

What is at stake here is not just a desire for the correct answer to a particular question, but the skillful appraisal of the range and capacity of an enterprise. Each person goes his or her own way anyhow, and one must see how far and whither one is going. In any case, I believe that Luhmann, with whom I have always found discussion to be instructive, has never operated with such a high degree of hermeneutical openness and given such scope to the principle of charity as he does here. Since discussions tend to be open-ended and ongoing, I limit myself here to a few comments on some of his remarks, trusting that the future will provide opportunity for further discussion.

"*Quod omnes tangit*"[189]: a lovely reminiscence, which is not quite correct. The issue of inclusive procedures in which all citizens may participate does not arise in matters of inheritance and certainly does not arise in lawsuits. It arises solely with respect to national legislation in a democratic state. In this regard, inclusiveness is guaranteed through the rights of communication and participation, including, *inter alia,* the universal right to vote. In courtroom discourses of application, which limit participation in familiar ways, the relation to the assumed "assent of everyone" is secured by the fact that *validly established* law must be applied. The validity of these norms depends upon the democratic procedure of a legislature that relies on discourses of justification to reach decisions affecting "everyone." With the recognition of this connection, I am not "externalizing" a problem of adjudication in a "political democracy." Rather, I address the problem of legitimation where it belongs according to the self-understanding of constitutional democracies. This notion allowed the democratic positivism of the Weimar period (the *Gesetzespositivismus* developed by Hans Kelsen and others) to eventually prevail in Germany against a legal tradition molded by constitutional monarchy. But that struggle is a matter for a chapter on law in the story of a "belated nation." This squabble does not touch the real question and the topic of much thought-provoking commentary: how can the system of institutions handle the unavoidable idealizations that are already built into communicative action and that already create social facts?

As one might expect, Luhmann puts his finger on the weakness of a detranscendentalizing operation that dissolves Kant's concealed ontological opposition between the supersensible realm and the empirical realm in the unconcealed idealizing surpluses of an *innerworldly* transcendence.[190]

188. *See generally* Luhmann, *supra* note 25.
189. *See id.* at 883.
190. *See id.* at 885.

This move leaves us with an unexplained tension between facticity and validity. Luhmann is primarily interested in how historically situated claims to universal validity overcome time. In other words, he is interested in the countertemporal sense of temporally situated ascriptions of invariance (i.e., ascriptions of accountability to speakers and of meaning-identity to words and sentences). In Luhmann's opinion, these idealizations "stop time," and he proposes that we replace them with descriptions that "dissolve" idealizations in temporal processes. Luhmann maintains, "[e]very identity— each and every one—is produced by a *selective* evaluation of past event-complexes and in its selectivity is continually reconstructed. In other words, identities *condense*, and in ever new situations they are *reaffirmed* and must be correspondingly *generalized*."[191] But what is the *right* description?

Oddly enough, Luhmann, whose reflective powers normally take in everything, does not reflect on a specific stratum of the premises. It is not so trivial as it appears to derive the tension between facticity and validity from the facticity of observable sequences of spatiotemporally constructed events. Nominalism, which underlies this conceptual formation, first focused attention on, and gave primacy to, contingent temporal particulars. In this theoretical universe all distinctions ultimately aim at the particular. Consequently, these contingent temporal particulars provide the basis by which universals can be understood as equally fleeting constructions.

In asking about the unity of facticity and validity, Luhmann assumes, *a priori*, that this unity is produced through an operation that (from the perspectives of other systems) can be observed as a temporal process. This nominalist strategy reveals a decision that operates as an unthematized preconception in Luhmann's thinking.[192] However, contrary to what Luhmann believes, systems theory has by no means left behind the conceptual alternatives of realism and nominalism, which emerged from the break with the ontological paradigm. This process of separation continued with each newly irrupting impulse of contingency, beginning with medieval nominalism through classical empiricism, and up to that second, historically-oriented empiricism which today is variously attired but always engaged in the same singularizing operation. Responding to the historical thinking that emerged in the late eighteenth century, empiricism not only dissolved observable nature in the contingent whirl of events, it also dispersed culture— which is accessible from the participant perspective but has become an alienated "second nature"—into the murmur of communicative events or the whirl of signifiers. It is evidently a hallmark of modernity—a modernity that still owes its victories for freedom to a passionate antiplatonism—

191. *Id.* at 888.
192. *See id.* at 887–90.

that the philosophies assembled under the banner of postmodernism have unconsciously abandoned themselves to the vortex of nominalist motifs.

However, the reduction of the universal to the particular has, in each case, sustained itself by paradoxically presupposing the universal. This began, at the latest, in the thirteenth century when the nominalists inconsistently held on to the determinate character of singular things existing in themselves. If the conceptual division of the world into species and kinds is supposed to be a subjective achievement, whereby the human mind operates with signs in order to process its impressions of individual entities into a knowledge of "things," then the work of abstraction cannot proceed in an absolutely arbitrary manner but must retain a *fundamentum in re* insofar as the subject's comparisons start with criteria that "hit" something in the things themselves. This inconsistency motivated the epistemological study of the constructive activity of an intellect that *brings* questions *to* nature, that no longer imitates nature but proceeds in an inquisitorial manner.

This study formed the common starting point for both empiricism and transcendental philosophy. When the linguistic turn on this mentalistic turn linked up with transcendental philosophy, there emerged once again an intelligent empiricism which is now geared for semantic universes and no longer gives an account of the paradoxical nature of its own nominalistic attempt to singularize even symbolic universals. When Luhmann emphasizes that "*[e]very* identity . . . is continuously reconstructed,"[193] he makes use of a generalization that can be reduced *without remainder* to the generalizing *process* as an event only if one considers the reference system (of science or of the person) capable of an ultimately paradoxical self-constitution of universals. But before one triumphantly makes a virtue out of this necessity, a reminder from the history of philosophy may give one pause and lead one to weigh the costs of the nominalist *a priori* against an alternative approach.

If one shakes off the obsession with an exclusively observational objectification and takes an internal, hermeneutical approach to symbolically structured worlds (to which the theorist pretheoretically belongs anyhow), then one can painlessly escape the nominalist's powers of suggestion. From this position one can see that the relations between universal, particular, and individual are built into the intersubjectively constituted communications of our symbolically structured forms of life and do not require any asymmetrical resolution, just as the tension between facticity and validity does not need to be asymmetrically relaxed in either a nominalist or a platonist direction.

193. *Id.* at 888 (emphasis added).

In a world where one cannot get something for nothing, this, too, has its price. It requires the provisional disconnection between, on the one hand, the statements one can (defeasibly) make from this participant perspective and, on the other, statements about matters that can appear only to the observer who adopts a nominalist strategy (such as objectifying statements about how cultural forms of life have arisen historically, or about the natural constancies under which alone cultures can reproduce). But why not leave this to different sciences? Must the empiricist dream of a unified science be dreamt once again in an obviously more ethereal and more comic form, the tulle of a systems-theoretic *poiesis* of distinctions? Under the conditions of postmetaphysical thinking, the price of renouncing such an overgeneralizing theory is no longer a burden.

If one carries out this shift in perspective, then the systematic compulsion to ask the questions that Luhmann finds so urgent disappears (such as, the question concerning the local nature of all argumentation, the question concerning the exclusionary effects of all discourse, the question concerning the normative content of the concept of rationality). As the gerund "idealizing" already reveals, idealizations are operations that we must undertake here and now, but *while performing them* we must not vitiate their context-transcending meaning. The civic discourse of freedom and equality is certainly constituted according to its own rules, but because its capacity for self-transformation distinguishes it from Foucauldian-type discourses, it still remains *intrinsically* open to internal criticism. Communicative rationality, which deciphers the mysterious genesis of legitimacy from legality, cannot "replace" the ruler, because in a democracy the ruler's seat is supposed to remain empty. This requirement is not meant only in a literal sense: the seemingly paradoxical achievement of law is to tame the conflict potential of unleashed individual freedoms through equality-guaranteeing norms, which are compelling only so long as they are recognized as legitimate on the unsteady basis of unleashed communicative freedoms.

Contributors

Robert Alexy is Professor of Public Law and Legal Philosophy at the University of Kiel, Germany. He is author of *A Theory of Legal Argumentation* (1989), *Theorie der Grundrechte* (1985), and *Begriff und Geltung des Rechts* (1994).

Andrew Arato is Professor of Sociology at the Graduate Faculty of the New School for Social Research. He is coauthor of *Civil Society and Political Theory* (1994).

Richard J. Bernstein is Vera List Professor of Philosophy at the Graduate Faculty of the New School for Social Research. He is editor of *Habermas and Modernity* (1985) and author of *Beyond Objectivism and Relativism* (1983), *The New Constellation* (1992), *Hannah Arendt and the Jewish Question* (1996), and *Freud and the Vexed Legacy of Moses* (forthcoming).

William E. Forbath is Angus Wynne, Sr. Professor of Civil Jurisprudence and Professor of History at the University of Texas at Austin. He is author of *Law and the Shaping of the American Labor Movement* (1991).

Klaus Günther is Profesor of Law at the University of Rostock, Germany. He is author of *The Sense of Appropriateness: Application Discourses in Morality and Law* (1993).

Jürgen Habermas is currently Professor of Philosophy at Northwestern University and Professor Emeritus of Philosophy at the Johann Wolfgang Goethe University in Frankfurt, Germany. His most recent work translated into English is *The Inclusion of the Other* (1998).

Arthur J. Jacobson is Max Freund Professor of Litigation and Advocacy at the Benjamin N. Cardozo School of Law of Yeshiva University. He is coauthor of *Justice and the Legal System: A Course Book* (1992) and coeditor of *Weimar: A Jurisprudence of Crisis* (California: forthcoming).

Jacques Lenoble is Professor of Law and Director of the Centre of Philosophy of Law at the Université Catholique de Louvain, Belgium. He is coauthor of *Dire La Norme—Droit, Politique et Énonciation* (1990) and author of *Droit et Communication—La Transformation du Droit Contemporain* (1994).

Niklas Luhmann is Professor Emeritus of Sociology at the University of Bielefeld, Germany. He is author of *The Differentiation of Society* (1982), *A Sociological Theory of Law* (1985), *Essays on Self-Reference* (1990), and *Social Systems* (1995).

Thomas McCarthy is Professor of Philosophy and John Shaffer Distinguished Professor in the Humanities at Northwestern University. He is author of *The Critical Theory of Jürgen Habermas* (1978) and *Ideals and Illusions* (1991), coauthor of *Critical Theory* (1994), and general editor of *Studies in Contemporary German Social Thought* published by MIT Press.

Frank I. Michelman is Robert Walmsley University Professor at Harvard University Law School. He has published extensively on constitutional law and deliberative democracy.

Michael K. Power is Professor of Accounting at the London School of Economics and a faculty member at the European Institute for Advanced Studies in Management, Brussels. He is author of *The Audit Society: Ritual of Verification* (1997).

Ulrich K. Preuss is Professor of Law and Politics at the Free University in Berlin, Germany. He has worked on constitutional transition in postcommunist states and on the development of a European constitution. He is editor of *Zum Begriff der Verfassung: Die Ordnung des Politischen* (1994), coauthor of *Constitutional Revolution: The Link Between Constitutionalism and Progress* (1995), and author of *Institutional Design in Post-Communist Societies: Rebuilding the Ship at Sea* (1997).

William Rehg is Associate Professor of Philosophy at Saint Louis University. He is author of *Insight and Solidarity: The Discourse Ethics of Jürgen Habermas* (California 1994), translator of Habermas's *Between Facts and Norms* (1996), and coeditor of *Deliberative Democracy* (1997).

Michel Rosenfeld is Professor of Law at the Benjamin N. Cardozo School of Law of Yeshiva University. He is author of *Affirmative Action and Justice: A Philosophical and Constitutional Inquiry* (1991) and *Just Interpretations: Law Between Ethics and Politics* (California 1998), editor of *Constitutionalism, Iden-*

tity, Difference and Legitimacy: Theoretical Perspectives (1994), and coeditor of
Hegel and Legal Theory (1991) and *Deconstruction and the Possibility of Justice*
(1992).

András Sajó is Professor of Comparative Constitutional Law at the Central
European University in Budapest, Hungary. He has also been a visiting pro-
fessor at the Benjamin N. Cardozo School of Law, the New York University
School of Law, and the University of Chicago Law School. He is past Deputy
Commissioner for Deregulation and past member of the Constitution
Drafting Committee for Hungary.

Bernhard Schlink is Professor of Constitutional and Administrative Law and
Philosophy of Law at Humbolt University in Berlin. He is also a Justice of
the Constitutional Court of the State of North Rhine–Westfalia in Germany. He is coeditor of *Weimar: A Jurisprudence of Crisis* (California: forthcoming).

Gunther Teubner is Otto-Kahn-Freund Professor of Comparative Law and
Legal Theory at the London School of Economics. He has taught at the
University of Michigan, Stanford University, and the European University
in Florence, Italy. He is author of *Law as an Autopoietic System* (1993) and
Droit et Réflexivité (1994), and editor of *Environmental Law and Ecological Re-
sponsibility* (1995) and *Global Law Without a State* (1997).

INDEX

Adjudication, 63–64; and legal consistency, 183–184, 415; and legislation, 23–24; quod omnes tangit problem, 157–158, 164, 169, 449; rationality of, 7, 226–227, 231–232

    application discourse and, 7, 43, 63–64, 67, 69, 177, 183, 226, 228, 230–231, 263, 312, 321–322, 430–431, 435–436, 444

    constitutional adjudication, 31–32, 44, 337–338, 343–344, 364–365, 367, 368, 369–370; criticism of, 340–341, 342–343, 350–351, 353–354, 356–357; and legal uncertainty, 363–364, 365; and political argumentation, 350–351; and politics, 345–346, 347–348, 349–350; and principles, 360–361, 362 (*See also* Principles); and public participation, 359–360; and reflexive law, 35–36 (*See also* Reflexive law). *See also* Constitution

    decision-making procedures and, 19, 33, 70, 78, 80, 117, 120, 128–129, 167–168, 171–172, 183, 264–265, 266, 268–269, 342, 354–355, 358–359, 385–386, 406–407, 415–416, 444, 446–447; and compromise, 136–137, 146. *See also* Majority rule

    judiciary and, 63–64, 70–71, 166, 167–168, 314–315, 349–350, 363–364. *See also* Judiciary

    justification discourse and, 7, 43, 63, 64–65, 67, 69, 228, 267, 311–312, 321–322, 403–404, 416–417, 430–431, 435–436, 447–448; direct as distinct from indirect, 117–118, 119–120, 146–147

Administration, 44 n.1, 62–63, 78, 284; administrative action systems, 223–224, 273–274; administrative steering, 19–20, 223, 273, 276–277, 332, 351; as autonomous sphere, 41–42; and communicative power, 19–20, 80, 275–276, 331–332; and context sensitive threshold, 29–30; evolution of, 37; and individual rights, 62–63, 71–72; and judicial review, 358–359; legitimacy of, 330–331; and public procedures, 31–32; rationalization of administrative power, 437–438; regulation of, 39–40; and separation of powers, 61–62, 69, 78; and strategic action, 60–61. *See also* Adjudication, application discourse and

Adorno, Theodor W., 207, 211

Apel, Karl Otto, 56, 427

Arendt, Hannah, 74, 235, 248, 276, 331

Autonomy, 183, 199; civic autonomy, 275–276; of discourses, 177; and law, 2, 75–76; of legal fields, 188–189; of the lifeworld, 175–176; of market, 282–283; of

ERRATA

Habermas on Law and Democracy: Critical Exchanges
Edited by Michel Rosenfeld and Andrew Arato

Page	For	Read
96, n. 32	17 CARDOZO L. REV. 771, 777 (1996)	Ch. 1 in this vol., 13, 19
96, n. 33	*See id.* at 778–79	*See id.* at 20
97, n. 34	*See id.* at 776–80	*See id.* at 17–21
382, n. 5	Sajó, *Constitutional Adjudication in Light of Discourse Theory,* 17 CARDOZO L. REV. 1193 (1996)	ch. 17 in this vol.
382, n. 6	Schlink, *The Dynamics of Constitutional Adjudication,* 17 CARDOZO L. REV. 1231 (1996)	ch. 18 in this vol.
382, n. 8	Forbath, *Short-Circuit: A Critique of Habermas's Understanding of Law, Politics, and Economic Life,* 17 CARDOZO L. REV. 1441 (1996)	Forbath, ch. 13 in this vol.
382, n. 9	17 CARDOZO L. REV. 1127 (1996)	ch. 14 in this vol.
382, n. 10	17 CARDOZO L. REV. 1163 (1996)	ch. 15 in this vol.
382, n. 11	17 CARDOZO L. REV. 1083 (1996)	ch. 5 in this vol.
383, n. 12	17 CARDOZO L. REV. 791 (1996)	ch. 4 in this vol.
383, n. 13	17 CARDOZO L. REV. 919 (1996)	ch. 8 in this vol.
383, n. 14	17 CARDOZO L. REV. 1147 (1996)	ch. 12 in this vol.
383, n. 15	17 CARDOZO L. REV. 1005 (1996)	ch. 9 in this vol.
383, n. 18	17 CARDOZO L. REV. 1027 (1996)	ch. 10 in this vol.
383, n. 19	17 CARDOZO L. REV. 901 (1996)	ch. 7 in this vol.
383, n. 20	17 CARDOZO L. REV. 1179 (1996)	ch. 16 in this vol.
383, n. 25	17 CARDOZO L. REV. 883 (1996)	ch. 6 in this vol.
384, n. 29	1129	289
384, n. 30	1130–31	290–91
386, n. 35	1143–44	302
387, n. 36	*Id.* at 1143	*Id.*
389, n. 43	1164–70	310–15
389, n. 44	1170–74	316–19
389, n. 45	1175	320
390, n. 47	1177	322
391, n. 51	1105	135
396, n. 57	1094	125
400, n. 64	1111–12	141

(continued)

ERRATA *(continued)*

Page	For	Read
400, n. 65	*Id.* at 1112	*Id.*
401, n. 66	1119	148
402, n. 69	1123	151
403, n. 72	1103	133
404, n. 74	*Id.* at 800	*Id.* at 90
404, n. 75	821	110
405, n. 76	800	90
405, n. 77	799	89
405, n. 78	794	85
405, n. 79	795	86
409, n. 86	792	83
410, n. 87	808	98
411, n. 88	816	105–06
411, n. 89	818–20	107–09
412, n. 90	820	108
412, n. 92	926	196
413, n. 94	*Id.* at 925	*Id.*
413, n. 95	928	199
418, n. 107	1014	215
418, n. 108	1012	213
419, n. 113	1010	212
429, n. 136	1033–34	232–33
431, n. 141	904	176
433, n. 144	907	179
433, n. 145	908–09	180–81
433, n. 146	910	182
435, n. 147	909–10	181–82
435, n. 148	910	182
435, n. 149	914, 915	185, 186
438, n. 155	1185	328–29
438, n. 156	1191	334
449, n. 189	883	157
449, n. 190	885	159
450, n. 191	888	162
450, n. 192	887–90	161–63
451, n. 193	888	162

Printed in the United States
106012LV00003B/91/A

9 780520 204669